THE DECLINE OF
COMPETITION

THE DECLINE OF COMPETITION

A Study of the Evolution of American Industry

by
ARTHUR ROBERT BURNS

Published under the Auspices of the
COLUMBIA UNIVERSITY COUNCIL FOR RESEARCH
IN THE SOCIAL SCIENCES

GREENWOOD PRESS, PUBLISHERS
WESTPORT, CONNECTICUT

Library of Congress Cataloging in Publication Data

Burns, Arthur Robert, 1895-
   The decline of competition.

   Reprint of the ed. published by McGraw-Hill, New York.
   Bibliography : p.
   Includes index.
   1. Trusts, Industrial--United States. 2. Monopolies--United States. 3. Trade and professional associations--United States. 4. Prices--United States. 5. Industry and state--United States. 6. Competition. I. Title.
HC103.B83 1974   338'.0973   74-136847
ISBN 0-8371-5281-X

Originally published in 1936 by McGraw-Hill Book Company, Inc., New York and London

Reprinted in 1974 by Greenwood Press,
a division of Williamhouse-Regency Inc.

Library of Congress Catalog Card Number 74-136847

ISBN 0-8371-5281-X

Printed in the United States of America

PREFACE

The rise of the "heavy industries," changes in methods of selling, and the widening use of corporate forms of business organization are bringing, if they have not already brought, the era of competitive capitalism to a close. These changes have swept across the industrial scene in America with remarkable speed since the closing years of the nineteenth century. Yet there has been astonishingly little analysis of their significance. Much has been written of the history of individual pools and trusts, and accusing fingers have been pointed at the increasing concentration of control over industry. This literature is founded upon naive conceptions of "competition" and "monopoly" and unreal assumptions concerning the possibility of reviving the competitive market. It has been too much concerned with judicial efforts to apply the anti-trust laws and too little with the underlying forces making for change and with the consequences of the manner in which they have been transforming the industrial system. On the other hand, the increasing practical importance of monopoly has been recognized in recent attempts to reconstruct economic theory in terms of "imperfect" or "monopolistic" competition.[1] This literature, still very young, is, however, written in terms of high abstraction. I have endeavored in the present work to throw a fragile bridge across the wide gulf between these abstractions and the realities which they must finally comprehend.

Commencing with the data available concerning the industries in which change has been most notable, I have sought to specify the causes underlying changes in market conditions and to draw conclusions concerning the manner in which the contemporary quasi-competitive, quasi-monopolistic industrial system is operating. The history of the National Recovery Administration not only revealed the extent of the transformation of the market and the vigor of the forces making for change; it also uncovered our unreadiness to control these forces and even more completely our failure to realize the issues at stake. I have, therefore, also tried

---

[1] CHAMBERLIN, *The Theory of Monopolistic Competition*, and ROBINSON, JOAN *The Economics of Imperfect Competition*.

PREFACE

to set out the far-reaching implications of any social control. As no satisfactory social control will be possible until we are ready to make a clear, deliberate, but exceedingly difficult selection of objectives, I have tried to set out the nature of the available choices, but I have attempted no more than a very general discussion of the means of control.

I now realize only too clearly that no individual can be sufficiently well acquainted with conditions in a large number of industries to escape the risk of misinterpreting the data. I have no doubt that, despite all efforts to avoid them, errors of interpretation will be discovered and I can only hope that the main outlines of the discussion, after these errors have been corrected, will have sufficient validity to be of value. I cannot, however, accept the entire responsibility for misinterpretation. The fog of secrecy and often of deception that hangs heavily over the activities of large corporate units is a serious barrier to accurate analysis. Fear of the anti-trust laws, and of misinterpretation by an uncomprehending public opinion, is a partial, but far from complete, explanation of this denial of access to the relevant facts. Government investigation has proved disappointing as a guide through this fog. Although the Federal Trade Commission Act of 1914 appears to vest in the commission all the powers necessary to enable it to bring the essential facts to light, political control and judicial "interpretation" have gone far to render it impotent. Political control has determined the personnel of the commission and its staff;[1] judicial decision has whittled away its investigatory power, its right arm, until as Professor Watkins has expressed it, "There remains nothing but an impotent stump."[2] In consequence "it is hardly too much to say that the commission throws the light of publicity upon such facts about the conduct of business as the business community chooses to have disclosed.[3] In at least partial extenuation of the resistance of business men to investigation it can, however, be said that the full complexity of their problems has not always been realized by government investigators. Although the past reports of the Federal Trade Commission have been far less helpful than they might have been had the spirit in which Congress established the commission also animated the executive and judicial arms, there are signs that it is pursuing

[1] *Cf.* BLAISDELL, *The Federal Trade Commission*, Chap. VIII.
[2] "The Federal Trade Commission," in *The Federal Anti-trust Laws*, Edited by Handler, 115.
[3] *Ibid.*, 117.

a more enlightening policy.[1] Finally, although the records of litigation under the anti-trust laws, and trade publications, throw some light upon the facts, it is usually an oblique and distorting one. I can only plead that the secrecy in which the industrial system operates be borne in mind when errors of omission or interpretation appear.

This study developed out of an investigation of the effects of the anti-trust laws commenced in 1926 when I was a Laura Spelman Rockefeller Memorial Research Fellow; since 1928 it has been continued concurrently with my duties as a member of the faculty of Columbia University. During the years 1932–1933 and 1933–1934 it has been facilitated by financial assistance from the Council for Research in the Social Sciences at that university, which has also made publication possible. I take the present opportunity of acknowledging my debt to both the Laura Spelman Rockefeller Memorial (now the Rockefeller Foundation) and the Council for Research in the Social Sciences. My indebtedness to other writers in the field I have attempted to discharge in the Bibliography of this volume. Miss Vera Shlakman assisted me during the year 1932–1933 with an ability and assiduity for which I express my gratitude. My colleague Dr. E. M. Burns stoically read the final manuscript as well as the proofs. Her criticism has enabled me to clarify many parts of the work. To others who have assisted with the spoken rather than the written word I am grateful and tender my thanks.

ARTHUR ROBERT BURNS.

COLUMBIA UNIVERSITY,
NEW YORK CITY,
April, 1936.

---

[1] *Cf.* F.T.C., *The Price Bases Inquiry*, 1932, and *The Practices of the Steel Industry under the Code*, 1934.

TABLE OF CONTENTS

	PAGE
PREFACE	v
LIST OF DIAGRAMS	xiii

CHAPTER I

COMPETITION IN TRANSITION	1
I. Introduction	1
II. The General Causes of the Growing Importance of Monopoly Elements in Industry	3
A. Technological Causes of the Decline in the Number of Sellers	8
B. Social Policy and the Decline in the Number of Sellers	9
1. Corporation Laws	9
2. Patent Laws	11
3. Anti-trust Laws	17
4. Other Laws	21
III. The General Influences Affecting the Operation of the Industrial System	25
A. Conditions of Sale	26
B. Conditions of Production	29
IV. Conclusion	40

CHAPTER II

THE TRADE ASSOCIATION AND INDUSTRIAL INSTITUTE	43
I. Introduction	43
II. Trade Association Policies 1912 to 1933	45
A. The Performance of Functions Most Economically Conducted on a Large Scale	46
B. The Cooperative Provision of Information	47
1. The Standardization of Forms of Cost Accounts	47
2. The Standardization of Methods of Calculating Costs	49
3. Statistics of Production	55
4. Statistics of Inventories	59
5. Statistics of Unfilled Orders	59
6. Statistics of Productive Capacity	59
7. Statistics of Selling Prices	60
C. Cooperative Control of Output	64
D. Cooperative Control of Types of Product	68
E. Cooperative Control of Methods of Selling	69
III. Summary	73

CHAPTER III

PRICE LEADERSHIP	76
I. The Definition of Price Leadership	76
II. The Evidence of Price Leadership	77
A. The Steel Industry	77
B. The Petroleum Industry	93
C. The Agricultural Implement Industry	109
D. The Anthracite Coal Industry	118
E. Other Industries	129
III. The Consequences of Price Leadership	140

TABLE OF CONTENTS

CHAPTER IV

SHARING THE MARKET 146
  I. The Definition of Sharing the Market 146
  II. The Evidence of Sharing the Market. 146
    A. Agreements between Sellers Affecting the Sharing of Business . . 146
      1. Pooling Agreements 146
      2. Cooperative Selling. 151
      3. Trade Association Activities. 152
      4. Agreements Concerning the Utilization of Plant 154
    B. Sharing the Market by Convention. 155
      1. The Meat Packing Industry. 156
      2. Anthracite 166
      3. Other Industries. 168
    C. Reciprocal Dealing and the Distribution of Business 170
  III. The Consequences of Sharing the Market. 175

CHAPTER V

THE STABILIZATION OF INDIVIDUAL PRICES 195
  I. The Definition of Stabilization of Prices 195
  II. The Evidence of Stabilization of Prices. 196
    A. The Detection of Stabilization of Prices. 196
    B. The Prevalence of Stabilization of Prices 197
      1. Conventions Concerning Price Policy. 197
        a. Price Setting 197
        b. Long-term Contracts. 200
        c. Guarantees against Decline in Price 200
      2. Trade Associations. 202
      3. Price Leadership. 204
        a. The Steel Industry 205
        b. The Anthracite Industry. 216
        c. The Agricultural Implement Industry 217
        d. The Petroleum Industry 218
        e. Other Industries. 220
      4. Duopoly and Monopoly. 225
      5. Other Examples. 233
      6. Summary of Evidence Concerning the Stabilization of Prices 241
  III. The Consequences of Stabilization of Prices. 243
    A. Price Setting for Short Periods. 243
    B. Stabilization of Individual Prices and the Business Cycle 245
    C. Stabilization of Prices over Long Periods 266

CHAPTER VI

PRICE DISCRIMINATION. 273
  I. The Definition of Price Discrimination and the Conditions Favoring It 273
  II. Discrimination According to the Use of the Product 274
  III. Discrimination According to the Trade Status of the Buyer. 277
  IV. Geographical Discrimination 280
    A. Zone Price Systems. 282
    B. Basing-point Systems. 290
      1. The Occurrence of Basing-point Systems 291
        a. Lumber and Miscellaneous Industries 291
        b. The Steel Industry 299
        c. The Cement Industry 317
        d. The Sugar Industry 322
      2. The Policy of the National Recovery Administration. . 325

TABLE OF CONTENTS

CHAPTER VII
PRICE DISCRIMINATION (continued) 329
    3. The Effects of Basing-point Systems 329
        a. The Interpenetration of Market Territories 329
        b. The Non-basing-point Producer 336
        c. The General Effects of Basing-point Systems 353

CHAPTER VIII
NON-PRICE COMPETITION 372
  I. The Origin and Nature of Non-price Competition 372
 II. The Effects of Non-price Competition 375
    A. Sales-promotion Activities 375
        1. Effect on the Organization of Production 376
        2. Effect on the Distribution of Goods and Services 385
    B. Competition in Quality and Service 394
        1. Effect on the Organization of Production 395
        2. Effect on the Distribution of Goods and Services 398
    C. Competition in Style 406
        1. Effect on the Organization of Production 407
        2. Effect on the Distribution of Goods and Services 409
III. The Changing Importance of Non-price Competition 412
    A. Evidence of Increasing Importance 412
    B. Evidence of Declining Importance 416

CHAPTER IX
THE INTEGRATION OF INDUSTRIAL OPERATIONS 418
  I. Integration and the Régime of Mixed Monopoly and Competition . . 418
 II. Imperfections in the Capital Market and Integration 419
III. The Principal Patterns of Integration 421
    A. Vertical Integration 421
        1. Influences Affecting Vertical Integration 421
        2. The Principal Consequences of Vertical Integration 431
    B. Integration of the Production of Commodities Requiring Similar
        Selling Organizations 446
        1. Influences Affecting Such Integration 446
        2. The Consequences of Such Integration 450
    C. Integration of the Production of Substitute Goods and Services . 453
        1. Influences Affecting Such Integration 454
        2. The Consequences of Such Integration 455
    D. Territorial Integration 456
        1. Influences Affecting Such Integration 456
        2. The Consequences of Such Integration 458
IV. Conclusions 460

CHAPTER X
INDUSTRIAL POLICIES UNDER THE NATIONAL INDUSTRIAL RECOVERY ACT, 1933 462
  I. The Provisions of the Law 463
 II. The Concentration of Power to Make Policy in the Hands of Industry
    Groups 464
    A. Control of Output 465
        1. Direct Control 465
        2. Indirect Control through Regulation of the Maximum Hours
           of Plant Operation 470

TABLE OF CONTENTS

B. Control of Prices.	471
1. Direct Control of Prices	472
2. The Prohibition of Sales at Prices below the Cost of Production.	479
3. "Open-price" Provisions	491
C. Control of Non-price Competition	500
1. Methods of Selling.	500
2. Quality and Service Competition.	508
D. Control of Long-term Investment.	509
III. Summary.	512

CHAPTER XI

THE PROBLEM OF SOCIAL CONTROL—OBJECTIVES. ... 522

I. The Requirement of Competition by Law.	523
A. Without Industrial Reorganization	524
B. Industrial Reorganization to Restore Competition	525
II. Acceptance of the Concentration of Economic Power.	526
A. Without State Participation.	526
B. Acceptance of Concentration of Economic Power and State Participation in its Exercise	529
1. Considerations of Productive Efficiency.	530
a. Shifts in Demand	532
b. Shifts in the Demand for Exhaustible and Irreplaceable Natural Resources	540
c. Cyclical Fluctuations in Demand	542
d. Changes in Methods of Production	546
e. Changes in the Conditions of Supply of the Means of Production.	550
f. Maintaining the Efficiency of Productive Units.	555
2. Considerations of the Distribution of the Produce between Different Classes and Individuals	560
a. Distribution within a Given Period of Time	561
b. Distribution over Time	563
3. Considerations of the Non-financial Burden of Productive Activity	564
III. Conclusions.	564

CHAPTER XII

THE PROBLEM OF SOCIAL CONTROL—MEANS. ... 566

I. The Problem	566
II. The Distribution of Authority Within the Administration of the State.	567
A. Control by Legislative Bodies	567
B. Control by Judicial Bodies.	570
C. Control by Administrative Bodies	571
III. The Sanctions.	579
A. The State as a Conciliator.	579
B. The State as Administrator of a Veto Power.	582
C. The State as Controlling Authority.	584
1. Types of Coercion	585
2. The Underlying Influences Determining the Effectiveness of Sanctions.	587
IV. Conclusion	589
BIBLIOGRAPHY.	591
INDEX	605

LIST OF DIAGRAMS

PAGE

1. Output of steel ingots and castings in the United States 1902 to 1932 and the proportion produced by the United States Steel Corporation . . . 86
2. Output of finished rolled steel products in the United States 1902 to 1932 and the proportion produced by the United States Steel Corporation . . 86
3. Average monthly price of iron and steel products 1886 to 1913 and their purchasing power in terms of an index of wholesale prices 91
4. Annual prices of pig iron and finished steel products 1905 to 1934 and index of wholesale prices 92
5. The prices of gasoline and crude petroleum and an index of wholesale prices 1913 to 1933. 107
6. Production of agricultural implements and the proportion manufactured or sold by the International Harvester Company, 1903 to 1911 and 1919 to 1923. 110
7. Prices charged by railroad-controlled and "independent" sellers of anthracite from January, 1923 to April, 1924 121
8. Capacity for production of anthracite, actual production and proportion of capacity in use 1890 to 1929. 125
9. The price of anthracite and an index of wholesale prices, 1913 to 1934 . . 128
10. Proportion of total slaughter of cattle, sheep and hogs slaughtered by each of the large packers 1913 to 1917. 157
11. Accumulated percentages of the shares of each large packer in total cattle purchases in 1916 158
12. Total slaughter by the five large packers and the percentage slaughtered by each, 1919 to 1924 162
13. The prices of livestock and meat products 1914, 1920 to 1922 and 1928 to 1931 187
14. The prices of writing paper, book paper and newsprint 1923 to 1931 . . . 203
15. Average monthly prices of bessemer pig iron, and bessemer billets at Pittsburgh and heavy bessemer rails at mills in Pennsylvania 1897 to 1911 . . 208
16. Average monthly prices of steel beams, plates, bars and sheets at Pittsburgh 1897 to 1911. 210
17. Monthly prices of pig iron, steel, and steel products 1915 to 1934 212
18. Monthly prices of iron and steel, steel products, finished goods and wholesale prices 1929 to 1934. 215
19. The price of stove sizes of anthracite 1903 to 1913 and 1923 to 1934 . . . 217
20. The price of crude petroleum and its products 1923 to 1933 219
21. Prices of cotton thread, rayon, nickel, newsprint and soda crackers, 1923 to 1933 221
22. Prices of sulphur, glass, salt, cement and bananas, 1923 to 1933 223
23. The price of tobacco leaf and tobacco products, 1914, 1920 to 1922 and 1929 to 1934. 226
24. The wholesale price of bread in five cities October 1923 to December 1929 234
25. The prices of wheat and flour 1922 to 1930 235
26. The prices of bread and flour in Minneapolis, Kansas City and Boston, 1913 to 1923. 236

xiii

LIST OF DIAGRAMS

	PAGE
27. Prices of sewing machines, matches, iodine, and shoes 1923 to 1933	239
28. Rigid and flexible prices, 1926 to 1933	241
29. The relation between frequency of price change and magnitude of price change during depression (1929 to 1934)	242
30. Production and prices of automobiles, 1929 to 1931	251
31. Consumption and prices of cigarettes, 1925 to 1931	252
32. Production and prices of textiles 1929 to 1931	253
33. Production and prices of leather products, 1929 to 1931	253
34. Prices and production in the agricultural implement industry, 1926 to 1933	254
35. Percentage of capacity for the production of cement in use 1907 to 1930	267
36. Location of maple flooring mills and of basing points in 1934	294
37. Location of southern pine lumber mills and of basing points in 1934	298
38. Correspondence between actual delivered prices and Pittsburgh-plus prices in 1919	303
39. Basing points and points of production of pig iron in December 1933	308
40. The differentials between the prices of soft steel bars, structural shapes, rolled annealed sheets and galvanized sheets at Pittsburgh and Chicago, 1920 to 1934	316
41. Annual average prices of cast iron pipe at New York, Chicago and Birmingham, 1920 to 1934	316
42. Annual average prices of pig iron at Pittsburgh, and Chicago, Birmingham and Valley Furnaces, 1920 to 1934	317
43. Location of basing points and points of production of cement on June 30, 1930	318
44. Net yields at base and non-base mills under a basing-point system	332
45. Net yields on bids for the sale of cement to the state of Illinois in 1929	334
46. Net yields on the sale of cement in 1927, 1928 and 1929	335
47. Productive capacity of steel ingots and castings and its geographical distribution, 1916 to 1931	342
48. Production of steel ingots and castings and the geographical distribution of output and capacity, 1916 to 1931	343
49. Location of productive capacity in the steel industry in relation to the basing points in 1934	351
50. Prices of cement in seven cities 1923 to 1932	360
51. The prices of commodities the output or prices of which were directly controlled under the National Industrial Recovery Act in 1933 and 1934	469
52. Industrial activity, payrolls, prices and profits, 1933 and 1934	515

CHAPTER I

COMPETITION IN TRANSITION

I. Introduction—II. The general causes of the growing importance of monopoly elements in industry—*A*. Technological conditions—*B*. Social policy—III. The general influences affecting the operation of the industrial system—*A*. Conditions of sale—*B*. Conditions of production—IV. Conclusion.

I. INTRODUCTION

Competitive capitalism was given a protracted and thorough trial in the United States after the Civil War. Although legal institutions were framed with a broad and consistent regard for the assumptions of competition, capitalism failed to preserve its competitive quality. The National Industrial Recovery Act of 1933 was a belated recognition of this failure.

In spite of notable caveats,[1] economic writings analyzing the implications of competition were read as beguiling briefs for laissez faire. Competition assured to buyers a supply of goods at prices just high enough to cover costs; it induced an allocation of resources between different uses that ensured the most efficient satisfaction of demands; the competitive struggle eliminated the least fit from each industry. It is true that the endorsement of competition meant the acceptance of the existing distribution of incomes, but this difficulty was easily swallowed; people must be allowed to enjoy the fruits of their competitive efforts to satisfy the consumer (with purchasing power). In its more dynamic aspects the competitive society was under the greatest possible urge to improve the methods of turning resources to the satisfaction of demand (backed by purchasing power).

Adam Smith's "obvious and simple system of natural liberty" has, however, never been fully accepted; slavery and the tariff constituted early and important exceptions. But exceptions soon began to increase in number; no amount of arguing that certain industries are "affected with a public interest" can conceal a growing doubt concerning the capacity of competition to survive or, where it survives, to produce satisfactory results. Even in

[1] *Cf.* MARSHALL, *Industry and Trade*, 736.

the larger fields regarded by the Supreme Court as not "affected with a public interest" the fruits of competition failed to ripen. At least as early as the eighties competition gave place to pools and agreements in the meat, steel, salt, whisky, coal, cordage, explosives, and a number of other industries. Single corporations secured control of a very large part of all the business in the sugar, starch, oil, tobacco, and many branches of the steel fabricating industries. Some of these corporations attained their position by methods both dramatic and ruthless. These phenomena were regarded, however, as manifestations of pathological tendencies in a few individuals. The possibility that they arose out of contradictions deep in the very nature of competitive individualism was ignored. It was said that "there ought to be a law about it" and there was.

For forty years the Supreme Court, armed with the phrases "restraint of trade" and "monopoly," sought to compel normal (in the sense of competitive) behavior. It sank into a bog of doubt concerning "intent,"[1] taking its frail gauges of normality with it. There bubbled up a few dicta that "mere size is no offense,"[2] that "the fact that competitors may see fit in the exercise of their own judgment to follow the prices of another manufacturer does not establish any suppression of competition or show any sinister domination,"[3] and that the stability of a price for some ten years must be ignored because "there is a danger of deception in generalities."[4] The court was doubtless wise not to look where it was going; any attempt to guide industrial evolution would have raised a multitude of problems with which it was both unwilling and unqualified to deal. The economists turned away to a tedious and fruitless analysis of the court's verbal rationalizations of its decisions. Meanwhile fear of price cutting has become increasingly pervasive. With increasing frequency price cutting is referred to as "cutthroat." Sellers have sought to establish relationships immune from attack under the law and yet capable of facilitating the making of prices without resort to short-term price cutting.

Only recently has it been realized that judgment of industries by reference to the categories of competition and monopoly is

---

[1] *Cf.* BURNS, "The Process of Industrial Concentration," *Quart. Jour. Econ.*, 47: 277 (1933).
[2] U.S. v. U.S. Steel Corp., 251 U.S. 417 (1920).
[3] U.S. v. International Harvester Co., 274 U.S. 693 (1927).
[4] U.S. v. U.S. Steel Corp., 251 U.S. 417 (1920).

impossible. Monopolies in the crude sense of single sellers of products for which there are no nearby substitutes are extremely rare. On the other hand industries in which there is more, and sometimes many more, than one seller fail to display all the qualities of competition. Attempts to resolve the problem by unearthing agreements concerning output and prices quickly disintegrate into detective work and innuendo; if business men have one tenth of the foresight attributed to them by economists they see to it that there is no written evidence of collusion. But, apart from collusion, business men seeking to maximize profits in the most rational and far-sighted manner no longer invariably choose lines of conduct calculated to yield the fruits of competition. Elements of monopoly have always been interwoven with competition but the monopoly elements have increased in importance. They can no longer be regarded as occasional and relatively unimportant aberrations from competition. They are such an organic part of the industrial system that it is useless to hope that they can be removed by law and the industrial system thus brought into conformity with the ideal of perfect competition.

The growth in relative importance of monopoly elements suggests three broad questions. Why have these monopoly elements thus developed? How does the resulting imperfectly or monopolistically competitive system work? How should the policy of social control be changed? This last question falls into two parts. What should be the objectives of policy? What are the most suitable means of seeking to attain these objectives? These are the questions with which the present work is concerned. The first of them will be discussed in the present chapter and the remaining two in those that follow.

II. THE GENERAL CAUSES OF THE GROWING IMPORTANCE OF MONOPOLY ELEMENTS IN INDUSTRY

Modifications of, or departures from competitive behavior cannot be discussed without a definition of competition. If competition is the opposite of monopoly, in the sense of a single seller, it means a market in which there is a number of sellers. But how many? And is there any requirement other than the number of sellers? Must there be a tendency for all sellers to sell at the same price at the same time and place? Obviously this last requirement is inadequate because uniformity of prices may arise out of agreement. In a perfect market, however, a slight increase in price by one firm must result in all business passing to other sellers.[1] Buyers consider prices alone and immediately learn of, and act upon, differences between sellers. The product need not be homogeneous nor need prices be uniform. Slight changes in the customary differential must, however, shift all business. It is also necessary that a slight change in output by one firm shall, although it must somewhat affect the price in the market, have a negligible effect upon the sales revenue of any one firm. The greater the number of sellers the more likely is the market to satisfy this condition. The necessary number depends, however, upon the elasticity of the total demand for the product, and the conditions of cost (which determine the reactions of other firms to the small change in price). Competition requires, therefore, a number of firms but a number varying with these conditions. A seller operating in a perfect competitive market takes no account of the effect of changes in his production policy upon the price of the product; he selects his production policy with regard to the market price and sells all his product; he acts as if the demand for his product were infinitely elastic.[2]

Few actual markets can meet these severe conditions. While it is important to realize that many producers are, by reference to these criteria, monopolists, it is convenient to group sellers together in order to analyze their mutual interaction. This grouping is made by reference to an arbitrarily defined "commodity"[3] of which the "product" of each manufacturer is a subvariety. The "market" thus constituted is imperfect; each seller is a monopolist for whose product there is a fairly nearby substitute.

In these markets changes in output by a seller not only affect the price at which the product is sold; the change in price also perceptibly affects the seller's revenue from sales. He acts as a monopolist in that, when deciding whether to change his output, he takes account of the price at which outputs of different sizes are likely to be sold.

He can pursue this policy only where an increase in price fails to reduce his sales to zero and a reduction fails to attract to

---

[1] ROBINSON, JOAN, "What is Perfect Competition?" *Quart. Jour. Econ.*, 49: 104 (1934).
[2] *Cf.* ROBINSON, JOAN, *The Economics of Imperfect Competition*, Chap. VII, and CHAMBERLIN, *The Theory of Monopolistic Competition*, Chap. II.
[3] *Cf.* ROBINSON, JOAN, *op. cit.*, 5, where a commodity is defined as one "bounded on all sides by a gap in the chain of substitutes."

him all the available business (which would frequently be more than he could accept). In taking account of the relations between output and price he aims at the greatest possible excess of revenue over the costs that must be incurred to secure that revenue. Within short periods of time he may be unable to obtain any profit, i.e., his best price may be one that falls short of average total costs. If he has unused plant no additional costs are incurred for plant when output is increased. In considering the addition to revenue resulting from the sale of another unit, however, he must allow for the lower price that will be obtained for the units already being sold. The most profitable output is such that the production of another unit would involve equal *additions* to both cost and revenue.[1]

Over longer periods failure of prices to cover total costs makes for a reduction in the number of firms; ability to make abnormally high profits attracts additional firms. But although total costs are covered by prices in the long run, firms produce less than the output which could be produced at the lowest average cost (*i.e.*, there will be unused capacity); prices are high enough to yield a normal return upon this unused as well as upon the used plant.[2] A reduction in price and an increase in output would increase costs more than revenue. If entry to the industry can be restricted in any way, prices may of course be maintained upon a level yielding abnormally high profits. But it is important to note that, in the absence of any such restrictions and, therefore, in the presence of a tendency to normal profits in the long run, plant may be less than fully utilized; resources are not even applied most efficiently to the satisfaction of the existing effective demand. It remains to discuss the extent to which business men behave in this way and the changes in conditions of demand and supply that have induced them to do so.

Just as a reduction in the number of sellers may prevent each from taking a purely competitive view, so also each of a small number of buyers is prevented from behaving competitively. The presence of a large number of sellers and a small number of buyers in the larger livestock and the tobacco leaf markets illustrates the difficulties of such situations. Buyers take into

---

[1] That is, marginal revenue equals marginal cost. *Cf.* ROBINSON, JOAN, *op. cit.*, Chap. III.

[2] ROBINSON, JOAN, *Economics of Imperfect Competition*, Chap. III; CHAMBERLIN, *The Theory of Monopolistic Competition*, 115. But see also KALDOR, "Market Imperfection and Excess Capacity," *Economica*, 2: 33 (1935).

account the direct effect of their buying policy upon market prices, and its indirect effect on prices through the reactions of their rivals thereto. The large interstate beef packers stated in response to the allegation that they shared the available supplies of livestock between them on an agreed basis[1] that they did not try recklessly to work up their percentages of livestock purchased, and argued that it would benefit no one if they did; it would merely cause an erratic market.[2] Each of the large packing houses was responsible for so large a proportion of the total purchases in the market that it could not ignore the direct and indirect effect of its decisions concerning the amount of livestock it would purchase upon the price at which it could obtain supplies. The reference by the packers to the avoidance of "reckless" attempts to improve their relative position in the industry suggests that they took account of the probable reactions of their rivals. Thus the smallness of the number of firms led to a policy which, however reasonable, was not competitive.

Contemplating the situation after the partition of the American Tobacco Company, under the Sherman Act, into four concerns (so far as the major tobacco products were concerned) the Federal Trade Commission asked[3] whether "true competition (can) be expected when four companies buy 90 per cent of the burley crop, when eight companies buy 76 per cent of the dark-fired crop, or when seven companies buy 80 per cent of the bright flue-cured crop?" By "holding off" the large buyers of tobacco are said to have "seesawed" the market.[4] A number of dealers believed very strongly that the price of tobacco leaf was seriously affected when large buyers used common agents.[5] The effect of this arrangement depends of course upon the extent to which it permitted the coordination of the buying policies of the manufacturers. If each made his own policy and used the buying agent

---

[1] See Chap. IV.

[2] SWIFT AND COMPANY, *Analysis and Criticism of the Federal Trade Commission's Report*, 28, 29. See also evidence offered by Morris and Company before a subcommittee of the Senate Committee on Agriculture and Forestry, pursuant to Senate Resolution 211, 1923, 1105.

[3] F.T.C., *Prices of Tobacco Products* 1922 (published as Senate Document 34, 69th Cong. 1st Sess.), 177.

[4] When the American Tobacco Company buyer withdrew from the Kentucky market in December, 1919, the Reynolds buyer made heavy purchases at lower prices. But when the American Tobacco Company reentered the market the Reynolds buyer was advised to "take things a little quiet for a few days, as it might have a tendency to steady things down to a lower level. . . . It might be a good time to seesaw the market" (*ibid.*, 181).

[5] F.T.C., *The Tobacco Industry*, 1920, 8, 88.

as an instrument for executing specific orders, the arrangement could have no effect upon prices. But conditions in the market are such that if the agent advised the manufacturers concerning market prospects, or communicated to them the buying policies of rivals, or facilitated the coordination of their policies, prices might be affected.[1]

The concentration of the business of milk distribution in many large cities in a very few hands has been accompanied by a concentration of selling in the hands of cooperative marketing associations of farmers with the result that the numbers on both the buying and the selling side of the market have been so far reduced that a double reason exists for the avoidance of price competition. In consequence of the impossibility of securing the determination of prices by competition the price of milk in Chicago has been determined by arbitration between distributors and producers since 1917.[2] In 1933 provision was made for the state control of milk prices in New York and New Jersey.[3] In 1933 the

[1] Sales of tobacco leaf are conducted by auction at a few points, and within only a few months of the year, and leaf is far from standardized in quality. The buying policy of a manufacturer over any short period is influenced by the anticipated level of prices over the remainder of the buying season; estimates of these future prices must be based upon the estimated demand to be satisfied during the same period. In the making of such estimates the manufacturers employing a common buying agent would have the benefit of the same point of view when they sought the advice of their agent. Further, some of the principals might receive from the agent knowledge of the instructions and general policy of others of his principals. The buying policy of each manufacturer would under such circumstances be expected to be somewhat different from his policy where he employed an agent separate from the agents of other manufacturers. The distribution of one manufacturer's buying over time might then be arranged to avoid clash with some of the other buyers by their taking turns in "holding off" the market. But even without such arrangements manufacturers would not go into the market on a particular day determined to buy a prescribed quantity whatever the price, and irrespective of the amount offered for sale; in so far as a rise in price causes some buyers to postpone their purchases, a redistribution of demand over time is to be expected without any disclosures by the brokers employed by a number of principals. The commission makes no reference to such disclosures by buying agents. The agent instructed to buy a prescribed quantity at a fixed average or maximum price over a period of time by two or more principals must, however, where instructed to buy the same grade for two or more manufacturers, determine the allocation of his purchases of that grade between them (ibid., 86). In so far as the instructions to the agent leave a margin of discretion, there is no doubt that his buying policy may be somewhat influenced by his knowledge of the amount to be purchased on behalf of all his principals. Whether the agent discloses the instructions of other manufacturers and the principal makes the decision as to buying policy, or whether the agent is in possession of discretionary orders to buy similar qualities, some adjustment of the buying of one manufacturer to that of another is possible, if not inevitable.

[2] DUNCAN, "The Chicago Milk Enquiry," *Jour. Polit. Econ.*, 26: 325; University of Illinois Agricultural Experiment Station Bulletin 269, *The Marketing of Milk in the Chicago Dairy District*, 1925.

[3] Laws of New York, Chap. 158 (1933); Laws of New Jersey, Chap. 169 (1933). By 1935 there were milk control boards in 22 states.

federal government, exercising its powers under the Agricultural Adjustment Act, 1933, placed all those handling milk in the Chicago metropolitan milk shed under federal license and established a minimum retail price for milk in the Chicago district, against the resistance of the Independent Milk Producers Association of Northern Illinois.[1]

A. Technological Causes of the Decline in the Number of Sellers

This difference in attitude between the perfectly and the imperfectly competitive business turns upon its size in relation to its market. It is a commonplace that the number of firms in many industries has been falling. In many markets, e.g., those for steel, automobiles, rubber tires, sugar, corn products, electrical products, air transportation, agricultural implements, the number is already too small for sellers to ignore the effect of changes in their output upon the price of the commodity and, therefore, upon their revenue. The reduction of the number of firms and their increasing size over the past half century are clearly due, in part, to the use of methods of production which are economical only if large quantities are produced under a single organization. These economies arise from plant reorganization, or from the reorganization of management or selling methods. The increased volume of business necessary to permit the utilization of these methods of production has been attained in part by price cutting; the largest firms, however, have more frequently attained their present size either by direct attacks upon rivals in the form of temporary or local price cutting aimed at destroying them, by defaming their products and the like, or by mergers. Whether or not such practices are approved, they may serve to adjust the productive system to the utilization of more economical methods of production, and they may be preferred to price competition because buyers are slow to respond to price cutting. Such methods of growth may, however, also be resorted to as a means of attaining a size larger than the most economical with the object of securing control of prices; they may merely satisfy the desire for size on the part of the managers. At least it is clear that, under a system once broadly competitive, methods of producing many commodities have changed in favor of the large firm; the very competition that induces the most economical utilization of the means of

[1] *New York Times*, Aug. 1, 1933.

production has induced the survival of firms so large and so few that perfect competition itself no longer survives in a number of industries.

B. *Social Policy and the Decline in the Number of Sellers*

1. CORPORATION LAWS

Although social policy is assumed to have been aimed in general at the maintenance of competition, it has in many ways reinforced the movement away from competition. The policies of states in the exercise of their powers to control the forms of corporate organization have fundamentally changed the environment in which price and production policies are made. The widespread adoption of the corporate form for organizing production has eliminated individual ownership from considerable portions of the industrial and commercial field.[1] Decisions concerning the utilization of the means of production no longer rest with those who "own" them and, therefore, receive the whole profits resulting from skillful and fortunate decisions, and suffer the whole losses resulting from unskillful or unfortunate decisions. The forces playing upon those who make policy within each group are no longer identical with those influencing the individual entrepreneur.

Corporation law has most directly contributed to the passing of competition, however, by providing for the transfer of business to small numbers of larger firms. This facilitation of the organization of large units has not only permitted the utilization of improved methods of production calling for units of large size; it has also facilitated the formation of units larger than those necessary to permit the most economical methods of production. Political power, having been in part illusory and in part distasteful, economic power has been sought. Its attainment may lead to attempts to overcome the inefficiencies of excessive size. Energy, initiative, and equipment are directed to making these aggregations of economic resources as efficient as smaller ones; if these efforts are successful, the tendency to smaller numbers of sellers is reinforced.[2]

---

[1] *Cf.* BERLE and MEANS, *The Corporation and Private Property, passim.*
[2] If the efficiency of the large unit is improved so that it yields normal profits upon a capital which does not include promotion profits, the large unit has been rendered economical, but no more so than the formerly existing small ones. Unless the changes introduced can be applied to smaller firms or to firms in other industries these activities of the management have resulted in the application of part of the aggregate social fund of skill and knowledge available for increasing the efficiency of production to no more economically valuable an end than increasing the range of

Corporate units tend to increase in size partly because of internal tendencies to expansion and partly because of external tendencies to grow by accretion. The separation within the group of the functions of management from those of ownership, and the concentration of the former in a few hands, have resulted in fact in a large share of profits being retained in the business; the "owners" have little opportunity to dispose of these profits as they would if the profit were all distributed in dividends; 29.4 per cent of their net income was retained within the larger corporations during the period 1922 to 1927.[1] This retention may be intended to avoid shortages of liquid resources in periods of restricted business or to permit the continued payment of dividends in the absence of adequate current profits.[2] But it also facilitates expansion without the necessity of issuing new securities; those managers who find size attractive can satisfy their desire without having to submit their plans to the test of the capital market. Mergers offer similar opportunities for satisfying the desire for size. They usually involve either the flotation of new securities or the exchange of securities with the owners of the corporation to be absorbed; investors in times of good business take such a very optimistic attitude toward the profitability of mergers 'that growth by accretion in this way is facilitated. Finally, the joining of corporation with corporation offers such large profits to those who arrange the matter that the corporation laws have provided a positive inducement to increase the size and reduce the number of firms in many industries.

---

the size of the most economical firm in the industry. If a normal return is obtained upon the capital of the consolidation *including* promoter's profits, these profits have stimulated an improvement of industrial organization; the methods thus developed would yield abnormally high profits upon a capital that did not include promotion profits. But even these improvements yield benefits only to promoters unless rivals are able to utilize them without resort to promoters, *i.e.*, if the rivals resort to price competition to obtain additional business.

In fact mergers have in the past often proved less profitable immediately after their formation than their constituent units had been immediately before their absorption (*cf.* DEWING, *The Financial Policy of Corporations*, IV, 224 *ff.*). Moreover Professor Dewing found as a result of a study of the profits of 29 industrial consolidations that the median aggregate earnings of the constituent companies exceeded by 6 per cent the median earnings of the consolidations during the tenth year of life "when the consolidation might be expected to have worked out its salvation after the addition of improvements and extensions" (*ibid.*, IV, 225). *Cf.* also DEWING, "A Statistical Test of the Success of Consolidations," *Quart. Jour. Econ.*, 36: 84. An inconclusive attempt to study the success of consolidations was also made by the N.I.C.B. (National Industrial Conference Board) in *Mergers in Industry*, Chaps. III and IV.

[1] MEANS, "The Large Corporation," *Amer. Econ. Rev.*, 21: 29 (1931).
[2] That is, stockholders are being converted into low-grade bondholders.

2. PATENT LAWS

The law with regard to patents rests upon a departure from competition. The prospect of monopoly profits protected by law for a prescribed period is held out as a bait to encourage the improvement of methods of production. The contribution of the patent law to the decline of price competition has passed far beyond the limits suggested by this principle. The owners of some patents have, by the exclusive exploitation of their rights, secured legal protection for the establishment of manufacturing units so large that they were impregnable by the time the patent expired, e.g., the Singer Sewing Machine Company,[1] the Aluminum Corporation,[2] the United Shoe Machinery Company.[3] The American Can Company[4] and the former American Tobacco Company[5] secured control of all the patents on the manufacture of the machinery they used. Patent protection has also determined the development of the motion picture, washing machine,[6] envelope, steel wire,[7] photographic materials,[8] cash register,[9] and Pullman car[10] industries.

The patent law itself may prolong the protection of the monopolist. Patents upon improvements cannot be exploited without license from the holder of the basic patent; those who patent improvements can often market their patents only by selling them to the holder of the basic patent, who can secure them at a relatively low price. The holder of the basic patent has a great advantage over any rivals who may arise after the basic patent has expired[11] because no rival can offer a product carrying all the most recent improvements. The United Shoe Machinery Company, for instance, has dominated the field in its products although the basic patents have long since expired. The General Electric Company is alleged to have maintained its control of the market in electric lamps after the expiration of the basic patents

---

[1] F.T.C., *House Furnishings Industries*, III, 155.
[2] U.S. v. Aluminum Corp., *Petition in District Court of Western Pennsylvania*, 31. The corporation's patents expired in 1909. F.T.C., *House Furnishings Industries*, III, 90.
[3] VAUGHAN, *Economics of Our Patent System*, 74.
[4] U.S. v. American Can Co., *Summary of Evidence*, 118; VAUGHAN, *op. cit.*, 85.
[5] COMMISSIONER OF CORPORATIONS, *The Tobacco Industry*, I, 66.
[6] F.T.C., *House Furnishings Industries*, III, 26.
[7] VAUGHAN, *op. cit.*, 77.
[8] *ibid.*, 90–97.
[9] *ibid.*, 100.
[10] *loc. cit.*
[11] *Cf.* VAUGHAN, *op. cit.*, 72

through its patent on the process for frosting lamps.[1] The Standard Oil Company of New Jersey, however, has transferred a patent upon the hydrogenation process of breaking down crude oil to a company controlled by the owners of about 80 per cent of the crude oil refining capacity of the country;[2] this policy is in marked contrast with those of patent owners in the industries just mentioned, partly, perhaps, because of the size and financial resources of the rivals to the patent owner.

While pooling agreements concerning output and prices have been held, until recently,[3] to contravene the anti-trust laws, patents have been pooled.[4] Pooling competing patents and licensing them with covenants concerning the price of the product was formerly upheld,[5] largely on the ground that patents were, in any event, grants of monopoly. Later, however, agreements to maintain the price of products made under patent were condemned[6] and more far-reaching attempts to control the trade in such products were held to contravene the Sherman Law.[7] More recently, however, the pooling of a number of competing patents concerning methods of "cracking" gasoline has been approved, partly because the court approved the pooling of complementary patents (which those concerned were not), and partly because there were "cracking" patents outside the pool.[8] The Radio Corporation of America acquired at its formation[9] exclusive divisible rights to sell and use the radio devices covered by practically all the patents covering radio devices of any importance (some 2,000). By May, 1930, this pool included some 3,500

[1] Charges by Senator Nye in *New York Times*, Jan. 4, 1934.
[2] *New York Times*, July 14, 1930.
[3] U.S. v. Appalachian Coals, Inc., 288 U.S. 344 (1933).
[4] See VAUGHAN, *op. cit.*, Chap. II. Pools of this type have been organized in relation to sewing machines, spring-toothed harrows, the seeding and processing of raisins, pneumatic straw stackers, liquid door checks, enameled bathtubs, the manufacture, distribution, and exhibition of motion pictures, coaster brakes for bicycles and motorcycles, the manufacture of gasoline by cracking processes, and the manufacture and use of radio devices.
[5] National Harrow Co. v. Bement, 186 U.S. 70; U.S. Seeded Raisin Co. v. Griffin and Skelly Co., 126 Fed. 364 (1903); Indiana Manufacturing Co. v. J. I. Case Threshing Machine Co., 154 Fed. 365 (1907).
[6] Blount Manufacturing Co. v. Yale and Towne Manufacturing Co., 166 Fed. 555.
[7] Standard Sanitary Manufacturing Co. v. U.S., 226 U.S. 20; U.S. v. New Departure Manufacturing Co., 204 Fed. 107; Motion Picture Patents Co. v. Universal Film Manufacturing Co., 243 U.S. 502 (1917).
[8] Standard Oil Co. of Indiana v. U.S., 283 U.S. 163 (1931).
[9] The Radio Corporation of America was organized in 1919 and then owned largely by the General Electric Company, the Westinghouse Electric and Manufacturing Company, the American Telephone and Telegraph Company, the United Fruit Company, and the former stockholders of the American Marconi Company.

patents[1] and it was attacked by the Attorney General on the ground that it restricted competition between members of the pool, as well as between them and their rivals.[2] The corporation and its principal stockholders denied the illegality of the pool but agreed to make the pooled patents available to all manufacturers on equal terms.[3] The General Electric, Westinghouse, American Telephone and Telegraph, and United Fruit companies were thus deprived of their exclusive advantages. A consent decree was signed which was expected to enable independent manufacturers to obtain patent licenses separately from each member of the pool[4] and also directed the ultimate complete divorce of the General Electric and Westinghouse companies from the Radio Corporation.[5] The former policy of permitting the pooling of competing patents facilitated the control of output and prices; even the power to fix royalty charges gives power over these matters. It is evident, however, that this policy has been modified; the courts have become increasingly critical of patent pools.

Restrictions upon pools suggest the consolidation of the ownership of patents in a single company. The United Shoe Machinery Company is the most outstanding example of this device. By mergers and otherwise[6] it secured control of most of the patents on

---

[1] Suit filed May 13, 1930, in Federal District Court for the District of Delaware (*United States Daily*, July 2, 1931); report of Attorney General to the Judiciary Committee of the U.S. Senate (*United States Daily*, Mar. 25, 1932); statement by Owen D. Young *New York Times*, May 14, 1930. It was stated that at that date about 95 per cent in value of all radio receiving apparatus was manufactured by licensees of the Radio Corporation of America patent pool; these licensees paid royalties of 7½ per cent of the value of all radio apparatus sold by them, with a minimum of $100,000 a year for manufacturers of apparatus and $50,000 a year for manufacturers of vacuum tubes. In 1929 the Radio Corporation received more than seven million dollars from this source. This royalty payment was "intended to represent the fair contribution of the licensees to the expense of the research and the cost of the original patents. It was intended to be less than the royalty payment would have been had the patents been in scattered hands." All the licensees had the benefit of all current research by the Radio Corporation and its associated companies as the licenses covered all new inventions. (*loc. cit.*)

[2] Release by Department of Justice, *United States Daily*, July 2, 1931. *Cf.* also Amended Petition in the Federal District Court for the District of Delaware, Mar. 7, 1932, *New York Times*, May 14, 1930, Mar. 8, 1932.

[3] *United States Daily*, July 3, 1931, Mar. 25, 1932.

[4] U.S. v. Radio Corp. of America *et al.*, Decree in Federal District Court of the District of Delaware, Nov. 21, 1932. See also *Preliminary Report on Communications Companies* (House Report 1273, 73d Cong. 2d Sess. (1934), 118, *United States Daily*, Nov. 22, 1932).

[5] *Cf. United States Daily*, Nov. 22, 1932.

[6] The United Shoe Machinery Company was formed in 1899 when it absorbed seven companies, each holding patents which gave them considerable, but rarely

shoe machinery. Under the protection of these patents, and by requiring the lessees of its patented machines to use them only in combination with other machines made by the company, it secured control of 95 per cent of the business in shoe machinery in the United States.[1] The Supreme Court decided that this consolidation did not contravene the Sherman Law,[2] apparently because it believed that the consolidation had increased efficiency, that the constituent firms made non-competing groups of machines (which was not the fact), and because the machines were patented. When efficiency and the prospect of maintaining a competitive number of firms in the industry conflict, the court has usually chosen the former.

In the absence of pooling or consolidation, patent rights have been used to exclude rivals from the market in other products purchased by the buyer or lessee of the patented product. The sellers of patented machines were formerly upheld in requiring the buyers to obtain supplies for use in connection with the machine only from the seller of the machine.[3] Considerably later, however, the seller of a patented motion picture projector was not upheld in requiring that the machine be used only with films leased by the patentee.[4] More recently the Radio Corporation of America, the General Electric Company, and the Westinghouse Electric Company were enjoined from licensing the right to manufacture and sell radio receiving sets made under patents held by them conditionally upon all the tubes needed for the initial equipment of the sets being bought from the Radio Corporation, the patents on these tubes having expired.[5] The Supreme Court upheld the United Shoe Machinery Company's policy of leasing its machinery with tying clauses concerning machines for performing other

---

complete, control of the market in one or more of the machines used for shoe manufacturing. Subsequently it acquired 57 more businesses engaged in the shoe machinery industry and contracted to secure the patents of professional inventors and its own employees.
 [1] U.S. v. United Shoe Machinery Co., 264 Fed. 138, 163 (1920).
 [2] U.S. v. Winslow, 227 U.S. 202 (1913); confirmed in U.S. v. United Shoe Machinery Co., 247 U.S. 32 (1918).
 [3] Heaten-Peninsular Button Fastener Co. v. Eureka Specialty Co., 77 Fed. 288 (1896); Henry v. A. B. Dick Co., 224 U.S. 1 (1912).
 [4] Motion Picture Patents Co. v. Universal Film Manufacturing Co. et al., 243 U.S. 502 (1917) (this decision was made without reference to the Clayton Act which the court regarded as merely confirming them in their view).
 [5] De Forrest Radio Co. v. Radio Corp. of America et al., 24 Fed. (2d) 565 (1928), 28 Fed. (2d) 257 (1928), 35 Fed. (2d) 962 (1929). Certiorari refused by Supreme Court, 283 U.S. 847 (1931). F.T.C., *Annual Report*, 1928, 48. See also terms of amicable settlement in *New York Times*, Sept. 23, 1931.

processes in the manufacture of shoes[1] largely because the patented commodity was leased and not sold.

Tying clauses have also been used to secure control of unpatented articles which have no necessary relation in use to the patented article. In 1911 the General Electric Company consented to a decree providing *inter alia* that it should cease selling tungsten lamps, which were covered by patent, on condition that all carbon lamps (which were not covered by patent) were bought from them.[2] The Clayton Act of 1914 prohibited the leasing or selling of goods or machinery, whether patented or unpatented, on condition that the lessee or purchaser neither used nor dealt in the commodities of competitors of the seller or lessor where such provisions would substantially lessen competition or tend to create a monopoly;[3] the contracts of the United Shoe Machinery Company were ultimately held to contravene this provision.[4] Tying clauses of this type have also been attacked by the Federal Trade Commission in the exercise of its power to prevent unfair competition.[5] Thus exploitation of a patent right by extending the application of the grant to other commodities more or less closely allied with the subject of the patent, while formerly regarded as a legitimate exploitation of a legal monopoly, has been subjected to increasing restriction.

Competitive conditions are also affected by the rights of patentees to "put their patents to sleep." Policy in this matter has also changed during the past 35 years. Until about 1898 patents were required to be utilized if the right was to be preserved.[6] In 1896, however, it was held[7] for the first time that the suppression of a patent was within the rights of the patentee, and the principle was acknowledged by the Supreme Court in 1908[8] and again in 1916.[9] Patents have been "put to sleep" by the

[1] U.S. v. United Shoe Machinery Co., 247 U.S. 33, 66 (1918) (this case was instituted before the passage of the Clayton Act of 1914).
[2] U.S. v. General Electric Co.; Decree of Circuit Court in U.S. Department of Justice, *Decrees and Judgments in Federal Anti-Trust Cases*, 271.
[3] Clayton Act, 1914, Sec. 3.
[4] U.S. v. United Shoe Machinery Co., 258 U.S. 455.
[5] F.T.C. Act, 1914, Sec. 5.
[6] Hoe v. Knap, 27 Fed. 204 (1896); Evart Manufacturing Co. v. Baldwin Cycle Chain Co., 91 Fed. 262 (1898).
[7] Heaten-Peninsular Button Fastener Co. v. Eureka Specialty Co., 77 Fed. 288 (1896). "His title is exclusive, and so clearly within the constitutional provisions in respect of private property that he is neither bound to use his discovery himself, nor permit others to use it."
[8] Continental Paper Bag Co. v. Eastern Bag Co., 210 U.S. 405 (1908).
[9] Motion Picture Patents Co. v. Universal Film Co. *et al.*, 243 U.S. 502 (1917).

American Tobacco Company, the United Shoe Machinery Company, the American Steel and Wire Company, the General Electric Company, and the American Bell Telephone Company;[1] patents covering the automatic telephone and paper bag making machinery were suppressed.[2] If the patent upon a new method of production is acquired by a new firm (which calculates that it can reduce prices and still cover total costs of production by the new method), prices are likely to be reduced to that level. As the demand for the output of the existing producers will be diminished as well as the price, a large producer can afford to pay up to the capitalized value of these threatened losses in order to acquire the patent. Unless total costs of production by the new method exceed the marginal costs of production by the old, the utilization of the new method will be postponed and prices maintained. The buyer of the patent is less well off than if he had not been compelled to buy the patent; but he may be better off than he would have been had the patent fallen into the hands of a producer not already committed to the old methods. If he does utilize the new patent the price of his product will probably be reduced; but the costs of production by new methods are always uncertain and a firm already committed to old methods is apt to be biased in favor of continuing to use the methods with which it is familiar. Thus a law intended to encourage the improvement of methods of production is interpreted so as to permit the obstruction of the utilization of new knowledge in order to protect those who have committed themselves to methods now obsolete. This difficulty arises out of the fact that producers must commit themselves for such long periods of time.[3]

Finally, the high cost of patent litigation places in the hands of financially powerful units a very effective weapon of attack upon small firms. They may be expelled, forced to merge, or prevented from exploiting patents which they have obtained but the validity of which they cannot afford to have confirmed by the courts; one million dollars are said to have been spent in preventing infringement of the patent of the Edison incandescent lamp.[4] Threats of patent suits are said to have assisted the National

---

[1] VAUGHAN, *op. cit.*, 73, 170, 172.
[2] VAUGHAN, *op. cit.*, 168, 169 *ff.*
[3] Patents may be taken out on a number of alternative methods of achieving the same end and all but one suppressed in order to secure undisturbed exploitation of the most efficient (VAUGHAN, *op. cit.*, 168).
[4] VAUGHAN, *op. cit.*, 72, 181.

Harrow Company, the National Cash Register Company, the National Binding Company, and the Eastman Kodak Company[1] to maintain their positions in their respective industries. Thus the patent law may enable a firm to obtain a powerful position in an industry, or to maintain such a position, by hampering the activities of smaller units. Even where patent holders are of considerable size, if they hold patents similar to those of rivals they may prefer a merger to patent litigation.[2] The expansion of the Eastman Kodak Company and the United Shoe Machinery Company was in part due to this cause. The high cost of patent litigation makes the holding and protection of patents a business possible only for large and well-financed corporations.[3] It sometimes tends to the consolidation of patent holdings, thus increasing and extending the monopolistic control granted by the patent law and inducing the emergence of large firms which, even apart from the patent law, cannot be expected to behave competitively.[4]

The patent law may also assist a manufacturer who has already attained considerable size to increase his business still further. By resorting to a device analogous to exclusive dealing, he may obtain a covenant from those supplying patented machinery not to supply that machinery to rivals. Large firms such as the Continental Wallpaper Company,[5] the American Tobacco Company,[6] the National Electric Lamp Company,[7] the American Can Company,[8] have adopted these tactics.[9]

3. ANTI-TRUST LAWS

None of the attempts at social control of industry has been more directly aimed at the preservation of competition than the anti-trust laws. Yet they have manifestly failed to achieve their

---

[1] VAUGHAN, *op. cit.*, 149–152, and N.I.C.B., *Public Regulation of Competitive Practices*, 181 ff.
[2] VAUGHAN, *op. cit.*, 70 ff.
[3] See VAUGHAN, *op. cit.*, 72.
[4] It is reported that the American Rolling Mill Company leased patents upon a new process for manufacturing steel to its rivals rather than incur the cost of expensive legal protection for them (FRASER and DORIOT, *Analyzing Our Industries*, 271).
[5] Continental Wallpaper Co. v. Voigt, 212 U.S. 227 (1909).
[6] COMMISSIONER OF CORPORATIONS, *The Tobacco Industry*, I, 67, 266.
[7] SEAGER and GULICK, *Trust and Corporation Problems*, 403.
[8] VAUGHAN, *op. cit.*, 87.
[9] The American Tin Plate Company sought to protect its position when it was making 90 per cent of all the tin plate in the country by making exclusive contracts with the manufacturers of rolls and rolling machinery (JONES, *The Trust Problem in the United States*, 193).

objective. They have reacted mainly upon the manner in which business men have responded to the underlying forces discouraging price competition.[1]

Until 1933[2] cooperation between producers to determine output and prices was illegal, no matter how small a proportion of an industry was affected. Other forms of concentration, such as resort to price cutting or sales promotion, the establishment of large corporate units or price leadership, were within the law provided the motives directing their use were acceptable.[3] This condemnation of price and output agreements tended to induce the development of large units wherever the dangers of price cutting were serious.

Ultimate reference to the criterion of motive leads the courts to regard very drastic price cutting as indicative of wrongful motives, with the result that they have, in some measure, accepted the view of the business men fearful of price competition.[4] Firms, realizing that larger-scale production would diminish their costs, may operate in a market so imperfectly organized that a larger volume of business can be obtained only by brief and drastic price cutting or moderate price cutting sustained for long periods of low prices and profits. Where the former is less costly but is likely to induce prosecution by the Attorney General, firms may continue to operate on less than the most efficient scale. They may resort to methods of non-price competition which, however morally repugnant, may be economically justified because they are the cheapest methods of attracting sufficient business to permit operation on a more economical scale. If these methods are regarded as evidence of wrongful motives or proscribed as

---

[1] The claim that price competition has been kept alive and has been destructive has probably some validity in fields in which the devices permitted by the law are inappropriate.

[2] A cooperative selling agency for soft coal was held not to contravene the Sherman Law (U.S. v. Appalachian Coals, Inc., 288 U.S. 344 (1933)).

[3] Cf. BURNS, "The Process of Industrial Concentration," Quart. Jour. Econ., 47: 303 (1933).

[4] In one of the most carefully reasoned decisions under the Sherman Act, but one which did not reach the Supreme Court, the dangers of short-run price cutting and the folly of overvaluing its advantages to the consumer were emphasized. "While the statute relies upon competition as a proper stimulus to the maintenance of industrial advance and as the chief protection to the consumer it takes a long view not a short. . . . It does not identify permanent capacity (i.e., efficiency) with the inability (? ability) to induce a transitory or local appeal to customers. Its presupposition is that there may well be competitors capable in the end of giving a service which will serve the public as well as their neighbors who may yet succumb to concerted competition apparently more serviceable but only because it is temporary and is put forward with no purpose of universal application" (U.S. v. Corn Products Refining Co. et al, 234 Fed. 1012 (1916)).

"unfair" under the Federal Trade Commission Act, the larger size must be sought by merger.

The extent of judicial interference with industrial consolidation has been small, but competitive conditions have been influenced by what business men and lawyers have believed to be the attitude of the courts to the permissible concentration of business in the hands of a single firm. After the Supreme Court had refused to partition the United States Steel Corporation, which had control of approximately one half of the business in its industry, there was a general belief (not justified by the text of the decision of the Supreme Court) that no firm possessing one half of the business in its industry need fear intervention by the Attorney General which would be upheld by the courts. To proceed beyond this degree of control was to enter upon a field of uncertainty. In an industry in which the most economical production could be obtained only by a firm controlling more than this percentage, this supposed attitude of the courts caused difficulties, more particularly where any large firm was equipped to deal with more business than it was in fact obtaining. Considerations of economy suggested a larger size, but regard for the assumed judicial policy discouraged the pursuit of economy. Where the large firm was already much more economical than the smaller firms in the industry, it was on the horns of a dilemma. If it reduced its prices to pass on the economies of large-scale production, it was likely to kill off some of its rivals and so increase its percentage of business as to risk being held to infringe the law. If it did not pursue this policy, it was likely to obtain high profits and attract unwelcome criticism.[1] Morris and Company claimed that continued pressure to prevent the large meat packers from increasing their control over the industry, if not to disintegrate them altogether, had tended to bring about a stable distribution of business between them.[2] The dictum of the Supreme Court that "the law does not make mere size an offense"[3] and its assent to the continued exist-

---

[1] It has been said that one such large firm made loans to prevent the failure of a smaller rival, although it knew that the loans were very unlikely to be repaid. The International Harvester Company for a time made parts for the machines of its rivals, the Avery, and Emerson-Brantingham companies, to enable brands which it had been required under the consent decree to transfer to them to be kept on the market, and these companies became indebted to the Harvester company in consequence (U.S. v. International Harvester Co., *Brief for the Harvester Co.*, 98).

[2] *Hearings on Senate Resolution* 211 before a subcommittee of the U.S. Senate Committee on Agriculture and Forestry, 1923, 1105.

[3] U.S. v. U.S. Steel Corp., 251 U.S. 417 (1920); reiterated in U.S. v. International Harvester Co., 274 U.S. 703 (1927) and U.S. v. Swift and Co. *et al.*, 268 U.S. 106, 116 (1931).

ence of the United States Steel Corporation (which controlled nearly half the business in rolled steel products) and of the International Harvester Company (with control of 64 per cent of the business in the industry in 1918)[1] have, however, diminished the importance of the anti-trust laws in this respect.

Where large concerns have been partitioned under the Sherman Law the courts have established three or four firms in each branch of the industry, as for instance when the American Tobacco Company and the DuPont de Nemours Company were partitioned. Other large concerns have been required to transfer to separate companies a small proportion of their business; such was the ultimate consequence of the prosecution of the International Harvester Company and the Corn Products Refining Company. Where only three or four large companies continue to exist, a régime approaching the competitive obviously cannot be expected; where the transfer of a small proportion of business permits the continued existence of a very large concern, or where failure to apply the anti-trust laws at all has the same effect, great differences in size of firms often result in the acceptance of the leadership of the large firm. The Supreme Court has explicitly stated that it cannot or will not interfere with such price leadership.[2]

The law has diverted the forces making for concentration of the control of economic resources in the direction of the merging of firm with firm to produce larger units. The merger provides a means of concentrating control of price and output policies where conditions have already arisen which cause price cutting to be costly to producers. It is now usually unnecessary for a firm to absorb all units in the industry. A firm securing a large proportion of all the business can influence the policies of its rivals; its superior size may enable it to compel rivals to accept its lead or rivals may be very willing to do so.[3] While the pool concentrates only those (very vital) functions of determining output and prices, the merger concentrates the whole range of the functions of the entrepreneur. The merger may for this reason permit economies of production unlikely to be made by a pool. Mergers may be used to remove troublesome price cutters and secure

---

[1] F.T.C., *The High Price of Farm Implements*, 1920, 679.
[2] "The fact that competitors may see fit in the exercise of their own judgment to follow the prices of another manufacturer does not establish any suppression of competition or show any sinister domination" (U.S. v. International Harvester Co., 274 U.S. 673 (1927).
[3] See Chap. III.

unanimity as to price policy. They may also facilitate the adoption of more economical methods of production on a larger scale than has prevailed but without resort to price competition likely to reduce prices to the new costs of production.[1]

4. OTHER LAWS

Since 1914 a number of fields of activity have been emancipated from the anti-trust policy of maintaining competition. The Webb-Pomerene Act of 1918 exempted the export trade from the provisions of the Sherman Act[2] and part of the Clayton Act.[3] Producers may, therefore, cooperate in controlling prices and sales in the export trade without any limitation upon their activities; the domestic prices of the commodities concerned must, however, remain unaffected (the full significance of this proviso has never become evident). In the marine insurance industry associations entered into "to transact a marine insurance and reinsurance business in the United States and in foreign countries and to reinsure or otherwise apportion among its membership the risks undertaken by such association or any of the component members,"[4] are exempted from the anti-trust acts. In both these fields sellers may unite in controlling prices without any state regulation.

In other fields reliance upon competition has been abandoned but at least a formal safeguard against excessive prices has been established. Agreements among shipping lines concerning traffic, rates, earnings, number and character of sailings, and other vital matters of policy existing at the time of the establishment of the United States Shipping Board were declared legal until disapproved by the board and were, therefore, exempted from the provisions of the anti-trust laws. Subsequent agreements were also subject to the approval of the board.[5]

---

[1] Cf. BURNS, op. cit., Quart. Jour. Econ., 47: 287, 299.
[2] Provided export organizations are "not in restraint of the export trade of any competitor of such association" and that "such association does not, either in the United States or elsewhere, enter into any agreement ... or do any act which artificially or intentionally enhances or depresses prices within the United States of commodities of the class exported by such association or which substantially lessens competition within the United States or otherwise restrains trade therein."
[3] Export associations are exempted from the prohibitions of Sec. 7 of the Clayton Act concerning corporate stock ownership "unless the effect of such ownership or acquisition (of stock or other capital) may be to restrain trade or substantially lessen competition within the United States."
[4] Merchant Marine Act, 1920, Sec. 29.
[5] Shipping Act, 1916.

Since 1914[1] increasing provision has been made for cooperation in agriculture. Beginning with a provision that the anti-trust laws should not be held to prohibit cooperative marketing associations (under prescribed circumstances), the federal government was by 1929 encouraging the organization of cooperative marketing associations and voting funds for the purpose.[2] These associations usually contracted with growers to take all their produce for a prescribed period of time, and to dispose of it at times and at prices determined by the management of the cooperative. Thus within the crop year competition between the members of the cooperative in selling their produce is eliminated if all the growers are also members of the cooperative; the cooperative is in a monopolistic position but its policy is narrowly limited if it is required in the course of the year to sell all the produce delivered to it by its members. Greater control can be obtained only by controlling planting by the members. Thus in agriculture, often regarded as the last stronghold of the system of small-scale production and of competition between large numbers of producers, the state provided a means of limiting competition. Cooperative associations operated, however, subject to the intervention of the Secretary of Agriculture where he believed that "such association monopolizes or restrains trade in interstate or foreign commerce to such an extent that the price of any agricultural product is unduly enhanced thereby,"[3] a power which, however, appears never to have been exercised. The Agricultural Adjustment Act established more far-reaching devices for controlling total output and prices; it replaced tentative and limited group planning by state control.

The National Industrial Recovery Act of 1933 made an open breach in the anti-trust laws and in the policy of preserving competition; it stimulated in most industries a more rigid control of methods of doing business and sometimes of methods of producing as well as of price and production policies. The act is, however, reserved for analysis at a later stage.[4]

The law concerning the ownership of natural gas and oil has given rise to a situation in which competitive behavior produces results disastrous alike to producers and consumers. Ever since a

---

[1] Clayton Act, 1914, as amended in 1916 and 1920, Sec. 6. This provision was elaborated and extended in the Capper-Volstead Act of 1922.
[2] Agricultural Marketing Act, 1929, Sec. 1; Cooperative Marketing Act, 1926.
[3] Capper-Volstead Act, 1922.
[4] See Chap. X.

Pennsylvania judge who was called upon in 1875[1] to lay down rules which would determine the ownership of crude oil, based his decision upon the resemblance between crude oil and wild game (on the ground that both were fugacious), it has been possible to obtain property rights in crude oil only by "capture." Once the existence of oil under the ground becomes known, the amount produced (*i.e.*, brought to the surface) is dominated by the fact that each owner of oil rights can obtain a share in the pool only if he drills a well and captures the oil before owners of other rights over the pool capture it. Although an owner of oil rights might prefer not to produce oil, but to await a higher price at a later date, he is unable to do so without a guarantee of cooperation from all other owners of similar rights over the same pool. He can, of course, capture the oil and store it on the surface, an obviously costly and wasteful method of postponing sale. The production of oil by reference to the best distribution of sales over time is hampered because postponement of capture means loss of the resource altogether. Once a well has been sunk, the marginal cost of production, consisting of labor to watch the well and power to pump it (if it needs pumping), is extremely small. The price at the well can, therefore, fall to almost nothing without discouraging production. Once the existence of oil is proven, it would be expected that wells would be drilled only if the anticipated price covered the total costs of drilling and operating. But in fact the aggregate output of the field (and therefore the price) is extremely difficult to estimate. The aggregate output of each well is equally uncertain because it depends partly upon the output of other wells. Those who complete their wells first expect a very high output. In consequence, there has frequently been a race to complete drilling and produce oil; natural gas has been wasted and excessive capital has been applied to the exploitation of the pool.

This combination of a large element of overhead costs with a grotesque legal principle[2] has resulted in attempts to avoid the resulting price competition. State governments, impressed by the obvious waste of both capital and natural resources, have enacted laws restricting competition. They aimed first at the prevention

---

[1] Westmoreland, etc., Co. v. Dewitt, 130 Pa. St. 235 (1875).
[2] The institution has been compared to a situation in which a number of boys each equipped with a straw competitively consume a glass of soda water (KIESSLING, *The Cooperative Development of Oil Pools*, II. Technical Publication 28 of 1927 of the American Institute of Mining and Metallurgical Engineers; this paper discusses more fully the economic aspects of legal institutions above analyzed).

of the waste of natural gas[1] but have proceeded to the control of waste arising out of production in excess of market demand.[2] The Supreme Court has confirmed the constitutionality of control aimed at the avoidance of waste.[3] No satisfactory device has yet been found, however, for coordinating the policies of the different states.[4] The powers granted to the President in the National Industrial Recovery Act of 1933 to control the interstate shipments of oil[5] have been held invalid as an unconstitutional delegation of legislative power.[6]

Occasionally state policy in the imposition of taxes and the granting of subsidies also reacts upon price competition. Annual taxes on standing timber tend to accelerate the rate at which timber is cut and marketed, and, if imposed or increased after timber has become privately owned, tend to magnify the pressure to sell and, by increasing the possible losses of holders of timber, press them on to find methods of avoiding price competition.[7] Taxes on unexploited mineral holdings tend to have a similar effect. In the whisky industry, on the other hand, the method of taxation was blamed for excessive investment in the industry;[8] the practice of announcing increases in taxation a considerable period before

---

[1] Oil and Gas Conservation Act of California, Stats. Cal., 1915, Chap. 718; 1917, Chap. 759; 1919, Chap. 536; 1921, Chap. 912; 1929, Chap. 535.

[2] Chap. 25, Laws of Oklahoma, enacted Feb. 11, 1915. The la ͏ includes in its prohibitions of waste the production of oil in excess of transporta͏ ͏n or marketing facilities or reasonable market demand, and has been interpreted to authorize the limitation of production to the reasonable daily market demand, and the rationing of the authorized production among producers.

[3] Bandini Petroleum Co. et al., v. Superior Court of the State of California, 284 U.S. 8 (1931), and Champlain Refining Co. v. Corporation Commission of the State of Oklahoma et al., 286 U.S. 210 (1932) (in this latter case the court found comfort in the belief that the powers conveyed by the act had not been exercised for the purpose of controlling the price of crude oil and had had no such effect; it noted that the price of crude oil had fallen during the period of control of output). The principal Texas statute has been sustained by the state and lower federal courts (Federal Oil Conservation Board, Report, V, 1932, 1). The authority of state governments to control "offset drilling," i.e., drilling by one owner to prevent wells on a neighboring area from draining away the crude oil which he might expect to obtain "is largely untested except for some successful efforts to control spacing of wells. No state has endeavored to declare an oil pool a unit and to require the development of it as a unit for the common protection of all owners. . . . In the main, efforts of the states have commenced with the production phase and have left the development phase relatively untouched." (Federal Oil Conservation Board, Report, V, 2.)

[4] Cf. Federal Oil Conservation Board, Report, V, 1932, 3; also evidence of Secretary of the Interior R. L. Wilbur in Hearings on Amendment of Federal Trade Commission Act before Senate Committee on Judiciary pursuant to S.R. 2626, etc., 1932, 221.

[5] National Industrial Recovery Act, 1933, Sec. 9c, and regulations issued by Secretary of the Interior, cit. New York Times, July 17, 1933.

[6] Panama Refining Co. v. Ryan, 55 Sup. Ct. 241 (1935).

[7] Cf. National Lumber Bulletin, June 7, 1925.

[8] JENKS, The Development of the Whisky Trust, Polit. Sci. Quart., 4: 297 (1899).

they came into operation induced investments to enable producers to expand their production prior to the operation of the increased tax.

The shipping industry offers the best example of state subsidies operating to induce the avoidance of price competition. Increased nationalistic feeling since 1918 has resulted in increased emphasis upon a mercantilist policy of encouraging national shipping. National governments have financed the shipping industry at less than the market rate of interest[1] and furnished ships at lower prices than those which would be offered by foreign buyers; they have directly subsidized shipbuilding; they have in many countries provided disguised subsidies through payments for carrying mail, and have frequently directly or indirectly borne the losses of unremunerative operation of shipping lines.[2] Excessive investment has thus been made in shipping with the result that many shipping companies have been unable to secure a normal rate of return. Rate agreements have been sought in order to avoid the worst consequences of price competition and in the United States such agreements have, as described above, been exempted from the general prohibition upon price agreements under the Sherman Act.[3]

III. THE GENERAL INFLUENCES AFFECTING THE OPERATION OF THE INDUSTRIAL SYSTEM

Technological change and social policy have both contributed to the decline in the number of firms. Each of the surviving firms considers the effects of any change in its output upon both its costs and its price; the most profitable output is, as we have already seen, such that an increase of one unit would add equally to costs and to revenue. This generalization is, however, a very broad truth. Its application to actual situations involves very great difficulties. The greatest of these arises out of the necessity for taking account of periods of time when making policy. The ideal output and price above described would change with every change in conditions of demand or supply, yet in fact prices are not incessantly changing. The policies of sellers depend also upon what they expect of their rivals. A description of the aspects of supply and demand that complicate the pricing problems of these

---

[1] *Cf.* the policy of the United States Shipping Board.
[2] *Cf.* the policy of the United States Shipping Board and the losses borne by the French, Italian, and many other governments.
[3] Shipping Act, 1916.

monopolists will help to explain the general origins of many of the policies later to be discussed.

A. *Conditions of Sale*

The larger the volume of business transacted by one seller the greater is the reaction upon its total sales revenue of a given increase in output and reduction in price; the greater therefore is the obstacle to price cutting. But the firm too large to ignore these considerations is influenced also by its estimate of the effect of a price reduction upon the volume of its sales. The estimated demand for the product of any one firm depends upon the price policy of other sellers of the "commodity." If each seller assumes that a reduction in his price will induce a similar change by his rivals, he may obtain a share of any increase in the total demand, but he can attract no business from his rivals. If he bears this fact in mind, and considers his own long-run interests, the price of the product will be the same as if there were one firm in place of the group (except for any differences in the cost of production in the two situations). The price of the "commodity" then depends upon its elasticity of demand as estimated by the sellers. This elasticity is important only because producers are few. But when they are few they are apt to resist demands for lower prices on the ground that a reduction would add so little to their sales that its principal effect would be to reduce the revenue obtained from the quantities they are already selling. The producers of steel and constructional goods, for instance, are probably correct in claiming, particularly during a depression, that the demand for their product is inelastic. The producers of milk and bread claim, similarly, that little increase in demand results from a reduction in price.[1] If a seller estimated demand to be much more elastic than did his rivals he would be more tempted than they to reduce his price. Producers, fearful of such reductions, frequently attempt to ward them off by propaganda to impress upon rivals the inelasticity of demand; estimates of the elasticity of demand by producers will, in these circumstances, be biased in the direction of assuming a greater inelasticity than exists. Since the assumptions of the producers determine their calculation of the most desirable price policy, prices are likely to be higher than they would otherwise be.

[1] *Hearings on the Price of Food Products* before the Senate Committee on Agriculture and Forestry, 1931, 124, 235.

The elasticity of the demand for the product of each seller depends on the willingness of buyers to turn from his product to nearby substitutes. This readiness of buyers to change their allegiance can be, and often is, reduced by devices for promoting sales and especially by advertising; buyers may be persuaded that rival products are less desirable. The greater the loyalty of buyers, the less elastic is the demand for the product of the seller, and the less the inducement to reduce prices.

If a seller in such a market, in deciding whether or not to cut his price, assumes that his rivals will not immediately cut theirs, he will arrive at a demand for his product which is more elastic than if he assumes his rivals immediately to follow his lead; some buyers transfer their business to him from his rivals. The inducement to reduce his price is increased and the inducement to raise prices is reduced. This policy assumes, however, a short view f the market; where firms are large, the period within which they are likely to permit business to be taken over by a rival who has reduced his price is usually short; they speedily counter with a similar reduction. Efforts to attract business within short periods of time by reductions in price in advance of similar reductions by rivals may lead to a series of reductions and counter reductions, *i.e.*, to a price war; in consequence there is a strong tendency away from price cutting based upon the short-term view.

The calculation of the most profitable price policy is seriously influenced by the reactions of purchasers over time. It is easy to say that the most profitable policy is one that takes account of the effect of a change in output upon costs and revenue. But how long a period do producers take into account in calculating the reactions of buyers? The slower the reaction of buyers to a price cut, the greater is the loss of revenue to the price cutter who is selling little more than before at a lower price; the longer the reaction time of buyers the more remote does the connection between the increase in business and the decline in price seem to the price cutter. In all these ways the slowness of buyers to respond to a price cut diminishes the willingness of sellers to seek business by price cutting.

The reaction time of buyers to a price reduction may be long because reallocation of purchasing power is a slow process. A reduction in the price of constructional goods in time of depression might attract additional business after a long lag; *i.e.*, demand over the longer period may be more elastic than it is during the shorter period. Planning to extend plant or to enter new industries takes a considerable time. The demand for a new product may increase slowly in response to a reduction in price because a considerable readjustment of habitual behavior is required; a reduction in the price of milk might induce a change in consumption habits if sellers would wait long enough. Demand may increase slowly because subsidiary facilities are needed before purchasers will adapt to the new product; in the earlier stages of the introduction of the automobile, such considerations were doubtless important. A price cutter aiming to attract business from rival firms must consider other influences affecting the speed with which business is shifted. Buyers may react slowly because information concerning the prices of the different sellers percolates through the market slowly. If price changes are widely published, the reaction of buyers is accelerated but so also may be the reaction of rival sellers. Where buyers believe that the quality of the goods sold by different sellers is not uniform, the transfer of business is apt to be retarded; they must evaluate the change in utilities resulting from the change in their source of supply. The branding of goods is intended to and does retard as well as obstruct changes of allegiance.

Changes in prices may also lead buyers to redistribute demand over time. If buyers anticipate that a reduction in price is temporary, they increase their purchases; but they accumulate inventories against the time when they expect the price to increase again. Producers who expect this reaction take account of the probability that a price cut will merely "spoil the market" in the future; the holders of the increased inventories sooner or later let them run off and while they are doing so they reduce their purchases. The belief that a price cut will merely mean selling now at a lower price what would otherwise be sold later at a higher price discourages price cutting; sellers believe that over the longer period demand is inelastic although within the shorter period it is more elastic.[1]

A reduction in price may in the short period result in a reduction instead of an increase in demand.[2] Buyers may regard the

---

[1] Sellers of anthracite have deliberately adopted a policy of seasonal discounts in order to redistribute demand over time and stabilize it.

[2] *Cf.* F.T.C., *Open Price Trade Associations*, 297. "The only cure for this sort of thing appears to be a better enlightenment of the public as to stocks, current productive capacity, and other market factors, and better commercial discipline" (*loc. cit.*). *Cf.* also CLARK, *Studies in the Economics of Overhead Costs*, 443.

COMPETITION IN TRANSITION

reduction as heralding further reductions; they reduce their inventories to the minimum by reducing their current purchases, and await what they regard as the lowest price to which the seller is likely to resort before again increasing their inventories. Again the anticipated behavior of buyers discourages price cutting. A reduction in price which may appear desirable in the short run may induce buyers to reform their standard of a fair price for the product. If conditions of demand or cost subsequently change, buyers may resist a rise in price with the result that the demand when the old price is restored may be less than before.[1] Immediately they may reduce their inventories although such action can be taken only for short periods; later they may vigorously seek and experiment with substitute products.

Conditions of demand are important, therefore, to those who sell in imperfect markets; they must calculate the effect of changes in output upon prices and revenue. Sellers take account of the elasticity of demand for both the commodity and their own product. They realize the unwisdom of price cutting that will evoke responses from rivals and depress prices unless the demand for the commodity as a whole is likely to increase sufficiently to yield them a net gain. The time taken for buyers to respond to price cuts and the far-reaching consequences of some of these reactions over longer periods of time introduce uncertainties as to elasticity of demand which result in widespread efforts to discourage short-term price competition.

B. *Conditions of Production*

The outstanding change in the conditions of supply affecting the price policies of producers is the great increase in the importance of overhead costs, *i.e.*, costs incurred for the production of a considerable volume of output and incapable of adjustment to changes in the scale of output below this volume. Large-scale production is economical because of the subdivision of labor, the specialization of tools and equipment, and the substitution of mechanical force for human labor. Subdivided labor must be integrated by a force of white-collar workers, and tools and equipment involve expenditure in anticipation of a considerable volume of output over a period of time. Investment in specialized equip-

---

[1] *Cf.* MARSHALL, *Principles of Economics*, 807. Marshall remarks that the demand prices that hold for the forward movement of prices will seldom hold for the return movement.

ment and organization is rarely so delicately balanced that the total output of the organization when fully employed can be sold at a price just sufficient to cover the full cost of production including a normal profit.

Where plant is not fully employed, the producer seeking the output at which the additional cost of producing another unit is just equal to the addition to revenue that would result takes account, on the side of costs, of only the additional costs, *i.e.*, mainly labor and raw material costs that vary with the volume of output. The most advantageous price frequently fails to cover the average total costs of production. If every seller ignored the effect of an increase in output upon the revenue obtained from the output he is already selling (*i.e.*, if he behaved competitively) the price would cover only the direct cost of producing another unit of output; the price might yield nothing at all toward the overhead costs although it would rarely be so low. If the number of firms is small enough for sellers to take account of the effect of changes in their output upon the price, and upon the revenue from their sales, the price will not fall so low; but there may still be a gap between the total revenue received and the total costs of production.

The larger the proportion of total costs that is made up of overhead costs, the wider this gap can be. The more elastic the demand for the output of each firm, in the estimation of that firm, the more nearly will the price approach that resulting from competition. If sellers believe that they can attract business from rivals by a price cut, they assume that the demand for their own product is very elastic, and reduce their price. But rivals are likely to follow and there is danger of a price war. Since most, if not all, the producers are anxious to find some way of avoiding price wars of this kind, price cutting is discouraged. The greater the relative importance of overhead costs the wider is the range within which prices may vary according to the attitudes of those in the industry to each other, and to the probable elasticity of total demand; the more may revenue fall short of total costs. The failure of prices to cover total costs tends to expel resources from the industry and to narrow the margin between total revenue and total costs, but the process of adjustment is so slow that producers attempt to minimize their losses by discouraging competitive price cutting.

Railroads offer an obvious example of an industry in which the dangers of price cutting are extreme; on the average two-thirds of railroad expenditures are said to be independent of the volume of traffic carried.[1] Such a statement must, however, be very broadly interpreted, because the extent to which expenses are dependent upon volume of traffic depends on the range within which traffic is assumed to change. If, for instance, traffic increased greatly, further rolling stock would be required, and, in relation to that addition of business, expenditures upon rolling stock would be a variable expenditure; there is also a point at which further track and terminal facilities are necessary to permit the acceptance of further traffic. Of the relative importance of overhead costs in other industries very little is known[2] except that they are usually much less important than in public utilities.[3]

The importance of the tendency for unused capacity to exert a downward pressure upon prices depends upon the extent to which unused capacity exists. It has been estimated that about 20 per cent of the manufacturing capacity of the United States remained out of use between 1925 and 1929.[4] This figure must be used with care because it rests upon a number of estimates and because also it is extremely difficult to calculate capacity for production at any time; it is necessary to decide which plants are still in the industry although they may not be operating; it is necessary to decide how many hours per day, days per week, and weeks per year of operation shall be regarded as "capacity."

Unused capacity is to be expected, as we have seen, even in the long run, wherever producers take account of the effect of changes in their production upon the revenue they obtain from the units they are already selling. But unused capacity develops in a variety

[1] RIPLEY, *Railroad Rates and Regulation*, 55.
[2] *Cf.* JONES, "Is Competition in Industry Ruinous? *Quart. Jour. Econ.*, 34: 477 (1920). Interest charges are, however, an inadequate measure of overhead costs; many firms issue no bonds but they may and do incur overhead costs. Capitalization in relation to annual output is also an unsatisfactory measure; capitalization is more arbitrary than most figures; it is affected by the value of raw materials and by the durability of equipment.
[3] The extent to which costs vary with output is dependent upon business practice. Where, for instance, it is possible to hire machinery in return for a royalty payment based upon output (as in the shoe industry), the cost of machinery is a variable cost; where machinery must be purchased or leased at a fixed rental it is an overhead cost. The system of contracts with employees may cause part at least of the labor costs to be fixed over considerable periods, and even where contracts do not necessitate this attitude, unwillingness to disband a sales force, for instance, in a period of slack demand, causes the expenses of maintaining it to fall into the category of overhead costs, a condition common in the merchandising industry. (FRASER, "The Readjustment of Retail and Wholesale Operating Expenses," *Harvard Bus. Rev.*, 1: 222, (1923); KING, *Employment Hours and Earnings in Prosperity and Depression*, 49–52; CLARK, *Studies in the Economics of Overhead Costs*, 341.)
[4] NOURSE and associates, *America's Capacity to Produce*, 416.

of other ways. Where the optimum or most economical scale of production is very large there may be no middle way between a certain number of firms securing an abnormal return and one more firm with all securing subnormal profits and only partially employed. Changes or anticipated changes in demand may lead to excess capacity; investment in new firms or the expansion of old firms must rest partly upon estimates of future demand, and as equipment is relatively durable, estimates of demand should cover the expected life of the equipment. These periods frequently stretch so far into the future, however, that unforeseen causes falsify estimates of demand. Because equipment can rarely be diminished in quantity as quickly as buyers can change their assessments of the utility of various products, industries frequently find themselves equipped to meet a demand in excess of the actual demand at the price anticipated when the investment was made. The difficulty of estimating demand tends to induce the provision of plant beyond that necessary to meet the demand that can be clearly foreseen, so that unexpected business opportunities can be grasped; producers assume that when demand increases sufficiently to call for the utilization of a certain percentage of existing plant, the safety margin has been passed; further investment is made and fear that producers will be tempted to use this unused capacity leads to efforts to instill codes of behavior that will prevent its use and eliminate the downward pressure upon prices.[1]

The development of new products which are durable tends to induce unused capacity. When the automobile or harvesting machine is placed upon the market, the initial demand arising out of the readjustment of the expenditures of buyers induces investment large enough to permit a very quick change in the habits of buyers. This equipment may, however, be excessive in relation to the subsequent period in which demand for the product shrinks to replacement proportions.[2] If investors took account of the probable decline in demand after the initial expansion, they would,

---

[1] *Cf.* statement that constructional steel firms "owe it to their buying public . . . to have available at all times at least a 25 per cent reserve capacity to take care of emergencies. It is the futile striving to keep this 25 per cent employed that ruins prices on the 75 per cent to which they are justly entitled." (*Aminsteel News*, November, 1931.)

[2] The lumber industry presents an analogous, but not quite similar, situation. So long as the population was shifting to new and hitherto uninhabited areas, the demand for lumber was very great compared to that in the subsequent period when the demand for building materials was much less.

of course, charge against their earlier output a sum sufficient to enable them later to abandon much of their plant before it was worn out, and might thereby avoid waste; but they would also retard the introduction of the new product by charging higher prices. Investment in each firm in the new industry is, however, stimulated by the hope of high profits in the period of initial activity and also of survival and possibly leadership in the succeeding period when replacement demand alone is to be met.

Where the geographical distribution of demand changes, similar forces operate. If it becomes profitable to produce shoes or steel in new areas in which a body of consumers has appeared, plant in the older areas of production is left unused, unless the shift in population has been anticipated. Changes in the location of industry may give rise to excessive capacity apart from changes in the distribution of population. It may be discovered that production is cheaper in some new area than in the old, as for instance when the textile industry moved to the South, meat packing moved westward nearer to sources of livestock supply, and flour milling to a few large centers and toward the Great Lakes. Changes in the location of supplies of pulp timber and in methods of production have induced changes in the localization of the newsprint industry and have contributed to the great excess of productive capacity in the industry.[1] The exploitation of timber in new areas doubtless accounts in part for the statement that ten per cent in number of the lumber mills could have produced more than the total output of lumber in the United States in 1929 and that the total capacity of lumber mills in 1932 was more than five times the production in that year.[2]

The development of new methods of production may also give rise to unused plant. Where the new methods involve production upon a larger scale, firms desirous of adopting the new methods may add to their investment at a time when the industry as a whole is capable of meeting all the current demand. If the old-fashioned producers continue to strive for some return upon their unexhausted investments in equipment, there is danger of cut-throat competition. In the soft coal industry the mechanization of mines, for instance, has tended to increase the output of the

[1] FRASER and DORIOT, *Analyzing Our Industries*, 322–324.
[2] *Hearings on the Amendment of the Federal Trade Commission Act* before Senate Committee on the Judiciary pursuant to S.R. 2626, 2627, 2628, 1932, 229. The decline in the demand arising from the settlement of new areas above referred to is clearly also a part of the explanation of this condition.

modernized pits and to increase the distress in the industry.[1] The displacement of sulphite pulp by cheaper sulphate pulp is said to have contributed to the unused plant in the newsprint paper industry. The building of large-scale flour mills has tended also to induce excess capacity in that industry, and there are, of course, countless other examples.

Cyclical fluctuations in general business activity also induce excessive investment; when an industry appears to be sufficiently profitable to attract new investment, existing producers extend their facilities and new firms enter the industry, but the collective response may be excessive; each may act upon the assumption that others do not recognize the desirability of new investment. This difficulty arises partly out of the fact that the process of increasing investment is itself extended over time. Within this period, therefore, there is opportunity for many producers to commit themselves to extensions of investment before the effect of any of these commitments has made itself evident in output and prices. Moreover, firms usually equip themselves to carry the peak load of years of great activity with the result that the burden of unused plant is concentrated in periods when demand is below the peak.

There are other minor causes of failure to make full use of plant but it is clear that there is a variety of forces making for a maladjustment between capacity for production and demand. The rate of interest has proved a very poor regulator of investment partly because of a persistent overestimation of probable profits in many fields of activity. Where the economy as a whole is expanding this overestimation is excessive in relation to information available at the time of estimation and less so in relation to subsequent events. But when expansion ceases or slows up, the old habits of optimism cause much more serious maladjustment. This stage has already been reached in England and will doubtless make its appearance in the United States.

The attitude of the seller in making his production and price policy may be complicated by the discovery that it is difficult or impossible to calculate the cost of producing outputs of different sizes. Few firms produce a completely standardized output and some produce a great variety of articles. A firm may produce more than one article because one cannot be produced without the others; where they must be produced in unvarying proportions,

[1] HAMILTON and WRIGHT, *The Case of Bituminous Coal*, 1926, 60.

and only one product is salable, the remainder costing nothing to dispose of, there are no complications. If all but one are unsalable and costly to dispose of, for example, ashes, the cost of disposal is part of the cost of producing the single salable product. But where more than one is salable and the production of more units of one is inevitably accompanied by a fixed amount more of the other, it is impossible to allocate the additional costs of production between the two products; the costs of producing different quantities can be calculated only for the two products taken together. The most profitable output of each is determined by considering the two products together in the proportion in which they must be produced; the best output is such that a slight addition to the set of products would increase costs as much as revenue. Joint products complying strictly with this definition over long periods of time are not common.[1] Over shorter periods they are important, especially for instance in the meat packing industry.

More frequently the output of each product can be varied independently of the others. The output of different grades and patterns of a product can be independently adjusted. The manufacture of a number of products under common management may be due to economies in the cost of production in the narrow sense; less materials may be wasted or machinery and equipment may be more fully utilized if more than one type of product is produced (*e.g.*, in the manufacture of furniture); it may also be due to the desire to make full use of selling or management units. The meat packers can adjust the output of lard and pork within limits. Petroleum refiners can change the proportions of gasoline, lubricating oil, and fuel oil that they produce although again within limits.[2] Smelting companies can vary the proportions of the various constituents of the ores that they will recover.[3] Lumber mills can vary the quantities of different sizes of timber that they produce.[4]

In any given situation a producer can calculate the effect of producing another unit of one of his products upon both his

[1] *Cf.* MARSHALL, *Principles of Economics*, 390.
[2] Between 1880 and 1932 the output of gasoline and naphtha per barrel of crude oil was increased from 4.3 to 18.8 gallons by the introduction of "cracking" and other improvements in technique.
[3] The Federal Trade Commission remarked upon the fact that the yield of calcium arsenate (important as an insecticide), which is a by-product of copper smelting, is limited by the nature of the ores (*Calcium Arsenate Industry*, 1923).
[4] Where considerations of economy dictate the cutting of all the timber of commercial sizes upon a tract, if any timber at all is cut, fir and cedar may be produced in proportions determined by natural conditions although one alone would not have been cut (U.S. TARIFF COMMISSION, *Red Cedar Shingles*, 1927, 61).

revenue and his costs. If at every stage the additional cost of adding to the output of any of the products is the same as the cost of similarly increasing the output of any of the others, changes in the proportions in which they are produced have no effect upon costs. The most profitable combination depends upon the nature of demand for each. The styles the demand for which is least elastic will be produced in the smallest quantities; each will be produced up to the point at which additions to revenue equal additions to cost (which are the same for all styles), but the prices of styles for which the demand is least elastic will be the highest.[1] This situation would arise where the same product is sold under different labels and some are more entrenched in the public favor than others although all are advertised together.

More often the different grades and patterns of a product involve some special costs. The addition to costs if the output of one product is increased is calculable on the assumption that the output of the others is fixed. If the facilities used in common for the production of a number of products are in full use, this assumption is unreal; the effect on total returns of reducing the output of some other product must be taken into account. If these facilities are not fully utilized, the cost of increasing the output of one depends upon the existing output of all the others. Calculations of the effect of increasing and reducing the output of each product in turn will enable the producer to decide the best combination of outputs. The calculation is obviously difficult; it depends upon the estimated demand for each product and the estimated cost of producing each under a variety of alternative conditions. Changes in the output of one may react moreover upon the demand for another.

This highly complex situation if combined with unused capacity increases the dangers of price cutting. If one producer differs from his rivals in his estimate of the demand or cost conditions for one type of product, he may be tempted to reduce the price of that product on the assumption that the price of the other products will remain unchanged. Other producers may reduce the price of other products for the same reason. The temptation to such a policy is increased by the realization that the cut in price will affect the revenue from only a portion of his existing sales;

---

[1] *Cf.* the discussion of discrimination, Chap. VI, and ROBINSON, JOAN, *Economics of Imperfect Competition*, 182.

the deterrent to price cutting is less than if he were compelled to reduce the prices of all his products. Yet there is a danger of all-round price cutting; rival producers may cut the price of other products or buyers may successfully contend that if one product can be reduced in price, all can be similarly reduced. Producers seek to reduce the risk of such action by controlling methods of cost accounting; they aim at the standardization of methods of distributing costs between different products. Cost accounts relate to average total, and not to marginal, costs and producers frequently find it unwise, if not impossible, to attempt to charge prices covering all their costs, but the standardization of methods of cost accounting is intended to maintain a fairly constant relation between the prices of all the products, and to avoid price cutting beginning with one product and spreading until "it gets out of hand" or "demoralizes the market."

Methods of production involving the greater use of specialized equipment have also reduced the speed with which the resources in an industry can be adjusted to conditions of demand. The resources in most industries can be increased far more speedily than they can be reduced. Whether or not firms are reconstructed, plant remains in use so long as it enables a seller to obtain revenue in excess of the other costs of production. The economic longevity of equipment prolongs periods when prices fail to cover total costs and the probability of such conditions is increased by the relative speed with which resources flow into industries when prices exceed total costs. This prolongation merely reinforces the efforts already mentioned to prevent sellers from reducing prices on the basis of estimates of the short-period advantages of such reductions. If their resources are imprisoned in the industry they seek a coordinated policy calculated to repay them the greatest possible proportion of their investment.

The most important factor determining the duration of this period of adjustment is, of course, the length of the physical life of the means of production, but if the probable life of a steel mill is twenty years[1] it does not follow that a reduction in price below the fully remunerative level will cause adjustments in the capacity for production only after a lag of twenty years. If there are firms whose equipment is approaching exhaustion, low profits or failure even to recover the whole of past investment are likely to dis-

[1] Evidence of Mr. Farrell, *Hearings on the Establishment of a National Economic Council* before a subcommittee of the Senate Committee on Manufactures, 1931, 349.

courage reinvestment, and, therefore, to cause a reduction in capacity. But in fact there are few industries in which there arises the opportunity to withdraw without abandoning some plant only partly exhausted. Most modern productive organizations consist of a great variety of forms of equipment which are exhausted at different times; they must decide year by year whether some assets should be replaced in order that the remainder may continue in use. If total anticipated future revenue exceeds total estimated additional costs, including the required new investment, they will make the new investment although total costs in the full sense may not be covered. The reduction of the resources in the industry is thus retarded.[1]

Investments in exhaustible natural resources have an effect upon price and production policy comparable with that where investment has been made in specialized equipment for production. Broadly speaking, the aim of the producer is to recover over a period of time as large a sum as possible from the realization of the resource. The investment is in a highly specialized form limited in its use. Investments of this kind are common in the steel industry (where holdings of iron ore, limestone, and other minerals are common), in the oil industry (where the large refining companies also control supplies of oil in the ground), the aluminum industry (the Aluminum Corporation owning large resources of bauxite), in mining enterprises generally, and in the lumber industry (where lumber mills often own standing timber which is only very slowly replaceable). Should competitive price cutting occur in such industries, and should existing producers be able to meet the consequent demand for their product, the price may continue to fall until neither capital nor interest is being recovered in respect of the investment in natural resources, a situation reported to exist in the lumber industry in 1931 and the immediately succeeding years.[2] The presence of such investment thus widens the range within which prices may fluctuate. But again the ownership of

---

[1] Where investment is in a form adaptable to other purposes, relief may be speedier according as transfer to new uses is speedier. That some machine industries can adapt themselves from one use to another is illustrated by the fact that parts for the early automobiles were made in shops set up to make parts for sewing machines and firearms.

[2] It was reported in 1932 that lumber prices had fallen to a level which yielded no return for timber and none upon overhead investment in sawmills, and in some cases did not even cover direct costs of conversion, production being maintained at the cost of a decline in working capital and increased borrowing (*Hearings on Amendment of Federal Trade Commission Act* before Senate Committee on Judiciary pursuant to S.R. 2627 and 2628, 1932, 230).

some exhaustible resources, *e.g.*, aluminum,[1] anthracite,[2] and copper,[3] is in the hands of a relatively small number of sellers. Concentration of control of standing timber in the hands of financially powerful owners is said to have enabled them to withhold timber from use, with the object of securing higher prices.[4] The fact that these concerns have a large proportion of their expenses falling in a category similar to that of overhead costs, and that they are relatively few, leads to efforts to avoid price competition. In the lumber industry[5] as well as in the anthracite industry,[6] concentration of ownership is expected to increase with the passage of time. While in the steel industry iron ore resources have been realized at prices at least equal to those at which they were optimistically capitalized, the owners of timber stands have been less fortunate; it has been evident since 1907 that the development of substitutes for lumber in building, and the decreasing demand for lumber in newly settled areas, have destroyed the prospect of continually rising prices upon the expectation of which the capitalized value of the holdings was calculated. The industry has, therefore, found it impossible to obtain a normal rate of return upon total investment. The danger of price cutting by some in order to realize as much as possible of their capital is increased, more particularly if there are some who believe that future prices will not exceed present prices by an amount sufficient to cover carrying costs.[7] It is not surprising, therefore, that lumbermen

---

[1] The Aluminum Corporation of America has been reported to own 90 per cent of the commercially available supplies of bauxite (from which aluminum is obtained) (U.S. v. Aluminum Corp. of America. *Petition in District Court of Western Pennsylvania*, 6, 7) and by agreements to control most of the remainder (F.T.C., *Report on House Furnishings Industries*, 1925, III, 90). Although the court decreed the abrogation of these agreements (*ibid.*, III, 287), the policy of the parties to the agreements remained unchanged (*ibid.*, III, 92); since 1921 secondary supplies of metal from scrap, sweepings, turnings, and junk have become an important rival source of ingots and alloys (U.S. Tariff Commission Tariff Information Survey, *Aluminum*, 1921, 26) and ore has been imported.
[2] Eight companies controlled 77.7 per cent of the recoverable anthracite in 1923 (F.T.C., *Wealth and Income in the United States*, 1926, 86).
[3] Ten companies controlled 71.5 per cent of the copper ore reserves (*ibid.*, 96) in 1923.
[4] COMPTON, *Organization of the Lumber Industry*, 61; STEPHENS, "Determinants of Lumber Prices, *Amer. Econ. Rev.*, 7: 296 (1917).
[5] F.T.C., *Lumber Manufacturers Trade Associations*, 1922, 87; F.T.C., *Southern Pine Lumber*, 1922. Concentration of the ownership of timber has, however, been checked since 1910 by the uncertain course of timber prices, some of the largest owners having reduced their holdings (U.S. DEPARTMENT OF AGRICULTURE, *Public and Economic Aspects of Lumber Manufacture*, 1917, 12).
[6] U.S. v. Reading Co. (1911), *Brief for U.S.*, 30.
[7] Secretary of Agriculture Houston, *cit. Brief for National Lumber Manufacturers Association*, 1916, 25.

who had made most of their profits from speculation in timber holdings rather than from the manufacture of lumber[1] should have been the first to experiment on a very large scale with trade associations as a means of maintaining prices by restricting the rate of realization of their lumber resources, and that they should have pressed for the assistance of the state in restricting output.[2]

IV. CONCLUSION

An industrial organization which was in the broad sense competitive has become diminishingly so during the past half century. Throughout this period outward professions of loyalty to laissez faire and competitive individualism were numberless and the courts have repeatedly expressed their belief that the underlying objective of the anti-trust laws was the maintenance of competition. The policy of the legislature and the courts has probably succeeded in eliminating price cutting and other tactics of the sort that carried the former Standard Oil Company, the American Tobacco Company, the National Cash Register Company, the American Sugar Refining Company, the DuPont de Nemours Company (the powder trust), the Corn Products Refining Company, and many others to positions of almost complete control in their industries. In consequence "trusts" of this type are now largely creatures of a past age. The modern problem is not that of the firm destroying practically all its rivals and controlling almost the whole of an industry. Nor is it that of the pool in the form of an agreement concerning prices and output, although the extent to which such agreements have been made is unknown.

The characteristic of industrial organization during the present century is the growth of firms large enough in relation to their industries as a whole for it to be irrational for them to disregard the effect of changes in their output, or their price policy, upon the market as a whole; they must take account of the effect of a reduc-

---

[1] DEPARTMENT OF AGRICULTURE, *Public and Economic Aspects of Lumber Manufacture*, 1917.

[2] Even before the passage of the National Industrial Recovery Act of 1933, the federal government had been persuaded to cooperate through the appointment by the President of the Timber Conservation Board of which the Secretary of Commerce was chairman. The Lumber Survey Committee of the board was recommending restriction of output in 1931 (*United States Daily*, July 31, 1931), but the board was restricted in its efforts to assist the industry to publicity and exhortation. Secretary of Agriculture Houston argued that as holdings of timber (apparently at existing capital values) could not yield more than two or three per cent "it appears obvious that the holdings of such a national resource should be a function of the state or national government" (*Cit. Brief for National Lumber Manufacturers Association*, 1916, 25).

tion in price not only upon the volume of their sales but also upon the total revenue from these sales. They find themselves in the position of a monopolist in that, in pursuit of the maximum of income, they must choose the best combination of price and sales, having regard for the effect of changes in output upon costs. The development of these large units is partly due to changes in the technique of production and distribution. Social policy has, however, contributed to this development in a variety of ways. Corporation laws have facilitated the concentration of the control of large quantities of the means of production. The patent law, partly directly and partly indirectly, has stimulated and protected concentrations in some industries, although the courts have progressively restricted the rights of patentees. The anti-trust laws have failed to prevent, but have not directly caused increasing concentration of control and the development of price and production policies appropriate to the new conditions; they have diverted the adaptation into particular channels.

These large units interested in the market for long periods of time are willing enough to behave as monopolists producing the most profitable output. But the calculation of this output is very difficult. The growing importance of overhead in total costs increases the range within which prices may fluctuate and the extent to which prices can be driven below total average costs. In consequence manufacturers seek to induce attitudes to demand and costs that discourage price cutting; but on the other side the behavior of buyers often deters price cutting. They may respond so slowly to price reductions as to impose heavy burdens upon any seller who is prepared to attempt to obtain business by lower prices. They may respond not at all, or very little, even when time is allowed, with the result that when firms become large enough to consider the probable sales at each price the inducement to reduce prices is small. Price reductions may merely redistribute business over time, an immediate response to a reduction in price being counterbalanced by a later decline. A reduction in prices may become an obstacle to a later increase. The producer on his side may seek to protect himself from attacks by rivals by advertising intended to attach buyers to him.

In this new environment price and production policies would be expected to differ from those associated with perfect competition. It remains, therefore, to look for broad patterns of behavior sufficiently common in the industries in which the conditions under discussion prevail, to justify their being cast into the form of generalizations. Some industries have resorted to sharing the market; many have sought to stabilize prices; some have resorted to price discriminations and a number to rivalry in matters other than prices. Tendencies to wider integration of industrial operations appear in various relations to these policies. The foregoing types of relationship between firms and the consequent price and production policies are each the subject of one of the succeeding chapters, where the conditions giving rise to each policy, its prevalence, and its probable consequences are discussed.

CHAPTER II

THE TRADE ASSOCIATION AND INDUSTRIAL INSTITUTE

I. Introduction—II. Trade association policies 1912-1933—*A*. The performance of functions most economically conducted on a large scale—*B*. The cooperative provision of information—1. The standardization of forms of cost accounts—2. The standardization of methods of calculating costs—3. Statistics of production—4. Statistics of inventories—5. Statistics of unfilled orders—6. Statistics of productive capacity—7. Statistics of selling prices—*C*. Cooperative control of output—*D*. Cooperative control of types of product—*E*. Cooperative control of methods of selling—III. Summary.

I. INTRODUCTION

A trade association or industrial institute is an organized group of producers of broadly similar commodities or services. Of such associations Adam Smith remarked that "people of the same trade seldom meet together even for merriment and diversion but the conversation ends in a conspiracy against the public or in some contrivance to raise prices."[1] The importance of such associations in the régime of mixed monopoly and competition depends, of course, upon the nature of their activities. Their mere existence does not indicate any far-reaching departure from competitive behavior or any particular type of departure. They are, however, potential instruments for the administration of new price and production policies. Yet in the United States trade associations increased in number and extended their activities in a period of alleged devotion to laissez faire. The state first ignored them, then encouraged them, then mildly restrained them, and under the National Industrial Recovery Act, virtually adopted them as its chosen instruments for the control of industry.

The activities of trade associations have varied greatly from time to time and from trade to trade. Associations of the modern sort began to appear in the United States soon after the conclusion of the Civil War. Until the passage of the Sherman Anti-Trust Act in 1890 they appear to have been frankly regarded by their promoters as a substitute for the trust in industries presenting

[1] *Wealth of Nations* (*Ed.* Cannan), I, 130.

serious obstacles to the concentration of production in very large units.[1] The passage of the Sherman Law resulted, at least temporarily, in some restriction of the range of their activities, although a number were subsequently charged with unlawful attempts to control the market.[2] They entered upon a new phase of their history, however, when Mr. A. J. Eddy, a Chicago lawyer interested in corporation and anti-trust cases, proposed a method of adapting them to the restraints of the Sherman Law. In *The New Competition*, published in 1912, Mr. Eddy emphasized the necessity for "open prices," *i.e.*, prices known to all sellers as well as all buyers. True competition, Mr. Eddy claimed, could exist only where each firm could "know and fairly judge what the others were doing. The essence of competition lies in the element of *knowledge;* it is real, true, and beneficial in proportion to its *openness* and *frankness*, its *freedom from secrecy and underhand methods.*"[3] This policy demanded concerted action and the trade association was recommended as the appropriate instrument for securing cooperation. In recommending this policy Mr. Eddy may well have been impressed by the "Gary dinners" at which the steel producers had revealed their prices to their rivals. As counsel for a number of trade associations he was influential in developing the "open-price policy" which became the core of trade association activities during the twenty years succeeding the publication of his book.

During this twenty years the extent to which industries organized trade associations was influenced by a number of factors.[4] The lumber industry stands out as the one in which the movement developed most rapidly. The industry was entering upon a difficult period of declining prosperity owing to over-optimistic capitalization of timber holdings, and declining demand, due to the decreasing importance of the settlement of new lands, and the competition of new building materials. The trade association

[1] U.S. DEPARTMENT OF COMMERCE, *Trade Association Activities*, 1923, 303.
[2] See N.I.C.B., *Trade Associations*, II.
[3] EDDY, *The New Competition*, 87. In his book he developed these principles for industries producing to specification and obtaining business by contract bidding. Having the anti-trust laws in view, Mr. Eddy recommended the free interchange of information concerning actual **and** not future transactions. *Cf.* also "The genuineness of competitive rivalry does not hinge upon the maintenance of ignorance. On the contrary, knowledge of the market is a necessary prerequisite to the effective operation of the competitive process." (N.I.C.B., *Trade Associations*, 119.)
[4] The earliest open-price trade associations are said to have been the Bridge Builders Society in the iron and steel industry which adopted the policy in 1911, and the Yellow Pine Association which followed in the next year (NELSON, *Open Price Associations*, 24).

THE TRADE ASSOCIATION AND INDUSTRIAL INSTITUTE 45

movement was encouraged after 1917 by the War Industries Board which desired to deal with industry in organized groups;[1] the number of associations increased between 1914 and 1919 from about 800 to 2,000.[2] The rapidity of the rise in the general level of prices after the conclusion of the war in 1918 and the equally rapid subsequent fall subjected the associations to a strain which proved fatal to many, largely because they had passed beyond the limited range of activities recommended by Mr. Eddy. Some, however, persisted long enough, and were apparently effective enough, to attract the attention of the Federal Trade Commission and the Attorney General; a few were charged with restraining trade in contravention of the Sherman Law, and a series of decisions by the Supreme Court placed some restrictions upon their activities. The trade association movement lost influence during the decade from 1920 to 1930 owing to the incompetence of the officers of many associations, the inadequacy of their programs, lack of support in many industries, and to dissatisfaction resulting towards the end of the period from unprofitable trade conditions.[3] In 1933, however, the National Industrial Recovery Act opened a new period in the history of trade associations which is separately discussed at a later stage.[4]

II. TRADE ASSOCIATION POLICIES 1912–1933

The twenty years between 1912 and 1933 stand apart, therefore, as a distinctive period in the history of trade associations. Overt control of prices and output was prohibited by the anti-trust laws. The forces making for the limitation of price competition and the concentration of the control of industry were deflected by Mr. Eddy into often vigorous and enthusiastic experimentation with the provision of information and indirect methods of influencing production and prices. Hopes of finding a middle way between a competition that was becoming increasingly dangerous,

---

[1] U.S. DEPARTMENT OF COMMERCE, *Trade Association Activities*, 304.
[2] *ibid.*, 304.
[3] Executive director of the American Institute of Steel Construction at *Hearings on the Establishment of a National Economic Council* before a subcommittee of the Committee on Manufactures of the U.S. Senate, 1931, 477. Director of Federal Employment Stabilization Board, *ibid.*, 5, 566. The trade conditions favoring the establishment of trade associations have been variously stated. On the one hand it has been suggested that periods of depression and disorganization, especially following wars and financial panics, have necessitated the formation of such associations for mutual protection (F.T.C., *Open Price Trade Associations*, 304). On the other hand it has been said that they have been formed mainly in periods of prosperity (N.I.C.B., *Trade Associations*, 7, 8).
[4] See Chap. X.

and a far-reaching state control were raised. What became of these hopes and efforts?[1]

The activities of trade associations fall into five classes, viz., (A) performance of functions most economically conducted on a large scale, (B) provision of information, (C) control of output, (D) the control of types of product, and (E) control of methods of selling.

A. *The Performance of Functions Most Economically Conducted on a Large Scale*

The principal activities undertaken by trade associations which are of a sort more economically performed upon a larger scale than the more directly productive activities of the individual members consist of industrial research (concerning the improvement of processes of production or the utilization of the product[2] and, occasionally, the best methods of selecting workers and organizing the conditions of work); commercial research (into the problems of distributing the product, an activity not very highly developed); the provision of credit information (concerning the records of customers in the matter of the volume of purchases and regularity of payment); the development of public relations (aimed at generally influencing public opinion in favor of the industry[3] and, occasionally, advertising[4] or exerting influence to secure favorable tariff legislation); the conduct of research into insurance legislation and, occasionally, the provision of facilities for insurance; negotiation with railroads concerning freight schedules, the classification of commodities, the allocation of cars,[5] and the provision of books of freight rates from one or more points of production.[6]

The general effect of these activities is to reduce the cost of these services to each member. Small firms may be enabled to

[1] No attempt will be made to give a full and balanced picture of the activities of trade associations: we are here concerned merely with their use as a means to the alleviation of the rigors of price competition.

[2] Activities of this type have been undertaken, for example, by such associations as the American Institute of Baking, the National Canners Association, the Institute of American Meat Packers, the Tanners Council of America, and the Portland Cement Association.

[3] For example, the activities of the Institute of American Meat Packers aimed at countering the effect upon public opinion of the Federal Trade Commission's report upon the industry in 1919.

[4] *Cf.* The advertising of lumber, sugar, and cement by trade associations.

[5] *Cf.* the activities of the National Coal Association and some of the lumber manufacturers' associations.

[6] For example, by the Cement Manufacturers Protective Association, the Maple Flooring Manufacturers Association, and the Sugar Institute.

secure services which otherwise they would be compelled to do without, and the most economical scale of production in the industry tends to be reduced.[1] Cooperative advertising might "eventually lead to some diminution of the social burden of competitive advertising and of the wild orgy of salesmanship which serves to keep many markets in turmoil,"[2] although there is no evidence that it has had this effect. The cooperative provision of services included in the above list may pass, and, indeed, has passed over to efforts to make decisions for the individual producer. The provision of credit information, for instance, has developed into efforts to eliminate competition in terms of credit[3] and freight rate books have been alleged to be devices for inducing uniformity of delivered prices.[4]

B. *The Cooperative Provision of Information*

The collection and dissemination of information likely to affect the production and price policy of members have been the core of trade association activities during the period under review.[5] The principal matters concerning which associations have provided statistics are costs, prices, production, sales, shipments, and inventories. The consequence of providing this information depends upon its interpretation by those in the industry. This interpretation depends in turn upon the completeness and accuracy of the information, the manner in which it is presented, and the nature and extent of the efforts of the association to induce any particular interpretation.

I. THE STANDARDIZATION OF FORMS OF COST ACCOUNTS

The desire to provide information concerning costs almost invariably led trade associations to provide standardized forms for

---

[1] *Cf.* for instance F.T.C., *The House Furnishings Industries*, II, 91: U.S. DEPARTMENT OF COMMERCE, *Trade Association Activities*, 1923, 8: JONES, *Trade Association Activities and the Law*, vii.

[2] N.I.C.B., *Trade Associations*, 306.

[3] See U.S. v. Tile Manufacturers Credit Association, U.S. District Court, S.D. Ohio, Decree of November 26, 1923; SEAGER and GULICK, *Trust and Corporation Problems*, 312.

[4] See Chap. VI.

[5] The mortality rate among associations supplying statistics has, however, been high (F.T.C., *Open Price Trade Associations*, 307). Although price reporting activities were held by the Supreme Court to be within the law, a number of associations resuming such activities after favorable court decisions had been made, subsequently abandoned them (*ibid.*, 135). About a hundred associations were reported as collecting statistics in 1927; these consisted almost entirely of manufacturers; price reporting activities were not popular in the distributing trades (U.S. DEPARTMENT OF COMMERCE, *Trade Association Activities*, 1927, 20).

the calculation of costs by their members. The Federal Trade Commission found in 1929 that 19 out of 85 open-price trade associations issued cost manuals.[1] The necessity for such a service arises, partly, from the fact that many, and especially the smaller, producers depart so far from the theoretical conception of an entrepreneur that they do not know their own costs,[2] and in large measure out of the desire to facilitate comparisons of costs.

In so far as this practice avoids the necessity of each firm employing an accountant to design a system of cost accounting, it falls within the class of activities already discussed, *i.e.*, those more economically performed on a larger scale than production in the narrow sense. Cost accounting stands, however, in a peculiar relation to the making of price policy. The establishment of uniform systems is expected, as we have seen, to eliminate price cutting arising out of the ignorance of sellers of their own costs. No firm can continue to sell below cost for long periods, even in the absence of cost accounts, but in industries operated on a small scale there may be a procession of firms quoting prices below cost because of their ignorance. Although they fail they seriously disturb the industry. Producers are, however, too ready to attribute price cutting to the ignorance of the price cutter rather than to his superior efficiency and vigor. The absence of adequate cost accounts is also important where each firm sells a number of products having significant elements of cost in common, as in the

[1] F.T.C., *Open Price Trade Associations*, 166. The secretary of the National Association of Cost Accountants reported in 1923 that 121 trade associations were known to have adopted a uniform system of cost accounts, and of these not more than 12 were exchanging cost data (*Yearbook* of National Association of Cost Accountants, 1923, 297, 298). Associations were especially active in providing uniform cost systems in the furniture manufacturing industry (F.T.C., *Household Furnishings Industries*, I, 224, 280, 365). Such systems were also provided by the National Association of Stove Manufacturers (*ibid.*, II, 94), the Washing Machine Manufacturers Association (*ibid.*, III, 44), and many of the associations in the lumber industry.

[2] After making investigations over a wide range of industry, the Federal Trade Commission reported in 1916 that its investigations "showed that a large percentage of the merchants and manufacturers of the country, particularly the smaller ones, had a very inadequate knowledge, either of their costs of production or of their selling expenses. Many of them kept their books in such a way that they were unable to supply the commission with even the simplest facts concerning their business." (F.T.C., *Annual Report* for year ended June, 1916, 15.) See also F.T.C., *Fundamentals of a Cost System for Manufacturers*, 1916; F.T.C., *The High Price of Farm Implements*, 291; F.T.C., *House Furnishings Industries*, I, 73, 75, 79, 208, 276, 305; F.T.C., *Open Price Trade Associations*, 163, 175, 176; F.T.C., *Wartime Costs and Profits of Southern Pine Lumber Companies*, 1922, 9, 18. It was estimated that in 1926 only 26 per cent of the mills in the cotton industry used correct cost procedure; by 1932 the percentage had risen to 61 per cent partly as a result of the activities of the Cotton Textile Institute (WHITNEY, *Trade Associations and Industrial Control*, 64).

THE TRADE ASSOCIATION AND INDUSTRIAL INSTITUTE 49

case of furniture, agricultural implements, and indeed most kinds of manufacturing.[1] More generally cost accounts are a means of suggesting a minimum price, it being assumed that prices should never fall below costs of production.

2. THE STANDARDIZATION OF METHODS OF CALCULATING COSTS

Standardization of the mere forms of accounting leaves room for wide differences in the methods of calculating costs. Trade associations have sought, therefore, to introduce uniformity of policy in these calculations, thus taking the first step in the direction of control of price policy. Differences in cost may arise out of differences in the price at which raw materials are included in costs in periods of changing prices. Raw materials may be entered at the actual price paid for them or at the price at which they could be replaced. During the period following the close of the war of 1914 to 1918 and throughout the subsequent period when the general level of prices was first rising and later falling, associations of cotton textile, stove, and furniture manufacturers attempted to induce their members to include raw materials at their replacement cost.[2] The actual amount to be included in costs for some purposes has been recommended by trade associations.[3]

The most difficult problem is that of determining the treatment of overhead costs. In so far as prices can be, and are, based upon average costs, suggestions concerning policy in this matter are of very great importance whenever plant is not fully utilized and, therefore, particularly during periods of general depression. If an attempt is made to distribute overhead costs equally over time, a decline in output causes an increase in average costs with a tendency to maintain or even raise prices.[4] A successful campaign to prevent prices from falling below costs so calculated would result in a normal return in periods when plant was not fully used.[5] A revival of business, increasing the proportion of plant in

---

[1] See p. 35.
[2] WHITNEY, *Trade Associations and Industrial Control*, 68; F.T.C., *House Furnishings Industries*, I, 186, 190, 208, 220, 245, 260, 267, 282, 342; II, 94, 175.
[3] The association of stove manufacturers, for instance, suggested percentages of the costs of material to be added for breakages, for processes such as plating, and for "general manufacturing expense," "loss and waste," "general distributing cost," "salesmen's costs," "discounts and rebates." In 1917 the association adopted such percentages for all expenses other than materials and labor. (F.T.C., *House Furnishings Industries*, II, 94 ff., 175.)
[4] *Cf.* CLARK, *Economics of Overhead Costs*, 435; also F.T.C., *Open Price Trade Associations*, 192.
[5] The Cotton Textile Institute warned against cost calculations based upon the

use, would bring a decline in average costs; it is doubtful, however, whether prices have in fact been cut in the face of an expanding demand. If a "normal" rate of operation be recommended in allocating overhead costs over output[1] and the "normal" is less than full operation, a smaller contribution will be obtained for overhead costs in years when plant is subnormally utilized, than in years when it is utilized at more than the "normal" rate. If prices are adjusted to costs so calculated, and direct costs do not change, prices remain constant; total revenue from sales just covers total costs when plant is actually operated at the "normal" rate, exceeds them when plant is more fully used, and falls short of them when it is less fully used. It is usually also necessary to distribute overhead costs over different types, grades, or sizes of product. There are usually some costs (at least management costs) that cannot be directly attributed to a single class of product. Trade associations have also attempted to introduce uniformity of policy in making this distribution.[2] This action was prompted by the desire to prevent price competition resulting from the meeting of a rival's price by selling a commodity not identical with his at the same price; it was also aimed at the elimination of types of product sold at a loss.[3]

A uniform method of cost calculation can be made to influence production and price policy more directly if manufacturers can be induced to standardize the amount of profit included in "costs."[4]

---

full use of plant in times when plant was not fully used (WHITNEY, *Trade Associations and Industrial Control*, 66).

[1] The National Council of Furniture Associations in June, 1921, when the industry was very depressed, recommended that manufacturers in their individual cost calculations should assume a normal rate of operation for the calculation of overhead cost (F.T.C., *House Furnishings Industries*, I, 210). The members of the Wool Institute said it was proposed that the members should "figure their costs on a basis of the average sales for the past two years" (*New York Times*, Feb. 16, 1928).

[2] For example, in the maple flooring industry (Maple Flooring Manufacturers Association v. U.S., *Petition by Attorney General for Rehearing*, 23, *Reply Brief for Maple Flooring Manufacturers Association*, 25). The stove manufacturers organized a trade association as early as 1871 and were engaged from its inception in discussions of costs. In 1889 they adopted a formula for the calculation of the cost of every type of stove. In 1907 when the formula was revised it was accompanied by a uniform system of cost accounting which was recommended to the members. The system not only described a system of ledger accounts but also recommended an arbitrary formula for the distribution over the goods produced of wages and all overhead expenses (including interest on investment at 5 per cent). (F.T.C., *House Furnishings Industries*, II, 94, 175.) *Cf.* also F.T.C., *Open Price Trade Associations*, 192.

[3] F.T.C., *House Furnishings Industries*, I, 225, 270, 318; *Open Price Trade Associations*, 192.

[4] Until 1922 the maple flooring manufacturers included 10 per cent on sales for profit and 5 per cent for contingencies (Maple Flooring Manufacturers Association

The resulting figure then becomes a desired selling price. But differences in "costs" thus calculated are likely to remain and encourage price cutting, although the standardization of methods of distributing overhead costs over time and over different types of product greatly reduces these differences. This increased uniformity of "costs" tends to induce a more uniform reaction on the part of producers to changes in conditions of demand or supply.[1]

In fact, however, associations have been unprepared to leave each seller to determine his policy in the face only of his own statistics of cost. "It is substantially true that the only trade association interest in uniform cost accounting is as a basis for cost comparison."[2] It is argued, with justification, that comparison of the detailed cost statements of different manufacturers is capable of increasing the efficiency of industry. Under competition it is assumed that the low-cost producer will, by reducing his price, bring pressure to bear upon the high-cost producers to improve their methods of production; if, however, the latter can compare their costs with those of the more efficient they can more speedily detect the origin of their relative inefficiency and improve their methods.[3] But, in fact, members rarely permit the publication and circulation of their individual costs and, therefore, this reason for the standardization of costs is of little practical relevance.[4]

Some associations published an average cost for the whole industry. As a means of increasing the efficiency of the industry this service cannot be very effective for it serves to stimulate only those whose costs are above the average; the publication of the lowest costs would provide a more general stimulus to efficiency as well as a rough basis for the criticism of prices. In fact, the average

---

v. U.S., *Reply Brief for the U.S.*, 83). Profit was also included in the cost calculation of the furniture manufacturers (F.T.C., *House Furnishings Industries* I, 210, 245).

[1] The secretary of an association of stove manufacturers referred to the "baneful influence on market conditions" of differences in opinion concerning the selling value of stoves resulting from differences in cost calculations (F.T.C., *House Furnishing Industries*, II, 175). Cf. also ibid., II, 124, 125.

[2] F.T.C., *Open Price Trade Associations*, 181. See also F.T.C., *House Furnishings Industries*, I, 276.

[3] The Federal Trade Commission argued, however, that "while it is clearly desirable that each producer should know his own cost it is very doubtful if any public interest is served by each producer knowing every other producer's costs" (*Canned Foods*, 1918, 93).

[4] The National Industrial Conference Board remarked that "in the absence of fairly precise knowledge of costs it is manifest that some of the basic data essential to the progressive development of efficiency in production are lacking" and also that "the market policies of producers are likely to be wayward and unstable"—a significant addition (*Trade Associations*, 230).

has served rather as a cost which should be adopted by members in place of their own separate calculations and used as the basis of calculating a selling price by the addition of the desired rate of profit.[1] Some furniture manufacturers found, for instance, that "the costs of individual factories cause varieties of prices and cause lack of stability in the furniture market" and therefore "average cost of production should control market prices."[2] There still remains, however, a possibility of differences in selling price owing to differences in the amount of "profit" added to cost and some associations have taken the final step and included an allowance for profit in the so-called "average costs." "Average costs" then become merely a suggested selling price, uniform for all,[3] and provide a means by which to define and detect price cutting and a stimulus to attempts to eliminate it.[4] Some stimulus to efficient operation may remain, but pressure to pass on the results of greater efficiency in the form of price reductions is eliminated; even the inducement to keep individual cost accounts is diminished.

The furniture manufacturers devoted much attention to the compilation and circulation of statistics of this type especially during 1920 and 1921. Bulletins containing the "selling values" or "basic costs" of selected products in most branches of the industry were periodically published. The products selected were of sizes, styles, materials, and finishes important in each branch. Supplementary figures to be added to or subtracted from those for the selected products were provided to facilitate the calculation of the "selling values" of other products. These selling values were calculated by committees or by a cost adviser or

[1] The Maple Flooring Manufacturers Association circulated statistics of "average costs" which the Attorney General regarded as a means to the reduction of price cutting; he argued that associations did not attempt to eliminate all price cutting but merely to establish a minimum price at which the most expensively produced goods could be profitably sold, members then competing to sell above this minimum; those who succeeded would make a good showing and be imitated by their rivals (Maple Flooring Manufacturers Association v. U.S., *Reply Brief for the U.S.*, 173). It was suggested to the southern furniture manufacturers that cost bulletins "should prove helpful to our membership to be used as a yardstick in checking against their individual cost systems" (F.T.C., *House Furnishings Industries*, I, 191, 211).
[2] Southern Furniture Manufacturers Association, *ibid.*, I, 186, 245.
[3] This uniformity is lacking as we have seen when a *rate* of profit is recommended as an addition to *individual* costs.
[4] U.S. DEPARTMENT OF COMMERCE, *Trade Association Activities* 6, 34, 36; F.T.C. *Open Price Trade Associations*, 164, 173. "Arguments against selling below cost are, unfortunately, too often not clear as to whether the reference is to average costs of the industry or the specific costs of the individual concern" (F.T.C., *House Furnishing Industries*, I, 176).

agreed upon at meetings.¹ The "selling values" were frequently said to be based upon actual costs² but they were also said to be based upon market value³ and it was never very clear how a single cost figure was obtained from the wide variety of actual costs. The treatment of overhead costs when demand changed was occasionally discussed.⁴ "Selling values" included an allowance for profit which was sometimes determined by the cost adviser and sometimes by the association.⁵ Urging the use of such "selling values" by his members, the secretary of one association argued that their adoption would bring about uniformity of prices.⁶

The investigation by the Federal Trade Commission revealed clearly that these "selling values" were regarded as minimum prices—as "average prices at which articles should be sold to yield a fair profit."⁷ Many similar phrases indicate how common was this interpretation of the figures.⁸ Recommendations in the bulletins that these "selling values" and "basic costs" be used as minimum prices were reinforced by the proceedings at the meetings of associations. Resolutions were passed approving and "adopting" the bulletins and recommending that the figures appearing therein be used as minimum prices.⁹ The bulletins were also used at the meetings as the basis for the discussion of future prices; occasionally members were required to state individually to the meeting their opinion of the "selling values," failure to oppose them being felt by the members to bind them to accept the recommended prices.¹⁰ Discussions of prices led to resolutions and expressions of opinion concerning the desirability of raising or maintaining the prices of various types of furniture.¹¹ In general, when sales were severely curtailed after the middle of 1920, the associations sought to maintain prices. During this period anxiety for uniformity of prices, *i.e.*, the prevention of price cutting, was intense and meetings were frequent.¹² Resolu-

---

[1] F.T.C., *House Furnishings Industries*, I, 219, 282, 318, 351, 369.
[2] *ibid.*, I, 219, 224, 244, 319, 352.
[3] *ibid.*, I, 212.
[4] *ibid.*, I, 244, 266, 267, 298, 342.
[5] *ibid.*, I, 244, 245, 282, 340. Occasionally profit was shown separately (*ibid.*, I 341).
[6] *ibid.*, I, 239.
[7] *ibid.*, I, 185.
[8] *ibid.*, I, 33, 187, 190, 191, 209, 212, 243, 244, 260, 318, 340.
[9] *ibid.*, I, 189, 190, 207, 267, 320.
[10] The procedure is similar to that at the Gary dinners in the steel industry.
[11] *ibid.*, I, 189, 198 *ff.*, 218, 226, 231, 233, 237 *ff.*, 251, 254 *ff.*, 289, 292, 293, 300, 320, 321, 324, 337, 342.
[12] *ibid.*, I, 201, 202, 209, 210, 232, 240, 253, 323, 338, 343, 354.

tions concerning the maintenance of prices occasionally implied that any future change would be upward.[1] It was doubtless hoped thus to strengthen the determination to maintain prices and also to discourage the postponement of purchases. A slight reduction might have encouraged hope of more reductions to come. It was also suggested that demand was so inelastic that reductions in price would bring out little new business.[2]

To these two types of pressure was added the persuasion of the officers of the associations. Members charging less than the suggested price were terrified by gruesome pictures of the fate of those who sold below cost, or shamed by references to "weak-kneed manufacturers who reduced prices and broke the market."[3] Rumors of price cutting were followed up and often denied.[4] In general this pressure, often subtle and difficult to trace, was successful,[5] but in times of strain it failed and was abandoned.[6]

In spite of these activities the associations of furniture manufacturers frequently denied any desire to make price agreements. They reiterated the right of every seller to fix his own prices while also stating it to be their purpose "to bring about an equalization of values and to prevent any individual from bringing down the whole market through a disregard of cost or market values."[7] This denial of any desire to control prices was partly stimulated by fear of prosecution under the Sherman Law, more especially during the period when the activities of the association of hardwood manufacturers were under investigation. But it was also partly due to the difficulty of enforcing agreements in an industry selling such a variety of styles, models, and grades of product. Broken price agreements disrupted the industry.[8] But while no association admitted the desire to control prices, none was content that its members should determine their prices in independent contemplation of their individual costs.

"Both in times of advancing and declining prices the purpose of the association's cost and price activities has been the control of price competition. The means used have been the adoption and recommenda-

[1] *ibid.*, I, 207, 296, 298, 299, 301, 353.
[2] *ibid.*, I, 206, 211, 267.
[3] *ibid.*, I, 188, 301, 323, 329, 330, 332, 336.
[4] *ibid.*, I, 246.
[5] *ibid.*, I, 332.
[6] *ibid.*, I, 237, 264. Occasionally the attempts of trade associations to show as large a cost as possible overreached themselves and members found themselves compelled to sell below the published figures (*ibid.*, I, 176).
[7] *ibid.*, I, 150, 208, 209, 227, 255, 260, 267, 283, 293, 306, 329, 341, 346, 356, 358.
[8] *ibid.*, I, 214, 264.

tion of costs and minimum selling values, the pricing of individual pieces, and the comparison of prices at meetings. From these activities have resulted resolutions recommending the advancement, maintenance, or reduction of prices, in accordance with bulletins or findings of price comparison meetings. These activities have resulted at different times and under varying conditions of demand and supply in varying degrees of price control.[1] . . . While the restraint involved appears loose, the very looseness of the plan and its lack of any drastic elements of compulsion constitute one of its elements of effectiveness. The considerable degree of freedom for individual action given by the adoption of minimum instead of fixed prices, and the emphasis on the common effort to reach the desired goal, probably resulted in greater success than could have been attained by methods of sharper control. The results suggest the inherent strength of a federation working loosely towards a common end as against the weakness sometimes inherent in unified, autocratic control."[2]

The commission concluded, therefore, that "among the many legitimate kinds of trade association activities which may easily and imperceptibly pass over from the stage of useful service to that of abuse and even illegality, few are more prone to this sort of transition than cost accounting work."[3]

3. STATISTICS OF PRODUCTION

Many associations and especially those in the lumber industry have collected and circulated information concerning the volume of production by their members. The repercussions of this information upon production policy have been influenced by the form in which the statistics have been made available and by suggestions concerning their proper interpretation. Statistics of output may be very confusing where the number of firms reporting is not constant, and it was partly for this reason that of the 35 associations providing such information which were studied by the Federal Trade Commission, 11 expressed output as a ratio of capacity and 3 as a ratio of normal production.[4] The selection of the "normal"

[1] *ibid.*, I, 214.
[2] *ibid.*, I, xvii. To this policy is to be attributed, at least in part, the fact that "the wholesale prices of furniture held up so long in 1920 and declined so gradually in 1921, though for a time in the spring of 1921 they broke below the reduced levels sanctioned by the manufacturers' associations." But "it is also to be said in fairness that the results indicate that the marked falling off in profits in 1921 was in part due to the fact that manufacturers and dealers did not reduce wages and salaries of employees as much, relatively, as they reduced prices." (*ibid.*, I, xxii.)
[3] *ibid.*, I, 176.
[4] F.T.C., *Open Price Associations*, 111. In general the commission believed that "the use of a 'normal' that is not objectively defined is not a favorable sign in connection with statistics" (*ibid.*, 26).

however, influences the interpretation of the statistics. The Southern Pine Association published in its bulletin a "barometer" of business which represented on three tubes side by side, orders, production, and shipments, "by which through concerted action the association instructs its membership how to restrict production and thereby to increase the price of lumber by an artificial control of supply as balanced against current demand."[1] The Federal Trade Commission contended that whenever the tube representing production was in advance of those representing orders and shipments members saw that production must be reduced unless inventories were to accumulate and prices were ultimately to fall; whenever production was falling behind orders and shipments members saw that supply was below demand and that higher prices could be obtained.[2] The commission's interpretation (which suggests that production could never increase) is not, however, the only one: it could be argued that when members saw production falling behind orders and shipments they would increase output. If members always adjusted production to orders, prices and inventories would remain unchanged, all changes in demand being met by equivalent changes in supply. The commission was, however, partly justified in its interpretation by the fact that until 1919 the "barometer" was accompanied by a comment that "experience indicates that whenever shipments or orders are above production, values increase provided production does not increase at a greater rate than shipments and orders."[3]

Statistics of production have also been presented in terms of a "normal" which was the actual production during some past period. The Southern Pine Association later adopted this principle; its "barometers" had, however, shown production below "normal" ever since 1916,[1] from which the Federal Trade Commission inferred that "the higher prices obtained for southern pine lumber have not been the result of unusual demand as such, but because the demand has constantly exceeded a less than normal supply."[2] It might have added that restriction of output had gone beyond any suggestion implied in the barometer and that the statistical activities of the association were not, therefore, a sufficient

---

[1] F.T.C., *Lumber Manufacturers Trade Associations*, 1922, 59.
[2] *loc. cit.*
[3] *ibid.*, 58. Early in 1925 the Southern Yarn Spinners Association commenced to remind its members weekly of the need to "regulate operations solely by the volume of orders" (F.T.C., *Open Price Trade Associations*, 280). The Wool Institute pursued a similar policy (WHITNEY, *Trade Associations and Industrial Control*, 124).

THE TRADE ASSOCIATION AND INDUSTRIAL INSTITUTE 57

explanation of the low volume of production. Indeed the commission reported in 1922 that the southern pine mills as a whole had lately curtailed output to nearly 50 per cent of "normal." The association of producers of Douglas fir lumber published a barometer in similar form and again the commission reported that since 1916 the production of Douglas fir had seldom approached the "normal" even under the influence of the enormous price increases of 1919 and 1920 and had for the most part remained well below it.[1] Again high prices were attributed to restriction of output but it is difficult to blame these particular activities of the association for the restriction. The selection of the output of a past period as a "normal" suggests a desire to prevent production in excess of that figure. Prices could be maintained at the level ruling during the period of "normal" output only if demand can be relied upon to attain the level during the period of "normal" output.

Where neither the form of the statistics nor the other activities of the association are aimed directly at any particular production policy the provision of such statistics is claimed to rationalize independent competitive conduct and render the competitive process more perfect because "it enables competing concerns to order their production policies intelligently on the basis of economic fact rather than blindly on the basis of hearsay or guesswork. And this is desirable from the public standpoint as well as in its private business aspect; for it serves to mitigate the dangers of misdirected production and to stabilize economic conditions."[2] This intelligent ordering of production often amounts, however, to adapting production to demand[3] and avoiding the accumulation of unsold stocks. It is implied that when demand declines there is only one proper response, *viz.*, an equal reduction of output.[4]

---

[1] *Lumber Manufacturers Trade Associations*, 77. The Western Pine Manufacturers Association was also accused of curtailing production with the object of maintaining agreed prices (*ibid.*, 93, 142).

[2] N.I.C.B., *Trade Associations*, 79.

[3] "Trade associations are better fitted than any other human agency to bring about closer adaptation of production and distribution to requirements of all concerned and to bring under control overproduction, business depression, and unemployment" (G. H. Montague, general counsel for the National Welded Chain Association, as reported in *New York Times*, June 30, 1928). *Cf.* the "eleventh commandment" referred to at a meeting of the Cement Manufacturers Association in 1913: "Don't be a hog—don't overproduce" (Cement Manufacturers Protective Association v. U.S., *Brief for U.S.*, 27).

[4] The Wool Institute, for instance, endeavored to induce members (*inter alia*) to "limit their stocks to a thirty days supply and manufacture only against orders" and to maintain prices throughout the season (*New York Times*, Feb. 16, 1928). The National Association of Hosiery and Underwear Manufacturers adopted a

One important further consequence of providing statistics of total production at very short intervals is that each member is enabled to calculate the extent to which changes in his volume of business are paralleled by changes in the total volume, *i.e.*, whether his share of the total is changing or not; the Department of Commerce approved of this use of the statistics.[1] The Sugar Institute when circulating statistics of total production calculated for each member his percentage of the total melt for the past week, and for the year to date, and provided a comparison with the previous year.[2] The Aluminum Wares Association, the Vacuum Cleaner Manufacturers Association, and the American Washing Machine Manufacturers Association made or facilitated similar calculations.[3] These calculations are aimed at deterring the firm whose sales have been falling from attempting to increase its sales by increased sales effort or price cutting at a time when the sales of all firms are falling. Thus a "demoralized market" is avoided. Such an interpretation of the statistics must tend to fix the distribution of business between firms. In so far as price cutting is deterred when business falls off there is also a tendency to maintain unchanged prices. The description of such statistics as a means of providing a "broad factual basis for independent judgment on economic conditions and market trends in the trade or industry"[4] clearly fails to reveal their more serious implications which will be discussed in connection with the policy of stabilizing prices.[5]

---

policy of "manufacturing only against orders and holding inventories to the lowest possible figure" (*New York Times*, Jan. 30, 1931).

[1] "Accurate information promptly distributed showing total production, shipments, orders received and unfilled, stocks on hand, etc., for the industry as a whole enables a manufacturer or a merchant to compare his own activity with that of the entire industry of which he is a part. If he finds that his own orders are increasing at a more rapid rate than those for the combined industry, he may congratulate himself and his organization. On the other hand if his orders are not increasing in volume while those for the whole industry are, he may wish to hold a conference with his sales manager. . . . A comparison of the activity in an individual unit with the industry as a whole enables the executive always to keep his organization in tune with current trends." (U.S. DEPARTMENT OF COMMERCE, *Trade Association Activities*, 1923, 23.) See also JONES, *Trade Association Activities and the Law*, 1922, 47.

[2] U S. v. Sugar Institute, *Brief for the U.S.* 176.

[3] F.T.C., *House Furnishings Industries*, III, 13, 44, 66. A discussion of the advantage of trade associations in the stove manufacturing industry produced the remark that the large firm did not wish to obstruct the small; it merely wished "to prevent the small man from taking away too much of his business and that's fair" (*ibid.*, II, 91). The Chicago Retail Lumber Dealers Association, however, published the percentage of the total business allotted to each member (F.T.C., *Lumber Manufacturers Trade Associations*, 1922, 52).

[4] N.I.C.B., *Trade Associations*, 121.

[5] See Chap. V.

THE TRADE ASSOCIATION AND INDUSTRIAL INSTITUTE 59

4. STATISTICS OF INVENTORIES

Some trade associations have circulated information concerning unsold stocks of goods. These statistics are likely to be used as a guide to production policy, production being diminished when stocks are accumulating, and increased when stocks are falling. Their use in this manner is likely to lead to results similar to those where statistics of production are circulated in a form inducing direct comparison of production with shipments. The existing price of the product tends to be maintained[1] and production adjusted to changes in demand at the unchanging price.

5. STATISTICS OF UNFILLED ORDERS

In industries in which little or no inventory can be kept, and goods are produced to order, statistics of unfilled orders have been compiled by some associations.[2] Unfilled orders resemble inventories in that they are a cushion between sales and production. Sales in excess of current output reduce inventories or increase unfilled orders according as the industry does or does not produce for stock. If the response to a decline in the total of unfilled orders resulting from an excess of production over current contracts for sale is a reduction of output, prices are maintained unchanged;[1] production is adjusted to changes in demand at the unchanging price.

6. STATISTICS OF PRODUCTIVE CAPACITY

Occasionally trade associations circulated statistics of the productive capacity of their industry.[3] These statistics were usually used to provide information concerning the proportion of productive capacity in use.[4] Calculations of capacity are, however, extremely treacherous. There are few industries in which products are homogeneous enough for measures of productive capacity to be calculated for the whole industry. It also is difficult to determine precisely what plants can still be regarded as "in the industry,"

---

[1] F.T.C., *Open Price Trade Associations*, 89.
[2] See JONES, *Trade Association Activities and the Law*, 47. Only some of the associations in the furniture industry compiled and circulated statistics of unfilled orders as well, usually, as those of orders shipped and orders cancelled (F.T.C., *House Furnishings Industries*, I, 27, 31, 183, 317, 357).
[3] *ibid.*, 156.
[4] The hardwood manufacturers, however, appear to have attempted to restrict the expansion of the industry (American Column and Lumber Co. v. U.S., *Brief for U.S.*, 2).

i.e., available for production. The general effect of circulating statistics concerning capacity is not easy to forecast. Where there is considerable excess capacity, such figures are intended to discourage potential new competitors, and thus avoid unjustified extensions of plant and long-continued unprofitable operation.[1] But such figures may be deceptive. Operation below capacity may be due to the restriction of production and it may be that not only all the existing equipment but more could be kept fully employed and secure a normal return. These figures also serve as a reminder to members of the extent of unused capacity and of the full possibilities of a campaign of price cutting.

7. STATISTICS OF SELLING PRICES

There were in 1927 about 100 associations administering the "open-price" policy propounded by Mr. Eddy, and their activities affected about 20 per cent of all the commodities for which the Bureau of Labor Statistics published wholesale prices.[2] The principal necessity for such a service is said to lie in the danger of "phantom competition," *i.e.*, pressure to reduce prices arising from untruthful reports by buyers concerning the offers made by other sellers.[3] Sellers wish to avoid shifts of business arising from price cuts before all firms have heard of and adjusted to them. They fear also that a downward change in prices once made may lead to a series of such changes.

Before 1914 statistics of this type "were doubtless in part developed as a substitute for outright agreements in restraint of trade."[4] The lumber industry was the first to make extensive use of them. Furniture manufacturers became interested in open-price activities in 1917,[5] partly, no doubt owing to the closeness of their relationships with the lumber industry. Open-price reporting has also been common in the constructional, textile, and paper and pulp industries, but it has aroused little interest in the machinery, vehicle, chemical, and clothing industries.[6] Trade associations have been ephemeral; partly for this reason the Federal Trade

[1] F.T.C., *Open Price Trade Associations*, 145 and 90.
[2] *ibid.*, 59, 69.
[3] *ibid.*, 82. *Cf.* the announcement that the Dow service was proposing to expand its weekly reports on building material prices by publishing actual sale prices of basic materials in the New York market in order to "diminish the hardships of ghost competition" (*New York Times*, Jan. 19, 1931).
[4] F.T.C., *Open Price Trade Associations*, 10.
[5] F.T.C., *House Furnishings Industries*, I, 227, 281, 335, 340.
[6] F.T.C., *Open Price Trade Associations*, 59.

THE TRADE ASSOCIATION AND INDUSTRIAL INSTITUTE 61

Commission had some difficulty in deciding whether trade associations persisted in open-price activities for long periods.[1]

As to the effect of open-price activities "it is implied practically without exception in the statements of those favoring open-price work that such work will mean an approach to uniformity of prices. This does not mean absolute uniformity or a fixed price, but merely a narrowing of the range of variation."[2] Whether the introduction of these activities raised the lowest or reduced the highest prices or both is not clear. It is doubtful whether the highest prices were reduced in view of the fact that the prices filed were rarely made available to buyers. It is even more doubtful whether open prices were intended to eliminate the highest prices. The Federal Trade Commission commented upon the possibility that the seller who fixed his prices without full knowledge of his costs (and presumably fixed them below those of his rivals) might be induced to raise his prices.[3] Where the identity of the firm filing each price is revealed pressure to raise prices might be brought to bear upon the firms filing the lowest prices. Where open-price reporting was combined with attempts to prevent sales at less than cost, pressure was applied to raise the lowest prices.[4] The Federal Trade Commission was unwilling to investigate the effect of open-price activities upon the level of prices;[5] the officers of a number of trade associations have claimed, however, that price reporting has somewhat raised prices.[6]

Open-price reporting probably tends toward the stability of prices by discouraging price cutting. The short-run inducement to price cutting, born of the hope of attracting business from rivals before they have similarly reduced their prices, is reduced to a

[1] Of 139 associations administering an open-price policy in 1921, only 33 appear still to have been doing so in 1927, even if successor associations be included; 44 were found to be no longer open-price associations, and the remaining 62 had passed out of existence for various reasons. The commission attributed this change partly to the fact that many associations were frightened out of open-price reporting by the decision of the Supreme Court in the hardwood case (American Column and Lumber Co. v. U.S., 257 U.S. 377). "On the other hand, if the practice had commended itself to the members of these associations as particularly valuable and important, it is proper to suppose that their memories of its benefits would have led to the reestablishment of price reporting after the cement and maple flooring decisions in 1925" (F.T.C., *Open Price Trade Associations*, 40).

[2] *ibid.*, 79. See also pp. 120, 182, 228, and 353. The commission made no special study of this matter but admitted that in some cases a great diversity of prices persisted (*ibid.*, 120). It is claimed that open prices prevent price concessions involving discrimination between buyers.

[3] *ibid.*, 79.
[4] F.T.C., *House Furnishings Industries*, I, 182.
[5] F.T.C., *Open Price Trade Associations*, 120.
[6] *ibid.*, 79; F.T.C., *House Furnishings Industries*, I, 225, 244, 352.

vanishing point when prices are open. Revelation of the identity of those filing prices,[1] by exposing those filing lower prices to pressure from their rivals, or from the officers of the trade association, not only tends to narrow the spread of prices by raising the lowest; it also tends to continuing efforts to prevent price cutting. These efforts merge into a policy of maintaining the level of prices obtaining at the time when the policy is introduced,[2] unless the association is powerful enough to exercise complete control of prices and output and secure unanimity and simultaneity in changing prices. In fact no association is known to have possessed such power. Their interest in stability was, in fact, mainly an interest in preventing reductions in price. This policy stands out clearly in the account of the activities of the trade associations in the furniture manufacturing industry in 1920 and 1921 and there is no reason to believe that this description is not typical of the activities of vigorous associations in other industries whose proceedings have been less fully analyzed.

The Federal Trade Commission found considerable stability of prices in some fields in which open-price activities also existed, but hesitated to attribute this stability to the activities of the trade associations.[3] Comparison of zero price changes (*i.e.*, the number of intervals of time in which prices in two successive intervals were identical) suggested, however, somewhat greater price stability in industries where there were no open-price activities than in those in which such activities were found but the difference was very small.[4] An examination of the maximum number of consecutive zero changes (*i.e.*, the maximum length of intervals of time in which no price change occurred) for the period after 1925 yielded similarly inconclusive results. The commission decided that the degree of stability of prices was most closely affected by the stage in the process of production between production of raw materials and of finished goods to which the prices related.[5] Other statistical

---

[1] The Federal Trade Commission opposed the identification of those filing prices. (*Open Price Trade Associations*, xviii.)

[2] *ibid.*, I, 192. Trade associations "followed up" reported price cuts in the wool and carpet industries among many others (WHITNEY, *Trade Associations and Industrial Control*, 82, 126).

[3] *Open Price Trade Associations*, 103, 120, and xix. The commission suggested that of the many causes that might induce such stability, price leadership was probably the most potent.

[4] *ibid.*, 101. "The exceptions are for cloths and clothing, consumers' goods; building material, raw products; house furnishings, consumers' goods, and miscellaneous consumers' goods."

[5] *ibid.*, 102.

measures led also to the conclusion that "there is no significant difference in degree of stability between the two groups,"[1] and that "it may be inferred that the open-price practice makes little or no difference as regards stability of prices.[2] This conclusion is not inconsistent with the idea that open-price associations of certain kinds work largely in the direction of uniformity and constancy of prices, but it does not appear that open-price work is the major and dominant factor in the situation generally."[3] It is possible that associations have developed in industries in which, owing to the lack of a price leader, or the fact that the industry was closer to the production of raw materials than to the production of finished goods, the dangers of price cutting were especially great. Associations may, therefore, have introduced a greater measure of stability than would otherwise have existed in the same industries, although not greater than in industries operating under conditions more favorable to the stabilization of prices. The success of the Copper Institute and Copper Exporters Inc. in stabilizing the price of copper at 18 cents per pound from April, 1929, to April, 1930, is a striking but not a typical example of the effect of association activities upon the stabilization of prices.[4] In so far as "open-price" activities tend to stabilize prices they tend to destabilize the volume of production.[5]

Associations setting out to provide a basis for the comparison of prices often meet with difficulties, owing to the fact that producers are located at different points and prices are quoted for delivery at a great variety of places. In the steel, lumber, and cement industries, for instance, comparison has been facilitated by reducing prices to one or a few geographical bases. Any attempt to narrow differences in prices as recalculated by reference to basing points

[1] ibid., 98.
[2] ibid., 97. The commission suggested caution in the interpretation of its results, owing to the smallness of the numbers of cases studied. It did, however, suggest that there had been an increase in the variability of the prices of commodities affected by open-price activities, but produced no comparable indexes for other commodities (ibid., 100).
[3] ibid., xix.
[4] WHITNEY, Trade Associations and Industrial Control, 92.
[5] See Chap. V. The effect of open-price activities upon production policy was not revealed by the investigation by the Federal Trade Commission. "It might be inferred that manufacturers in this group more than others let production take the brunt of fluctuations in business instead of adapting their prices to conditions of demand . . . but the inexactness of the data, together with the closeness of the difference, permits only the conclusion that open-price associations produce no very distinctive results for their industries" (ibid., 116). For contrary opinions see U.S. DEPARTMENT OF COMMERCE, Trade Association Activities, 1923, 3. See also F.T.C., Open Price Trade Associations, 35.

tends to the coordination of the price policies of producers in different areas and possibly to the development of a "basing point system."[1] A somewhat less definite means of producing the same result was revealed in the furniture industry, where producers in different parts of the country sought advice concerning costs and prices from a single "cost adviser."

It is evident, therefore, that the extent to which the provision of information concerning prices places an industry more nearly in the position of one in which there is an organized market is very uncertain. Trade associations in fact commonly provided information only to their members and not to buyers, although such was not the original intention of the founder of the movement.[2] An industry in which there is an organized market differs from one in which a trade association carries on open-price activities, moreover, in that in the former there is an interest in having the maximum amount of business done, "while the trade association is not interested in increasing the volume of buying and selling."[3]

C. *Cooperative Control of Output*

The discussion of the effects of the statistical services of trade associations suggests the difficulty of drawing a distinction between services which merely facilitate rational conduct by producers and attempts to concentrate in the hands of the association or its leaders power to determine the production and price policy for the whole industry. The Federal Trade Commission believed, however, that "emphasis on restriction of output, though of course on its face without any element of concert or agreement, is the control idea back of a good deal of trade association work."[4]

---

[1] See Chap. VI.

[2] EDDY, *The New Competition*, 115, 151. The Federal Trade Commission believed that trade associations may even have acted against their own interest in attempting to keep such information private. "It may be that in many cases the buyer adopts undesirable tactics and forces hard bargains, largely because he is not better informed as to the conditions as regards the cost of production of the commodity he is buying. . . . If the publication and dissemination of trade statistics were to be made a government function, then the expense and trouble to which individual manufacturers have been put in making returns would become a minor incident and not sufficient ground for giving sellers a preference as regards the possession of the information. The fact that the buyers should be given substantially the same information as the seller is a further important argument for government participation." (F.T.C., *Open Price Trade Associations*, 145.) The Department of Commerce has also emphasized the necessity for making such information available not only to buyers but also to non-members of the association (U.S. DEPARTMENT OF COMMERCE, *Trade Associations*, 1927, 34).

[3] F.T.C., *Open Price Trade Associations*, 77.

[4] *ibid.*, 358, 365.

This end has been sought by presenting statistics in a form suggesting a particular interpretation or by the exertion of pressure, through bulletins, at meetings,[1] or through the officers of the association, to secure the desired reaction.

Some trade associations have influenced the price and production policy of their members by manipulating the statistics they circulate. If, in calculating the summary figures circulated to their members, some bargains are arbitrarily excluded on the ground that they are "abnormal," and the bargains excluded are those at low prices, the reported average price is, of course, increased; in so far as the figures circulated have any effect, this practice tends to raise prices.[2] Individual members have apparently also excluded from their returns bargains at the lower prices.[3] Occasionally trade associations have suspended the publication of statistical information where it was expected to have an unfavorable effect upon the industry.[4]

On some occasions, however, trade associations have gone beyond the mere presentation of data and the application of pressure to secure a desired response.[5] The hardwood manufacturers collected in elaborate detail, statistics of output, sales, and shipments, and after 1920 sent circulars pressing for the curtailment of output in order to avoid overproduction. The Supreme Court held that these activities disclosed a clear purpose to restrain trade; so minute was the disclosure of business transactions that it could have been induced by only most attractive prospects; excessive increases in price, moreover, actually followed, and "the uniting action of this large and influential membership of dealers contributed greatly"[6] to this outcome. Drastic efforts to control

---

[1] The Federal Trade Commission remarked that the records of the associations contain fewer references than formerly to such activities. This change may be due, however, to more caution in recording such proceedings in view of the attitude of the courts to the activities of trade associations, or to the fact that better statistical information has rendered meetings less necessary. (*ibid.*, 266.)

[2] U.S. DEPARTMENT OF COMMERCE, *Trade Association Activities*, 34.

[3] F.T.C., *The Northern Hemlock and Hardwood Manufacturers Association*, 30; NELSON, *Open Price Associations*, 112.

[4] F.T.C., *Open Price Trade Associations*, 351.

[5] As early as 1904 the Southern Lumber Manufacturers Association is said to have brought about considerable restriction of operations in time of slump. (COMMISSIONER OF CORPORATIONS, *The Lumber Industry*, 1914, iv, 76) by the issue of offic ! price lists and, later, market reports (F.T.C., *Lumber Manufacturers Trade Associations*, 1922, 10).

[6] American Column and Lumber Co. v. U.S., 257 U.S. 377 (1921). The absence of the identification of members in the activities of the Maple Flooring Manufacturers Association was favorably commented upon by the court in Maple Flooring Manufacturers Association v. U.S., 268 U.S. 563.

prices and output were also made by the Northern Hemlock and Hardwood Manufacturers Association.[1] The way in which the provision of cost information developed into the recommendation of minimum prices in the furniture manufacturing industry has already emerged. Efforts to maintain these prices inevitably developed into discussions of the restriction of output to prevent the accumulation of inventories during the depression after the middle of 1920. Resolutions were passed favoring reductions of output, the extent of the reduction being occasionally stated.[2]

In the cotton textile industry curtailment of production has been the central objective of the Cotton Textile Institute. Meetings to form opinion on the subject were succeeded by organized plans. Early in 1930 an attempt was made to limit the hours of plant operation and later in the same year discontinuance of the employment of women and children at night was recommended with the object of increasing the cost of night work. In 1932 agreements for the curtailment of output were negotiated, although with difficulty.[3]

The effect of the transfer of the making of production policy from a number of independent economic units to a trade association turns upon the circumstances in which the concentrated power is exercised. An association including all those in the industry and sure of complete allegiance to its policy might be expected to aim at the maximum of monopoly profit, but there is a marked difference between conditions of production in such circumstances and those of a single monopolist. Trade associations moreover, rarely, if ever, operated under these conditions between 1912 and 1932. Their membership usually covered less than the whole of their industry.[4] The power of a trade association over prices does not, however, depend entirely upon the percentage of the total output

[1] This association appointed a committee to decide by majority vote prices which should be observed by all members, and on occasion attempted to restrict output (F.T.C., *Northern Hemlock and Hardwood Manufacturers Association*, 1923, viii, 24, 30, 33).
[2] F.T.C., *House Furnishings Industries*, I, 204, 254, 255.
[3] See WHITNEY, *Trade Associations and Industrial Control*, 72, and below, Chap. IV.
[4] The Federal Trade Commission reported that of the 74 open-price trade associations supplying information, 34 or nearly one-half included three-fourths or more of the total number of establishments in the industry. The proportion of the total volume of business in the industry done by members of the associations was generally larger than the percentage of the total number of firms belonging to the association, although in some industries the largest unit remained outside the association as a matter of policy. Only one association reporting included all producers in the industry among its members. (F.T.C., *Open Price Trade Associations*, 64.)

of the industry produced by its members. Manufacturers who do not join an association may nevertheless be prepared to accept the leadership of the association. Where the largest concern in an industry does not join the association it is possible that there is no conflict between the policies of the large firm and the members of the association; the large firm may accept the lead of the association but it is more likely that the association is a means for securing the acceptance of the large firm's policy by a number of small firms in the industry.[1] Where non-members are not expected to follow the policy of the association, the capacity of the non-members to accept additional business limits the power of the association to raise prices above those charged by non-members. Finally, mere membership of an association may give an exaggerated impression of its influence, because the association may have only a very poor hold over its members. It may, moreover, be conscious of the ease with which potential could be translated into actual competition by a policy of raising or maintaining prices.

The outstanding characteristic of trade association policies has been their attempt to restrict price cutting. This policy, except in times of generally rising prices, is likely to result in an increased stability of prices. Associations, like cartels, have proved poor instruments for dealing with an excess of productive capacity.[2] They have been more inclined to maintain or raise prices so as to make the operation of all or nearly all their members profitable than to pursue a price policy likely to eject firms from the industry. They were unable to compel members to acquiesce in a policy that meant economic death to some of them. Threatened members would fight for survival by price cutting. In fact, therefore, a

[1] The National Association of Tin Plate Manufacturers circulated the prices of the American Sheet and Tin Plate Company (which the members followed) (F.T.C., *Brief on Pittsburgh Plus*, 44, 225) The United States Industrial Alcohol Company belonged to the Industrial Alcohol Institute and announced its prices at meetings of the institute; the company was responsible for about 40 per cent of the sales of industrial alcohol (WHITNEY, *Trade Associations and Industrial Control*, 132).

[2] Experience in Germany during the period from 1924 to 1928 revealed that cartels tended more to hinder than to facilitate the reorganization of industry because of their efforts to secure the survival of all firms (WARRINER, *Combines and Rationalisation in Germany*, 48). In general, agreements between large units internally reorganized proved the best means of rationalization. *Cf.* also Report of a Committee of the Progressive Conference presented as an appendix to the *Hearings upon the Establishment of a National Economic Council* before a subcommittee of the Senate Committee on Manufactures (S.6215), 1931. *Cf.* also the tendency of rationalization in Germany to increase the rigidity of the economic system by separating marketing from production (sometimes placing the former in the hands of a syndicate) (DERNBURG, HECHT, and NEU, *Erzeugungs- und Absatzbedingungen der Deutschen Wirtschaft*, 138).

policy that will secure the survival of all or nearly all their members[1] is all that can be expected of such associations. Prices tend to be maintained upon a level that will keep even the highest cost firms in existence and give to others abnormally high returns.[2] In consequence where the demand for a product is declining, the trade association, if successful, raises the level of prices so that the income from the restricted output is sufficient to allow returns upon the investment which has become excessive owing to the change in the attitude of consumers. Pursued with rigor this policy would prevent any firm from failing but for the effect of rising prices upon the volume of demand. In fact, it tends to retard but not altogether prevent adjustments of the allocation of investment. Furthermore, the pressure existing under competition to raise the efficiency of all firms to the level attained by the most efficient is eliminated. The inducement to reduce costs remains but is modified by the withdrawal of the opportunity to follow up reductions in costs by price cutting campaigns aimed at improving the relative position of the innovator in the industry. In consequence, the transmission of the benefits of reductions in costs to purchasers is retarded. This same policy of reducing price cutting and maintaining prices tends during periods of depression to a restriction of output, a policy not, however, peculiar to trade associations. Nevertheless many a claim has been made that trade association activities have already mitigated or will mitigate the violence of cyclical fluctuations in business activity.[3] There is yet no evidence to support these claims; in fact the contrary effect is more probable.[4]

D. *Cooperative Control of Types of Product*

During the years from 1920 to 1930 the Department of Commerce actively and often successfully urged trade associations to use their influence to reduce the number of sizes, dimensions, grades, and patterns of products.[5] Such activities tend in obvious

---

[1] *Cf.*, F.T.C., *Open Price Trade Associations*, 175.
[2] *Cf.* American Column and Lumber Co. v. U.S., *Supplementary Brief for U.S.*, 162; F.T.C., *Open Price Trade Associations*, 78.
[3] Herbert Hoover as Secretary of Commerce concluded that "there is no question but that the curves in the business cycle from activity to depression have been less disastrous in those industries or trades where accurate and lawful statistical data have been available to all" (U.S. DEPARTMENT OF COMMERCE, *Trade Association Activities*, 1923, 3). See also F.T.C., *Open Price Trade Associations*, 35; SHARFMAN, "The Trade Association Movement," *Amer. Econ. Rev.*, 16: 1, Supplement, 203 (1926); NELSON, *Open Price Trade Associations*, 201.
[4] See Chap. V.
[5] In 1931 it was reported that about 115 of such simplification programs were in effect, of which about one third related to various building materials, and a large

THE TRADE ASSOCIATION AND INDUSTRIAL INSTITUTE 69

ways to reduce the cost of production in some industries.[1] They reduce the range of consumer choice, a matter of little importance in some, but not all fields. They tend to hinder experimentation with new variations of the product and obstruct competition in quality and type of product; standardized products are more difficult to change than unstandardized. Their effect upon price competition is not clear; they may, by reducing the number of varieties of the product offered by different sellers, present buyers with a simple choice in terms of price alone, and thus concentrate rivalry into the channels of price competition. But by so concentrating rivalry they may render it more susceptible of control and facilitate price leadership.[2]

E. *Cooperative Control of Methods of Selling*

Many associations have sought to limit the devices by which sellers may seek to attract business, by drawing up codes of ethics which set agreed limits to methods of selling. The Federal Trade Commission having been established *inter alia* to prevent "unfair competition" interested itself in these codes. As early as 1919 it

---

[1] part of the remainder to paper, textiles, and containers (Letter from the Federal Trade Commission in *United States Daily*, Apr. 17, 1931). Trade Associations in the lumber industry have for long been interested in the standardization of sizes and grades (F.T.C., *Northern Hemlock and Hardwood Manufacturers Association*, 1923, 29). The Southern Lumber Manufacturers Association was standardizing the grades and sizes of lumber before 1906 (COMMISSIONER OF CORPORATIONS, *The Lumber Industry*, 1914, IV, 76).
  The National Industrial Conference Board claims that heterogeneity of products constitutes a "source of instability in the economic process. It narrows the market for each type of product, thereby increasing the violence of fluctuations in effective demand and rendering productive operations less regular," and trade association activities aimed at standardization of products "look to the mitigation of this evil as well as to greater industrial economy and, within proper limits, these efforts need not nullify the acknowledged advantages of permitting the character of industrial activity to be shaped by competitive forces." (*Trade Associations*, 306.)

[2] "The exclusion of some methods of competition and the simplification of the situation often means an intensification of competitive effort. In general a complex situation in the marketing of goods puts the seller at an advantage as compared with the buyer because the seller may in general be presumed to be the more expert," although where sales are made to expert buyers this presumption is rebutted. Where style is important sellers are generally content to retain and emphasize it owing to "the fact that the style factor complicates the situation as to the selection and pricing of goods and that this complexity, in the long run, redounds to the benefit of the seller. If a product or a group of products is well standardized the buyer or consumer can afford to concentrate his attention on price competition; but he cannot consider price merely or even chiefly if he has to select between a great variety of brands of somewhat different quality and of very different reputation." (F.T.C., *Open Price Trade Associations*, 350.) In a number of industries varieties in style, changes in design, lack of standardization of products, and differences in methods of marketing have been cited as obstacles to the control of prices (F.T.C., *House Furnishings Industries*, I, 314, 359; Maple Flooring Manufacturers Association v. U.S., *Brief for Maple Flooring Manufacturers Association*, 66, 70).

held Trade Practice Submittals; those engaged in each business might submit a code of business ethics agreed upon by them. In 1926 the commission greatly increased the attention given to these submittals which were rechristened Trade Practice Conferences. Between 1926 and 1931 the practices most commonly proscribed were willful interference with the contractual relations of rivals, misrepresentation of products, misrepresentation of the products of rivals, giving secret rebates and commissions, selling below cost as a means of competition, price discrimination, false advertising, and bribery.[1] The United States Chamber of Commerce[2] and the trade associations showed increasing interest in these codes, but their effectiveness varied greatly; some have been effective[3] but "many association members consider codes of ethics as mere bluff or worse"; some were said to be mere smoke screens for illicit activities, and others a mere gesture having no practical significance.[4] Each member of the American Bakers Association, for instance, was required to "recognize my duty to the American home, my employees, and my fellow bakers."[5] Early in 1931, however, the Federal Trade Commission decided upon a rigorous revision of the codes adopted with its cooperation because it believed that in a number of industries they had induced behavior in contravention of the anti-trust laws.[6] The holding of Trade Practice Conferences virtually ceased. In March, 1931,[7] new codes were offered to some eighty industries forbidding secret rebates, price discrimination, malicious inducement of breaches of contract, sales below cost with the intention and effect of injuring a competitor, bribery, defamation of competitors, malicious enticement of the employees of competitors, shipment of goods not conforming to samples, deceptive advertisements, and shipments on consignment.[8] Representatives of industry objected, however, that the rules were being so standardized that the Trade Practice Conference had been deprived of most of its value as an instru

---

[1] For a summary of these rules see JAVITS, *Business and the Public Interest*, 202 ff., 220 ff.
[2] *Cf.* Hon. Edwin B. Parker, president, in a speech of Oct. 17, 1927.
[3] The Federal Trade Commission believed that the development of such codes with the assistance of the commission would make the marketing of goods "a more open and aboveboard affair" and that much of the machinery needed to find out what competitors were doing might be dispensed with. What was needed in its stead was more comprehensive trade statistics. (*Open Price Trade Associations*, xxi.)
[4] *ibid.*, 306.
[5] F.T.C., *Competition and Profits in Bread and Flour*, 1928, 63.
[6] WHITNEY, *Trade Associations and Industrial Control*, 54.
[7] *United States Daily*, Mar. 31, 1931.
[8] *New York Times*, Mar. 31, 1931.

ment for the self-regulation of industry[1] merely in order to simplify the work of the commission. This difficulty was temporarily resolved by the passage of the National Industrial Recovery Act of 1933, which is discussed at a later stage.[2]

Cooperative control of methods of obtaining business was most vigorously applied to methods of sales promotion that might be regarded as disguised price cutting.[3] Granting larger discounts than rivals to one class of customers or granting the same discounts as rivals to a wider classification of customers is not far removed from price competition. Many trade associations therefore attempted to standardize the conditions under which trade discounts were granted and the amount of such discounts.[4] Conduct with regard to quantity discounts was sometimes standardized by eliminating these discounts altogether, with the result that "the differential incidence of costs of selling" is ignored.[5]

---

[1] Commissioner Humphrey of the Federal Trade Commission in *United States Daily*, June 30, 1931.

[2] See Chap. X.

[3] "The present tendency of trade associations is to attempt to stabilize prices by agreements and regulation relating to credit terms, period of forward delivery contracts, methods of computing prices, and other trade customs and practices, especially such elements in the contract of sale as are susceptible of being used covertly as a means of granting what are in effect price concessions to buyers" (F.T.C., *Open Price Trade Associations*, 36). The commission concluded that there was a certain justification for such policies, as they had some of the advantages of standardization, but remarked that "trade associations should probably not be allowed to go ahead of their own frequently too limited point of view. If, however, the public is adequately represented, it would seem that standardization is no more objectionable here, and is indeed quite as desirable, as it is for the physical commodities. Machinery for public participation in such regulation of trade practices is afforded by the trade conference division of the Federal Trade Commission."

[4] Attempts were made in the oil industry to insure a uniform basis of classification among different sellers for the purpose of determining discounts to be allowed (F.T.C., *Pacific Coast Petroleum Industry*, II, 92). The Attorney General charged that the Asphalt, Shingle, and Roofing Institute violated the Sherman Law by fixing uniform and non-competitive prices, requiring its members to adhere to those prices, and also by agreeing concerning uniform maximum discounts to various classes of the trade and definitions of the classes of customers to be allowed discounts at each rate (*New York Times*, Dec. 31, 1930). Somewhat similar charges were made 'against the Bolt, Nut, and Rivet Manufacturers Association (*New York Times*, Mar. 18, 1931). The Sugar Institute was also alleged to have attempted to standardize all discounts (see page 72).

[5] The Federal Trade Commission concluded that the standardization of trade practices as regards terms was in itself desirable, but that "the prorating of selling expenses of all goods sold regardless of their occasioning such expenses may sometimes involve such important amounts as to be uneconomic and unfair." It lamented "that the majority sentiment in certain industries is so often absolutely against quantity discounts and in fact against any departures from fixed prices. Price concessions, where granted generally, and in recognition of economic conditions properly entitling the buyer to such consideration, are a dynamic and progressive illustration of rapid development in industry and should not be suppressed"; it referred to the probable influence upon the development of the public utility industry of low rates to special classes of customers. (*Open Price Trade Associations*, 81.)

The removal of all possible disguises for price competition and all possible types of rivalry other than price competition leads very far afield. How far it leads is well illustrated by the activities of the Sugar Institute.[1] The Attorney General alleged that the institute had so standardized prices and selling practices that the only function left to the purchaser was that of deciding how much sugar to buy. The amount of cash discounts and the terms upon which they were allowed were standardized. Quantity discounts were eliminated,[2] together with credits for sugar bags returned, and the packing of sugar in bulk, or in paper containers. Sales of damaged sugar or "frozen stocks" at prices below those generally announced were required to be reported if they were not regulated. The acceptance of assignments of contracts for the purchase of sugar before the sugar had been delivered was declared to be "wasteful and unbusiness-like." The institute endeavored to eliminate guarantees against a decline in the price of sugar between the date of the contract and the date of delivery. It discouraged long-term contracts with manufacturers using large quantities of sugar, and the sale of sugar packed under private brand names. It endeavored to reduce the number of points at which stocks of sugar were held; the holding of local stocks permitted more speedy delivery and reduced the stocks which dealers and retailers found it necessary to hold, although it increased the costs of the refiners. The institute attempted, on some occasions, to maintain a system of charging delivered prices based upon the cost of railroad transportation, even where cheaper methods of transportation were used.[3] It attempted to eliminate tolling contracts (*i.e.*, contracts to refine raw sugar owned by others).

The institute also found it necessary to secure considerable control over sugar between the time it left the hands of the refiners and the time when it reached the retailer. It sought to fix general brokerage charges including those for reselling sugar on behalf of owners other than refiners. It sought to avoid the "splitting" of brokerage charges between brokers and buyers. It required distributers to choose whether they would act as brokers, warehousemen, or jobbers and obstructed the integration of these activities as well as the integration of transportation and broker-

---

[1] U.S. v Sugar Institute, *Brief for U.S.; Brief on the Facts for the Sugar Institute;* decision of Circuit Judge Mack (mimeographed).

[2] The refiners contended that there was no economic justification for quantity discounts in the sugar industry (see Chap. VI).

[3] See Chap. VI.

age. The refiners claimed that their main objective was the elimination of discrimination between buyers, whether secret or open. They alleged that many of the above practices gave advantages only to some buyers, often the larger buyers. They implied, however, that any difference in price to different buyers involved discrimination, whereas in fact it is discriminatory *not* to permit differences in prices where there are differences in the cost of doing business with different buyers. The prevention of differences in the allowances made for various special types of business by different sellers, and the fear that such allowances would be made as a substitute for price reductions, were doubtless the main reasons for attempts to secure uniformity of treatment upon a simple basis. The profits resulting to refiners on some occasions, the obstruction of the development of the most economical organization for distributing sugar, and the losses imposed on some established firms, were often a cause of difficulty to refiners and were not the main objective of their policy. They desired above all to eliminate disguised price competition and non-price competition.

Like the standardization of products, the standardization of methods of selling is capable of diverting all rivalry into channels of price competition. But rivalry thus concentrated is more easily brought under control than when it takes a multitude of separate forms. As the description of the policy of the Sugar Institute has revealed, standardization of selling methods may have important incidental consequences in obstructing improved methods of selling and distribution, in which respect it is comparable to the standardization of products. It may result in reductions of cost but is less likely to do so than is standardization of products.

III. SUMMARY

The trade association does not necessarily involve any change in economic behavior. During the period from 1912 to 1932, however, these associations were enthusiastically welcomed as a means of coordinating the policies of sellers in a variety of industries; the movement sought, it was said, to "coordinate competitive forces without relinquishing the fruits that spring from individual initiative."[1] The evolution of trade association policies, on the one hand, reveals an underlying urge to modify the com-

[1] SHARFMAN, "The Trade Association Movement," *Amer. Econ. Rev.* 16: I, Supplement, 203 (1926). See also *ibid.*, 205, and N.I.C.B., *Trade Associations*, 307.

petitive process, and, on the other, suggests the particular type of modification that appealed to business men. The reasons for the increasing fear of price competition have already been discussed.

Setting out under the leadership of Mr. Eddy, trade associations claimed that their function was to contribute the knowledge and rationality that were essential to competition yet lacking in so many industries. But the associations found that fuller information concerning methods of cost accounting, actual costs, prices, production, shipments, and the like did not meet their needs. They were impelled to devise methods of replacing individual decisions concerning price and production policy (no matter how broad their factual basis) by cooperative control. The provision of information bred a desire to secure unanimity in the interpretation of that information. Information concerning the best bookkeeping forms for calculating costs passed over into suggestions concerning policy in the matter of distributing costs over production at different times and over different types of product. Suggestions concerning amounts to be added for contingencies and profits developed this policy into one of suggested prices. The use of average instead of individual costs suggested a uniform price for the whole industry. Statistics of production were accompanied by suggestions concerning future production policy; output was compared with current sales and it was suggested that production, and not prices, called for adjustment when production exceeded sales. Statistics of production were used as a tentative basis for the sharing of the market. Statistics of inventories and unfilled orders supplemented these efforts. Direct statistics of prices developed the desire to induce uniformity of prices and thus restrict price competition; price cutters were sought out and cajoled or threatened. Occasionally these aims found their final expression in direct attempts to control output and, therefore, reduce the pressure to cut prices.

The consequences of these policies are far from clear. Associations varied in the degree of their control over their members. They were hampered by producers who refused to join or who joined without fully accepting the policies of the association. They lacked any legal means of enforcing their policies, some of which indeed were in contravention of the law; they were cartels emasculated by the anti-trust laws. It is evident, however, that their policies were narrow and shortsighted partly, but not wholly, because of their limited power. They sought to hamper price cutting with the result that they pressed vaguely, and with varying success, for the stabilization of prices. They aimed in general at securing profits for all their members by maintaining prices and restricting output[1] rather than by pressure to reduce the number of firms or increase the internal efficiency of producers. They were without any long-run vision of the consequences of their policies and contributed little to the adjustment of industrial policies to the changing techniques of production and selling.

The policies of trade associations are, however, indicative of new forms of behavior which were becoming popular in industry at large, *viz.*, price leadership, sharing the market, the stabilization of prices, and the standardization of products and of the non-price aspects of the sale of goods. The consequences of these policies are analyzed in the succeeding chapters where also the history of trade associations after 1932 is discussed.

[1] "In trade association circles emphasis on seeking profits rather than volume of business is current and conspicuous" (F.T.C., *Open Price Trade Associations*, 365, 568).

CHAPTER III

PRICE LEADERSHIP

I. The definition of price leadership—II. The evidence of price leadership—*A*. The steel industry—*B*. The petroleum industry—*C*. The agricultural implement industry—*D*. The anthracite coal industry—*E*. Other industries—III. The consequences of price leadership.

I. THE DEFINITION OF PRICE LEADERSHIP

The concentration of power through the establishment and acceptance of leadership has been a notable feature of social history since the close of the war of 1914 to 1918. The economic field has not escaped this general tendency. Especially in the United States have there been increasingly frequent demands for the appointment of a "czar" to regulate methods of obtaining business (*e.g.*, in the moving picture and anthracite[1] industries) or to coordinate production and price policies. This chapter is concerned with leadership in the matter of output and prices.

Price leadership exists when the price at which most of the units in an industry offer to sell is determined by adopting the price announced by one of their number. Changes in offer price must be initiated by one firm even under competition; such changes react, moreover, upon the offer prices of rivals; but under conditions of competition changes in price are not initiated throughout long periods solely by one firm.

Leadership is merely a relation between sellers and, in this respect, resembles a trade association. We have seen that both types of relation may, and do, occur in the same industry, the trade association administering and perfecting the policy of leadership. The large firm may stand outside the trade association in its industry, the association circulating information concerning the prices of the leader, or it may be a member of the trade association which facilitates the acceptance of its lead.[2]

[1] *New York Times*, June 5, 1935.
[2] The United States Steel Corporation and the Corn Products Refining Company are or have been members of the trade organizations in their respective industries. The United States Industrial Alcohol Company, which has led in making prices for industrial alcohol, announced its prices at the meetings of the Industrial Alcohol Institute (WHITNEY, *Trade Associations and Industrial Control*, 131).

II. THE EVIDENCE OF PRICE LEADERSHIP

Leadership in absolute compliance with the foregoing definition is rare and its existence difficult to prove. But where one firm in an industry is large[1] in relation to the others, that firm usually exercises considerable influence upon the price policy of the industry. There may be departures from leadership, strictly defined, in that other firms may not always change their price simultaneously with the changes announced by the large unit or they may even occasionally initiate changes in price. The mantle of leadership may pass from the shoulders of one firm to those of another. There may also be narrow limits to the policy a leader can pursue if he is to remain a leader. Leadership is not in practice, therefore, a simple and uniform relationship; leaders vary from industry to industry, in both the duration of their leadership and the range of action within which they can rely upon the loyalty of their followers.

Leadership would be expected to fall to the largest firm in an industry where there is any leader at all. The largest unit has the greatest interest in preventing price cutting. It is likely to be most able to enforce its policy upon others because it is likely to command the greatest amount of unused productive capacity and financial resources. Rivals are, moreover, likely to regard the large unit as better equipped than themselves to frame a satisfactory policy for the whole industry. The subtle variations in the powers of leaders are best revealed by an examination of conditions in industries in which leadership is said to exist. The most notable of these industries are steel, petroleum, agricultural implement manufacturing, and anthracite.

A. *The Steel Industry*

The United States Steel Corporation is more frequently classified as a price leader than any other American corporation. Yet the steel industry well illustrates the difficulty of establishing the existence of absolute leadership; complete domination of the industry by the United States Steel Corporation is hard to prove and probably has not existed. It is rarely denied, however, that the

---

[1] It has been suggested that possession of 40 to 60 per cent of the business in an industry is sufficient to induce rivals to adopt the prices of the large unit (Commons, cit. F.T.C., *Statement on Pittsburgh Plus*, 765, *Brief on Pittsburgh Plus*, 233).

corporation exerts great influence over the price and production policy of the industry.[1]

Conditions in the steel industry are peculiarly calculated to induce attempts to avoid price competition. Overhead costs represent a very high proportion of total costs; the range between prices that will attract new capital and those which will not cover direct costs is, therefore, dangerously wide. In many branches of the industry firms are large and few in number. The demand for steel is subject to wide fluctuations with the result that there is frequently a large amount of unemployed plant. Demand for many steel products is probably very inelastic. In these difficult conditions the presence of so large a unit as the United States Steel Corporation suggests the acceptance of its lead in the making of policy in order to avoid the dangers of price competition.

The history of the development of leadership in the industry is of considerable significance; it illustrates the impact upon the forces making for the avoidance of price competition of policies of social control of industry. One form after another has been used for securing coordinated policies. During the last two decades of the nineteenth century escape from price competition was sought in the organization of pools[2] which had for the most part been abandoned by 1904.[3] Trade meetings for the control of prices appear to have taken the place of pools until 1907.[4] During the panic of 1907 the need for organized occasions for coordinating policy, and particularly for preventing price cutting in times of reduced demand, made itself felt. Largely as a result of pressure exercised by the United States Steel Corporation, these occasions were provided in the "Gary dinners" which were not finally abandoned until 1911.[5] Since the abandonment of both pools and dinners such leadership as exists has been secured without any

[1] *Cf.* MARQUAND, *The Dynamics of Industrial Concentration*, 175.
[2] COMMISSIONER OF CORPORATIONS, *The Steel Industry*, I, 68 *ff*.
[3] Some pools continued to exist after the formation of the United States Steel Corporation in 1901 and the corporation for a time participated in some of them (U.S. v. U.S. Steel Corp., 223 Fed. 173 (1915), *Brief for U.S. Steel Corp.*, 208).
[4] U.S. v. U.S. Steel Corp., 223 Fed. 173 (1915).
[5] One member of the industry thought that the Gary dinners had almost made a panic worth while and topped off his eulogy of Mr. Gary's success in removing distrust from the industry with a lyric:

"The melancholy days have gone,
We're feeling light and airy,
We're not a-cussing anyone
But just a-blessing Gary."

(U.S. Steel Corp. Record D.E. 3, 347 (speech of J. T. Drummond on June 19, 1913) in U.S. v. U.S. Steel Corp., *Petition of the Attorney General for Rehearing*, 13.)

formal organization other than the American Iron and Steel Institute. The "Gary dinners" probably inculcated into members of the industry a realization of the benefits of leadership. As will later be seen, however, the industry has not been without a hankering after a more formal control of price cutting.

The nature of the influence exerted by the corporation has varied from time to time. The president of the United States Steel Corporation was motivated in holding the Gary dinners by the desire "to prevent if I could, not by agreement, but by exhortation, the wide and sudden fluctuation of prices which would be injurious to everyone interested in the business of the iron and steel manufacturers."[1] In 1908 rivals were reminded that if they refused "to assist each other by the friendly interchange of views" and resorted to "unreasonable and destructive competition" they would compel the "application of the law of the survival of the fittest."[2] The demand for steel was so small in 1909 that some producers failed to respond to the exhortation of the corporation thus administered and had to be brought to heel by a threat of secret price cutting by the corporation (except in the market for rails).[3] By October, 1909, steel producers were again lunching and dining together and continued to do so until 1911. At a meeting in that year the president of the United States Steel Corporation stated that he believed that it would be undesirable to reduce prices at that time: other manufacturers called upon in succession to express themselves upon the subject were almost unanimous in agreeing with the president of the corporation.[4]

[1] U.S. v. U.S. Steel Corp., *Brief for U.S.*, II, 149. Judge Gary's exhortations were administered through a series of committees at which attempts were made to secure general acceptance of the prices announced by the corporation (*ibid.*, 168, 169. See also JONES, *The Trust Problem in the United States*, 225 ff.).

[2] *Iron Age*, Feb. 6, 1908, 443, cit. FETTER, *The Masquerade of Monopoly*, 129.

[3] They were told that as they were selling at prices below those "generally maintained" the leading manufacturers had "determined to protect their customers and for the present at least sell at such modified prices as may be necessary with respect to different commodities in order to retain their fair share of the business. The prices which may be determined upon and the details concerning the same will be given by the manufacturers to their customers direct as occasion may require." (*Iron Age*, Feb. 25, 1909, cit. FETTER, *op. cit.*, 130, and F.T.C., *Statement on Pittsburgh Plus*, 409.) See also U.S. v. U.S. Steel Corp., *Brief for U.S.*, II, 200.

[4] U.S. v. U.S. Steel Corp., *Brief for U.S.*, II, 993, 998. On this occasion, Judge Gary contemplating this harmony among the steel manufacturers rejoiced that we have "something better to guide and control us in our business methods than a contract which depends upon written or verbal promises with a penalty attached." Having been "in close communication and contact during the past few years" they had "reached a point where we entertain for one another respect and affectionate regard and the position each has reached in his line is such that we are almost bound to protect one another," each realizing that "his honor is at stake" and that "even more than life itself is concerned"; each had therefore reached a position "more

80   THE DECLINE OF COMPETITION

A Circuit Court decided that the prices of steel products had been maintained between 1901 and 1911 by cooperation between the corporation and its rivals and that the offense of the corporation differed from that of its rivals only in that it had assumed leadership in perfecting and promulgating the policy;[1] the corporahad not compelled its rivals to accept its prices.[2] The Supreme Court[3] concluded that the only attempt at a fixation of prices was "through an appeal to and confederation with competitors"; it dismissed the suggestion that the rivals of the corporation rose to opulence by accepting its leadership in price policy. At least rivals could not obtain higher prices than those of the corporation except when the productive capacity of the corporation was in full use.[4]

During the depressed year 1921, the corporation was again forced to resort to secret prices,[5] a step which the *Iron Age* expected to exert a restraining influence on the indiscriminate cutting of prices.[6] The death of Judge Gary was expected to remove a restraining hand from the policies of the corporation and to result in a more aggressive attitude toward rivals by the officials of the corporation.[7] The growth of the larger rivals to the corporation since 1920 also affected the relations between the corporation and these rivals. In 1928 it was the president of the corporation's largest rival who was telling members of the American Iron and Steel Institute that "the avoidance of uneconomic price cutting" was necessary to the stabilization of the industry.[8] However, in 1930 "price shading" was reported to be widespread and it was felt at Youngstown "that the Steel Corporation will be more vigilant henceforth in meeting price cuts. The independents have always been able to meet periods of lean buying

---

binding on him than any written or verbal contract." (U.S. v. U.S. Steel Corp., *Brief for U.S.*, II, 989.)
 [1] U.S. v. U.S. Steel Corp., 223 Fed. 55 (1915), Judge Wooley.
 [2] U.S. v. U.S. Steel Corp., 223 Fed. 89–92.
 [3] U.S. v. U.S. Steel Corp., 251 U.S. 417.
 [4] See F.T.C., *Brief on Pittsburgh Plus*, 186, 187.
 [5] "When the subsidiaries of the Steel Corporation ascertain to a certainty that large and important independents are selling at prices lower than those which have been heretofore announced, our subsidiaries meet new prices. They do not precipitate a lead in making new prices for they are aware that the prices which have prevailed for some time past are lower than the actual cost of production by most, if not all the producers." (F.T.C., *Statement on Pittsburgh Plus*, 84.)
 [6] F.T.C., *Brief on Pittsburgh Plus*, 171.
 [7] "Many men felt that Judge Gary carried his policy of tolerance too far and that advantage was taken of the Steel Corporation by its competitors," and that a more aggressive attitude by the corporation would lead to "a more careful adherence to prices and trade practices" by its rivals (*New York Times*, Nov. 7, 1927).
 [8] Charles M. Schwab, president of the Bethlehem Steel Corporation, in a speech before the American Iron and Steel Institute, *cit. ibid.*, Oct. 27, 1928.

by shading the market and the Steel Corporation has more or less winked at such acts"; the merging of independents was expected to stimulate the corporation to more aggressive price cutting.[1] The appointment of Mr. R. P. Lamont as executive head of the institute in 1932 in the hope of stabilizing the industry and eliminating practices that "create bitter competition under perilous circumstances"[2] indicated a tendency to turn more to the American Iron and Steel Institute as a means to the control of competitive conditions.

These references to "price shading" and the necessity for bringing it under control suggest that the leadership of the corporation has been only partial. Measurement of the degree of leadership prevailing from time to time is impossible. Comparison of the prices charged for similar products at the same time by the corporation and its rivals suggests itself as a measure of the success of leadership but the test is unsatisfactory. Complete uniformity has been claimed as evidence of both perfect competition and perfect leadership; it is equally evidence of complete agreement. Complete uniformity is, however, in practice more likely to indicate the modification than the perfection of competition. When the market is imperfect in that either buyers or sellers are incompletely informed concerning all aspects of the offers available (as to the quality, time, and conditions of delivery as well as price), or when such information percolates slowly through the market, differences in price would be expected at any moment. Differences in the prices of different sellers do not, however, necessarily indicate competitive behavior in an imperfect market. These difficulties are well illustrated by the efforts of the Federal Trade Commission to prove the existence of the Pittsburgh Plus practice in the steel industry (*i.e.*, the adoption by all the sellers of the practice of quoting only delivered prices for steel, and of calculating such prices by adding to the price announced by the United States Steel Corporation for delivery in Pittsburgh the freight thence to the point of delivery).[3] Published prices are often list prices; it was testified that the quotations of different sellers (reduced to a Pittsburgh base) agreed very closely[4] but that actual

---

[1] *ibid.*, Apr. 30, 1930. A reduction of $4.00 a ton in the price of pipe by the corporation on Apr. 1, 1930, in response to price cutting by rivals is referred to below (p. 90*n*).
[2] *ibid.*, Aug. 5, 1932.
[3] See Chap. VI.
[4] F.T.C., *Statement on Pittsburgh Plus*, 512–516.

prices did not always agree with these list prices.[1] It was difficult to decide whether to use the prices of the subsidiaries of the corporation in Pittsburgh, or those published in the *Iron Age*, as those likely to be accepted by followers; these two prices differed at times, partly no doubt because the *Iron Age* quotations could be changed no more frequently than once every week.[2] There was also a question whether the *Iron Age* quotations represented merely the actual prices at which past business had been done or the offer prices at which future business would be accepted. As deliveries were often made under contracts made at varying intervals before the date of delivery, the price on the date of invoice or delivery often departed from the base price on that date. Finally many prices were for bargains peculiar in some respect, for example, as to the time of delivery, size of order, destination of product, conditions under which scrap would be repurchased, or special qualities of the articles. In spite of all these difficulties, both the corporation and the Federal Trade Commission agreed, after analyzing a great number of contracts over a long period of time, that about 91 per cent of the tonnage of steel products was sold at prices deviating by five cents or less per hundred pounds from the Pittsburgh base price.[3] The corporation argued, and with obvious justification, that differences of five cents per hundred pounds (one dollar per ton) were considerable.[4]

Some of these departures from uniformity of prices are doubtless due to gaps in the data and lack of uniformity in the contracts. But some are due to actual price differences; in 1912, 1913, 1916, and 1920, for instance, premium prices over those of the corporation were paid to rivals of the corporation for speedy delivery.[5] On the other hand, the tension that arises during periods of depression, evidenced by some of the events above alluded to, and by frequent references in the technical press to "price shading" and "price concessions," indicates that the industry has not completely freed itself from price cutting. In 1928 the president of the Ameri-

---

[1] F.T.C., *Brief on Pittsburgh Plus*, 56.
[2] F.T.C., *Statement on Pittsburgh Plus*, 345.
[3] *ibid.*, 363. These calculations are amended in view of an evident error in the commission's statement. The total tonnage analyzed by the corporation was greater than that investigated by the commission. The extent of the agreement is illustrated diagrammatically in Fetter, *Masquerade of Monopoly*, 173. (From F.T.C., Docket 962, on Bethlehem-Lackawanna Steel Companies' Merger.) The more detailed results of this investigation are discussed in Chap. VI.
[4] *Brief on Pittsburgh Plus for U.S. Steel Corporation*, 91; F.T.C., *Statement on Pittsburgh Plus*, 358.
[5] F.T.C., *Statement on Pittsburgh Plus*, 77, 82, 331, 532.

can Iron and Steel Institute took the members severely to task, stating that if they had ever learned "the economic necessity of maintaining a single price open to all" they had forgotten it and were charging "many prices, often quoting different customers different prices for the same product on the same day." This policy was harmful to steel producers, he alleged, because it involved discrimination between buyers and induced them to haggle over prices and misrepresent the prices charged by competitors in order to coax lower prices out of sellers. He recommended as a means of stabilizing the steel industry "the avoidance of uneconomic price cutting."[1] Later in the same year he told the members of the American Institute of Steel Construction that "a one-price policy in the steel industry, if generally adopted by the mills, would go far toward stabilizing the industry."[2] In 1930 intensified competition and the "shading" of the prices of the corporation were reported and it was said that a reduction of the corporation's prices would "only be a recognition of conditions that have existed for some time."[3] Discontent with existing conditions was presumably implied in the statement of President Farrell of the United States Steel Corporation in connection with the Sherman and Clayton acts that "it is just as offensive to undersell, sell below cost, as it is for manufacturers to get together and fix prices."[4] We have already seen that by 1932 "trade practices that destroy profits, disorganize trade, and create bitter competition under perilous circumstances" were sufficiently serious to induce the appointment of Mr. R. P. Lamont as the executive head of the American Iron and Steel Institute in the hope of stabilizing the industry and eliminating such practices.[5] Yet many passages in the technical press[6] even as late as 1930 and 1931[7] suggest that

[1] *New York Times* Oct. 27, 1928. Nevertheless he believed that "there is more confidence among members of the steel industry today than there has been since the war . . . that we may pull together and observe the ordinary principles that obtain in most other businesses . . . that we are going to have an increased return and that we are entering upon the greatest era of prosperity since 1920."
[2] *New York Evening Post*, Nov. 16, 1928. He said that it was not contrary to the public interest for producers to divide territory and customers among themselves under supervision.
[3] *New York Times*, Apr. 30, 1930.
[4] *Hearing on the Establishment of a National Economic Council* before a subcommittee of the Senate Committee on Manufactures, 1931, 346.
[5] *New York Times*, Aug. 5, 1932.
[6] See F.T.C., *Brief on Pittsburgh Plus*, 167 ff.
[7] A simultaneous increase in the prices of the more important rolled steel products by all producers early in December, 1930, at a time when the prices of most other products were falling suggested a "suspicious case of conspiracy" and gave rise to a demand that the Department of Justice investigate the matter (*New York Times*,

steel manufacturers accepted speedily and in detail changes in price announced by the corporation.

The code of fair competition under the National Industrial Recovery Act, 1933,[1] suggested a desire to replace what informal leadership had existed by formal arrangements calculated to bring about complete uniformity.[2] The code provided (Art. VII) that the minimum prices of all sellers should be filed with the code authority (*i.e.*, the board of directors of the American Iron and Steel Institute) which might (Schedule E, Sec. 5) investigate any base price; if it judged the price to be unfair, having regard to the cost of manufacturing the product, the code authority might require the member concerned to file a new and fair base price.[3] The code appears to have resulted in substantial uniformity of prices. The Navy Department resorted, in the face of identical tenders by all producers, to the allocation of orders by lot;[4] the president of the United States Steel Corporation agreed that the code provided for a "one-price policy"[5] and the executive secretary of the American Iron and Steel Institute rejoiced in the elimination of secret price cutting and the restriction of competition to quality, service, and convenience of delivery.[6] The extent to which this uniformity arose out of acceptance of the leadership of the corporation, reinforced by the code, is, however, not clear.[7] A committee appointed under the National Industrial Recovery Act decided that there was no consistent leader for all steel products in 1934; some producers more or less habitually took the lead in some products and others in others.[8]

The consequences of price leadership depend upon the policy pursued by the leader. The dominant element in the policy of the

---

Dec. 5, 1930). In 1931 it was said that the announcement of higher prices (usually by a subsidiary of the United States Steel Corporation) was generally followed by all the producers (*New York Times*, Mar. 19, 1931).
[1] Approved Code No. 11 of Aug. 19, 1933.
[2] Mr. Lamont believed that the code submitted would eliminate sales below cost and under-cover price cutting (*New York Times*, June 17, 1932).
[3] This clause was annulled when the code was revised (Approved Code No. 11, Amendment No. 1, May 30, 1934).
[4] *New York Times*, Jan. 6, 1934.
[5] *ibid.*, Feb. 9, 1934.
[6] *ibid.*, Jan. 2 and 21, 1934.
[7] While the prices of steel products were raised by all producers in April, 1934, a reduction initiated in June by the National Steel Company caused consternation and general uncertainty in the industry because manufacturers had no warning of the reductions. These reductions canceled about one half the increases made in April and were attributed to pressure by the automobile manufacturers. (*New York Times*, June 30, July 1, July 2, July 15, 1934.)
[8] N.R.A., *The Operation of the Basing Point System in the Iron and Steel Industry*, 139.

Steel Corporation appears to have been the maintenance of prices in times of diminished demand accompanied, however, by efforts to restrain increases in times of increasing demand.[1] The payment of premiums over the corporation's prices, in times of increasing demand, to obtain more rapid delivery from rivals, indicates, not only that higher prices could have been charged by the corporation, but also that its rivals did not follow dutifully in its footsteps at such times. The "shading" of its prices in times of depression indicates both its attempt to maintain prices and the incomplete loyalty of its rivals. The broader effects of these efforts to stabilize prices will be discussed at a later stage.[2]

Attempts by a leader to stabilize prices might be expected, especially if rivals resist its policy, to affect the relative position of the leader in the industry. The share of the total sales of steel products made by the United States Steel Corporation has indeed shown a downward trend but the extent to which this decline is due to the policy of the price leader is difficult to judge. Between 1900 and 1929 the total output of steel ingots and castings in the United States increased about 450 per cent and that of finished rolled steel products about 230 per cent.[3] Figures 1 and 2 indicate that the proportion of the increasing output produced by the United States Steel Corporation has shown an almost continuous decline in spite of the acquisition of a number of rivals, including the Tennessee Coal and Iron Company and the Union, Sharon, and Clairton companies. In 1902 the corporation produced about 65 per cent of the total output of steel ingots and castings, and in 1931, 39 per cent: of the total output of finished rolled steel products it produced in 1902 about 51 per cent, and in 1931, about 34 per cent. This decline in its share of business has, of course, not been so great as to involve a decline in the absolute volume of its business which has greatly increased; its rivals have, however, expanded even more.[4]

Attempts by a leader to stabilize prices might be expected to react differently upon its position in the industry according as

[1] Mr. Charles M. Schwab stated that, while he was president of the corporation, its prices "as a rule were somewhat above the other prices in depressed times, and below the other prices in prosperous times. In other words, we endeavored to keep them more uniform." (*Cit.* U.S. v. U.S. Steel Corp., 223 Fed. 91.)

[2] See Chap. V and also BERGLUND, *The United States Steel Corporation and Price Stabilization*, Quart. Jour. Econ., 38: 1 (1933).

[3] American Iron and Steel Institute, *Annual Statistical Reports*.

[4] The Bethlehem Steel Corporation was 20 to 25 per cent larger in 1926 than was the United States Steel Corporation at its formation (Charles M. Schwab, *New York Times*, Dec. 14, 1926).

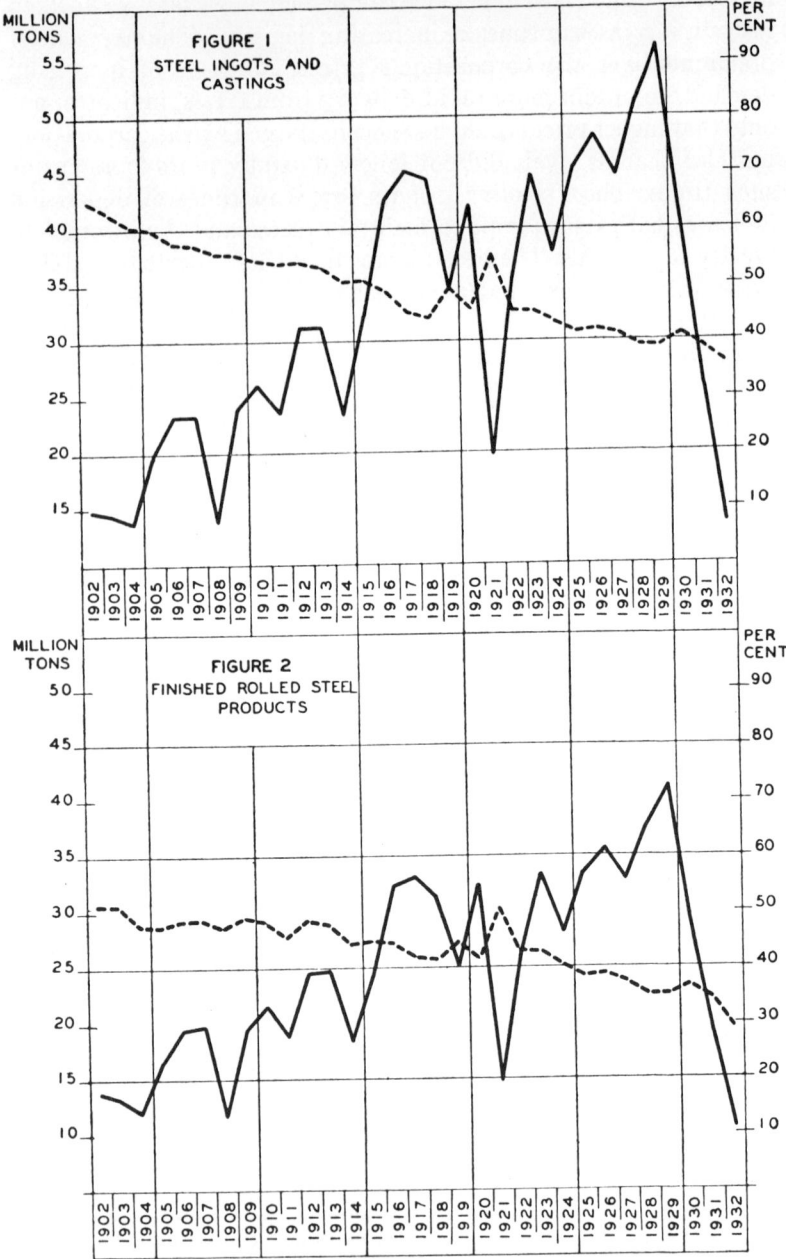

FIGS. 1 and 2.—The output of steel ingots and castings and of finished rolled steel products in the United States, 1902 to 1932, and the proportion produced by the United States Steel Corporation. (*American Iron and Steel Institute: Annual Statistical Reports.*)

demand is rising or falling. The relationship between changes in the corporation's share of business and changes in the total volume of business is presented in the following table:[1]

TABLE I

Period	Annual percentages of aggregate business done by U.S. Steel Corp.		Percentage of *all* annual changes which fell to the U.S. Steel Corp.		Percentages of annual changes of *more than* 10 *per cent* which fell to U.S. Steel Corp.	
	Low	High	Decreases	Increases	Decreases	Increases
1902 to 1911	45.7	51.3	57.0	50.2	54.2	43.8
1912 to 1921	42.0	48.5	40.7	42.5	38.4	43.8
1922 to 1931	34.2	42.9	41.7	33.0	46.1	26.1

Only in the first decade did it maintain its proportion of business in years of increase and then not in years of large increase. In the second and third decades it lost ground in years of increase, and especially in years of large increase in the third decade. In years of declining total sales it lost heavily in the first decade, gained in the second, and lost again in the third (especially in years of large decrease). These figures suggest that in the first decade of its existence the corporation secured its full share of business in good years but was not altogether successful in bad years in preventing price cutting that undermined its position: in the second and third decades it did not succeed in maintaining its position in good years, possibly because of a more cautious policy of expansion of plant; whereas in the middle decade it bore less than its share of declines in business in bad years (possibly owing to greater ability to keep rivals in hand), in the third decade failure to prevent price cutting or other methods of securing business thrust upon it more than its share of declines in business.

The corporation's policy of stabilization is not, however, the only possible reason for its declining proportion of the total business.[2] The corporation was, at its formation, so large that it is

---

[1] Calculated from American Iron and Steel Institute, *Annual Statistical Reports.*
[2] *Cf.* the evidence of Charles M. Schwab before the Industrial Commission in 1901, that the proportion of business secured by the United States Steel Corporation was smaller in prosperous than in slack times (*Cit.* U.S. v. U.S. Steel Corp., *Brief for U.S.*, II, 553). It has been said, however, that the United States Steel Corporation operates with more stability than its rivals, (*Iron Age*, Mar. 31, 1927, 952) and that the establishments with less than 100 workers show the greatest declines in employment in times of depression (MacCallum, *The Iron and Steel Industry in the United*

possible that, in spite of subsequent improvements in methods of organizing units of increasing size, it was unable to expand at the same rate as the industry as a whole without loss of efficiency involving increasing costs and declining profits. It is well known that the corporation has been highly successful from the standpoint of the investor. The Commissioner of Corporations, after adjusting data concerning profits and investment, concluded that during the whole period from 1901 to 1910 the corporation had secured an average rate of return of 12 per cent.[1] The directors, reviewing the career of the corporation up to the end of 1926, calculated that it had made aggregate net profits of 2,345 million dollars of which common stockholders had received 667.1 million dollars (representing 131.25 per cent on their stock) and 1,005.2 million dollars[2] had been accumulated in reserves. If it is true that the costs of the corporation exceed those of its leading rivals[3] and are considerably in excess of those of some of its rivals, the latter must have benefited greatly from the price policy of the corporation. That fact may explain the greater rate of expansion by rivals than by the corporation, their high profits having both encouraged and enabled them to expand.[4] While this relatively more rapid expansion by the smaller units in the industry has been viewed with disquiet by the larger firms,[5] partly, no doubt, because they felt that the aggregate capacity of the industry was being excessively increased, they did not seek to discourage the expansion by reducing the prices of steel products. But the code of fair competition for the industry under the National Industrial Recovery Act provided (Art. V, Sec. 2) that no member might construct any new blast furnace, open hearth, or Bessemer steel capacity. It appears

---

States 62). This state of affairs may be due to the complete closing of small plants. It is not known whether this relationship holds as the establishments increase in size beyond 100 workers.

[1] *The Steel Industry*, I, 51.

[2] *Annual Report for* 1926, 6. The chairman of the board of directors of the Crucible Steel Company, however, stated at the annual meeting of the American Iron and Steel Institute in 1928 that "the steel industry was not receiving a fair return at $3\frac{1}{2}$ to $4\frac{1}{2}$ per cent on its investment" (*New York Times*, Oct. 27, 1928).

[3] U.S. v. U.S. Steel Corp., *Summary of Evidence*, 855, *Brief for the U.S.*, 481.

[4] During the period from 1919 to 1927, of about 5.1 million dollars spent upon additions to the steel plants of the country only a little more than 25 per cent was spent by the four largest companies (*i.e.*, the United States Steel Corporation, the Bethlehem Steel Corporation, the Inland Steel Corporation, and the Republic Steel Corporation) (MacCallum, *The Iron and Steel Industry in the United States*, 173).

[5] Mr. Charles M. Schwab as president of the American Iron and Steel Institute told the members in 1928 that one of the ways of stabilizing the industry was "by discouraging by every lawful means the construction of additional capacity at times when the capacity is already overexpanded" (*New York Times*, Oct. 27, 1928).

therefore, that the leader, probably not the lowest-cost producer, has set prices profitable to itself after allowing for cyclical depressions; it has thereby provided rivals with profits sufficient to tempt them to expand and presumably to attempt to obtain business by some price cutting but mainly by other methods. Lower prices which would have been less profitable both to the corporation and to its rivals would have been less encouraging to investment in the industry. Leadership by a firm which is not the most economical (possibly because it is uneconomically large[1]) may be unstable in the long run unless a more complete control of production can also be secured: the leader's percentage of the business in the industry may decline, the disparity between the sizes of firms diminish, and leadership may decay.

Wider distribution of power to control the price policy in the industry has, however, been facilitated not only by new investment by rivals of the United States Steel Corporation. Mergers of some of the smaller firms in the industry with others have strengthened the position of the rivals of the corporation by rendering them more integrated, and by giving them access to new market territories.[2] At the conclusion of a series of mergers in 1930 the Republic company had attained an ingot capacity of about 4.9 million tons (compared with 8.19 million tons of the Bethlehem Steel Company and 24.5 million tons of the United States Steel Corporation, the only two larger companies); the three companies together con-

[1] Its size may be due to mergers stimulated by the hope of acquiring control over prices.

[2] In 1922 the Bethlehem Steel Corporation secured plants in the eastern states by absorbing the Lackawanna Steel Company; in 1924 it entered the Chicago territory by absorbing the Sheet and Tube Company of America; in 1931 it was negotiating with the Pittsburgh Steel Company which had access by water to the south and middle west. Both the United States and Bethlehem Steel companies purchased steel companies in California in 1930. The acquisitions by the Bethlehem company were said to have "materially strengthened the company through putting it in a position to compete with the United States Steel Corporation on the Pacific coast" (*New York Times*, Mar. 10 and 23, 1930). In 1930 the Republic Iron and Steel Company absorbed the Central Alloy Steel Corporation, Donner Steel, Inc., the Bourne-Fuller Company, and a number of their subsidiaries to which it was said at the time the Jones and Laughlin Steel Company, the Youngstown Sheet and Tube Company, and the Gulf States Steel Company might later be added. The new company was fully integrated; its activities extended from mining to the manufacture of finished steel. In March, 1930, it was announced that the Corrigan, McKinney Steel Company had been purchased by interests representing the Republic company. (*New York Times*, Mar. 25 and Apr. 9, 1930, July 8, 1934.) Had the Bethlehem Steel Corporation succeeded in acquiring the Youngstown Sheet and Tube Company in 1930 the Bethlehem company would have entered the middle west and western territory. It is said that the Bethlehem company had formerly tacitly agreed with the United States Steel Corporation to refrain from entering this territory. Interests associated with the Republic company succeeded in preventing the merger. (*New York Times*, Mar. 10, 1930.)

trolled about 60 per cent of the industry.¹ The attempt to regulate the industry through the American Iron and Steel Institute, even before the National Industrial Recovery Act, has already been mentioned. This attempt may be in part the outcome of this wider distribution of influence over the vital aspects of the policy in the industry, or it may merely indicate the use of the machinery of the institute to make leadership more effective.²

The price policy of the industry has frequently been defended on the ground that the prices of steel products have over long periods moved more favorably to buyers than the average of all wholesale prices. Figure 3 shows that indices of the prices of steel products moved in this manner between 1886 and 1898 and, after a brief but sudden reversal, resumed the movement up to 1915.³ Figure 4 shows a similar movement. Between 1923 and 1929 the movement was similar but between 1929 and 1932 steel prices fell less than the average of wholesale prices.⁴ This movement of steel prices contrary to movements of general prices, more especially during the earlier years, has been cited as evidence of the "effects of competition passing on to users of iron and steel the savings arising out of improved technique,"⁵ and of the absence of control of prices by the United States Steel Corporation.⁶ It does not, of course, prove the absence of control; but it does indicate failure to maintain unchanged prices; prices may, however, have fallen less than they would have, had the relations between sellers been different.

Information concerning costs in the industry over periods of time is practically nonexistent. It is known that between 1901 and

---

¹ The promoters of the merger announced that one of their chief purposes was "to bring a new stabilizing influence into the industry (*New York Times*, Dec. 18, 1929).

² It was said by a rival of the corporation at Youngstown in 1930 that the growth of the size of the rivals of the corporation, partly as a result of mergers, was "recognized by the Steel Corporation which is meeting new price situations more aggressively than ever before in its history." This new policy was evidenced by a reduction of $4 per ton in the price of pipe by the National Tube Company, a subsidiary of the corporation. "This was the most drastic cut in pipe prices for ten years and was retaliation for price cutting by independents," and it was believed "that a serious war for steel business might develop in times when there is not enough business to go round." (*New York Times*, Apr. 30, 1930.)

³ In February, 1915, the index of general prices was about twenty per cent higher than the average for 1902 while the composite price of finished steel calculated by the *Iron Age* was about 37 per cent lower.

⁴ Between January, 1929, and June, 1932, the U.S. Bureau of Labor Statistics Index of wholesale prices fell from 97.2 to 63.9 and that of all finished products from 96.5 to 70.0 while that of iron and steel prices fell from 96.7 to 79.8 and the composite of iron and steel prices published by *Steel* fell from 94.4 to 77.2.

⁵ VANDERBLUE and CRUM, *The Iron Industry in Prosperity and Depression*, 10.

⁶ U.S. v. U.S. Steel Corp., *Brief for U.S. Steel Corp.*, 140.

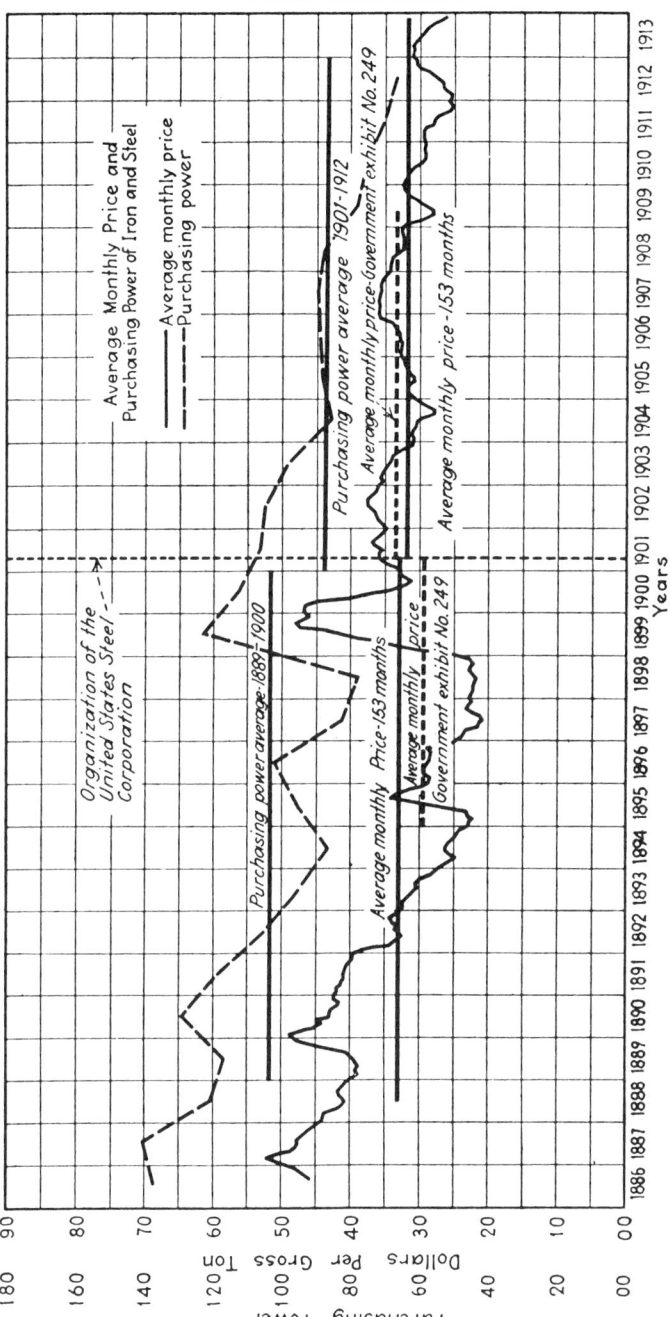

FIG. 3.—The average monthly price of iron and steel products, 1886 to 1913, and their purchasing power in terms of an index of wholesale prices. (*U.S. v. U.S. Steel Corp., Defendant's Exhibit*, "Smith 212.")

1915 wages were rising but costs were greatly reduced by improvements in methods of production; many processes were mechanized and the open hearth process was increasingly utilized.[1] Figure 4[2] shows that the price of pig iron also declined in the face of a slight increase in the general level of prices between 1901 and 1915 owing

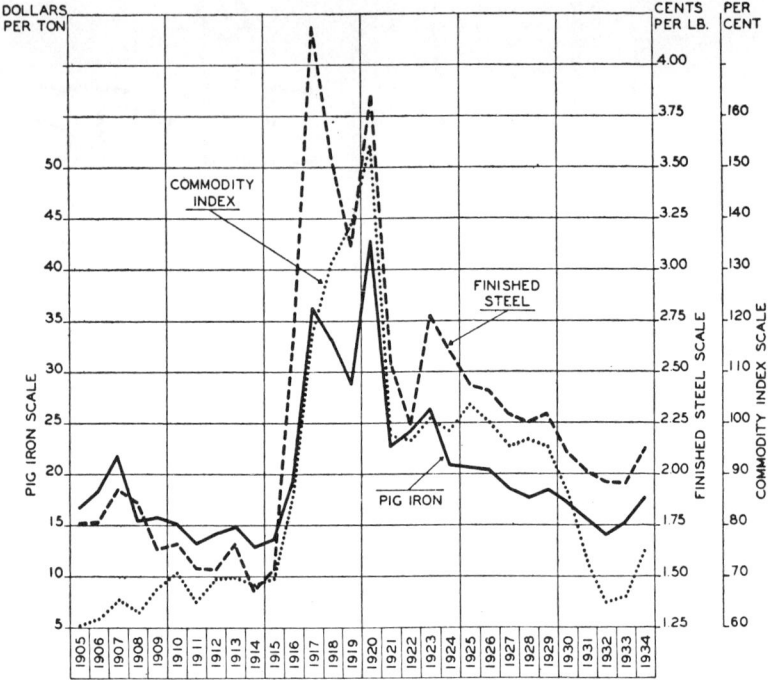

FIG. 4.—Annual prices of pig iron and finished steel products, 1905 to 1934, and an index of wholesale prices. (*Drawn from data in "Iron Age" and U.S. Bureau of Labor Statistics: Wholesale Prices.*)

partly to improvements in methods of production (largely in the form of increases in the size and efficiency of blast furnaces). Between 1915 and 1921 the price of pig iron rose much less than the general average of prices, and since 1921 its purchasing power in commodities generally has fallen below the level of 1914.

The price of finished steel products also increased more than the price of pig iron after 1915 and remained upon a higher level at least until 1930, the margin between the two being fairly constant

---

[1] In 1903, 40 per cent of all the steel manufactured was made by this process; by 1915, 74 per cent was so made (VANDERBLUE and CRUM, *op. cit.*, 8–10; also BERGLUND, *Proceedings of the American Economic Association*, December, 1930, 102).

[2] See also VANDERBLUE and CRUM, *op. cit.*, 24.

between 1921 and 1930. The rate at which the smaller firms have expanded, and the known profitability of the United States Steel Corporation, indicate that although prices have fallen there has been a comfortable margin between costs and prices.

B. *The Petroleum Industry*

In 1911 the former Standard Oil Company of New Jersey was partitioned in conformity with the decision of the Supreme Court under the Sherman Act. It has been repeatedly stated that since that time the leading successors to the former Standard Oil Trust have been leaders in the markets for crude oil and petroleum products. The conditions under which the industry operates are certainly calculated to induce the modification, if not the avoidance, of price competition. Overhead costs are a large part of total costs owing to heavy investments in oil lands, pipe lines, refineries, and marketing facilities. Most producers are too large for rivals to be able to ignore their policy and each is glad of a basis for forecasting the policies of its rivals.[1] More especially since 1912 probable future conditions of demand and supply have been very difficult to predict. The rapid development of the automobile was not clearly foreseen. The discovery of new supplies of crude oil was, particularly in earlier years, very uncertain; changes in the technique of utilizing crude oil have been important but difficult to anticipate. More recently social control of the output of oil, and world trade conditions have also introduced elements of uncertainty. These uncertainties induce fear of the consequences of attempts by each firm to make price, inventory, and production policies upon its own estimate of the future. Even if one man's guess is as good as another's it is better *for the producers* that one man's guess should be accepted than that prices and profits should be the outcome of the guesses of many in conflict in the market. The presence of the Standard Oil companies, each controlling a large proportion of the total business in their territories,[2] and generally regarded as very well informed concerning conditions in the industry, suggests them as best qualified to pro-

---

[1] "The price cutting can always be met and if necessary one company can cut as low as its competitor, and, of course, will, if forced. It would be bad business for the one and equally bad business for the other, but if necessary it will be done." (R. W. Stewart of the Standard Oil Company of Indiana at American Petroleum Institute, 1922.)

[2] *Cf.* Senate Committee *Report on the High Cost of Gasoline*, 1923, 41; F.T.C., *Prices, Profits, and Competition in the Petroleum Industry*, 1928, 230.

94   THE DECLINE OF COMPETITION

vide the effective guesses. In short, "It is God's blessing to the industry that they have a Standard Oil Company to set the price."[1]

The evidence of price leadership is to be found in the numerous reports of the Federal Trade Commission. Already in 1915 the commission reported that prices posted for crude oil by the Standard companies constituted, with rare exceptions, the market price in the Appalachian and mid-continent fields.[2] In 1920 it reported that the Standard companies made the price in all fields.[3] In 1922[4] and again in 1928[5] it reported that "the Standard Oil Company of California is the largest purchaser of crude petroleum and the acknowledged price leader in California." Similarly in the markets east of the Rockies in 1922 the Standard companies commonly took the initiative in making price changes; other companies frequently followed although occasionally one of the larger independent companies, such as the Texas or Gulf company led the way.[6] In 1928 the commission reported that in the Appalachian field there was only one large purchasing company; in the mid-continent field, while for many years the Prairie Oil and Gas Company had been recognized as the price leader, "within the past three years other buyers have frequently assumed price leadership." Of 39 changes in crude oil prices in this field between January, 1922, and June, 1927, however, only two were made by a non-Standard company.

[1] Cit. F.T.C., *Prices, Profits, and Competition in the Petroleum Industry*, 1928, 230. The National Petroleum Marketers Association referred to the Standard Oil Company as the "logical organization to take the initiative in making intelligent and constructive markets to conform properly with the laws of supply and demand" (*ibid.*, 230).
[2] F.T.C., *The Price of Gasoline in* 1915, 5. "While . . . the Prairie Oil and Gas Company apparently fixes the price of mid-continent crude oil no evidence has been found showing the alleged purpose of that company to manipulate crude prices to the injury of independents" (*ibid.*, 122).
[3] "The prices for crude oil for the bulk of the production in each field are . . . the prices announced and posted by the large crude oil marketing companies or refiners which purchase the oil. Generally the Standard purchasing company takes the initiative in posting the price and other large purchasing companies generally follow its lead. . . . The large companies in the field say that they pay this price to all producers without discrimination, and that it is indeed necessary for them as a matter of business policy. The small companies, on the other hand, often pay premiums, partly to get oil from particular pools of superior quality, and partly because the producers generally prefer to sell to the large purchasing companies unless some extra price inducement is offered to them." (F.T.C., *The Advance in the Prices of Petroleum Products*, 1920, 32.)
[4] F.T.C., *The Pacific Coast Petroleum Industry*, 1922, II, 77, 78, 127. Premiums were often paid for oil with an unusually high gasoline content.
[5] F.T.C., *Prices, Profits, and Competition in the Petroleum Industry*, 1928, 195, 201.
[6] F.T.C., *The Pacific Coast Petroleum Industry*, 1922, II, 129.

In the market for petroleum products, at least since 1915, similar conditions have prevailed. The Federal Trade Commission reported that in 1915 the price of gasoline announced by the Standard companies fixed the market price, with unimportant exceptions.[1] The Independent Petroleum Marketers Association in the Pacific states agreed at that time to charge the prices announced by the Standard Oil Company of California, and the larger companies which were not members of the association pursued the same policy.[2] The Western Oil Jobbers said in 1915 that they followed the price announced by the Standard Oil Company of Indiana.[3] Again in 1922 the commission reported that the Standard Oil groups were the dominating factor in the oil business in every section of the country.[4] The president of the Union Oil Company, speaking of the Pacific states, agreed that prices "have been regulated by the prices fixed by the Standard Oil Company and that other marketing concerns in that territory have fixed their sales prices so as to correspond with the prices established by that company. This is a natural and unavoidable situation arising from the fact that a large percentage of the oil refining and marketing business has been in the hands of that corporation and has not been brought about by any agreement between the marketing companies for the fixing of prices."[5] The Standard marketing companies at that time usually took the lead in announcing price changes in the territories east of the Rockies and the other companies usually followed although they occasionally took the initiative.[6] In 1924 the commission stated that the independent marketers in the territory of the Standard Oil Company of Indiana recognized the Standard Oil Company as a price leader, that they endeavored to secure immediate information concerning its price policy in order to follow it, and that they exchanged information and held formal conferences

[1] F.T.C., *The Price of Gasoline in 1915*, 6.
[2] F.T.C., *The Pacific Coast Petroleum Industry*, 1922, II, 127.
[3] F.T.C., *The Price of Gasoline in 1915*, 157.
[4] F.T.C., *The Pacific Coast Petroleum Industry*, 1922, II, 129. See also Senate Committee on the *High Cost of Gasoline*, 1923, 41; U.S. FUEL ADMINISTRATION, *Prices and Marketing Practices for Gasoline*, 1919, 13; F.T.C., *The Advance in the Prices of Petroleum Products*, 1920, 53.
[5] F.T.C., *The Pacific Coast Petroleum Industry*, 1922, II, 76. The Standard Oil Company of California sold about 61 per cent of the gasoline sold by the five large companies (which between them sold about 90 per cent of the refined products sold in the territory).
[6] *ibid.*, II, 129. The prices of the different sellers in Montana and neighboring states moved together in 1921 (F.T.C., *The Petroleum Industry in Wyoming and Montana*, 1922, 1).

with the officials of the Standard Oil Company with this end in view.[1]

Furthermore the amount added to tank wagon wholesale prices to arrive at retail prices was throughout the greater part of the country the differential set by the Standard company.[2] Again in 1928 the commission repeated that it made no charge of price agreements but that "the consensus of opinion in the trade based upon experience is that the Standard Oil companies establish the tank wagon and filling station prices of gasoline, which other marketers follow as a general rule and which the various associations endeavor to have their members maintain."[3] Although other concerns occasionally led in making price changes such occasions were regarded as exceptional.[4]

The acceptance of the leadership of a single company is apparently often entered explicitly in contracts both for the purchase of crude oil and for the sale of petroleum products. In the Pacific states in 1915 it was a common practice for even such large rivals of the Standard company as the Union Oil Company (then the second largest firm in the territory) to make contracts for the purchase of crude oil over considerable periods of time to be paid for at the price announced by the Standard Oil Company of California and in force at the time of delivery of oil under the contract; any change in the price announced by the Standard company automatically applied, therefore, to these contracts made by its rivals.[5] Jobbers sometimes contracted to buy oil at a price to be arrived at by deducting a prescribed amount from the announced tank wagon price of the Standard Oil Company at the time of

---

[1] Associations of independent sellers aimed at avoiding price cutting and the maintenance of the announced price of the Standard company because they regarded it as futile to sell at any other price (F.T.C., *Letter of Submittal, Report on Gasoline Prices in* 1924).

[2] F.T.C., *The Price of Gasoline in* 1915, 157, 158. The secretary of the American Oil Men's Association said that the margin was high because it was set by the Standard Oil Company (F.T.C., *Prices, Profits, and Competition in the Petroleum Industry*, 1928, 230).

[3] *ibid.*, xix, 229, 239. *Cf.* also 168, 240.

[4] *ibid.*, 240. The chairman of the board of the Texas Company stated that "price changes were usually made first by the Standard Oil Company because the Standard Oil companies, taken together, cover the entire territory of the United States" but also (in the next sentence) that "taking all the Standard Oil companies in one group, and all the other companies in another group, price changes would be made first by each group about an equal number of times" (*ibid.*, 234). The vice president and general manager of the Sinclair Oil Company said that his company followed the prices published by the Standard Oil Company (*ibid.*, 235).

[5] F.T.C., *Pacific Coast Petroleum Industry*, II, 30. Fixed premiums above the announced price of the Standard company were provided where oil had a higher gasoline content (*ibid.*, II, 79).

delivery, which meant that in selling they were compelled to keep to the announced tank wagon price of the Standard company although the open market price might be below it.[1] Contracts for the sale of gasoline at wholesale in tank cars were commonly made for periods of a year or more and, while the approximate or precise amount to be delivered under the contract might be prescribed, "in many cases the prices instead of being fixed are based upon certain prices current at the time of shipment such as the tank wagon market prices of the Standard Oil companies or the open tank car prices as reported in *Platt's Oilgram*,[2] *The National Petroleum News, The Chicago Journal of Commerce*, and the *Oil and Gas Journal* together with variations of these methods."[3] In fact the Standard Oil Company's price was apparently the basic price in many of these contracts.

As in the steel industry, however, the leadership of the large firms was not absolute and continuous. The Federal Trade Commission has rarely claimed complete loyalty by the independents to the Standard companies. Reference has already been made to the initiative occasionally taken by independent companies in making changes in crude oil prices as early as 1922,[4] to the payment by small refiners of higher prices for crude oil than were paid by the large firms in 1920 (thereby causing the larger firms to advance their prices),[5] and to the assumption of price leadership in the mid-continent field by non-Standard companies from time to time.[6]

---

[1] F.T.C., *Prices, Profits, and Competition in the Petroleum Industry*, 1928, 230. Such contracts are said to have enabled the Standard Oil Company of Indiana to maintain the price of gasoline in its territory when it was falling elsewhere (*ibid.*, 215). On the other hand, the commission stated that the use of long-term marginal contracts based upon the tank wagon or service station prices of the leading marketing company in a given region tends apparently to stabilize prices on the basis of the leading company's quotations, but does not definitely fix the selling prices of the purchaser on such contracts (*ibid.*, 218).

[2] A private reporting service, the tank wagon prices in which "come from the chief price makers in each district. Of course, these are the Standard Oil companies because they are the largest single distributors, although they do not have a predominating volume. The Standard Oil companies do not make the price. The trade looks for and follows their prices usually." (W. C. Platt, *ibid.*, 223.)

[3] *ibid.*, 214.

[4] F.T.C., *The Pacific Coast Petroleum Industry*, II, 129.

[5] "When oil is relatively scarce the small purchasers often offer higher premiums than usual to get it and this often leads the large purchasing companies to advance their prices. . . . On the other hand, when there is a glut of oil and stocks are piling up small purchasers have been often able to get the oil they needed at a discount." The South Penn Oil Company (the Standard purchasing company in the Pennsylvania field) was repeatedly forced by the offer of premiums by small buyers in 1919 to raise its prices. (F.T.C., *The Advance in the Price of Petroleum Products, 1920*, 32.)

[6] F.T.C., *Prices, Profits, and Competition in the Petroleum Industry*, 1928, 201.

Similar imperfections in leadership have appeared in the markets for petroleum products. "Within recent years a large independent, such as the Gulf Oil Corporation, occasionally assumes leadership."[1] The president of the Gulf Refining Company stated in 1927 that the Standard company usually led in making advances but its rivals usually led in making reductions,[2] and the chairman of the board of the Texas Company, in the contradictory evidence already quoted, stated that price changes were initiated with about equal frequency by Standard and non-Standard companies.[3] Furthermore, although the prices announced by the Standard Oil companies were generally adhered to, "price concessions" were frequently given in certain localities for brief periods and to certain customers or classes of customers.[4]

The Attorney General's attempt in 1931 to prevent the merger of the Vacuum Oil Company with the Standard Oil Company of New York resulted in a discussion of the leadership of the Standard company of New York.[5] The Attorney General produced witnesses who testified that the retail price of gasoline set by the Standard company was followed by its rivals who accepted changes in its price within a day or two.[6] Officials of the Richfield Oil Company, the Warner-Quinlan Oil Company, and the Texas Company testified, however, that they did not invariably accept the price announced by the Standard company;[7] the company itself denied that it did or could dictate the retail price of gasoline in New York and New England.[8] It produced evidence showing that on specified days, and at specified places, there was a considerable number of rivals selling at prices lower than its own;[9] that suggestions

---

[1] A number of examples of price reductions initiated by non-Standard companies are quoted at *ibid.*, 239.
[2] *ibid.*, 235.
[3] *ibid.*, 234.
[4] *ibid.*, 240. "In the early part of 1927 the average concessions from such prices to all classes of customers were estimated by the representatives of important refiners and marketers from one half cent to one cent per gallon, based on their total sales. In some cases, however, local temporary cuts amounting to three or four cents per gallon have been noted, especially when the larger companies are endeavoring to establish themselves in new territory. Concessions take the form of straight price reductions of so much per gallon, of allowances, service, equipment, rental, etc., equivalent to bonuses, and of discounts based on gallonage." (*loc. cit.*)
[5] The Attorney General contended that the Standard company already did twice as much business as its largest rival and that the absorption of the Vacuum company (another successor of the former Standard Oil "trust") would increase its dominance (U.S. v. Standard Oil Co. of New York *et al.*, *Brief for U.S.*, 54).
[6] *ibid.*, 8. See also *New York Times*, July 8, 1930.
[7] *Brief for the Standard Oil Co. et al.*, 63.
[8] *Rejoinder Brief for Standard Oil Co. et al.*, appendix, 17.
[9] *ibid.*, 14.

were made by its officials that the company's price should be reduced unless it was prepared to lose business;[1] and that on various occasions the Standard company was in fact compelled to reduce its price owing to competitive conditions.[2] Because the Standard Oil Company usually made the first open-price reduction the impression had arisen that it initiated price reductions; in fact, however, the company was frequently forced to make such reductions by actual but not openly announced reductions by its rivals or by local reductions.[3] The fact that a reduction in its price was so frequently followed by its rivals was attributed to competition: "if its competitors do not meet this price the natural effect will be for their customers to turn to Socony for their supply. But in precisely the same sense any other substantial competitor controls the price of Socony and its other competitors"; such were "the ordinary laws of competition."[4] The principal question, however, is whether rival companies ever initiated changes in price up or down. That smaller firms sold oil products at prices below those set by the larger is indicated by the protest of smaller firms against the setting up of a minimum price by the Secretary of the Interior exercising his powers under the National Industrial Recovery Act. It was said that the smaller companies that did not advertise had secured business only because they had sold at prices below those set by the larger refiners.[5]

The commission believed that in 1928 price competition was only sporadic, local, or temporary.[6] Since the date of the report there has, however, been increasing evidence of price competition. Independent sellers were reported, for instance, to have initiated price cutting in the New York area in the middle of 1932[7] and the

[1] *ibid.*, 2.
[2] Price reductions were said to have been made under these conditions on 32 different dates between July 19, 1928, and June 20, 1930 (*Summary of Evidence by the Master*, 14). The Attorney General replied that "Socony's control of prices is not negatived by the fact that in certain local areas it from time to time made reductions to meet the low prices of local competitors. These reductions which were brought about by local conditions were (not) maintained for any appreciable time." (*Brief for U.S.*, 55.)
[3] *Brief for Standard Oil Co. of New York and Vacuum Oil Co.*, 61.
[4] *ibid.*, 57, 61.
[5] *New York Times*, Oct. 2, 1933.
[6] F.T.C., *Prices, Profits, and Competition in the Petroleum Industry*, 1928. An analysis of press announcements of changes in the price of gasoline in New York City, Newark, N.J., and Philadelphia, Pa., during the period from the beginning of 1920 until the middle of 1929 revealed that of 146 changes in which the name of the firm first making the changes could be identified, about four fifths were initiated by Standard companies (NICHOL, *Partial Monopoly and Price Leadership*, 52 ff.).
[7] *Oil and Gas Jour.*, Aug. 25, 1932, 29.

increase in price of gasoline in New York and New England announced on Oct. 21, 1932, resulted from the initiative of th Sinclair company.[1] In 1933 price cutting was prevalent in many eastern markets where it was reported that the "race for gallonage continues unchecked with profit margins being ruthlessly slashed."[2] Non-Standard companies appear increasingly frequently to lead in making price reductions. The Standard Oil Company of New York, for instance, insisted that it was often forced to accept a competitor's price even though it did not consider it justified by economic conditions.[3]

From the industry itself have come frequent denials of leadership. The secretary of the American Petroleum Institute believed that he had "conclusively demonstrated that supply, demand, and competition are the 'combination' which is controlling the oil business."[4] No combination of all or a part of the industry could control it. The Standard Oil Company of New Jersey claimed in 1922 that "the price is not fixed by the Standard Oil Company (New Jersey) or by any other large company or by any association or group of companies."[5]

If the Standard companies each operate as leaders in their respective territories the relations between the various Standard companies are important. Does competition occur between these companies in any form, and, if not, how are their policies coordinated? Until about 1922 interlocking stock ownership between the Standard companies was held to provide a basis for the sharing of territory and the coordination of price policies.[6] As a result of this coordination great inequalities existed in the price of gasoline in the different territories which were "not in accordance with the cost of transportation or marketing nor generally with differences in demand and supply."[7] This interlocking ownership has now, however, almost disappeared.[8] The Standard companies have moreover begun to invade each other's territories;[9] this move-

[1] *New York Times*, Oct. 22, 1932.
[2] *Oil and Gas Jour.*, Mar. 2, 1933, 23. The Sun Oil Company made disturbing reductions in the price of oil in Brooklyn in February and, when general increases in the price of crude oil were made in August, 1933, the Sun Oil Company made larger increases than any of its rivals (*New York Herald Tribune*, Aug. 26, 1933).
[3] F.T.C., *Prices, Profits, and Competition in the Petroleum Industry*, 1928, 167.
[4] WELCH, R. L., *The Recent Increases in the Prices of Petroleum and its Products*, American Petroleum Institute, 1920.
[5] *The Lamp*, June, 1922.
[6] F.T.C., *The Pacific Coast Petroleum Industry*, 1922, II, 132, 149.
[7] *ibid.*, 149.
[8] F.T.C., *Prices, Profits, and Competition in the Petroleum Industry*, 1928, 72.
[9] U.S. v. Standard Oil Co. of New York and Vacuum Oil Co., *Answer to Supple-*

ment had not, however, proceeded far by 1928, when it was reported that "as a rule the Standard Oil companies have less than 1 per cent of the sales of gasoline in territories other than their own" although the proportion was as high as 74 per cent in one case. "No Standard company is the second largest seller of gasoline in the territory of any other Standard company."[1] Doubtless the fact that few of the non-Standard companies limit themselves to territory as narrow as that of the Standard companies has made it increasingly difficult to maintain wide differences of price between different territories.[2] It appears, however, that, at least until recently, it has been possible to pursue a somewhat independent policy in the Pacific coast territory: the commission found that the changes in the price of crude oil in California coincided in neither time nor amount with the changes east of the Rockies.[3] During the general decline in business activity between June, 1929, and February, 1933, the price of crude oil fell only 24.2 per cent in California compared with 66.1 per cent and 70.7 per cent in the Pennsylvania and Kansas-Oklahoma fields respectively. The price of gasoline fell 44.9 per cent in California, 54.8 per cent in Pennsylvania, and over 70 per cent in north Texas and Oklahoma.

The extent to which the price policies of firms in the industry are determined by the lead of the Standard Oil companies in their respective territories is, therefore, difficult to gauge. The actual initiative in making price changes may not always be indicated by precedence in announcing prices, especially where changes in announced prices follow rather than precede actual price reductions. Moreover, there is little evidence that the Standard companies have forced their policy upon unwilling rivals. It is true

---

mental Petition. 14. The Atlantic Refining Company initiated this new policy when it entered the territory of the Standard Oil Company of New York. Subsequently the Standard Oil Company of New York entered the territories of the Standard Oil Company of New Jersey, the Continental Oil Company, and (in 1926) of the Standard Oil Company of California. The Standard Oil Company of Indiana has invaded the territories of the New York, New Jersey, Kentucky, and Louisiana companies through the acquisition of control of the Pan-American Petroleum and Transport Company. (F.T.C., *Prices, Profits, and Competition in the Petroleum Industry*, 1928, 54.) An abortive attempt was made to merge the Standard Oil companies of New Jersey and California.
[1] *ibid.*, 228.
[2] The chairman of the Texas company stated, however, that the reason for the acceptance of changes in price of the Standard companies by their rivals was that "taken together they cover the entire territory of the United States (*ibid.*, 234). This argument was endorsed by the National Petroleum Marketers Association (*ibid.*, 230).
[3] *ibid.*, 135. In the other fields the price of crude oil moves generally in unison, but changes by the different Standard companies are not simultaneous (*ibid.*, xix).

that a representative of a Standard company is reported to have mentioned on one occasion to a meeting of independents that he had full authority to reduce the retail price of gasoline to a level that would oust all competition;[1] but evidence of such an attitude is rare. Of course rivals know that the productive capacity and financial resources of the Standard companies would enable them to cut prices below those of their rivals and accept a great deal of additional business if the rivals did not follow them. They also know that the Standard companies could maintain the low prices for a considerable period if the rivals did follow them.[2] In general, however, "the Standard Oil companies do not initiate local price reductions but they are able to detect instances of price cutting on the part of local marketers"[3] and generally meet such competition by making local price concessions. The repressive tactics reported by the commission in 1928 revealed *jobbers* boycotting a refiner who had sold gasoline below the price announced by the Standard Oil Company and *retailers* exerting pressure upon a fellow retailer selling below the price announced by the Standard Oil Company.[4]

The measure and nature of leadership in this industry are so uncertain that its consequences are extremely difficult to identify. In more recent years acceptance of the prices set by the Standard companies, in so far as it has occurred, appears to be mainly due to a desire to avoid cutthroat competition and also to the greater hope of survival and profit from following the lead. The Federal Trade Commission concluded that the lead of the Standard Oil companies consisted more in registering the effects of uncontrollable elements of supply and demand upon prices than in any control of supply and prices; writing in 1928 of the power of the Standard companies to dictate the price of crude oil, it concluded that "there can be little doubt that the major price swings were generally the result of supply and demand conditions, but, owing to the limited number of large purchasers who must determine severally their own prices (or follow the price of some other company), the element of arbitrary human judgment becomes an important factor in the changes in a more conspicuous degree than where there is a great number of both buyers and sellers. To that

---

[1] *ibid.*, 231.
[2] The Federal Trade Commission attributed the dominance of the Standard companies to their large production, investment, financial resources, and credit (*The Pacific Coast Petroleum Industry*, 1922, II, 132).
[3] F.T.C., *Prices, Profits, and Competition in the Petroleum Industry*, 1928, 241.
[4] *ibid.*, 243 *ff.*

extent at least it is evidently true that crude prices only lamely, and . . . only through comparatively infrequent changes, reflect the constantly altering relations of supply and demand."[1] As to their power to control the price of gasoline it stated that they have such power "as long as they follow the general trend of market conditions,"[2] which suggests that prices have not departed widely from what might have been expected had competition existed. On the other hand, the commission held that this power to make the market price gave the Standard companies an opportunity "to obtain all the financial advantages which accrue to those having advance knowledge of price changes in trade and the capital profitably to exploit that knowledge."[3]

No more than an oblique light is thrown upon the price policy in the industry by an analysis of the changing relative importance of the Standard companies in the industry as a whole. As in the steel, so in the petroleum industry, the sellers charged with leading the industry have suffered a considerable decline in the proportion of the total sales which they have controlled. The percentage of the total output of refined oil which was produced by the Standard Oil Company began to decline as early as 1900. In 1899 the company's proportion was 90.1 per cent;[4] by 1906 it had fallen to 84.8 per cent[5] and by 1911 to 80 per cent,[6] which decline was much emphasized by the company in the proceedings against it under the Sherman Act.[7] The changes in the distribution of business have been most striking, however, since the partition of the former Standard company. Whereas in 1911 the Standard company possessed about 80 per cent of the business in refined products in the United States, by 1913 successor companies as a group controlled 75 per cent, by 1914, 69 per cent,[8] by 1915, 65 per

[1] *ibid.*, 135.
[2] F.T.C., *The Pacific Coast Petroleum Industry*, 1922, II, 133.
[3] *loc. cit.* The commission offered no proof, however, that the companies had profited from such knowledge. If a large company attempted to accumulate crude oil before announcing an increase in the price of refined products, the price would be expected to rise owing to its abnormal buying. In so far as the companies announce a price and then take all the crude oil offered at that price, the price would not rise, but it would be difficult to see how they could accumulate oil. Similarly it is difficult to see how the leader could benefit from prior knowledge of a decrease in prices.
[4] This calculation related to the whole North American market but the proportion is believed to have been very similar for the United States alone (U.S. v. Standard Oil Co., *Brief for U.S.*, I, 144).
[5] This figure excludes the territory of the Waters-Pierce Oil Company but this exclusion appears to affect the figures little (*loc. cit.*).
[6] WAR INDUSTRIES BOARD, *Bulletin*, No. 36, *cit.* AMERICAN PETROLEUM INSTITUTE, *Recent Rises in the Price of Petroleum*, 13.
[7] *Brief (Circuit Court) on the Facts for the Standard Oil Co.*, I, 238.
[8] F.T.C., *Prices, Profits, and Competition in the Petroleum Industry*, 1928, 262.

104   THE DECLINE OF COMPETITION

cent,[1] by 1919, 49 per cent,[2] and by 1926, 43.1 per cent[3] of the business.

The distribution of the production of crude oil has changed somewhat differently. The Standard Oil Company produced in 1898, 33.5 per cent of the total crude output of the country, the highest percentage it attained;[4] by 1906 its percentage was reported to be no more than 17 per cent.[5] By 1919 the successor companies as a group produced 21.3 per cent[6] and by 1926 about 24.5 per cent, or, including associated companies, 29.3 per cent.[7] The percentage of oil lands in the hands of the Standard company and its successors has changed even more sharply in contrast with the control of refined products. While the former Standard Oil Company controlled little oil acreage, the successor companies controlled in 1925, 47.4 per cent of the proven acreage and this percentage has subsequently increased.[8] The increasing relative importance of the Standard companies as a group in the production of crude oil and the control of oil reserves, in contrast with their continued decline in relative importance in the marketing of gasoline, is, of course, due to a rapid integration of crude oil production with refining and marketing.[9] All the Standard companies have shared in this reduction in the proportion of business in refined oil products falling to them as a group.[10]

[1] F.T.C., *The Price of Gasoline in* 1915, 143.
[2] Records of Bureau of Mines, *cit.* American Petroleum Institute, *loc. cit.*
[3] F.T.C., *Prices, Profits, and Competition in the Petroleum Industry*, 1928, 76. The proportion was 51.5 per cent if associated companies be included.
[4] *Brief (Circuit Court) on the Facts for the Standard Oil Co.*, 569.
[5] COMMISSIONER OF CORPORATIONS, *The Petroleum Industry*, I, 8. The Attorney General set the figure at 11 per cent (*Brief for U.S.*, I, 139).
[6] F.T.C., *Prices, Profits, and Competition in the Petroleum Industry*, 1928, 27.
[7] *ibid.*, 77.
[8] *ibid.*, 78.
[9] See Chap. VIII.
[10] The Federal Trade Commission reported (F.T.C., *op. cit.*, 225) that the proportion of the sales of gasoline in the marketing territory of each of the important successor companies in the hands of the successor company in 1926 was:

	Per cent
Standard Oil Company of New York	46.1
Standard Oil Company of New Jersey	43.2
Atlantic Refining Company	44.5
Standard Oil Company (Ohio)	37.6
Standard Oil Company (Indiana)	35.5
Standard Oil Company (Kentucky)	33.3
Standard Oil Company of Louisiana	35.5
Magnolia Petroleum Company	18.1
Standard Oil Company (Nebraska)	23.6
Continental Oil Company	47.2
Standard Oil Company of California	28.7

The Standard Oil Company of New York testified that its proportion of the total sales of gasoline in New York and New England fell from about 85 per cent in 1911 to 60 per cent in 1918, 46 per cent in 1926, 34 per cent in 1929, and 32.7 per cent in the first four months of 1930 (U.S. v. Standard Oil Co. of New York *et al, Answer to Supplemental Petition*, 14, 15; *New York Times*, July 2, 1930).

This decline in the relative importance of the successor companies[1] may be, and probably is, partly due to the efforts of these companies to maintain prices. But there is no doubt that other and more powerful forces have also operated to cause a decline. The demand for gasoline has increased very rapidly with the rapid increase in the use of automobiles. Sales of gasoline increased from 1,099 million gallons in 1913[2] to 10,996 million gallons in 1926,[3] an increase of almost exactly 900 per cent. In order to maintain their relative position, the Standard Oil companies would, therefore, have been required to increase to ten times their former size in thirteen years, and it is more than likely that expansion at such a pace was impossible without a great decline in efficiency. They did, however, increase their sales by about 475 per cent. They may even have hesitated to increase their investment upon the assumption of a more rapid expansion of the industry. The expansion of the rival companies was facilitated by the fortunes made as a result of the good luck of some of those who discovered rich supplies of crude oil. They sought to establish integrated companies and entered the business of refining and marketing. It is evident, however, that the successor companies, with a large volume of business relatively to that of any rival, have been either unable or unwilling to prevent the establishment and rapid growth of new firms, as well as the rapid growth of small firms existing at the time of the partition.[4] It is equally

---

[1] The significance of the decline in the relative importance of the former Standard Oil Company, although emphasized by the company itself appears to have received little consideration from the Commissioner of Corporations, who was most concerned with the large percentage of business remaining in the hands of the company.

[2] F.T.C., *The Price of Gasoline in 1915*, 31. These statistics are, however, not complete.

[3] F.T.C., *Prices, Profits, and Competition in the Petroleum Industry*, 136.

[4] An analysis of the origin of the capital invested in the industry by firms with a published investment at the end of 1926 of one hundred million dollars or more affords an indirect measure of the growth of the various types of firm. Of this investment 9 per cent was invested by Standard Oil companies in or before 1911 and another 50 per cent was invested by such companies subsequently to 1911, making a total of 59 per cent of the 1926 investment in the hands of companies that were already established on a considerable scale in 1911. Three per cent of the 1926 total was invested by other companies in or prior to 1911, and 17 per cent was invested by these companies subsequently; thus 20 per cent of the 1926 investment was controlled by companies already existing on a small scale in 1911. The remaining 21 per cent of the 1926 investment was made by firms established since 1911. (Calculated from Federal Trade Commission, *op. cit.*, 61.) These figures must be interpreted very broadly as they are based on uncorrected figures published by the corporations concerned; they exclude all companies with less than one hundred million dollars capitalization in 1926; associated companies have not been included with the Standard companies. Two of the independent companies in 1911 had a capitalization of 71 million dollars which exceeded that of all but two of the Standard companies. Capitalization is moreover a very indirect measure of the distribution of business

evident that profit prospects in the industry (including any prospective influence exerted over prices by the Standard companies and any prospective obstacles they might place in the way of rivals) have attracted new investment. In fact, much of the increase in capital having been supplied out of profits, these profits have evidently been considerable.[1] They were, however, on a higher level before and during the war of 1914 to 1918 than subsequently, which decline the Federal Trade Commission attributed "in part to the development of a greater degree of competition," in turn stimulated by the period of high profits.[2] In so far as statistics of profit throw any light at all upon the differences in the costs of firms of different sizes (which is very doubtful) they do not suggest any great differences in efficiency between the larger and the smaller units.[3]

Figure 5 indicates that the value of gasoline has declined in terms of commodities generally at wholesale. The relationship between changes in the price of crude oil and gasoline since 1913 is also shown. These statistics throw little light, however, on the

---

because of the probability of differences between companies in their accounting practices and in the degree of integration of each.

[1] Such statistics of profits as are available suggest a high rate of profit but little is known of the profits of smaller companies and no account can be taken of the losses of the many firms that have disappeared. Between 1922 and 1925 the average rate of profit of the five Standard companies in their crude oil producing business was 5.1 per cent while that of the independent companies was 16.5 per cent, although during the first half of 1926 the rate of return of the Standard companies was reported to be 20 per cent and that of the independents 14.8 per cent (calculated upon a comparable basis) (F.T.C., *Prices, Profits, and Competition in the Petroleum Industry*, 271). In petroleum refining during the period from 1912 to 1925 the average rate of return for 10 or 11 Standard companies (varying from year to year) was 13.8 per cent while that of companies representative of the industry as a whole (the number of companies varying between 18 and 26) was 12.4 per cent, and ranged between 5.6 per cent in 1921 and 24.5 per cent in 1917 (*ibid.*, 303).

[2] *ibid.*, 303-304.

[3] Statistics of crude petroleum production in 1925 reveal that companies with an investment of $25,000,000 and over earned on the average 15.5 per cent, those with an investment of $5,000,000 to $25,000,000, 15.9 per cent, those with an investment of $1,000,000 to $5,000,000, 16.4 per cent, and companies with an investment of less than $1,000,000, 13.4 per cent. Only 5 of the 90 companies included in the study were in the investment group with the highest rate of return. (*ibid.*, 278.) Returns by about 60 companies engaged in petroleum refining (*ibid.*, 297) showed for the year 1925 that companies with an investment in that business of $100,000,000 and over earned 11.3 per cent, those with an investment of $25,000,000 to $100,-000,000 earned 10.6 per cent, while the highest return (11.5 per cent) was earned by companies with an investment of $5,000,000 to $25,000,000. Only ten of the 63 companies included in the study for that year were in the class obtaining the highest return. Investment was calculated by adding together capital stock, surplus and reserves, long-term borrowings, and advances from affiliated and associated companies, and deducting outside investments. Income was obtained by adding together net income before payment of bond interest or taxes, interest paid on long-term advances and borrowings, and advances including amortization, and deducting income from outside investments. (*ibid.*, 267.)

question whether leadership has resulted in prices emancipated from the influence of costs. The profitability of production in 1913 is not revealed. Costs have subsequently changed greatly owing to changes in the supply and price of crude oil, changes in methods of refining, and also changes in conditions of demand for oil products; there is no means of judging whether all these changes have been reflected in prices.

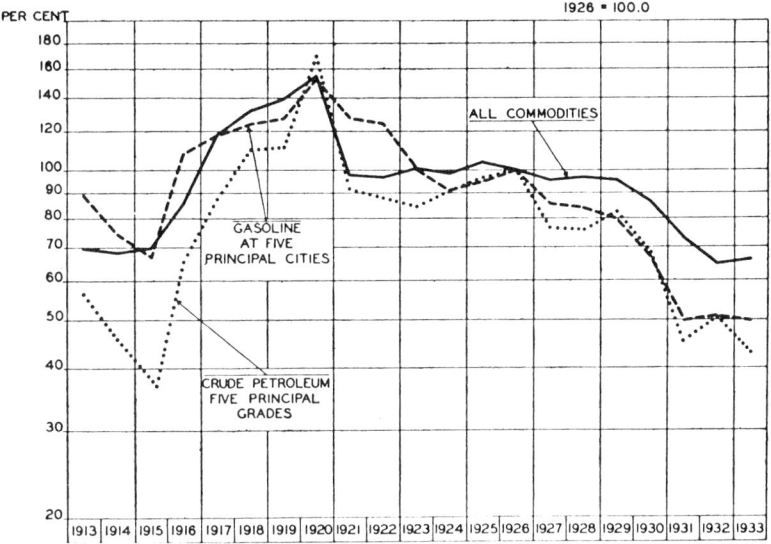

FIG. 5.—The prices of gasoline and crude petroleum and an index of wholesale prices 1913 to 1933. (*Drawn from statistics in "Oil Paint and Drug Reporter" and U.S. Bureau of Labor Statistics: Wholesale Prices.*)

The picture of price leadership is, therefore, again a confused one. The announcements of changes in price[1] by the Standard Oil companies are naturally of great importance in the industry. Most increases appear to have been initiated by these companies and few reductions by them fail to be accepted by their rivals. But rivals do from time to time initiate price reductions, thus suggesting that the policy of the Standard companies, if in complete command of the industry, would have been to maintain prices higher than those that have often prevailed. It is perhaps partly on account of this desire of the Standard companies to maintain prices that rival companies have grown so rapidly. As the Standard companies usually meet local price cutting, rivals have

[1] The industry has not been characterized by great stability in prices at least partly owing to the rapidly changing conditions of supply of crude oil.

not to any great extent obtained business by charging prices lower than those of the Standard companies[1] in the same areas. It is more probable that the prices that have prevailed have provided a liberal margin of profit (especially in retailing) which has provided both a powerful inducement to and a means of making new investment. New firms have obtained business largely from the great numbers of new purchasers of gasoline and partly by resort to non-price competition.[2] There has been rivalry in the purchase of oil lands proven and unproven; heavy expenditures on advertising and particularly heavy expenditure upon retail outlets (both by providing expensive equipment for roadside gas stations and securing, by various devices, the control of great numbers of these stations). This policy is doubtless partly the outcome of the rigid differential between the tank wagon price and the retail price of oil. Thus the industry is competitive in the sense that the various firms attempt to secure business at each other's expense but price competition is only sporadic and temporary and other forms of competition are more important.[3] The burden of non-price competition led, when the time came for the submission of a code of fair competition under the National Recovery Act, to serious efforts to regulate competition in the provision of facilities to and the control of retailers.[4] On the other hand, the tendency for Standard companies to operate in nation-wide markets,[5] together with the growth in the size of rival firms, and the apparently diminishing power of the Standard companies in their own territories,[6] raises even more acutely the question which developed also in the discussion of the steel industry, *viz.*, is price leadership a transitional form for the concentration of control of price and output policy in industry? A general survey of recent events in the

[1] Unadvertised gasoline has, however, been sold at less than the prices of the Standard companies.

[2] See Chap. VII.

[3] F.T.C., *Prices, Profits, and Competition in the Petroleum Industry*, 198, xx. *Cf.* also, "Price initiative today seems to be left generally to the Standard companies and competition is apparently more directed to developing facilities for getting business than to seeking to obtain it by underselling" (F.T.C., *The Advance in the Price of Petroleum Products*, 1920, 53).

[4] *New York Times*, July 15, 1933.

[5] The desire to merge the Standard Oil companies of California and New Jersey was attributed to the fact that geographical limitation of their markets handicapped them because they were able to meet only locally the competition of rivals operating in a nation-wide market (STANDARD OIL COMPANY OF NEW JERSEY, *The Lamp*, October, 1931). The proposed merger has since been abandoned (*New York Times*, Oct. 20, 1933).

[6] The commission noted that the Standard companies no longer treat the independent companies as intruders (F.T.C., *Prices, Profits, and Competition in the Petroleum Industry*, 1928, 204).

industry suggests that the power of the Standard companies over prices is diminishing partly owing to the lack of harmony between the Standard companies themselves. The division of opinion in the industry after the passage of the National Industrial Recovery Act concerning the desirability of complete federal control of prices suggests not only dissatisfaction with the conditions affecting prices in the past but also differences of opinion between the major Standard companies.[1]

C. *The Agricultural Implement Industry*

There is some evidence that the International Harvester Company was accepted as a leader in making the prices for agricultural implements prior to 1910. Competitors of the company are said to have "generally admitted that they got what competition, *i.e.*, the competition of the International Harvester Company, would allow." There was substantial uniformity in the wholesale prices of the more important harvesting machines although Deere and Company charged slightly higher prices than the Harvester company.[2] The Federal Trade Commission, observing that the percentage of increase in the price of dump hay rakes made by the Harvester company prior to 1920 was the same as that made by its rivals, believed that a "follow the leader" policy was indicated.[3] The small companies probably also followed the lead of the Harvester company in making the price of other implements;[4] the Attorney General argued, therefore, that to permit the development of a company as large as the International Harvester Company was to "overawe its small competitors and cause them not to act upon their own initiative but to follow the lead in all important matters affecting the trade."[5] One court decided that the Harvester company had such an advantage over its rivals in the matter of financial resources, organized selling mediums, production costs, ownership and manufacture of raw materials, and in the volume and distribution of business that it was able completely to dominate the industry, which "it does so control and dominate by regulating prices," the rivals of the

[1] *New York Times*, Aug. 4, 1933. The majority of firms in the industry were prepared moreover to countenance a reduction of the margin between the wholesale and retail prices of gasoline (*ibid.*, June 27, 1933), which margin had probably played a large part in shaping the recent development of the industry and inducing sporadic and temporary price wars.
[2] U.S. v. International Harvester Co., *Brief for U.S.*, 93.
[3] F.T.C., *The High Prices of Farm Implements*, 1920, 196.
[4] *Brief for U.S.*, 224.
[5] *Brief for U.S.* (Reargument) (1916), 88.

110   THE DECLINE OF COMPETITION

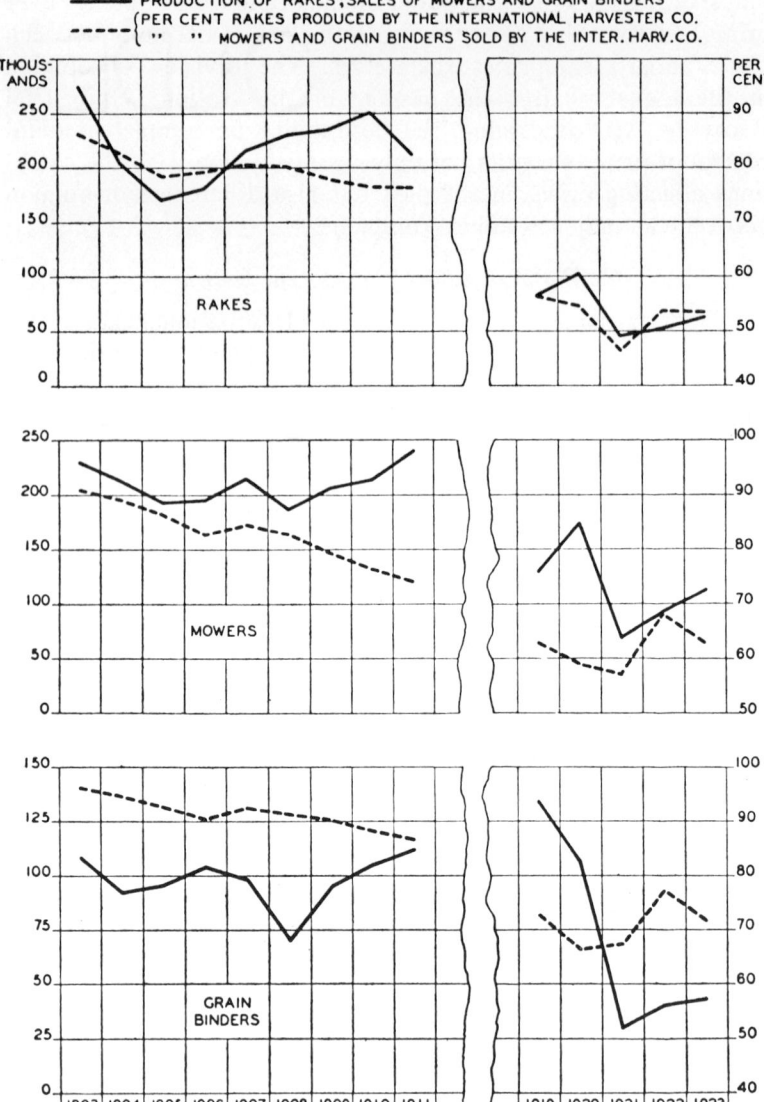

Fig. 6.—The production of agricultural implements and the proportion manufactured or sold by the International Harvester Company, 1903 to 1911, and 1919 to 1923. (*Compiled from Commissioner of Corporations: The International Harvester Company*, 180 ff., and *U.S. v. International Harvester Co., Brief for U.S.* 146 to 164.)

company prudently governing their prices by those made by the company.[1] The Harvester company, on the other hand, denied that its competitors usually accepted its prices.[2] It argued that in 1921, for instance, prices were first reduced by one of its rivals and that the price reduction was then accepted by the company[3] in order that it might continue to get business. The Supreme Court expressed no opinion on the question whether the Harvester company was generally accepted as a price leader in the industry; it remarked, however, that "the fact that competitors may see proper in the exercise of their own judgment to follow the prices of another manufacturer does not establish any suppression of competition or show any sinister domination."[4]

Perfect uniformity between the prices of different sellers was not secured. The ability of Deere and Company to secure prices higher than those of the Harvester company has been mentioned. In a list of the high and low prices prevailing in 1918 for a variety of implements there is always some spread between the high and the low prices; for some of the lower priced implements the highest price was some 30 per cent above the lowest.[5] It is to be remembered, however, that lack of homogeneity in the products of different companies, and the probability that the prices relate to machines delivered at different points, make comparison of their prices especially difficult. It is possible that at least some of the higher prices were those quoted by rivals of the International company.

Yet again the firm alleged to be a price leader suffered a decline in its proportion of total sales.[6] Figure 6 shows that during the

[1] U.S. v. International Harvester Co., *Brief for U.S.*, 17.
[2] U.S. v. International Harvester Co., *Brief for International Harvester Co.*, 158, 161.
[3] *ibid.*, 47, 161.
[4] U.S. v. International Harvester Co., 274 U.S. 693 (1927).
[5] F.T.C., *The High Prices of Farm Implements*, 137.
[6] The Commissioner of Corporations reported (*The International Harvester Company*, 179) the following changes in the Harvester company's share of business between 1904 and 1909 in the manufacture of the more important harvesting machines:

Implements	1904		1909	
	Output for U.S. (thousands)	Percentage produced by Harvester Co.	Output for U.S. (thousands)	Per cent produced by Harvester Co.
Binders and headers	108.8	86.7	129.2	85.9
Mowers	267.6	82.6	359.2[a]	77.8
Reapers	60.9	74.9	58.2	77.2
Rakes	236.2	71.0	266.2	69.1[b]
Tedders	35.7	52.6	34.3	73.2
Corn harvesters	6.9	70.1	19.6	75.5

[a] Includes combined mowers and reapers.
[b] Includes side delivery and sweep rakes.

The table excludes the foreign business of the International Harvester Company. The acquisition of the Osborne company's business in 1903 raised the proportion of

112   THE DECLINE OF COMPETITION

period from 1904 to 1909 its proportion of the sales of binders, rakes, and mowers fell somewhat, while its proportion of the sales of reapers, corn harvesters, and tedders rose. The commissioner commented that at the end of the period the company still retained its dominant position and that it appeared to be the policy of the company to use its strong position in the manufacture of these implements to build up a business in the manufacture of others.¹ Of the next period from 1911 to 1918 the Federal Trade Commission reported "a considerable decrease in the production of the harvesting machines made by the International Harvester Company in 1918 as compared with 1911, which was partly due to the growth of several of its largest competitors and partly to the cutting off of export trade in 1918, in which the International Harvester Company was by far the largest factor. Broadly speaking the control of the International Harvester Company in the harvesting machine trade declined from roughly 80 per cent in 1911 (taking account of quantity and value of machines) to about 64 per cent in 1918. While there was, therefore, a considerable decline in its proportion of this business the percentage remaining in its hands is so great that it still retains its dominating position in the industry on the basis of quantity produced."² During the period from 1919 to 1923, when the International Harvester Company was operating under a consent decree, its percentage of the sale of the larger implements taken as a group declined from about 66.6 to 64.1.³

---

binders made by the company to 94.2 per cent in that year. The company's proportion of *sales* in the United States declined fairly steadily from 96.3 per cent in 1903 to 87.2 per cent in 1911 (*ibid.*, 180).
    ¹ *ibid.*, 36, 184.
    ² F.T.C., *The High Prices of Farm Implements*, 679, 34. Little emphasis is placed upon the declining trend in the proportion of business in the hands of the Harvester company. The proportion of the total production of the more important harvesting machines manufactured in the United States which was produced by the Harvester company during the period from 1911 to 1918 was:

	1911		1918	
Implement	Total output of United States (thousands)	Percentage produced by Harvester Co.	Total output of United States (thousands)	Percentage produced by Harvester Co.
Grain binders................	168.9	87.0	81.5ᵃ	65.3
Corn binders.................	19.6ᵇ	75.5	37.2	72.5
Mowers.......................	315.1	76.6	187.3ᵃ	59.5
Side delivery and dump hay rakes..........................	228.2ᶜ	72.0	99.8	57.5ᵈ

    ᵃ Includes estimated production from one small company.
    ᵇ Production for 1909, figures for 1911 not available.
    ᶜ Of these 14,400 are estimated.
    ᵈ Including estimated production for side delivery rakes.

(F.T.C., *The High Prices of Farm Implements*, 679.)
    ³ The percentage of total sales made by International Harvester Company was:

PRICE LEADERSHIP

This downward trend in its share of the total business must be interpreted, however, in the light of the changes in the total output of the industry. Over considerable periods the total output of most implements has followed a downward trend. Between 1903 and 1913 the average annual sales (for five-year periods) by the Harvester company of grain binders, corn binders, and headers increased, although less quickly than the aggregate sales of the whole industry; even during that period, however, sales of reapers, mowers, and sulky hay rakes declined, usually more sharply than the decline of the aggregate output of the industry. During the subsequent period from 1914 to 1923, the output of all these products by the Harvester company declined as well as its percentage of the whole industry.[1] In the prosecution of the company its counsel emphasized the decline in its percentage of business,[2] and remarked that "an increasing per cent of trade built up by the present owner surely indicates more present power than a diminishing percentage, acquired by purchase from several former owners. And if the greater power does not prevent competitive conditions how can the less?"[3] He contended that if the International Harvester Company had power and intention to control the trade its share of trade would have increased.[4] For all agricultural implements (harvesting machines and other implements) its output had declined 22.5 per cent while that of its rivals had increased by 158 per cent.[5]

Implement	1919	1923
Grain binders	72.7	71.2
Corn binders	65.8	70.6
Mowers	63.8	65.4
Reapers	84.7	57.7
Headers and push binders	90.0	73.7
Sulky rakes	56.3	55.4
Side delivery and sweep rakes	58.6	45.3
Tedders (including combined side rakes and tedders)	90.6	93.1
Harvester threshers	73.1	33.8
	66.6	64.1

(U.S. v. International Harvester Co., *Brief for U.S.*, 146 to 154.)

[1] *Brief for the International Harvester Co.*, 120.
[2] He described the decline in a variety of terms. Speaking of the period of 1903 to 1912, he pointed out that while its total sales of binders had increased by 5 per cent those of its rivals had increased about 900 per cent; its total sales of mowers had declined 21 per cent while those of its rivals had increased 238 per cent; its sales of rakes had declined 42 per cent while those of its rivals had increased by 54 per cent. (*Brief for the International Harvester Co.* (Reargument), 117.) These statements, however, must be interpreted with care; the large percentages of increase in output by rivals were partly due to their very small output at the beginning of the period.
[3] *Brief for the International Harvester Co.*, 182.
[4] *Brief for the International Harvester Co.* (Reargument), 117.
[5] Analyzing these figures further, he pointed out that (excluding one company) the smallest increase in sales by any competitor was 12.7 per cent; in the output of

The company attributed the decline in the aggregate sales of implements in 1921 and 1922 to the decline in the purchasing power of farmers, due to the fall in the prices of agricultural products and not to the monopolistic policy of the company. The Attorney General, on the other hand, claimed that the failure of 150 of the rivals of the Harvester company was due to the dominance of the company;[1] only three rivals of the Harvester company survived this period when the Harvester company was greatly prospering. The company replied that the number of new manufacturers established during the period for the production of the more important implements was about equal to the number withdrawn from the industry;[2] new firms did not enter a field they believed to be closed against them, or from which they have seen other firms eliminated by impossible conditions.

The "domination" of the International Harvester Company was due partly to its efficiency. It has never been seriously charged with price wars aimed directly at the destruction of rivals; apparently prices satisfactory to it were inadequate to support many of the smaller firms, pressure upon which was increased by the shrinkage of demand. Had prices sufficed to keep all its rivals alive they would have yielded a still larger profit margin to the Harvester company. The average cost of manufacturing binders (the most important harvesting machine), in the two years 1910 and 1911, in the domestic plants of the Harvester company, ranged from $54.11 to $73.78 (excluding general and selling expenses but including raw materials supplied by subsidiary companies at market prices), the average for all its plants being $56.32. The average factory cost for the four largest independent companies was $70.83, although the machines produced by the different companies were not identical in type or quality. Only two independents manufactured at a cost appreciably below the highest costs of the Harvester company.[3] The output of the independent companies was smaller than that in any of the plants

---

mowers only one competitor suffered a decrease and that of 19 per cent; in the output of rakes the largest decrease in output by a rival was 30 per cent.

[1] The Attorney General, comparing the position of the International Harvester Company with that of the United States Steel Corporation, remarked that while the U.S. Steel Corporation had been engaged in efforts to keep its competition in line the Harvester company had dominated its rivals with the result that some of them had been unable to continue in operation (U.S. v. International Harvester Co., *Brief for U.S.*, 130).

[2] *Brief for the International Harvester Co.*, 37.

[3] COMMISSIONER OF CORPORATIONS, *The International Harvester Company*, 27, 260–265.

of the Harvester company except one, and the size of the companies was evidently a large factor in the determination of costs. The inclusion of general expenses placed the independents generally at a still greater disadvantage in comparison with the Harvester company; the average cost of binders to the independents was $76.18 against $58.57 for the Harvester company. In the manufacture of mowers and rakes[1] the situation was similar. The Harvester company probably also had an advantage in relation to its rivals in the production of the newer lines although the information on this point was not conclusive.[1] The Attorney General[2] and the Federal Trade Commission[3] agreed that the dominance of the Harvester Company arose from its tremendous advantage in manufacturing costs as compared with its competitors, and therefore, that the consent decree would fail in its purpose to "restore competitive conditions in the United States in the interstate business in harvesting machines."[4] The company denied that the government had proved that the company possessed permanent advantages[5] in costs of production but also claimed

[1] *ibid.*, 28.
[2] He offered (U.S. v. International Harvester Co., *Brief for U.S.*, 73, 77) the following statistics:

Implement	Advantage over nearest competitor		Advantage over competitor with highest costs	
	1916 dollars	1918 dollars	1916 dollars	1918 dollars
Grain binders	11.10		55.18	82.96
Harvesting machines	28.08			
Corn binders	16.77	17.69	63.43	103.63
Mowers	3.52	3.41	13.20	25.80

[3] The commission, commenting in 1920 upon the effects of the consent decree requiring the Harvester company to dispose of three of its brands of machines, reported that the company's cost of manufacturing two of the brands to be sold was greater than that of the brands to be retained; that the costs of manufacturing the third brand to be disposed of, while comparing favorably with those of brands retained, was reduced by being manufactured at one of the large plants of the company. Moreover the costs of the brands retained were much lower than the costs of the brands of rivals. In consequence, although the proportion of the business in the hands of the company had decreased between 1911 and 1918 "the company still retains a sufficient proportion of the business to give it a dominating position in the industry, especially as it has additional advantages in low costs of manufacture and in the reputation in the trade of the brands retained." (*The High Prices of Farm Implements*, 34.)
[4] After pointing to the large proportion of all the business that would remain in the hands of the company after the separation of the three brands to be sold the commission added, "when consideration is also given to the costs of production of its two great harvesting machine plants, the McCormick and Deering works, it is evident that the independents are unable to offer any serious competition in harvesting machines (*ibid.*, 680).
[5] The company contended that the differences in cost probably represented the differences in cost systems (the commission admitted that some rivals of the company had no cost system or poor ones); that some considerable elements in costs were

that any such advantages were the result of greater efficiency;[1] the advantage of size had been exaggerated as, beyond a certain point, an increase in the volume of business required multiplication of similar producing units: "the quantity which affects costs is not the absolute quantity but the relative quantity to the capacity of the plant as laid out."[2]

A leader able to produce at lower costs than its rivals may select a price policy that will drive rivals out of business without reducing its own rate of return to a normal level. In fact the prices charged yielded considerable profits both to the Harvester company and to a number of its much smaller rivals. The adjusted rate of return upon investment obtained by the Harvester company showed an upward trend from 5.34 per cent in 1904 to 13.43 per cent in 1909, after which it fell to 12.77 per cent in 1910 and 11.51 per cent in 1911.[3] Subsequent calculations by the Federal Trade Commission revealed that the percentage of profit on the investments[4] of the International Harvester Company and 21 rival companies (so far as their business in implements was concerned) was as shown in Table II.[5]

Thus the Harvester company secured a higher rate of return than the average for the whole industry in each year except 1918; its average return for the whole period was also above that for the industry. The commission concluded that over the whole period "the average for the whole industry was little, if any, above what might be considered a normal return."[6] An attempt to segregate the profits of the Harvester company upon its domestic sales

---

merely estimates; that some differences were due to fluctuations in the cost of materials during the war. Other differences were due to factors which were not continually operating, companies operating at the lowest costs in some years giving place to others in other years. It also claimed that the returns on all agricultural implements should be taken together as some firms produced some lines at lowest costs and others other lines. (*Brief for the International Harvester Co.*, 66, 149.)

[1] *ibid.*, 138, 149.

[2] *ibid.*, 148. The company remarked that if the commission was correct in claiming an existing and permanent difference in costs of production "it should have gone on and drawn the conclusion that all manufacturers of implements would be eliminated because of the market advantage of cost of some other competitor" (*ibid.*, 149).

[3] COMMISSIONER OF CORPORATIONS, *The International Harvester Company*, 238.

[4] Actual cash or equivalent invested by stockholders or others; goodwill was excluded owing to the difficulty of valuing it.

[5] *The High Prices of Farm Implements*, 103. Except during the years 1913 and 1914, the smallest companies (with an investment not exceeding $1,000,000) generally made a higher rate of return upon their implement business than the larger companies, including the Harvester company (*ibid.*, 109). These companies, however, did not all produce the same series of implements; those producing mainly harvesting machinery were relatively unprofitable (*ibid.*, 111).

[6] *ibid.*, 102.

suggested, however, that the rate of return on this section of its business in the period from 1913 to 1917 was considerably higher than that on its business as a whole; the rate varied from 10.35 per cent in 1914 to 28.21 per cent in 1917, and for the period from 1913 to 1918 averaged 16 or 17 per cent, which the commission regarded as "considerably more than an adequate return on the capital

TABLE II

Year	International Harvester Co. and Corp.	21 other companies	Average all companies
1913	10.67	8.62	9.82
1914	7.60	4.97	6.57
1915	7.84	5.19	6.79
1916	10.62	8.31	9.72
1917	18.59	13.43	16.60
1918	19.59	20.34	19.88
Average	12.48	10.03	11.52

employed," particularly in view of the fact that "the dominant position of the International Harvester Company makes the element of risk for this company very much smaller than for any other implement company."[1]

The course of prices in the industry during the period from 1914 to 1918 was analyzed in great detail by the Federal Trade Commission, which reported that the most used sizes of the more important implements increased in price on the average by 75 per cent,[2] in comparison with an increase in the index number of all wholesale prices of 97 per cent and of farm products of 112 per cent.[3] The Attorney General argued that the International Harvester Company had power to raise prices (as it had during the war) to a point which ensured prosperity to its competitors; it was also able to lower them (as it did in 1921) so as virtually to eliminate competition; he concluded lamely that "such price changes may be responsive to economic conditions and not the result of deliberate purpose to suppress competition, but the effect on competitors and the public is the same."[4]

[1] *ibid.*, 104.
[2] *The High Prices of Farm Implements*, 77. The less commonly used sizes increased somewhat less so that the average increase in the price of implements of all sizes was 73 per cent (*ibid.*, 79).
[3] *ibid.*, 646.
[4] *Brief for U.S.*, 96. In those lines in which its advantage in the matter of costs was greatest (*i.e.*, in the manufacture of the more complicated **implements**) its

118   THE DECLINE OF COMPETITION

The picture presented by the farm implement industry in recent years is, therefore, one in which one firm is vastly larger than any of its rivals and produces more cheaply than most of them. Total sales of many implements have been declining but prices have been such that new firms have been willing to enter the business and existing firms have been able to expand in spite of their apparently high costs. The Harvester company appears, therefore, to have elected to maintain prices in a time of declining demand and thereby secure profits sufficiently high for rivals to be able to obtain business from it; some rivals have secured considerable profits in spite of their higher costs. It has suffered a decline in its share of the shrinking total business, although that decline does not yet appear to have proceeded so far as to threaten the company's leadership, as it has in the steel and petroleum industries. The Attorney General remarked that such a decline in the percentage of business done by the largest unit, which had also occurred in the oil and tobacco industries, was so common in such cases "as to excite the suspicion that combinations of this character, having found that they can dominate the trade with a smaller proportion than they started with, voluntarily yield part in the belief that they put themselves in a better position to face the law."[1]

D. The Anthracite Coal Industry

In the market for anthracite of domestic sizes the prices of the large sellers were substantially uniform between 1902 (shortly after the acquisition of the Central Railroad of New Jersey by the Philadelphia and Reading Company) and 1920. This uniformity was attributed to the acceptance by other large companies of the announced prices of the Philadelphia and Reading Company.[2] The president of the Reading company agreed that the prices announced by his company were generally followed by its rivals. He attributed this practice to the fact that the Reading company was mining in an area in which costs were higher than in the Wyoming area where there was less water and where the seams were more conveniently mined; if the market price failed to cover

---

margin of profit was probably high, but the average return on its whole investment was brought down by lower margins of profit in other lines (F.T.C., *High Price of Farm Implements*, 192).

[1] *Brief for the U.S.*, 198.

[2] JONES, ELIOT, *The Anthracite Coal Combination*, 172; U.S. v. Reading Co. (1920), *Brief for U.S.*, 193.

the costs of the Reading company it would cease to operate, with the result that there would be a shortage of anthracite, a rise in price, and then a resumption of its activities.[1] The Attorney General, however, raised the question whether prices were not *above* the level necessary to keep the company's mines in operation and claimed that its size and dominant position enabled it to control prices.

Uniformity of anthracite prices is said to have appeared after the strike of 1902.[2] Even after May, 1901, prices below those of the Reading company became much less important than they had been and were very small between 1902 and 1908.[3] The monthly average of prices *above* those charged by the Reading company reveals no such sharp reduction.[4] There was, therefore, considerable uniformity of prices but there were differences,[5] and

[1] U.S. v. Reading Co. (1911), *Record III*, 1060. He stated that producers in the Wyoming area took the same prices as the Reading company "because it would be foolish for them to undercut it when there is a market for the reasonable output of existing mines taking it year in and year out." The Attorney General replied that such arguments were irrelevant where a few have power to control production and even prevent the operation of the ordinary laws of trade and where the limit of production had not been reached. "It is not applicable merely because there is a demand for all that is produced—the very reason why production is not larger may be control by a combination" (*Brief for U.S.*, 202).

[2] In 1899 there was no month in which the monthly average of actual selling prices of all sellers reported by the Bureau of Labor Statistics coincided with the list price of the Lehigh and Wilkes-Barre Coal Company for stove coal at New York; the actual price ranged from 15 to 48 cents below the list price (the average list price being about $4.00 per ton). After the strike of 1902 list prices for all companies became uniform and actual prices agreed closely with list prices. Counsel for the Reading company contended, however, that there were differences even in October, 1902, when the conspiracy was said to have been put into operation and "when presumably it must have been fresh in the minds of the alleged conspirators" (U.S. v. Reading Co. (1911), *Brief for Reading, Co. et al*, 84). In 1903 the monthly average of actual selling prices departed from the list price in only one month and then by only one cent (JONES, *The Anthracite Coal Combination*, 167).

[3] The average of the monthly unweighted average of the amounts by which the prices charged by rivals for stove coal fell short of the Reading company's prices was 7 cents between November, 1900, and May, 1901, and 1.5 cents between June, 1901, and September, 1908.

[4] The average having been 7.8 cents from November, 1900, to May, 1901, and 6.3 cents from June, 1901, to September, 1908. Prices above those of the Reading company show a regular seasonal variation, the greatest differential being in April and May, April being the month in which the regular annual reduction in prices was made to induce "off peak" summer buying.

[5] The total additional sums which the five larger companies would have received on sales of coal of prepared sizes had they charged the list prices from the period from November, 1900, to December, 1908, were computed at 2.8 million dollars (U.S. v. Reading Co. (1911), *Record VI*, 559); these sums are the product of the volume of sales and the amount of the differential. The extent of the lack of uniformity of prices was also displayed by a calculation that if each company had sold each size of coal at the lowest average reported for any company in each month the nine largest companies would have received in the whole period from 1900 to 1908 7.28 million dollars less than they in fact received (U.S. v. Reading Co. (1911),

these differences tended to increase. They have been magnified, however, partly by the inclusion of sizes other than stove sizes of coal.[1] On the other hand, as counsel for the Reading company pointed out,[2] the use of monthly averages of the prices of different companies tends to eliminate day to day differences in price where there is a general tendency for prices to come to a common level although this level may never be completely attained. Some differences, moreover, were due to differences in the conditions affecting different bargains.[3] Nor does the presence of differences preclude the possibility of a well-understood minimum price.

More information is available concerning the prices charged by the smaller sellers for the period since 1913. The prices of the independents were much more erratic and usually higher than those of the railroad-controlled companies: the independent companies usually published no list price, although after 1917 the larger of them announced prices usually 75 cents or more per ton above the highest railroad price. In times of shortage the prices charged by the railroad companies were such that the independents were able to charge considerable premiums over those of the railroads, while in times of plenty the prices charged by the independents were often driven down to the prices of the railroad-controlled companies.[4] Figure 7, showing the prices for different sizes of coal charged by the larger companies and by the independents between January, 1923, and April, 1924, reveals that the price obtained by the independents for steam sizes was rarely above and frequently below the prices obtained by the railroad companies, in contrast with the conditions above described in the market for the larger domestic sizes. The prices announced annually by the larger railroad-controlled companies were fairly

---

Record VI, 508). These figures accumulated upon all sales over long periods of time magnify the differences in price that occurred.

[1] The company itself pointed to the absence of any charge by the Attorney General that the uniformity of prices between the different sellers extended to the smaller sizes of anthracite (U.S. v. Reading Co. (1911), *Brief for Reading Co. et al*, 84), but it included these other sizes when calculating the magnitude of the differences that existed in practice.

[2] *loc. cit.*

[3] The Attorney General admitted some variations from the schedule of prices but attributed them to differences in the quality of coal and favoritism in selling and argued that the companies had not attempted to prove that the bulk of sales were made at prices varying materially from the schedule prices (U.S. v. Reading Co. (1911), *Brief for U.S.*, 201).

[4] F.T.C., *Premium Prices of Anthracite*, 1925, 4. During the period 1913 to 1925 the prices charged by the railroad-controlled companies were such that price differentials appeared almost annually (*ibid.*, 11).

PRICE LEADERSHIP 121

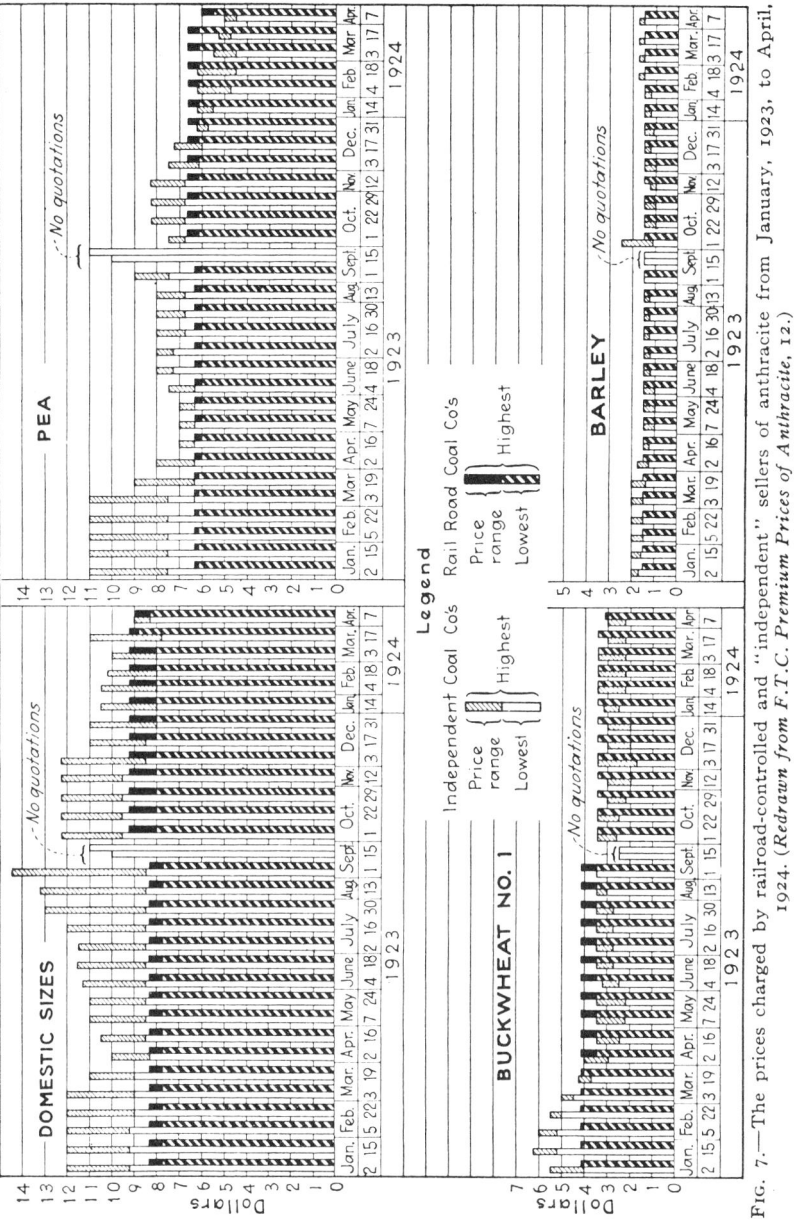

FIG. 7.—The prices charged by railroad-controlled and "independent" sellers of anthracite from January, 1923, to April, 1924. (Redrawn from F.T.C. Premium Prices of Anthracite, 12.)

uniform,[1] differences in quality being responsible for some differences in price.

Complete uniformity of prices was not, therefore, attained, but it was closely approached within the group of railroad-controlled companies. The higher prices charged for domestic sizes by independents in times of activity suggest an unwillingness or inability on the part of the large producers to increase their output sufficiently to adjust supply to demand at the current price but also an unwillingness to adjust demand to supply by raising the price. On the other hand, the fact that independents undercut the large producers in times of diminished demand suggests that the large producers then attempted to maintain prices. Again the influence of the leader, supported by other large producers, was exerted in the direction of stabilizing prices.[2]

The proportion of business controlled by the leader was a much smaller percentage of total sales in the whole industry than in the case of the industries already discussed; the Philadelphia and Reading Company was responsible for only 18.99 per cent of the output of anthracite in 1890. The acquisition of control of the Central Railroad of New Jersey in January, 1901, raised this percentage which was reported in 1912 to be 29.16 per cent.[3] The company claimed[4] that this percentage was not sufficient to give it control of prices or power to dominate the industry.[5] The industry is also notable in that leadership aimed at maintaining and stabilizing prices was not accompanied by a serious decline in the relative position of the leader. During the whole period from 1890 to 1913 its percentage moved in a narrow range between 18.70 and 21.29 per cent,[6] and the range narrowed further with

[1] When, in 1922, the Pennsylvania Fuel Commission required an announcement of prices by the large producers the prices of only three railroads varied by more then 0.6 per cent (5 cents per ton) from the price announced by the Reading company and the extreme range of all their prices was 4.5 per cent (*ibid.*, 6).
[2] See Chap. V.
[3] U.S. v. Reading Co. (1920), *Brief for U.S.*, 166.
[4] *Brief for the Reading Co.*, 280.
[5] *ibid.*, 280. The Supreme Court, however, held that even control of about 20 per cent of the total output gave it power to influence the price of coal and condemned the acquisition of control of the Central Railroad of New Jersey which increased its share of the total business to over one third (U.S. v. Reading Co., 253 U.S. 57 (1920)). This decision is in marked contrast with the complacency of the court toward the United States Steel and International Harvester companies, each of which controlled a much larger share of their respective industries. The concentration under the control of the Lehigh Valley Railroad of 20 per cent of the output of anthracite was similarly condemned (U.S. v. Lehigh Valley Railroad Co., 254 U.S. 270 (1920)).
[6] The Reading company reported (*Brief for Reading Co.* (1914), 262) its own percentage of business for the whole period for 1890 to 1911 to have been:

the passage of time.¹ This stability is doubtless in part due to the control of most of the anthracite reserves by a few companies; new competitors cannot enter the industry and undermine the position of the leader. The absence of new firms is, therefore, not evidence of low rates of return upon capital already invested. The failure of other existing firms to increase their proportion of the business² is probably due to leadership being reinforced by a policy of sharing the market.³ Prices have sufficed, however, to maintain in existence large firms paying annual interest and tax charges upon heavy investments in resources not being exploited.⁴ The larger companies have been exploiting their reserves at a slower rate than the smaller.⁵ Up to the end of 1922 the eight railroad companies estimated originally to have controlled 76.5 per cent of the

1890	18.99	1901	17.13
1891	19.29	1902	15.81
1892	17.44	1903	16.60
1893	17.30	1904	16.75
1894	17.92	1905	17.58
1895	18.87	1906	17.19
1896	17.61	1907	17.32
1897	16.11	1908	15.34
1898	16.34	1909	14.75
1899	17.22	1910	14.10
1900	17.10	1911	14.30

The percentage of business done by the Reading company and the affiliated Wilkes-Barre Coal Company together was reported (*ibid.*, 265) to have been:

1901	25.02	1907	24.47
1902	23.22	1908	23.01
1903	24.44	1909	21.87
1904	24.26	1910	21.23
1905	25.25	1911	21.40
1906	24.53		

¹ Its average yearly variation of production from its ten-yearly average of its percentage of total shipments was 2.15 per cent in the decade 1871 to 1880, 1.33 per cent between 1881 and 1890, 0.57 per cent between 1890 and 1900, and 0.57 per cent between 1901 and 1910 (JONES, *The Anthracite Coal Combination*, 149).

² The company claimed that there had been a sufficient decline in its proportion (of the business in *all* sizes of anthracite, however) to rebut any charge of monopoly or restraint of trade (*ibid.*, 26; also 262, 279).

³ See Chap. IV.

⁴ The United States Coal Commission commented that "the peculiar difficulty of the Reading company has apparently been to pay the taxes and interest on its enormous reserve of coal lands" (*cit.* F.T.C., *Premium Prices of Anthracite* (1925), 52).

⁵ The Attorney General calculated for each of the large holders of anthracite reserves the life of their reserves if they continued to be exploited at the rate current in 1895, with the result that the life of the Reading company's reserves was calculated to be 216 years, that of the reserves of the Lehigh and Wilkes-Barre Coal Company (which later came under the control of the Reading company) 163 years, against 116 years for the company with the next longest expectation of life, and 63 years for the remainder (U.S. v. Reading Co. (1911), *Brief for the U.S.*, 30). The United States Coal Commission, speaking of the heavy reserves of the Reading company, said, "had the anthracite business been an ordinary competitive business and the Philadelphia and Reading Coal and Iron Company an ordinary competitive business enterprise, one of two things would have happened long ago. The company would either have been forced out of business or else forced to sell part of its coal lands to someone else (*cit.* F.T.C., *op. cit.*, 52).

resources in the ground had produced only 71.7 per cent of the output of anthracite with the result that at that date they controlled 77.7 per cent of the estimated recoverable supply.[1] This basis of sharing the market may be attributable to the inducement offered by the level of prices. The sharing of the market to avoid price competition has been largely confined to the major units in the industry. Technical considerations must, however, also have been important. Smaller reserves can be exploited without additional overhead investment in mines, while the more extensive reserves cannot. Nevertheless the policy of sharing the market offered sufficient gains to the large units, in the form of profits to be gained and losses to be avoided, to induce them to postpone the marketing of their anthracite resources. Furthermore, if the president of the Reading company was correct in claiming that its mining costs were greater than those of its rivals, its leadership would have made for higher profits by its rivals even if its own profits were normal.[2]

Whether by restriction of output producers have maintained prices on a level above that necessary to cover costs and a normal rate of profit is difficult to determine. The capacity of the industry to produce, judged simply by the capacity[3] of the mines existing from year to year, and the extent of actual production since 1890, are shown in Fig. 8. The mines have been worked to 90 per cent of their capacity in only three years during the whole period from 1890 to 1929, the average percentage of capacity in use for the whole period being 70.7 per cent. The United States Coal Commission, however, in 1923 attributed the recent market shortage and high prices for anthracite to insufficient development and inadequate production.[4] The commission concluded that production had been kept below demand for many years with the result that high profits had been obtained; coal companies should not be

---

[1] *Cit.* F.T.C., *Wealth and Income in the United States*, 1926, 86. The Attorney General pointed out that, at the current rate of mining, the supplies of the Reading company would outlast those of all competitors, and that there was no possibility of the monopoly being broken up by the influx of new capital attracted by high prices (U.S. v. Reading Co. (1920), *Brief for the U.S.*, 22).

[2] FRAZER and DORIOT, *Analyzing Our Industries*, 404. It has been said that the concentration of control has resulted in the maintenance of prices and the avoidance of overproduction during the periods of declining demand with the result that profits have remained stable and satisfactory.

[3] Calculations of capacity in use are based upon the number of days worked in relation to an annual number of days regarded as a maximum (a crude method of calculation).

[4] Separate reports on anthracite industry, July 5, 1923. *Cit.* F.T.C., *Premium Prices of Anthracite*, 1925, 52.

allowed to hold large reserves without developing them; private property institutions appropriate to other economic resources operated, in its opinion, much less satisfactorily when applied to natural resources. In fact throughout the period 1890–1911 (during the last half of which the coal combination is alleged to

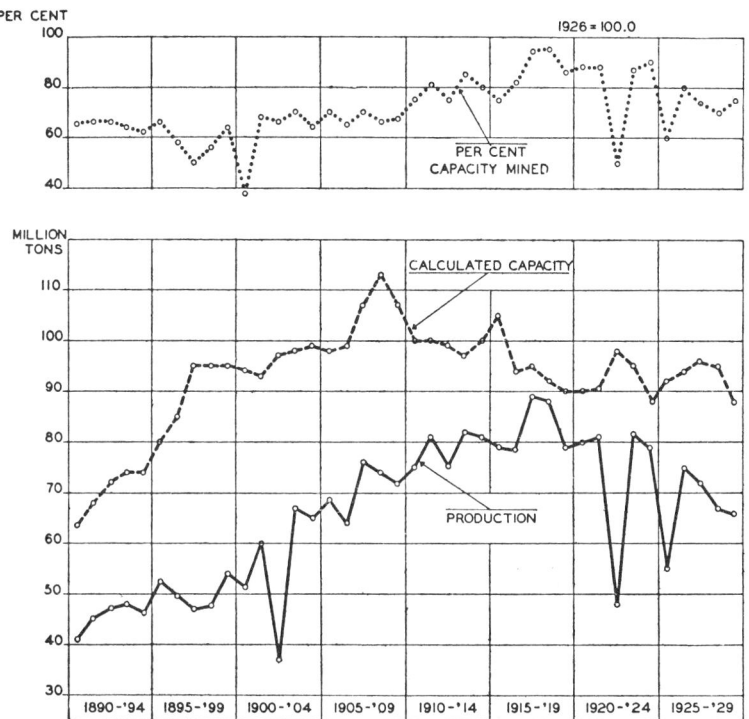

FIG. 8.—Capacity for production of anthracite, actual production and proportion of capacity in use, 1890 to 1929. (*Drawn from data in Mineral Resources of the United States* 1929, II, 695.)

have been in existence), the production of anthracite increased from about 41 to about 81 million tons per annum, and the average value of anthracite per ton (*i.e.*, the value of all sizes) increased from $1.50 to $2.16 per ton. The output of anthracite was evidently insufficient to meet the demand at an unchanging price. Inspection of Figure 8 reveals that capacity for production began to decline in 1907, and, that, while the percentage of capacity in use declined until 1900, it slowly increased thereafter at a time when prices were rising. Between 1911 and 1921 the output remained substantially unchanged, although the average value per ton increased from $2.16 to $5.58. Changes in the general level of prices and, therefore, in the cost of mining must, of course, be taken into account in judging this increase of prices. Between 1921 and 1929, however, the output of anthracite declined from 80 million tons to 66 million tons per annum, although the price increased from $5.58 per ton in 1921 to $5.84 in 1929. During this period the capacity for production showed neither an upward nor a downward trend but the percentage in use declined. Counsel for the Reading company in 1920 contended that the output of anthracite had kept pace with the increase in population, "which is the logical criterion of normality," and therefore that the industry had enjoyed an entirely normal growth.[1] This defense could not be made for the period since 1920, and is not strictly true of the period since 1911. He claimed, furthermore, that 40 per cent of all the anthracite was of the smaller sizes which must compete with soft coal for a market, while the remaining 60 per cent competed with gas and fuel oil for central heating. It is evident, however, that in so far as there was any preference on the part of buyers for anthracite over the substitute products, or inability on the part of sellers of substitutes to sell equivalent quantities at the same price as anthracite, there was a limited monopoly available to any group of firms able to control the output of anthracite. No monopoly, of course, is absolute.

The anthracite producers have incurred considerable criticism because "the boasted stabilization of prices has not prevented frequently recurring premium markets with resultant instability of prices to the ultimate consumer."[2] The commission stated that high prices and frequently recurring premium prices, together with almost stationary production, were viewed by the public generally as evidence that production was too restricted owing to the fact that operators made no provision for developmental work or storage facilities designed to meet an emergency: in consequence wholesalers and retailers had been able to secure excessive profits during periods of temporary or apparent shortage.[3] The Federal Trade Commission attributed the recurrence of premium prices to the failure of mine operators to increase output in keeping with demand since 1913.[4] The presence of premium prices from time to time is, however, simply an indication that the prices charged by the anthracite producers were not so high as they might have

[1] U.S. v. Reading Co. (1920), *Brief for Reading Co.*, 262.
[2] F.T.C., *Premium Prices of Anthracite*, 54.
[3] *ibid.*, 55.
[4] *ibid.*, 5.

charged for the quantities of anthracite that they decided to produce. Had they frequently adjusted prices so that demand at the prices set equalled the supply, the few smaller producers would have been unable to charge premiums over the prices set by the combination. The premium prices, taken alone, therefore, suggest clumsiness in price setting, but nothing more and probably were incidental to the effort to stabilize prices.

The failure of the output of anthracite to increase with increasing prices remains, however, to be explained. The Federal Trade Commission, contemplating the premium prices above mentioned, reported that the railroad producers of anthracite voluntarily restricted price increases, apparently to prevent undesirable inroads of other fuels and to avoid regulation, which conduct, it was said, "strengthens the argument against burdening present consumers with high prices in times of shortage merely because such high prices can be obtained."[1] The commission also reported that a greater production of anthracite was possible at more moderate costs and prices, and questioned the desirability of prices which covered the costs of very high cost producers. "Before it becomes necessary to advance prices to a point justifying such mining methods, substitution of other fuels or technical improvements may gradually take place which might relieve the public of the necessity of ever paying such prices."[2] The policy of the producers has undoubtedly been influenced also by their high funded obligations resulting from their efforts to purchase control of deposits.[3] Furthermore, as the unmined deposits of a small number of companies are likely to be exhausted within a short period of time, the trend of output of anthracite is a serious matter.

Comparison of the behavior of prices of anthracite with the movement of the index of wholesale prices suggests that general monetary conditions do not wholly explain the movements in the price of anthracite. The price of anthracite did not rise between 1903 and 1907, during which period the index number of general prices rose from 85.5 to 93.5. This stability was regarded by the president of the Lackawanna Railroad as the reason why anthracite "should remain in the control of the few hands where it now is."[4]

[1] *ibid.*, 19.
[2] *loc. cit.*
[3] JONES, "Is Competition in Industry Ruinous?" *Quart. Jour. Econ.*, 34: 503 (1920).
[4] Lackawanna Railroad, *Annual Report*, 1907, 11.

Between 1899 and 1911, however, the price of anthracite rose 29.8 per cent while the general index of commodity prices rose 27.1 per cent.[1] But Professor Eliot Jones has pointed out that the rise in the price of anthracite can hardly be regarded as a reflex of the rise in all prices, because the increase in the price of anthracite occurred almost entirely between 1899 (when the relative was

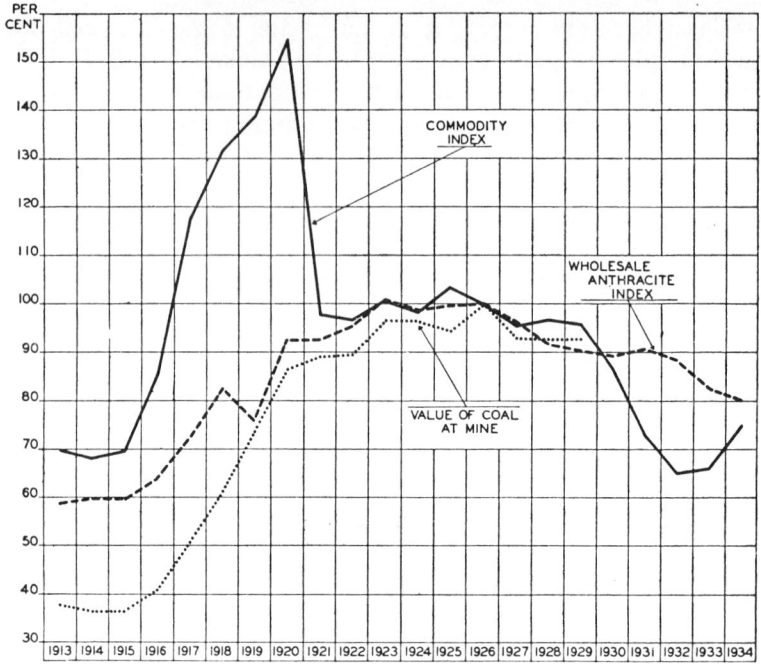

FIG. 9.—The price of anthracite and an index of wholesale prices, 1913 to 1934. (*Drawn from data at U.S. Bureau of Labor Statistics: Wholesale Prices.*)

97.6) and 1903 (when the relative was 127.1); there was practically no change during the period in which the price of all commodities rose from 85.5 in 1903 to 93.0 in 1911. Evidently the anthracite coal combination did not endeavor after 1903 to raise the price in harmony with changes in the general level of prices. Figure 9, showing the movements in the wholesale price of anthracite and in the index of general prices since 1913, indicates that the price of anthracite rose during the period from 1915 to 1920 by considerably less than the index of general prices: it rose from 59.5 to 92.5 while the index of general prices rose from 69.5 to 154.4. Between 1920 and 1926 the price of anthracite continued to rise

[1] JONES, *The Anthracite Coal Combination*, 140.

during the period when the general commodities index was falling perceptibly and then rising more slowly. Between 1923 and 1929 the value of anthracite at the mine (all sizes) tended downward slightly more than the index of general prices although in 1929 it was higher in relation to prices in general than in 1913.

In the anthracite industry, therefore, the Reading company appears to have had considerable influence as a leader and its large rivals appear to have acted in harmony with it. Smaller producers have at times sold at prices below those of the larger companies, but they have also sold at higher prices. Moreover, smaller producers have been realizing their reserves more quickly than the larger firms, which, therefore, have been meeting out of the prices charged heavier costs for carrying unused reserves; these costs have been further enhanced by the much greater scale of their reserves. The power of rivals to oppose the policy of the larger units is limited by the relatively small amount of their reserves and the rate at which they can be marketed: opposition from new competitors is excluded by the concentrated control of resources. In consequence the share of the leader appears not to have fallen; high prices have probably, however, facilitated the expansion of the sales of rival fuels. Increases in output have been induced only by considerable increases in prices, possibly because of differences in the cost of exploiting resources in different areas. During the period between 1921 and 1929, when sales were decreasing considerably, prices rose. Full analysis of conditions in the industry is, however, hampered by lack of information concerning the sales and profits of each producer in recent years.

E. *Other Industries*

In the prosecution of the American Can Company evidence was offered that "the company's rivals usually followed the published price of the American Can Company for 'packer cans'"; indeed, there were few sales of cans until the American Can Company had announced its price for the season.[1] Some smaller competitors,[2] however, regularly sold at a price slightly lower than that of the American Can Company.[3] The price of "general line cans" varied considerably from seller to seller but the variations were probably due to differences in specifications: one witness testified that the

---

[1] U.S. v. American Can Co., *Summary of Evidence*, 174.
[2] These competitors were not more than one twentieth as large as the American Can Company in output (U.S. v. American Can Co., 230 Fed. 892).
[3] U.S. v. American Can Co., *Summary of Evidence*, 168.

price of the American Can Company was the balance wheel in making the price.[1] In consequence the Attorney General argued that the presence of the company had substantially eliminated price competition. The company replied that its largest, as well as its smaller, rivals did not always follow its prices; the fact that they cut very little below its prices indicated the impossibility of selling at much lower prices.[2] The court decided, however, that since 1901 the American Can Company had largely fixed the price of packer cans throughout the United States, although there was no evidence of price agreements: the largest rival to the American Can Company followed the prices of the latter very strictly; the smaller concerns were unable to cut prices further because by so doing they would attract more trade than they could handle; to attempt a sudden expansion of facilities might bring them face to face with ruin if the American Can Company reduced its price; on the other hand the price policy of the American Can Company was limited by the potential competition of these smaller rivals.[3] Again therefore complete uniformity of prices was not attained.

There is no satisfactory evidence concerning the price policy of the industry under this leadership. The price of cans was raised after the formation of the American Can Company, although the amount of the increase is uncertain, partly because of the lack of records and partly because there was a variety of bases of comparison. A very considerable increase had been made over prices three years before the formation of the company, but the increase was less if comparison was made with prices in the period after it became known that the company was to be formed.[4] The chief of the cost estimating department of the company testified that the

---

[1] *ibid*. 180.
[2] *Brief for American Can Co.*, 13.
[3] U.S. v. American Can Co., 230 Fed. 891, 892.
[4] U.S. v. American Can Co., 230 Fed. 879. A considerable number of new plants was set up partly in response to the high prices and partly in the hope of selling out to the company. The price of "Number three packer cans" during the period 1896 to 1898 had been about $15.00 to $16.70 per thousand. In 1899 and 1900 it rose to $23.00 to $24.00 (U.S. v. American Can Co., *Summary of Evidence*, 201). The average annual price of tin plate had been between $2.99 and $3.63 per base box in the period 1896–1898 and between $4.41 and $4.82 between 1899–1900. Tin plate is said to represent from 60 to 80 per cent of the cost of cans. A very rough calculation suggests that an increase of $1.50 per thousand in the price of cans might be explained by the change in the price of tin plate. (If $16.00 per thousand be taken as the price in the first period and 70 per cent ($11.20) of this be taken as the price of tin plate, and if $4.60 be taken as the price in 1899–1900, an increase in cost of 14 per cent of $11.20 or about $1.50 would be expected.) Between Mar. 28 and Aug. 1, 1901, all prices were said to have increased about 25 per cent (U.S. v. American Can Co., *Summary of Evidence*, 129).

company raised the price of "general line cans" after it was formed by about 60 per cent, for which advance he knew of no economic reason.[1] In the period following this initial change in prices, the price of "number three packer cans," which had been about $24.00 a thousand in March, 1901, fell fairly steadily until by January, 1914, the price was $17.00. Meanwhile the price of tin plate fell from $4.35 per base box to $3.89 in 1913.[2] Thus the price of cans in 1914 was apparently not very different from what it had been in 1896. Although wages increased somewhat, labor costs were said to have fallen,[3] but the quantity of solder used was said to have increased greatly.[4] The court concluded that, prices being about the same when fixed by the company as they had been when fixed by a number of competitors, and the manufacturing costs having been reduced, the company had not conferred the benefits of this reduction upon the buyers of cans.[5]

That this price policy was remunerative, at least to new producers,[6] is suggested by the decline in the relative importance of the American Can Company in the industry although its business has expanded. At its formation in 1901 (by the combination of some 95 plants) it produced about 90 per cent of all the cans made in the United States.[7] By 1913, however, the company was producing

[1] The general manager of the New England plants stated that prices were advanced immediately by 25 to 33 per cent and sometimes as much as 50 per cent. Other evidence quoted increases of 15 to 50 per cent which were said often to have been made against the advice of those who had formerly run the business, to which advice, however, the new owners responded that they had spent a lot of money and had to get it back (*Summary of Evidence*, 121–124). It was pointed out that prices in 1900 had been above those in preceding years and that after the promoters of the company obtained options upon plants they had advised maintaining prices (U.S. v. American Can Co., 230 Fed. 867).
[2] U.S. v. American Can Co., *Summary of Evidence*, 202 and 203.
[3] *ibid.*, 205.
[4] The capacity of can-making machinery was said to have increased from 25,000 to 50,000 per day in 1901 to 75,000 in 1909 (*ibid.*, 205). The capacity of machinery is, of course, irrelevant unless it can be shown that the cost of production was substantially reduced by increases in capacity; the machinery may have been introduced because of the rising wages or because it made possible an absolute fall in costs.
[5] It admitted that cans were now more uniform, but remarked that the machinery now in use made it no more costly to make good than bad cans. The company claimed to have conferred other benefits upon the trade: it offered to contract for the whole amount of cans required by the packers, the former practice having been to contract for a fixed quantity of cans and, in seasons when demand exceeded the quantities provided for in the contract, to supply the balance at higher prices. The company required exclusive contracts in return for this concession, but kept stocks of cans in warehouses in different parts of the country to enable it to supply speedily all the demands of the packers.
[6] The reported profits of the American Can Company ranged in the decade 1923–1933 between 10.4 million dollars (in 1923) and 22.8 million dollars (in 1930). Reported profits in 1933 were 15.3 million dollars.
[7] U.S. v. American Can Co., 230 Fed. 867.

only 50 per cent of all cans made for sale. During this period a large rival, the Continental Can Company, grew rapidly in size and prospered. Moreover, some packers began to make their own cans: of all cans made (including the output of these integrated manufacturers) the company made only 33 per cent in 1913.

In the newsprint industry "the International Paper Company really makes the market price for newsprint paper for the entire United States except the Pacific coast," the price in the latter territory being made by the Crown Zellerbach Corporation.[1] The sales manager of the Great Northern Paper Company stated to the Federal Trade Commission that no seller could charge a higher price than the International Paper Company without losing business, or a lower price without inviting further reductions by the International Paper Company.[2] The leadership of the International Paper Company is evidenced by the fact that in long-term contracts for sale of newsprint (which are common in the industry) the price at which paper is to be supplied is frequently determined by reference to an average of the announced prices of three large companies at the time of delivery; this price is in fact that of the International Paper Company.[3] The International Paper Company controlled only 20 per cent of the business in the industry.[4] Although the North American producers were equipped in 1932 to produce about 30 per cent more newsprint than had ever been sold, and were able to meet demand based upon the most optimistic estimates of consumption until 1940,[5] and although there have been repeated reductions of price, the available data do not suggest that the industry has been particularly unprofitable.[6]

In the corn products industry, the Corn Products Refining Company "set the prices of the staples of the industry, published

[1] F.T.C., *Newsprint Paper Industry*, 1930, 81.
[2] *loc. cit.*; *cf.* also *New York Times*, Oct. 31, 1928.
[3] *ibid.*, 31, 81, 90.
[4] *ibid.*, 81. Three companies produced about 50% of the production of the United States. Imports have, however, been considerable.
[5] FRAME, "Planning for the Newsprint Industry," *Harvard Bus. Rev.*, 1932, 447.
[6] During the years from 1927 to 1932 (the figures for the last year being partly estimated) percentages of net profits after payment of tax to book value of stock equity in the paper pulp and products industry were 6.7, 7.1, 6.4, 2.9, −0.5, −3.8; the comparable figures for manufacturing industry in general were 6.2, 7.6, 8.3, 2.6, −1.0, −2.5 (National Bureau of Economic Research, *Bulletin* 50, April, 1934). The declared profits of the International Paper Company ranged in the period from 1923 to 1928 between 2.6 million dollars and 5.1 million dollars: it declared a deficit of 9.5 million dollars in 1932.

them, and the rest of the trade generally followed."[1] A court decided that the company, having a productive capacity capable of meeting the whole demand at the price ruling in 1913 and 1914, had the power to manipulate prices; after 1907, however, the capacity of the independents was sufficient to prevent the raising of prices. The Federal Trade Commission reported that the price of gluten feed in 1919 was uniform for all manufacturers. The rivals of the Corn Products Refining Company (which was responsible for the production of 63 per cent of the total output) explained frankly that this unanimity was the result of "the dominant position which the Corn Products Refining Company occupies in the industry." Immediately upon receiving notice of a change in the prices of the Corn Products Refining Company "each of the smaller concerns institutes a similar change in prices." There was no agreement concerning prices but the price announced by the Corn Products Refining Company was consistently followed.[2] For a considerable period after 1890 the Corn Products Refining Company and its predecessors sought to destroy or absorb their rivals and not to lead them. Their attempts to keep prices on a level high in relation to costs repeatedly attracted new firms which in turn were absorbed. In the opinion of the court the company manipulated the price of glucose and starch independently of the price of corn, "alternately raising and lowering it as the immediate occasion seemed to require."[3] They had raised prices to a level that encouraged rivals and then "lowered prices to a sum less than a fair profit for the purpose of securing trade for themselves and harassing and annoying and, if possible, driving out their competitors." "They never meant to keep the prices so low . . . and could not have done so. . . . All their conduct illustrates the kind of competition which tries to prevent the development of new-

---

[1] "A distinction must be, however, taken here between actual control by the leader and voluntary following by the independents. A producer may still be the largest in the market and yet be unable to force others to follow his lead. That would depend upon his capacity to fill the larger demand which would arise from his lower prices. If, for example, he was producing nearly up to his capacity, he would be unable with a drop in price to increase more than that limit; indeed it would be hard to imagine any purpose in lowering his price, for it would result in the economic solecism of two prices in the same market. If, however, the elasticity of the largest producer's capacity of production were so great that he could accommodate it to the increased demand as the price fell, then he has the absolute power to compel all other producers to follow him down when he lowers his prices." (U.S. v. Corn Products Refining Co., 234 Fed. 975, 993 (1916)).

[2] F.T.C., *Commercial Feeds*, 1921, 163, 173. This uniformity of prices between sellers was achieved by the use of a basing-point system (see Chap. VI).

[3] U.S. v. Corn Products Refining Co., 234 Fed. 971.

comers who might permanently secure their own position."[1] In more recent years, however, the industry appears to have settled down to a régime similar to that in other industries where leaders exist. In particular it has achieved a considerable stability in the price of corn starch, and glucose.[2]

The Federal Trade Commission also reported a very modified kind of price leadership in the fertilizer industry. The Virginia-Carolina Chemical Company issued printed price lists for each spring season for the states of Virginia, North Carolina, South Carolina, Georgia, and Alabama; these prices were adopted by practically every other fertilizer concern doing business in these states. Competitors awaited the publication of these lists and adopted them because if they tried to charge more, they got no business, and if they charged less the Virginia-Carolina Chemical Company would meet their prices. In the northern states the prices of the American Agricultural Chemical Company were followed by other companies.[3] The use by competitors of the price lists of the Virginia-Carolina Chemical Company gave rise to the belief that there was a secret agreement concerning prices, but although list prices and certain discounts were uniform, actual prices were not; allowances and concessions were made in different amounts

---

[1] *loc. cit.*, 1010 The National Starch Manufacturing Company, a predecessor of the Corn Products Refining Company (formed in 1890 by consolidating 20 concerns), controlled from 75 to 80 per cent of the starch output of the country (see WATKINS, *Industrial Combination and Public Policy*, Chap. X; U.S. v. Corn Products Refining Co., 234 Fed. 968) but from 1895 onward its percentage fell seriously. In 1900 the company was reorganized and absorbed many important rivals; it thereby secured control of 95 per cent of the box starch sold in the United States and about 80 per cent of the lower grade bulk starch (the president of the company told the United States Industrial Commission (XIII, 673) that it produced 85 to 86 per cent of all the starch then produced). This percentage fell during the next two years and the company got into difficulties, which ended in a further consolidation, which concentrated control of both starch and glucose manufacturing. The Glucose Sugar Refining Company, which controlled about 85 per cent of the glucose output of the country in 1897, also suffered a decline in percentage owing to the development of new rivals and the expansion of old ones. The Corn Products Refining Company, formed in 1902, controlled practically the whole output of both starch and glucose in the United States but by 1906 its percentage of control had fallen to 50 per cent or less: a further absorption of rivals in 1906 increased the company's percentage of control to about 100 per cent of the glucose and 64 per cent of the starch output of the country. Its percentage of starch rose from 64 per cent in 1906 to 70 per cent in the period of 1907-1911 but thereafter fell to 67 per cent in 1912 and 63 per cent in 1913 and 58 per cent in 1914. Its percentage of glucose manufacture had also fallen by 1914 to 53 per cent. The company, which had in 1906 consumed 95 per cent of all the corn used in wet milling, was by 1914 using less than 65 per cent. Owing to the growth of the industry as a whole, however, the company ground about the same amount of corn in 1916 as in 1910 and a little less than in 1906.

[2] See Chap. V.

[3] F.T.C., *The Fertilizer Industry*, 1916, 218, 219.

from the list prices by different competitors.[1] In 1923, however, the commission reported that for some years the announced price list of the American Agricultural Chemical Company had been adopted by the Virginia-Carolina Chemical Company in its northern territory, while the published price list of the latter had been adopted by the former in its southern territory. These lists were also adopted by smaller concerns, "that is, the list prices are regarded as maximum prices, and independent companies usually have to shade these prices by a margin of a dollar or a dollar and a half a ton."[2] The lists being regarded merely as maximum prices, the large companies cannot be regarded as leaders.[3] In fact, the commission reported "that competition in the sale of fertilizer was keen in both 1921 and 1922 and that the list prices made by the large manufacturers were not maintained."[4]

The United States Industrial Alcohol Company is said to have been the price leader in the market for industrial alcohol.[5] By 1930, 99 per cent of the ethyl alcohol marketed in the United States was sold by six firms. Of this output the United States Industrial Alcohol Company manufactured 40 per cent and controlled the sale of a larger percentage. The company consolidated its leadership after the formation of the Industrial Alcohol Institute in 1928; the company's announcements of its prices at meetings of the institute were received with "significant silence."[6] A notable degree of control appears to have been secured only during 1928 and 1929 when prices became markedly more uniform from seller to seller; at the end of 1929, however, deviations from official price lists became so frequent that the lists became a mere formality. Such leadership as existed appears to have reduced both the frequency and the amount[7] of price changes. But between March, 1928, and December, 1932, the amount of price changes increased again partly owing to the increased range of movements of prices in general; it is probable that the diminished frequency of price

[1] *ibid.*, 243.
[2] F.T.C., *The Fertilizer Industry*, 1923, 58.
[3] The above two fertilizer companies were reported in 1923 to be selling one third of all the fertilizers sold in the United States (*ibid.*, 58).
[4] *ibid.*, 87.
[5] An excellent brief analysis of conditions in the industry between 1922 and 1932 will be found in WHITNEY, *Trade Associations and Industrial Control*, 129 ff.
[6] *ibid.*, 132.
[7] The price remained unchanged for an average of 1.61 months between January, 1922, and February, 1926, 1.71 months between March, 1926, and February, 1928, and 3.63 months between March, 1928, and December, 1932; the average amount of price changes was 3.13 cents per gallon in the first period, 2.86 in the second and 3.60 in the third (*ibid.*, 213, also 211).

changes dammed up the forces making for reduction with the result that the changes were larger than they would have been had they been made more frequently. Over longer periods no great measure of stability of prices was attained[1] but changes were not closely correlated with changes in the price of the principal raw material and considerable changes occurred in the margin between the price of alcohol and that of blackstrap molasses.[2] The published income of the United States Industrial Alcohol Company reflected these changes in margin with some lag.[3] If the year 1926 be excluded, the movements in the margin suggest a steady upward pressure until 1929. Exploration of the possibility of monopoly profits was facilitated by the exclusion of new competitors; the Commissioner of Industrial Alcohol imposed a system of production quotas with the object of preventing the accumulation of inventories and reducing the temptation to sell through illegal channels. By 1929, however, the development of rival products was restricting the possible monopoly profits.

Of the cement industry it is reported that the five largest companies, which together controlled about 40 per cent of the output in the United States in 1931, "are the leaders in the industry and are generally followed by the smaller companies in matters of policy and price,"[4] *i.e.*, that, as in the oil industry, there was a number of leaders. The industry sells a product homogeneous in a high degree; considerable uniformity in the prices of different sellers is therefore to be expected. The Federal Trade Commission reported that of sales of 22 million barrels of cement in 1927, 1928, and 1929 (about 4.2 per cent of all sales in the United States) 94 per cent were made at uniform prices by different sellers at each point of delivery; in 13 of the 21 cities to which the cement was delivered there was complete uniformity of prices by all

[1] The annual average of the monthly high and low prices of alcohol rose from 25.1 cents per gallon in 1922 to 48.8 in 1925, then fell to 29.1 in 1926, rose again to 48.0 by 1929, and fell to 27.0 in 1931.
[2] The margin between the price of alcohol and that of blackstrap molasses (multiplied by two and a half) rose from 22.0 cents per gallon in 1922 to 32.5 in 1925, the price of alcohol rising more than the price of molasses; a fall in the price of alcohol then reduced the margin in 1926 to 11.6; a sharp decline in the price of molasses and an equally sharp increase in the price of alcohol restored the margin to 31.4 in 1927 and 33.6 in 1929, after which year, largely owing to the fall in the price of alcohol, the margin fell to 15.1 in 1931 (*ibid.*, 219).
[3] Its published income rose from 1.3 million dollars in 1922 to 3.2 million dollars in 1923, declined to 2.2 million dollars in 1927, rose to 4.7 million dollars in 1929: in the three succeeding years it incurred losses of between one and two million dollars (*ibid.*, 222).
[4] F.T.C., *The Cement Industry*, 1933, xi.

sellers.[1] Similar results were revealed by investigation of the prices at which 2.9 million barrels were sold to Wisconsin dealers in 1927 and of the prices in 8,000 bids to five state highway commissions in 1929. Even here, however, it is notable that complete uniformity was not revealed.

The analysis of prices for cement is confused, however, by the custom of selling only at delivered prices; *i.e.*, prices calculated by adding to the price at a basing point in each territory the cost of railroad transportation to each delivery point. Many manufacturers calculate their delivered prices by reference to a point other than the point of manufacture. The five large companies above referred to, or their predecessors, operated, in 1927, 47 plants, all but two of which were located in strategic points east of the Rockies; they produced together 47 per cent of the output in this territory. A further 18 per cent of this output was produced in rival mills at or near the basing points of one of the larger companies, and a further 30 per cent was produced at mills at points which were not basing points. If these five companies chose to cooperate they could, therefore, influence directly the price of 95 per cent of the cement sold in this territory.[2] The largest firm in the industry, the Universal-Atlas Company, controlled about 17 per cent of the domestic shipments of cement.[3]

Realization of the dangers of price cutting in the industry might be expected to predispose sellers to the acceptance of leadership. A considerable proportion of the cost of production is in the form of overhead costs; demand is subject to wide cyclical fluctuations, and for this and other reasons capacity for production has recently been greatly in excess of demand at current prices.[4] Mergers have increased the power of the large units,[5] facilitated unanimity by reducing the number of policies to be brought into harmony, and eliminated recalcitrant producers.[6] Resistance has, however, been encountered. The Federal Trade Commission reported the application of various forms of pressure to firms refusing to adopt the pricing structure conventional in the

[1] F.T.C., *Price Bases Inquiry*, xvi. These statistics allow for changes in the price of cement from time to time.
[2] F.T.C., *Price Bases Inquiry*, 89.
[3] *ibid.*, 94, and Exhibit I.
[4] The percentage of capacity in use declined from 85.3 in 1924 to 65.9 in 1929; capacity for production increased every year up to 1930 (*ibid.*, 19). In 1932 the percentage had fallen to 29.7 (F.T.C., *The Cement Industry*, xi).
[5] The largest firm in the industry resulted from the merger of the Universal and Atlas companies in January, 1930.
[6] *ibid.*, 92.

industry.[1] The broad consequences of leadership in the industry are so much entangled with the consequences of the particular basis upon which uniformity in prices was secured, *viz.*, the use of a number of basing points, that they are best left for analysis in connection with the discussion of geographical price discrimination.[2]

It is reported that since 1899 sellers of non-ferrous metals have customarily contracted to sell at prices equal to those of the American Smelting and Refining Company in force on the date of shipment.[3] To the extent that this practice is followed, the American Smelting and Refining Company obviously becomes the price leader in the industry. It is also stated that when the National Lead Company announces a change in price, others usually follow.[4]

Manufacturers of crackers "must and do follow the lead set by the National Biscuit Company and the Loose-Wiles Biscuit Company."[5] Counsel for the Quaker Oats Company stated that the price in the market was much influenced by the small millers, who might cut prices because they needed business, but that the largest producer, having the largest number of orders and contracts to deliver, was generally the first to advance in price and the last to reduce it. When he advanced the price he took the chance of losing business to smaller rivals, who sold heavily at the former price until they had obtained sufficient orders to satisfy them. On the other hand, if the largest producer reduced his price, other mills generally accepted at once. Other millers "sooner or later follow the price made by the largest producer and attempt to get his price, and in the business it will naturally be expected that the asking and list prices will be either the same or about the same as those of the miller producing the best quality of oats."[6]

It was reported that in the sugar industry the beet sugar manufacturers follow the price of the cane sugar manufacturers,[7]

---

[1] *ibid.*, xix, 84, 125 (footnote), 130.
[2] See Chaps. VI and VII.
[3] FETTER, *Masquerade of Monopoly*, 202.
[4] SAKOLSKI, "Price Making and Price Stability," *Harvard Bus. Rev.*, 3: 207 (1925).
[5] F.T.C., *Open Price Trade Associations*, 78. The National Biscuit Company was reported to have sold 51.6 per cent of all the biscuits and crackers sold in the United States in 1914 and 55.7 per cent in 1921, and the Loose-Wiles Biscuit Company sold in 1914 about 15 per cent of the crackers and biscuits (National Biscuit Co. v. F.T.C., 299 Fed. 735, and ALSBERG, *Combination in the American Bread Baking Industry*, 6).
[6] U.S. v. Quaker Oats Co., *Brief for Quaker Oats Company*, 170.
[7] U.S. v. Sugar Institute, *Brief for Sugar Institute on the Facts*, District Court 177; U.S. v. Sugar Institute, Decision of Judge Mack (mimeographed), 44.

but there is little evidence of price leadership in the market for cane sugar.

The Federal Trade Commission reported in 1918 that about 90 per cent of the pack of canned salmon was sold at the "opening prices," that is, prices set in the late summer, when it is possible to make some reliable estimate of the size of the catch for the year.[1] Although no cooperation or agreement has been proved to exist among the canners, there has been great uniformity in the opening prices charged by the canners since 1905; nearly all canners follow the prices of one or two large companies, and refuse to quote prices until those of the large firms have been announced. The Alaska Packers Association has taken the lead in declaring the prices of all grades except one and its prices have been followed by nearly all the other canners in declaring their prices. The price for the remaining variety (which is mainly caught on Puget Sound) is usually declared by a firm of brokers much interested in packing in the district. Many packers wrote inquiring when the opening price was likely to be declared and whether it was possible to give an advance estimate of the prices.[2] A great number of canners do not declare opening prices but arrange with their brokers to sell their whole product for them. Both the uniformity of the prices declared and the uniformity of time of declaration suggest that the prices of one or two leading firms are used as a guide.[3] Control over the opening price involves possible control of output; as the price is announced before the end of the season it may be difficult to increase the catch if the opening price is high but a low price may cause a restriction; in fact, the catch is said to have been so restricted in 1921.

[1] F.T.C., *Canned Salmon*, 1918, 49.
[2] A practice which the Federal Trade Commission regards as suggesting "an implied agreement to fix or maintain prices" (*loc. cit.*).
[3] *ibid.*, 54. There is a number of conditions peculiar to the industry which may account for this procedure: the industry is carried on by a considerable number of companies (128 reported to the Federal Trade Commission in 1917) but the marketing of the product is concentrated to the extent that in 1917, five companies or groups of companies handled 53.4 per cent of the total pack. (*ibid.*, 70). A great number of packers have a small output and are working in locations far from the market, of which they are ill informed; their size and the smallness of the variety of products they have to offer make it unprofitable for most of them to attempt to market their product directly. "The limited number of [fishing] locations and the large amount of capital needed for an undertaking have led to an important degree of centralization of control" (*ibid.*, 78). The supply of the product is determined mainly by natural conditions (which cause very wide fluctuations in supply) but also by federal and state government action in limiting the territory and the frequency of fishing. The product though supplied during a portion only of the year can be stored for a considerable period and carried over from one year to the next. For the method of price fixing in the industry see *ibid.*, 21, 49 ff. 70, and 79.

140   *THE DECLINE OF COMPETITION*

The Federal Trade Commission reported that intrastate wholesale slaughterers accepted the leadership of the large packers in making the prices of meat products.[1] It has also been alleged that there is a leader stabilizing the market in the packing industry,[2] but there is no evidence of one among the large packers acting as a leader in price making. The presence in the industry of two large packers of approximately equal size (Swift and Company and Armour and Company) probably makes it difficult for either to secure leadership. The principal charge against the industry has been that the large firms have shared the market.[3]

The tobacco manufacturing industry presents a somewhat similar situation in that there is a small number of companies all of very considerable size. There is, however, little evidence of price leadership. The list price of the principal brands of cigarettes has invariably been uniform for all the four large companies, but while the R. J. Reynolds Company has initiated more changes than any of its rivals,[4] it has not invariably been the first to announce changes in price.

The rubber tire industry is also one in which there is a small number of fairly large firms but it has been seriously unsettled by repeated price cutting, which has contributed to the regret that "unlike the more experienced, older, and wiser industries, it had no opportunity to work out a solidarity and group consciousness."[5]

III. THE CONSEQUENCES OF PRICE LEADERSHIP

The foregoing summary of the available data suggests that some kind of price leadership is present in many of the industries in

[1] F.T.C., *The Meat Packing Industry*, I, 114.
[2] F.T.C., *Prices, Profits, and Competition in the Petroleum Industry*, 1928, 232.
[3] See Chap. IV.
[4] At the beginning of 1917 the P. Lorillard Company was the first to attempt to adjust the price of cigarettes to the rising general level of prices, but "lost its courage and restored its earlier prices" (Cox, *Competition in the Tobacco Industry*, 204, 205). After the passing of the Revenue Act of that year R. J. Reynolds Tobacco Company led in the first real advance. The wholesale price of popular brands of cigarettes reached its highest point in 1919 ($8.00 per thousand) and remained steady for the next two years, at the end of which period the American Tobacco Company reduced its list price by 25 cents. R. J. Reynolds Tobacco Company responded by reducing its price 50 cents and made two further reductions in the same year, each of which was accepted by the other companies. After minor adjustments the price remained unchanged until April, 1928, when the R. J. Reynolds Tobacco Company was again the first to announce a reduction (*ibid.*, 204, 207) and was followed by its competitors. In 1929 this company was the first to announce an increase in price, but a reduction in January, 1933 was initiated by the American Tobacco Company (*New York Times*, Jan. 3, 1933). The increase in January, 1934, was, however, again initiated by the R. J. Reynolds Tobacco Company (*New York Times* Jan. 10, 1934).
[5] *New York Herald Tribune*, Mar. 22, 1931. The steel industry may well have been the "older and wiser" industry in view.

which production is concentrated in large units. Leadership is most likely to occur where one firm far exceeds any of its rivals in size, although the alleged leaders in the newsprint and anthracite industries did not control more than 20 and 33 per cent of the total output of their respective industries.

Leaders vary so widely in their power that it is difficult to generalize concerning the effect of leadership on price and production policies. The proportion of the industry accepting the price of the leader is not, as may appear at first sight, an element determining the price policy of the leader. This proportion indicates whether or not the apparent leader is in fact a leader, but no more. The policy of the leader depends upon his estimates of the reactions of his rivals and potential rivals to each possible line of policy; there are limits of policy within which rivals are likely to be loyal and potential competitors discouraged. The probability of attracting new firms into the industry turns upon the profits being made in the industry and the extent to which these profits are known to potential competitors; potential competitors must also estimate the probable effect upon prices of their entry into the industry. Among potential competitors, moreover, must be numbered industrial purchasers who may produce their own materials if they believe that prices charged them are too high. Even if new firms entering the industry accept the price leadership of the large firm, their entry involves sharing the existing volume of business between a larger number of sellers, with the result that the profits of each tend to be diminished.

A leader, able to assume that his followers will loyally accept any price policy he may select, and that any new firms will do likewise, must be expected to set the price upon the same level as a monopolist; the total amount of investment in the industry may, however, be very much greater than would be made by a monopolist, particularly if potential competitors become actual competitors. Monopoly prices may be charged, but the rates of return upon investment (itself excessive in relation to actual output) may be normal.[1] In practice, however, there are serious difficulties in the way of calculating the output for the whole industry which will yield the maximum net return. Future demand, especially in new industries, is difficult to calculate and the relation between demand

---

[1] A monopolist might be able to make more efficient use of the means of production and also to obtain them at a lower cost than a group of semi-independent producers (*Cf.* ROBINSON, JOAN, *The Economics of Imperfect Competition*, 143, also Chaps. XI, XXVII).

and price at each moment of time is imperfectly known. Finally, leadership in prices, even though it results indirectly in control of output such as will prevent the accumulation of stocks, may well lead to increasing expenditure upon efforts to secure additional business at existing prices; monopoly prices may encourage expenditure upon advertising and other forms of sales pressure and diminish the profits resulting from such prices.

In practice the leader is able to rely upon the loyalty of his rivals only within limits; he is also conscious of the possibility that a policy of high prices may attract new competitors. Leaders appear in consequence to confine themselves to the exertion of a general pressure in the direction of maintaining prices; this influence is especially evident in times of diminished demand and suggests a widespread policy of stabilizing individual prices upon a higher level than might occur without leadership,[1] but without always yielding high profits. But even this policy has met with at least intermittent resistance in most industries. Complete uniformity in the prices of different sellers is rare. This lack of uniformity is in part apparent rather than real and arises from imperfections in price data; it is in part also real and due to smaller rivals charging lower prices than the leader. The declining tendency of business firms to resort to the drastic economic warfare of the type indulged in by the former Standard Oil and American Tobacco companies has made it easier for smaller firms to sell at prices a little below those of the leader.[2]

It appears to be the common fate of leaders to suffer a decline in their proportion of the total business in the market. Sporadic and intermittent price cutting by smaller firms and expenditure on sales promotion by them are doubtless partial explanations of this fate. When leaders elect to maintain prices and raise the margin of profit they stimulate rivals to one or both of these policies. The leader may from time to time absorb rivals but in none of the

---

[1] See Chap. V.

[2] It has been suggested that the large companies are the victims of unfair methods pursued by the smaller, that, for instance, the large firm is less able to contravene the prohibitions upon price discrimination in Sec. 2 of the Clayton Act than the small competitors, who are able to obtain business from it by this means (GORDON, in *The Federal Anti-Trust Laws* (edited by Handler), 1932, 215). *Cf.* also argument of counsel for the Standard Oil Company of New York, "that a concern which has the largest part of the business in a particular area is particularly sensitive to lower prices by even small competitors. Having the larger business it is more vulnerable to attack and has to follow the price made not only by the larger of its competitors but even by relatively small ones." (U.S. v. Standard Oil Co. of New York and Vacuum Oil Co., *Brief for Standard Oil Co. et al.*, 58.)

industries discussed has the leader succeeded in maintaining his superiority by this means.

Changes in the relative position of the leader in his industry have not been, however, necessarily or even usually the result of efforts to control the market: in the industries discussed changes in the aggregate demand for the product appear to have been more effective. Where the industry is contracting and the leader's share of business is declining, its absolute volume of business must be declining faster than that of rivals. Rivals must be protecting themselves against the general decline in demand either by price cutting (indicating limited acceptance of price leadership), by the offer of a better quality of product (indicating indirect or disguised price competition), or by expenditure upon the promotion of sales. Expenditure upon the promotion of sales suggests that the level of prices is sufficient to permit such expenditures by the smaller firms. The leader presumably expects that the maintenance of prices will be profitable even though the leader must carry more than its proportionate share of the restriction of output necessary to support its price policy. Where new firms enter the declining industry the restrictive policy must offer considerable profits to new units. The leader's policy may offer a wide margin of profit in general; some branches of the industry may remain profitable; or some portions of the marketing territory may offer good profits to new firms more advantageously located with regard to such areas than the existing firms.

In expanding industries (such as the steel and oil industries in the period under review) a deterioration in the relative position of the leader implies neither imperfect leadership nor high profits. Price leadership may be complete but the leader may be unable, because of its great size, to accept a volume of business increasing as rapidly as the industry as a whole; such rapid growth may give rise to serious inefficiencies. The leader may even be more cautious than smaller rivals in calculating the future rate of expansion of demand upon which it bases its investment policy. Smaller firms (previously existent or new) are thus enabled to obtain business without resort to price cutting. Their growth may enable them to organize on more nearly the same technical lines as the leader. But while they grow without resort to price competition their growth increases their ability to challenge the leader.

The power of the leader is frequently also circumscribed by differences in the costs of different firms. If the leader is a high-cost producer he is likely to aim at prices remunerative to himself; more efficient producers may thus be stimulated to expand or enter the industry. But if he is a low-cost producer he may be tempted to aim at prices which yield more than a normal return. Apart from his desire to maximize profits, he may wish to secure the continued allegiance of his followers; charging a price likely to cover their costs is one way of buying that allegiance. In fact leadership approaches the trade association and cartel in this respect. Imperfect and limited control of the market fortifies itself by avoiding any irritation of rivals. Otherwise short-term price cutting may begin. Again control may be purchased at the expense of a deterioration of the leader's position.

Leadership tends to replace pressure to reduce costs by pressure to keep prices comfortably above costs. Pressure upon the less efficient to adopt the methods of the more efficient is reduced. Each is protected from the risk that rivals, finding better methods of production, will seek to benefit from them by cutting prices and improving their relative position in the industry.

Leadership, if it be restricted to matters of price and production policy, leaves open a considerable field for rivalry. The leader may be able to maintain his position without meeting the price reductions of his rivals if he can secure loyalty among his customers by filling orders more promptly than rivals or being less ready than they are to raise prices as soon as demand increases.[1] In fact, however, leadership in price policy alone more commonly concentrates rivalry into various methods of promoting sales other than by price reductions. In this manner also leadership tends to increase costs. Leadership may thus by raising costs in a variety of ways deflect criticism from prices that yield no more than a normal return largely because manufacturing and marketing costs have been raised incidentally to efforts to control price competition.

Price leadership is a step in the direction of replacing the rule of industry through the conflict of many individual decisions by rule in accordance with a plan for the whole industry. But it suffers from most of the disadvantages of association control. It is true that it is not in itself contrary to the anti-trust laws[2] but it lacks any power of enforcement. For this reason it may be a transitional form for the concentration of control. In the steel industry it

[1] *Cf.* F.T.C., *Open Price Trade Associations*, 78.
[2] U.S. v. U.S. Steel Corp., 251 U.S. 417 (1920); U.S. v. International Harvester Co., 274 U.S. 693 (1927).

replaced pools and meetings to control prices, largely, no doubt, because these were illegal forms of control. But leadership requires considerable disparity between the largest firms and its rivals. Rivals are apt to learn from the career of the large firm of the advantages of size and they too are apt to look to mergers or vigorous business tactics to increase their size. With the reduction of disparities in size, and increasing social control of crude methods of coercion, other methods of unifying policy are likely to be sought. The trade association may be the means to the solution of this problem. Price leadership being no more than a form of relationship between sellers, further discussion of its consequences must be in terms of the outcome of the policies leaders are apt to pursue; *e.g.*, sharing the market, the stabilization of prices, and the inducement of non-price competition. These policies are the subject of the succeeding chapters.

CHAPTER IV

SHARING THE MARKET

I. The definition of sharing the market—1I. The evidence of sharing the market— *A*. Agreements between sellers affecting the sharing of business—1. Pooling agreements—2. Cooperative selling—3. Trade association activities—4. Agreements concerning the utilization of plant—*B*. Sharing the market by convention—1. Meat packing—2. Anthracite—3. Other industries—*C*. Reciprocal dealing and the distribution of business—III. The consequences of sharing the market.

I. THE DEFINITION OF SHARING THE MARKET

"Sharing the market" occurs when output is controlled by reference to the share of the total sales of the product obtained by each firm. Where market conditions stimulate a fear of short-term price cutting aimed at changing the existing distribution of business in favor of the price cutter, sellers may endeavor to avoid this danger by resort to the contention that each firm is entitled to a "fair share" of the market but no more. It is assumed that everyone knows what is a "fair share"; in practice, it often means the share possessed by each firm at the time when price cutting was abandoned. Instead of endeavoring to increase this share, each firm should "live and let live," *i.e.*, avoid conduct likely to drive out rivals.

II. THE EVIDENCE OF SHARING THE MARKET

The evidence concerning the prevalence of the policy may be arranged by reference to the forms of relationship between producers from which it has arisen. Explicit agreements to share production, cooperative selling agencies, trade associations, conventions aimed at the stabilization of the distribution of business, and conventions involving the distribution of business by reference to a formula applied by buyers, may all involve the sharing of the market, and each will be separately discussed.

A. Agreements Between Sellers Affecting the Sharing of Business

1. POOLING AGREEMENTS

Pooling agreements or cartels aimed at the control of prices generally provide also for the control of output. If they do not, some members may too optimistically estimate the amount of the product they can sell at the price fixed by the agreement; the accumulation of inventories may lead to the abandonment of the agreed price. It is not sufficient to determine the permissible output for the whole industry: the output of each member must be fixed.[1] Price competition can no longer determine the distribution of business between firms and a quota is usually set for each. These quotas may be set either by allocating specific shares of business or by allocating markets.

Specific quotas of sales are frequently expressed as a percentage of total output. Decisions concerning changes in the total output are then automatically applied to the quota of each firm. The distribution of quotas is the most difficult stage in the negotiation of cartel agreements. Quotas are usually calculated by reference to some arbitrary criterion such as the total output of each firm in some past period of time, or the capacity of each firm for production. Provision is rarely made for changing the quotas of each firm; such adjustments are usually made by abandoning the pooling agreement and reestablishing it upon a new basis.[2]

Pooling agreements appear to have been the first device to which large-scale industries turned during the last third of the nineteenth century in order to regulate prices. Price and output agreements were relatively infrequent before the Civil War, when also they must have been restricted to local markets. After the Civil War,[3] with the development of wider marketing territories consequent upon the improvement in transportation facilities, they increased in number and importance, agreements being made in the cordage industry in 1861 and more formal pools having appeared in 1875.[4] Pools existed in the seventies and eighties in the salt, whisky, coal, cordage, and nail markets and in the nineties (when they became larger and more important) in the explosives, iron and steel, beef, and anthracite markets.

Specific pooling agreements were made in the anthracite industry during the seventies and tentative agreements during the eighties, but none was satisfactory, partly because the member-

[1] *Cf.* VON BECKERATH, *Modern Industrial Organization*, 239.
[2] In more recent years quotas have often been made transferable in countries where they are permitted; the rigidity of the distribution is thus relieved. Quotas are generally regarded as having been transferred whenever two firms each possessing a quota are merged.
[3] A pool existed in the brass industry as early as 1853 (JONES, *The Trust Problem in the United States*, 6).
[4] DEWING, *Corporate Promotions and Reorganizations*, 114.

ship was not sufficiently comprehensive,[1] and partly because of dissatisfaction with quotas. In 1892 the Reading company attempted a large combination but the venture resulted in bankruptcy for its promoters.[2] Between 1897 and 1902 shipments of anthracite were apparently regulated according to the mining capacity of each producer in the territory of each railroad in 1896.[3] The large railroads after 1900 secured control of the output of the independent operators through uniform contracts to purchase, in perpetuity, all the output of the independents, at a price equal to 65 per cent of the tidewater price.[4] By 1907 about half the output of the independent operators was disposed of under these contracts,[5] which subsequently the Supreme Court ordered to be abrogated.[6] These pooling agreements were superseded by sharing of the market by convention.[7]

Pooling agreements existed in the market for dressed meats after 1885. Between 1885 and 1893 there was an agreement fixing the quantity of dressed meat to be shipped to the east by each packer; between 1893 and 1896 there was a similar agreement providing for the payment of fines in respect of business in excess of each firm's quota and for the receipt of bonuses in respect of deficiencies from each firm's quota.[8] These agreements are said to have been abandoned in 1902,[9] after which date the market appears to have been shared in accordance with an unwritten convention.

Pooling agreements were common in the steel industry in the eighties and nineties of the last century. A steel rail pool established in 1887 lasted until 1893 when it collapsed owing to disagreements concerning quotas; it was renewed until 1897 when it again collapsed owing to unfavorable trade conditions which induced infractions of the pooling agreement.[10] It set the total output of business and its distribution between the parties to the

---

[1] The pool formed on Dec. 31, 1884, did not include the Pennsylvania Railroad which, moreover, did not even act in harmony with the pool (JONES, *The Anthracite Coal Combination*, 47).
[2] *ibid.*, 57.
[3] Cooperation was facilitated by the formation of the Temple Iron Company, the directors of which were the presidents of the five anthracite railroads, and the meetings of whose board of directors offered opportunities for the discussion of many matters other than the business of this insignificant company (*ibid.*, 151).
[4] U.S. v. Reading Co. (1911), *Brief for U.S.*, 63, 65, 192.
[5] U.S. v. Reading Co. (1911), "*Enterprise*" *Brief*, 45.
[6] U.S. v. Reading Co., 226 U.S. 324 (1912).
[7] See below p. 166.
[8] F.T.C., *The Meat Packing Industry*, II, 12 ff.; WELD, *The Packing Industry*, 92.
[9] WELD, *op. cit.*, 92.
[10] COMMISSIONER OF CORPORATIONS, *The Steel Industry*, I, 68 ff.

agreement. Even after the formation of the United States Steel Corporation, there was a friendly agreement between the producers of rails concerning the output of each producer and providing for uniform prices.[1] A wire nail pool, formed in 1894, survived for one and a half years, which was considerably longer than its promoters had anticipated.[2] A steel billet pool formed in 1896, under the name of "The Bessemer Steel Association of the United States," provided for the maintenance of prices and the distribution of the available business, with penalties and bounties for those who exceeded or fell short respectively of their allotted shares. The pool was undermined by a few of the members who used their billets for further manufacture and sold the secondary products at prices which their non-integrated competitors could not meet if they paid the pool price for billets. Several important manufacturers also failed to join the pool and it collapsed within a year.[3]

The Bessemer Ore Association was a pool formed by iron ore producers in the Lake Superior district. Profits had fallen seriously as a result of the panic of 1893, and they sought to control the price and production of ore and to allocate output between operators. The pool was threatened with extinction in 1896 but managed to survive on the basis of an agreement between some of the leading producers who reduced the price of ore to $2.75 per ton.[4] A structural steel association was formed in 1897 by nine manufacturers who agreed to share the available business among themselves, according to fixed percentage allotments.[5]

The producers of cast iron pipe in a territory from which the cost of transportation excluded outside competition (within a considerable price range) devised in 1895 a complicated method of distributing business without resort to price competition. Producers of two thirds of the pipe produced in the territory formed the Southern Associated Pipe Works, which set the price to be charged for the pipe over more than three quarters of the United States. Members of the association bid against one another

---

[1] U.S. v. U.S. Steel Corp., *Brief for U.S.* (before the District Court of New Jersey), II, 122.
[2] The pool was abandoned owing to difficulties encountered in fixing quotas and enforcing them as well as owing to the establishment of outside competition; new manufacturers could very easily enter the industry and were induced to do so by the price policy of the pool.
[3] COMMISSIONER OF CORPORATIONS, *The Steel Industry*, I, 73, 74.
[4] *ibid.*, I, 74.
[5] STEVENS, *Industrial Combinations and Trusts*, 211–213.

privately for the right to tender at the fixed price, the firm paying the highest price for the privilege of tendering obtaining an understanding from his rivals that they would tender only at a price above that agreed upon. The proceeds of these private auctions were distributed among the members of the association.[1] In the course of much spurious argument intended to prove that this device had no effect upon price competition (because only one firm could in any event secure each contract) it was claimed that the arrangement was aimed at securing a "fair division" among the members of the association of the business secured by all of them.[2]

Between 1886 and 1891 there was a pooling agreement fixing the total production of explosives and the production by each firm, with provision for payment of fines for exceeding the quota, and receipt of premiums for failure to produce a full quota, the agreement being substantially continued for a further five years after 1891. In 1895, however, pooling gave place to consolidation.[3] A cotton bagging pool was formed in 1888 providing also for the regulation of the output of individual producers.[4]

Sharing the market by sharing sales territory has occurred in the markets for cast iron pipe and nails. Division of territory is more commonly employed, however, to share the international market between national groups; market agreements of this type have been made at various times in the tobacco, steel rail, cotton thread, glass bottle, aluminum, gunpowder, calcium carbide, and meat industries. This method of sharing does not secure a constant distribution of business, but leaves the rate of expansion of different firms or groups of firms to be determined by the rate of growth of demand in the different territories and the price policy pursued in each.

It is evident that the urge to a cartel movement was present in the United States as in other countries and that the movement attained considerable proportions. Information concerning pools

[1] Addyston Pipe and Steel Co. *et al.*, v. U.S., 175 v. U.S. 237 (1899).
[2] *Brief for Addyston Pipe Co. et al*, 28, 29; *Supplemental Brief*, 7; *Brief for U.S.*, 62. In 1896 the price paid to the association for the right to tender at the lowest price for public contracts in the so-called "pay territory" rose as high as $7 to $8 a ton, which suggests the difference between the profitability of contracts inside and outside the restricted areas, after taking account of freight rates. In consequence some firms chose to sell most of their product outside the restricted area and take their share of profits arising from the high prices inside the restricted area. (*Brief for U.S.*, 70.)
[3] U.S. v. DuPont de Nemours Co., *Pleadings.* 26, 34, 45.
[4] JONES, *The Trust Problem in the United States*, 8.

fades away at the turn of the century when their illegality became evident.[1] Probably the pools themselves also faded away except as temporary and often as local agreements.

2. COOPERATIVE SELLING

The cooperative selling organization, frequently resorted to in Germany to enforce adherence to agreed quotas, has also been tried in the United States. If a cooperative selling agency secures power to dispose of all the output of its members it can compel adherence to quotas as well as fix the price of the product and, therefore, the total volume to be sold. One of the first experiments of this type was made in the Michigan salt industry as early as 1876.[2] A brief experiment in cooperative selling was also made in the oil industry after the collapse of the South Improvement Company in 1872. The Standard Oil group formed the National Refiners' Association, which was succeeded in 1875 by the Central Association of Refiners, a selling agency dominated by the Standard Oil Company; the Standard company determined the output of each member, purchased all crude oil, and sold all oil products and negotiated all transportation for its members.[3] By 1879 it controlled 90 to 95 per cent of all the oil refining capacity and was replaced by the first trust agreement.

The Continental Wall Paper Company is a more typical example of the cooperative selling agency. Formed in 1898, it was controlled by the producers of 98 per cent of the wall paper manufactured in the United States. It purchased the whole output of its members, determined the selling price of wall paper and the output of each member, and regulated the activities of jobbers. Its profits were distributed according to the productive capacity of its members.[4] The emphatic condemnation of the company by the

---

[1] The decision in U.S. v. Addyston Pipe Co. (175 U.S. 211) made their status clear.

[2] The Michigan Salt Association was formed, the stock in the association being held by manufacturers of salt in proportion to their productive capacity. The members agreed to deliver to the association all the salt produced or to lease their plants to the association, except that, on payment of a sum of 10 cents a barrel, members might market their own salt. It appears, however, that no restriction was placed upon the output of the members. The operations of the association were very successful for some time, although competition had to be met from the New York and Ohio fields. The pool finally collapsed in 1882 when it reduced prices in an attempt to gain control of the Chicago market. [RIPLEY (Editor), *Trusts, Pools, and Corporations*, 6–12.]

[3] The Standard interests were occupied during this period in driving out or absorbing most of their rivals (*cf.* JONES, *The Trust Problem in the United States*, 52).

[4] Continental Wall Paper Co. v. Voigt and Sons, 148 Fed. 947 (1906).

Supreme Court[1] put an end to such experiments for twenty years.

In 1932, however, the bituminous coal industry sought relief from long-continued low profits by a cooperative selling agency; it may have been encouraged by the fact that the federal government was by this time vigorously encouraging cooperative selling by agricultural producers. 137 operators producing about 54 per cent of the soft coal produced in the Appalachian and surrounding territory formed Appalachian Coals, Inc. This company was to seek purchasers of soft coal and allocate orders between its members[2] and determine the selling price, but not the output, of the members. For the first time the Supreme Court accepted the cartel as a legitimate form of organization, largely because it was deeply impressed with the distress in the industry,[3] and implied its preparedness to rest its judgment upon the policy pursued rather than the nature of the industrial structure.[4]

3. TRADE ASSOCIATION ACTIVITIES

The statistical activities of trade associations have been discussed. Statistics of the volume of business of each firm in relation to the total sales of the industry tend, although often ineffec-

---

[1] Continental Wall Paper Co. v. Voigt and Sons, 212 U.S. 227 (1909).

[2] The members, however, reserved the right separately to seek orders, it being provided that orders obtained by their solicitors should be allocated to them.

[3] Remarking that "realities must dominate the judgment" the court noted that the industry had a capacity for production in excess of current demand by about 40 per cent, and that the demand for coal had been declining owing to the competition of oil, gas, and water power, with the result that the industry was in a "chaotic condition." In consequence "if some improvement can be effected it will be better for all concerned." The court held that the law did not preclude the operators from "making an honest effort to remove abuses, make competition fairer, and thus to promote the essential interests of commerce." The mere establishment of machinery for cooperative selling "did not unduly restrain trade, and if this latter should follow as the result of the agreement then the government would be able to apply for relief." (Appalachian Coals, Inc., v. U.S., 288. U.S. 344 (1933).) The court provided that the case should remain open in order that evidence of any attempt by the company to abuse its position might be brought before it. The lower court remarked upon the fact that not all the producers in the Appalachian field had joined the association, and that no such association had been established in other fields (U.S. v. Appalachian Coals, Inc., F. Suppt., 339). As the company was set up in order to ascertain its legal status and with the intention of establishing similar agencies in other fields if they were held not to contravene the law, the fact that operators in only one field had adopted the device was unimportant. The code of fair competition for the industry under the National Industrial Recovery Act empowered marketing agencies in each area to establish "fair market prices" for each grade and size of coal in the area, provided the agency represented at least two thirds of the commercial output of the area.

[4] In 1927 the same court explained the impossibility of judicial control of the policies of trade associations controlling output and prices (U.S. v. Trenton Potteries Co., 273 U.S. 392 (1927)).

tually, to induce a sharing of the market upon a constant basis. Attempts to control the hours of plant operation point in the direction of sharing the market in proportion to the productive capacity of each firm.

More recently, however, schemes have been proposed for the more effective use of the trade association for the purpose of sharing the market. The members of the American Institute of Steel Construction were in distress because of a "fear on the part of some that they would not get their share of the available business."[1] It was proposed, therefore, that members whose business exceeded a "reasonable ratio" of the total business available (such "reasonable ratio" being based upon the productive capacity of each member) should pay additional dues to the institute on the ground that they were enjoying a greater share of the benefits of its research and promotional work.[2] "The principle on which this plan is based is that a member of the Institute is entitled to his proper share of the business available";[3] "competition would be more widely distributed and the public benefited" by this scheme because it would keep many businesses in existence which would otherwise fail; it was not proposed to control prices but merely to "live and let live."[4] Unless small businesses were protected there would be a series of mergers which the institute desired to prevent. The scheme proposed was in fact an agreement to distribute quotas, to impose fines for exceeding the quota and presumably bonuses for failure to attain the quota; these latter bonuses, however, were limited to the remission of the institute fees.[5]

The legality of this device being highly questionable, those interested in promoting the use of trade associations for industrial regulation have been more interested in the amendment of the law. Mr. Gerard Swope recommended[6] the amendment of the Sherman Law to permit two or more producers to make contracts "in order to balance production and consumption to so divide

---

[1] *Aminsteel News*, November, 1931.
[2] Hearing *on the Establishment of a National Economic Council* before the Senate Committee on Manufactures, 1931, 468.
[3] *Aminsteel News*, November, 1931.
[4] *Hearings on the Establishment of a National Economic Council*, 468.
[5] No such remission was prescribed but presumably the greater the special dues the less would the ordinary dues be.
[6] *Hearings on the Establishment of a National Economic Council*, 1931, 302, 308–309. Mr. Swope's recommendations were in harmony with those of the American Bar Association and the United States Chamber of Commerce.

between them the demands of the given time."[1] It was hoped thus to stabilize business activity. In order to protect purchasers against unreasonable prices, the contract was to be operative only after a prescribed period, and then only if no objection had been raised or a federal supervising commission had taken no action; Mr. Swope contended, however, that the plan involved no control of prices by the state.[2]

4. AGREEMENTS CONCERNING THE UTILIZATION OF PLANT

The distribution of business between producers may also be controlled by agreements concerning the rate of operation of plant. During the period from 1879 to 1884 the large railroad producers of anthracite are said to have closed their mines for an agreed number of days when the market weakened; the number of days of non-operation varied from 88 in 1880 to 107 in 1884. This policy stimulated the opening of new mines[3] and increased the labor force attached to the industry. The introduction of mechanical methods of producing window glass increased the productive capacity of the industry which sought to protect itself by an agreement to curtail the period of operation of furnaces to four and a half months a year; the Supreme Court took no exception to this restriction of output.[4] The fir lumber manufacturers sought to curtail production by suspending operations for at least one day a week in 1916.[5]

The Cotton Textile Institute, which began operations in 1927, endeavored to rehabilitate the cotton industry by restricting the hours of plant operation. In January, 1930, the institute attempted to pledge the industry to the limitation of day shifts to 55 and night shifts to 50 hours per week, in the hope of reducing fluctuations in output.[6] About 75 per cent of the industry accepted but

---

[1] *ibid.*, 167, 168, 185.
[2] *ibid.*, 308–309. Mr. Javits, a trade association counsel, stated that Mr. Swope's proposals clearly rested upon price fixing and restriction of output and remarked that such a plan tended to keep the marginal producer in business (*ibid.*, 547). The chairman of the committee of the Chamber of Commerce agreed that it would indirectly involve such control of prices (*ibid.*, 185). A committee of the Chamber of Commerce reported that "many producers would prefer to gauge their output to the consuming capacity and divide the volume of such production among the different units of industry on an equitable basis," a proceeding which was hindered by the anti-trust laws. (Report of Committee on Continuity of Business of the United States Chamber of Commerce, *cit. ibid.*, 1931, 185.)
[3] JONES, *The Anthracite Coal Combination*, 46.
[4] WATKINS, *Industrial Combinations and Public Policy*, 159 ff., and U.S. v. National Association of Window Glass Manufacturers, 263 U.S. 403 (1923).
[5] F.T.C., *Lumber Manufacturers Trade Associations*, 1922, 77.
[6] *New York Times*, Mar. 28, 1930.

"in 1932 only 49 per cent of the southern mills were actually observing the 50-hour night shift, and the average time worked by each employee in approximately 160 mills throughout the country was still, as it had been in 1928 and 1930, 53.4 hours a week."[1] In June, 1932, when operations were at a low ebb, the Institute endeavored to discourage night operations by increasing their cost; it recommended the abandonment of the employment of women and children at night. The proposal appears to have been abortive[2] and was abandoned when business increased.[3] The policies of the Cotton Textile Institute were important, however, because the industry obtained the first code of fair competition under the National Industrial Recovery Act and the code included restrictions upon the weekly hours of plant operation; similar clauses were subsequently accepted in the codes for many branches of the textile industry.[4]

Restrictions upon the hours of plant operation tend in the direction of sharing the market according to the productive capacity of each producer. They may, therefore, cause considerable changes in the distribution of business. The restriction may also result in a reduction of the total output of the industry. In general it increases the average costs of all firms whose output is reduced. It may increase obsolescence charges by retarding the replacement of plant and it must increase interest charges per unit of output. If night work is less efficient than day work and is eliminated there is an offset to the tendency to increase costs.[5]

B. *Sharing the Market by Convention*

Although until 1933 agreements to share markets were clearly contrary to the anti-trust laws, some markets appear to have been shared by convention. The sentiment that "we must recognize the ethical distinction between necessary price reductions and price cutting which is inspired by a selfish desire to obtain more

---

[1] WHITNEY, *Trade Associations and Industrial Control*, 71; COTTON TEXTILE INSTITUTE, *Annual Report*, 1932, 3-4; *Monthly Labor Review*, July, 1932, 151.
[2] WHITNEY, *op. cit.*, 72.
[3] MURCHISON, "Stabilization in the Cotton Textile Industry," *Proceedings of the American Economic Association*, 1932, 77.
[4] See Chap. X.
[5] The policy adopted by the Federal Farm Board in 1930 when it attempted to reduce the output of cotton and wheat by appealing to all producers to reduce their output by a uniform percentage (FEDERAL FARM BOARD, *Annual Report*, 1931, 62) and the subsequent policy of the Agricultural Adjustment Administration involved the sharing of the market on the basis of previous output; it was also aimed at the restriction of total output.

than a reasonable proportion of business,"[1] suggests regard for the reactions of price policy upon the distribution of business. In the beef and anthracite industries this attitude has apparently been translated into action although whether by explicit agreement or tacit convention is uncertain. As these two industries are important and afford the only available information concerning a probable conventional sharing of the market, they call for analysis in some detail.

1. THE MEAT PACKING INDUSTRY

Conventional sharing of the market appears to have succeeded the meat pools which were abandoned in 1902. The market for packing house products is said to have been shared as early as 1903 by sharing the purchases of livestock in the large stock markets.[2] In 1918, after a prolonged investigation, the Federal Trade Commission reported that the large packers were "in an agreement for the division of livestock purchases throughout the United States according to certain fixed percentages,"[3] which allegation the packers denied. The amounts of cattle purchased by each of the large packers as a percentage of the total purchases of the group are shown in the following table:[4]

TABLE III

Year	Swift	Armour	Morris	Wilson	Cudahy
1913	33.90	27.18	17.80	11.74	9.38
1914	34.01	27.16	17.97	11.56	9.30
1915	34.47	27.57	18.14	10.15	9.67
1916	34.59	27.04	17.86	10.94	9.57
1917	35.07	26.96	17.14	10.85	9.98

The commission remarked upon these figures that "the first glance . . . reveals such a remarkable uniformity in the percentages purchased by each of the big packers from year to year as to convince any disinterested person that such results could be obtained only by agreement." Figure 10 shows the distribution

[1] Address by the executive director of the American Institute of Steel Construction at the Conference of Iron, Steel, and Allied Industries, cit. *New York Times*, Feb. 13, 1931.
[2] U.S. v. Swift and Co., 196 U.S. 375 (1905). In 1910, however, a number of packers were acquitted of this charge (U.S. v. Louis F. Swift *et al.*, indictment in Northern District of Illinois, September, 1910, and U.S. DEPARTMENT OF JUSTICE; *The Federal Anti-trust Laws*, 86).
[3] F.T.C., *The Meat Packing Industry*, I, 226.
[4] *ibid.*, I, 52.

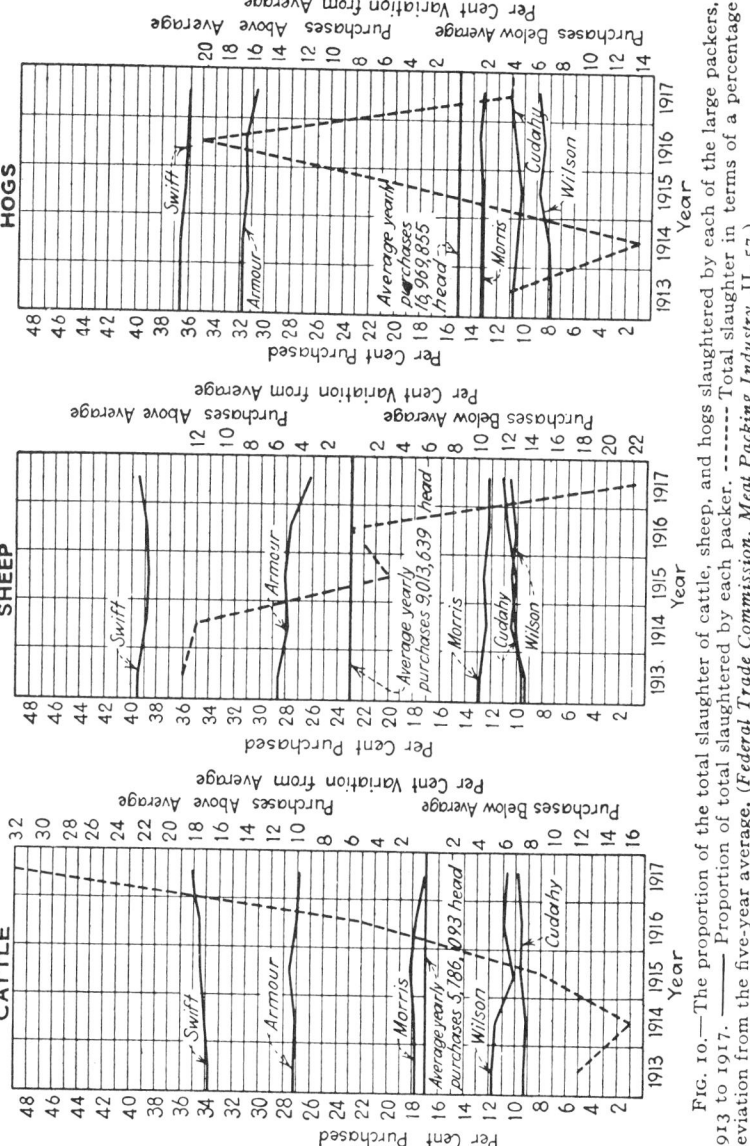

FIG. 10.—The proportion of the total slaughter of cattle, sheep, and hogs slaughtered by each of the large packers, 1913 to 1917. ——— Proportion of total slaughtered by each packer. ------ Total slaughter in terms of a percentage deviation from the five-year average. (*Federal Trade Commission, Meat Packing Industry*, II, 57.)

between the large packers of their total slaughter of cattle, sheep, and hogs during the period 1913 to 1917. It is evident that "the percentages for hogs, sheep, and calves displayed the same uniformity." "Even more significant, the figures for the separate markets also were consistently maintained." The commission also reported that approximate stability in the distribution of business was maintained even from week to week.[1] Accumulated per-

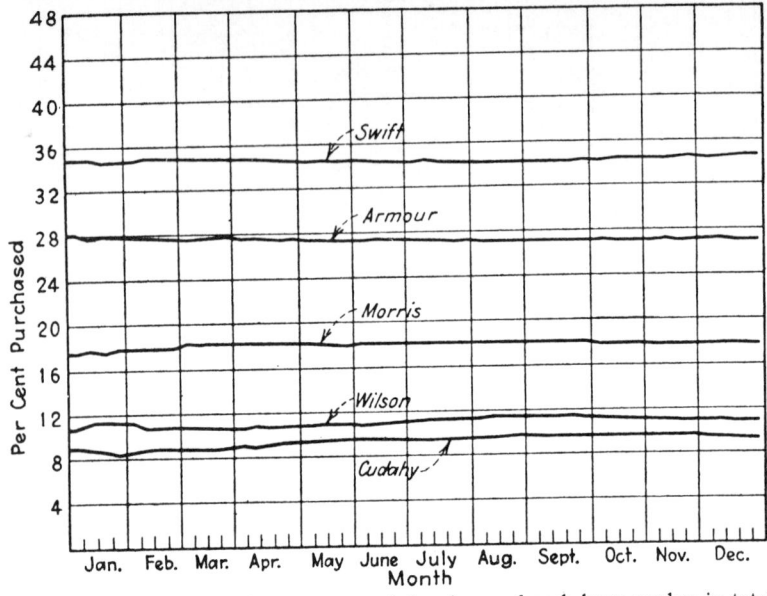

FIG. 11.—Accumulated percentages of the shares of each large packer in total cattle purchases in 1916. (Redrawn from *Federal Trade Commission, Meat Packing Industry*, II, 50.)

centages of the shares of cattle purchases up to the end of each week during the year 1916 are shown in Fig. 11. The stability of these curves of accumulated percentages is undeniable: it is the more remarkable in view of the very great seasonal and weekly changes in the total volume of cattle purchased by large packers; the smallest weekly purchase during the period was 62,006 cattle and the largest 190,686.[2] "With this variation in the number of animals purchased, the maintenance of such percentage uni-

[1] When in one week "one of the companies exceeds or falls behind its percentage, it restricts or expands its purchases during the succeeding weeks so that by the end of the year a close approximation to the agreed division is secured" (*ibid.*, II, 50).

[2] See also *Hearings on Government Control of the Meat Packing Industry* before Senate Committee on Interstate and Foreign Commerce, 1919, 79.

formity could not be expected without agreement."[1] The commission claimed that this statistical evidence (together with documents found in the records of the packers) proved the existence of an agreement to share business.[2]

The large packers, vigorously denying the commission's allegations, contended that the distribution of business was not completely stable. They failed, however, to rebut the commission's charges concerning the facts.[3] They also argued that such stability in the distribution of business as had existed was the outcome of competition and of no particular significance "as these businesses have been many years in developing, and each company now has its regular organization, its territory and usual trade, and its plant capacity and distributing system."[4] It was argued[5] that businesses

[1] F.T.C., *op. cit.*, II, 50.

[2] It believed that the agreement was administered through the rigid control of all purchases from Chicago, irrespective of conditions in local markets or at local plants (each local buyer knowing his share of local supplies and buying that share in the absence of special instructions), and the keeping of daily records by each packer of the purchases of other packers (with the aid of the stockyard companies and often of the other packers) (*ibid.*, 42 *ff.*).

[3] It was argued that the percentage of animals purchased varied greatly from week to week in most markets. During the period from Sept. 1, 1917, to Sept. 1, 1918, the proportion of the total purchases of hogs by the five large packers which was bought by Swift and Company varied from 32.5 per cent to 40 per cent; the average variation from week to week was 25,000 hogs; their percentages of cattle varied between 32 per cent and 39.8 per cent (with an average variation of 12,000 cattle per week) (SWIFT AND COMPANY, *Rejoinder*, Oct. 29, 1918). These absolute figures do not, however, touch the allegations of the commission, nor do the variations in weekly percentages; the commission agreed that daily and even weekly compliance with the agreement would be difficult in view of the short period of the daily markets and the actions of individual buyers and speculators (F.T.C., *op. cit.*, II, 46). The commission rested its case mainly upon the stability of the accumulated percentages for the whole set of major livestock markets. Swift and Company also contended that their percentage of purchases had increased between 1913 and 1917 by about 3.5 per cent or 90,000 cattle and claimed that there had been a further increase in 1918 (SWIFT AND COMPANY, *Analysis of the Federal Trade Commission Report*, 30). The figures presented by the commission showed, however, an increase of only 1.17 per cent. The packers also contended that the form in which the statistics were presented suggested a greater uniformity of distribution than existed in fact. Owing to the tremendous volume of purchases, a difference of one per cent meant a difference in purchases of several hundred thousand head of cattle. (Testimony on behalf of Morris and Company in *Hearings on Packer Consent Decree Pursuant to Senate Resolution* 211 before a subcommittee of the Committee on Agriculture and Forestry of U.S. Senate, 1923, 1105.) A difference of one per cent in the purchases of Morris and Company for the period from 1913 to 1917 represented, it was said, 76,000 cattle, equal to ten weeks' kill in Chicago and three weeks' kill at all the Morris plants. Where the unit of measurement is small in relation to the aggregate to be measured, a change of one per cent represents a large number of units, but this fact does not diminish the significance of the stability to which attention was called.

[4] Evidence on behalf of Morris and Company at *Hearings on Packer Consent Decree Pursuant to Senate Resolution* 211, 1923, 1105.

[5] Evidence of L. D. H. Weld at *Hearings on Anderson Bill* before the Committee on Agriculture of the House of Representatives, Mar. 11, 1920, xiv, 124.

160   THE DECLINE OF COMPETITION

of all kinds reach an equilibrium in the course of their development, and that stability in the distribution of business represents their relative plant capacities, facilities for distribution, and established trade. After examining this contention "in the light of comparative plant capacities and the purchase figures" the commission rejected it; in Denver, where the plant capacity of Armour and Company was less than that of Swift and Company, and where the aggregate purchases of the two firms ranged within wide limits, purchases were shared between the two firms on a substantially equal basis.[1] If the plants of all the firms were fully occupied the available business would naturally be distributed according to their capacity for production; but over periods of considerable length in relation to the time necessary to establish new plants, if plants were fully occupied some firms would be expected to increase plant facilities in order to provide for taking over still more business. Little information is available concerning the productive capacity of the packers;[2] it is believed, however, that their plants have been occupied at considerably below their capacity owing to the decline in the export demand for their products after the conclusion of the war of 1914 to 1918.[3] Failure fully to exploit plant, taking the form either of the exploitation of all plants to the same percentage of their capacity, or of an equal sharing from year to year of the business available, suggests that the distribution of business is determined by other than competitive conditions.[4]

[1] F.T.C., *op. cit.*, II, 75.
[2] The commission produced no further information concerning the relative productive capacities of the packers, nor did it examine the proposition that business might be expected to be distributed according to the capacity of each packer, *i.e.*, that all firms would employ their plants to an equal percentage of capacity.
[3] Between 1925 and 1929, 86 per cent of the capacity for meat packing is said to have been occupied on the average, seasonal slackness not being regarded as employment below capacity. The proportion of unoccupied plant was less than in manufacturing in general. (NOURSE and associates, *America's Capacity to Produce*, 303.)
[4] The larger packers insisted that stability in the distribution of business was evidence of competitive behavior in that it was to be found in many other industries such as railroads (an unfortunate example), paper manufacturing, insurance, and merchandising. (L. D. H. Weld, evidence at *Hearings on the Anderson Bill* before the Committee on Agriculture of the U.S. House of Representatives, Mar. 11, 1920, xiv, 124). Subsequently it was claimed that in any stabilized business operating under competition there is more uniformity of purchase by leading interests than there is in the packing industry (evidence on behalf of Morris and Company at *Hearings on Packer Consent Decree Pursuant to Senate Resolution* 211 before subcommittee of the Committee on Agriculture and Forestry of the U.S. Senate, 1923, 1105). The packers do not appear, however, to have presented any statistics to support their contention.

The large packers also explained the stability in the distribution of business between them as the outcome, not of agreement or convention, but of the equipoise of vigorous efforts by every packer to secure business from every other packer. They agreed that they kept records of the percentage of total amounts of livestock bought by them, but contended that they did so for competitive reasons:[1] there was no agreement concerning prices in the industry, "in fact, there is no agreement whatever as to the division of receipts. . . . The fact is that the packers are in such active competition with each other that not one of them is willing to lose ground to the other in volume of business handled, accordingly they watch each other so closely that no single packer is able to increase his purchases inordinately."[2] Swift and Company claimed that they measured their success in this keen competition by reference to their percentage of business, which percentage they were constantly striving to increase. They also stated, however, that they did not attempt recklessly to work up their percentages, and that if they did so, no one would benefit and the market price of livestock would be more erratic.[3] They referred to "cooperative competition" to regulate cutthroat competition and compared their activities to those of open-price trade associations collecting and distributing information as to costs, output, and selling prices; records of past transactions were reasonably used as a basis for future operations without any price agreement.[4] They stated that the closer the contact between competitors and the more watchful they were of each other's activities, the more likely was this constant distribution of business. The stable distribution of livestock was, therefore, "merely an indication of keen competition and rivalry among the several large packers."[5] The larger

---

[1] SWIFT AND COMPANY, *Analysis of the Federal Trade Commission Report*, 27.
[2] SWIFT AND COMPANY, *Statement*, Aug. 19, 1918, 2. *Cf.* also the statement "Each packer watches the others so closely that no one of them is able to gain appreciably on the others" (SWIFT AND COMPANY, *Analysis of the Federal Trade Commission Report*, 28 *ff.*).
[3] *ibid.*, 28, 29.
[4] *ibid.*, 27.
[5] SWIFT AND COMPANY, *Statement*, Aug. 19, 1918, 18. Mr. Edward Morris of Morris and Company testified to the same effect, denying any formal agreement to distribute purchases and stating that "it must be self-evident that it would be an absolute impossibility to give instructions in any possible manner to attain a definite and fixed percentage and not have these buyers know it" (*Hearings on House Resolution* 13324. IV, 1038). Evidence of reference by buyers to agreed percentage distribution of business in certain markets has, however, been offered (F.T.C., *op. cit.*, II, 30, 72). See also *Hearings on Senate Bill* 5305, I, 655, 664, *Hearings on House Resolution* 13324, IV, 724. The commission also quoted letters by some of the

packers also claimed that the "law of general average" tended to bring about constancy in the distribution of business[1] but did not elaborate the contention.

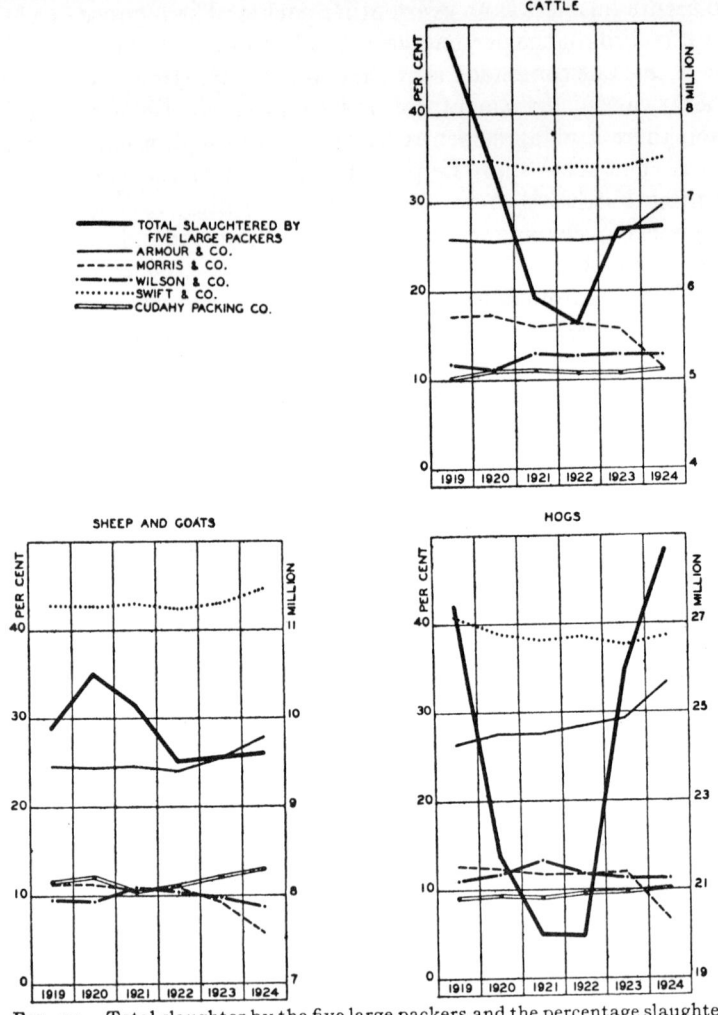

FIG. 12.—Total slaughter by the five large packers and the percentage slaughtered each, 1919 to 1924. (*Drawn from statistics in F.T.C. Packer Consent Decree, 1924*, 18, 19.)

The only reply to the argument that this stability in the distribution of business is due to an equipoise between vigorous large packers complaining that others were not buying their quota (F.T.C., *op. cit.*, II, 60 *ff.*).

[1] Evidence on behalf of Morris and Company, *Hearings on Packer Consent Decree Pursuant to Senate Resolution* 211, 1923, 1105.

competitors is that where the conditions of demand are changing, and where the personnel of each company is changing, it is odd that efforts on the part of each firm to discover some better means of appealing to customers than they have formerly used, and better than their rivals are using, do not result in at least temporary displacements. In this industry such displacements would result in changes in the proportions in which they purchase raw materials. The truth of the matter appears, however, to have been stated more than once by the packers themselves, *viz.*, that they did not endeavor to secure any great increase in their share of the business at the expense of their large rivals, for fear of setting in motion a price-cutting campaign. As each possessed considerable capacity for production in excess of that in use, each could take over a considerable amount of business from the others. They chose, however, to keep up their percentage but not to increase it "recklessly."[1]

The distribution of business between the five large packers between 1919 and 1924 is indicated in Fig. 12. It is evident that very considerable, but not complete, stability in the distribution of business persisted also during this period. The purchase of the business and assets of Morris and Company by Armour and Company in March, 1923, raised the percentage of Armour and Company from 17.4 in 1923 to 24.2 in 1924; as Swift and Company controlled 24.2 per cent of all interstate slaughter, the Federal Trade Commission remarked that the "Big Five" had given place to the "Big Two"[2] and that the future of the meat packing industry depended upon the relations between the large packers. Subsequent statistics[3] show that between 1920 and 1929 Swift and Company somewhat increased its percentage of federally inspected slaughter while Armour and Company (including Morris) suffered a slight reduction.[4]

---

[1] SWIFT AND COMPANY, *Analysis of the Federal Trade Commission Report*, 30.
[2] F.T.C., *The Packer Consent Decree*, 20.
[3] Having been deprived of jurisdiction over the industry by the Packers and Stockyards Act, 1921, the commission had no recent information concerning the conduct of the industry.
[4] The percentages of federally inspected slaughter were:

	Swift and Company		Armour and Company	
	1920	1929	1920	1929
Cattle	23.8	25.8	30.0	27.0
Calves	31.1	33.4	24.8	24.6
Sheep	30.1	36.6	29.1	28.8
Hogs	17.7	19.5	21.2	17.1

(U.S. v. Swift and Co. *et al.* (1931), *Brief for U.S.*, 36.)

164   THE DECLINE OF COMPETITION

This policy of attempting to maintain but not increase their shares of business has been variously explained. "One fundamental reason why no single packer is going to lose business to the other if he can help it is that the expense of operating plants and distributive machinery is more or less fixed. Hence a decrease in volume would raise his expenses and help to lower the expenses of his rivals."[1] It is equally true, however, that an increase in volume reduces the expenses of the packer improving his relative position, while increasing the expenses of those whose share is reduced; in this form the argument suggests very forcefully the desirability of attempts to increase the proportion of business done by each packer. It was stated, however, that a packer could increase his proportion of business only by paying higher prices for livestock; "but since, due to competition, dressed meat is handled on a profit of only a fraction of a cent a pound, it would be a disastrous thing for us to attempt."[2] Furthermore, other packers would be likely to meet such competition, "suffering losses rather than permit us permanently to get part of their trade."[3] In other words the avoidance of price competition is partly due to the smallness of the number of buyers in the market and the consequent impossibility of any one ignoring the effects of his action upon that of his rivals.[4] Wide seasonal variations in the volume of packing house activities give rise to a considerable amount of unemployed plant in some months. Whenever the amount of livestock is insufficient to keep all plants fully occupied, the packers may either indulge in cutthroat competition or restrain themselves, assuming that others will do the same. The presence in many livestock markets of only two or three packers operating on a large scale increased the probability that price competition would become cutthroat competition.[5] Speaking of local markets where livestock purchases were shared equally between two large packers, Mr. Morris of

[1] SWIFT AND COMPANY, *Rejoinder*, Oct. 29, 1918, 11.
[2] SWIFT AND COMPANY, *Statement*, Aug. 29, 1918, 18.
[3] *loc. cit.*
[4] *Cf.* the opinion of U.S. Food Administrator Herbert Hoover, that "Entirely aside from any conspiracy to eliminate competition amongst themselves and against outsiders, it appears to me that these five firms closely paralleling each other's business as they do, with their wider knowledge of business conditions in every section, must at least follow coincident lines of action and must mutually refrain from persistent sharp competitive action towards each other. They certainly avoid such competition to a considerable extent." (An opinion given to President Wilson on Sept. 11, 1918.)
[5] WALLACE, H. C., "Livestock, the Basic Raw Material of the Packing Industry," 42, in INSTITUTE OF AMERICAN MEAT PACKERS, *The Packing Industry;* WELD, L. D. H., *ibid.*, 82.

Morris and Company stated that "when you get down to cold facts, you will find that it is in the interests of the producers that the little markets near the sources of production be maintained, and they cannot be maintained by ruinous competition."[1]

The anti-trust laws have also been blamed for this stability in the distribution of business; efforts to enforce these laws had involved a "very determined fight for several years from certain quarters to hold these companies to their present volume and not to permit them to grow or extend, if not to disintegrate them altogether. All of this would tend to bring about an even greater uniformity of purchases than the law of general average."[2]

The reason why attempts to control cutthroat competition took the form of a sharing of livestock purchases, rather than some more direct form of control of price cutting, is doubtless that in both the markets in which the packers buy and those in which they sell there is no single price to be controlled; both their raw materials and their products lack homogeneity. Their products are so numerous that they would be difficult to control. Packing house products are also sold in a very great number of places; again price control would be difficult. There is, however, some direct evidence of sharing the market in finished products. Swift and Company have stated that, in order to prevent gluts and scarcities in city markets, the packers learned from each other the amount of fresh meat in each market and regulated shipments by reference to the stocks of rivals.[3] Whatever may have been the effect or the objective of these arrangements, they suggest a sharing of local markets which may indeed have been necessitated because control of purchases of livestock proved too distant and crude a regulator of competition in the selling of products in the larger cities. No packer would be likely to reduce his shipments to a market to enable his rivals to dispose of their inventories there without reducing prices unless there were some understanding that the burden of maintaining prices would be distributed among the different sellers on a satisfactory basis. Shipments to a market influence subsequent stocks and provide a reason for restriction. Unless this restriction were shared, there would be a temptation to increase stocks in order to thrust the burden of restriction upon others.

[1] *Hearings on House Resolution* 13324, IV, 1026.
[2] Mr. Edward Morris of Morris and Company, at *Hearings on Packer Consent Decree Pursuant to Senate Resolution* 211 before a subcommittee of the Senate Committee on Agriculture and Forestry (1923), 1105.
[3] U.S. v. Swift and Co. *et al.*, 196 U.S. 375, and *Brief for Swift and Co.*, 69–71.

2. ANTHRACITE

Conventional sharing of the market appears to have developed in the anthracite industry in much the same way as in meat packing. It was adopted as a substitute for the pooling agreements already mentioned when, at the turn of the century, they were challenged by the Sherman Act. Efforts to distribute coal tonnage between the carriers on a stable basis began as early as 1896.[1] The president of the Reading Railroad Company admitted before the Industrial Commission in 1901 that in a general way each railroad tried to maintain its proportion of the traffic in anthracite coal.[2]

TABLE IV

Railroad	Highest percentage of aggregate business in any year	Lowest percentage of aggregate business in any year
Philadelphia and Reading	21.29	18.70
Central Railroad of New Jersey	15.66[a]	11.04
Lehigh Valley	18.88	14.84
Lackawanna	16.51	11.31
Delaware and Hudson	10.30	8.67
Pennsylvania Railroad[b]	13.57	7.67
Pennsylvania Coal Company	4.92	3.98
Erie Railroad[c]	12.58	2.87
Ontario Railroad	5.22	1.72
Delaware, Susquehanna, and Schuylkill	4.02	0.11[d]
New York, Susquehanna, and Western	3.22	1.75[e]

[a] Since 1893, 13.18.
[b] No statistics after 1900.
[c] Since 1899 includes New York, Susquehanna, and Western, and since 1901 includes Pennsylvania Coal Company.
[d] No statistics after 1906.
[e] 1894 to 1898 only.

The carriers feared that any relative expansion by one company would lead to demoralization of the industry and cutthroat competition. Seasonal variations in activity increased the risk of cutthroat competition, the demand for domestic sizes of anthracite being heavier in the winter than in the summer.[3]

The stability of the leader's share in the total output has already been discussed; it was, however, part of a broad stability in the distribution of business between the major producers. The

[1] U.S. v. Reading Co., 226 U.S. 344 (1912).
[2] JONES, *The Anthracite Coal Combination*, 150.
[3] The practice of granting regular discounts during the summer months distributed the demand more evenly and, therefore, reduced this risk (*ibid.*, 167).

range within which the percentages of the total market enjoyed by the major sellers varied during the whole period from 1890 to 1913 was extremely narrow as will be seen from Table IV.[1] Changes in the control of producers during the period, however, somewhat obscure the meaning of this table. The average yearly variation of production by the more important producers from the ten-yearly average of their percentage of total shipments during the forty years from 1871 to 1910 was:

TABLE V[1]

	1871–1880	1881–1890	1891–1900	1901–1910
Philadelphia and Reading.........	2.15	1.33	0.57	0.57
Central Railroad of New Jersey...	0.93	0.65	0.86	0.44
Lehigh Valley..................	1.21	0.89	0.58	0.61
Lackawanna....................	1.51	0.79	1.10	0.60
Delaware and Hudson............	1.38	0.36	0.33	0.30
Pennsylvania Railroad...........	0.89	1.13	0.68	0.73
Total variations...............	8.07	5.15	4.12	3.25

[1] JONES, op. cit., 149.

The distribution of business was not only highly stable over these ten-yearly periods; it also increased in stability from decade to decade, more especially when the pools were established.[2] In the year 1902, when total shipments declined to 50 per cent of those of the previous year, the distribution of business remained unchanged.[3]

The Reading company and the other large anthracite carriers emphasized both the magnitude of the departures from the percentage distribution of output said to have been agreed upon by the presidents of the railroads, and the decline in the percentage of the Reading company. The excesses and deficiencies of the tonnage actually shipped by the more important companies above or below the "presidents' percentages"[4] of the output for the

[1] JONES, *The Anthracite Coal Combination*, 147ff. See also U.S. v. Reading Co., *Brief for U.S.*, 32.
[2] Pooling is said to have existed since 1876 (U.S. v. Reading Co. (1912), *Brief for U.S.*, 53).
[3] JONES, op. cit., 147, 155.
[4] That is, those alleged to have been agreed upon by the presidents of the railroad-controlled companies in 1896 (U.S. v. Reading Co. (1912), *Brief for U.S.*, 53; *Brief for Reading Co.*, 39).

whole period from 1896 to 1908[1] were emphasized, but they accounted for only 5.5 per cent of the total output for the whole period.

Since 1921 there have been many shifts of corporate control and figures concerning the sales of the different companies are not available; in 1930, nevertheless sale of anthracite was still in the hands of a small number of railroad-controlled companies.[2] The Reading company has, however, ceased to be the largest producer. In the main this stability in the distribution of business has been attained in a period of expanding output. The total output in the industry increased from 41 million tons in 1890 to 89 million tons in 1917, and then declined to 66 million in 1929.[3]

3. OTHER INDUSTRIES

There is sporadic evidence of attitudes favorable to sharing the market in a few other industries. There is occasional evidence of such attitudes in the steel industry, although, as we have seen, no stability has been attained in the sharing of the market. The repre-

[1] The excesses and deficiencies were reported to have been (in millions of tons):

Company	Excess	Deficit
Reading company		2.490
Lehigh		1.705
Jersey Central	3.241	
Delaware, Lackawanna, and Western	10.730	
Delaware and Hudson		0.934
Pennsylvania		12.185
Erie		1.570
Ontario and Western	7.069	
Delaware, Susquehanna, and Schuylkill		2.150
	21.040	21.034

(*Brief for Reading Co. et al.*, 53.)

[2] FRASER and DORIOT, *Analyzing Our Industries*, 400. The Glen Alden Company was incorporated in 1921 to take over the anthracite properties of the Delaware, Lackawanna, and Western Railroad and merged with the Wilkes-Barre Coal Company in 1929. The Hudson Coal Company took over the anthracite properties of the Delaware and Hudson Railroad in 1927, the latter retaining stock control. The Pittston Company was formed in 1930 to lease the properties of the Erie Railroad.

	Proportion of Total U.S. Output (per cent)
Glen Alden Coal Company	18.8
Philadelphia and Reading Coal and Iron Company	12.5
Hudson Coal Company	10.4
Lehigh Val'ey Coal Company	9.4
Pittston Company	6.3
Lehigh Navigation and Coal Company	5.1
	62.5

[3] *Mineral Resources of the United States*, 1929, II, 695.

sentatives of the steel producers were convinced in 1907 that "demoralization harmful to all must follow any efforts to capture an undue share of business or an invasion of a rival's territory."[1] Judge Gary stated that he believed that every business man knew what constituted his fair share of the market and that when he sought to get more than this share he delayed progress: to struggle over the business in sight blinds the participants in the struggle to the bigger business in the future. In consequence it was not a good policy to run an industrial machine, particularly a large one, at maximum speed all the time. It was necessary to provide reserves for emergencies, and opportunities for the maintenance of equipment as well as its continual improvement.[2] Mr. Schwab, addressing the American Iron and Steel Institute on Oct. 28, 1927, insisted upon the necessity of a "live and let live" policy; emphasizing the tremendous investment in the industry, he said that "we have our customers, our trade, and our position, and, therefore, must try and respect our relative positions."

The Federal Trade Commission has reported orders by the large tobacco manufacturers for the purchase of leaf expressed in terms of percentages of the offerings of leaf,[3] and there have been complaints that the few buyers who had a dominant position in the tobacco leaf market bought "only a certain percentage of the offerings."[4] Unless, however, this percentage is kept rigid throughout the season, instructions in this form do not lead to sharing the market to any important extent. The wide fluctuations in the distribution of business, particularly in the cigarette market,[5] between the large successor companies, indicate that sellers have not succeeded in sharing the market between them upon any constant basis.

The Federal Trade Commission has also reported that grain elevators frequently endeavor to maintain what they regard as a fair share of the business of the locality and will cut the price when they feel they are not obtaining that share of the receipts of grain.[6] The commission also reported that fruit brokers "got together in the matter of ordering goods" and agreeing upon the share to be taken by each, an arrangement which it thought "might be

---

[1] Meeting on Nov. 21, 1907, cit F.T.C., Statement on Pittsburgh Plus, 401.
[2] McGarry, W. A., Saturday Evening Post, Oct. 15, 1927.
[3] F.T.C., Tobacco Industry, 1920, 62, 64, 89, 96, 147, 149.
[4] F.T.C., Prices of Tobacco Products, 1922, 9.
[5] See below, p. 225.
[6] F.T.C., The Grain Trade, 1920, I, 277, 282.

open to suspicion as a possible means of unduly limiting supply."[1] The president of the National Association of Window Glass Manufacturers in 1915, when the industry was operating at 50 per cent of capacity, said that "most producers have recognized the fundamental law of supply and demand and demonstrated a willingness to exact his [sic] share and be satisfied," but lamented that "a few manufacturers . . . propose to operate full capacity for a full year, furnace conditions permitting."[2]

C. Reciprocal Dealing and the Distribution of Business

Sellers who restrict price competition may place themselves in a position in which the distribution of business between them is determined by the buyers. If the different sellers offer their goods at a uniform price and buyers abandon hope of price competition they must select the firms from whom they buy on some basis other than price. They may cast lots.[3] They may, however, look for benefits less direct than price or quality advantages.

Price cutting being largely absent from the railroad industry, many of these arbitrary devices are found there. The career of the South Improvement Company (formed in 1871, 45 per cent of the stock being held by persons later prominent in the Standard Oil Company) indicates the lengths to which those interested in building up a monopolistic position in the oil industry were prepared to go. The company, as an important purchaser of transportation services, contracted with the interested railroads to share its oil traffic between them on condition that the railroads paid to the South Improvement Company a rebate on all petroleum and its products carried by them (whether the property of those interested in the South Improvement Company or their rivals). The railroads also agreed to furnish the South Improvement Company with waybills for all petroleum products transported by them. It has been contended,[4] however, that the South Improvement Company was not a completely new and outrageous device

[1] F.T.C., *Wholesale Food Marketing*, 157.
[2] *Cit.* WATKINS, *Industrial Combinations and Public Policy*, 158.
[3] The Navy Department is reported to have been receiving identical tenders from different steel producers as a result of the operation of the code under the Recovery Act and to have awarded contracts by lot (*New York Times*, Jan. 6, 1934). *Cf.* also F.T.C., *Basing Point System in the Steel Industry*, 5, 45, 65; *Cement Industry*, 73.
[4] MONTAGUE, *The Rise and Progress of the Standard Oil Company*, 20 ff.

and that it originated with the railroads rather than with the oil interests.¹

In general outline the contract was very like those subsequently made with the grain elevator owners in the northwest and with the cattle shippers in Chicago. Throughout this period it was the policy of the railroads to bind to themselves growing industries in which, as in the elevator and refining industries, considerable capital and much enterprise were necessary in order to succeed and by granting to these concerns special rates to build up trade for the industries and traffic for themselves.²

In short, they selected the firm most likely to succeed and assisted it to drive out rivals by giving it secret rebates;³ the railroads required, however, that traffic be distributed between them on an agreed basis.⁴ But the South Improvement Company does not appear, however, to have been intended to act as an "evener,"⁵ controlling the distribution of traffic between the railroads; it would have controlled the largest single volume of traffic, and if it continued to share this business among the railroads its contract would have controlled practically all railroad transportation of oil. The South Improvement Company was, however, stillborn; when its relationships with the railroads became known public criticism caused it to be abandoned.

Steel rails are purchased by railroad companies by reference to the amount of freight traffic in steel products obtained by the railroad from each mill.⁶ This situation is of peculiar interest because

¹ BOYLE in *Report of the Industrial Commission*, 1900, 421. Mr. Boyle's impartiality has been questioned (*Report of the Industrial Commission*, 1900, 398) but Mr. Montague claims that it has never been disproved (MONTAGUE, *op. cit.*, 22).
² *ibid.*, 27.
³ The railroads also contracted to maintain the business of the South Improvement Company "against loss or injury by competition to the end that the [South Improvement Company] may keep up a remunerative and so a full and regular business," and to secure this end the railroads agreed to "lower or raise the gross rates of transportation over its railroads and connections as far as it legally may, at such times and to such extent as may be necessary to overcome such competition" (*ibid.*, 26). The railroads reserved the right to give the same privilege to any other concern offering the same volume of traffic as the South Improvement Company, but the chances of any other seller attaining the position of the South Improvement Company were very much diminished by its arrangements with the railroads.
⁴ "Where the competition for traffic was keen, the railroads usually contracted with the strongest shipper or group of shippers to carry freight at a special rate or else—as in the case of the large cattle shippers of Chicago and the South Improvement Company in the oil regions—appointed the group 'evener,' and, in return for a special rate, required it to apportion traffic among the roads according to a fixed ratio" (*ibid.*, 28).
⁵ *ibid.*, 32.
⁶ U.S. INTERSTATE COMMERCE COMMISSION, *Reciprocal Purchasing Agreements* 1932, Docket Number 22455, 433.

it brings together as buyer and seller firms in the two industries in which the danger of cutthroat price competition is probably greater than in any others. There are only five or six manufacturers of steel rails, and fixed costs are a very high percentage of total costs; broadly similar conditions apply to the railroads. Steel manufacturers are said to have threatened to reroute traffic to avoid as far as possible any railroad purchasing rails from abroad or changing its distribution of business between domestic manufacturers. In consequence the distribution of business in steel rails and the routing of steel traffic tend to become stabilized for long periods; an attempt to secure rails at a slightly lower price is not worth the risk of loss of traffic.[1] Purchases of cement are also distributed approximately according to the distribution of freight traffic by the manufacturers.

Railroads serving coal mines occasionally adopt a policy of purchasing only from those providing them with a minimum volume of tonnage, varying from 17,000 to 20,000 tons a year.[2] Their purchases of coal are

. . . apportioned in most instances to the commercial traffic controlled by the seller, and this practice of purchasing traffic usually results in the payment of prices higher than necessary. Some of the railroads that do not serve coal mines also admittedly pay higher prices to commercial shippers than those at which coal of equal quality is offered by the operators not shipping the tonnage required by reciprocal practices to entitle them to orders.

Furthermore,

. . . railroads with mines on their line pay more in practically every case than those not serving but buying from the same mines. They generally pay a uniform price reached by agreement with the operators throughout a particular district for the same sizes of coal irrespective of the inherent differences therein. They maintain it is to their interest from the standpoint of commercial traffic to have the mines in opera-

[1] In 1929 steel rails represented only 7.8 per cent of the total cost of supplies for Class I railroads. This arrangement is said to have had one peculiar consequence; it was one of the inducements to the attempted merger of the Youngstown Sheet and Tube Company and the Bethlehem Steel Company. The Youngstown company did not produce rails, and its freight transportation of steel products did not secure to it, therefore, a share in orders for rails; but the merged company by securing control of the transportation of other steel products from the plant of the Youngstown company would thereby secure a larger proportion of the orders for rails. (FRASER and DORIOT, *Analyzing Our Industries*, 257.)

[2] INTERSTATE COMMERCE COMMISSION, *op. cit.*, 427.

SHARING THE MARKET 173

tion and that their orders at fair prices are a backlog enabling the mines to continue operation. Some carriers try to distribute their coal orders among as many operators as practical, having regard in most instances for commercial traffic.[1]

The meat packing industry also provides the railroads with a very large volume of transportation and a reciprocal purchasing relationship has been deliberately established with this industry. Railroads cannot be expected to purchase meat products in any considerable volume, but senior officers of both Swift and Company and Armour and Company have, since 1920, been directly or indirectly interested in companies producing minor railroad equipment. The Mechanical Manufacturing Company, said to represent officials of Swift and Company, has been ordered by the Federal Trade Commission to cease threatening to withdraw the freight traffic of Swift and Company from railroads unwilling to purchase equipment from the Mechanical Manufacturing Company.[2] The members of the Swift family who were officers and directors of Swift and Company, together with three employees of Swift and Company (two of whom were manager and assistant manager respectively of the transportation department) made up the board of the Mechanical Manufacturing Company. The Waugh Equipment Company, closely related with the traffic officials of Armour and Company, was ordered on Oct. 12, 1931, to cease using the threat to withdraw Armour and Company's freight traffic as a means of coercing railroad companies to purchase equipment.[3] This integration between meat packing and the manufacture of railroad equipment is explicable only as a device for securing disguised transportation rebates from the railroads; it is notable that the companies to whom rebates would have been payable in the form of high prices for railroad equipment were owned, not by the companies controlling the freight traffic, but by a few strategically situated members thereof. A large manufacturer of radios and radio equipment, who controlled considerable competitive railroad traffic, was also interested in minor transportation

---

[1] *ibid.*, 426. Payment of higher prices to firms controlling freight traffic constitutes an indirect rebate on transportation rates. It is notable also that the effort by each railroad to keep in operation as many mines as possible operates to prevent the closing of mines as the result of competitive pressure.
[2] *United States Daily*, Apr. 4, 1932.
[3] F.T.C., *Annual Report* for year ending June 30, 1932, 24. Since that date the Swift estate has also become interested in the Waugh Equipment Company. See also U.S. v. Swift and Co. *et al.* (1931), Brief for U.S., 68, 69, 25.

equipment; the traffic in radio equipment was an effective inducement to carriers to purchase the equipment.[1]

The Interstate Commerce Commission stated that

> ... while the practice of reciprocity in purchasing and routing is not new it is clear ... that never before have traffic considerations assumed such an important place as at present.[2] ... The shippers use their tonnage in soliciting purchases from the carriers and the carriers use their purchases in soliciting tonnage from the shippers. Under such practice the greater the tonnage controlled by the shippers and the larger the purchasing power of the carriers the greater the pressure that can be exerted. Obviously, where the business is competitive, the concern or carrier which exerts the greatest pressure usually obtains the greatest share of the business.[3]

Where purchases are made by tender the higher bidders are frequently advised of the amount of the low bid;

> ... after the final bids are in, the purchases are usually divided between a number of the lowest bidders, the division being dependent upon the bidders' traffic value as demonstrated by past shipments. There are exceptions to this general practice in the case of some carriers and as to some commodities, but in practically all cases, the amount of traffic controlled by the seller is of considerable if not controlling importance.[4]

The commission concluded that the practice, "sound and logical when indulged in in a strictly private business," was "a matter of concern when transplanted to a quasi-public enterprise." It resulted mainly in a shifting rather than an increase in traffic and succeeded "only in making the handling of existing traffic more expensive"; costs were considerably increased and although the public benefited little, it had to bear the cost through the charges it paid to the railroad companies.[5]

Large quantities of cement have been purchased since 1920 by highway commissions. Price competition has been so effectively restricted that bid prices have often been completely uniform. The commissions must then find some means of selecting suppliers.

---

[1] INTERSTATE COMMERCE COMMISSION, *op. cit.*, 432.
[2] *ibid.*, 433; see also 420, 425.
[3] *ibid.*, 423.
[4] *ibid.*, 422. The commission reported that manufacturers controlling a large volume of freight traffic had suggested to carriers that the carriers could afford to pay a higher price for their commodities than they paid to other manufacturers offering little or no traffic. While the payment of such higher prices was generally denied, some instances were disclosed (*ibid.*, 424).
[5] *ibid.*, 433-434.

Non-price competition is restricted both because specifications are uniform and because of the method of purchasing. In Indiana an attempt has been made to distribute orders in proportion to the purchases by the cement manufacturers of coal mined in the state. Others have distributed orders in proportion to the amounts of taxes paid by different cement manufacturers in the state; in Oklahoma a statute requires preference to producers in the state; yet others distribute contracts in such a manner as to maximize the profits of the manufacturers (by minimizing transportation costs).[1] The code of fair competition for the cement industry under the National Industrial Recovery Act prohibited the purchase of fuel or other supplies at above the market price, or the shipment of cement by any transportation agency for the purpose of increasing sales, thus suggesting that reciprocal selling arrangements had affected the sale of cement to railroads, mines, and other purchasers. Reciprocal selling arrangements were also prohibited in the codes of a number of other industries.[2]

III. THE CONSEQUENCES OF SHARING THE MARKET

Sharing the market removes any incentive to any firm to increase its volume of business, except at the rate at which the sales of the industry as a whole are increasing. Price and non-price competition, in so far as they continue to exist, merely attract to each firm a share of any new business. Prices tend to uniformity, except in so far as buyers believe that products differ, or sellers market in different places, under conditions permitting differences in price without inducing any net shift of business from firm to firm. A constant distribution of business could be secured by the maintenance of prices at the level at which they happened to be at the time the policy of sharing the market was introduced, but it could also be obtained as the result of raising or reducing the price level in the market provided all buyers changed their prices simultaneously and equally. The market can be shared at any price level. Similarly the relative expenditure of different firms on non-price competition must be so adjusted that there is no net shift of business from one to another: expenditure on non-price competition might be on any level provided the expenditures of the different firms were adjusted to be mutually neutralizing.

[1] F.T.C., *Price Bases Inquiry*, 61, 62.
[2] Waterproofing and compounds, crushed stone, sand gravel and slag, machined waste.

If sellers aim at the maximum of income and have no fear of attracting new competitors, their price and production policy will be that of a single monopolist.[1] Each will endeavor to regulate his output and price so that the total output of the whole industry (calculated on the assumption that his proportion of the total is known and fixed) is that which yields the maximum return. A producer who knows that his share of the profits in the industry is fixed will cooperate to maximize the aggregate profit to be shared.

The calculation of the monopoly policy is often extremely difficult. This difficulty may be enhanced by differences in the methods of organizing different firms, changes in aggregate output reacting differently upon the costs of different firms. The total output for the industry as a whole which would maximize the profits of one firm may not, therefore, be identical with the total output which another would prefer. In consequence there may be differences of opinion concerning the price level at which business should be shared on the accepted basis, *i.e.*, as to the absolute amounts of business each will seek. Short-term changes in conditions of demand and supply due to seasonal, cyclical, and other causes further complicate the practical problem.

Producers are rarely able to ignore the probability of new firms entering the market if a monopoly price is charged. If new firms appear, at least the former basis of sharing the market must be abandoned. If the basis of sharing is repeatedly modified for this reason the whole market is not shared although the original firms may maintain the same relative positions.[2] Those sharing the market may select a price policy with the object of attracting no new firms. Each must then calculate the total output that can be sold at a price that will offer no more than a normal rate of return to a firm operating at the lowest costs technically possible at each moment. Each can then calculate its share of this output. There are, however, many obstacles to the adoption of such a policy. Calculations of the proper price and of the sales that each firm can

[1] Unless costs are different from what they would have been had there been a single producer.
[2] A monopoly price policy might continue under these circumstances with the monopoly profits of each firm continually declining owing to the widening basis of their distribution. Where overhead costs are important, and the aggregate demand for the product is not increasing rapidly, the slowness with which equipment can be curtailed to adjust the investment of each firm to the amount technically necessary to produce its diminished output may cause profits to fall although the monopoly *price* is maintained. Even in the long run the reduction in the output of all firms may cause increases in cost where firms are compelled to produce on less than the most economical scale.

expect at that price may vary from firm to firm. Producers must estimate the conditions of demand and of production in the most modern plants and unanimity in such estimates is unlikely. Prices covering the average costs of a completely up-to-date plant in full operation involve losses whenever plant is not fully occupied. The only advantage of this policy over a purely competitive one is that it protects the industry from great reductions in price due to cutthroat competition where there is a considerable amount of unemployed plant. In times when the demand for the product is rapidly expanding the price that will attract no new firms may cause so great a demand for the product that if the existing firms attempt to meet it they will become uneconomically large. Their average costs may increase owing to their inability to handle the greater volume with the same efficiency as the smaller. In rapidly growing industries like petroleum, steel, and automobiles, it would probably for this reason have been impossible to maintain a rigid sharing of the market. Finally, the calculation of such a policy involves estimating the information available to potential competitors and their probable reaction to it, a further source of difference of opinion between the firms sharing the market. Doubts concerning the loyalty of existing firms to the prevailing basis of sharing the market further obstruct uniformity of price and output policy.

Sharing the market is not in itself and alone a determinant of price policy nor does it offer more than the most uncertain basis of calculating such a policy. It tends in the direction of a restriction of output because it holds down the firms most likely to expand to the rate of expansion of the industry as a whole.[1] Pooling agreements almost invariably involve also direct control of total output. Prices then depend upon the policy of output control. Conditions in the markets said to have been shared by convention illustrate these uncertainties.

The Federal Trade Commission contended that the

. . . prearranged division of livestock purchases forms the essential basis of a system by which the big packers are relieved of all fear of each other's competition and, acting together, are able to determine not only what the livestock producers shall receive for their cattle and hogs, but what the consumer shall pay for his meat.[2]

---
[1] *Cf.* Von Beckerath, *Modern Industrial Organization*, 240.
[2] F.T.C., *Meat Packing Industry*, I, 49; II, 26, 77.

As the relative amounts of fresh meats each could offer for sale were fixed none could flood the market,

> . . . nor is it likely that there will be a general glut as a result of all the members of the combination buying more livestock than the market for fresh meat can absorb, for, with the price held down by the division of purchases, the shipments will tend to fall off as soon as general oversupply is threatened. All that is necessary to complete the control of dressed meat sales is an exchange of information as to margins (together with an understanding of each company's method of figuring test costs) and a personal inspection of the supplies in one another's coolers at the principal distributing points.[1]

If it were true that the price of livestock was "held down by the division of purchases" the quantity of livestock brought to market could be controlled and general gluts prevented, but there is no evidence that the division of purchases had this effect. Swift and Company appear to be more correct in their claim that, even if there were an agreed division of livestock receipts, it would not carry the power to control the price of livestock in the various markets or the price of dressed meat.[2] If a meat packer discovers that his purchases represent an increasing percentage of the total business in the market he may reduce the price offered for livestock and thus allow his percentage of business to fall; but on the other hand, a meat packer discovering that his purchases represent a decreasing proportion of all businesses may increase the price offered for livestock. A stable distribution of business can be secured at any level of prices for raw materials or finished goods, provided all packers are paying and charging the same prices, or prices differing merely by a sufficient amount to neutralize imperfections of the market. The commission was on much firmer ground, therefore, in considering that an agreement to share the market would give rise to uniformity in the prices paid by those attempting to maintain their proportion of the total volume of business.[3]

Concerning the level of prices likely to result from this policy, the Federal Trade Commission stated that in a market in which the large buyers purchased 95 per cent of the product "the common price comes inevitably to be that offered by the low bidder.

[1] *ibid.*, II, 77.
[2] SWIFT AND COMPANY, *Analysis and Criticism of the F.T.C. Report on the Meat Packing Industry*, 41.
[3] F.T.C., |*The Meat Packing Industry*, II, 77; F.T.C., *Meat Packing Report of July 3, 1918*, 24.

SHARING THE MARKET

Thus without collusion beyond the agreement to divide purchases, the market price is bound, in the long run, to be the lowest price which will keep the producers raising cattle, hogs, and sheep and sending them to the stockyards."[1] It is not clear why the market price should be set by "the low bidder," and there is a very wide range of prices within which some cattle, hogs, and sheep will be sent to the market. The commission also stated that "in the long run the highest prices which the packers can pay for livestock are those which would equal the prices which they are able to get for the products minus the actual cost of operating the packing business and a small profit on investment", and "in the long run the lowest prices which it is advantageous for the large packers to pay for livestock are those which will yield the maximum amount of profit, considering the cost of slaughtering livestock and the price of its products, together with the volume of business."[2] Having set these limits to livestock prices, the commission stated that, in general, the large meat packers would "endeavor to keep the actual prices of livestock as near as practicable at the level which yields them maximum profits. However, in making the daily livestock market they continuously change their prices according to variations in the receipts of livestock at the different markets, according to the trend of animal product prices, and according to prospective market changes."[3] In other words, according to the commission, the meat packers aimed at a monopoly policy; in order to calculate these prices they estimated the demand for each of the meat products at different prices and the supply of livestock that could be expected at each price offered for it. In fact, however, the calculation of a monopolistic policy would be extremely difficult in this industry; the range of products sold by the packers is so very wide that it would be very difficult to estimate the conditions of demand for all products; both the supply and the demand of many of these products are mutually dependent; the supply of livestock over long periods of time is difficult to calculate. The monopoly policy would also be limited by the probability that any success which the large packers might have in widening the margin between costs of production and selling prices would induce the establishment of local packers and the expansion of those already existing.

[1] F.T.C., *The Meat Packing Industry*, II, 77.
[2] *ibid.*, III, 105, 106.
[3] *loc. cit.*

180   THE DECLINE OF COMPETITION

The commission, however, concluded that the large packers having covered the whole country with their branch houses and peddler car routes, had given the local packer the impression that he could "not maintain himself against their distribution system if he should attract their unfavorable attention by aggressively trying to increase his volume of business. The local packer, though able to compete in the local market, fears to exert his full powers. His strong tendency is to come in 'under the umbrella' of the big packer prices and to content himself with a modest share of the nearby business."[1] If he did so the umbrella must have been very ineffectual; 23 meat packing companies secured profits equal to only 1.9 per cent of their investment throughout the whole period from 1919 to 1928 when the average rate of return for all manufacturing firms of moderate size was about 10.8 per

TABLE VI
PERCENTAGE OF INTERSTATE SLAUGHTER IN HANDS OF FIVE LARGE PACKERS

	Year ended June 30, 1908	Year ended June 30, 1917
Cattle	74.9	80.8
Calves	63.0	73.6
Sheep	71.6	86.6
Swine	53.2	60.2

cent.[2] It is necessary, however, to examine the changes in the position of the large packers as a group in the industry as a whole.

The large packers obtained an increasing proportion of the total interstate slaughter[3] until about 1918, since which date the percentage appears to have declined. The percentage of the total

[1] ibid., I, 114, also 108.
[2] Epstein, *Industrial Profits in the U.S.*, 242.
[3] There was much controversy upon the question whether the position of the large packers should be calculated by reference to the total slaughter in the United States or by reference only to the intrastate slaughter. The commission preferred not to include the intrastate slaughterers because their importance was "by no means in proportion to the number of animals they slaughter" (*The Meat Packing Industry*, I, 114). It definitely rejected the proposal to include the slaughter in retail butcher shops and on farms because there was no reliable estimate of the aggregate slaughter and because "the fact that the farmer has an opportunity to raise and slaughter cattle for his own use or for the use of an adjacent town or village has little bearing on the question of the monopolistic position of the big packers as regards their control of the prices which the great majority of the urban population must pay for meats" (*ibid.*, 18). (See also the *Hearings on H.R.* 13324 before the Committee on Interstate and Foreign Commerce of the House of Representatives, 65 Cong. 2d Sess., 1919, 81.) In fact, therefore, the commission's inquiry and conclusion relate only to the sale of meat products in large cities.

SHARING THE MARKET 181

federally inspected slaughter in the hands of the five large packers increased between 1907–1908 and 1916–1917 as shown in Table VI.[1] During this period, however, the total volume of "interstate slaughter" was also increasing as follows:[2]

TABLE VII

	1907–1908 (millions)	1916–1917 (millions)
Cattle	7.11	9.29
Calves	1.99	2.67
Sheep	9.70	11.34
Swine	35.11	40.21

The large packers increased their percentage of the total business partly by purchasing smaller packers; these purchases were regarded by the commission as evidence of "rapid progress by the Big Five in perfecting their control."[3] Since 1917, however, this trend has been reversed; the percentage of all animals included in "interstate slaughter" handled by the five large packers as a group having increased from 59.7 in 1908 to 70.5 in 1917, fell to 69.3 in 1919, and 60.6 in 1924;[4] between 1919 and 1924, however, the total interstate slaughter increased from 70.7 millions to 79.8 millions.[5]

The cause of this improvement in the relative position of the large packers as a group in the earlier period is not clear. The commission reported in 1918 that the large packers were relatively inefficient.[6] Although they obtained their principal raw material, viz., livestock, more cheaply than the independents (because of their control of the centralized markets), enjoyed transportation

[1] F.T.C., *The Meat Packing Industry*, I, 129.
[2] ibid., I, 128, 129.
[3] ibid., 130.
[4] F.T.C., *The Packer Consent Decree*, 17, 18.
[5] It has been stated that between 1920 and 1929 the five (later four) large packers increased their collective share of the total (interstate and intrastate) slaughter of the United States as follows:

	1920 (per cent)	1929 (per cent)
Cattle	44.4	47.2
Calves	32.2	38.6
Sheep	59.8	65.8
Hogs	31.4	31.0
Meat and lard	38.2	38.3

(U.S. v. Swift and Co. *et al* (1931), *Brief for U.S.*, 37.)

[6] F.T.C., *The Meat Packing Industry*, III, 123.

advantages,[1] and were able to grade their hides and obtain better prices for them,[2] they possessed no appreciable advantage over the large or even medium-sized rivals in the utilization of by-products.[3] They enjoyed great advantages, however, in the distribution of their products; the small meat packers were at a great disadvantage in distant markets because they owned few refrigerator cars.[4] The small packers owned relatively few branch houses and those they owned were generally near to their plants or in sparsely populated areas; those of the large packers were generally distant from their plants and in areas of dense population.[5] Lack of adequate refrigerated transportation facilities obstructed the development of branch houses by the smaller units: while formerly meat brokers and commission houses had furnished an outlet for the smaller packers, the absorption of such independent dealers by the larger packers or their departure from the business had cut off this outlet, "so that the principal remaining outlet for the small independent, aside from his local trade, is the big packer, and in utilizing this outlet, he largely delivers himself over to the influence of the big packer upon whom he depends for a substantial part of his business and ceases to be a competitor of moment."[6]

The peddler car routes of the large packers, which in 1918 reached 25,361 towns (including duplication where more than one packer reached the same town) in the territory of chief production and slaughter and its adjacent marketing area, served "a double purpose of reaching an extensive market not otherwise open to the Big Five and of checking in this market the development of local slaughtering and of advantageous sales by the nearby independent interstate slaughterers."[7] But the control of such a widespread organization by the large packers was not maintained without cost: overhead costs for general management and advertising expense were very much heavier for them than for the packers selling in local markets, where also the smaller packers often obtained higher prices than the large packers (partly because of a reputation for selling fresher products).

[1] *ibid.*, III, 116.
[2] *ibid.*, III, 121.
[3] *ibid.*, III, 120.
[4] Ninety-two per cent of the beef refrigerator cars were owned by the large packers, and the supply of cars in the hands of the railroads and private car lines available for leasing to smaller packers was inadequate and irregular (*ibid.*, III, 193).
[5] *ibid.*, III, 129.
[6] *ibid.*, 131.
[7] *ibid.*, III, 125.

The packers attribute the decline in the relative importance of the large packers in the interstate business during the period up to 1922 to the fact that the smaller packers were not burdened with a widespread selling organization (which, however, the Federal Trade Commission regarded as an advantage), to high freight rates (which favor local firms), and to the ability of smaller packers to pay lower wages and work longer hours.[1]

Recent changes in methods of distributing meat products have greatly diminished the earning power of the elaborate system of branch houses, refrigerator cars, and car routes organized by the large packers. The rise of chain grocery stores, controlling, by 1930, 50,000 retail outlets for the sale or consumption of meats, has increased large-scale buying by chain store organizations. These firms have meat products shipped to their warehouses whence they distribute to their stores without resort to the branch houses of the large packers; this method of operation conforms to the customary method of doing business by small packers but has reduced the profits on operating the branch houses of the large packers.[2] Some of the chain stores have established their own slaughtering plants[3] and a number have bought meat in carcasses and operate their own dressing plants, thus, according to the large packers, depriving the latter of the most profitable of their operations.[4] The increasing use of automobile trucks has also widened the territory of operations of the smaller packers, both because of the capacity of the small packer to distribute cheaply over a wide area, and because of the developing tendency of local dealers to make purchases in neighboring towns, thus again depriving the large packers of business.[5] These inroads upon their business forced the packers to solicit smaller orders than formerly and consequently to increase the cost of doing business through branch houses.[6] The development of chain stores in the territory served by the car routes of the large packers has reduced the amount of

---

[1] WELD, *The Packing Industry*, 76.
[2] U.S. v. Swift and Co. et al., *Brief for Swift and Co. and Armour and Co.*, 105, 106.
[3] *ibid.*, 107. There were 30 processing plants under federal inspection owned by chains in 1930, compared with 8 in 1920 (*ibid.*, 15).
[4] *ibid.*, 108.
[5] *ibid.*, 109.
[6] The average sales ticket at branch houses of Armour and Company fell from 156 pounds in 1920 to 126 pounds in 1929 (*ibid.*, 112) and for Swift and Company from 117 pounds per sales ticket in 1923 to 93 pounds in 1930 (*ibid.*, 113). Swift and Company's cost of doing business is said to have increased from $0.845 per hundredweight in 1923 to $0.991 in 1930 (*ibid.*, 113).

business done by these cars with the result that here also the packers have been forced to accept smaller orders,[1] and also that the number of cars shipped has been reduced.[2] It appears, however, that the development of the quick-freezing process may again reverse this trend; "it will deprive local packers of the advantage that they now have in that their meats are freshly slaughtered."[3]

This decline in the relative importance of the large packers as a group has affected the two largest of the group. Whereas in 1916 the business of Armour and Company and Morris and Company together accounted for 36.5 per cent of the federally inspected slaughter of cattle, 31.8 per cent of the slaughter of sheep, 29.7 per cent of the slaughter of calves, and 25.0 per cent of the swine, in 1925, after the two were merged, it was said that the new unit controlled less than 25 per cent of the federally inspected slaughter.[4] If all livestock be reduced to a dressed meat basis and lard be included, the percentage in the hands of Armour and Company, including Morris and Company, between 1920 and 1929 fell from 15.8 per cent to 14.1 per cent, and of Wilson and Company from 5.2 per cent to 4.3 per cent, which decline, the packers argued, was "not suggestive of any monopolistic control at the present time."[5] Furthermore the large packers alleged that, with one exception, all of their rivals increased their business between 1920 and 1930 at a time when each of the four large packers suffered a decline in absolute volume of business[6] and argued that the large packers were obviously not dominating the industry.[7]

These more recent changes in conditions in the industry are said to have been accompanied by an increase in the number of "independent" packers. The number of packers reporting under the Packers and Stockyards Act increased from 494 in 1923 to 832

[1] The average weight per car route order for Swift and Company fell from 206 pounds in 1923 to 165 pounds in 1929 (*ibid.*, 114).
[2] In 1925 Swift and Company despatched 8,146 cars from its East St. Louis plant and in 1929, 4,341 (*ibid.*, 115).
[3] U.S. v. Swift and Co. *et al.* (1931), *Brief for U.S.*, 18, 25, 58.
[4] U.S. Secretary of Agriculture v. Armour and Co. before Secretary of Agriculture, *Conclusion and Order*, Docket 19, 1925, 7.
[5] U.S. v. Swift and Co., *Brief for Swift and Co. and Armour and Co.* 49. The percentage of Swift and Company rose from 13.2 to 15.2 and that of Cudahy from 4.0 to 4.7.
[6] *ibid.*, 50–52.
[7] "Obviously it is not true that either the power to monopolize or to crush competitors exists in those who have been unable to hold their own strength and who occupy part of a field wherein flourish increasingly successful and strong competitors—competitors who testified without exception that they have no fear of defendants' competition" (*loc. cit.*).

in 1929.¹ This increase is, however, partly due to increasing efforts by the Packers and Stockyards administration to secure complete returns.² It might be partly due also to the maintenance of prices upon a level which offers, at least to smaller scale packers, a rate of return sufficient to induce new investment. The Federal Trade Commission reported that during the three years from 1914 to 1916 the profits of the five large packers had averaged 13.5 per cent of their capitalization, while those of 65 independent packers had averaged 16.3 per cent.³ The commission concluded that the large packers were either less efficient than the small packers in meat packing in the narrow sense, or that their profits on non-meat packing activities were lower than those on meat packing; it decided that they were investing profits from meat packing in new fields in which they were not securing a normal rate of return.⁴ In 1921, however, the five large packers are said to have suffered a loss of 10.8 per cent upon their net worth while the independents as a group made a profit of 3.2 per cent of their net worth.⁵ The returns of the large packers are said to have been poorer than those of the independents since the consent decree;⁶ the earnings of the four largest packers appear in every year between 1920 and 1929 to have been very much less than those of the fifteen largest rivals; during the whole period the average earnings of the four largest packers were 2.6 per cent of their net worth, while those of the smaller packers were 9.2 per cent:⁷ the larger packers are now evidently at a disadvantage as compared with the smaller.⁸

---

[1] *Hearings on Food Prices*, 1930, 318.
[2] The Attorney General contended that the increase in the number of federally inspected slaughterers was only 17.
[3] The commission emphasized, however, that the functions performed by the large packers differed from those of the small packers; the former operated branch houses, car routes, and a number of enterprises other than meat packing in the narrow sense; the smaller packers generally undertook a smaller variety of activities and sold locally or through brokers.
[4] F.T.C., *The Meat Packing Industry*, I, 16; V, 94 and 95.
[5] It has also been reported that the smaller meat packers suffered losses of 5.8 per cent of their net worth in 1921 (Swift and Co. *et al.* v. U.S. 286 U.S. 106 (1931)).
[6] The Federal Trade Commission was not prepared to say whether the decree was the cause of this decline and remarked that the big packers probably made heavy losses on their export business during the period 1919 to 1922 (F.T.C., *Packer Consent Decree*, 20, 43. See also *Hearings on Senate Resolutions* 4110 *and* 389 before Senate Committee on Agriculture and Forestry, 1933, 9).
[7] Swift and Co. *et al.* v. U.S., 276 U.S. 311 (1928), *Brief for Swift and Co. et al.*, 9, 52.
[8] Much higher earnings per dollar of sales by a number of rivals of the large packers were quoted as evidence of the higher operating costs of the large packers in 1929 (*ibid.*, 56). The Attorney General, however, denied that the profits of the large packers have been small compared to those of their rivals; he compared the propor-

Although the larger packers must exercise considerable control over prices the fact that their costs are higher than those of their smaller rivals has enabled rivals to prosper and expand under price conditions yielding low returns to the larger packers. Sharing the market between them has not, therefore, meant even a constant share of the total market, nor has it meant prosperity to the larger packers.

Criticism of the prices they have charged is not easy owing to the close interdependence of supplies of various meat products the demands for which may be altogether unrelated. Figure 13 suggests that the price of beef rose in relation to the price of cattle between 1913 and 1926 and that between 1926 and 1928 the price of cattle rose more than the price of beef. During the first period, however, the price of hides fell relatively to the prices of beef and cattle and during the second it rose again.[1] During a depression the demand for some meat products falls off more than that for others; in consequence the relationship between the prices of different products obtained from a single

---

tion of total business which they did with the proportion of total profits obtained by them with the following results:

Year	Percentage of business	Percentage of profits
1924	69.42	63.27
1925	63.27	75.97
1926	66.22	75.91
1927	70.99	103.27[a]
1928	70.87	69.13
1929	71.89	77.63

[a] Apart from the defendants there was a combined net loss for this year. About 70 per cent of the losses were sustained by six concerns.

These statistics, however, presumably include the low profits of a large number of small firms. The large packers were said to be operating in 1929 on a much more profitable basis than at the time of the decree, combined earnings having been 0.18 per cent of total sales in 1920 and 1.06 per cent in 1929 and for the years 1923 to 1929 inclusive they averaged 1.30 per cent (U.S. v. Swift and Co. *et al.* (1931), *Brief for the U.S.* 39). These returns, however, include the profits on foreign business and the operations of subsidiaries using by-products.

[1] The relation between the price of by-products and the spread between the prices of cattle and beef for the years 1919 and 1921 is analyzed in Swift and Company, *The Effect of By-product Values on the Spread between Cattle and Beef Prices*, 1921. A similar comparison of the price of hogs and hog products is presented in U.S. Bureau of Labor Statistics, *Bulletin 493*, p. 50. The export of hog products tends to stabilize the price of hogs and some hog products (SWIFT AND COMPANY, *The Effect of Pork Exports on the Production and Price of Hogs*, 1922). For a comparison of the relative movements of livestock prices and the prices of their respective products, see Letter from Department of Public Relations and Trade of the Institute of American Meat Packers, *United States Daily*, Apr. 14, 1932, where it was argued that there was "a close correspondence between live prices and product prices"; product prices in general fell somewhat less, however, than the price of live animals.

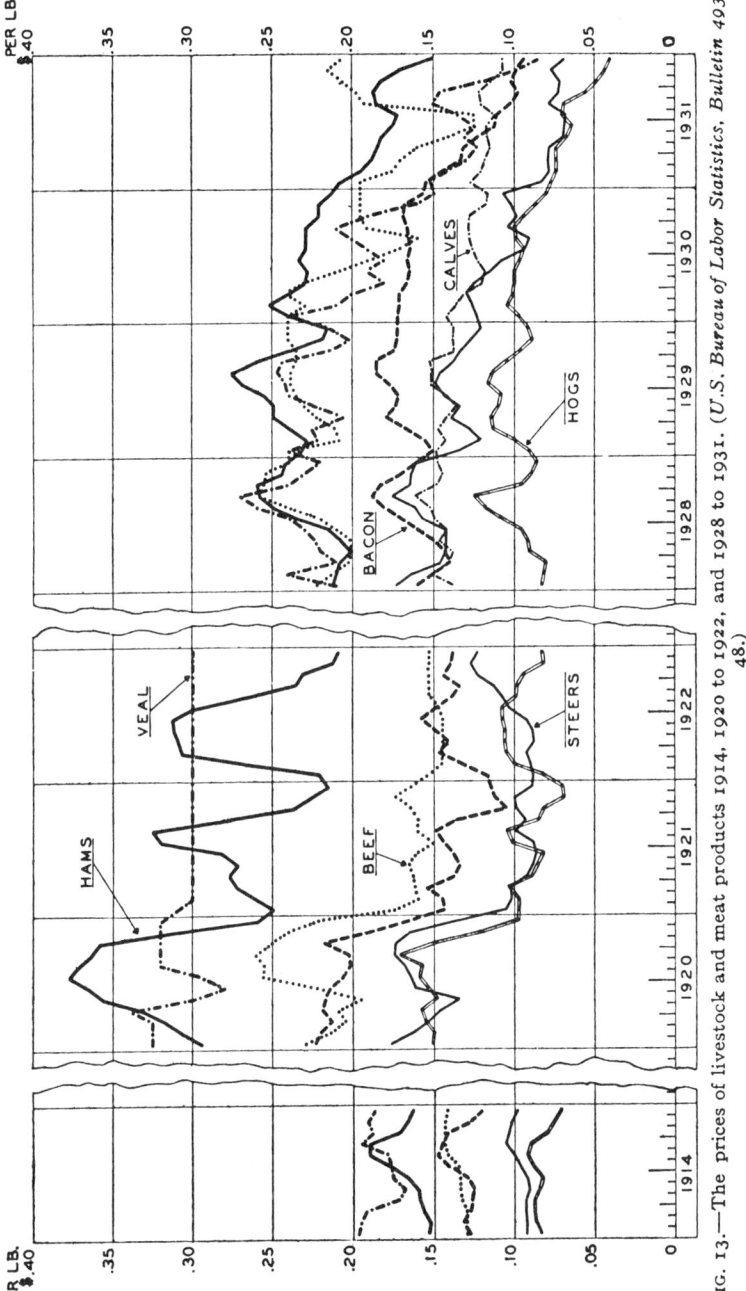

FIG. 13.—The prices of livestock and meat products 1914, 1920 to 1922, and 1928 to 1931. (*U.S. Bureau of Labor Statistics, Bulletin 493, 48.*)

animal changes.[1] The prices of meat products declined sharply during the period of declining wholesale prices from June, 1929, to February, 1933, owing largely to still sharper declines in the price of livestock.

Although the meat packing industry presents more information concerning sharing the market than any other, the effects of such a policy are not evident. It was never the whole market that was shared, and lack of satisfactory statistics obstructs any conclusion concerning the change in the relative position in the industry of the large packers as a group. Their relations with other packers were more in the nature of those between a group of leaders and followers. Important changes in the conditions of production and distribution have affected differently the large integrated manufacturers and the small packers. It is difficult to prove any attempt to obtain monopoly profits, if for no other reason, because the monopoly profits available cannot be calculated. New firms have appeared and smaller firms have increased their share of the total interstate business, a fact which indicates that prices have exceeded the cost of production, at least by the smaller firms, by an attractive margin. Possibly the large meat packers with their higher costs have exerted pressure to maintain prices upon a level higher than would otherwise have prevailed but the growth of the smaller packers must have placed serious limitations upon their policy.

The anthracite industry has shared the market under more favorable conditions than the meat packers. During the period of most definite market sharing there was little obstruction to leadership, partly no doubt because demand followed an upward trend from 1890 to 1917. The proportion of the whole industry collaborating to share the market was greater than in meat packing. Leadership has moreover enjoyed more scope because the industry is less exposed to competition from new firms. Ten railroad-controlled companies owned 90.3 per cent of the unmined anthracite in 1896[2] but only 78.04 per cent in 1907;[3] in this latter

[1] Hides vary in price much more widely than cattle and the price does not appear to be very closely related to that of the cattle from which they are produced, but of which they are a relatively unimportant joint product (U.S. Bureau of Labor Statistics, *Bulletin 493*, 48). The prices of different hog products are affected by the fact that the relative quantities of them are capable of adjustment: when the price of fat backs is low in relation to the price of lard more lard and less fat backs are sold (SWIFT AND COMPANY, *The Price of Pork Products: Lard*, 1923).

[2] JONES, *op. cit.*, 109.

[3] *ibid.*, 105; U.S. v. Reading Co. *Brief for the U.S.* (1911), 36; *Brief for Reading Co.*, 82.

SHARING THE MARKET 189

year, however, the railroad-controlled companies controlled about half the output of the independents through perpetual selling contracts. In 1923 the eight principal railroad-controlled companies controlled 79.8 per cent of the recoverable anthracite supplies.[1] Harmony between the existing producers was secured, as we have seen, upon a basis which involved slower marketing of the unmined reserves of the leader than of those of its followers and the imposition upon the leader of heavy carrying charges in respect of its unmined resources.[2]

There is evidence that since 1917 prices have been raised as a result of a decline in output. Output declined by about 26 per cent between 1917 and 1929 while the price of stove sizes had risen by the end of 1928 nearly 100 per cent. The general level of wholesale prices fell about 17 per cent and the prices of other sizes produced jointly with stove sizes did not increase, and some fell. The average wholesale price of anthracite, however, rose by almost 20 per cent. During the depression which began in 1929 anthracite was one of the few commodities to increase in price; it rose 0.7 per cent between June, 1929, and February, 1933, during which period the index of all wholesale prices fell 37.2 per cent. These policies, while not attracting new anthracite producers, have doubtless undermined the position of the industry in the general market for fuel and power resources.

"Live and let live" policies are said to

... tend not to the strict rationing of opportunity practiced by guilds and communism, but to a milder form of socialization of the opportunity in which working rules are laid down to protect the individual in the enjoyment of his share so long as he proves himself the most worthy candidate for that share. Behind the individual are the rules that fit him into his sharing of the opportunity, and behind the rules are measurement and observation telling us what the opportunity is and how individuals make use of it.

[1] F.T.C., *Wealth and Income in the United States*, 86.
[2] Statistics offered by the Reading company (and based upon the output of all sizes) suggested that the percentage of business done by the largest company had declined, the smaller firms having benefited more than the larger; the percentage of total production marketed by the principal companies in 1901 and 1911 having been:

Company	1901	1911
Philadelphia and Reading and Lehigh and Wilkes-Barre companies.	25.02	21.40
Delaware, Lackawanna, and Western	12.09	12.51
Lehigh Valley Coal Company	14.08	14.26
Pennsylvania Coal Company	8.13	11.47
Delaware and Hudson	9.36	10.11
Susquehanna Coal Company	4.85	5.54
Lehigh Coal and Navigation Company	2.98	4.88

(*Brief for the Reading Co.*, 265.)

Such a policy

. . . admits of the pursuit of self-interest but concedes that the force of group opinion tends to limit that pursuit to methods which do not unduly disturb trade. It looks upon efficiency as an informed and sustained ability to sell at a reasonable price, and to stand back of the product even after it has been sold. It gives first consideration to the fit, leaving the elimination of the unfit to the effect of the average group price over a period of time.[1]

But is the "group opinion" of producers the most suitable medium for control of a whole industry when concentrated control is permitted? Will group opinion protect producers only so long as they are the "most worthy candidates"? Is the average group price (whatever that may be) a suitable test of worthiness? Is it true that, in the opinion of the industrial group, efficiency is sustained ability to sell at a "reasonable" price? Is the group the best judge of the reasonableness of prices? Is the group to be trusted to decide what changes in industrial conditions constitute "undue" disturbances in trade? Will group control of this kind and no other device induce sellers to "stand back" of the product even after it has been sold?

Sharing the market, as we have seen, may affect costs of production through its effect upon total output. It also affects the cost of production through its effect upon the inducement to improved methods of production. That part of the competitive stimulus to greater efficiency which consists of rewards in the form of improvements in the relative position of the innovating firm is eliminated. The extent of the remaining stimulus to the reduction of costs turns largely upon size of the firms in the industry. Where the firm is large, the benefit to be obtained from reducing the cost of producing its existing output may be great enough to stimulate attempts to increase efficiency, but where the firm is small the stimulus is correspondingly small. Pressure to improve methods of production in the form of fear of losing ground to more efficient rivals is also removed where it is understood that the market is to be shared. The contention that a "live and let live" policy assures a seller that he "will not be deprived of his customers by price cuts so long as he can keep up to the average efficiency of the industry,"[2] assumes that

[1] MONTGOMERY, "The Government and the Theory of Competition," *Amer. Econ. Rev.*, 15: 449, 446 (1925).
[2] *ibid.*, 447.

prices will be set so as to yield a normal profit only to those who attain "average efficiency"; the diminution of the stimulus to improve this average is, however, of great importance. If each firm is assured, when demand declines, of its old percentage of whatever business is available, the pressure to eliminate firms is reduced. The adjustment of investment to changing demand is thus retarded.[1] Sharing the market tends to obstruct those improvements in methods of production requiring a larger scale of operation; where the merger of two firms entitles the new firm to a quota equal to the sum of the quotas of the two firms disappearing, this objection is partly avoided; smaller adjustments of scale of production may, however, be difficult to make by mergers.[2] As the cost of acquiring additional business in this manner may be less than the cost of acquiring it by price competition the transferable quota may facilitate the adoption of more economical large-scale methods of production and the transfer of business from the less to the more efficient firms.[3] But on the other hand, it may operate merely to facilitate expansions dictated by the desire for size even when it is inefficient.

The effect of cartel arrangements for control of output by the imposition of fines upon producers in excess of agreed quotas and the payment of subsidies to producers falling short of agreed quotas depends in part upon the amount of the fines and subsidies. Where the reductions in cost accruing from larger-scale production exceed the fines a firm may increase its output sufficiently to permit it to operate more nearly at the optimum size. The fines and subsidies virtually set the prices at which quotas are transferred: firms losing all business may cease production and without selling their quotas become automatically "cartel rentiers." When the fines exceed any reductions in cost likely to be obtained from larger-scale production, firms are unlikely to expand beyond the quota allowance, but if the subsidies are equally high firms may be increasingly prepared to become mere rentiers, thus production tends to be diminished below the aggregate fixed amount. But as fines are usually expected to provide all the funds

---

[1] *Cf.* WARRINER, *Combines and Rationalization in Germany*, 48. Also the *Hearings on a National Economic Council*, 1931 (168, 341, 482), where Senator La Follette and the president of the General Motors Corporation contended that agreements to share the market would tend to maintain in existence the least efficient firms.

[2] Some pooling agreements permit the sale of quotas. The opportunity to obtain a prescribed share of the business is sufficiently protected by agreement or convention to be treated as a property right to be bought and sold.

[3] *Cf.* VON BECKERATH, *Modern Industrial Organization*, 241.

to pay the subsidies, subsidies requiring more revenue than is yielded by the fines are not likely to persist for long. Cartels which provide compensation to firms closed down or unable to fulfill their quotas tend to keep prices low in order to reduce the number of firms to be compensated for not filling their quotas and to distribute the cost of compensation as widely as possible.[1] High prices reduce demand and any increased profit is offset by increased subsidies to those unable to sell.

The particular basis upon which the market is shared may also affect costs. Sharing according to capacity for production tends to excessive investment, especially where the market is shared by an agreement which must be periodically renewed. When the date of expiry of the agreement approaches, additional investment may be made to reinforce a demand for an increased quota.[2] The excessiveness of prices may be concealed by high costs which reduce profits. Sharing market territories diminishes the opportunities for dumping goods at distant points more economically reached by rivals and thereby reduces the total transportation costs of the industry. In this respect it is superior to simple control of output or prices.

The meat packers have claimed that "sharing the market by pools has been undoubtedly a benefit to the public at large in that they helped to avoid recurrent gluts and scarcities in eastern markets and tended to steady markets."[3] They contended[4] that when a number of firms ship long distances to a city with only limited demand, "if each acts without the knowledge of what the other is doing in that market, there will be an oversupply of fresh meat at their warehouses there." This meat cannot be reshipped easily and must be sold quickly, and unless demand responds quickly to a fall in price, some of the meat may spoil before it is sold; prices would have to be cut below cost to dispose of the meat. It has already been suggested, however, that the sharing of local markets may have been necessary to support the more general sharing of the market through control of the purchases of livestock. Otherwise, the packers might have failed to make the best distribution of their products between local markets and therefore to obtain the full benefits of their policy.

[1] *ibid.*, 265.
[2] VON BECKERATH, *op. cit.*, 240. BRADY, *The Rationalization Movement in Germany*, 96.
[3] SWIFT AND COMPANY, *Statement*, Aug. 19, 1918.
[4] U.S. v. Swift and Co. *et al.*, 196 U.S. 375.

The consequences of the kind of market sharing that arises out of reciprocal dealing require separate discussion. Reciprocal dealing does not discourage attempts to attract buyers by offering benefits in matters other than price. It encourages such efforts, their form being determined by the criterion adopted by the buyer in distributing business. Purchasers faced with identical offers by sellers turn to formulae that will yield them indirect benefits. Sellers who refuse to compete openly and directly tend to be driven into indirect competition which benefits the buyer. It is of the essence of such a device, therefore, that the distribution of business, although governed by an unchanging formula, is capable of change. Steel manufacturers by adjusting their distribution of freight between railroads could bring about changes in the distribution of steel rail orders. Cement manufacturers by changing the location of their plants or the distribution of their purchases of coal could change the distribution of orders for cement. If different purchasers use different formulae the situation is complicated but remains fundamentally unchanged.[1] If only some buyers are able to resort to such formulae the distribution of business is determined only in part thereby.

The price policy of an industry treated by its customers in this manner remains to be explained mainly in other terms. The very identity of offers which drives buyers to such a policy betokens the presence of some device by which the harmony is maintained. If there is price leadership then it is necessary to investigate the policy of the leader. But the policy of the buyers, being aimed at changing the behavior of the sellers, is likely to affect their costs. If steel rail orders are distributed between manufacturers according to the proportion in which they have provided traffic to each railroad buying rails, there is presumably an inducement to each manufacturer to direct his freight in each year to the railroad likely to be planning the largest orders for rails. In so far as such diversions involve costs to railroads they may be regarded as expenditures on non-price competition. They increase the total costs of sellers, and thereby tend to provide a reason for maintaining prices through their tendency to diminish profits. They bring the profits of railroads under the influence of causes other than technical efficiency and their suitability to meet demands for transportation. The effect of inducing cement manufacturers or railroads to purchase coal where they

[1] Formulae adopted by different purchasers might conflict.

would not otherwise purchase it is similar. Where the cement producers are induced to locate plants in states where a large demand for cement for highway construction is expected, costs may also be increased with similar consequences. This policy may, however, merely speed up a geographical redistribution of production that would occur in its absence though more slowly.

In general, therefore, the desire to avoid destructive price competition expresses itself more or less definitely in some industries in the form of preparedness on the part of producers to abandon opportunities of improving their relative position in their industry; it is assumed, of course, that rivals will take the same attitude. One element of risk in industry is thus eliminated. The knowledge that sellers have adopted this policy is not sufficient to permit the calculation of the level of prices or the level of expenditure on non-price competition. All that can be said is that at any moment of time prices tend to be equal and the selling costs of different firms mutually neutralizing. In consequence such policies must be accompanied by some other objective, such as the pursuit of monopoly profit or the pursuit of a reasonable profit. If the latter be the objective, then it is necessary to inquire how a reasonable profit is likely to be calculated. Sharing the market diminishes the pressure to improve methods of production and eliminates the necessity for passing on to purchasers any of the advantages of reduction in cost. Any tendency to excessive investment arises rather from the price policy pursued than from sharing the market.

CHAPTER V

THE STABILIZATION OF INDIVIDUAL PRICES

I. The definition of stabilization of prices—II. The evidence of stabilization of prices—*A*. The detection of stabilization of prices—*B*. The prevalence of stabilization of prices—1. Conventions concerning price policy—*a*. Price setting—*b*. Long-term contracts—*c*. Guarantees against decline in price—2. Trade associations—3. Price leadership—*a*. The steel industry—*b*. The anthracite industry—*c*. The agricultural implements industry—*d*. The petroleum industry—*e*. Other industries—4. Duopoly and monopoly—5. Other examples—6. Summary of evidence concerning the stabilization of prices—III. The consequences of stabilization of prices—*A*. Price setting for short periods—*B*. Stabilization of individual prices and the business cycle—*C*. Stabilization of prices over long periods.

I. THE DEFINITION OF STABILIZATION OF PRICES

The phrase "stabilization of prices" is used in a number of senses of widely differing economic significance. Occasionally, but altogether illegitimately, it is used synonymously with uniformity of prices between different sellers at a moment of time; such uniformity may or may not involve absence of change over periods of time. Legitimately used, the phrase relates to the behavior of a given price over time. Complete stability means the absence of changes of price. Prices that never change do not exist; in consequence the phrase is used in practice in a wider sense, implying degrees of stability. Such degrees may be measured in terms of the length of the periods in which complete stability occurs or in terms of the number of changes in longer periods of time. Degrees of stability may also be measured by the amplitude of fluctuations in price instead of their frequency in time. The influences giving rise to reductions in the amplitude of price changes are very different from those causing reductions in their frequency; stabilization in the latter sense is the principal subject of the present chapter.

No citations are necessary to show that pleas for the stabilization of prices have become increasingly widespread among business men in recent years. Their pronouncements at meetings of trade associations and in the press lean increasingly heavily upon the necessity for stabilization. This widespread desire is traceable to a number of causes. It springs in part merely from the desire to avoid any lowering of prices in the crude belief that higher prices always mean greater profits. Where there is unused plant and overhead costs are a large part of total costs price competition is costly, and the avoidance of changes in price eliminates dangerous price cutting. The desire to prevent "cutthroat" competition leads, however, to the elimination of all price cutting, "cutthroat" competition being difficult to distinguish from other price competition. Sellers able to coordinate their policies may reduce the frequency of price changes because of assumptions concerning the behavior of buyers. Where they fear, for instance, that reductions in price will stimulate the hope of further cuts, or where they believe that demand is inelastic in a more general sense, they are likely to reduce the number of price changes. Stability may also be sought because of uncertainty as to the policy that will be most profitable in the industry, particularly if the effect of high profits upon investment in the industry is taken into account. Finally stability of prices may be sought merely because it is a simple policy and because the wisest policy is hard to discover.

II. THE EVIDENCE OF STABILIZATION OF PRICES

A. *The Detection of Stabilization of Prices*

The proof of the prevalence of policies aimed at stabilizing prices is beset with the same type of difficulty as the proof of price leadership and sharing the market. Considerable periods of unchanging price can be shown to have existed in a number of industries for periods of increasing length. As early as 1897 the Joint Committee of the Senate and Assembly of New York State concluded that trusts had secured a greater stability of prices and doubted whether the stability had benefited the consumer.[1] Types of relationship between sellers likely to give opportunities for the attainment of stability can also be shown to exist, frequently in the same industries. It is then fairly clear that producers whose policies are coordinated have chosen a policy of price stabilization. But as the interval of unchanging price diminishes in length, and as the evidence of the existence of interrelationships between producers calculated to facilitate

[1] New York Senate Doct. 40, 1897; JENKS, "Recent Legislation and Adjudication on Trusts," *Quart. Jour. Econ.*, 12: 462 (1898).

such a policy becomes more shadowy, it becomes increasingly difficult to determine how far such periods of stability as occur can be attributed to any deliberate policy.

The inadequacy of statistics of prices also obstructs definite conclusions. The statistics most easily available and most often used in official compilations are statistics of quotations, or offer prices. In many industries, however, it is almost customary to depart, at least from time to time, from these offer prices. The market reports concerning steel prices, for instance, refer frequently to the "shading" of the official price and to "concessions"; the sugar refiners pointed out that offer prices and actual prices after 1928 were not identical; the prices of rubber tires are notoriously subject to a number of discounts. The so-called "official" price becomes then a point of reference from which to measure actual prices which may vary from time to time, from seller to seller, or even between the different buyers from a single seller. Nevertheless, so long as statistics of quoted prices are all that are available, analysis must be applied to them, with, however, the constant realization of their inadequacy. Constancy of offer prices alone is, moreover, not without significance; widespread departures from the "official" price usually compel an adjustment of "official" to actual prices. The available price statistics are often inadequate also because they relate to a given day in each month or to an average of quotations for a given period. It is conceivable that such series should follow a horizontal line although the actual prices vary from day to day, but only a rare coincidence would cause daily variations to neutralize each other over long periods.[1]

B. *The Prevalence of Stabilization of Prices*

The evidence of stabilization of prices may conveniently be marshaled by reference to the forms of behavior that appear to facilitate it, *viz.*, conventions concerning price policy, trade associations, price leadership, and duopoly and monopoly, each of which will be discussed in turn.

1. CONVENTIONS CONCERNING PRICE POLICY

a. Price Setting. The most important convention affecting the frequency of changes in price is that of price setting. In an increas-

---

[1] The Federal Trade Commission found that the apparent stability of some prices was partly due to the nature of the statistics but concluded that there was "a good deal of apparently undue stability" (*Open Price Trade Associations*, 120).

ing number of industries sellers set an offer price likely to remain open for a considerable period of time. Within the period in which the offer remains open production is adjusted to the amount sold at the price set. This situation differs markedly from that in a competitive market to which sellers bring their output to be sold at prices determined as a result of conditions of demand and supply at each price.[1]

Where there is a seasonal concentration of either sales or production, prices are frequently set at the beginning of the season and maintained throughout most if not the whole of the season. "Opening prices" which are commonly maintained for a considerable portion of a whole season are prevalent in the canning,[2] agricultural implements,[3] anthracite,[4] tin plate,[5] woolen fabric,[6] carpet,[7] various dress goods, oil, and automobile industries.[8] Some trade associations have attempted to introduce this practice into industries where it has not previously prevailed. When the Wool Institute was established one of its objectives was "the maintenance of prices throughout the season."[9] The price of dried beet pulp (used as a fertilizer) also frequently remained unchanged for several months and generally for the whole crop year;[10] one concern had contracted for the purchase of a great part of the whole output of this pulp, the price of which it endeavored to set for the whole year. When the price was set too low to equate supply and demand, supplies of the product were exhausted before the end of the year. On occasion, apparently, the company rationed the supply in preference to raising its price.[11]

The practice of setting prices irrespective of the season is obviously prevalent in a great many other markets, particularly

[1] The president of the Millers National Federation, enumerating a number of methods of selling which he regarded as undesirable, included the practice of "selling flour on the basis of bids rather than naming a price at the home office and maintaining it" (F.T.C., *The Flour Milling Industry*, 1926, 136).
[2] F.T.C., *Canned Salmon*, 49. 90 per cent of the total pack was sold at the opening price. *Cf.* also *Open Price Trade Associations*, 78.
[3] U.S. v. International Harvester Co., *Brief for International Harvester Co.*, 161; F.T.C., *The High Prices of Farm Implements*, 135.
[4] *Mineral Resources of the United States*, II, 453.
[5] The steel makers customarily adhere for nine months to the price announced at the beginning of the season in the sense that they do not advance it: can manufacturers making seasonal contracts with packers are thus protected (*New York Times*, Nov. 5, 1934).
[6] U.S. v. Wool Institute, Inc., *Petition*, 4, 5.
[7] WHITNEY, *Trade Associations and Industrial Control*, 80.
[8] F.T.C., *Open Price Trade Associations*, 78.
[9] *New York Times*, Feb. 16, 1928.
[10] F.T.C., *Commercial Feeds*, 1921, 126.
[11] *ibid.*, 166.

THE STABILIZATION OF INDIVIDUAL PRICES 199

those for branded goods sold at retail, the prices of which are well known not to fluctuate from day to day. The prices of oil, gasoline, bread, sugar, drugs, and many other products sold at retail also have been freed from any tendency to continuous change. This setting of prices involves stability for the season or other period and injects a degree of rigidity into the price structure varying with the length of the intervals between changes.

The convention of setting prices for a number of months arises out of imperfections in the market. To obtain the maximum of profit a manufacturer must charge a price such that the sale of one more unit would result in a greater addition to total costs than to revenue and the sale of one less unit would involve a greater reduction in total revenue than in total costs.[1] But it would be both impossible and absurd to readjust prices on this basis from moment to moment. A seller operating upon a large scale in relation to the total market realizes that changes in his policy affect the price in the market; if changes in his price are immediately accepted by his rivals his share of the market is not increased; a price cut initiated by him and immediately becoming general may, however, increase total sales. But a reduction may cause a greater reduction by a rival and generate a price war. An increase may be more difficult to make than a reduction because rivals are tempted to delay following the lead of a firm initiating an increased price; for this reason reductions expected to be temporary are discouraged. Some of the reactions of purchasers to price changes are slow, far-reaching, and uncertain. A price reduction may result in a purely speculative increase in demand, *i.e.*, an increase due to the anticipation of the demands of a future period when prices are expected to be higher; demand is then merely shifted forward from the future period. A reduction may induce increased purchases only after long-delayed adjustments to the new price level. A reduction may create in the minds of buyers a notion of what is a "fair" price which later becomes an obstacle to attempts to raise the price; buyers may let their inventories run down or experiment with rival products. When prices move downward more easily than upward, price changes continue to reverberate throughout the industry for a considerable time, and when costs must be incurred on a large scale for long periods producers attempt to limit readjustments of prices to rare occasions when fundamental changes in conditions of demand or supply

[1] That is, marginal cost is equal to marginal revenue. *Cf.* Chap. I.

exert themselves. If demand or supply is subject to wide seasonal fluctuations prices tend to be set for whole seasons; seasonal prices are, however, not always free from competitive pressure; midseason price reductions may be made.[1] Where seasonal fluctuations in demand or supply are not pronounced, offer prices may prevail for longer periods; price setting merges into long-period price stabilization.

b. Long-term Contracts. The frequency of transactions influences the frequency with which it is possible for prices to change. In organized markets in which transactions occur almost continuously, rapid changes are at least possible; speculation increases the number of transactions and, therefore, the opportunities for change. Wherever sales are made by contract to supply goods over considerable periods of time, as in the market for steel rails, newsprint,[2] book paper, and crude oil,[3] the number of transactions is thereby diminished. If it is customary for such contracts to be made by most buyers, at about the same time, particularly at about the same time in each year (*e.g.*, steel rails), the apparent lack of change in prices throughout the year may be due to the lack of transactions; the offer price is ineffective. Long-term contracts tend to prevent price reductions, if not price increases, because of the pressure to modify existing contracts if prices are seriously reduced and because the reduced price will apply to business for a long period in the future. In 1909, for instance, Judge Gary resisted a reduction in the price of steel products because a reduced price would apply to many long-term contracts.[4]

c. Guarantees against Price Decline. In some industries sellers have guaranteed that, should their price be reduced during the currency of the contract, the lower price would apply to all deliveries made under the contract; postponement of orders by buyers who anticipate that selling prices will be reduced in the near future is thus discouraged. This practice has frequently been followed in the steel industry. A reduction in price necessitates the repayment of a part of the sums received for past sales under contracts still in force, the amount of the refund depending

[1] In the carpet industry sellers jockeyed for position at the seasonal openings, endeavoring to delay declaration of their prices until those of their rivals were available, but the Carpet Institute attempted to eliminate the practice (WHITNEY, *Trade Associations and Industrial Control*, 80).
[2] F.T.C., *Newsprint Paper Industry*, 1917, 48.
[3] F.T.C., *Prices, Profits, and Competition in the Petroleum Industry*, 1928, 101.
[4] F.T.C., *Statement on Pittsburgh Plus*, 410.

upon the duration of contracts; the reduction of prices is obstructed. In the market for iron ore this practice is said to have favored the large manufacturers who own ore deposits as against those who buy ore in the market, presumably because of its tendency to maintain the price of ore.[1] A somewhat different type of guarantee against price decline was granted by manufacturers of canned milk who undertook, whenever they reduced the price, to pay a rebate to the jobbers upon all canned milk bought at the higher price and still unsold. This practice tended to encourage speculative buying by wholesale grocers when the price fell; if the price increased again the buyer made a speculative profit, but if it fell further he suffered no loss.[2] Manufacturers are discouraged from making price reductions, although possibly less than by the first form of guarantee; they must carry the losses upon the inventories held by jobbers as well as upon those held by themselves.[3] Guarantees against a decline in prices tend to stabilize prices only when other influences make for reductions; they do not discourage increases in price.[4] Even where sellers do not guarantee against price declines but habitually make a reduced price applicable to all subsequent deliveries under contracts in force at the time of the reduction (*e.g.*, in the cement and steel industries) price reductions are discouraged. The reduced prices attract little business from rivals in the short run; they merely compel rivals to deliver more cheaply under existing contracts.[5] As increased prices apply only to new business[6] they

[1] F.T.C., *Digest of Replies in response to an inquiry by the Federal Trade Commission relative to the pracitce of giving guarantees against price decline*, 1920, 45.

[2] F.T.C., *Canned Milk*, 1921, 55.

[3] Adopted on any large scale these guarantees must lead to control of jobbers' inventories by manufacturers, and probably also to attempts to control their resale policy.

[4] In the months immediately preceding the post-war boom in business the Federal Trade Commission issued eleven complaints against this practice, but subsequently decided that the practice was not unfair and abandoned the proceedings (WATKINS, "The Federal Trade Commission," *Quart. Jour. Econ.*, 40: 572 (1926)). The majority of the codes under the National Industrial Recovery Act, however, proscribed the practice as unfair.

[5] "In the old days the steel trade had a marketing style of its own. . . . The steel trade throve on 'buying movements' for forward deliveries, when at intervals prices advanced for successively further forward deliveries. During such periods the seller's skill lay in limiting his obligations until the top was reached. At that time all buyers were covered and prices were automatically protected because in essence contracts were guaranteed against price declines, and for months more specifications for actual shipment could be squeezed out of contracts than could be secured by cutting prices. A buyer offered a cut price would merely require his original vendor to readjust the contract. Eventually the market would break and then a dip would lead to a natural recovery." (*New York Times*, Nov. 7, 1927.)

[6] F.T.C., *Price Bases Inquiry*, 83, note 9.

may have little effect upon sales revenue for a considerable time.

2. TRADE ASSOCIATIONS

The manner in which the statistical activities of trade associations may reduce the frequency of changes in price has already been analyzed.[1] Statistics of production are often presented with suggestions that supply must be adjusted to demand at current prices. More direct campaigns to induce restriction of output and a feeling of shame in those who cut prices tend in the same direction. Open-price policies increase the speed and accuracy with which the prices quoted by any seller are communicated to others, and thereby reduce the interval within which any price cutter can expect greatly to increase his volume of business because of a difference between his prices and those of his rivals; one inducement to price cutting is removed. Furthermore, "it is probable that trade associations foster an attitude that is favorable to such stability of prices through instilling into the members the idea that the lowering of a price will merely tend to demoralize the market."[2] The Supreme Court agreed in 1923 that the association of the linseed crushers of the country with the Armstrong Bureau of Related Industries (which organized the speedy exchange of very detailed information concerning prices) had rendered the price of linseed oil more stable.[3] Trade associations

---

[1] See Chap. II.

[2] " ... Perhaps the form of price reporting that most directly conduces to this end is that wherein deviations from announced net prices are reported and distributed to competitors as soon as made. This system does not involve any element of conspiracy or restriction of the liberty of the individual to make his own prices as he will. Yet it may not only be effective in causing substantial uniformity in prices in a market at the same time, at least for a homogeneous commodity, but it may also tend to maintain a constant level of prices from month to month, somewhat regardless of changes in cost, especially, for example, in the cost of raw materials." (F.T.C., *Open Price Trade Associations*, 353–354.)

[3] U.S. v. American Linseed Co. *et al.*, 262 U.S. 371 (1923). The Attorney General regarded periods of stability in the price of linseed oil as the effect of the operations of the Linseed Oil Council; the longest of these periods during the twenty-one months of the life of the association was a little over two months and most of them were of about two or three weeks, duration (U.S. v. American Linseed Co., *Brief for the U.S.*, 125). The crushers replied, however, that during the twenty-nine years from 1889 to 1917 (immediately before the establishment of the Linseed Oil Council) there was one period during which the price remained unchanged for five months, one period of unchanging price of four months, three of three months, twelve of two months, and twenty-seven of one month (*Brief for Ankeney Linseed Co. et al.*, 150; also Government Exhibit 6). It does not appear, therefore, that prices were rendered more stable by the association if the length of the periods of unchanging price is the criterion of stability. The crushers admitted that fluctuations in prices had been reduced, partly owing to the elimination, through the operations of the council, of price reductions induced by false representations by buyers that they had received

have been very active in collecting and disseminating statistics of the prices, output, and sales of paper of various kinds; Fig. 14 shows that the price of writing paper changed only once between 1923 and 1931 and that the prices of book paper and newsprint changed infrequently. Between 1922 and 1932 the capacity of the industry was repeatedly increased although production

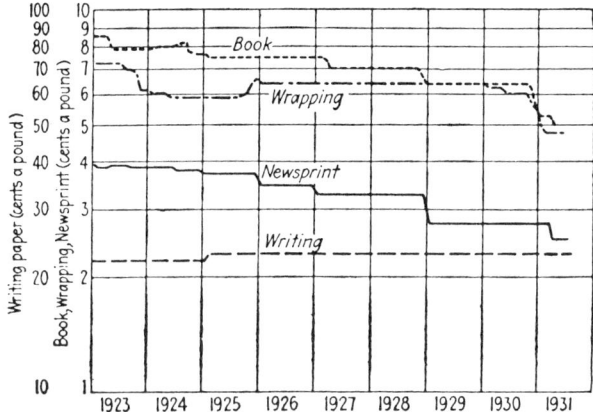

FIG. 14.—The prices of writing paper, book paper, and newsprint, 1923 to 1931. (*Reproduced from Fraser and Doriot, Analysing Our Industries, 320.*)

continuously fell short of capacity by 20 per cent or more.[1] During the period from June, 1929, to February, 1933, when the price of wood pulp of various kinds fell 34 to 44 per cent, the price of wrapping paper remained unchanged, that of tissue paper fell 20 per cent, and that of book paper 30.4 per cent:[2] in January, 1932, the price of tub-sized writing paper which had been $10 for eight years fell to $4.50.[3]

---

offers to sell at reduced prices (*Brief for the Ankeney Linseed Co. et al.*, 235) but they appear to have referred to the amplitude of fluctuations. It was said that during the twenty-seven and three quarter years prior to the formation of the council there had been, on the average, 4.86 months per annum in which the difference between the high and low price during the month did not exceed one cent per gallon, while during the twenty-one months during which the council was in operation this average had been 4.0 months per annum (*Brief for the Ankeney Linseed Co. et al.*, 151). According to this criterion also, therefore, prices had been more stable prior to the formation of the council than during the period of its operations. The court neither approved nor disapproved of such stabilization as had occurred. The two judges dissenting from the decision of the court condemning the activities of the Hardwood Lumber Manufacturers Association concluded that if the activities of the association had substituted stability of prices for violent fluctuations "its influence in this respect is not against the public interest" (American Column and Lumber Co. v. U.S., 257 U.S. 418).

[1] CONSUMER ADVISORY BOARD, *Paper Complaints*, 5, 8.
[2] U.S. Bureau of Labor Statistics, *Wholesale Prices*.
[3] CONSUMER ADVISORY BOARD, *Paper Complaints*, 8.

The inconclusiveness of the Federal Trade Commission's attempt to discover the extent to which the prices of commodities manufactured by firms belonging to trade associations were more stable than the prices of other products has already been mentioned. It has been pointed out, moreover, that the absence of correlation between stability of prices and the presence of active trade associations does not indicate that trade associations fail to secure a greater degree of stability than would otherwise occur in the same industries.[1]

3. PRICE LEADERSHIP

The most notable characteristic of the price leaders already discussed is the wide variation in the limits within which their leadership is accepted by their followers. A leader assured of unquestioning and unswerving allegiance in the matter of prices might be expected to pursue the same price policy as a monopolist.[2] He must, however, consider the effect of such a policy upon the rate of expansion of his existing rivals and upon the appearance of new ones. But neither a monopoly policy nor one aimed at avoiding undue stimulation of existing or potential rivals would be expected to involve an unchanging price. The price would change with changing conditions of cost and of demand. Yet stable prices have found great favor in the eyes of leaders. The Federal Trade Commission commented that the leadership of the United States Steel Corporation has "tended toward constancy of prices through considerable periods, even though there might be lack of uniformity of prices at various particular times. Something similar has possibly been achieved in various other industries, in steel pipe, for example, and possibly in tin cans."[3]

This desire to stabilize prices is probably due to the instability of the relations between leaders and their followers.[4] Fear that

---

[1] See page 63. The prices in industries without trade associations may also be influenced in varying degrees by the fact that they buy from industries in which such associations exist and have succeeded in introducing some measure of stability.

[2] The cost of production is likely, however, to be different in the two situations.

[3] *Open Price Trade Associations*, 77. The commission also stated that the observed undue stability of some prices might be due to price leadership (*ibid.*, 103) and that "price leadership is probably a more important cause of stability or undue stability in prices than any other factor" (*ibid.*, 121). See also *ibid.*, 354.

[4] *Cf.* the remark of the Federal Trade Commission that "in this country . . . it appears to be difficult to discourage in any important line of business for long the expression of independence and the exertion of individual initiative" (F.T.C., *Open Price Trade Associations*, 103).

changes in price will unduly strain the delicate bond between the leader and his followers may lead to the avoidance of price changes. The leader may doubt his capacity to secure the acquiescence of his rivals in what he believes to be the wisest policy and decide, therefore, to "let sleeping dogs lie" and seek to protect his investment and profit in some other way. He may be uncertain as to the wisest policy and for this reason lack the conviction to initiate a change: where, for instance, a few sellers deal with a few buyers (as in the market for steel rails, or in a number of urban markets for fluid milk), it is very difficult to arrive at a proper price. Even where the leader feels himself moderately secure he may aim at stable prices; he may fear to disturb buyers who may hold off the market if the price is reduced a little, or who may be stimulated into criticism of prices if they are raised; he may believe demand to be inelastic. Stabilization may also be an incidental consequence of the avoidance of price cutting during periods of diminished demand, a period of danger in any industry and of great danger in those the demand for whose products fluctuates widely with cyclical changes in general business conditions. Evidence that leaders have in fact secured stability of prices is available for a number of industries and this evidence will now be considered.

a. The Steel Industry. The steel industry provides the most notorious example of a price unchanged for long periods, *viz.*, the price of steel rails. Before May, 1901, the price of rails fluctuated with the price of pig iron and steel billets[1] and during the period from 1880 to 1891 ranged between $8.50 and $16.50 per ton.[2] Since 1901, however, the price of rails has remained stable for long periods. Less than sixty days after the formation of the United States Steel Corporation a price of $28 a ton was announced and it remained in force from May, 1901, until April, 1916, (180 months). After a number of changes[3] the price was again

[1] During a period of sixteen years subsequent to 1887, prices are said to have been fixed by a pool except during the years 1897 and 1898 (BELCHER, "Industrial Pooling Agreements," *Quart. Jour. Econ.*, 19: 117 (1904); U.S.v. U.S. Steel Corp., *Brief for U.S. Steel Corp.*, 210).
[2] BERGLUND, "The U.S. Steel Corporation and Price Stabilization," *Quart. Jour. Econ.*, 38: 1 (1923).
[3] Between May, 1916, and October, 1916 (6 months), rails were quoted at $33, in November, 1916, at $36, from December, 1916, to December, 1917 (13 months), at $38, from January, 1918, to February, 1919 (14 months), at $55, in March, 1919, at $52.50, from April, 1919, to February, 1920 (11 months), at $45, in March, 1920, at $49, from April, 1920, to November, 1920 (8 months), $55, December 1920, $50, January, 1921, to September, 1921 (9 months), $45, October, 1921, $43.75, and from November, 1921, to September, 1922 (11 months), $40.

stabilized at $43 from October, 1922, to October, 1932 (121 months).[1]

This remarkable stability has been variously explained. Firstly, it is said that before 1900 the railroads purchased rails whenever they needed them at the best price obtainable, but about 1900 they began to make purchases of rails at the end of each calendar year for the succeeding year, partly as a consequence of the adoption by the Pennsylvania Railroad of an annual budget[2] and the acceptance of the practice by other railroads. If annual purchases were concentrated within a very short period steel companies might have no inducement to change their quotations during the remainder of the year:[3] but the absence of changes from year to year cannot be thus explained. Secondly, it was said that orders for rails were usually distributed among sellers "something along lines of their respective freight tonnages."[4] This method of distributing rail orders, as we have seen, is more likely to be a result than a cause of lack of price competition among sellers of rails. Thirdly, the manufacturers claimed that the cost of manufacturing Bessemer rails had increased owing to the high quality required by railroads.[5] But why, then, was the price of rails not raised during the period? The only answer offered was that the corporation had refused to increase its price, with the result that other sellers were unable to increase theirs.[6] Fourthly, it was said that the price of $28 which prevailed for fifteen years applied only to standard Bessemer rails, the demand for which, however, declined during the period and the price of which was used merely as a convenient base for calculating the price of more expensive open hearth rails which

[1] AMERICAN IRON AND STEEL INSTITUTE, *Annual Statistical Report*. Quotations since October, 1921, relate to Bessemer or open hearth rails.

[2] It has been said, however, that the Pennsylvania Railroad adopted this practice as early as 1885 (*Hearings before Stanley Committee*, I, 308. *Cf.* SEAGER and GULICK, *op. cit.*, 255).

[3] Reductions during the year were also said to be discouraged by the practice of granting rebates on all purchases under a contract if the price was reduced during its currency. (See p. 201.)

[4] U.S. v. U.S. Steel Corp., *Brief for U.S. Steel Corp.*, 210.

[5] *ibid.*, 211. The average price of pig iron during the period 1901 to 1910 was said to be $4.29 per ton above its level in the immediately preceding years, while the average price of steel rails rose only $2.40 a ton.

[6] *loc. cit.* It has been pointed out that in 1899, just after the reformation of the rail pool, and before the corporation was formed, the price of steel rails had been $35 a ton, whereas the price maintained for ten years had been $28 a ton. It was said that in 1902, 1905, and 1906–1907 prices could have been raised without exciting any comment. (MEADE, "The Price Policy of the United States Steel Corporation," *Quart. Jour. Econ.*, 22: 454 (1908).).

the railroads were demanding in increasing proportions.[1] Whatever the validity of this explanation of price stability during the earlier period, it does not apply to the period since 1921, when the quotations were for open hearth rails.

The stability of the price of rails attracted public attention again in April, 1931: it was suggested that railroads failed to press for changes in the price of steel rails partly for fear of a rerouting of the freight traffic of the steel companies; for the same reason they feared to import rails from abroad. Steel companies, on the other hand, presumably avoided price cutting because, in view of the small number of producers, any price cut would inevitably be accepted by rivals and would fail to bring much additional business to the price cutter.[2] The president of the United States Steel Corporation[3] claimed that the price of rails was attributable to increases in the cost of production; the price could not be excessive when the price per pound was no more than the cost of two Connecticut cigars of his favorite brand; the price of rails should be $49 a ton instead of $43. The maintenance of the price of steel rails was regarded in other quarters, however, as "a striking example of a kind of trade restraint that constitutes an important obstacle to business recovery. The pegging of prices at artificially high levels exercised an important influence in causing the depression and the maintenance of such a pegged price is a barrier against the return of prosperity."[4] Meager reductions followed[5] but without much effect upon the volume of business. In 1933, however, the federal government sought to provide employment in the steel and railroad industries by making part of the funds voted for public works available for the purchase of 700,000 tons of rails.[6] The railroads were not prepared to pay $40 per ton for rails nor was the Transport Coordinator prepared to authorize loans for purchases at that rate. In pressing for competitive bidding and a lower price, he remarked upon the great stability in the price

[1] *Brief for U.S. Steel Corp.*, 214.
[2] RIPLEY, *Letter to New York Times*, Apr. 5, 1931.
[3] Speech at a meeting of the American Iron and Steel Institute, *cit. New York Times*, May 23, 1931.
[4] *Cleveland Trust Bulletin*, Mar. 15, 1931.
[5] To $41.80 in October, 1932, and $40 per ton in November, 1932.
[6] The funds were to be lent at a low rate of interest to the railroads which, however, were not anxious to increase their obligations at a time when their revenue was poor and their general financial condition unsatisfactory. Some railroads, moreover, had made purchases in 1930, also in response to a presidential exhortation, and, traffic having been very light, these rails were still in good condition.

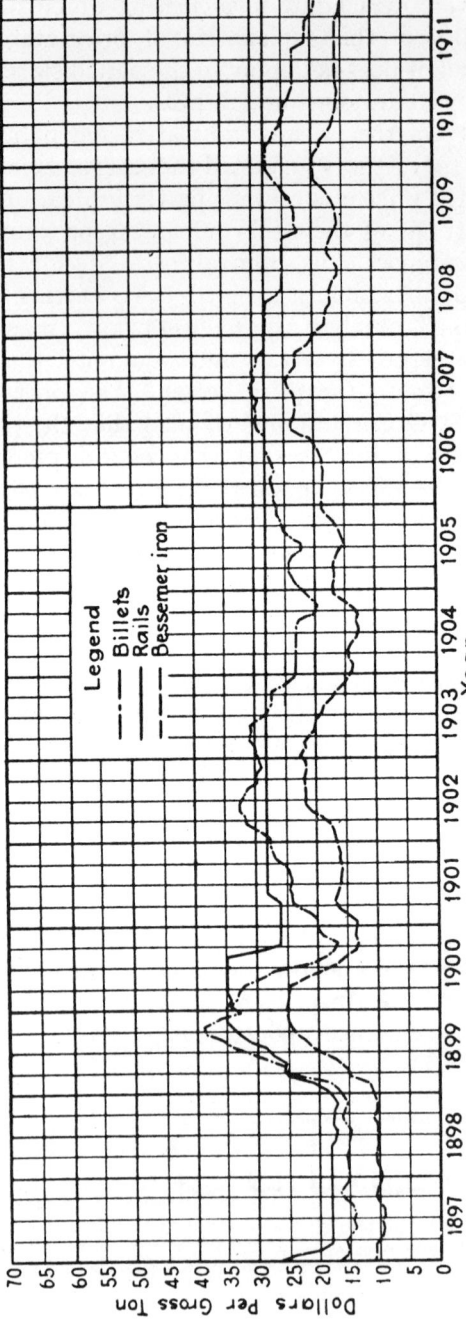

FIG. 15.—Average monthly prices of bessemer pig iron, and bessemer billets at Pittsburgh, and heavy bessemer rails at mills in Pennsylvania, 1897 to 1911. (Redrawn from U.S. v. U.S. Steel Corporation. Government Exhibit "Walker 245.")

of rails in the past, the uniformity in the prices of all sellers, and the fact that since 1926 an international agreement between manufacturers had prevented the importation of rails although the price of rails in other countries had declined with the price of other steel products. Railroads had changed their specifications for steel rails since 1922, but these changes had not materially increased costs and had been offset by improvements in methods of iron and steel production. He also remarked that while the code of fair competition recently adopted (under the National Industrial Recovery Act) had increased the labor costs of steel producers, these costs were not higher than those prevailing prior to the depression, and the large orders offered could be executed under favorable conditions, particularly as the number of types of rail required was being reduced. In consequence "the available information warrants a conclusion that the base prices to be submitted should be below rather than above $35 per ton"; he suggested that the best method of refuting this claim would be to give government agents access to the cost records of the companies. The companies displayed no haste either to justify their prices[1] or to reduce them. After much hesitation the companies cut the price to $37.75 per ton, not, however, by competitive bids but by the simultaneous filing of the revised price by all the manufacturers with the American Iron and Steel Institute.[2]

The market for steel rails is obviously very far from competitive: in the presence of only five or six sellers and of extremely high overhead costs of production and a very inelastic demand, price competition cannot be expected.[3] Stability has been secured in the face of wide fluctuations in the price of pig iron, which equaled or even exceeded the price of rails on more than one occasion between 1901 and 1907 and again in 1917.[4] The Attorney

---

[1] The vice president and general manager of sales for the Carnegie Steel Company (a subsidiary of the United States Steel Corporation) thought that the existing price was "right." He pointed out that the price of steel rails should not be compared with the price of other steel products without allowing for the fact that quotations for rails were for a ton of 2,240 pounds while a ton of 2,000 pounds was used for all other products. The price of rails adjusted to the unit used for other steel products was $35.70 a ton while merchant bars of a similar grade sold for $45 per ton. He also emphasized the increasing cost of coal. (*New York Times*, Sept. 26 and 27, Oct. 5 and 16, 1933.)

[2] *ibid.*, Oct. 22, 1933.

[3] While the Transportation Coordinator appealed for competitive bidding he at the same time announced that the firm making the lowest bid would *not* thereby secure the business; it would simply set the price for all.

[4] During 1917 when the price of steel rails was maintained at $38 per ton the price of pig iron was on some occasions $20 a ton above the price of rails (BERGLUND,

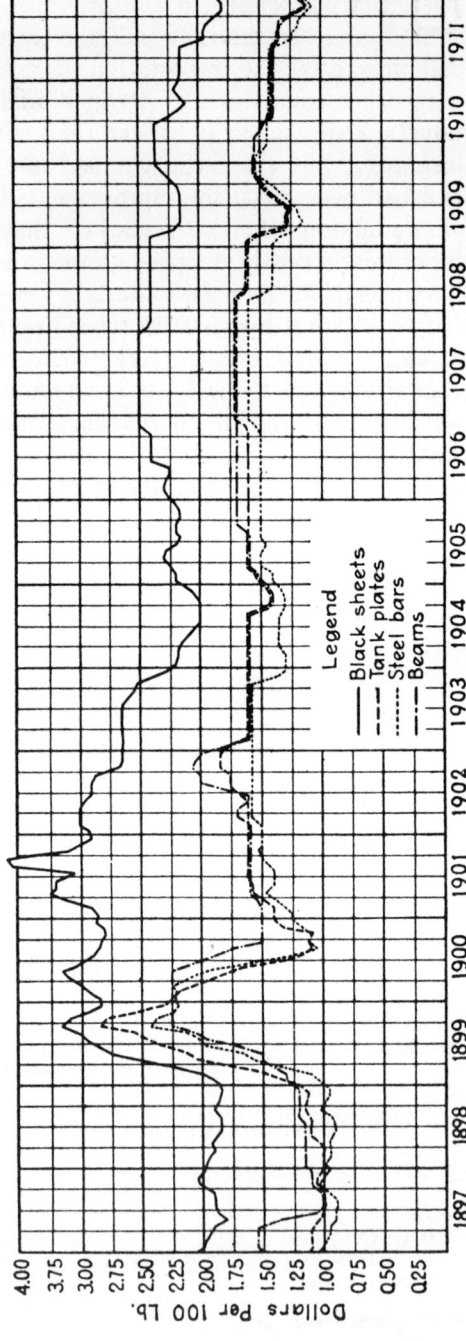

FIG. 16.—Average monthly prices of steel beams, plates, bars, and sheets at Pittsburgh, 1897 to 1911. (Redrawn from U.S. v. U.S. Steel Corporation. Government Exhibit "Walker 246.")

General contended, however, that, at the price of $28 a ton that prevailed for so long, the corporation made a profit of $13 a ton,[1] although the basis of the calculation was not disclosed. The policy of price stability may have been chosen because of the difficulty of agreeing upon changes; it is doubtless also partly due to the importance of the reciprocal relations between the railroads and the steel manufacturers.

The prices of other steel products have never attained a stability comparable with that in the steel rail market. Figures 15 and 16, however, indicate that prices have remained unchanged for considerable periods, and this tendency has been more pronounced since the formation of the United States Steel Corporation than it was before; it has been most evident in the course of the prices of sheets, tank plates, bars, beams, wire, and wire nails.[2] This stabilization of the price of steel products was often accomplished in the face of wide fluctuations in the price of raw materials. There were times when the price of wire nails was lower than the price of the wire rods out of which they were made, the price of skelp was higher than the price of pipe, and the price of galvanized sheets was lower than the price of spelter.[3] After the general disruption of prices owing to the war of 1914 to 1918 (*i.e.*, mainly after 1922), the prices of a number of steel products, *e.g.*, bars, billets, tank plates, and rails, again showed periods of unchanging price for considerable periods (*cf.* Fig. 17). The price of iron ore remained unchanged from 1925 to 1928[4] and again from 1929 until the end of 1933.[5]

"The United States Steel Corporation and Price Stabilization," *Quart. Jour. Econ.*, 38: 24). Cf. Fig. 17.

[1] U.S. v. U.S. Steel Corp., *Brief for U.S.*, I, 174, 181.

[2] The Attorney General claimed that the price of beams had fluctuated remarkably little since the formation of the United States Steel Corporation (U.S. v. U.S. Steel Corporation, *Brief for U.S.*, I, 181). The price of tin plate, which fluctuated monthly before the formation of the American Tin Plate Company (at the end of 1898), also showed little fluctuation between 1898 and 1911. A similar change in the behavior of the price of plain wire followed upon the formation of the wire combination, the price of wire having remained uniform for many months at a time (*ibid.*, I, 185). The price of sheets changed much less frequently after the formation of the corporation, although in the years 1897, 1898, and 1899 the price had changed every month (*ibid.*, I, 186). While the price of wire nails had risen to $70 in 1899, it had remained between $40 and $38 a ton during the period from 1900–1907 (MEADE, "Price Policy of the United States Steel Corporation," *Quart. Jour. Econ.*, 22: 455 (1908)). The price of plates showed a similar lack of change for periods of a number of months between 1902 and 1909.

[3] BERGLUND, "The United States Steel Corporation and Price Stabilization," *Quart. Jour. Econ.*, 38: 23, 24 (1923).

[4] READ, T. T., "Valorization in the Metal Industry," *Polit. Sci. Quart.*, 47: 238 (1932). The integration of iron ore and steel production renders the price of iron ore relatively unimportant however.

[5] CONSUMER ADVISORY BOARD, *Brief on Steel Complaints*.

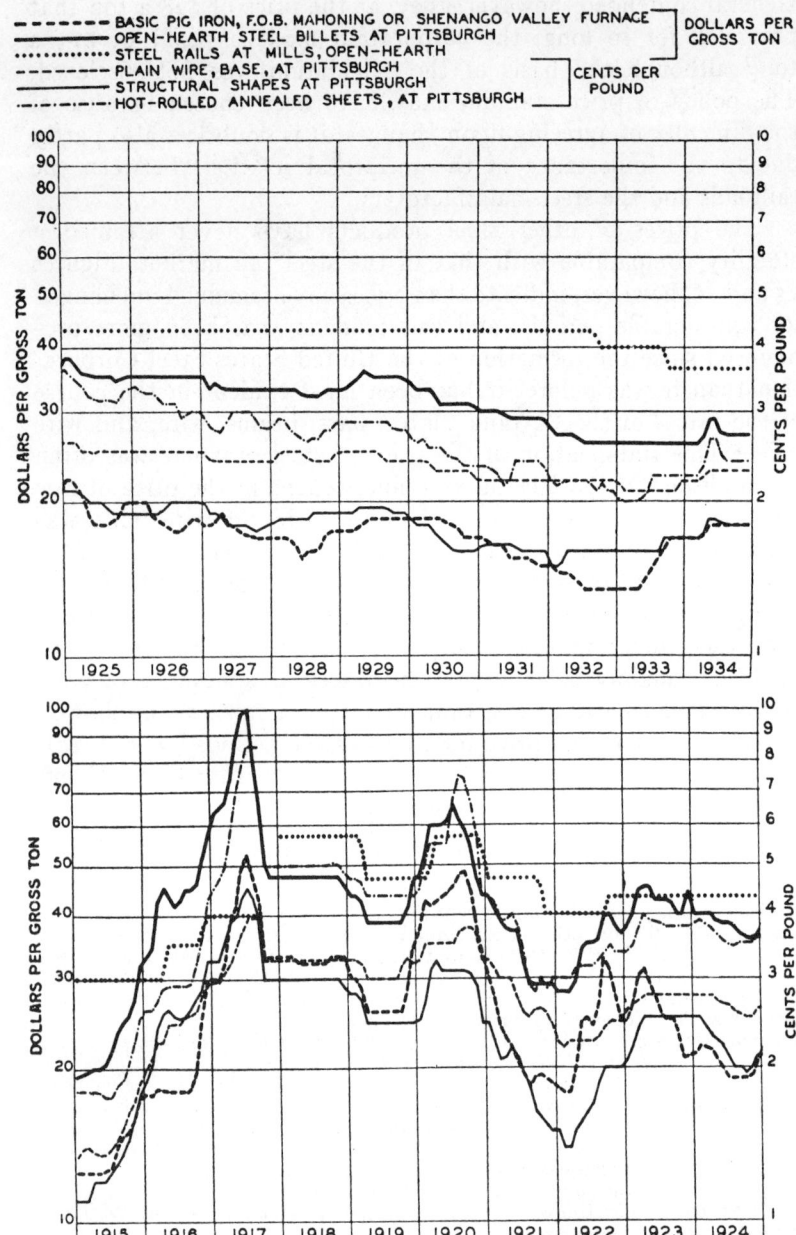

FIG. 17.—Monthly prices of pig iron, steel, and steel products at Pittsburgh, 1915 to 1934. (*Drawn from statistics in Iron Age.*)

THE STABILIZATION OF INDIVIDUAL PRICES   213

The general policy of the United States Steel Corporation has been to avoid very great increases in price during periods of increased demand for steel products and to oppose reductions during periods of decreased demand and in this way to stabilize prices. This point of view has frequently been expressed. At the meeting of representatives of the steel industry in 1907 it was said that as prices had not been advanced in the recent prosperity they should not then be reduced, that "stability of prices is the greatest consideration from the standpoint of the personal interests of the producer and that buyers generally cordially approve it when they have the assurance that others do not have advantages over them."[1] Similar views were expressed at a second conference in 1908.[2] Figures 16 and 17 suggest that in 1907 attempts were being made to maintain prices on the level to which they had been raised since 1904 and that the effort was in general unsuccessful: the price of billets fell even during 1907 and during the succeeding four years never regained the level it had attained in 1907; while the prices of sheets, bars, plates, and beams were maintained throughout 1907, they declined in the subsequent years; the price of wire and wire nails was even raised during 1907 but was also subsequently reduced to a lower level. The corporation agreed in the course of the proceedings against it under the Sherman Act that its policy of keeping prices down in good times and maintaining them in bad times was in sharp contrast with that of its predecessors and was partly responsible for the diminished fluctuations in the price of its principal products since its formation. It contended, however, that the use of the "asking prices" quoted in the trade journals, gave an impression of greater stability than had in fact occurred;[3] these figures took no account of the rebates and allowances which were commonly made from the quoted prices.[4] During the decline in general

---

[1] Meeting on Nov. 21, 1907 (F.T.C., *Statement on Pittsburgh Plus*, 401).
[2] "While no agreements for the maintenance of prices were made or suggested, it was the expressed belief of all that maintenance would result in benefit to the manufacturers, to their customers, to the employees, and to business interests generally; that stability of prices if and when reasonable is desirable; that violent fluctuations resulting in abnormally high prices when the demand exceeds the supply and in unreasonably low prices when the reverse is true are to be deplored. . . . It was also remarked that the present disposition to assist one another by the free interchange of views rather than resort to unreasonable and destructive competition which would ultimately result in the application of the law of the survival of the fittest is in accordance with the present state of public sentiment." (*Iron Age*, Feb. 6, 1908; cit. F.T.C., *Statement on Pittsburgh Plus*, 403.)
[3] U.S. v. U.S. Steel Corp., *Brief for U.S. Steel Corp.*, 140.
[4] The average price of beams in 1906 received by the United States Steel Cor-

business which began in 1920 the price of steel products fell, although less than the index of the prices of manufactured goods. The index of the price of iron and steel products fell by only 2.2 per cent between June and October, 1920, while the index of the price of manufactured goods fell 7.8 per cent; by June, 1921, however, the former index had fallen 30 per cent while the latter had fallen 35 per cent.[1]

Figure 18 indicates that during the depression which began in 1929 the prices of the principal products were maintained until about the middle of 1930, after which they fell, although considerably less than the average of wholesale prices.[2] Thus prices were not stabilized, and yet output declined until only 12 per cent of the blast furnace capacity of the country was in use in August, 1932. Indeed the power of the United States Steel Corporation to stabilize prices appears to have been less than formerly. There were many complaints of secret rebates in 1931[3] and efforts to maintain prices.[4] Finally Robert P. Lamont

---

poration had been $36.36, whereas the charts based on published prices showed an unvarying price in 1906–1907 of $38.08 per ton (*Brief for U.S. Steel Corp.*, 335).

[1] *Steel* and *Standard Statistics Base Book*, 1931. The prices of some steel products fell more than the general index of manufactured goods. Between June and December, 1920, the latter fell 19 per cent while the price of billets fell 30 per cent and that of shapes and plates, 24 per cent; the price of wire nails remained unchanged.

[2] Between June, 1929, and February, 1933, the following percentage declines in wholesale prices occurred (U.S. BUREAU OF LABOR STATISTICS, *The Trends of Wholesale Prices, June, 1929, to 1933* (mimeographed)):

	Per cent		Per cent
All commodities	37.2	Tie plate steel	18.6
Metals and metal products	23.5	Tin plate	20.6
Iron and steel	19.1	Reinforcing bars	22.0
Bar iron, Pittsburgh	0.0	Billets	26.2
Bar iron, Philadelphia	4.0	Bars sheet steel	26.8
Pipe, galvanized	5.2	Pig iron	27.0
Pipe, black steel	6.9	Sheets steel	28.5
Steel rails	7.0	Barbed wire	29.0
Terne plate	15.2	Sheets, galvanized	29.7
Wire, plain annealed	16.7	Nails, wire, 8 penny	30.0
Wire, galvanized	17.4	Strips, cold rolled	35.7
Steel merchant bars	17.9	Auto body sheets	39.0
Structural steel	18.0		

The price of iron ore remained completely unchanged from the beginning of 1929 to the end of 1934 (*New York Times*, Apr. 22, 1935). Little ore is, however, sold in the open market.

[3] *Cf.* J. A. Farrell of the United States Steel Corporation at a meeting of the American Iron and Steel Institute, cit. *New York Times*, May 23, 1931.

[4] In December, 1931, the leading producers were "as strongly committed to price maintenance as formerly. In the three heavy rolled products, bars, shapes, and plates, representing in 1930 38 per cent of the total production of the steel industry, the Pittsburgh mills are insisting on the long prevalent price of 1.60 cents a pound in the matter of first quarter contracts. . . . Wire products are being held at prices representing an advance of $3.00 a ton over the minimum price of this year." (*New York Times*, Dec. 28, 1931.) "With price structures weakened by the practice of granting concessions to get volume in the early months of 1932 the industry sought

resigned his Secretaryship of the Department of Commerce to become active president of the American Iron and Steel Institute and bring about "closer cooperation among the various producing units of what has been one of the most highly competitive indus-

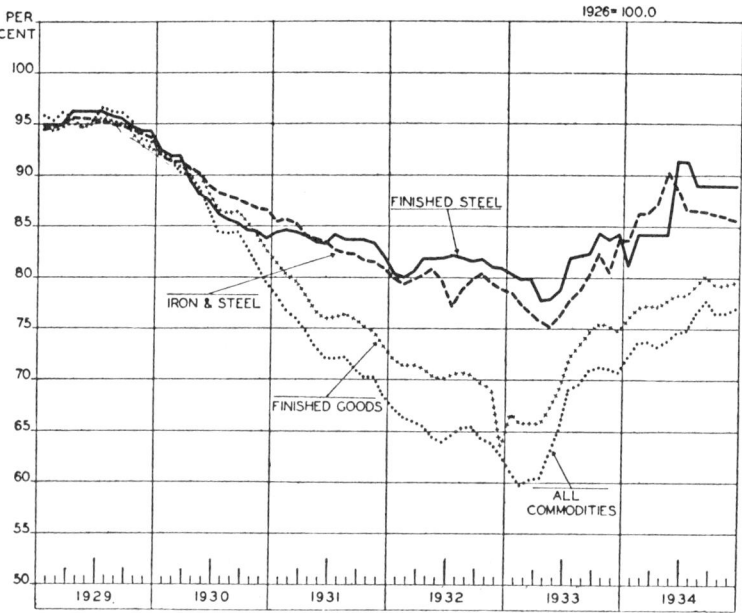

FIG. 18.—Monthly prices of iron and steel, steel products, finished goods and an index of wholesale prices, 1929 to 1934. (*Drawn from data in U.S. Bureau of Labor Statistics: Wholesale Prices.*)

tries in the country. Mr. Lamont will in effect become dictator in the industry."[1] Those in the industry regarded this appointment as part of a move "to eliminate the price cutting rebates and bitter competition which have long caused dissension among the steel producers," and it was expected that Mr. Lamont

---

aggressive measures to correct this situation through price stabilization. While such a campaign usually takes the form of 'pegging' a declining market or stimulating an advance in prices, in the case of the steel industry the primary objective has been the elimination of destructive concessions. So far price stabilization has been a failure in that it has not revived buying confidence to the extent where increasing orders have poured in from manufacturers abandoning hope of concessions. In the view of most steel men, stabilization is impracticable without full collaboration of the steel makers" (*loc. cit.*).

[1] *ibid.*, Aug. 5, 1932. "Important steel executives expressed distaste for that term" (*ibid.*). The institute did not seek agreements to partition markets or fix prices; it desired to "seek stabilization of the industry in as forceful a manner as possible and endeavor to stamp out trade practices that destroy profits, disorganize trade, and create bitter competition under perilous circumstances."

would "recommend steps to control overproduction and to develop the export market, and urge detailed studies of the tariff rates. He may perhaps propose the absorption of some of the other steel associations into the larger and more powerful organization."[1] The code of fair competition under the National Industrial Recovery Act gave the industry in 1933 the powers it was seeking.

The desire for stability of prices is clear. Some measure of stability has been attained. The statements of the steel producers indicate fairly clearly the origin of their desire for stable prices. The demand for their products is subject to wide cyclical fluctuations; they are anxious above all to avoid price cutting in times of diminished demand because of their heavy overhead costs and their (doubtless well-founded) belief that in any given condition of business the demand for steel products cannot be greatly stimulated by price reductions. They also appear to pin some faith to the belief that if they maintain their prices buyers can be discouraged from holding off the market in the hope of further reductions.[2] The policy of stable prices springs, therefore, from a dual source, the hope of eliminating price cutting from a situation in which it may be very costly, and the hope of mitigating the cyclical fluctuations in demand which lead to undue price competition. The extent to which this latter hope is justified will be discussed below.[3]

b. The Anthracite Industry. Prices have attained considerable stability in the anthracite industry, as will be seen from Fig. 19. This stability applies, however, to the domestic and not to the smaller (steam) sizes of coal.[4] Allowance must, moreover, be made for the regular seasonal fluctuations in the price of anthracite for domestic use; the price is reduced in the summer months with the object of reducing seasonal fluctuations in demand. Prices remained stable after the strike of 1902 until 1912; after 1923 seasonal discounts reappeared, the price tending upward, and after 1926 the seasonal discounts became less regular but prices followed a horizontal trend.[5] Between June, 1929, and

---

[1] *ibid.*, Aug. 6, 1932.
[2] It has been argued that this policy has enabled steel purchasers to plan for the future in the light of fair certainty as to the policy of the United States Steel Corporation and to protect themselves from surprises in its policy (MEADE, "The Price Policy of the United States Steel Corporation," *Quart. Jour. Econ.*, 22: 455).
[3] See footnote, p. 245.
[4] Steam coal is sold in competition with bituminous coal; it is also sold on contracts running from year to year (U.S. v. Reading Co. (1911), *Brief for U.S.*, 119).
[5] The Federal Trade Commission noted in 1925 that the prices announced by the

February, 1933, however, the price of chestnut sizes fell 3.2 per cent and egg sizes, 5.1 per cent.[1] Here, too, therefore, leadership has resulted in considerable stability modified by a conventional seasonal variation.

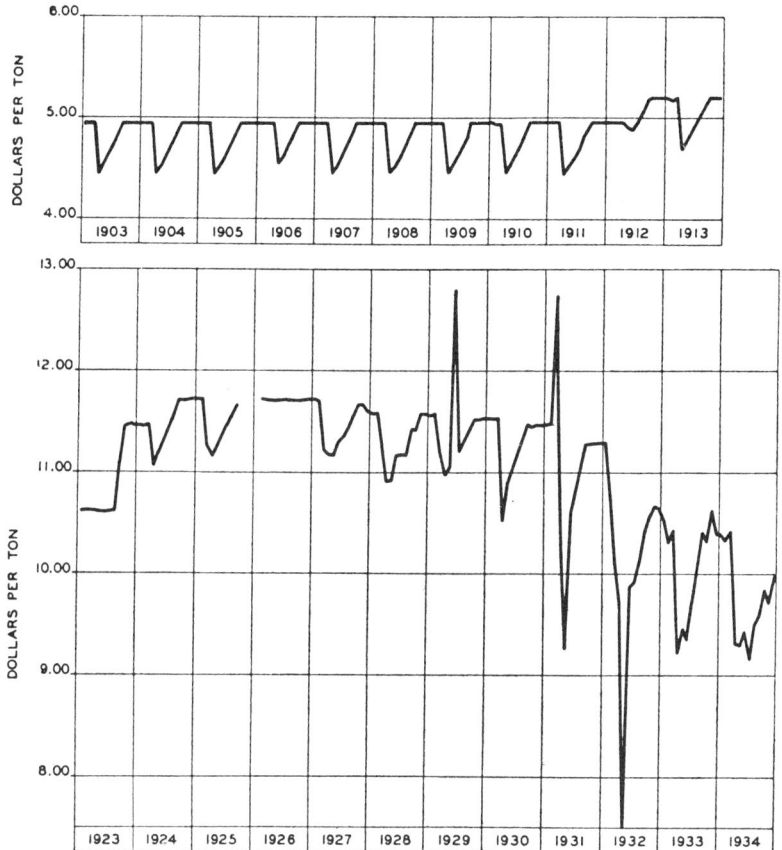

FIG. 19.—The price of stove sizes of anthracite 1903 to 1913, and 1923 to 1934. (*Drawn from U.S. Bureau of Labor Statistics: Wholesale Prices.*)

c. *The Agricultural Implements Industry.* The practice, already noted, of announcing prices for the whole season has resulted in seasonal stability of the prices of agricultural implements; stability

---

railroad companies remained in force for some time and did not fluctuate with demand, except for the regular seasonal variations (*Premium Prices of Anthracite,* 1925, 4). The prices of the larger independent companies appear also to have been stable (*Mineral Resources of the United States,* II, 453, 462).

[1] U.S. BUREAU OF LABOR STATISTICS, *The Trend of Wholesale Prices, June,* 1929. *to* 1933 (mimeographed).

has, however, been secured for even longer periods. The wholesale contract prices charged by the International Harvester Company for 6 foot and 7 foot binders and for 5 foot regular and 5 foot vertical and 6 foot mowers and for corn binders remained unchanged for five years from 1903 and 1907 and for at least four years from 1908 to 1911.[1] Actual prices depart somewhat from these list prices, however, owing to the granting of concessions which vary from year to year.[2] The monthly prices of most implements as quoted by the Bureau of Labor Statistics show practically no changes from January, 1927, until the second half of 1931, when prices were reduced, although considerably less than the average of wholesale prices. Between June, 1929, and February, 1933, the average of all wholesale prices fell 37.2 per cent while the prices of agricultural implements in general fell 16.1 per cent; the prices of some important implements remained unchanged or changed very little.[3]

d. *The Petroleum Industry.* The prices of crude oil, gasoline and a number of oil products have remained unchanged for considerable periods as will be seen from Fig. 20. The quoted price of crude oil has remained unchanged for periods of some months: the quotations used are, however, often the posted or offer prices of large buyers and do not always represent the actual prices being paid.[4] The prices of fuel oil in particular and also gasoline and kerosene on the Pacific coast have been notably stable.[5] The price of medium grade automobile lubricating oil

---

[1] COMMISSIONER OF CORPORATIONS, *The International Harvester Company*, 254. For one implement the company required payment for attachments which had previously been supplied gratis. Statistics of average net prices for a number of implements are given at *ibid.*, 248, and show slight variations from year to year: these variations are, however, due to the granting of concessions from year to year in varying amount, to variations in the proportion of machines of various sizes sold, and to differences in the proportions sold in each region.

[2] *ibid.*, 248.

[3] The percentage decline in the prices of the separate implements during the period from June, 1929, to February, 1933, was:

	Per cent		Per cent
Grain drills	0.0	Threshers, grain	6.2
Corn planters	0.0	Rakes, side delivery	8.0
Tractors	0.0	Harrows	8.4–9.0
Rakes, self dumping	0.0	Tractors, 10/20 hp	11.4
Shellers, corn	0.0	Wagons, farm	11.4
Harvester threshers	2.6	Plows, one-horse	11.8
Cultivators	4.6	Manure spreaders	12.5
Hay mowers	5.2	Rakes, hand	14.1
Grain binders	6.1	Plows, two-horse	17.4
Hay loaders	6.5	Tractors, 15/30 hp	29.3

[4] F.T.C., *Report on Petroleum Industry*, 1920, 5.

[5] F.T.C., *Pacific Coast Petroleum Industry*, 1922, 48.

f.o.b. refinery on the Atlantic seaboard was at times remarkably stable; it remained unchanged between January, 1924, and

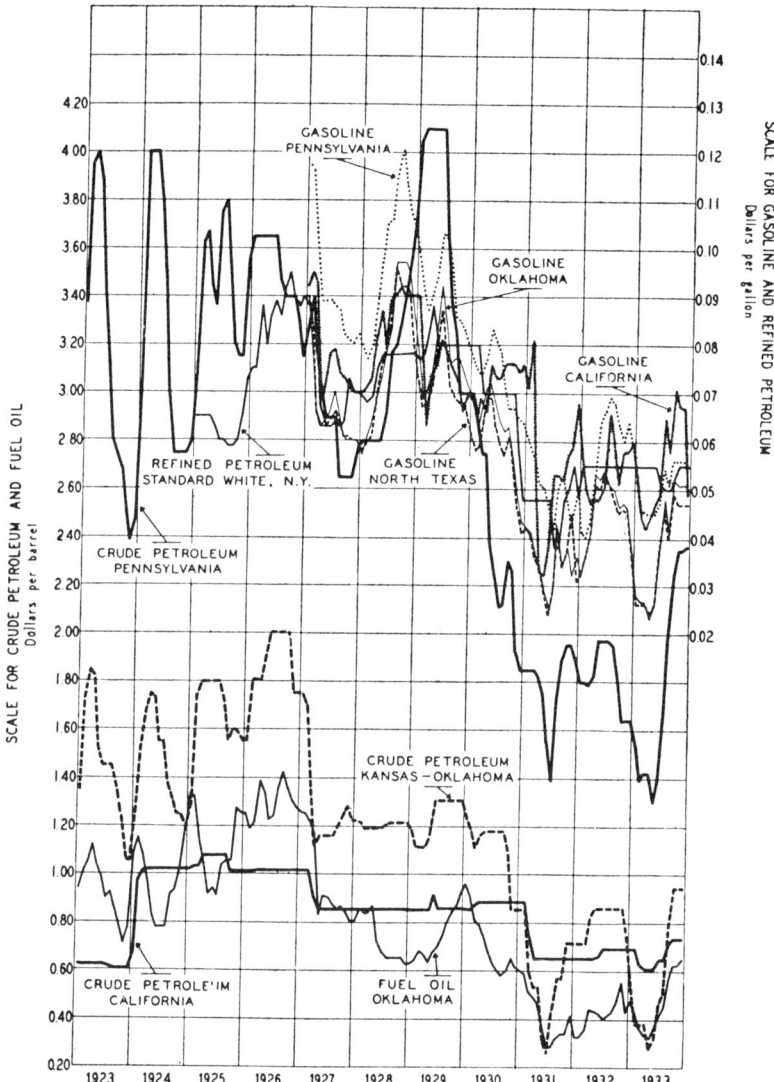

FIG. 20.—The price of crude petroleum and its products 1923 to 1933. (*Drawn from data in U.S. Bureau of Labor Statistics: Wholesale Prices.*)

March, 1925, and between May, 1925, and June, 1926: similar periods of unchanging price occurred on the Pacific coast and in the central western states.[1] During the period of the general decline in prices between June, 1929, and February, 1933, the prices of oil and oil products declined more than the index of wholesale prices, partly owing to increases in the supply of crude oil. The principal decreases were:

	Per cent		Per cent
Crude Oil:		Fuel Oil:	
California	24.2	Pennsylvania	31.7
Pennsylvania	66.1	Oklahoma	37.0
Kansas-Oklahoma	70.7	Kerosene:	
Gasoline:		Refined	36.1
California	44.9	Water White	31.2
Pennsylvania	54.8		
North Texas	70.5		
Oklahoma	72.2		

e. Other Industries. Newsprint as we have seen is commonly sold on contracts for considerable periods of time, not infrequently longer than one year; as these contracts usually provide for a fixed price throughout the period of the contract, prices tend to be stabilized for considerable periods.[2] Prices are also said to be guided by a leader with the results shown in Figs. 14 and 21. The announced price of the International Paper Company remained unchanged for the three years 1926 to 1928 although, in fact, allowances from the published price changed.[3] The average price of newsprint quoted by the U. S. Bureau of Labor Statistics remained unchanged for four years, from January, 1927, until January, 1931: the price was reduced in January, 1931,[4] January, 1932, and twice in the late months of 1932. Between June, 1929, and February, 1933, the price of newsprint declined 27.4 per cent while the index of wholesale prices fell 37.2 per cent and the price of wood pulp between 34 and 41 per cent.

[1] F.T.C., *Prices, Profits, and Competition in Petroleum*, 1928, 182. The Federal Trade Commission regarded the more frequent changes in the price of lubricating oil on the Gulf coast than in the other territories and the downward trend there compared with an upward trend elsewhere as an indication of keener competition (*loc. cit.*).
[2] F.T.C., *Newsprint Paper Industry*, 1917, 48.
[3] F.T.C., *Newsprint Paper Industry*, 1930, 32, 33.
[4] The announcement of reduced prices by the International Paper Company in May, 1931, established a schedule of prices and provided for the extension of contracts for a period of five and a half years, which announcement was regarded as establishing the maximum prices for newsprint for the whole of that period (*New York Herald Tribune*, May 11, 1931).

The Corn Products Refining Company is said to have led in making prices[1] in the corn products industry and there is some

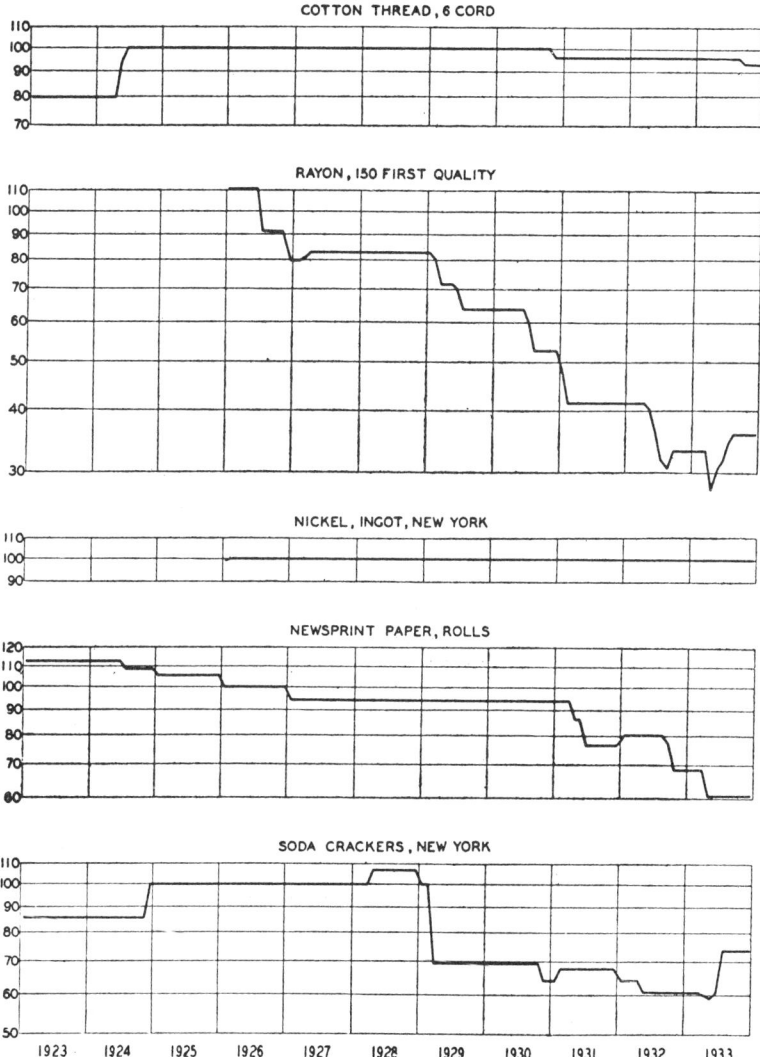

FIG. 21.—The prices of cotton thread, rayon, nickel, newsprint, and soda crackers 1923 to 1933. (*Drawn from data in U.S. Bureau of Labor Statistics: Wholesale Prices.*)

indication of success in stabilizing prices. The monthly price of cornstarch quoted by the U. S. Bureau of Labor Statistics remained

[1] There is also an active trade association in the industry which requires all reports to be made by telegraph (F.T.C., *Open Price Trade Associations*, 126).

unchanged at 7.3 cents per pound from July, 1923, until October, 1930. The price of laundry starch was similarly stable; the price of glucose, however, has been less stable although it has recently remained steady for at least a few months in each year. This stability is attained in the face of wide fluctuations in the price of corn: the price of corn fell between June, 1929, and February, 1933, about 74 per cent while the price of cornstarch fell 47.4 per cent and glucose 39.1 per cent; the average of wholesale prices fell 37.2 per cent.

Figure 22 suggests that the price of cement has remained unchanged for considerable periods. There has been notable stability in some cities. According to statistics offered to prove the competitiveness of the industry, the price of cement in New York remained unchanged for 24 consecutive months, beginning in January, 1913, 11 months beginning in December, 1915, 9 months beginning in April, 1917, and 13 months beginning in April, 1919;[1] it was admitted that cement prices changed only infrequently.[2] More recent investigation of the industry has shown that the basing-point system has been accompanied by considerable periods of practically unchanging prices. In Washington, Wilmington, and New York City there had been only one change in 1927; during 32 months between 1927 and 1929 only two changes were made in Chicago and Minneapolis, four in Cleveland and Indianapolis, and three in St. Louis and Madison; in Birmingham, Alabama, there had been only three changes in 24 months.[3] Prices remained unchanged at basing points in the Lehigh Valley between January, 1927, and November, 1930 (except during the period August to November, 1929) and in the Hudson Valley there was similar stability except during the period from November, 1929, to November, 1930, when they were 10 cents higher than they had been prior to August, 1929. At Buffington, Indiana, they had also been stable except that during the last year of the period the price was 10 cents lower than prior to August, 1929. These forms of statement magnify the stability of prices but the duration of periods of unchanging price is nevertheless striking. The Federal Trade Commission concluded that delivered prices of cement in the 21 cities studied appeared to change less frequently than would be expected for

[1] WILLIS and BYERS, *Portland Cement Prices*, 39.
[2] *ibid.*, 4.
[3] F.T.C., *Price Bases Inquiry*, 81. *Cf.* also FRASER and DORIOT, *Analyzing Our Industries*, 295.

THE STABILIZATION OF INDIVIDUAL PRICES 223

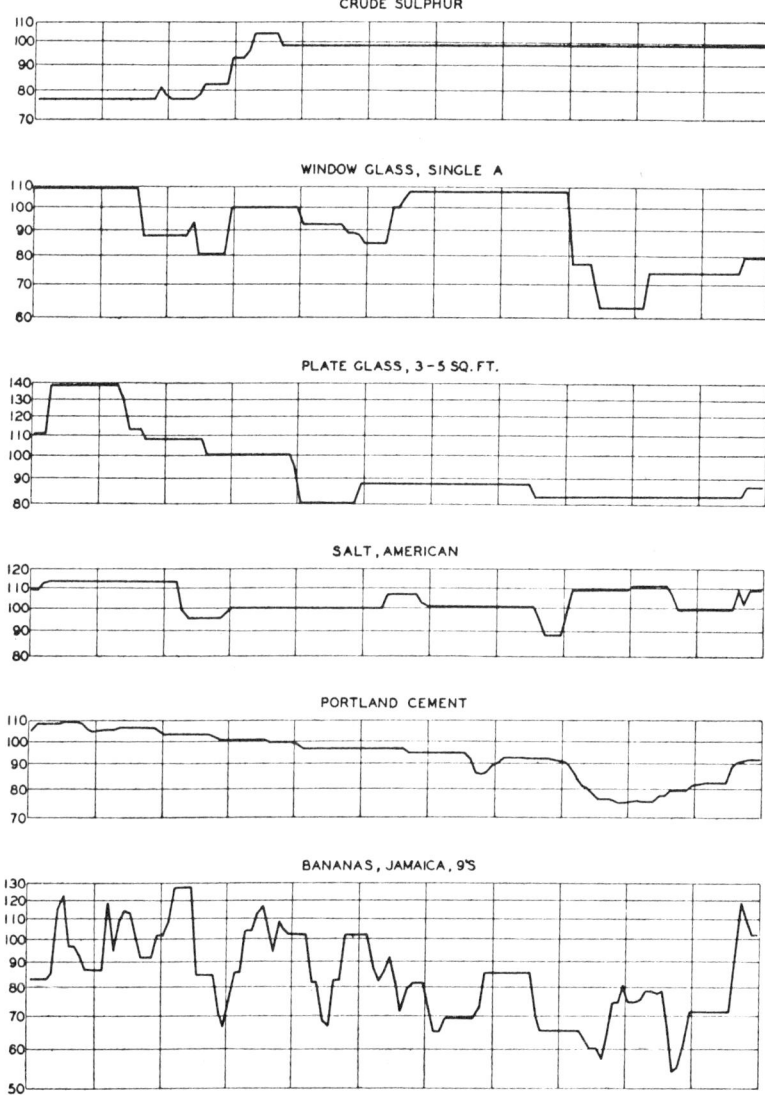

Fig. 22.—The prices of sulphur, glass, salt, cement, and bananas, 1923 to 1933. (*Drawn from data in U.S. Bureau of Labor Statistics: Wholesale Prices.*)

a commodity the demand for which is sensitive to changing industrial conditions and which is supplied by a number of presumably independent producers. Moreover, between 1927 and 1930 the percentage of plant capacity in use was declining. Between June, 1929, and February, 1933, the price of cement reported by the U.S. Bureau of Labor Statistics fell 13.5 per cent.

The glass industry is one in which the distribution of business between firms is similar to that in the steel industry; the Pittsburgh Plate Glass Company (formed in 1895 by the consolidation of five firms) produced in 1895 at least 80 per cent of the total output of plate glass; but by 1913, in spite of considerable expansion of its capacity for production, the company produced only 47 per cent of the total output of plate glass, the remainder being produced by eleven companies. During the subsequent decade the company raised its percentage to about 50 per cent, at which point it appears to have been maintained. The great increase in building activity after 1920 induced heavy imports and the percentage of total sales made by the Pittsburgh Plate Glass Company appears to have fallen from about 48 per cent in 1920 to 39 per cent in 1923.[1] That prices have been stable for considerable periods is indicated by Fig. 22. The wholesale price of plate glass of sizes from 5 to 10 square feet published by the Bureau of Labor Statistics remained unchanged from December, 1927, to June, 1930, and from January, 1931, until at least August, 1933. The wholesale price of plate glass fell only 5.2 per cent during the period from June, 1929, to February, 1933.

In the window glass industry the American Window Glass Company (formed in 1899, when it controlled about 85 per cent of the productive capacity of the industry) made abortive attempts to drive out rivals; by 1918 it was apparently pursuing a policy of "live and let live . . . not only in production but in prices,"[2] with the result that production appears to have been curtailed at times far below the productive capacity of the industry.[3] Figure 22 indicates that the wholesale price of grade A window glass published by the Bureau of Labor Statistics has remained

---

[1] Calculated from approximate figures quoted by WATKINS, *op. cit.*, 166. Professor Watkins contends that as the period 1920 to 1923 was abnormal there is no evidence that the Pittsburgh Company is "slipping" further.
[2] U.S. TARIFF COMMISSION, *The Glass Industry*, 1918, 74–83. Cit. WATKINS, *op. cit.*, 157.
[3] WATKINS, *op. cit.*, 160, 163.

unchanged for considerable periods. During the decline in general prices from June, 1929, to February, 1933, however, the price of grade A window glass fell 31.5 per cent.

Leadership in the can manufacturing industry has also been accompanied by considerable stability of prices.[1]

The National Biscuit Company, which produces about half the crackers in the country, is said to be accepted as a leader in the setting of prices.[2] Figure 21 indicates that the wholesale price of crackers published by the Bureau of Labor Statistics remained unchanged, e.g., from September, 1921, to November, 1924, December, 1924, to March, 1928, and that changes have been infrequent. During the period from June, 1929, to February, 1933, the wholesale price of sweet crackers fell only 3.3 per cent and that of soda crackers 12.8 per cent, while the price of flour fell between 36 per cent and 46 per cent.

4. DUOPOLY AND MONOPOLY

There is a number of industries in which neither leadership nor the existence of a trade association can be definitely pointed to as a means of controlling prices but where the smallness of the number of firms, or the overwhelming proportion of the total business being in the hands of one of them, is accompanied by price stability.

The partition of the former American Tobacco Company by the Supreme Court placed the greater part of the tobacco products industry in the hands of three or four large firms. There is little evidence of price leadership and positive evidence of the absence of any successful sharing of the market.[3] The American

---

[1] N.R.A., *Charts on the Operation of the National Industrial Recovery Act*, 12.
[2] National Biscuit Co. v. F.T.C., 299 Fed. 735 (1924).
[3] "The four companies formed by the decree to which most of the domestic cigarette business was passed have developed among themselves a considerable degree of competition, in so far as the existence of competition is proved by changes in the distribution of control over the country's output" (COX, *Competition in the American Tobacco Industry*, 71). The American Tobacco Company produced 36 per cent of the national output of cigarettes in 1912, but its proportion dropped to 20 per cent in 1921, after which it appears to have regained its former position as the largest manufacturer of cigarettes in the country (*ibid.*, 69); its proportion of the total output of cigarettes since 1926 has been estimated as follows:

Year	Share (per cent)
1926	20.14
1927	22.44
1928	29.59
1929	34.16
1930	38.10

The R. J. Reynolds Tobacco Company produced 0.2 per cent of the country's cigarettes in 1913 (COMMISSIONER OF CORPORATIONS, *The Tobacco Industry*, 1915, III,

Tobacco Company, which set out with the largest percentage of the sales of cigarettes, had by 1926 suffered a severe decline, but by 1930 had recovered its former position. Lorillard, the next

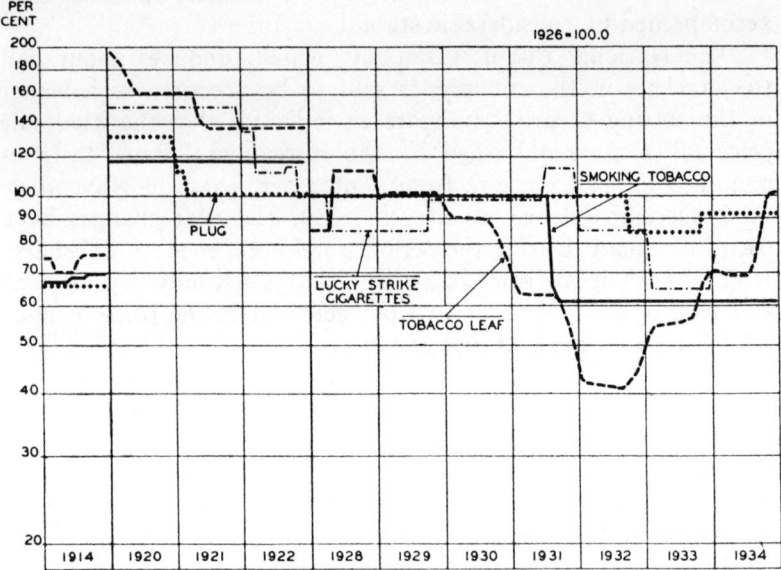

FIG. 23.—The price of tobacco leaf and tobacco products, 1914, 1920 to 1922, and 1929 to 1934. (*Drawn from data in U.S. Bureau of Labor Statistics: Wholesale Prices.*)

largest firm at the partition, had declined to the position of least relative importance by 1928. Liggett and Myers, which set out with one third of the total output in 1912, produced only one sixth in 1922 but by 1930 it was again producing about one third, while the firm with no output at all at the time of the partition

---

2) but its "Camel" brand proved popular, and by 1924 its production was reported (SEAGER GULICK, *op. cit.*, 181) to be about 50 per cent, in 1928 about 35 per cent, and in 1930 about 29 per cent of the country's total output of cigarettes (COX, *op. cit.*, 67–71). The share of the business held by Liggett and Myers is estimated (*ibid.*, 70) to have changed as follows:

Year	Share (per cent)
1912	37
1913	34
1922	15 ("Chesterfield" alone)
1927	29
1930	24.2

The P. Lorillard Company, which was awarded brands accounting for 18 per cent of the total sales in 1912 and 22 per cent in 1913, suffered severely from the decline in the popularity of Turkish cigarettes; the introduction of its "Old Gold" cigarette has failed to restore its former position, its share of total sales in 1928 being estimated at less than 11 per cent (*ibid.*, 71).

had acquired one half of the total business by 1924 but by 1930 was producing less than one third of the total.¹ These fluctuations in the distribution of business have not been due, however, to price competition; Fig. 23 reveals long periods of unchanging price for tobacco products. Plug tobacco remained unchanged in price from September, 1921, to December, 1923, and from February, 1924, until September, 1932. Smoking tobacco remained unchanged in price from January, 1920, until January, 1924, and from February, 1924, until July, 1931. The price of the four popular brands of cigarettes ("Camel," "Chesterfield," "Old Gold," and "Lucky Strike") has also remained constant for long periods, for example, throughout 1920 and 1921, from November, 1922, to April, 1928; thereafter it was changed in October, 1929, June, 1931, January, 1932, February, 1933, and January, 1934. In 1931 the wholesale price of smoking tobacco was reduced by 16 per cent but that of cigarettes increased. This latter increase was regarded, even in Wall Street, as ill-timed and unexplained;² a reduction in price was regarded as more reasonable, a view in which the Federal Farm Board concurred.³ Leaf prices had been falling for nearly three years and demand was stationary, if not actually declining; the price of a number of tobacco products had been notably stable between 1923–1928 when leaf prices were changing considerably. When the price of the four well-known brands of blended cigarettes was reduced in January, 1932, it fell only to the level ruling until 1929.

The prices of tobacco products do not, however, move in any simple and constant relation with the prices of leaf tobacco. The price of leaf fluctuates more than the price of products. The price of leaf has fallen more during the depressions that began in 1921 and 1929 than have the prices of the principal manufactured products[4] but leaf prices also rise more quickly with a rising general level of prices than the price of tobacco products;[5] tobacco product prices follow increases in the price of leaf more quickly than decreases.[6] One of the principal explana-

[1] Little is known concerning changes in the distribution of the business in other tobacco products.
[2] BARNEY AND COMPANY, *Tobacco Industry*, 1931.
[3] FEDERAL FARM BOARD, *Annual Report*, 1930, 15.
[4] Cox, *Competition in the American Tobacco Industry*, Chap. VIII.
[5] *ibid.*, 195.
[6] *ibid.*, 198. The average warehouse price of leaf in Kentucky began to rise in 1916 and by 1919 its price was represented by a relative of 260 as compared with a relative of 82 in 1915 (base year 1926). During the same period the relative for dark red burley at Louisville rose from 61.4 to 162.8. During these periods, however, the

tions of the failure of cigarette prices to decline concurrently with the decline in leaf prices is that leaf is purchased by manufacturers two or three years prior to its utilization in manufactured products. When the price of leaf falls, therefore, cigarettes and other manufactured products must continue to be made from leaf purchased at the prices of two or three years earlier. New competitors being unable to take advantage of the current leaf prices to manufacture at lower costs than the producers already in business, a reduction in leaf prices cannot be expected to cause immediate reduction in the prices of products. On the other hand, during a fall in general prices pressure to reduce the price of products would be expected to come mainly, and in this industry first, from a decline in the power of purchasers to buy the product. During the period between 1918 and 1930 or 1931 this influence was, however, partly offset by a general extension of the demand, particularly for cigarettes. Presumably these two factors would, even in a fully competitive industry, have prevented a decline in product prices simultaneously with a decline in leaf prices.

The fact that increases in leaf prices have been more speedily reflected in the price of products than reductions is again partly due to a steady upward trend in the demand for the product. The increase in price in 1931 is, however, beyond explanation, and the stability in the prices of products over long periods of time in the face of considerable changes in the price of the principal raw material doubtless indicates that the few important producers in the industry are unwilling to resort to price competition. But even here, it is to be remembered that the price of leaf tobacco is not a large part of the price of the finished product.[1]

---

price of manufactured plug tobacco rose from a relative of 58.2 in 1915 to 107.9 in 1919 and continued to rise during 1920. The price of smoking tobacco rose from a relative of 69.2 to 110.3 in 1919 and continued to rise in 1920. But whereas the price of tobacco leaf in Kentucky fell from 260.9 in 1919 to 139.1 in 1921 and that of burley from 144 to 130.2, the price of plug tobacco fell only from 107.9 to 102.5 after a rise in 1920, and that of smoking tobacco rose from 110.3 to 119.2. During the period 1922–1931, the average price of leaf at Kentucky sales fluctuated, falling from 170.6 in 1922 to 100 in 1926 and rising again to 197.4 in 1929, but the price of plug tobacco was approximately constant; the price of smoking tobacco remained approximately unchanged between 1924 and 1930 and the general course of cigarette prices after allowing for changes in taxation was about the same as that for smoking tobacco, although the increase from $6 to $6.40 a thousand in October, 1929, was attributed to an increase in the cost of leaf (*New York Times*, Oct. 6, 1929). The price of smoking tobacco declined in 1931 when that of cigarettes increased.

[1] In 1914 the cost of leaf to the successor companies to the American Tobacco Company was about 40 per cent of the net receipts from the sale of plug tobacco (after deduction of taxes); for smoking tobacco the percentage was 36, for snuff 26,

The stability of prices persisted during the depression which began in 1929; the Bureau of Labor Statistics reports that between June, 1929, and February, 1933, while the price of leaf fell 46.2 per cent the wholesale price of snuff remained unchanged, that of cigarettes fell 6.7 per cent, cigars 12.2 per cent, plug tobacco 15.5 per cent, and smoking tobacco 38.5 per cent.

The sewing thread industry was reported in 1927[1] to be in the hands of three large firms; 90 per cent of the production of household thread and handwork cottons, and between one half and two thirds of the total production of these types of thread, together with manufacturers' thread, was in the hands of these three firms; they held a "dominant position" in the field of household spool thread production and by their international affiliations influenced the amount of foreign importation. The price of thread apparently remained unchanged from 1890 to 1900, 1900 to 1906, and 1909 to 1913.[2] Figure 22 shows that the wholesale price of thread quoted by the Bureau of Labor Statistics[3] was unchanged from September, 1921, to April, 1924, and June, 1924, to October, 1930; during the decline in prices from June, 1929, to February, 1933, it fell only 4.1 per cent.

There are only two important producers of sulphur in the United States and the coordination of price policy in the industry is said to have been secured through an export corporation organized under the Webb-Pomerene Act.[4] Both before and since the organization of this corporation prices have been stable for long periods (see Fig. 22); the average price of crude sulphur reported by the Bureau of Labor Statistics was unchanged from January, 1927, throughout the period of the depression to at least February, 1933.

The dominant position of the Aluminum Company of America in its industry is well known. It attained its superior

and for cigarettes 42 (COMMISSIONER OF CORPORATIONS, *The Tobacco Industry*, 15 226, 255, 312, 334).
[1] U.S. TARIFF COMMISSION, *Cotton Sewing Thread and Cottons for Handwork*, (Tariff Information Survey) 1927, 15.
[2] *ibid.*, 43. The American Thread Company, formed in 1898, had by 1912 secured control of 90 per cent of the domestic thread business, and 60 to 70 per cent of the manufacturers' thread business. As a result of a suit in equity a decree was issued in 1913 aimed at the establishment of three independent units in place of a single unit resulting from interlocking stockholding (*ibid.*, 21).
[3] Six-cord 200 yard spools, J. and P. Coats, freight paid spool mill.
[4] Read, "Valorization in the Mineral Industry," *Polit. Sci. Quart.*, 47: 238. Moreover "the Sicilian sulphur pits and the American sulphur producers divided up the world sulphur market long ago" (VON BECKERATH, *Modern Industrial Organization*, 226).

position by control of patents which expired in 1909. It has subsequently maintained its position through its control of supplies of bauxite (the mineral from which aluminum is manufactured) aided by a protective tariff. While it has produced practically all the crude and semifinished aluminum it has somewhat less control of some branches of the fabricating industry.[1] In 1925, however, the Federal Trade Commission decided that the company controlled the price of sheet aluminum to the manufacturers of kitchen utensils because the latter were dependent upon it for supplies of either sheet or ingots, and that the consent decree under the anti-trust laws had failed to restore competitive conditions.[2] This position remained unchanged in 1934[3] when it was reported that the "price policy of the Aluminum

[1] In the prosecution of the Aluminum company in 1912 the Attorney General claimed that the corporation controlled 90 per cent of the raw material (bauxite); it produced practically 80 per cent, and consumed substantially 100 per cent of the alumina (the intermediate concentrate used for metal production); it manufactured substantially 100 per cent of the crude and semi-finished aluminum; it controlled and manufactured more than 50 per cent of all the aluminum castings manufactured and sold in the United States; it manufactured and sold more than 70 per cent of the aluminum cooking utensils in the United States (U.S. v. Aluminum Co. of America, *Petition*, 26, 27). The company replied admitting that it used about 100 per cent of the bauxite used in the United States for manufacturing aluminum and that it manufactured 100 per cent of the crude aluminum, but it contended that there were large importations of ingot and semi-finished aluminum products and that there were other manufacturers of cooking utensils and "dozens" of manufacturers of aluminum castings (*Reply Brief for the Aluminum Co. of America*, 18, 33). The courts expressed no opinion on this situation as the company consented to a decree (*Decrees and Judgments in Federal Anti-Trust Cases*, 341) which was aimed at diminishing the power of the company over the bauxite supplies of the country and eliminating unfair practices.
[2] F.T.C., *House Furnishings Industries*, III, xxvi. "The manufacturers of aluminum kitchen utensils in the United States are almost entirely dependent upon the Aluminum Company of America for their supply of raw materials, the quantity imported being relatively small. With the exception of three companies which operate rolling mills, these utensil manufacturers buy aluminum sheet in various forms. Of the three concerns operating rolling mills which are dependent upon the Aluminum Company of America for their supply of ingot, one is owned and another largely controlled by the Aluminum Company of America. . . . The Aluminum Company of America, with its complete control of the production of aluminum in the United States, fortified by a high protective tariff upon imports, controls the price of sheet aluminum to utensil manufacturers." The commission concluded that the company had repeatedly violated the prohibitions upon unfair practices in the decree and that "the original decree is obviously insufficient to restore competitive conditions in harmony with the anti-trust laws, especially with respect to the monopolization of high-grade bauxite lands" (*ibid.*, III, xxxii). In 1926 the Attorney General reported that the control of bauxite lands was not in itself illegal and that he knew of no reason why the company should be prosecuted for violation of the decree (Senate Doc. 67, 69th Cong. 1st Sess. (1926), vii, x).
[3] The company controlled the distribution of 90 to 95 per cent of the normal imports and domestic production of high-grade bauxite ores and produced 100 per cent of the alumina, and had 100 per cent of the virgin aluminum ingot plant capacity. A duty of four cents per pound on imported ingots kept down imports during the period 1928 to 1932 to 11 per cent of the total supply of ingots used; 32 per cent of

THE STABILIZATION OF INDIVIDUAL PRICES 231

Company is the dominant factor in the American aluminum market."[1] This control "proved to be sufficient to maintain the basic level for ingot prices at a more stable and relatively higher point than for other basic commodities during the depression period";[2] the price of pig aluminum had followed a very slow downward trend since 1924 with unchanging prices from June to September, 1927, from January, 1928, to July, 1930, and thence until March, 1933. Between June, 1929, and February, 1933, the price fell only 4.2 per cent.

The world output of nickel is controlled by very few firms and in recent years has been largely in the hands of the International Nickel Company, said since 1928 to control about 90 per cent of the world output.[3] The price of nickel ingots has been stable for considerable periods. It remained practically unchanged throughout the period of the war of 1914 to 1918, in spite of heavy increases in demand, particularly for military use.[4] The price of nickel ingots remained completely unchanged from 1925 throughout the period of the depression until at least February, 1933 (see Fig. 21).

The Federal Trade Commission reported in 1924 that the Singer Sewing Machine Company handled 80 per cent of the world output of sewing machines and on this account dominated their price.[5] The prices of electric and treadle machines both remained completely stable from January, 1925, to May, 1927, June to August, 1927, September, 1927, to December, 1928, and were practically so from January, 1929, to December, 1930. During the period from June, 1929, to February, 1933, the price of treadle machines fell 17.8 per cent and that of electric machines 25.6 per cent.

The importation of bananas is in the hands of a very small number of firms and little is known of the industry; Fig. 22 indicates that the average wholesale price published by the Bureau of Labor Statistics changes only at intervals of a few

---

ingot used was from scrap sold for a little less than virgin aluminum, the price of which it followed closely. (N.R.A., *The Aluminum Industry*, 1935, 4, 5.)
[1] *ibid.*, 9.
[2] *ibid.*, 4.
[3] BECKERATH, *op. cit.*, 231.
[4] TAUSSIG, *Price Fixing as Seen by a Price Fixer*, Quart. Jour. Econ., 33: 217 (1919). The Bureau of Labor Statistics reports an increase in the average wholesale price from 42.5 cents per pound in 1913 to 44 cents per pound in 1918 with no subsequent increase.
[5] F.T.C., *House Furnishings Industries*, III, 173.

months. During the period from June, 1929, to February, 1933, the price fell only 3 per cent.

The sale of fluid milk for consumption in large cities presents an interesting market situation. A large majority of farmer producers of milk are cooperatively organized, the marketing association negotiating selling prices on behalf of all its members. The number of distributors in many of the larger cities is also very small. The price of milk has remained unchanged in many parts of the country for increasingly long periods in recent years. The price published by the Bureau of Labor Statistics has remained unchanged for periods of two, three, and four months since 1927.[1] This average may change, however, while the price in many cities remains unchanged for long periods. The president of a large milk distributing company in Washington, D.C., stated in 1931 that the basic price of milk had not changed for three and one half years.[2] There were only four changes in the retail price of milk in Chicago during the decade 1921–1931.[3] The price of milk remained unchanged in Boston for considerable periods between 1917 and 1926,[4] although some instability appears to have been caused by the use of milk as a price leader by chain stores prior to 1926. The retail price of milk in New York City changed ten times during the five years from 1926 to 1930, although on one occasion it remained unchanged for 21 months.[5]

This stability of prices has been defended on the ground that retail milk prices have so small an effect upon the demand for milk that "if prices were fixed by the interplay of immediate supply and demand, prices would be erratic beyond measure."[6] In months of increased output of milk, the price of fluid milk would drop perceptibly, while in months of shortage it would increase. The unwillingness of farmers to face these fluctuations, together with the inconvenience of periods of milk shortage, and the necessity for some control of the hygienic conditions under which milk is produced, stimulate the organization of cooperative marketing associations. These associations elect to

[1] *Cf.* BUREAU OF LABOR STATISTICS, *Bulletin* 493, 60. See also *Hearings on Food Prices,* 1931, 210.
[2] U.S. Senate Committee, *Hearings on Food Prices,* 1931, 238, 262.
[3] *ibid.,* 222, and UNIVERSITY OF ILLINOIS AGRICULTURAL EXPERIMENT STATION, *The Marketing of Milk in the Chicago Dairy District,* Bulletin 269, 1925, 462.
[4] U.S. DEPARTMENT OF AGRICULTURE, *Some Economic Aspects of the Marketing of Milk and Cream in New England* (Circular 16), 31.
[5] U.S. Senate Committee, *Hearings on Food Prices,* 1931, 211.
[6] U.S. DEPARTMENT OF AGRICULTURE, *op. cit.,* 50.

set the price for considerable periods of time, thus adopting a selling policy comparable with that developing in many manufacturing industries. The seasonal variations in output of milk result, of course, in fluctuating surpluses which cannot be sold at the retail price based upon the wholesale price set by the association. Some cooperative associations deal with the situation by charging lower and more fluctuating prices for milk for other than fluid consumption.[1]

The shoe machinery industry, in which a very large proportion of all the available business is in the hands of the International Shoe Machinery Company, publishes no information concerning prices, many of which are, moreover, in the form of rentals and royalties.

The automobile tire industry is one in which there is a small number of large firms and a fringe of smaller ones. The wholesale quotation for tires frequently remains unchanged for a few months but rarely longer than 9 or 10 months. The list prices are subject, however, to large and fluctuating discounts. In fact, there have been many complaints of destructive competition.[2] During the general fall in prices between June, 1929, and February, 1933, the price of cord automobile tires fell 19.2 per cent, that of balloon tires, 23.2 per cent, and that of truck and bus tires, 28 per cent: the price of rubber, however, fell about 85 per cent and that of finished goods generally, 30.8 per cent.

The production of rayon is in the hands of a small number of firms and it will be seen from Fig. 21 that its price[3] has been stable for considerable periods: between June, 1929, and February, 1933, however, its price fell 52.4 per cent (doubtless partly as a result of a fall of 71.9 per cent in the price of silk yarn). It is notable that 85 to 90 per cent of all productive capacity in the industry was in use in July, 1933.[4]

5. OTHER EXAMPLES

There remain a number of products the prices of which reveal periods of stability but where information concerning the nature

[1] See Chap. VI. These other uses have a much more variable supply of milk, but as they make products such as cheese and butter which can be stored, the arrangement need not be uneconomical (U.S. Senate Committee, *Hearings on Food Prices*, 1931, 237).

[2] The average ratio of net income (before payment of federal taxes) to capitalization for 26 companies was, however, 5.9 per cent for the ten-year period 1919 to 1928 (NATIONAL BUREAU OF ECONOMIC RESEARCH, *Bulletin* 44, January, 1933).

[3] The price of 150 A denier quoted by the U.S. Bureau of Labor Statistics.

[4] *New York Times*, July 31, 1933.

of the relationships between the firms in the industry is too sparse and vague to justify their inclusion under any of the foregoing headings.

The production of bread for sale in large cities is frequently in the hands of one or a few large bakers and a fringe of smaller ones. These larger bakers frequently sell bread over very large territories and might be expected, because of the proportion of the business in their hands, to exercise considerable influence

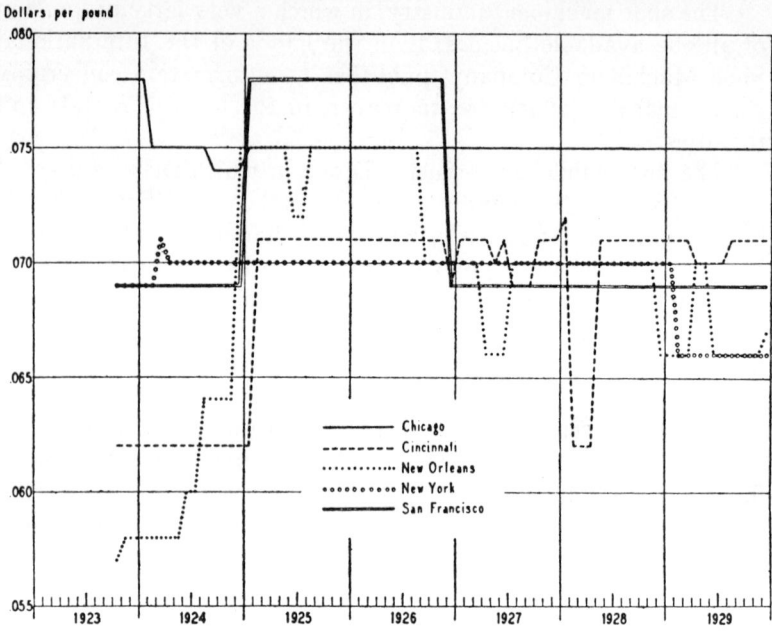

FIG. 24.—The wholesale price of bread in five cities October, 1923 to December, 1929. (*Drawn from data in U.S. Bureau of Labor Statistics Wholesale Prices:*)

in the determination of bread prices, the smaller firms accepting the prices of the larger.[1] Complaints have been made, however, that price cutting has been initiated by the large bakers.[2] The price of bread in fact shows considerable stability especially in the presence of a decline in the cost of flour. Figure 24 shows the course of the wholesale price of bread in a number of large cities since January, 1921. These prices show a high degree of stability:[3] in Cincinnati the price was fixed at 6.2 cents per pound

[1] ALSBERG, *Combination in the American Bread Baking Industry*, 113.
[2] F.T.C., *Competition and Profits in Bread and Flour*, 192.
[3] U.S. Senate Committee, *Hearings on Food Prices*, 1931, 36. See also U.S BUREAU OF LABOR STATISTICS, *Bulletin* 493, 42.

during 1922, 1923, and 1924, and at 7.1 cents from February, 1925, until December, 1926; in New York the price was 7.0 cents from March, 1924, until December, 1928, and 6.6 cents from February, 1929, until January, 1932; in a number of other large cities a similar stability is evident. Even the average of retail prices in 51 cities,[1] remained unchanged for 17 successive months

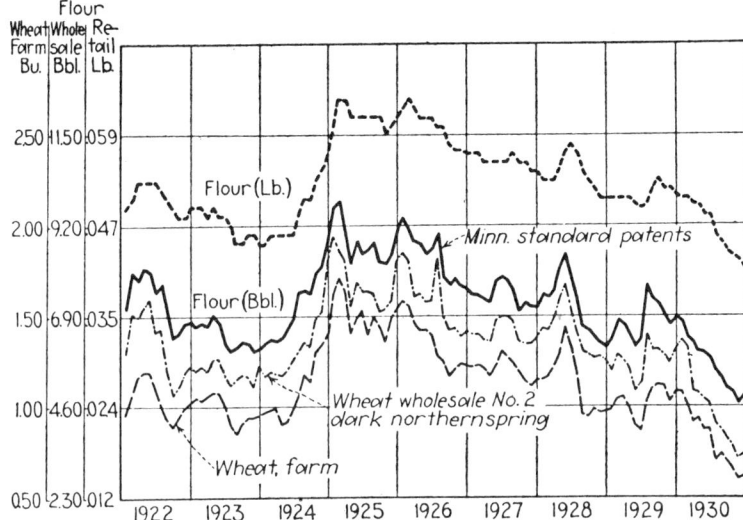

FIG. 25.—The prices of wheat and flour 1922 to 1930. (*Senate Committee on Agriculture and Forestry, Hearings on the Price of Food,* 1931, 8.)

on one occasion, 9 successive months on another, 6 on two others, 3 on another, and 2 on two others.[2]

The Senate Committee inquiring into food prices in 1931 was informed that the wholesale price of wheat and the wholesale price of flour move in fairly close correspondence;[3] the relationship between the prices of wheat and flour between 1922 and 1930 is shown in Fig. 25. During the period of falling wheat prices[4] there was a slight increase in the spread between the price of wheat and that of flour. It was remarked that the decline in wheat prices which had been so disastrous to the farmer had benefited

[1] This average obscures changes in price in particular cities.
[2] F.T.C., *Competition and Profits in Bread and Flour,* 222.
[3] *Hearings on Food Prices,* 1931, 8.
[4] Although the cost of production of flour was said not to have changed much during this period the price of the by-products (used mainly for feeding stock) fell sharply owing to the decline in the price of dairy products, in which form the stock feed was ultimately marketed (*ibid.,* 14, 27).

the purchaser of bread very little.[1] The Federal Trade Commission inquired into the relationship between wholesale flour

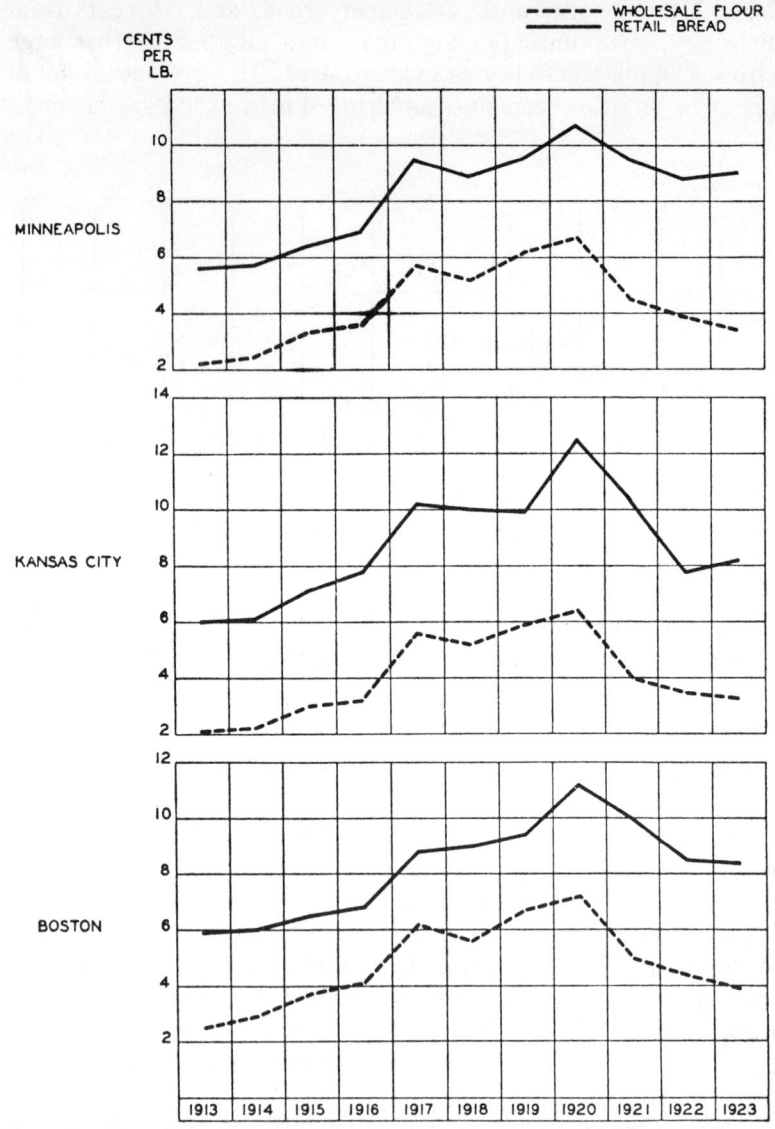

FIG. 26.—The prices of bread and flour in Minneapolis, Kansas City, and Boston, 1913 to 1923. (*F.T.C.*, *Wheat Flour Milling*, 1924, 82.)

and retail bread prices between 1913 and 1923 in Minneapolis, Kansas City, and Boston and reported the price movements

[1] *ibid.*, 83.

presented in Fig. 26 which showed "one thing very definitely, that is that the development of the bread baking industry has not lowered the price of bread, and that the price of bread is not sensitive to a reduction in the cost of flour. In other words, the bread baking industry has developed a power of resistance to conditions of supply and demand in flour."[1] Subsequently the Senate Committee in 1931 discovered that, in spite of the drastic decline in the price of wheat to the lowest point reached in 23 years, and the general reflection of this reduction in the wholesale price of flour, the price of bread had not fallen at the same rate.[2] The price of bread failed, however, to advance as rapidly as the price of flour between 1916 and 1920 but between 1920 and 1924 the price of flour fell much more than the price of bread; between 1924 and 1927 the price of flour increased more than the price of bread, and between 1927 and 1930 the price of flour was again falling more quickly than that of bread.[3] During the period of general decline in prices from June, 1929, to February, 1933, while the price of various grades of flour fell from 36 to 46 per cent, the wholesale price of bread in different cities (as reported to the U.S. Bureau of Labor Statistics) behaved in remarkably different ways. In Cincinnati it fell 38.4 per cent and in Chicago 33.6 per cent; in New York, however, it fell only 8.9 per cent while in San Francisco it rose 2.6 per cent.

Any criticism of bread prices must take into account the stability of such prices at times when the price of flour is rising as well as at times when the price of flour is falling. The bakers have offered two explanations of the behavior of bread prices. Improvements in the quality of bread[4] and the production of new varieties are said to account for the increased spread between flour and bread prices. The bakers arbitrarily insisted that the consumer was better off in getting better quality bread than he would be if he were able to buy the same quality of bread as

[1] F.T.C., *Wheat Flour Milling*, 1924, 82.
[2] *Hearings on Food Prices*, 1931, 36. Senator Wagner in proposing the hearings pointed out that between October, 1929, and October, 1930, the price of number two hard winter wheat in Chicago had fallen from $1.28 a bushel to 78 cents, that is, by 39 per cent. The price of hard winter 95 per cent patent flour at Chicago had fallen from $6.10 a barrel to $4.30, that is, by 29 per cent. The price of bread reported by the Department of Labor had fallen from a relative of 158.9 to 153.6, that is, by 3.3 per cent. (*New York Times*, Jan. 20, 1930.)
[3] *Hearings on Food Prices*, 36.
[4] A representative of the American Bakers Association and the chairman of the General Baking Corporation argued that the price of bread did reflect a decrease in the cost of materials and that the profits of the bakers were two million dollars less than they had been in the previous year. They denied that bakers dictated the price of bread and argued that "plain bread" out of plain flour, "the kind that we had in 1900," cost 5.4 cents a pound in 1931 compared with 5.6 cents in 1913. (*Hearings on*

238   THE DECLINE OF COMPETITION

before at lower prices.¹ Stability in the price of bread has also been attributed to the fact that if large bakers contract ahead for flour and the price of flour subsequently rises, their rivals, whose costs are increased, suffer serious losses if the larger bakers keep down the price of bread. If they raise the price of bread they are charged with profiteering, although their abnormally high profits arise from successful speculation in the flour market rather than from their baking operations. If the price of flour falls, large bakers may be able to resist a reduction in prices and permit the smaller firms to gain. Consequently the large bakers may use their resources to stabilize prices, resisting reductions when the price of flour falls and resisting increases when the price of flour rises.² Pressure of public opinion and the possibility of adverse legislation are also said to lead to the stabilization of prices.³

The prices of shoes show considerable stability,⁴ as will be seen from Figure 27.⁵ During the general decline in prices from June, 1929, to February, 1933, the prices of shoes published by the U.S. Bureau of Labor Statistics declined on the average 21.5 per cent, the decline in the price of various types varying from 3.0 to 41.0 per cent. The price of leather fell 49.9 per cent and of hides and skins 63.1 per cent.

The production of matches has been in the hands of a small number of companies and the wholesale price reported by the

---

Food Prices, 65.) The average retail price of bread in 51 cities on January 15, 1931, as quoted by the Bureau of Labor Statistics, was 8.2 cents per pound (*ibid.*, 50) but that price did not relate to "plain bread." It was contended that price reductions had occurred and that if further reductions were made they would involve the use of inferior flour (*ibid.*, 115).

¹ Legal limitations upon the weight of the loaf were said also to hinder price adjustments.

² ALSBERG, *Combines in the American Bread Baking Industry*, 111, 120.

³ The Federal Trade Commission discovered, however, that statistics of the retail price of bread must be used with care. They do not represent the price obtained for the whole output of the baker because a proportion of his output must always be sold as stale bread at lower prices. They do not allow for samples given away (which, however, must be regarded as advertising expenditure) and they do not take proper account of differences in transportation and delivery costs. (F.T.C., *Competition and Profits in Bread and Flour*, 1928, 211.) It is notable in this connection that this lack of harmony between the movements of the prices of bread and of flour have attracted attention in England and that the Food Council, in attempting to bring pressure upon the bakers, has suggested reasonable maximum prices from time to time which are calculated by reference to the price of flour (Food Council *Report* of Nov. 14, 1925).

⁴ Shoes have obviously not been homogeneous throughout the period; there has, moreover, been a tendency in the clothing industries to adapt the product to conventional "price lines."

⁵ The quotation was also unchanged for some years prior to 1894 and from 1897 to 1903 (U.S. BUREAU OF LABOR STATISTICS, *Bulletin* 440, 1927, 106).

THE STABILIZATION OF INDIVIDUAL PRICES 239

Bureau of Labor Statistics (not however, in unvarying units owing to changes in the number of matches per box) has shown

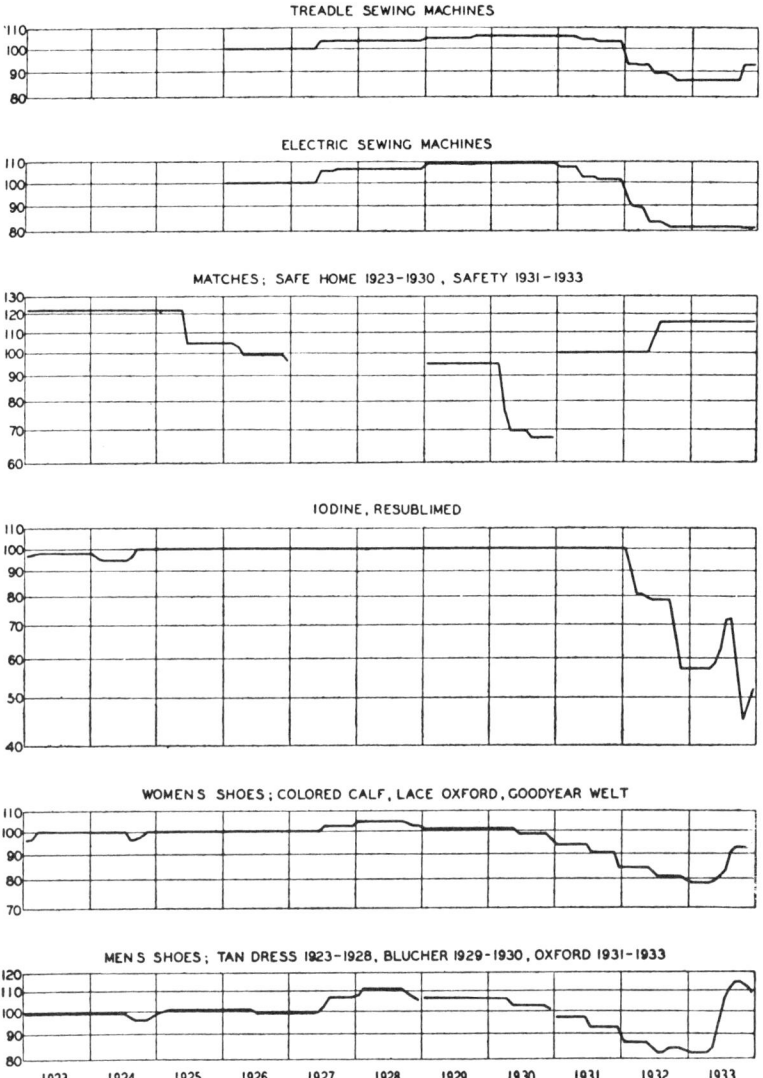

FIG. 27.—The prices of sewing machines, matches, iodine, and shoes, 1923 to 1933. (*Drawn from data in U.S. Bureau of Labor Statistics: Wholesale Prices.*)

unusual stability: it was unchanged between 1891 and 1893, 1896 and 1901, 1903 and 1914, 1917 and 1919, 1921 and May,

1925; subsequent changes are shown in Fig. 27. During the period of declining general prices from June, 1929, to February, 1933, the price of safety matches *increased* 27.8 per cent and that of "strike anywhere" matches 38 per cent. Changes in the price of salt are shown at Fig. 22; the price of salt *rose* 4 per cent between June, 1929, and February, 1933. The prices of a number of drugs were highly stable during the period from 1924 to 1929;[1] the prices of some but not all of them resisted the general decline after 1929.[2] Similar conditions prevailed in the chemical[3] and fertilizer industries.[4]

[1] The drugs whose reported prices were unchanged for long periods were: Citric acid, cream of tartar, epsom salts, ether, iodine (September, 1924, to January, 1932), Opium (September, 1924, until June, 1929, and from August, 1929, to March, 1931), peroxide of hydrogen (May, 1926, until March, 1932), quinine (May, 1926, until July, 1931), soda phosphate (1924 until December, 1929), and zinc chloride.

[2] The changes in the prices of these products between June, 1929, and February, 1933, were:

	Per cent		Per cent
Citric acid	−37	Peroxide of hydrogen	−12.9
Cream of tartar	−44.7	Quinine	0.0
Epsom salts	+ 4.0	Soda phosphate	−30.8
Iodine	−43.0	Zinc chloride	−17.2
Opium	− 0.8		

[3] The chemical products whose prices remained stable for long periods were: acetic acid (January, 1927, until July, 1928, January, 1929, until May, 1930), boric acid, liquid carbonic acid (1924 to at least the end of 1931), muriatic acid, nitric acid, oleic acid, salicylic acid (October, 1926, until at least February, 1934), sulphuric acid (June, 1926, until at least February, 1934), alum, aluminum sulphate (March, 1924, until November, 1930), anhydrous ammonia, anilin oil, white arsenic, bleaching powder (November, 1925, to July, 1931), calcium chloride, coal tar colors, copperas (August, 1926, to February, 1930), acetate of lime, caustic potash, soda ash, bicarbonate of soda, carbonate of soda (sal soda), caustic soda, silicate of soda, toluene. The behavior of the prices of these products during the decline in general prices from June, 1929, to February, 1933 (when the price of chemicals in general fell 19.2 per cent), is summarized below:

	Per cent		Per cent
Acetic acid	−31.7	Calcium chloride	−10.0
Boric acid	−21.7	Coal tar colors	− 0.0
Carbon dioxide	0.0	(Nigrosine)	− 3.0
Muriatic acid	0.0	Copperas	− 7.6
Nitric acid	0.0	Calcium acetate	−44.5
Oleic acid	−47.4	Caustic potash	−12.3
Salicylic acid	0.0	Soda ash	− 8.9
Sulphuric acid	0.0	Bicarbonate of soda	− 7.5
Aluminum sulphate	−10.7	Carbonate of soda (sal soda)	−11.1
Anhydrous ammonia	+10.7	Caustic soda	− 1.7
Anilin oil	+ 6.6	Silicate of soda	− 7.1
White arsenic	0.0	Toluene	−25.0
Bleaching powder	−12.5		

Over the whole period of ten years from 1919 to 1928 nine corporations producing crude chemicals secured an average return of 11.1 per cent on their capitalization (excluding bonded debt) (NATIONAL BUREAU OF ECONOMIC RESEARCH, *Bulletin* 44, January, 1934).

[4] The fertilizer products whose prices remained unchanged for long periods were: Kainit (from the beginning of the quotations in July, 1927, until April, 1929), manure salts (1926 until April, 1929), muriate of potash (December, 1926, until April, 1929). During the fall in general prices between June, 1929, and February,

6. SUMMARY OF EVIDENCE CONCERNING THE STABILIZATION OF PRICES

The foregoing evidence, unsatisfactory as it is, abundantly proves that many manufactured, and occasionally unmanufactured products (e.g., fluid milk) are no longer sold in markets in which prices are incessantly changing[1] in response to actual

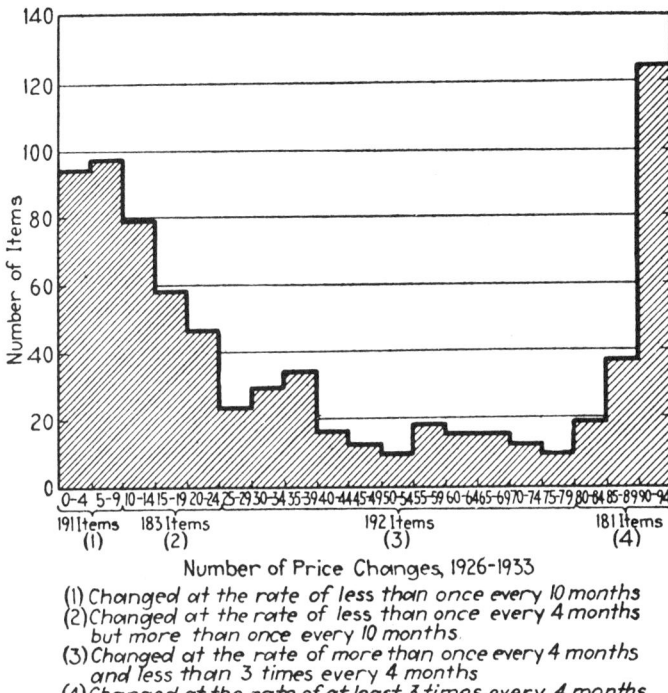

Number of Price Changes, 1926-1933

(1) Changed at the rate of less than once every 10 months
(2) Changed at the rate of less than once every 4 months but more than once every 10 months.
(3) Changed at the rate of more than once every 4 months and less than 3 times every 4 months
(4) Changed at the rate of at least 3 times every 4 months

FIG. 28.—Rigid and flexible prices 1926 to 1933. (Redrawn from Means, Industrial Prices and Their Relative Inflexibility, 2. [Senate Document 13, 74th Congress, 1st session].)

and anticipated changes in conditions of supply and demand. That this new type of market in which prices remain unchanged from day to day and even year to year, is now sufficiently common to require investigation is suggested by Fig. 28 which indicates 1933, the prices of these products changed as follows:

	Per cent		Per cent
Kainit	+1.1	Phosphate rock	0.0
Manure salts	−4.0	Sulphate of potash	−0.6
Muriate of potash	+1.1		

[1] Cf. also F.T.C., *Open Price Trade Associations*, 449.

the relative importance of commodities whose prices change with different degrees of frequency. In general, markets in which prices are stable for considerable periods are those in which there is a firm with a quasi-monopoly, a price leader, or a small number of firms. A measure of stability occurs even in the absence of these conditions where short-term price cutting is avoided by convention; long-period contracts and guarantees against price decline tend to produce this result but the more frequent con-

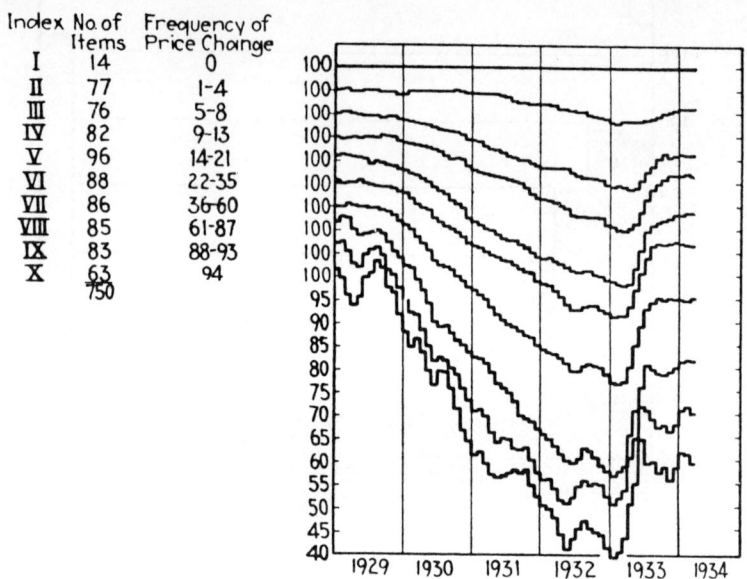

Fig. 29.—The relation between frequency of price change and magnitude of price change during depression (1929 to 1934). (*Redrawn from Means, Industrial Prices and Their Relative Inflexibility*, 4. [*Senate Document* 13, *74th Congress, 1st Session*].)

ventional cause is the practice of setting prices for a season or some other period not necessarily predetermined.

Although stability is here defined in terms of the duration of periods of unchanging price, sufficient information has been given to indicate that the conditions of price making that permit the stabilization of prices in times of relatively small change in the volume of business also very commonly permit in times of business recession (such as the period from June, 1929, to February, 1933) considerable resistance to the general tendency to declining prices. A remarkable number of the products that decreased little, remained stable, or even increased in price during this period of depression are to be found in the industries in which, prior to the decline in business activity, prices were infrequently changed.[1] Figure 29 reveals the close relation between the frequency and amount of price changes during the years from 1929 to 1933 among the prices included in the index of wholesale prices compiled by the U.S. Bureau of Labor Statistics.

III. THE CONSEQUENCES OF STABILIZATION OF PRICES

The importance of the substitution of a price unchanging for an interval of time for one varying from minute to minute in response to conditions of supply and demand lies in the elimination of the mutual dependence of supply, price, and demand. Price is less influenced by actual or anticipated changes in supply and demand but more influential in determining supply and demand. The operation of this type of market depends, therefore, upon the factors determining prices. It is obviously unreal to assume that, but for a mischievous conspiracy on the part of business men, ever-changing prices would induce speedy and happy equilibria between demand and supply in every market; the desire for stability springs in large part from fundamental changes in the conditions of both demand and supply. But it is equally unreasonable to assume that these stable prices are the happiest possible response to the unhappy conditions in which producers find price competition so dangerous. The effects of stabilization depend *inter alia* upon the periods over which stability is secured. It is impossible to establish a sharp classification of these periods but three type situations present themselves, *viz.*, price setting for a few months or a season, price stabilization for periods long enough to include cycles of business activity, and stabilization over long periods of years. Actual problems must be discussed by applying a mixture of the considerations present in each type case.

A. *Price Setting for Short Periods*

Stability for many months or even a season may and does occur in such industries as automobiles and furniture without any suggestion of stability over longer periods. The price setting which brings about this result greatly diminishes resort to price

[1] A chart of the wholesale prices of raw materials and semi-finished goods the prices of which were regulated by cartels in Germany shows that such prices declined little in 1929 and 1930 while unregulated prices declined in Germany by about 25 per cent (N.I.C.B., *The Rationalization of German Industry*, 51).

cutting, which, as we have seen, is one of the reasons for its adoption. No firm can for long maintain an openly published offer unless it is identical with the offers of rivals, or differs from them only by an amount accounted for in terms of difference in place of delivery or in the real or assumed nature of the product.

The exclusion of price competition affects the cost of production in a number of ways. It may cause increased expenditure upon non-price competition as a means of changing both the aggregate demand for the product and the share obtained by the seller incurring the expenditure. It necessitates the adjustment of output to demand at the unchanging price and, if demand at a constant price fluctuates, either output or (as in the automobile industry) inventories must be destabilized. If buyers assume that a newly announced offer price will remain unchanged for a considerable time the inducement to speculate on changes in price is removed; they plan their orders so as to create a more stable demand than would otherwise exist; they are also more willing to hold inventories and therefore to accept less speedy delivery of orders. If the output of the manufacturer can be thus stabilized costs of production can be reduced; stabilization of output by the accumulation of inventories by manufacturers, however, requires additional capital and involves additional costs.

The setting of a price for a period of time affects the level at which the price is set, apart from its effect upon costs of production. The selection of a price is a matter for delicate calculation. The trend of costs and demand throughout the future period in view must be calculated. If the calculation is made with considerable allowance for "contingencies" (*i.e.*, it is realized that the basis of the estimate is slender) and the estimate is biased in favor of the producer prices are likely to be somewhat higher than will cover technically necessary costs. But each seller must take into account the probable prices of rivals. The nature of the relations between sellers which enable each to take account of the probable policies of others doubtless varies, but, having attained a relationship which avoids at least the minute to minute and day to day price cutting, there is a tendency to set higher prices than would otherwise prevail. Such a policy tends, however, to induce additional investment in longer periods and to adjust investment to prices until only a normal return is available upon an investment abnormal in relation to output.

B. Stabilization of Individual Prices and the Business Cycle

Stabilization of prices over periods of a few years implies stability over periods long enough to include cyclical fluctuations in demand, and long enough to permit increases in investment in the industry in response to the level of prices maintained. If the demand for a product is at all elastic the maintenance of an unchanged price throughout cycles of increasing and decreasing demand must increase the amplitude of fluctuations in the volume of production beyond what it would be if the price were increased in times of increasing demand and reduced in times of falling demand. Price stabilization operates most devastatingly to increase the amplitude of fluctuations in the sales of those products the demand for which is most fluctuating and most elastic. The wider the cyclical fluctuations in demand the greater is the scope for attempts to stabilize; the more elastic the demand for the product the greater the possibility of remedying the instability of output by destabilizing prices. Unfortunately, however, products for which demand is subject to the widest cyclical fluctuations have also a relatively inelastic demand (within each short period of time); the opportunities for stabilizing the output of steel, cement, and most construction goods by destabilizing prices are thereby greatly diminished.

The relationship between prices and output has been more thoroughly investigated in the steel industry than in most others. Attempts to maintain the price of steel in periods of falling demand have been based primarily on the assumption that the volume of sales is largely independent of price within short periods of time. Price competition resulting in declines in prices prior to 1901 (when the United States Steel Corporation was formed) is alleged to have failed to increase the demand for the various products and to have achieved merely an increasing uncertainty among buyers.[1] During the depression of 1907–1908 the demand for steel products the prices of which were not stabilized is said to have declined as much as the demand for those that were. It was pointed out, for instance, that the price

---

[1] MEADE, "The Price Policy of the United States Steel Corporation," *Quart. Jour. Econ.*, 22: 452 (1908). At a meeting of representatives of the steel industry in 1907 it was stated that the prices of steel products had not "in the past boom times risen to a point where prices checked consumption, nor would now a slaughter of values stimulate buying" (meeting on Nov. 21, 1907, *cit.* F.T.C., *Statement on Pittsburgh Plus*, 401).

of pig iron was greatly reduced without calling forth any response in the form of increased business;[1] but so long as those who manufactured pig iron into steel and steel products were maintaining their prices, it is difficult to see how reductions in the price of pig iron could call forth an increased demand for pig iron; such reductions could do no more than increase the profit margin of those steel manufacturers who bought pig iron; furthermore, the demand for different commodities shrinks by different amounts during a depression; allowance must be made for these differences before inferring from similar reductions in demand that dissimilar reductions in price have left demand unaffected; in other words, the demand for the products the prices of which were not stabilized might have fallen much more had the price been stabilized.

The desire to maintain prices is reinforced by the fear that reductions in price will induce an expectation of further reductions, and, therefore, reduce the volume of business rather than increase it: sellers fear the "uncertainty of buyers." The stabilization of prices is intended to discourage speculation and distribute demand more evenly over time. To achieve this end, however, it is necessary to eliminate only those reductions in price which induce an expectation of further reduction; the maintenance of prices when purchasers consider continued maintenance impossible merely induces the postponement of purchases while reductions sufficiently great to convince buyers that no further reductions can be expected discourage the postponement of demand. A halfway policy of making grudging reductions when there is a general shrinkage in business activity and reduction of the prices of other products is the one most calculated to induce a general expectation of more severe cuts,[2] and a postponement of purchases. Yet attempts to stabilize the prices of steel products appear often to have operated in just this way; prices have been maintained during the earlier part of the contraction of business activity, but have ultimately been reduced. The reduction in the price of steel rails in October, 1932, from $43 a ton (the price that had prevailed for the previous ten years) to $40 a ton, "in the hope of inducing the railroads to place orders which have been long deferred,"[3] was abortive partly because a reduction of 7 per cent

[1] MEADE, *op. cit.*, 461.
[2] CLARK, *The Economics of Overhead Costs*, 406; also Thompson in NATIONAL BUREAU OF ECONOMIC RESEARCH, *Business Cycles and Unemployment*, 167.
[3] *New York Times*, Oct. 21, 1932.

appeared inadequate in view of the fact that the index of the prices of steel products generally (including steel rails) had declined since October, 1922, by 25 per cent, and the index of prices of finished steel products had declined 20 per cent. It has been said that business men would act more intelligently in times of depression if they made a cut in price that equates "the new demand with the short-period supply"; this being "the maximum possible cut . . . cannot lead, so far as people understand the facts, to the expectation of a further cut later on—apart, of course, from a further independent fall from the side of demand."[1] There are, however, many obstacles to intelligent action of this kind. The "short-period supply" is the supply the marginal cost of which is equal to the marginal revenue obtained from sales.[2] This price is difficult to calculate, more especially where the reaction of demand to a change in price is uncertain. The reaction of buyers is likely, moreover, to depend upon the period of time taken into account: the immediate reaction may be small but as time goes on a greater response may be made. But attempts to take account of longer periods are complicated by the possibility that demand is progressively declining (apart from the effect of changes in price); this progressive decline suggests a succession of reductions which, if expected by buyers, may lead to bear speculation by them in the form of reductions of inventories and purchases. Moreover the adjustment of prices to a declining demand so that marginal costs and marginal revenue are equal may suggest an increase in price[3] which for practical reasons producers cannot make. Finally an announcement of a reduction in the price of, say, steel, like the announcement of a change in a discount rate, operates indirectly as well as directly; it is apt to be interpreted as an indication that observers well qualified to judge have decided that prices in general must fall; business men are deprived of what optimism they had and pursue a more cautious policy, with the result that the demand for steel products, as well as many other commodities, is reduced.

It is impossible to prove that if prices had been less stable production would have been more stable. Information concerning the volume of sales at prices other than those that have prevailed is, of course, not available. The secondary reactions of policies

[1] *Cf.* PIGOU, *Industrial Fluctuations*, 1929, 170.
[2] That is, the additional cost of producing one more unit is equal to the addition to total revenue resulting from the sale of one more unit.
[3] For example, if marginal costs rise with the decline in output.

of stabilization or other possible policies are far from clear. Two approaches to an approximate judgment are, however, worth examination, *viz.*, the changes in the behavior of production in the steel industry over a period in which price policies have changed, and the differences in the behavior of production in different industries in which prices have varied in their stability. Analysis of the fluctuations in the volume of output before and after the formation of the United States Steel Corporation suggests, but does not prove, that less stability in prices would have been accompanied by more stability in output. The average of annual deviations of the output of the steel industry from a five-year moving average was 10.5 per cent for steel ingots and castings between 1887 and 1901 (that is, before the establishment of the United States Steel Corporation) and 14.7 per cent between 1902 and 1922; for rolled iron and steel the comparable percentages were 8.5 and 14.9, and for pig iron 7.7 and 13.5.[1] Thus annual fluctuations in total output of the industry measured in this way have been greater in each of these three classes of product since the formation of the corporation than they were before.[2] "Inferentially, price stabilization has required frequent and, in some cases, drastic adjustments with respect to output to meet market conditions."[3] The price of steel rails having been more stable than the price of any other steel product, considerable interest attaches to changes in the amplitude of fluctuations in output of this product as compared with those of others. During the period 1902–1915 the average of the percentage of annual deviations from a five-year moving average was 17.9 for steel rails, 15.0 for steel castings, 14.8 for steel ingots, and 13.6 for pig iron.[4] Fluctuations in the output of rails (measured in the same manner) for the period 1880 to 1901 and 1902 to 1922

[1] BERGLUND, "The United States Steel Corporation and Price Stabilization," *Quart. Jour. Econ.*, 38: 614, 615.

[2] BERGLUND, "The Modern Merger Movement" (discussion), *Proceedings of the American Economic Association*, 1931, 102. Professor Berglund added that periods of depression in the industry appear to have been shorter but more severe than before the organization of the corporation.

[3] BERGLUND, "The United States Steel Corporation and Price Stabilization," *Quart. Jour. Econ.*, 38: 618. Subdivision of the period 1902–1922 into two intervals revealed a slight decrease in the annual deviation of production from the five-year moving average in the period 1915 to 1922 compared with that from 1902–1914 (*ibid.*, 617); the percentages of annual deviation from the five-year moving average were as follows:

Date	Pig iron	Steel ingots and castings	Rolled iron and steel products
1902–1914	13.7	15.0	15.1
1915–1922	13.1	14.2	14.6

[4] *ibid.*, 622.

resulted in an average annual percentage deviation in the former period of 13.1 and in the latter of 14.9. Thus fluctuations in output were wider in the latter period than in the former, but the increase is much less than for the output of the industry generally. The smallness of this difference is said to be due to the presence in the earlier period of a special influence making for fluctuations in output which was not present in the latter, namely large variations in demand from year to year during the decade 1880–1890 owing to the building and completion of new railroads.[1] It has been reported, on the other hand, that cyclical fluctuations in the output of pig iron were more pronounced in the period 1879 to 1896 than in the period 1897 to 1913. The standard deviation of percentage deviations of annual output from the trend, adjusted for seasonal variations, was 19.30 for the first period and 15.63 for the second. Thus it appears that while the output of iron and steel products was subject to wider cyclical variations, the output of pig iron was less variable.[2] The explanation of these differences in behavior may lie either in a change in the fluctuations of inventories or very probably, in differences in the methods of statistical analysis used.[3] It is notable that the general tendency for the amplitude of fluctuations in the output of steel products to increase is not explicable in terms of a tendency for the amplitude of fluctuations in business activity in general to increase.[4]

[1] *ibid.*, 619.
[2] "An Index of Business Conditions, 1875–1917," *Review of Economic Statistics*, 1927, 28.
[3] It has been stated that there is some reason to think that the amplitude of fluctuations in production in the iron and steel industry "is tending to decrease in recent years . . . in spite of the destabilizing effects of a policy of price stabilization" and that "it is advisable to look to factors other than industrial combination alone for the explanation of the situation," as the attribution of changes in the stability of production in the industry to the formation of the United States Steel Corporation or other combinations "involves too great a dependence upon the argument *post hoc ergo propter hoc*" (MACCALLUM, *The Iron and Steel Industry in the United States*, 163, 164). Professor Berglund concluded that the average percentage annual deviation of the number of workers employed by the United States Steel Corporation compared with the five-year moving average was 8.9 per cent, which is much less than the 13.5 to 14.9 per cent fluctuations in the output of the corporation during the period 1902 to 1922 (*op. cit.*, 623).
[4] The decline of business activity from crest to trough as a percentage of the trend after allowing for seasonal variations during the period since 1890 has been:

1890–1891	24		1906–1908	35
1892–1894	34		1910–1911	15
1895–1897	23		1912–1914	28
1899–1900	15		1916–1919	25
1901–1904	20		1919–1921	38

(AMERICAN TELEGRAPH AND TELEPHONE COMPANY, *Business Index, cit.* MITCHELL, *Business Cycles*, 347.)

The extent of reductions in the price of steel billets during periods of declining demand is compared with the contemporaneous changes in the percentage of the total capacity of the industry in use in the following table:

TABLE VIII

Period	Percentage reduction in the price of Bessemer billets[a]	Percentage of ingot capacity in use		Decline in percentage of ingot capacity in use[b]	Percentage changes in the index of the price of manufactured goods
		1st date	2d date		
Nov. 1907–Jan. 1909	10.7	no data		no data	
May 1913–Nov. 1914	30.0	91	42	49	− 1.1
Jan. 1919–Oct. 1919	11.4	81	45	36	+ 4.2
Oct. 1920–July 1921	41.3	77	19	58	+31.0
Mar. 1924–July 1924	5.0	85	36	49	− 3.2
Mar. 1927–Nov. 1927	2.9	90	62	28	+ 0.6
Oct. 1929–Dec. 1932	25.7	82	19.8	26	−28.0

[a] *Standard Statistics Bulletin Base Book,* 1932, and June, 1933.
[b] Percentage of ingot capacity in use from 1913 to 1932 calculated by dividing ingot production for the month specified into one twelfth of the annual capacity as published by the American Iron and Steel Institute and expressing the result as a percentage.

Large price reductions have apparently failed to prevent large reductions of output; the largest percentage reduction in price (of 41.3 per cent in 1920 to 1921) was accompanied by the second largest decline in the percentage of capacity in use (of 58 per cent); the largest decline in percentage of capacity in use (of about 62 per cent in 1929 to 1932) was accompanied by the third largest percentage reduction in price (of 25.7 per cent). The price of billets fell about 27 per cent more in 1920–1921 than in 1913–1914, yet output declined by 58 points in the former and only 49 in the latter period. In view of the fact that the magnitude in the decline in demand (apart from differences in price policy) differed from depression to depression these figures are, however, inconclusive.

Differences in the relation between the price and production policies of different industries during the depression which began in 1929 are very evident. The correlation between stability of price and instability of production is indicated by Table IX[1] shown on page 252. These relationships are denoted in Figs. 30 to 34. But

[1] MEANS, *Industrial Prices and Their Relative Inflexibility,* 8.

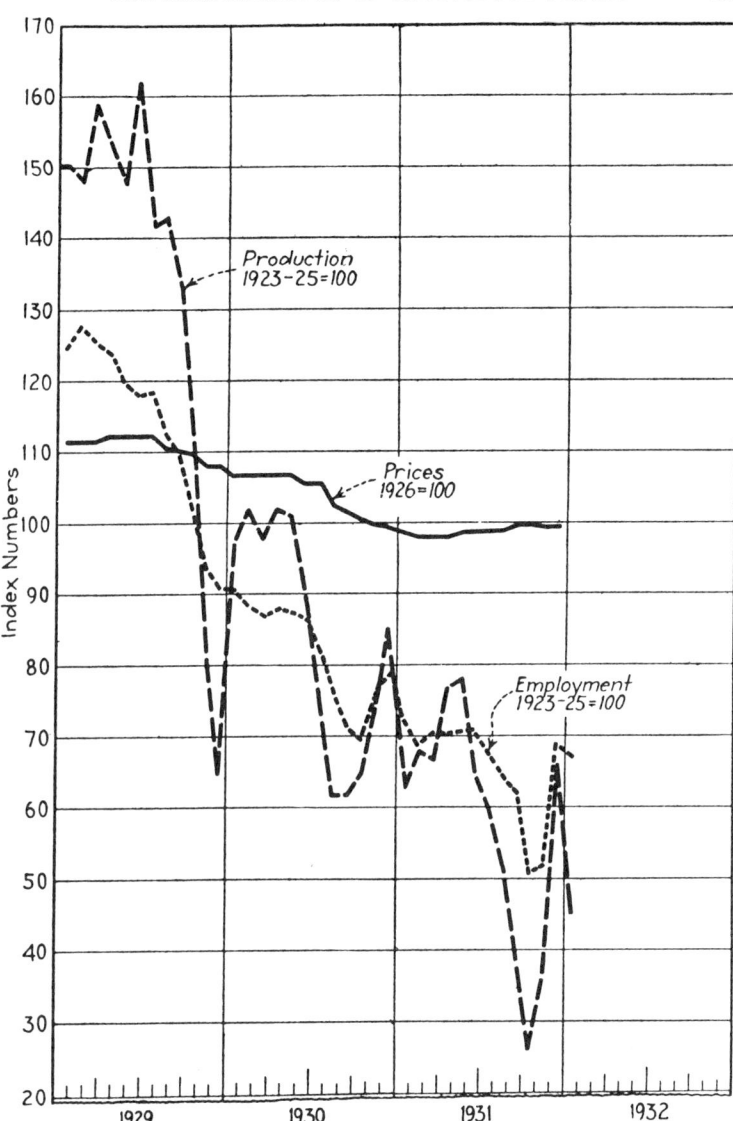

FIG. 30.—Production and prices of automobiles, 1929 to 1931. (*Redrawn from Senate Committee on the Judiciary Hearings on Amendment of the Federal Trade Commission Act*, 1932, 17.)

TABLE IX

	1929 to spring of 1933	
	Decline in price (per cent)	Decline in production (per cent)
Agricultural implements............	6	80
Motor vehicles....................	16	80
Cement..........................	18	65
Iron and steel....................	20	83
Automobile tires..................	33	70
Textile products..................	45	30
Food products....................	49	14
Leather..........................	50	20
Petroleum.......................	56	20
Agricultural commodities..........	63	6

it cannot be inferred that, if the prices which changed little had been reduced more drastically, output would have been maintained

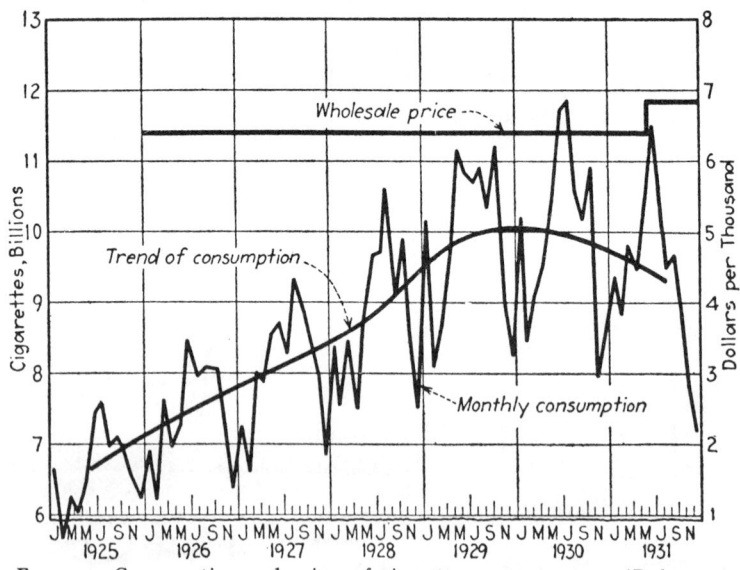

FIG. 31.—Consumption and prices of cigarettes, 1925 to 1931. (*Redrawn from Senate Committee on the Judiciary, Hearings on Amendment of the Federal Trade Commission Act,* 1932, 17.)

as it was by the group of industries whose prices fell; it is more likely that if this latter group had maintained its prices its produc-

THE STABILIZATION OF INDIVIDUAL PRICES 253

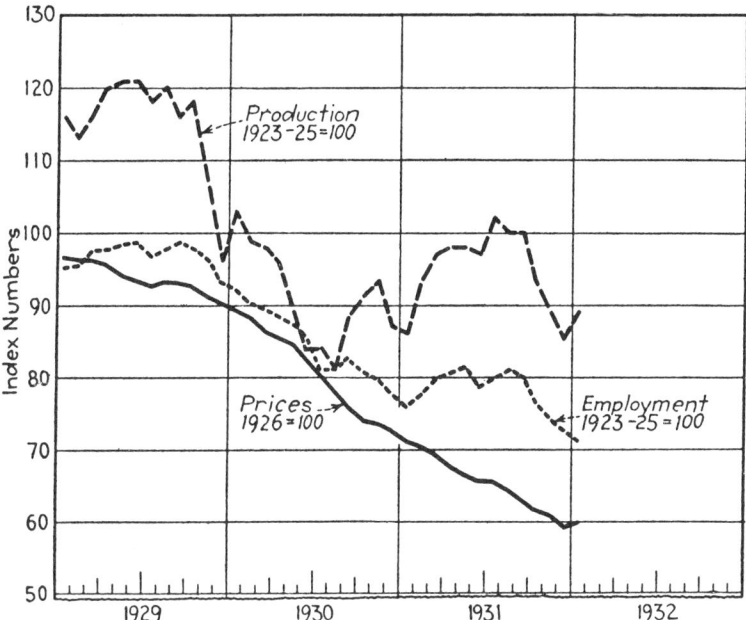

FIG. 32.—Production and prices of textiles 1929 to 1931. (*Redrawn from Senate Committee on the Judiciary, Hearings on Amendment of the Federal Trade Commission Act*, 1932, 17.)

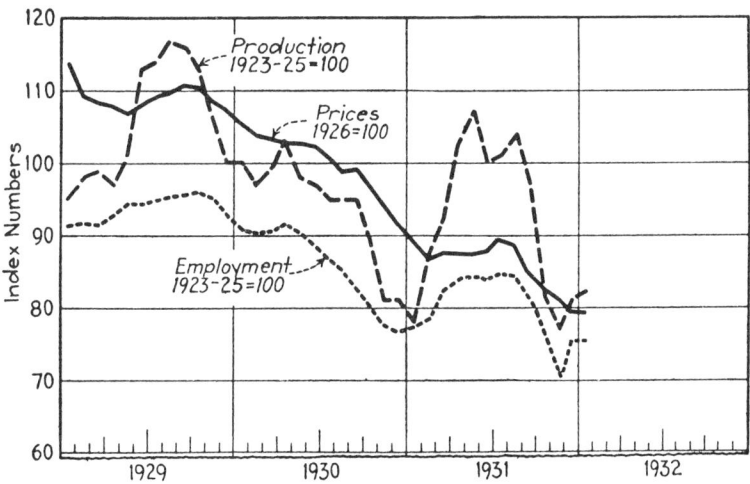

FIG. 33.—Production and prices of leather products, 1929 to 1933. (*Redrawn from Senate Committee on the Judiciary, Hearings on Amendment of the Federal Trade Commission Act*, 1932, 17.)

tion would have fallen more nearly as did that of the first group. The products the output of which fell most are, in the main, durable products the life of which can be prolonged when incomes are curtailed (*e.g.*, automobiles and tires) or constructional goods the demand for which is known to fluctuate more widely than

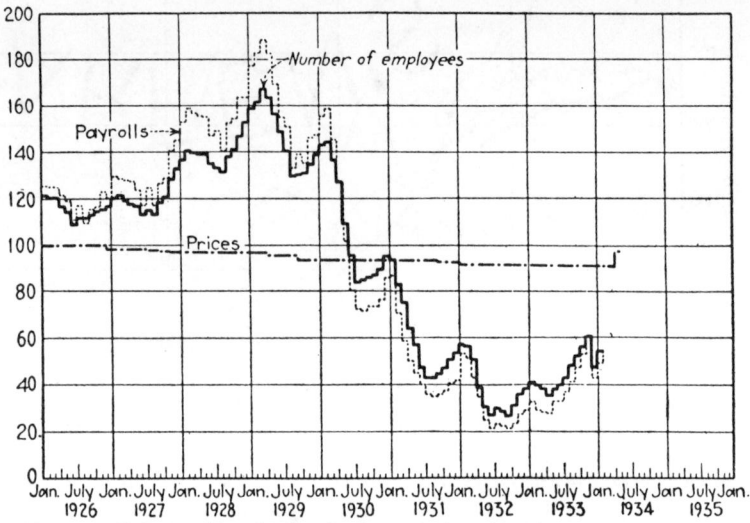

FIG. 34.—Prices and production in the agricultural implement industry, 1926 to 1933. (Redrawn from Means, *Industrial Prices and Their Relative Inflexibility,* 5. [*Senate Document* 13, 74th *Congress* 1st *Session*].)

that for other products (*e.g.*, steel, cement). It appears that "prices for open-price trade associations are much more stable than output," but that "this is doubtless true for manufactures generally."[1]

The stabilization of prices might, conceivably, while increasing the amplitude of cyclical declines in demand, curtail the period of

[1] A comparison of the fluctuations in the output of industries in which there was an open-price policy with those in which there were merely statistical services without an open-price policy led to the conclusion that "it does not appear that industries with open-price associations are better in respect to stability or regularity of operation than those that merely have trade statistics; indeed the comparison, although on too narrow a basis, is more in favor of the latter" (F.T.C., *Open Price Trade Associations*, 357, 358). It will be remembered, however, that a comparison of the stability of wholesale prices in industries in which there were open-price trade associations and in those in which there were none, yielded no positive results. "If open-price associations effectively stabilize prices, that effect is brought about in other ways by equally important factors whatever they may be, so that the open-price commodities show no greater stability or no more undesirable stability, as the case may be, than other commodities. In fact they appear to show a trifle less consistency in their movements from month to month" (*ibid.*, 357). "Possibly open-price work is more often undertaken in industries where instability forces remedial action of this sort" (*loc. cit.*).

such declines. Professor Berglund remarked that, since the formation of the United States Steel Corporation the very drastic curtailments in the output of steel in times of depression have been associated with rapid business increases which are "seemingly associated, to some extent at least, with a general price policy which experience has apparently proved to be a factor in any permanent financial prosperity."[1] The average duration of periods of declining business was about 19 months between 1878 and 1904 and about 15 months between 1904 and 1923.[2] Such results turn largely, of course, upon the delimitation of cycles of business activity but, in so far as periods of declining business have become shorter there is a number of influences other than the price policy of the United States Steel Corporation to which the curtailment may reasonably be attributed. The period from 1873 to 1896 was one in which prices generally were falling and that from 1896 to 1920 was one in which prices were rising; it is well known that periods of prosperity are prolonged and periods of depression curtailed by an upward trend of prices.[3] As it is not claimed that the duration of cycles as a whole has been curtailed by the policy of the corporation, this behavior of the general price level offers a plausible explanation of the curtailment of the period of recession. Moreover, changes in the size of the population and in the technique of production caused an especially rapid increase in the demand for steel in the second period and probably one more in advance of the expansion of investment in the industry than in the first; recession would also be curtailed by such conditions. It is also possible that the curtailment of periods of recession has been more a cause than an effect of the policy of stabilizing prices; the difficulties of such a policy are diminished as periods of recession are curtailed. In so far as demand revives because of the "rusting out" and obsolescence of plants in other industries, a price policy which causes a severe decline in the output of steel during the decline in general business might, however, by postponing renewals and replacements for a time, cause a piling up of potential demand. This potential demand is likely to become actual when business revives and thus cause an increase of demand greater than would have occurred had

[1] BERGLUND, "The United States Steel Corporation and Price Stabilization, *Quart. Jour. Econ.*, 38: 628.
[2] Derived from AMERICAN TELEPHONE AND TELEGRAPH COMPANY, *Index of Business Activity*, cit. MITCHELL, *Business Cycles*, 338.
[3] *Cf.* MITCHELL, *Business Cycles*, 411.

some replacements been induced by greater price reductions during the period of recession. But only if "rusting out" and obsolescence proceed so fast as to reduce usable plant below that needed during the depression would failure to replace during the recession be likely to advance the moment when replacements begin.

A policy of price stabilization involves the avoidance of increases in price in periods of increasing business activity as well as the avoidance of reductions during a recession. The absence of fear of increases in prices during periods of increasing demand is said to discourage speculative increases in purchases and inventories beyond the amount justified by immediate increases in business. It is probably easier to remove fear of an increase in price in times of expanding business than to remove hope of a decrease in times of depression. The stabilization of prices is occasionally accompanied, however, by premium prices for speedy delivery; purchasers must then choose between higher prices and delayed delivery and this situation may stimulate speculative increases in purchases. This consequence is, however, the outcome not of stabilization but of failure to stabilize. Unless the demand for the product is completely inelastic in times of business activity the failure to raise prices must induce a greater demand than would otherwise exist. If producers endeavor to expand their investment to enable them to meet the whole of this demand they facilitate the cyclical expansions of demand which prepare the way for subsequent cyclical contractions. Failure to raise prices in good times is not so meritorious as is often alleged; and may not even be so profitable as it is thought to be. The desire to stabilize prices during depressions arises out of a threatening condition of the market which is the outcome, in part, of success in stabilizing prices in times of active business.

There is in fact a tendency in industries in which prices are stabilized to increase investment to permit the industry to meet the peak of demand.[1] This tendency not only prepares the way for later declines in demand; it also tends to increase the cost of

[1] The fact that in times of peak demand in the steel and anthracite industries, for example, the smaller producers are able to charge premiums over the prices of the larger firms (F.T.C., *Brief on Pittsburgh Plus*, 12; *Statement in Pittsburgh Plus*, 82, 537; *Premium Prices of Anthracite*, 4) suggests that larger firms do not adjust their investment to the absolute peak of demand; these firms ration their output while the smaller raise their prices. But the increasing volume of unfilled orders of the large firms and the higher prices obtainable by the smaller stimulate increased investment; the premiums are thereby usually kept within small limits.

production by the industry. If over the longer period prices cover total costs, prices must be higher than they would be if there were less investment in the industry and it were more fully used. Whether the prices of commodities subject to wide cyclical fluctuations in demand do yield only a normal profit over long periods is uncertain. It is even uncertain whether the price policy pursued in fact maximizes profits; it has already been suggested that perhaps even higher prices would be charged during periods of reduced demand if short-term considerations of profit dominated policy. Steel manufacturers believe that profits would be lower or losses higher in times of depression if prices were reduced[1] and if they are correct in their belief more new investment is doubtless attracted in years of increasing demand than would be if years of depression brought heavier losses.

The stabilization of prices affects not only the industry the price of whose products is stabilized; it reacts also upon those who sell to and those who buy from the industry. Those who sell to the industry with stabilized prices may be somewhat protected from pressure to reduce their prices. It is very evident, however, that the stabilization of the price of tobacco, bread, and corn products, for example, has not stabilized the price of the principal raw materials of which they are made. Firms selling their own product at a stable price continue to strive to minimize their costs (including the cost of materials). The demand for the raw material being restricted by the policy of the manufacturers its price may fall far if the sellers compete. If, however, sellers of the raw material are few, or have succeeded in discouraging price cutting, the realization that buyers have stabilized the price at which they resell greatly strengthens the resistance of sellers of the raw material to attempts to obtain lower prices. If they reduce their prices to buyers who will not in turn reduce their prices the sellers of raw materials can expect no increase in demand; they simply increase the profits or reduce the losses of those to whom they sell. Sellers to an industry in which prices are stabilized are forced to accept a reduction in volume of business; if they reduce their prices they suffer a still further

[1] When in 1909 the United States Steel Corporation announced its abandonment of an open-price policy to enable it to deal with price cutters it was remarked that price stabilization by maintaining the price in times of diminished demand, maintains profits or reduces losses, and that "the wiping out of profit in the manufacture of steel may have its sinister side in checking the development of further facilities for production for some time to come" (*Iron Age*, Feb. 25, 1909, cit. F.T.C., *Statement on Pittsburgh Plus*, 410).

reduction in revenue. They are deprived of the choice between increased sales at a lower price and existing sales at the existing price; they can secure only existing sales even at a lower price. They are likely, therefore, to stabilize their own prices.[1] Stabilization of prices is often said to benefit industries using the product the price of which is stabilized: its adoption is not infrequently attributed to the desire of those engaged in a subsequent stage of production to avoid losses owing to fluctuations in the price of their raw materials or factors of production. The stabilization of the price of steel products is said, for instance, to have protected customers against sudden increases and decreases in price and to have been highly appreciated by them.[2] The stabilization of an important element in the costs of the industry using the product of which the price is stabilized tends to stabilize the price policy of the second industry; the quantitative effect of the inducement depends upon the relative importance of the cost of the product the price of which is stabilized in the total costs of the industry using it. Those in this latter industry realize that attempts to increase the aggregate sales of the industry by price cutting will be more expensive if one element of costs is fixed than they would be if that element could be reduced.

[1] "It has long been recognized that the stability or inertia of prices to the consumer has involved a certain inefficiency in the machinery of distribution. If producers of foodstuffs, for example, have unusually large crops, the consumer feels very little of the effect in the form of reduced prices and has very little inducement to increase his consumption, so that the surplus, instead of being worked off by lower prices to the users, is in large part simply wasted. If through a stabilization of manufacturing industries that involves a disinclination to sell larger quantities at lower prices, there is no disposition on the part of the manufacturer to take increasingly large quantities of raw materials even at much lowered prices, then the price difference between the raw materials and the finished products is increased by stabilization at the latter end, and the difficulties of the producer of raw materials intensified. . . . If the producer of raw materials cannot make effective any reductions in price to the consumer and has nothing to say as to how much the market will take, the consumer, of course, will take only the usual quantity and the surplus merely goes to waste." (F.T.C., *Open Price Trade Associations*, 353. See also 363.)

[2] COMMONS, "Delivered Price Practice in the Steel Market," *Amer. Econ. Rev.*, 14: 507. A further reason for maintaining prices during the period following the panic of 1907 was given by Judge Gary at a meeting of the American Iron and Steel Institute on Feb. 25, 1909. He stated that "jobbers and consumers throughout the country had purchased large stocks at the prices prevailing when prices were favorable and these were undisposed of. Pending contracts for construction which involved iron and steel were extensive, contracts for new furnaces, mills, and equipment and for raw and semi-finished material had been made by large numbers. An immediate and radical reduction of prices would have meant bankruptcy to multitudes. To prevent disaster and ruin and at the request of scores who were interested, a large percentage of the leading men connected with the industry met to advise each other in regard to the best interests of all concerned including the general public." (*Cit.* F.T.C., *Statement on Pittsburgh Plus*, 408.)

These considerations lead to wider questions concerning the relation between policies of price stabilization and fluctuations of general business. The stabilization of prices in a single industry may react upon general business conditions in two important ways: it may affect general business conditions because of the far-reaching influence of the industry whose price is stabilized; or because stabilization is adopted in a large number of industries.

That the policy of a single industry may seriously influence general business conditions because it impinges upon a large number of industries is the assumption underlying attempts to control business activity through control of banking. This policy is applicable to any industry the cost of whose product enters into the costs of most industries:[1] e.g., coal, gas, electrical energy, and transportation. The prices of gas, electrical energy, and transportation are, however, relatively stable; during the period from June, 1929, to February, 1933, the quotations of the Bureau of Labor Statistics for electricity *increased* 9.0 per cent and those for gas 2.3 per cent; freight rates on a number of staple products were raised 15 per cent and even the price of bituminous coal fell only 11.4 per cent while the index of wholesale prices fell 37.2 per cent.

Stabilization of prices in one industry might seriously affect general business conditions also because the industries which it touched most closely were those subject to the widest cyclical fluctuations in activity. Industries providing materials to the constructional industries are the principal examples of this second class; during the period from June, 1929, to February, 1933, they also generally declined in price less than the index of wholesale prices as is indicated by the following list:[2]

	Percentage Decrease in Price, June, 1929, to February, 1933
Cement	13.5
Structural steel	18.0
Iron and steel	19.1
Brick and tile	19.3
Other building materials	19.4
Lumber	40.0
Average of all wholesale prices	37.2

[1] MACGREGOR, "Rationalization of Industry," *Econ. Jour.*, 37: 538 (1927).
[2] ibid.

The steel industry falls in both classes because of the considerable demand for steel products for the manufacture of consumers' goods as well as producers' goods.

The effect of the stabilization of prices by an industry whose product is demanded by a large number of industries involves merely a more general application of the argument already presented concerning the effect of the stabilization of the price of raw materials upon the price policies of the industries using them. In general, all industries using the product are presented during a depression with more forceful arguments against reductions in price than would be present if the costs of their materials were falling. A general tendency to maintain prices during a period of falling demand increases the contraction of business. If when demand began to contract every producer maintained his price his sales would decline; he would reduce his direct costs as nearly as possible in proportion to the reduction in sales. In the entirely imaginary case of *all* costs being direct costs capable of exact adjustment to changes in output, every producer's expenditure upon costs would decline by the same amount as his receipts; an initial decline in sales would cause an equal reduction in disbursements on costs which would cause an equal reduction in sales and so on. Production in this simply and rigidly organized world could be brought to a standstill by a small but sustained initial fall in demand. The presence of overhead costs prevents the speedy[1] reduction of all costs in the same proportion as output. But it is not costs as calculated by reference to bookkeeping conventions that are important: it is disbursements out of business revenue. Disbursements in respect of overhead costs are made intermittently and in irregular amounts; they can in fact be reduced in proportions greater than reductions in output. When demand falls by a considerable amount it is possible to stop replacements of plant altogether for a time,[2] thus causing a contraction in the demand for producers' goods, unemployment, and contracted demands in other fields. Price stabilization does not, however, enhance this tendency; if the decline in demand is such that, even if the price of the product were drastically

---

[1] Over longer periods, reorganization of whole industries owing to the failure of firms and decisions not to replace assets tends to reduce total costs more nearly in proportion to demand than is possible in short periods.

[2] Such reduced disbursements may result in the repayment of bank debts or the purchase of securities and thus indirectly permit a reduction of bank debts and deposits.

reduced, replacements of plant must still be completely suspended, a greater reduction in sales owing to the stabilization of the price of the product can do no more; it is more likely to prolong the period of suspension of demand for producers' goods than to increase the magnitude of the reduction in demand.

The stabilization of the price of a commodity demanded by a large number of industries also affects the rate of expansion in periods of increasing general business activity; it has been said that it "without doubt moderates the impact of crises on society if the stable prices of syndicalized [cartelized] producers' goods, especially of raw materials and fuels, diminish the tendency of industrialism to sudden speculative expansion of productive equipment."[1] But does the stabilization of such prices tend to diminish the tendency to expansion? The absence of increases in the price of producers' goods, *i.e.*, the absence of increases in costs in times of increasing demand for finished goods, is more likely to magnify the expansion of the finished goods industries.

The stabilization of the prices of some products while the prices of others move freely affects the incidence of the burden of depression; both the Federal Farm Board[2] and the Federal Trade Commission[3] contend that the burden borne by industries

[1] VON BECKERATH, *Modern Industrial Organization*, 256.

[2] "Agriculture is an industry which in this depression has maintained production and employment but has done so at the cost of very much reduced prices for its products." While the volume of industrial production was reduced about 42 per cent between 1929 and 1932 the price of manufactured goods fell less than the general index of prices. (Evidence on behalf of the Federal Farm Board at *Hearings on the Amendment of the Federal Trade Commission Act*, before U.S. Senate Committee on the Judiciary, 1932, 170–172.)

"During a period in which the prices of the products obtained from slaughtering a hog had fallen about $4, the price of hogs fell by almost the same amount: in other words practically all the cut in price was passed back to the farmer and the distributors and those in between were able to maintain their margin unchanged. . . . The reason for the maintained margin was that wages, freight rates, and other costs which are paid by the wholesaler and the distributor of farm products did not decline rapidly. . . . As it is now the prices of half of the [economic] system may be controlled as, for example, through set freight rates or agreed prices or customary margins." (*ibid.*, 167.)

"If you permit certain prices in your economic structure to be controlled and at the same time other prices are not controlled that means the industries which are not able to control their prices have to bear the entire strain of economic readjustments which take place" (*loc. cit.*).

[3] "Stabilization in a single line of business may be obtained at considerable expense to the rest of society. Stabilization for manufacturers in general may be achieved at the cost of agricultural producing interests." It was added that the extent to which stabilization had been achieved in manufacturing "may be considerably exaggerated and manufacturers, not being able to reduce wages as fast as prices fall, the difference in the incidence of deflation upon manufacturers and agriculturalists was partly due to factors beyond the control of the former." (F.T.C., *Open Price Trade Associations*, 366.) The commission believed that "if there is to be

in the hands of large numbers of relatively small producers (*e.g.*, in agriculture and the cotton textile industry) is increased by the ability of others to take shelter from price competition and stabilize prices; the prices of the goods they sell decline more than the prices of their raw materials and consumption goods. Wage earners in the sheltered industries suffer a greater reduction in employment than those in the unsheltered; whether those who retain work secure higher wages than they otherwise would depends partly upon the behavior of sales revenue and other costs. Farmers receiving returns in the form of wages and profits combined have probably suffered little unemployment but have suffered a drastic reduction in returns.

Stabilization of prices does not necessarily maximize the profits of investors; we have seen that on some occasions higher prices might yield higher profits in a depression; doubtless on other occasions reductions during a depression and increases during periods of activity would be more profitable. If the secondary effects of price policies are taken into account it is difficult to decide what policy is likely to be most profitable. It is difficult to decide, therefore, whether the profit receivers in industries that have stabilized their prices have thus improved their position compared with what it would have been had they reduced their prices; doubtless many industries have thus benefited. But the magnitude of the restriction of output in many industries is, as we have seen, mainly due to causes other than their price policies, *e.g.*, to the directions in which entrepreneurs and consumers economize in a depression.

In the effort to avoid short-term price cutting aimed at shifting business from firm to firm in a world in which more rigid and formal control of prices and output has been prohibited, business men turned in a number of industries to a policy that has eliminated almost all price cutting. They have paralyzed the mechanism of response to declining demand; claiming to benefit industries purchasing from them, they have failed to realize the extent to which their policy magnifies reactions to a decline in business. Major adaptations to changing conditions of supply are hindered. Not only is pressure to increase efficiency diminished

stabilization of prices through regulation of output, it is worth considering whether the beginning of the application of this method should not be at the raw product end. If applied first to finished products it means sheer waste of raw products. If applied first to raw products then the waste not only of material but of labor in planting and harvesting is avoided."

THE STABILIZATION OF INDIVIDUAL PRICES 263

but also positive pressures towards decreasing efficiency and increasing costs are set in motion.

Banking is the only industry which has hitherto been expected to frame its price policy with reference to its effect upon general business activity; it is argued that if one element in the cost of many businesses (*viz.*, interest charges) can be controlled the volume of business activity as a whole is capable of control. Current interest charges on short-term loans are a small element in the total costs of most businesses but changes in long-term interest rates affect the volume of general business through their effect upon the profitability of new investments, and, therefore, upon the demand for producers' goods. Control involves, however, *not* the stabilization of this element of cost but a deliberate and calculated destabilization, a destabilization calculated to neutralize the effect of other elements in the industrial organism making for instability. If the United States Steel Corporation were in a position to control the prices of steel and cement which enter largely into the costs of producers' goods, the output of which is subject to wide cyclical fluctuations, and if it wished to stabilize general business, it would seek to destabilize and not to stabilize steel and cement prices. It would endeavor to damp down the demand for producers' goods when it was believed that business was approaching a condition of unstable activity and reduce them when business appeared to be declining to an unhealthy degree. Stabilization of prices may, however, discourage speculation in inventories by its customers that would further destabilize business. The stabilization of prices which enter into costs over a wide field of industrial activity tends, therefore, to destabilize industrial activity as a whole. Price control by industry groups springing from fear of short-run price competition is not yet sufficiently emancipated from its origin to be used as an instrument for the control of general business activity. Indeed it is doubtful whether it can ever be so used.

If key prices are used as a means of general stabilization they must be frequently adjusted in the light of changes in economic conditions; industries vary in their power to influence general conditions because the importance of their prices in the costs of other industries varies: if attempts are made by more than one industry to stabilize general business, conflicts must occur; stability in general business activity moreover may not be identical with the interests of the industry whose price is to be used as a means of control. Finally, it is questionable whether the stabilization of general business can be left in the hands of those managing key industries; knowledge is so inadequate that policy must rest largely upon judgment.

Price stabilization has become effective over an increasingly wide industrial field, partly no doubt because it tends to spread from industry to industry in the manner already explained, and partly because similar conditions in different industries have produced a similar response. The general consequences of such a rigidity of prices have already been analyzed in connection with stabilization by vital or key industries. To this analysis must be added some consideration of the effect of stabilizing prices when industrial efficiency is increasing. This combination of circumstances has been held to be the major cause of the collapse of business after 1929.[1] If prices are stabilized while costs are falling profit margins widen as they probably did between 1923 and 1929;[2] the index of the prices of manufactured goods declined by 7 per cent or about 1.2 per cent per annum,[3] policies aimed at the stabilization of prices being common, but not universal. The stability of prices may have been due in some industries to the absence of significant changes in conditions of demand and supply. The efficiency of business operation was, however, increasing; the national income increased 24.9 per cent during the period 1923 to 1929,[4] without any general increase in prices or

---

[1] *Cf.* "The rapid technical progress and organizatory rationalization, combined with easy credit, did not lead to the price fall objectively possible. Instead it promoted both the stock market boom and an overinvestment in real estate, factories, transport facilities (automobile industry), the radio trade, etc. The overinvestment was made possible by the accumulation of vast new capital from the extraordinary profits many entrepreneurs realized from the profit margin widened through more efficient machinery and human organization despite rising wages and salaries. This disproportionate investment of capital could have been avoided only by a sharp restriction of credit and by high interest rates. Actually, however, credit was easy as a result of a rather expansive credit policy which caused the stabilization of the price level virtually equivalent to raising it." (VON BECKERATH, *Modern Industrial Organization*, 270.)

[2] The rate of return upon capitalization for 2046 corporations of medium and large size and responsible for over half the manufacturing by corporations was for each of the years from 1919 to 1928: 18.3, 12.3, 2.9, 10.2, 11.2, 10.0, 12.1, 12.4, 9.5, 11.0 (EPSTEIN, *Industrial Profits in the United States*, 242). As, however, the book capitalization is used as a basis for these figures they are difficult to interpret.

[3] MILLS, *Economic Tendencies*, 333; CURRIE, "The Failure of Monetary Policy to Prevent the Depression of 1929 to 1932," *Jour. Polit. Econ.*, 42: 162 (1933); COPELAND, "How Large Is Our National Income?" *Jour. Polit. Econ.*, 40:1 (1932) Changes in the prices of the more complex manufactured goods (such as various types of machinery) are not reflected in these figures owing to the difficulty of securing series that are homogeneous.

[4] COPELAND, *loc. cit.*

any great change in the proportion of labor and plant unemployed. This widened profit margin is obtained by the displacement of labor or capital or both; the sales of the goods with fixed prices can be maintained although unemployment is increased if profit receivers as a class apply their added purchasing power at the points from which it has been withdrawn by the workers and interest receivers (if any) whose incomes have been reduced. If profit receivers save part or all of their increased incomes, and prices are stable, the demand for goods *may* fall. If the workers discharged, and capital freed, are reemployed during the period in which more equipment is being produced, and they receive the same income as before and spend it as before, and current incomes from profits remain unchanged, again no disequilibrium need occur. But if prices are stabilized the demand for goods is maintained only so long as the increased purchases of equipment continue. When new equipment becomes available for use the continued high profits of the industries with stable prices will not suffice to purchase the products of the new plants; the annual payment for the use of the plants can be only a fraction of the expenditure upon their equipment. The continued building of plants is discouraged; cessation of building causes both labor and equipment to be thrown out of employment (although some labor will be needed to operate the new plant). If all prices were stabilized this reduction in demand would cause a progressive decline in production and a progressive increase in unused resources; profits then decline and reduce the supply of funds available for investment. If wages and selling prices are fixed workers can buy no more goods when the efficiency of production increases; if the receivers of increased profit do not wish to consume more they can temporarily maintain sales and profits by increased investment but they cannot permanently do so. As investors they refuse to take account of their own policy as employers, sellers, and consumers.

Increases in wages tend to divert incomes from those who save much to those who save less; they increase the demand for consumers' goods and offset the above tendencies. Some such offset probably occurred in the period under discussion. During the period from 1920 to 1926 the share of the national income going to workers is reported not to have changed significantly:[1] the

---

[1] COPELAND, in NATIONAL BUREAU OF ECONOMIC RESEARCH, *Recent Economic Changes*, II, 769.

annual rates of increase in wages judged by various indexes from 1922 to 1929 varied from 0.8 per cent for woman factory labor to 4.3 per cent for hourly union rates, even farm wages increasing 1.6 per cent per annum.[1] Incomes from work increased about as quickly as incomes from property, partly because wage rates are increased with less reluctance in times of increasing profit margins and partly because piece rates tended to increase the money earnings of workers.[2] If the collapse of business from 1929 to 1933 is attributed to the stabilization of prices while costs were falling the above diversion of incomes to workers must have been insufficient to offset the tendency to diminish spending on consumers' goods.

C. Stabilization of Prices over Long Periods

The analysis of the effects of the stabilization of the prices of individual commodities over long periods of time provides an opportunity for investigating the consequences of stabilization apart from the business cycle.

Price stabilization tends in a variety of ways to a higher level of costs than would otherwise occur. The level upon which prices are stabilized is likely to be one that subjects no important firm to great pressure; the most efficient firms probably receive a relatively high rate of return. As the efficiency of production is increased the stable price becomes increasingly profitable. Wide margins of profit provide the means for, as well as induce, new investment either by new firms or by those already in the industry; increased investment may be induced by the hope of securing business by non-price competition or very profitable business at times of peak demand. Profits are reduced (unless demand at the unchanging price increases sufficiently to keep the expanding equipment fully occupied) but the reduction comes not from any reduction in price which benefits consumers, but from an increase in costs which has benefited nobody except, possibly, those engaged in the provision of productive equipment. The extent to which such unused plant is becoming a permanent characteristic of industries that stabilize prices is impossible to measure. It has been calculated that about 20 per cent of manufacturing capacity in general was unused during the period from 1925 to

[1] MILLS, *Economic Tendencies*, 477.
[2] HANSEN and TOUT, "Investment and Saving in Business Cycle Theory," *Econometrica*, 1: 147 (1933). See also CURRIE, "The Failure of Monetary Policy to Prevent the Depression of 1929 to 1932," *Jour. Polit. Econ.*, 42: 162.

THE STABILIZATION OF INDIVIDUAL PRICES 267

1929 and that there was no tendency for this proportion to increase between 1900 and 1929.[1] The statistics available for the industries discussed in the present chapter are:[2]

	Percentage of Capacity in Use 1925 to 1929
Boot and shoe	80
Paper	92
Pig iron	85
Steel	93
Rolled steel products	73
Tin plate	68
Wire	74
Window glass	62
Plate glass	85

These figures are inconclusive; the measurement of capacity is notoriously difficult, and reliable factual material is often lacking.

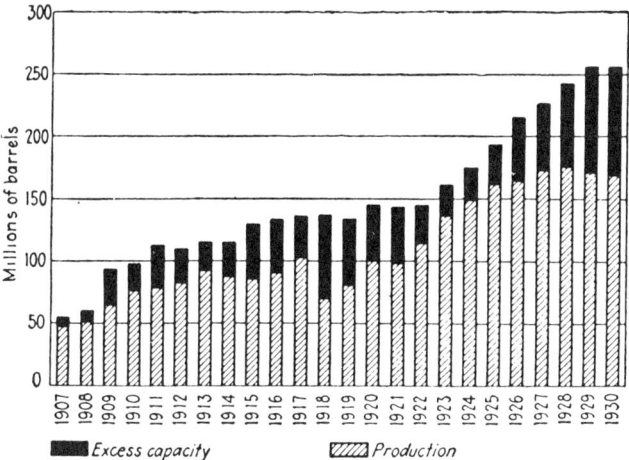

FIG. 35.—Percentage of capacity for the production of cement in use 1907 to 1930. (*Fraser and Doriot, Analysing Our Industries*, 288.)

We have seen, moreover, that stabilization tends to expand both demand and capacity in times of business activity such as the years investigated; the extent of the unemployed plant the cost of which tends to be included in prices appears, therefore, in years of depression. It has been remarked, for instance, that

---
[1] NOURSE and associates, *America's Capacity to Produce*, 416, 421.
[2] *ibid.*, 303.

the prices of steel products in 1934 sufficed to yield profits as soon as plants were employed at more than 50 per cent of capacity.[1] In the cement industry except for a few months in the latter half of 1929 the price of cement was maintained throughout the four-year period beginning with 1927.[2] During this period, however, productive capacity in use showed a continuous decline from 83.5 per cent in 1926 to 65.9 per cent in 1929 and 61.5 per cent in 1930.[3] It is evident from Fig. 35 that the amount of equipment available in 1911 was not equaled by actual output until 1922; during the whole period from 1923 to 1928 capacity for cement production increased about 50 per cent, while sales increased about 28 per cent; although the volume of production declined in 1929, investment in the industry continued to increase for a time.[4] Many influences have contributed to this result; production has been established in a number of new areas; railroads have induced the building of plants on their lines; local pride has led some states to build their own cement plants to provide cement for public buildings and highway construction.[5] But there is little doubt that if the price of cement had been lower, the apparent profit prospects of plants in new areas would have been diminished. Furthermore the establishment of plants by state governments is attributable not only to local pride, but also to a suspicion that state plants could produce at costs below the prices being paid.[6] Again in the paper industry capacity was constantly increased between 1923 and 1933 although production continuously fell short of capacity by 20 per cent or more.[7]

The elimination of the less efficient is retarded by price stabilization in a variety of ways: prices are unlikely, as we have seen, to be stabilized upon a level likely to drive firms out of business; prices being uniform for all sellers (apart from differences in grade of product or places of delivery) the low-cost firms are prevented from driving the high-cost firms out of business by

[1] *New York Times*, Aug. 15, 1934.
[2] F.T.C., *Price Bases Inquiry*, 82.
[3] *loc. cit.*
[4] Probably owing to the completion of projects initiated earlier.
[5] FRASER and DORIOT, *op. cit.*, 288.
[6] The manufacturers have been very conscious of this threat to the maintenance of prices in the industry; in one case at least they quoted a base price for cement at a point at which the only producer was a state plant; the price being low, this action has given the impression that the state plant is an unprofitable enterprise (F.T.C., *Price Bases Inquiry*, 122).
[7] CONSUMER ADVISORY BOARD, *Paper Complaints*, 5.

price cutting.¹ The pressure to reduce costs is also diminished; it is not removed because reductions in cost widen the profit margin. Where improvements require considerable expenditure for their discovery and development and the expenditure will be about the same for a large as for a small firm the stimulus to improvement is proportionate to the volume of business done by each firm; the larger firm may incur the cost, but if it succeeds in increasing its efficiency, the absence of price competition reduces the pressure upon the smaller firms to adopt the new methods. The larger firm may reduce profits by expenditure on non-price competition or overexpansion. The minimum level of efficiency possible in the industry depends (apart from expenditure upon non-price competition) upon the level at which prices are stabilized; it is a matter of administrative decision in the industry, freedom of decision being limited by the fear that if the price set will not permit the survival of most firms it may precipitate a struggle for survival in which price competition will again raise its ugly head.²

The minimization of price competition by resort to price stabilization tends to divert rivalry into other forms of competition. Individual firms prevented from attracting additional business by price cutting attempt to obtain such business by increasing their expenditure on sales promotion.³ Selling costs in the cement industry, for instance, are said to have reached a high level.⁴ In the cement, sugar, and steel industries the main-

---

[1] The Federal Trade Commission concluded with regard to the stabilization of the price of cement during the four years beginning with 1927 that "had there been keen competition in price during these four years, and so price flexibility, low cost producers would have forced the high cost and disadvantageously located producers out of production by lowering their prices" (F.T.C., *Price Bases Inquiry*, 82).

[2] The Federal Trade Commission has argued that, just as large firms which have stabilized prices have suffered a decline in relative importance in their industries, so whole industries that succeeded in stabilizing (*e.g.*, through the activities of a trade association) might be expected to lose ground in relation to industries with less rigid price policies (*Open Price Trade Associations*, 364). The analogy is, however, not altogether proper; we have seen that the declining relative position of leaders has been due in a number of cases to the growth of the industry as a whole at a rate with which already large firms would have difficulty in keeping up. Moreover, the more successful smaller firms do not appear to improve their relative position because their policies are less rigid than those of the leaders. However, the commission suggested that "some of the loss of importance observed in the case of the trusts and to be expected in the case of too highly stabilized lines of business is probably due to comparative inefficiency. The benefit of competition is not merely in the lowering of prices but still more in the stimulus to efficiency." (*loc. cit.*)

[3] See Chap. VIII.

[4] The selling and administrative costs of the Lehigh Portland Cement Company in 1930 were reported at 18.3 per cent of sales and those of the International Cement Company at 12.2 per cent of sales (FRAZER and DORIOT, *op. cit.*, 309).

tenance of mill prices has been accompanied by efforts on the part of producers to increase their sales by enlarging their sales territory; they reach out into territory in which, to sell at the same price as producers who have easier access, they must accept prices which yield at the seller's mill less than sales to buyers nearer the plant. This policy tends to increase transportation costs; buyers may pay higher prices than are necessary although producers may make only normal profits.[1] This practice may go so far, where there is a large excess capacity, that producers finally turn to price cutting, as they did in the cement industry in the spring of 1931; a price war following upon increasing freight absorptions carried the price of cement to about one dollar a barrel at the mill, a price said to be below the cost of production for the great majority of plants.[2]

Price stabilization reduces the risks of investment in the industry to the extent that it excludes price cutting in periods of reduced demand. Risks are diminished, however, only if the return above direct costs is greater when prices are stabilized than when prices are not: whether or not such is the fact depends upon the extent to which demand might be increased by a reduction in prices and the extent to which average costs are increased by a reduction in output. The possible tendency to reduce costs in this way is, however, more than counterbalanced by the tendency to increase them.

Stabilization of prices leading to high profits over the longer period of time also stimulates integration: state governments building roads and public buildings have undertaken the manufacture of cement; the International Harvester Company makes its own steel and the automobile manufacturers have contemplated the same policy. The broader aspects of this matter are, however, discussed in a later chapter.[3]

The effect of price stabilization upon the distribution of economic well-being between the principal classes in the community is extremely difficult to discover; the ultimate effect of stabilization upon both the level of the price stabilized and upon cyclical fluctuations of business is uncertain. Stabilization of prices is intended to reduce the risks of capital, but it is doubtful whether this is achieved; price competition tends to be replaced

[1] See Chap. VI.
[2] FRAZER and DORIOT, *op. cit.*, 310.
[3] See Chap. IX.

by non-price competition. It is also doubtful whether over long periods of time a stable price policy is more profitable than one of adjusting prices to conditions of demand and supply. The benefits to investors are doubtful except in comparison with an economic system in which there is continuing cutthroat competition. The following statistics of the average rate of profit (before payment of federal taxes) to capitalization (excluding funded debt) from 1919 to 1928 suggest that over this period the industries whose prices were relatively stable were also more profitable than most:[1]

TABLE X

	Number of corporations	Profit as per cent of investment (1919-1928)
All manufacturing	2046	10.8
Boots and shoes	25	17.3
Glass	18	16.9
Bakery products	17	16.8
Carpets	18	15.6
Portland cement	21	14.2
Tobacco	23	14.2
Crude chemicals	9	11.1
Wire and nails	20	10.9
Paper	111	9.6
Petroleum refining	52	8.7
Sheet metal	20	7.1
Rubber and rubber products	26	5.9
Castings and forgings (including iron and steel plants of all kinds)	99	5.8

These figures relate, however, only to medium and large-sized producers who remained in operation throughout the whole period.[2] Their relatively high profits, moreover, were due in part to other consequences of the conditions that enabled them to stabilize prices. Their profits might have been even higher had they not aimed at price stabilization.

Purchasers of the product are unlikely to gain from any reduction of risk that is achieved: price stabilization attracts

[1] EPSTEIN, *Industrial Profits in the United States*, 242 ff.
[2] The corporations included were responsible for over one-half of all the manufacturing by corporations.

excessive amounts of capital to the industries concerned and probably magnifies cyclical fluctuations of business: selling and transportation costs may increase thus reducing profits without reducing prices: the stimulus to increase the efficiency of production is diminished as well as the pressure to transmit the benefit of lower costs to purchasers. Workers may secure some greater measure of stability of income; they may share in the benefits of the reduction of risks. Producers may have pursued a "high-wage policy" in the sense that they have paid wages higher than they would otherwise have paid simply because of a fear that if costs were reduced without any equivalent reduction in prices there would be increased difficulty in disposing of their product. These higher payments to workers represent another tendency under a régime of stabilized prices for costs to increase, but they serve also to pass on to workers some advantage from the discovery of more efficient technical methods of production. But it is doubtful whether a high-wage policy has been adopted for these reasons. Moreover, stabilization of prices, in so far as it increases the amplitude of cyclical fluctuations in business, increases the burden thrown upon workers in the form of unemployment.

CHAPTER VI

PRICE DISCRIMINATION

I. The definition of price discrimination and the conditions favoring it—II. Discrimination according to the use of the product—III. Discrimination according to the trade status of the buyer—IV. Geographical discrimination—*A*. Zone price systems—*B*. Basing-point systems—1. The occurrence of basing-point systems—*a*. Lumber and miscellaneous industries—*b*. The steel industry—*c*. The cement industry—*d*. The sugar industry—2. The policy of the National Recovery Administration.

I. THE DEFINITION OF PRICE DISCRIMINATION AND THE CONDITIONS FAVORING IT

Price discrimination occurs whenever a seller sells a homogeneous commodity at the same time to different purchasers at different prices. If sellers attempt merely to sell at the best prices offered, discrimination tends to disappear. Even if sellers take account of the purpose for which the product is to be used, or the place at which it is to be used, there will be little difference in the prices paid by different buyers unless there is only one seller or unless the sellers adopt a common basis of discrimination. Even in these circumstances, however, different prices can be maintained for different classes of buyers only where the commodity is not easily transferable by buyers in one class to those in another.[1]

The profitability of discrimination in price rests upon differences in the elasticities of the demand of different groups and, ultimately, of different individual buyers. If a producer is selling at a uniform price in a number of markets the sale of another unit in the market in which demand is most elastic will yield a greater net revenue than the sale of another unit in markets where demand is least elastic. He will gain by restricting sales in the markets with the least elastic demand and increasing them in those with the most elastic demand. The most profitable total output will be such that the marginal revenue upon sales in all markets is equal, and equal to the marginal cost of production.

[1] Medical men are able to treat the poor more cheaply than the rich partly because the service cannot be sold at second hand by the poor to the rich.

The price will be highest in the market with the least elastic demand.[1]

Discrimination would be profitable in the sale of practically all commodities. Interest centers, therefore, upon the extent to which past changes in the organization of production (and particularly in the scale of production) have facilitated discrimination, and the extent to which facilities for discrimination have been used to maximize profits. In any strict definition discrimination occurs wherever there are higgling and bargaining and where temporary local price cutting occurs but it is unsystematic and unlikely to maximize profit. Systematic discrimination aimed at maximizing profits is most likely where the same product is sold at different prices according to the use to which it is to be put. The limitation of discrimination to dealings in homogeneous articles is, however, unnecessarily narrow. It may also occur when the prices at which different combinations of commodity and service are sold at prices which do not correspond to the difference in the identifiable cost of producing each. It is more difficult to identify under these conditions; there are, however, two important types of such discrimination, *viz.*, discrimination according to trade status, and geographical discrimination. The three types of discrimination call for separate discussion.

II. DISCRIMINATION ACCORDING TO THE USE OF THE PRODUCT

Uniform products have for long been sold by public utilities at prices varying with the use to which they are to be put. Water, gas, electricity are often sold at one price for domestic use, another for commercial use, and possibly another for public use. Electricity is commonly sold at different prices for lighting and heating. The monopolistic position of the seller, and the relative ease with which sales intended for one purpose can be prevented from flowing into other uses, make this discrimination possible.

Discrimination similar in type is beginning to make its appearance in other markets, of which that for milk is the most important. Cooperative associations of dairy farmers commonly sell milk identical in quality at a variety of prices according as it is to be used for fluid consumption, cream, butter making, cheese making, or canning as condensed or evaporated milk.[2] This

---

[1] *Cf.* ROBINSON, JOAN, *The Economics of Imperfect Competition*, Chap. XV.

[2] *Hearing on the Prices of Food Products* before the Senate Committee on Agriculture and Forestry, 1931, 206. When the Milk Control Board of the State of New

policy is possible only because of a considerable element of monopoly on both sides of the market. The cooperative prevents farmers from attempting to take advantage of the higher-priced markets, thus bringing prices in all to a common level. Buyers can be prevented from diverting low-priced milk into higher-priced uses. The policy is profitable because in each area the demand for milk for fluid consumption is relatively inelastic while that for other uses is more elastic, owing partly to the ease with which demand can be postponed (*e.g.*, cheese can be manufactured and stored when prices are low) and partly to the availability of supplies from other areas (*e.g.*, butter can be economically transported longer distances than fluid milk). There is, however, no means of deciding how nearly the price of fluid milk approaches the monopoly price. The profits of dairy farmers depend upon their numbers. So long as there is freedom of entry, increased numbers mean a smaller share for each in the high-priced market and a greater proportion of their product sold in the lower-priced markets at falling prices.

The grape growers of California were encouraged by the Federal Farm Board to seek relief in the formation of a Grape Control Board which was to purchase in each year "the estimated surplus of grapes above the quantity which could be marketed at adequate prices and remove it from the grape and raisin market channels, either by leaving the fruit on the vines, or disposing of it to by-product industries."[1] The board claimed as one of the merits of cooperative marketing associations their ability "to market an entire crop so as to return the producers the most that the crop viewed as a whole can be made to yield."[2]

York established minimum prices to be paid by dealers it fixed prices separately for some seven categories of this kind (*Official Order* 17 by Milk Control Board of the State of New York, May 12, 1933).

[1] FEDERAL FARM BOARD, *Annual Report*, 1931, 59. The control board was to determine the probable amount of surplus grapes and to purchase them out of a levy on the grapes sold. The board in the year 1930 bought 337,000 tons of raisin grapes (about a quarter of the total crop), most of which were left on the vines, although some were sold for manufacture into by-products. The control of the fresh-grape market was less successful.

[2] FEDERAL FARM BOARD, *Annual Report*, 1932, 9. The board approved of the "principle of the diversion of excess supply to lower-value uses, so that the remaining quantity could be sold in remunerative channels at the usual price. With fluid milk the surplus may be dried, condensed, or churned; with lemons it may be made into by-products; with grapes or peaches for canning the grower may be paid to leave it unpicked. The grower benefits from a stabilizing of prices when the increased return for 'basic disposition' more than offsets the decreased return from the surplus quantities. So long as the weighted average price received by the grower exceeds the price which would prevail if the surplus was permitted unduly to depress prices, he gains." (*ibid.*, 61.)

But power to control the number of producers and their planting programs is a prerequisite to monopoly profits although not to monopoly prices.[1] The approval by the World Wheat Advisory Commission of the proposal to denature part of the wheat supply to prevent its use for human consumption while leaving it available for use as cattle food[2] suggests the possibility of a discriminatory policy in the wheat market.

Discrimination according to the use of the commodity occurs in the markets for industrial products but information upon the subject is very scarce. The price of plate glass per square foot varies considerably with the size of the piece sold, the smaller pieces being sold very much more cheaply than the larger.[3] Small pieces are as costly to produce as the larger, because glass is most cheaply made by being first ground in large sheets and later cut up into smaller pieces. The maintenance of this policy must depend upon at least a common determination by all sellers to protect the market for the larger pieces even though they must "dump" their remaining output into the market for smaller pieces.[4] The fact that small pieces cannot be recombined into large sheets prevents the former from finding their way into the market for large sizes. These larger sizes are used in large buildings and for store fronts where a considerable resistance to wind pressure is necessary and where, the cost of glass constituting but a small part of the total cost of the building, the demand for it is inelastic. Smaller sizes, however, have to be sold in competition with window glass and the price that can be charged is limited by the difference in quality of the two products.

The Aluminum Company controls the price of pig aluminum by virtue of the fact that it produces all the aluminum made in the United States.[5] Prior to 1935 the company apparently sold aluminum ingots at 23.0 cents per pound but sold aluminum made into cable (at a fabricating cost of 6 cents per pound) at 17.5 cents per pound. The price obtainable for aluminum cable

[1] Monopoly profits are prevented if high prices induce unnecessary expenditure upon the production of commodities not sold.
[2] *New York Times*, Apr. 6, 1934.
[3] The average price per square foot in 1906 was $0.1875 for a piece from three to five square feet and $0.45 for a piece of fifty to a hundred square feet. The corresponding prices in 1915 were $0.17 and $0.35. (WATKINS, *Industrial Combinations and Public Policy*, 170.) In February, 1935, plate glass in pieces of 3 to 5 square feet cost $0.245 per square foot and in pieces of 5 to 10 square feet $0.260 (Bureau of Labor Statistics).
[4] WATKINS, *op. cit.*, 171.
[5] N.R.A., *Report on the Aluminum Industry*, 20. Imports occur, over a tariff duty of 4 cents per pound, and must exercise some restraining influence.

was limited by the price of copper cable. This differential could be maintained only by requiring purchasers of cable to agree to use it only for transmission purposes.[1]

Somewhat similar discrimination occurs in the sale of coal. In some areas the price paid for coal is dependent upon the type of building in which it is burned.[2] Discrimination also occurs in the markets for steam and domestic sizes.[3]

Discrimination of this type is in the interests of all concerned where it permits a scale of production more economical than would be possible if a uniform price were charged and, consequently, results in lower prices. The price of plate glass of large sizes might be higher than it is if none were sold in competition with window glass. But where there is more than one producer this argument is unlikely to apply; if there were fewer producers they could sell at the same *average* price as they get under discrimination and obtain equally high profits while selling large sizes at lower prices. Discrimination is also a means of avoiding the consequences of excessive investment. It may yield only normal profits but on an excessive investment. If it yields more than normal profits it may perpetuate itself by inducing increased investments until profits are normal even under discrimination, and discrimination is necessary to maintain normal profits.

III. DISCRIMINATION ACCORDING TO THE TRADE STATUS OF THE BUYER

Manufacturers commonly sell their products even where completely homogeneous at different prices according to the trade status of the purchaser, *i.e.*, according as he is a wholesaler, jobber, retailer, or final purchaser. The goods and services supplied to these different classes are, however, not uniform. The wholesaler takes commodities in large quantities, and performs a number

---

[1] *ibid.*, 14. Fabricators for other purposes would have bought cable at 17.5 cents in preference to ingots at 23.0 cents and melted the cable had they been permitted to do so.

[2] N.R.A., CONSUMERS ADVISORY BOARD, *Fixing Coal Prices* (statement at Price Hearing, Jan. 9, 1935), 4, 9.

[3] *ibid.*, 9. Differences could be classified as discriminatory, however, only if the process of production is such that the quantities of each size are subject to control. The British coal industry has been sharply divided concerning the desirability of differentiating in price according to the use to which the coal is to be put. Many producers contend that they should be permitted to quote lower prices to the bunker trade than to other buyers. The Coal Mines Act of 1930 does not permit such discrimination. (MINES DEPARTMENT, *Coal Mines Act 1930: Report on the Working of Schemes. . . . During the Year 1932*, 10, *cit* LUCAS, "The British Movement for Reconstruction," *Quart. Jour. Econ.*, 49: 220 (1935).)

of distribution services (including, possibly, carrying inventories) that would fall upon the manufacturer if he sold direct to the consumer. In a smaller measure the jobber and the retailer also perform part of the service of distribution. Discrimination occurs, therefore, only where the differences in price (or the trade discounts) do not correspond to differences in the cost of doing business with each class, *i.e.*, where the net yield upon sales to those in each class, after deducting costs of selling directly attributable to differences in the trade status of buyers, is not uniform.

Departure from this uniformity has occurred. Chain and department stores and cooperative buying associations of retailers, having integrated the services of wholesaling and retailing, have claimed the full trade discounts allowed by manufacturers to wholesalers who buy under similar conditions. Some manufacturers have refused to grant these discounts and have been upheld in their refusal by the courts.[1]

Differences in the prices charged to wholesalers, jobbers, and retailers turn partly upon differences in the size of orders. In so far as large orders involve lower bookkeeping, credit, and selling costs, they can be executed at a lower price per unit of product. Quantity discounts frequently, however, exceed the differences in costs arising from these sources. They are often granted because the manufacturing cost of executing large orders is believed to be lower than that of executing small orders. Where a seller has unoccupied capacity for production, an additional large order *may*, but does not necessarily, involve lower costs per unit than a number of small orders. Where a large order is placed for delivery over a considerable period of time, the manufacturer can frequently execute the order by utilizing his plant at times when other orders, smaller and for more immediate delivery, do not occupy it. Where the buyer is supplying such an "off-peak load" it can be accepted at a lower price, just as a public utility is properly permitted to charge lower prices for such business. But a large order requiring immediate delivery may involve costs greater than are involved in smaller orders coming in over a period of time, because it requires an extension of plant or the utilization of present plant beyond its most economical rate.

[1] Great Atlantic and Pacific Tea Co. v. Cream of Wheat Co., 227 Fed. 46 (1915); F.T.C. v. Mennen Co., 288 Fed. 778 (1923); F.T.C. v. National Biscuit Co. and Loose-Wiles Biscuit Co., 299 Fed. 739 (1924) (in which case refusal to treat a co operative organization of buyers as favorably as a chain-store buyer was upheld).

In the steel and oil[1] industries large orders appear to have been generally accepted at lower prices than smaller ones before 1933, but in the cement[2] industry quantity discounts were rarely given. In the sugar industry it was denied[3] that large orders could be executed at lower costs than smaller ones and contended that discounts unaccompanied by savings equivalent to the discount allowed were "purely arbitrary price discrimination."[4] It appears, however, that some large orders could be executed more cheaply than smaller ones because of lower delivery, storage, and bookkeeping costs.[5] Large contracts for delivery by equal installments over long periods of time also involved lower indirect costs.[6]

[1] F.T.C., *The Petroleum Industry*, 1928, 241.
[2] F.T.C., *Price Bases Inquiry*, 23.
[3] U.S. v. Sugar Institute, *Brief on the Facts for the Sugar Institute*, 86–102.
[4] *ibid.*, 90. Large orders permitted no savings in the purchase of raw sugar (which accounted for 80 per cent of the cost of the refined product) nor did they permit any savings in indirect costs. They did not permit a more even distribution of production over the year. It was said that "a large purchaser who takes from 50,000 to 100,000 bags of sugar during the year contributes no more to the production volume of the refiner to whom he throws that business than would be contributed by 50 or 100 customers who took 1,000 bags apiece during the year" (*ibid.*, 100). It was agreed, however, that economies could perhaps be realized if delivery could be made at the option of the seller, that is, if orders could be executed at times when there was little other business and immediate delivery could be made to the purchasers, but contended that in fact such arrangements were not possible. Such discounts did not permit longer "runs" through the plant because sugar was a completely standardized product. Finally, no savings in the costs of selling, carrying, storage, delivery, and handling were obtainable because, when a large quantity of sugar was sold on a single contract, delivery was usually taken in a series of installments within a period of thirty days. Nor did such discounts induce large jobbers to stock the product and press it upon the market as they did in some industries, thus increasing total sales and reducing average costs. Quantity discounts attracted business to a refiner only if they were secret; if given openly rivals would immediately grant similar discounts and thus leave all parties where they were. (*ibid.*, 103.) "As surely as the door is open to quantity discounts in the sugar refining industry it is also open to secret and irregular price concessions in favor of large customers to the disadvantage of small customers. This is why quantity discounts are condemned in the code of ethics of the institute. . . . If the trade is not permitted to eliminate quantity discounts it is impossible to hope for the elimination of secret price discriminations which will put some purchasers of sugar, and particularly the smaller purchasers, at an unfair disadvantage in their competition with other purchasers and particularly with the larger purchasers" (*ibid*, 103).
[5] U.S. v. Sugar Institute, *Decision* of Circuit Judge Mack in Southern District of New York, 1934 (mimeographed), 99.
[6] *loc. cit.* In reply to the argument of the refiners that, the demand for sugar being inelastic, the encouragement of large sales by quantity discounts would not build up production, Circuit Judge Mack remarked that one third of the sugar sold was used for the manufacture of other products and "as these may well have 'a market capable of indefinite expansion' a quantity discount to a manufacturer of such a product would in turn enable him to dispose of more of his product; increased demand for sugar would necessarily follow." That the refiners did not, in fact, regard the demand for sugar as inelastic was held to be evidenced by heavy expenditure on advertising "ice cream, cereals, and various other things with which sugar would be consumed" (*ibid.*, 101). The court decided that the attempt of the refiners to eliminate quantity discounts was intended to preserve the uniformity of the price

Opposition to the adjustment of prices to differences in the cost of selling to different classes of buyers arises from two sources. The efforts of the sugar refiners to eliminate discounts based upon the quantity sold[1] arose from a desire to eliminate a potential disguise for price competition. Similarly where discrimination arises out of an over-rigid classification of buyers adopted in order to secure a uniform trade discount policy on the part of all sellers it facilitates, as it is intended to, the elimination of differences in prices to different buyers in the form of higher trade discounts to some.

In many industries discounts based upon the status of the buyer and not in accordance with the cost of selling to each maintain a hierarchy of distributors. If wholesalers buy in the same quantities as chain stores and require no less service but obtain lower prices, they can survive although they, and their dependent retailers, operate on a higher level of other costs than the chain stores. In fact, this outcome is partly the aim of manufacturers who prefer the survival of numbers of wholesalers and retailers to the passing of distribution into the hands of a few large firms who may later bargain harshly with them. Whether discrimination based on trade status arises out of a desire to regulate competition between sellers or maintain a number of buyers it obstructs the improvement of methods of distribution.

IV. GEOGRAPHICAL DISCRIMINATION

Geographical discrimination, like the type of discrimination just discussed, arises where the combination of goods and services sold is not uniform; the amount of transportation service provided varies. The cost of this service is, however, usually capable of easy calculation. Geographical price discrimination occurs, therefore, when any seller disposes of his products at prices which, after deduction of any transportation expenses incurred by the seller on the finished product, yield net prices at the point of production (often called "mill-net realization" or "mill net") varying with the geographical location of buyers.

---

structure and prevent refiners from using such discounts as a cloak for price concessions, and that, to attain this end, they were prepared to obstruct economies in the sale and distribution of sugar (*ibid.*, 102). It is possible, however, that the demand for sugar is extensible by sales-promotion activities without being very elastic within practicable ranges of price.

[1] The efforts of other industries to eliminate quantity discounts under the National Industrial Recovery Act doubtless arose from a similar cause. See Chap. X.

Geographical price discrimination is absent only when this mill net realization is uniform for all the sales of each product at a given time. The simplest selling policy resulting in this uniformity is that of selling on a "shipping-point" or "f.o.b. mill" basis uniform for all buyers. When prices are so declared, they are announced for delivery at the plant (or on rail or truck near the plant) and purchasers at a distance may either purchase at the plant and arrange their own transportation or pay a delivered price which exceeds the declared shipping-point price by the actual cost of transportation. Prices are, however, commonly referred to as "f.o.b. point of origin" when in fact they are not shipping-point prices in the above sense. Although the title to the goods (and the risk of loss in transit) may pass to the buyer at the point of origin[1] the seller may make "freight allowances" or charge "freight pickups," *i.e.*, he may pay a part of the freight or charge an amount in excess of the actual freight. These practices convert the apparently shipping-point pricing system into some other system the nature of which depends upon the pattern of the freight "allowances" or "pickups."

The only data available concerning the frequency of the use of "shipping-point prices" were obtained by the Federal Trade Commission, which, in 1928, collected information from about 3561 representative manufacturers in the principal industries in the country. It found that 44 per cent of all the firms reporting sold exclusively on an f.o.b. point-of-origin basis, with a further 38 per cent adopting both this basis of selling and others.[2] Of all firms included in this inquiry 82 per cent made at least some sales upon an f.o.b. point-of-origin basis, and of this total 15 per cent made some sales on an f.o.b. point-of-origin basis coupled with partial freight allowance.[3]

[1] F.T.C., *Price Bases Inquiry*, 1932, 5.
[2] Of the fifteen industry groups into which the returns were classified, eight showed more than 50 per cent of the reporting firms selling exclusively on the f.o.b. point-of-origin basis. These groups were textiles and their products (68 per cent), paper and paper products (52 per cent), printing and publishing and allied industries (62 per cent), petroleum and coal products (53 per cent), leather and its finished products (65 per cent), machinery except transportation equipment (59 per cent), transportation equipment (81 per cent, and miscellaneous industries (60 per cent). In all but two (food and kindred products, and rubber products) of the fifteen groups, the percentage of reporting firms in the exclusively f.o.b. point-of-origin class was higher than the proportion in the exclusively delivered-price class (F.T.C., *Price Bases Inquiry*, 1932, 10). Where firms were engaged in more than one industry group they were counted more than once.
[3] The industry groups in which the greatest percentage of firms made such allowances were iron and steel and their products except machinery (35 per cent), nonferrous metals and their products (32 per cent), paper and paper products (20 per

The practices that result in departures from this uniformity of "mill-net realization" fall into a few general patterns, viz., zone prices, basing-point systems, and systems in which local differences in price are correlated with local variations in the distribution of business between sellers (local price cutting). Local price cutting is usually unsystematic and temporary and is excluded from further discussion. The remainder of this chapter is concerned with the nature of the remaining two practices, the extent of their adoption, and the reasons for their adoption.

A. Zone Price Systems

A zone system of prices occurs when sellers charge delivered prices (*i.e.*, prices including the cost of transportation) uniform for all points in a territory which may be that of the whole country or of some lesser area. This practice involves discrimination wherever transportation costs from the place of production to all points of equal delivered price are not uniform. The net realization at the mill is smallest upon sales for delivery at points to which the cost of transportation is greatest.

The Federal Trade Commission discovered that of all firms selling any product on any delivered price basis, 30 per cent sold at prices uniform for all destinations (*i.e.*, a single-zone system), this percentage being higher than that for any other form of delivered-price system.[1] Uniform-price zones are to be expected where costs of transportation are uniform or where they are nearly so and account for only a small part of the final cost of the product (*e.g.*, in the sale of tobacco products and cotton thread[2]). They require more explanation, however, in the sale of stoves,[3] mahogany,[4] and asphalt and mastic tiles.[5]

---

cent), leather and its finished products (19 per cent), stone, clay, and glass products (18 per cent), and machinery except transportation equipment (18 per cent) (*ibid.*, 11).
 [1] *ibid.*, 12. The practice was most prevalent in the rubber products industry, where 86 per cent of firms using delivered prices sold on a single-zone price basis. It was also used by 64 per cent of firms selling leather and its finished products, 59 per cent of those in the printing and publishing and allied industries, and 53 per cent of those in the textile and textile products industries.
 [2] *Cf.* TARIFF COMMISSION, Tariff Information Survey, *Cotton Thread*, 1927, 44.
 [3] *Cf.* F.T.C., *House Furnishings Industries*, 1923, II, 89.
 [4] The code authority for the lumber and timber products industry under the National Industrial Recovery Act established a uniform price throughout the country for African and American mahogany (CONSUMER ADVISORY BOARD, *Statement at Hearing on the Operation of the Lumber Code*, Jan. 9, 1934).
 [5] The code of fair competition for this industry under the National Industrial Recovery Act required uniformity of prices throughout the United States.

Multiple-zone systems of selling are also common; of all firms selling some or all products on any delivered-price system in 1928, 27 per cent sold at prices uniform in each of a number of zones.[1] The practice has been used in the salt industry[2] and in the sale of bath tubs by the so-called "bath tub trust."[3] "Freight zoning plans" are also reported to have been used successfully in the alcohol,[4] coffee, and soap industries and to have been contemplated in the cane sugar industry.[5] In the corn products[6] and steel industries such zoning preceded the use of basing-point systems.[7] Sellers of steel divided the country into seventeen zones a short time after the United States Steel Corporation was formed in 1901, and sold in each zone at uniform delivered prices based upon the Pittsburgh price plus the average freight to all points in the zone. Their declared object was "to have everybody get his fair share of the business."[8] Sharp differences in price to buyers on either side of the zone boundaries caused friction[9] which resulted at the end of 1903 in the zone system being replaced by the "Pittsburgh plus" practice.[10]

[1] In the chemical and allied products industry (presumably including petroleum products) 33 per cent of firms sold on a zone basis; in the stone, clay, and glass products industry this percentage was 33 per cent, in non-ferrous metals and their products, 32 per cent, and in the paper and paper products industry, 32 per cent (F.T.C., *Price Bases Inquiry*, 12).

[2] RIPLEY (Editor), *Trusts, Pools, and Combinations*, 11. The code of fair competition for the industry under the National Industrial Recovery Act delimited market areas and provided that the minimum price in each should be the lowest price announced by any seller in the field. Any change in market territories was thus prevented.

[3] U.S. v. Standard Sanitary Manufacturing Co., *Brief for U.S.*, 31.

[4] WHITNEY, *Trade Associations and Industrial Control*, 133.

[5] U.S. v. Sugar Institute, *Brief for the U.S.*, 245, 246; FETTER, *Masquerade of Monopoly*, 242.

[6] U.S. v. Corn Products Refining Co., 234 Fed. 994 (1916); F.T.C., *Commercial Feeds*, 1924, 163.

[7] It was apparently in turn preceded in the steel industry by a basing-point system which was abandoned because of the use of water transport from Buffalo which enabled prices to be quoted at Duluth below the prices that could be quoted by mills having access only by rail transportation (F.T.C., *Statement on Pittsburgh Plus*, 632. FETTER, *op. cit.*, 148).

[8] F.T.C., *Statement on Pittsburgh Plus*, 632.

[9] A producer at Council Bluffs, for instance, on one bank of the Mississippi River, paid two to three dollars per ton more for steel than a rival on the opposite bank of the river at Rock Island. Buyers objected to this situation and a large Minneapolis consumer bought for delivery in one zone and arranged for the goods to be carried on to another without transshipment, and without any additional payment for freight, with the result that he saved $5,000 on one shipment (COMMONS, "Delivered Price Practice in the Steel Market," *Amer. Econ. Rev.*, 14: 505).

[10] See page 300. Zone prices for boiler and tank steel plate and structural steel were the first to be abandoned with the result that the price of structural steel at points near to Pittsburgh was reduced by $0.50 to $1.00 per ton, but raised $0.30 at Chicago, $0.70 at Milwaukee, and from $1.50 to $2.00 at some other points (F.T.C., *op. cit.*, 705; *Iron Age*, Jan. 7, 1904). In September, 1904, zone prices for billets,

The proceedings against the American Linseed Company revealed that twelve linseed crushers had agreed, through their membership in the Armstrong Bureau of Related Industries, to divide the United States into eight zones, throughout each of which prices were uniform; all sellers sold in different zones at the same differentials.[1] Two explanations of the practice were offered, *viz.*, that it avoided troublesome freight calculations[2] and that it facilitated the intelligent exchange of market information by "establishing a uniform basis for the reports of all council members."[3] It appears, however, that pressure from two large crushers of flaxseed, between them doing 50 per cent of all the business, was instrumental in causing uniformity of practice.[4]

The practice of announcing prices at the shipping point but "absorbing" part of the cost of transporting the goods to the delivery point can be, and has been, used to produce delivered prices uniform for large zones. This result is attained if on all sales for delivery within a territory freight charges in excess of a fixed sum (less than the actual freight rate to any point in the territory) are paid (or "absorbed") by the seller. The zones of uniform delivered price thus created may be large or small and they may exist in a geographical price structure which is not wholly divided up into zones. For instance, the Quaker Oats Company and at least one competitor are said to have made a uniform freight charge from their points of production to a group of cities, although the actual freight rates to those cities were not uniform. These cities were said to be places from which wholesale houses were competing against each other for sales in common territory, and the policy was supported on the ground that it "did not put the wholesaler at a disadvantage in competing with some other wholesaler at a different point in common territory who, by reason of a somewhat lower freight rate, might resell goods at a lower price from the same mill if this arrangement were not in existence."[5] The potency of such a policy to

---

sheets, and iron bars were also abandoned, with the result that the excess of the price of bars in Chicago over that in Pittsburgh was increased from $1.00 to $3.00 (F.T.C., *op. cit.*, 707; *Iron Age*, Sept. 22, 1904).

[1] It was "stipulated that each member should quote a basic price for zone number one and should add thereto one, two, four, six, seven, eight, and eleven cents respectively for others" (U.S. v. American Linseed Co. *et al.*, 262 U.S. 371 (1923)). For map of zones and prices see FETTER, *Masquerade of Monopoly*, 225.

[2] *Brief for U.S.*, 23; *Brief for Ankeney Linseed Co.*, 56.
[3] *Brief for Ankeney Linseed Co.*, 36; *Brief for American Linseed Co.*, 12.
[4] *Brief for Ankeney Linseed Co.*, 20; *Brief for U.S.*, 142.
[5] U.S. v. Quaker Oats Co., *Brief for Quaker Oats Co.*, 71.

counteract the advantages of superior location and, therefore, to influence the location of buyers is indicated by this argument.

The newsprint industry, at the beginning of 1928, adopted a policy of quoting mill prices with part of the freight to destination "allowed" to the purchasers. "For convenience in applying the freight absorption plan the territory east of the Mississippi River was divided into zones on the basis of the freight charges to be borne by the purchasers."[1] There were four such zones, one of which comprised only the city of Boston, but others of which were of considerable area.[2] A fixed amount (four dollars per ton in the most extensive zone) was payable for freight by the purchaser, and the whole balance by the seller. As freight rates to all points in the territory exceeded four dollars,[3] all buyers in the territory paid the shipping-point price plus four dollars and the seller received net prices at the mill varying with the amount by which the actual freight to each delivery point exceeded this four dollars, that is, varying approximately according to the distance of delivery points from the mill. Thus a uniform zone price was established. In 1929 the International Paper Company made its prices on a similar basis[4] and the Great Northern Paper Company was reported to be making a uniform price to all buyers in the same zone.[5]

The partition of the former Standard Oil Company gave rise to a series of price zones for gasoline, although the relations between the prices in different zones differed from those in the industries discussed up to this point. The former Standard company was succeeded by a number of companies selling in territories for the most part geographically separate.[6] It was the practice in the industry for sellers to charge a "uniform price in a state or marketing territory regardless of freight rates." During 1915

[1] F.T.C., *Newsprint Paper Industry*, 1930, 37.
[2] One, for instance, included the New England states (except Boston), New York, Pennsylvania, New Jersey, Maryland, Delaware, District of Columbia, Ohio, part of Michigan, Indiana, a part of Illinois including Chicago, and parts of West Virginia and Kentucky.
[3] Had the freight rate to any part of the zone been less than four dollars the seller would have absorbed no freight on sales to such points and buyers would have paid a freight rate varying with their distance from the mill.
[4] F.T.C., *op. cit.*, 44.
[5] *ibid.*, 80.
[6] The value of sales of oil products (except lubricating oil) by Standard companies in the territories of other Standard companies was reported in 1915 to be negligible (F.T.C., *The Price of Gasoline in 1915*, 1917, 149). The territories of the Magnolia Petroleum Company and the Standard Oil Company of Louisiana overlapped those of other successor companies.

there were great differences between prices in the various Standard territories, which differences varied from time to time, but not in accordance with cost of transportation or marketing, nor generally with differences in demand and supply.[1] These zone prices appear at first sight to differ from those in the other industries hitherto mentioned, in that in the newsprint, steel, and linseed industries each seller sold in more than one zone (and at different prices in each zone) whereas each Standard company selling petroleum products confined its sales to a single zone. Considerable quantities of gasoline did, however, pass from one zone to another "but the sales were made by one Standard company to another so as to minimize their tendency to equalize prices."[2] Thus in effect companies were selling in different zones and at different prices, although the prices received by each company for sales in different zones were not related to differences even in average transportation costs thereto or to differences in cost of production.[3] The Federal Trade Commission attributed this policy to the determination of the successor companies to avoid competition between themselves,[4] owing to the interlocking stockholding resulting from the method of partition ordered by the court.[5] The companies stated that invasion of the territories of other successor companies would merely invite retaliation[6] and would involve heavy investments upon which there was no prospect of adequate return. It is clear, therefore, that these price zones arose out of consideration by each seller of the effect of changes in his policy upon those of rivals, and the peculiar basis upon which business was distributed by the court among the successor companies in the forlorn hope of speedily restoring competition.

This situation has, however, greatly changed with the passage of time. Interlocking stockholding had so far diminished by 1923 that stockholders holding one per cent or more of the stock outstanding in two or more producing, refining, or marketing companies held, in the aggregate, only 30.4 per cent of all the stock in the former Standard companies and in 1926, 23.7 per cent.[7]

[1] *ibid.*, 149, 113, 121; also F.T.C., *The Advance in the Price of Petroleum Products*, 1920, 54.
[2] F.T.C., *The Price of Gasoline in 1915*, 149.
[3] *ibid.*, 6.
[4] *loc. cit.*
[5] *ibid.*, 129, 150.
[6] *ibid.*, 153, 154.
[7] F.T.C., *Prices, Profits, and Competition in the Petroleum Industry*, 1928, 71. The

PRICE DISCRIMINATION 287

No body of stockholders holding a controlling interest in any company held a majority interest in any other. Inquiry into the changes in stockholdings in pipe line companies yielded substantially the same result.[1] There was little community of stockholding in the industry outside the group of former Standard companies.[2] Concurrently with this change in the control of the successor companies, the sharp separation of marketing territories began to disappear. Some of the Standard companies began to sell gasoline to jobbers for marketing outside the territory of the seller.[3] More recently, however, the Standard companies have invaded each other's territories, usually by the acquisition of independent companies,[4] and there have been signs of an attempt by these companies to extend their marketing territories to cover the whole country.[5] In 1926, however, "no Standard company was the second largest seller of gasoline in the territory of any other Standard company."[6] Nevertheless zone prices were

---

extreme percentages for any company were 41.6 (South Penn Oil Company) and 10.8 (Standard Oil Company of Kentucky) in 1923 and 39.8 (South Penn Oil Company) and 5.3 (Standard Oil Company of Kansas) in 1926. The percentage holdings of these shareholders declined in every company between 1923 and 1926 with the single exception of the Standard Oil Company of Kentucky.

[1] *ibid.*, 75. There were 20 stockholders who, on Dec. 31, 1923, or June 30, 1926, held as much as one half of one per cent of the voting stock in each of two or more pipe line companies of the Standard group and if the two holders who appear on only one of these dates be eliminated "in 1923 the combined holdings of 18 stockholders average 35.2 per cent of all the outstanding voting stock per company for all these companies. In 1926 the average combined holdings in each of these companies by these same eighteen holders was a little less than 33 per cent of their total voting stock."

[2] *ibid.*, 81.

[3] *ibid.*, 57. Products other than gasoline were sold over a wider territory by some of the companies than was their gasoline, although trade in gasoline between Standard companies continued on a large scale.

[4] " During the past few years, particularly through the acquisition of independent companies, there have been some important changes in the gasoline tank-wagon marketing territories of certain Standard companies" (*ibid.*, 54, where details of the more important changes are set out); while the boundaries of the Standard marketing territories for tank-wagon deliveries coincided with state lines in most cases, those of independents "are extended apparently to any point that can be reached advantageously" and without any attempt to reach every part of any state in which they make tank-wagon deliveries (which seemed to be the policy of the Standard companies) (*ibid.*, 57).

[5] *Cf.* the statement that the Standard Oil Company of New York has "followed the general tendency of the integrated companies towards nationwide distribution" (U.S. v. Standard Oil Co. of New York (Socony-Vacuum Merger), *Brief for Standard Oil Co. et al.*, 38). Between 1925 and 1930 the Standard Oil Company of New York absorbed 15 companies 13 of which gave it additional distribution facilities (*Brief for U.S.*, 26, 57) with the result that in 1930 the company had 23,351 retail outlets in New York and the New England states and 13,556 retail outlets located in all the states west of the Mississippi except Idaho. Furthermore, the company sold gasoline in states in which it had no retail outlets (*ibid.*, 7).

[6] F.T.C., *Prices, Profits, and Competition in the Petroleum Industry*, 1928, 228.

slow to disappear; until 1930 gasoline was generally sold in the wholesale market at tank-wagon prices which were uniform, usually for state-wide territories, but which covered the average freight from refineries to all points in the zone. In the eastern states this system was replaced in January, 1930, by one of delivered prices at each point equal to the cargo price for gasoline at seaboard plus freight to destination.[1]

Zone prices arise in a number of ways. In the first place, they arise even out of uniform mill-net realizations where transportation costs are upon a zone basis but they then involve no discrimination. Zone prices would be expected, for instance, where goods are distributed by mail. In the second place, where transportation costs are a relatively unimportant part of total delivered costs, even to distant points, sellers may prefer to sell at uniform delivered prices rather than calculate the delivered cost of each shipment.[2] The departure from uniform mill-net realizations may also be too small to induce any buyer to take delivery at the plant and arrange for the transportation of the commodity. In the third place, where transportation costs are heavy, zone prices facilitate the limitation of price competition. They aid in the comparison of prices by reducing the number of price quotations. They facilitate the discovery of price cutting and the acceptance of price leadership.[3]

One of the immediate consequences of the use of zone systems is to produce uniformity between the prices of different sellers; delivered prices for large zones are unlikely to vary from seller to seller. As differences in price no longer determine the distribution of business between sellers this distribution must be determined by other causes. Rivalry may remain in speed of delivery, credit facilities, or other incidents to the sale, or in sales promotion. In the absence of rivalry in any of these forms, the distribution of business may depend upon an open or tacit sharing of market

[1] *New York Times*, Jan. 29, 1930, Feb. 2, 1930.
[2] In the course of its decision concerning the Corn Products Refining Company, which had sold on a zone basis, the court decided that such a system was not objectionable if "the zones are fairly organized and not too large and the radial difference from the routing point of places within the same zone is not too great." It concluded that the practice made for economy and convenience. (U.S. v. Corn Products Refining Co., 234 Fed. 994 (1916).)
[3] That such is the purpose of at least some zoning systems is indicated by the fact that the zone price systems in the steel and corn products industries gave place to basing-point systems, which also facilitate price comparison and leadership while avoiding some of the difficulties of zoning (arising out of the sharp differences in price at the edges of the zones).

territories. Producers may regard business in some areas as their own, provided that rivals take a similar point of view with regard to other areas, after the manner of the successor companies to the former Standard Oil Company. The volume of business done in the territory served by each plant is then a matter of positive control by sellers rather than the outcome of competition. Even then there may be bands of territory approximately equidistant freightwise from more than one point of production, in which some of the above forms of rivalry persist.

The level of prices is likely to be influenced by a leader who, not improbably, induces the acceptance of zone prices as a means of facilitating both the following of its prices and the detection of departures from them. This situation probably prevailed when zone systems were in use in the steel, linseed, corn products, and newsprint industries. The relation between the prices set in the different zones may be determined by the desire to maximize aggregate net returns, in which event the differences in price from zone to zone would depend upon differences in the elasticity of demand in the different zones (should such differences exist), and differences in the cost of doing business in each (including differences in the cost of transportation). Conditions in the oil industry after the dissolution of the Standard Oil Company were such as to permit the pursuit of separate monopoly policies in each territory; the successor companies confined their direct sales to their own territories and sold to other territories only through the Standard Oil company there. Indeed the Federal Trade Commission claimed that these companies, closely interlocked as to ownership and control, were able to obtain "the highest price possible for the output of the group as a whole."[1] It has been claimed, however, that at least some of the zone systems above described, e.g., steel, provide for prices in each zone based upon the average freight costs to all points in the zone from the nearest point of production. This policy precludes discrimination between zones based upon differences in the elasticity of demand in each.

Zone prices exert a particular influence upon the location of production. The industry charging zone prices is seriously affected only where conditions of supply and demand are such that one plant customarily sells in more than one zone, and, even then, only if the prices in the different zones are unrelated to trans-

[1] F.T.C., *Prices, Profits, and Competition in the Petroleum Industry*, 1928, 69.

portation costs from production points. In these circumstances production is pulled in the direction of the zone in which prices yield the highest net returns at the point of production. Industries purchasing the product sold upon a zone basis are more affected; the extent of their reaction depends upon the importance of the product in their total costs, and the amount of the departure of the zone prices from those which would result from sales at prices yielding uniform mill nets. In general, zone prices diminish the importance of nearness to the point of production of the material sold on a zone basis. Where conditions of production and the nature of demand in each zone are such that there is in each zone a number of plants, each being *economically* equally near to supplies of the raw material, *physical* nearness to such supplies ceases to affect the location of the industry. Where a single plant delivers to points in more than one price zone it is drawn to the edge of a zone and the direction of the zones of highest price. It thus diminishes the cost of transporting its finished goods to the areas in which rivals must pay a higher price for the material sold on a zone basis without increasing the cost of these materials to itself. These influences operate, however, only over long periods, *i.e.*, where a zone system is expected to persist.

B. Basing-point Systems

A basing-point system of selling exists whenever goods are sold at delivered prices calculated by adding together the price at a basing point and the cost of transportation from that point to the point of delivery. In the country as a whole there may be one or a number of basing points.

This practice may give rise to discrimination for two reasons. Firstly, the mill-net yields of sales from points of production that are not basing points vary with the differences between the cost of transportation from the basing point and that from the actual point of production.[1] Secondly, even though every point of production be a basing point, sellers often "absorb freight" on sales to points more cheaply reached by rivals; sales involving

[1] For example, if the base price is $5.00 and a producer not at the basing point pays $1 to send the goods there, the net realization on sales at the basing point will be $4.00. If he sells for delivery at his point of production and the cost of transportation from the base to his point of production is $1.00 he sells for, and secures a net realization of, $6.00.

freight absorption yield less than sales which involve no such absorption.

1. THE OCCURRENCE OF BASING-POINT SYSTEMS

The Federal Trade Commission found that, where sales were made at delivered prices, basing-point prices were less common than zone prices.[1] They occur in industries in which transportation costs comprise a large part of the cost of the delivered product, overhead costs are important, the number of producers is fairly small, and production and demand widely scattered. They appear in their most developed form in the lumber, metal, and cement industries but are beginning to appear in others.

a. Lumber and Miscellaneous Industries. Single-basing-point systems have been used in a number of branches of the lumber industry. The Attorney General contended[2] that the actual prices of maple flooring corresponded to those that would have resulted had Cadillac, Michigan, been used as a base, and that this correspondence was due to the circulation by the Maple Flooring Manufacturers Association of a bulletin showing freight rates on flooring from Cadillac. This freight rate book, together with calculations of average cost at the basing point, was intended to be used, and had in fact been used, to secure the quotation of uniform prices by all members at each point of delivery. The manufacturers denied that Cadillac had been generally accepted as a basing point, suggesting that, had it been generally used, the great differences in delivered prices which had existed in the same centers of consumption would have been impossible.[3] They claimed,[4] moreover, that although only three of the plants were actually located in Cadillac most of the mills were in Michigan and Wisconsin and were so distributed geographically that the average freight rates from the various mills to the centers of consumption were approximately the same as the rate from Cadillac.[5] This argument inclined the Supreme Court to accept

[1] The five industry groups having the highest percentage of reporting firms making any sales upon basing-point prices were iron and steel and their products (except machinery), 26 per cent, stone, clay, and glass products, 18 per cent, food and kindred products, 12 per cent, chemicals and allied products, 6 per cent, lumber and allied products, 5 per cent. In the iron and steel industry alone of all firms selling on any delivered-price system a higher percentage sold at basing-point prices than on either single- or multiple-zone systems. (F.T.C., *Price Bases Inquiry*, 13.)
[2] U.S. v. Maple Flooring Manufacturers Association *et al.*, 268 U.S. 563 (1925).
[3] U.S. v. Maple Flooring Manufacturers Association, *Brief for Appellants*, 290.
[4] *ibid.*, 282.
[5] Mere correspondence of *average* freight rates from all points of production with that from Cadillac is, of course, a matter of little importance. In fact, it is possible

the freight rate books partly on the ground that, while they caused divergences from the price structure that would result if each mill were used as a base, the divergences were small. Professor Fetter claims, however, that purchasers in Minnesota paid to the lumber mills "130 per cent more for freight than the amount which the common carrier may legally charge."[1] The Attorney General contended that this structure of prices was maintained partly by the refusal to sell at other than delivered prices, to which the manufacturers responded that although 90 to 95 per cent of maple flooring was sold at a delivered price, prices f.o.b. mill were quoted whenever buyers desired them.[2] But if, as appears probable, the f.o.b. price was computed by first calculating the delivered price based on Cadillac and then deducting the actual freight rate from the point of production to the point of delivery, the buyer gained nothing from the use of the mill price.

One effect of the use of the basing-point system was suggested by the plea in extenuation of the practice that "no member could take advantage of his geographical position if all members were using the Cadillac freight rate."[3] It prevents geographical advantages in the location of plants from being expressed in prices. Geographical advantages are not, however, eliminated as an element determining profits which are enhanced by proximity to areas of high delivered prices.[4] In general, purchasers nearer to a mill than to Cadillac probably paid higher prices than they would otherwise have done, while those near to Cadillac paid somewhat lower prices. The Attorney General also pointed out that the practice, together with that of publishing the "average costs" of each grade of product, caused uniformity in the delivered prices of different sellers, a uniformity which the manufacturers

---

to imagine an industry like sugar refining in which production is carried on in New York, New Orleans, and San Francisco claiming that all sales should be made with St. Louis as a base, on the ground that the freight charges from St. Louis (where no sugar is refined) are equal to the average freight charges from each of the points of production, thus producing a completely arbitrary geographical price structure.

[1] FETTER, *Masquerade of Monopoly*, 234. On shipments to Chicago the Cadillac freight rate used to calculate prices was 24.5 cents, while the average of actual freight rates from the seventeen mills delivering to Chicago was 19.8 cents and from the two nearest mills 14 cents (*ibid.*, 449).

[2] *Brief for Appellants*, 282.

[3] *Brief for Appellants*, 289.

[4] It was admitted that the system gave an advantage to those situated west of Cadillac in shipments westward and to those east of Cadillac in making shipments eastward (*ibid.*, 287).

admitted, but which they attributed to "the operation of economic law."

Other branches of the lumber industry also used single basing points. The Western Red Cedarmen's Information Bureau used Sand Point, Idaho, as a basing point when circulating price information.[1] The hardwood manufacturers used Wassau, Wisconsin, in much the same way; as many sellers had a considerable freight advantage over Wassau, the magnitude of the departure from a mill-price price structure was greater than in the maple flooring industry. The Federal Trade Commission concluded that the policy of the Northern Hemlock and Hardwood Manufacturers Association, "being in the interests of price uniformity, lays the basis for price enhancement."[2] The Western Pine Manufacturers used Spokane as a basing point; again some sellers secured added profits because of a freight advantage in regard to markets as compared with Spokane, and here too the Federal Trade Commission concluded that this policy had been an incident in the organized activities of the manufacturers aimed at eliminating or restricting price competition.[3] Similarly, New Orleans has been used as a basing point for selling cypress lumber, Norfolk for North Carolina pine, and Minneapolis for northern pine.[4]

The code of fair competition for the lumber industry under the National Industrial Recovery Act specifically provided for f.o.b. mill prices. Nevertheless "the lumber code authority has established and announced through its bulletin a wide variety of basing-point systems.[5] For most divisions of the industry it orders that those subject to the code shall quote only delivered prices, and that these delivered prices shall be composed of the f.o.b. mill price plus freight from a specified basing point."[6] Cadillac, Michigan, was still the basing point for maple flooring in 1933, Wassau, Wisconsin, for northern hemlock, and Duluth, Minnesota, for northern pine.[7] The Consumer Advisory Board remarked that, buyers being quoted identical prices by all sellers, dealt with distant mills as readily as nearby ones, with the result

[1] F.T.C., *Western Red Cedar Association, etc.*, 1923, 6.
[2] F.T.C., *Hemlock and Hardwood Manufacturers Association*, 1923, ix.
[3] F.T.C., *Lumber Manufacturers Associations*, 1922, 121.
[4] COMPTON, *The Organization of the American Lumber Industry*, 1916, 50.
[5] This action may have been thought to be justified by the requirement in the code that the code authority in fixing prices have regard to competition between areas and species.
[6] COMSUMER ADVISORY BOARD, *Statement at Hearing on Operation of the Lumber Code*, Jan. 9, 1934, 14.
[7] *ibid.*, 16.

that the total transportation costs of all the mills were increased. Figure 36 shows the long distance between some of the maple flooring mills and the basing point in 1934.

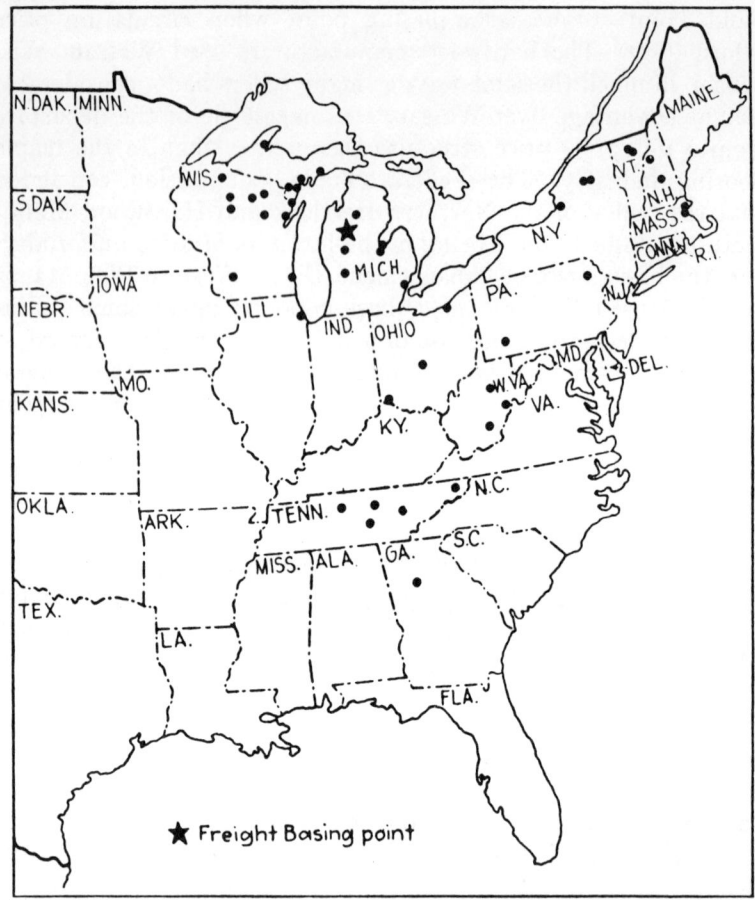

FIG. 36.—Location of maple flooring mills and of basing points in 1934. (*Redrawn from N.R.A., Consumer Advisory Board, Statement at Lumber Hearings, January 9, 1934, 16.*)

Corn gluten feed has been sold by reference to Chicago as a basing point.[1] A petition by the Attorney General for an injunction against the fifteen manufacturers who were members of the Corn Derivatives Institute,[2] and who manufactured more than 98 per

[1] F.T.C., *Commercial Feeds*, 1921, 163, 120 note.
[2] *United States Daily*, Apr. 8, 1932.

cent of the aggregate output of corn products in the United States, suggests that this practice was facilitated by the institute which maintained a system of reports concerning prices, production, terms of sale, and the like, aimed at maintaining uniformity of practice in selling corn products.[1] The use of the basing point was naïvely explained by manufacturers as arising from the desire to avoid discrimination between their customers, but their rambling explanations of the practice[2] resolve themselves into two contentions, *viz.*, (1) that sellers must naturally be expected to exploit the advantages of their location and buyers must be protected by them from the temptation to do likewise, and (2) that the abandonment of the basing-point system would involve cutting the prices of rivals in some places.

Zinc has been sold for many years at prices based upon the price in East St. Louis, Illinois, plus freight therefrom to the delivery point.[3] The freight from middle western zinc smelters west of the Mississippi River is generally equal to the sum of the freights from the smelter to the base and thence to the delivery point. This system of pricing is used, however, even when sales are made from a smelter several hundred miles from the base and zinc is shipped direct without touching East St. Louis. In so far as smelters are generally west of East St. Louis and the markets are a considerable distance east therefrom, such a system is likely to result in conditions similar to those that would exist if mill prices were quoted. Indeed, it is comparable to the "gate-

[1] The institute consented to a decree requiring the dissolution of the institute and enjoining *inter alia* agreements to refuse to quote except in accordance with the basing-point system. This decree could not, of course, compel the abandonment of the basing-point system.

[2] "In order best to conserve the consumer, the industry has to hold itself in a position to serve all buyers in every part of the country differing only in differences in price by differential freight rates. Did we do anything else you can plainly see that we would be discriminating against certain classes of buyers. As a matter of fact we would be cutting other manufacturers' prices and the amounts involved would be so infinitesimal that it would not cut any ice—it is so ridiculously small. If by virtue of our location we are able to get into certain points at a lower rate of freight and at a lower cost than our competitors why should we relinquish that advantage?" It was insisted with a great show of public spirit that if a manufacturer in Clinton, Iowa, did not sell on a Chicago base, buyers near the plant would be able to buy at lower prices than those more distant and the manufacturers felt it "essential to protect all buyers in all parts of the country according to their geographical location . . . in other words, they would not be called upon by virtue of a disadvantageous location to pay a higher price for their goods than people who might be more advantageously located." (F.T.C., *op. cit.*, 164.)

[3] SPURR and WORMSER (Editors), *The Marketing of Metals and Minerals*, 216, 221, 223. Delivered prices are uncommon, prices being quoted f.o.b. East St. Louis although that is the point neither of production nor of delivery; quotations f.o.b. smelter are rare, except upon sales for export.

ways" used in some branches of the lumber market.[1] Smelters in Pittsburgh, however, also sell on an East St. Louis base; although they are nearer to consuming markets than the middle western smelters they are farther away from ore supplies.[2] East St. Louis is said to have been used as a base because of its proximity to the most important zinc field in the country in the Missouri-Kansas-Oklahoma territory.

Copper is sold from smelters in Arizona, Montana, Michigan, New Mexico, California, and Tennessee upon a New York basis.[3] Some 53 per cent of the smelting capacity of the country in 1925 was, however, in New York and New Jersey, and a further 28 per cent in Maryland, only about 8 per cent of the smelting capacity being in each of the states of Washington and Montana and little over 2 per cent in Michigan.[4] By far the largest consumption of copper occurs in the eastern states, a fact which presumably explains the geographical distribution of smelting plants. In so far, however, as the Montana and Washington plants sell at New York prices plus freight, unless their costs of production exceed those in the east by the cost of transportation (which appears very improbable) they are exploiting the local market to the full extent possible without losing all business to the eastern smelters.

Where production occurs at a number of points distant from each other there is a strong tendency for the number of basing points to increase. Multiple basing-points systems then develop.

Some branches of the lumber industry have for many years used more than one basing point. Savannah, Jacksonville, Hattiesburg, Beaumont, and Houston have been used as basing points for southern yellow pine, and Baltimore and Puget Sound cities for fir.[5] In the hardwood industry sales were made at a delivered price calculated for territory east of a line from Chicago to New Orleans upon Cincinnati as a base, and, for territory west of that line, upon Cairo, Illinois, as a base.[6] The hardwood trade association issued a weekly report of sales in which the delivered price

---

[1] See p. 297.
[2] SPURR and WORMSER, loc. cit.
[3] FETTER, Masquerade of Monopoly, 198.
[4] SPURR and WORMSER, op. cit., 46.
[5] COMPTON, The Organization of the American Lumber Industry, 1916, 50.
[6] FETTER, Masquerade of Monopoly, 222. Special basing points apparently also existed in about 1920 south of Memphis. The difference between Cairo and Cincinnati prices ranged from $3.00 to $10.00 a thousand feet according to the kind and grade of lumber.

at which each transaction was made was "audited back" to the basing point by deducting the official railroad tariff between the destination and the "gateway" of Cincinnati. An average price for all sales at the "gateway," supposedly based upon actual statistics, was set beside the actual prices. As, however, the "average" was always stated in even dollars,[1] the elimination of differences in prices by different mills appears to have been the object of the arrangement. In so far, however, as the actual freight rates paid by mills departed from freight rates from Cincinnati for the eastern territory, the net return on sales at the various mills varied with the point of delivery.[2] When the code of fair competition was approved under the Recovery Act of 1933, multiple basing points continued in use. Johnson City, Tennessee, was used as a basing point by producers of oak flooring for sales in Pennsylvania, Maryland, Michigan, and Ohio, while producers in Florida used Alexandria, Louisiana, as a basing point, and a producer in Chicago used Memphis, Tennessee. Shippers of southern pine to New England from Florida used Jacksonville as a base, while those in Virginia, North Carolina, South Carolina, Georgia, and eastern Alabama used Goldsboro, North Carolina. Producers of southern hardwood were classified into groups according to the freight cost from their mill to Toronto, Ontario. Those falling in each group used a single basing point.[3] Figure 37 shows the long distance between many of the mills producing southern pine lumber and the basing points.

In December, 1926, the Department of Justice complained that 39 producers of fertilizers, producing about 85 per cent of the total output in the United States, had during the previous three years agreed *inter alia* upon the sale of fertilizers at prices calculated by reference to certain ports. Delivered prices were calculated by adding an arbitrary sum to prices, equal to the freight rate therefrom to the point of delivery, although the shipments were not in fact made from the ports upon which the price was calculated.[4]

[1] *ibid.*, 223.
[2] Had Cincinnati been a "gateway" in the sense that all transportation routes from the mills to points of delivery passed through it, there would, even under competition, have been a tendency to uniformity in the delivered prices adjusted to the "gateway." In fact, however, lumber cut in northern Ohio and shipped to Boston or Philadelphia and lumber cut in West Virginia and shipped direct to Baltimore was paid for as if it had passed through Cincinnati.
[3] CONSUMER ADVISORY BOARD, *Statement at Hearings on Operation of the Lumber Code*, Jan. 9, 1934.
[4] *New York Times*, Dec. 11, 1926. The companies concerned were fined, the court

298   THE DECLINE OF COMPETITION

In 1930 the practice of selling gasoline at prices uniform over considerable zones gave place, as we have seen, to a basing-point system. The first notice of this new practice was given by the

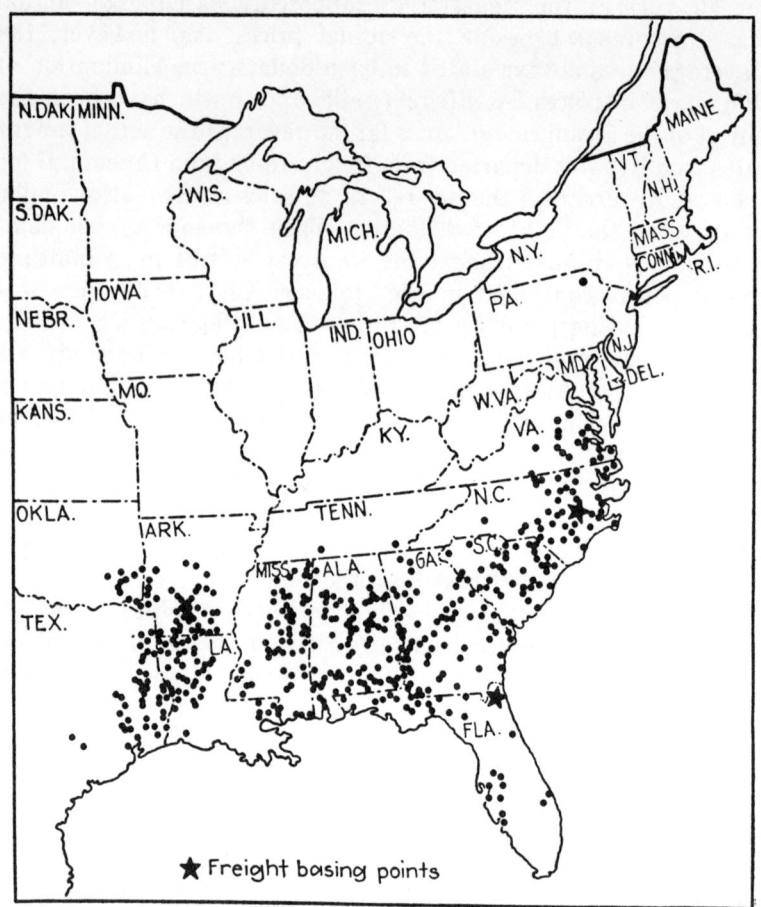

FIG. 37.—Location of southern pine lumber mills and of basing points in 1934. (Includes only mills with an average monthly production of over 500,000 board feet.) (*Redrawn from N.R.A. Consumer Advisory Board, Statement at Lumber Hearings, January 9, 1934.*)

Standard Oil Company of New Jersey, which announced that in the future the price of gasoline at each point would be calculated by adding to the cargo market price for gasoline in tank-

---

taking into account the period of severe losses through which the industry was still passing. The code of fair competition for the industry under the National Industrial Recovery Act provided for the zoning of prices in the industry.

steamer quantities a fixed differential together with the actual cost of transportation to each selling point. This change of practice resulted, of course, in considerable reductions in price to consumers near ports and much lower reductions to more distant points.[1] The practice was apparently introduced to deal with the sporadic but effective competition of small distributors[2] originating in increasing importance of shipments of oil from California to eastern ports by way of the Panama Canal. A similar method of pricing was adopted by the Magnolia Petroleum Company, a subsidiary of the Standard Oil Company of New York, selling in southern territory,[3] and by the Standard Oil Company of New York for sales in New York and New England. Whether all prices are calculated by reference to the port through which the oil actually passes, and whether oil passes to each point through the point offering the lowest delivered cost is not known.

Lead is sold generally at delivered prices based apparently upon prices in the New York, St. Louis, and Chicago markets. These markets were regarded as "gateways"; New York handled lead from San Francisco, Utah and Idaho (by way of the Panama Canal), Spain and Mexico; St. Louis handled lead from Missouri, and Chicago lead from Utah, Idaho, and Colorado when sent overland.[4] Professor Fetter[5] has alleged that some form of basing-point system has been used also in the markets for asphalt shingles and roofing, sewer pipe, hollow building tile, expanded metal laths, and bolts, nuts, and rivets,[6] but he has offered no evidence in support of the statement.

b. The Steel Industry. The steel and cement industries afford the most detailed information concerning the development and effects of basing-point systems. In the early part of the nineteenth century the bulk of the rolling mills in the iron and steel industry were east of the Alleghenies and Philadelphia prices were dominant

---

[1] *New York Times*, Jan. 3, 1930. The change in price apparently also involved a general reduction in the margin between wholesale and retail prices.

[2] In announcing its prices, the company implied that the zone prices had not been uniform: "local competitive conditions have caused prices to vary in different neighborhoods. At times comparatively wide variations have existed between nearby communities causing the public to be confused and the dealer dissatisfied" (*New York Times*, Jan. 29, 1930). The new price schedules were intended to meet this local price cutting; the company announced prices calculated to tenths of a cent.

[3] *New York Times*, Jan. 9, 1930.

[4] Spurr and Wormser, *op. cit.*, 93 *ff.*

[5] *Masquerade of Monopoly*, 242.

[6] See U.S. v. Bolt, Nut, and Rivet Manufacturers Association *et al.*, in equity No. 53-383, District Court of U.S. for Southern District of New York. *Petition*, May 17, 1931. Consent decree filed.

THE DECLINE OF COMPETITION

in the industry. By about 1875, however, production in western Pennsylvania had increased in importance[1] and producers there began to dominate the market.[2] Prices based upon Pittsburgh appeared in the market for rolled steel products in 1876[3] and in the nail trade in 1894[4] and by the end of the century applied to all important steel products. The temporary resort to zoned prices has already been mentioned; after quoting on a Pittsburgh base was resumed in 1904 about 90 per cent of the sales of plates, shapes, bars, wire products, and sheets were on a Pittsburgh-plus basis until 1921.[5]

Steel rails[6] and pig iron were the principal products not sold on a Pittsburgh base. The railroads could arrange to take delivery at least at the nearest point on their tracks to the mill, and often at the mill itself, and they were not expected to pay prices that covered transportation from Pittsburgh when no such transportation had taken place. In 1900 for the first time an identical price was quoted for rails in both Chicago and Pittsburgh, and this uniformity of mill price continued. Judge Gary attempted to

[1] The opening up of the Lake Superior iron ore fields was the principal reason for the relocation of the industry (N.R.A., *The Operation of the Basing Point System in the Iron and Steel Industry*, 19).
[2] See *ibid.*, 36. *Cf.* also 18, 41.
[3] *ibid.*, 37.
[4] F.T.C., *Statement on Pittsburgh Plus*, 262. It was said that "the Pittsburgh-plus system was unknown as a general practice in the steel trade prior to 1901 as to any but possibly wire products" (*Brief for Amici Curiae*, 87; EDGERTON, "The Wire Nail Association," *Polit. Sci. Quart.*, 12: 251). It appears, however, that rails were quoted on a Pittsburgh basis as part of a price-fixing scheme toward the end of 1895 (*Iron Age*, Oct. 31, 1895, *cit.* F.T.C., *Brief on Pittsburgh Plus*, 19). Wire products generally are said to have been quoted on a Pittsburgh base in 1899. Testimony was also offered, however, that Pittsburgh was used as a basing point for steel beams as early as 1880, when the first steel beam association was formed, the practice being extended to plates, shapes, bars, sheets, tin plates, and wire toward the end of the century (Colonel H. V. Pope, *cit.* FETTER, *Masquerade of Monopoly*, 147. See also F.T.C., *The Practices of the Steel Industry under the Code*, 60). The Bessemer billet pools of 1896 and 1900 based their prices on Pittsburgh (*Brief on Pittsburgh Plus*, 50).
[5] F.T.C., *Statement on Pittsburgh Plus*, 311. Certain specialty products to which the United States Steel Corporation gives little attention were not sold on a Pittsburgh base (F.T.C., *Statement on Pittsburgh Plus*, 330) nor were semi-finished products such as billets, wire rods, sheet bars, or railroad track materials consistently sold on a Pittsburgh basis (*ibid.*, 291). Nails were always sold on both a Chicago and a Pittsburgh base. In 1908 the method of quoting for billets was modified in order, it was said, to put the consumer of billets located at points distant from the supply on an equitable basis in competition with finishing mills located nearer Pittsburgh and which, therefore, had the advantage of lower freight rates. This modification had the effect of making delivered prices at all points at which the freight rate from Pittsburgh exceeded one but fell short of three dollars, the Pittsburgh basing price plus only half the freight. In so far as finishing mills at Pittsburgh had to pay full freight upon their finished goods, this modification gave a definite advantage to finishing mills at a distance from Pittsburgh.
[6] F.T.C., *Brief on Pittsburgh Plus*, 52.

establish a basing-point system for pig iron during the war of 1914 to 1918, but was unsuccessful[1] and there were in fact almost as many pig iron markets as producing districts.[2] A Pittsburgh price for pig iron would, of course, have transferred any profits arising from the Pittsburgh-plus system from producers outside Pittsburgh to suppliers of pig iron. Where, as in the case of the large units in the industry, pig iron production was carried on by the steel manufacturer, no shift of profits would have occurred.

Before the Federal Trade Commission began its investigation Judge Gary had admitted that the Pittsburgh-plus policy had been "practically universal in adoption and practice,"[3] but the attitude of the United States Steel Corporation changed after proceedings were begun. With great labor the commission sought to prove that the actual geographical structure of prices was consistent with prices calculated by adding to the published Pittsburgh price the cost of transportation from Pittsburgh to the point of delivery. Some of the admitted departures from Pittsburgh basing have already been indicated.[4] It was also contended that while quotations were on a Pittsburgh-plus basis they were seldom strictly adhered to, the corporation and its competitors selling in different localities "at the market prices prevailing therein as determined by the law of supply and demand and the competition among manufacturers."[5] Although there were many statistical difficulties[6] it appeared that over 90 per cent of a large number of contracts were at prices within 5 cents per hundred pounds of the Pittsburgh-plus price.[7] The extent of this correspondence is represented diagrammatically in Fig. 38.

[1] F.T.C., *Brief on Pittsburgh Plus*, 189. This end was achieved after the passage of the National Industrial Recovery Act in 1933 (see p. 309).
[2] Pig iron was quoted at the furnace, and the differences between different producing points had no relationship to transportation costs between them (*ibid.*, 53).
[3] *ibid.*, 58.
[4] See p. 300.
[5] F.T.C., *Statement on Pittsburgh Plus*, 27.
[6] It was not always clear exactly what had been the base price and especially whether the prices quoted in the *Iron Age* were the prices at which past transactions had been completed or offer prices (*Cf. ibid.*, 345). The date of the contract was often not the date of the quotation by the seller. Commodities were not always identical with those for which base prices were quoted.
[7] *ibid.*, 353, 363. The commission examined contracts for 3765 sales, of which at least 379 were of doubtful comparability as they represented concession prices, jobber sales, future prices, Chicago base price, export prices, or special goods, and found that 69.75 per cent agreed with the *Iron Age* quotations, while another 19.10 per cent deviated by five cents or less per hundred pounds therefrom (*ibid.*, 345). The corporation examined the same underlying documents and, having rejected some, found that of 2877 sales on contract 61.9 per cent agreed with the *Iron Age*

The corporation claimed that the margin of departure from the Pittsburgh-plus price structure admitted by the commission, *viz.* 5 cents per hundredweight, or $1 a ton, was very substantial,[1] to which the commission replied that while such a difference would affect the profits of fabricators, it was not sufficient to cause the abandonment of sales territory.[2] The corporation did not, however, prove that the deviations were not equally distributed over contracts for a variety of products for delivery at a variety of points. In other words, they did not disprove the charge that the geographical structure of delivered prices was explicable by reference to a Pittsburgh base. The deviations were probably due to a number of causes. Some were due to cutting below the base price of the corporation, especially during periods of reduced demand,[3] although some were due to small producers charging premiums over the prices of the United States Steel Corporation in return for prompt delivery in years of great activity in the industry.

---

quotations for the date next before the sale while 5.4 per cent deviated by less than five cents. Such discrepancies as existed were due to differences in the basis upon which contracts were rejected as non-comparable, arising out of lack of information concerning dates of sale, uncertainty as to the amount to be deducted for "extras," and similar matters. The corporation, however, objected to the exclusion of some contracts by the commission, arguing that only by such exclusions could the high measure of correspondence between actual and Pittsburgh-plus prices be obtained (*Brief for U.S. Steel Corp.*, 91). The Federal Trade Commission also calculated that of the *tonnage* for which information was available, about 66.5 per cent was sold at prices which agreed with those quoted in the *Iron Age*, whereas the corresponding figure calculated by the corporation was only 24 per cent (F.T.C., *Statement on Pittsburgh Plus*, 363). (These calculations are amended because of an evident error in the commission's statement. The total tonnage analyzed by the corporation was greater than that considered by the commission.)

[1] *Brief for U.S. Steel Corp.*, 91.
[2] F.T.C., *Statement on Pittsburgh Plus*, 358.
[3] During the depression year 1908 in which the output of steel ingots fell about 40 per cent below the output in 1906 and 1907, conferences of steel manufacturers discussed prices but no reductions were made. In February, 1909, however, individual companies broke away from the agreed basing-point prices, with the result that the United States Steel Corporation declared an open market (*ibid.*, 78). Business revived, however, and by May, 1909, mills were again quoting uniformly on the old basis. In May, 1911, the Republic Iron and Steel Company cut below the official prices in the industry, and a meeting of other steel producers decided upon a reduction in the price. In December of that year, Judge Gary told the Senate Committee on Interstate Commerce that his corporation could keep down prices if it wished, and significantly added that the Republic company which had cut the price of bars in the preceding May would be glad at that time to increase them (F.T.C., *op. cit.*, 81; *Annual Report*, 1924, 36). Prices on a Pittsburgh base were restored in 1912 (*Statement on Pittsburgh Plus*, 92). Again, in February of the depression year 1921 the Midvale Steel Corporation, whose mills had been closed for some months, announced a price reduction, with the result that the United States Steel Corporation refused fully to cooperate with independents as it had done before; the United States Steel Corporation in July, 1921, met local competition in Chicago by departing from the Pittsburgh-plus prices (*ibid.*, 93), and prices fell below the level set by the Midvale company (F.T.C., *Statement on Pittsburgh Plus*, 84).

PRICE DISCRIMINATION 303

The United States Steel Corporation charged no such premiums but sold for delivery from sixty days to six months ahead.[1] Prices

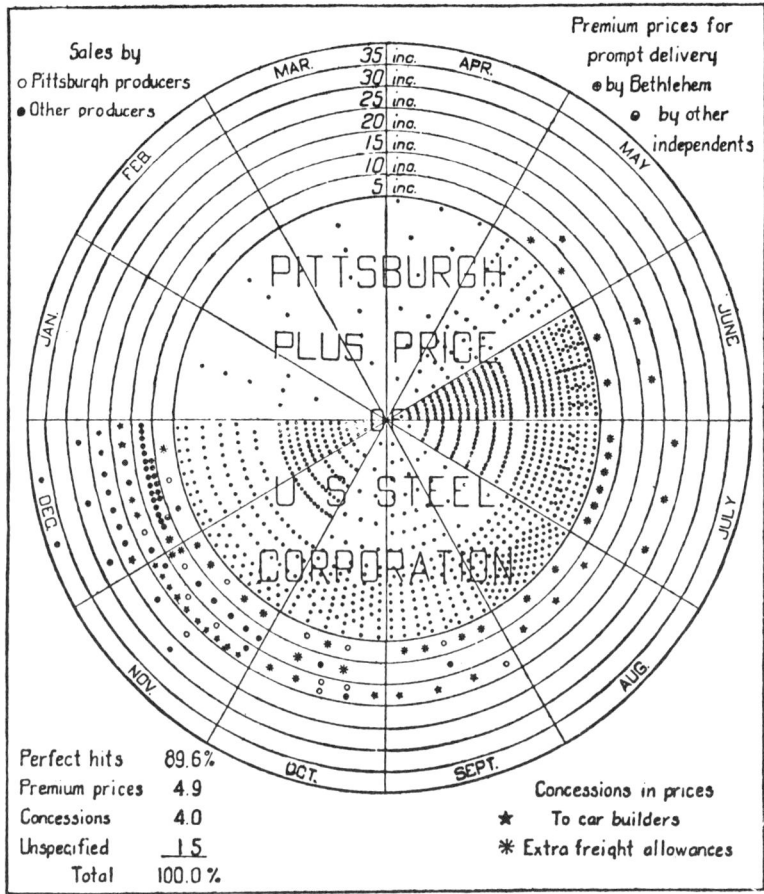

FIG. 38.—Correspondence between actual delivered prices and Pittsburgh plus prices in 1919 for steel plates, structural shapes, and bars sold by some sixty corporations for delivery to various points east of the Rocky Mountains. (*From F.T.C., Docket 962; Bethlehem-Lackawanna merger; cit. Fetter "Masquerade of Monopoly," 173.*)

NOTE: Each dot or other character represents a single sale of a carload or more (some sales were of over 10,000 tons). Characters in the area marked "Pittsburgh Plus Price of U.S. Steel Corporation" represent sales at delivered prices equal to those obtained by adding together the Carnegie Steel Company's "base Pittsburgh" price and the cost of transportation *from Pittsburgh* to the delivery point. Characters in the successive outer zones represent sales at delivered prices differing (up or down) from these Pittsburgh plus prices by the number of cents per hundred pounds indicated within each zone.

were generally, therefore, in conformity with the Pittsburgh-plus system with exceptions as to certain products and certain areas;

[1] *ibid.*, 77, 82, 331, 532. Such premium prices were being charged for bars in the latter months of 1912 and in 1913. In 1916 premium prices again appeared, but the

such price cutting as existed did not destroy the main outlines of the basing-point system.

The basing-point system was, however, under constant pressure and has been repeatedly modified; indeed, the Pittsburgh-plus system has probably never applied throughout the whole industry. The development of new centers of production resulted in pressure to increase the number of basing points. In about 1909 the United States Steel Corporation yielded to complaints against the sale on a Pittsburgh basis of steel products manufactured at Birmingham, Alabama, by the Tennessee Coal, Iron, and Railway Company (which the corporation had acquired in 1907).[1] It decided to sell steel bars manufactured at Birmingham at a Birmingham base price which was arbitrarily fixed at $3.00 per ton above the Pittsburgh price.[2] The corporation explained this local departure from Pittsburgh plus as a temporary concession to Birmingham manufacturers to enable them to develop industries which would be of great benefit to the south and would furnish an additional market for the products of the Tennessee company;[3] it proved, however, to be a permanent concession.[4] This argument reveals the power in the hands of the corporation to control the rate of development of steel using industries in different parts of the country, and raises the question why other parts of the country, and particularly the middle west, did not obtain similar consideration. When the concession was made at Birmingham the president of the corporation admitted that ultimately Chicago would also have to be made a basing point.[5]

---

government, following the advice of the steel producers, fixed a uniform price "at a height intended to bring out maximum production." Premium prices appeared again, however, in 1920.

[1] When these complaints were under consideration it was reported to a meeting of sales managers of the United States Steel Corporation that freight rates on bars and plates from Birmingham were at least as favorable as those from Pittsburgh or Chicago to about 46 per cent of the area of the country containing about 29 per cent of the total population. In the matter of heavy and light rails, Birmingham was at least as favorably situated as Pittsburgh or Chicago in relation to about 35 per cent of the area of the country including about 26 per cent of its population. (*ibid.*, 620.)

[2] *ibid.*, 127. The delivered price of bars from Birmingham was calculated, therefore, by adding to the Birmingham base price the actual freight from Birmingham.

[3] *ibid.*, 28.

[4] The arrangement continued until August, 1920, when the differential was raised to $5.00 a ton simultaneously with an increase in freight rates (*ibid.*, 12). This rise in the differential was not, of course, required by the change in the cost of transportation, but presumably represented in part a desire to take advantage of the possibility it offered for raising prices for goods delivered from mills distant from Pittsburgh, and in part an effort to avoid a disturbance of the market territories served respectively by mills at Pittsburgh and Birmingham.

[5] *ibid.*, 620.

For brief periods prior to 1921 products manufactured in Chicago were also sold on a local base price.[1] Most of these temporary deviations occurred in times of diminished demand when sellers were tempted to cut prices at Chicago, where demand was large and mill nets on local business were high. In 1909, when the United States Steel Corporation failed to prevent serious price cutting, a Chicago base was established, and the demand for the output of Chicago mills was stimulated, but after only a few months the Pittsburgh basis of pricing was restored.[2] Temporary selling on a Chicago base again occurred for about six months toward the end of 1911.[3] In 1917 the War Industries Board established Chicago as a basing point with steel prices in Chicago the same as in Pittsburgh.[4] The price structure for steel products over a wide area was changed with the result that fabricators in the west enlarged their plants and extended their sales territories.[5] But again, after about nine months, the Pittsburgh pricing system was restored at the request of Mr. Gary.[6] The users of steel in the middle west refused however, to accept the Pittsburgh base and pressed the Federal Trade Commission to take action, which it unwillingly did.[7] In January, 1922, shortly

[1] Prior to 1901 light sheets had been sold on a local price, the district having been favorite fighting ground for sales of this product. The consolidation of the sheet mills, however, resulted in local products being sold upon a Pittsburgh basis (F.T.C., *Brief on Pittsburgh Plus*, 26); the American Tin Plate Company announced in 1903 that all products would in the future be sold on a Pittsburgh basis, owing to "the higher cost of delivering steel and other raw material to the mills in that district, and to the heavy additional expense incurred through the substitution of coal for gas as fuel in the various plants" (*ibid.*, 23). This argument implies that more costly methods of production had been substituted for less costly.
[2] F.T.C., *Statement on Pittsburgh Plus*, 181.
[3] *ibid.*, 81. Prices dropped from $1 to $3 per ton below the Pittsburgh-plus price (*Iron Age*, Jan. 4, 1912, 59).
[4] F.T.C., *Costs and Profits in the Steel Industry*, 1925, 20.
[5] FETTER, *Masquerade of Monopoly*, 153.
[6] COMMONS, "Delivered Price Practice in the Steel Market," *Amer. Econ. Rev.*, 14: 509.
[7] Consumers of steel in the Chicago district protested to the commission in 1919 that this method of selling was contrary to Sec. 2 of the Clayton Act (which prohibits sales at discriminatory prices where the result of discrimination may be to lessen competition (except where the discriminatory price is made in good faith and to meet competition)). After a protracted hearing the Commission concluded that the practice was *not* illegal and declined to issue a complaint (F.T.C., *Annual Report*, 1924, 36). Apparently as a result of protests to the president of the United States Steel Corporation by the Western Association of Rolled Steel Consumers, supported by the American Association of Ultimate Consumers of Rolled Steel (who agitated through legislatures, attorneys general, and the governors of some 32 states), Mr. Gary himself approached the Federal Trade Commission and in April, 1921, it issued a formal complaint. Thirty of the states formed an organization known as "The Associated States Opposing Pittsburgh Plus" and filed a brief. After almost continuous hearings from January, 1922, to March, 1924, the commission on July 21, 1924, ordered the abandonment of the practice by the United States Steel Corpora-

after the commission issued its formal complaint, the corporation voluntarily commenced selling bars, plates, and shapes (the principal heavy rolled steel products other than rails) on a Chicago base; the Pittsburgh-plus practice continued to apply, however, to sheets, tin plates, wire, and wire products.[1]

The order of the commission in July, 1924, resulted, however, in the abandonment of Pittsburgh base prices for sheets, wire, and pipe,[2] and the establishment of bases at Duluth, Cleveland, and a number of other points.[3] Pittsburgh basing continued in the eastern states although there was much complaint of price cutting; it was said that it continued, "if at all, only because there was nothing better."[4] The independent companies adapted themselves to the new conditions, "here and there creating an additional basing point as competitive conditions required."[5] In 1927 the Bethlehem Steel Corporation announced f.o.b. prices for structural shapes, plates, and bars at its mills at Bethlehem, Pennsylvania, Coatsville, Pennsylvania, Sparrows Point, Maryland, and Lackawanna, New York.[6] This further modification of the basing-point

---

tion and certain of its subsidiaries, an order which the corporation did not contest. This order of July 21, 1924, prohibited the sale of steel products on a Pittsburgh-plus basis, the sale of such products upon any basing point other than that at which they were manufactured or from which they were shipped, selling without a clear indication upon the invoice of the f.o.b. mill or shipping-point price of the product and of the charge for actual freight, and discrimination in the price at which sales were made to different buyers. Professor Fetter reports that in 1905 the Commissioner of Corporations took the view that freight absorptions by firms at points outside Pittsburgh to enable them to dump products under conditions yielding them less than the net realization they were obtaining at the mill were not discriminatory against local buyers, and, where factories were large and widely scattered such price cutting was the only means of preserving competition (FETTER, *Masquerade of Monopoly*, 13).

[1] COMMONS, *op. cit.* 509. *Cf.* also N.R.A., *The Operation of the Basing Point System in the Iron and Steel Industry*, 40. At various times prior to the order by the Federal Trade Commission there had been minor concessions from the basing-point system. The Colorado Fuel and Iron Company was said to have departed from Pittsburgh base prices from time to time in selling wire products in the southwest, especially in Texas (F.T.C., *Statement on Pittsburgh Plus*, 66). In 1922 a special price was established for wire products in the city of Cleveland only. Strip and sheet steel was also sold on a Youngstown base price identical with that of Pittsburgh. This price appears to have been quoted only locally in Youngstown and to have affected about 10 per cent of the business of the mills in the immediate territory (*ibid.*, 66, 533).

[2] *Iron Age*, Jan. 1, 1925, 3, 48, 54.

[3] *ibid.*, Sept. 25, 1924. The Colorado Fuel and Iron Company, which manufactures at Pueblo, Colorado, and enjoys in western markets a very high freight advantage over eastern plants, adjusted its prices at many points to the new Chicago and Birmingham base prices, although it continued to sell at some points at prices involving the absorption of part of the freight (FETTER, *Masquerade of Monopoly*, 323).

[4] *New York Times*, Nov. 20, 1927.

[5] N.R.A., *op. cit.*, 43.

[6] *New York Times*, Dec. 8, 1927.

system[1] was accepted as offering a more stable price arrangement in the east than had existed since 1924.[2]

When the code of fair competition under the National Industrial Recovery Act was drawn up for the iron and steel industry, all questions concerning the existence of the basing-point practice were dispelled. Explicit provision was made in the code for the legal enforcement of the practice. The code provided that all prices[3] should be delivered prices and set out the basing points for each product. Members were required to file their price lists using only the prescribed basing points.[4] Excluding four peculiar and two very minor classes of product, the average number of basing points for each of the remaining 32 steel products was 4.6, the range being from a minimum of one to a maximum of eleven.[5] While no attempt was made to make every producing point a basing point, the number of bases was increased.[6] The industry offered the code as being in substantial conformity with existing practice as to the number and location of basing points[7] but this claim was challenged[8] and there is no doubt that the code introduced a number of important departures from previous practice.

One of the most remarkable changes was the abandonment of Youngstown, Ohio, as a basing point for sheets. Youngstown

---

[1] The change may have been due to the acquisition by the Bethlehem Steel Corporation of plants throughout the eastern territory, or to its knowledge that the Federal Trade Commission was inquiring into the desirability of the merger between the Bethlehem and Lackawanna companies.

[2] By this time bars were being sold by reference to Pittsburgh, Chicago, Birmingham, Cleveland, and on a zone system in Michigan; shapes by reference to Pittsburgh, Chicago, Birmingham, Bethlehem, and Buffalo; plates by reference to Pittsburgh, Chicago, Buffalo, Sparrows Point, Maryland, and Coatsville, Pennsylvania; sheets by reference to Pittsburgh, Chicago, and Birmingham; pipe by reference to Pittsburgh, Gary, and Lorain, Ohio; tin plate by reference to Pittsburgh and Gary, and wire products by reference to Pittsburgh, Cleveland, Chicago, Worcester, Birmingham, Ironton, Anderson, Indiana, Duluth, DeKalb, and Joliet.

[3] Except for steel rails and oil pipe materials.

[4] The basing point to be used was to be the point of production where that point was also a basing point recognized by the code and otherwise "the basing point for such product nearest in terms of all-rail freight rates to such plant," or in the case of basing points on the Gulf or Pacific coast "f.o.b. cars dock such port." Steel rails, however, were to be quoted f.o.b. mill or port of destination when shipped from any Atlantic or Gulf port to any Gulf or Pacific coast port. Other basing points might be used with the permission of the code authority (*i.e.*, the board of directors of the American Iron and Steel Institute). Substantially similar provisions appeared in the code for the reinforcing materials industry (except that both zone and basing-point prices were provided for).

[5] F.T.C., *Practices of the Steel Industry under the Code*, 1934, 17.

[6] A list of the new bases is given in N.R.A., *The Operation of the Basing Point System in the Iron and Steel Industry*, 46.

[7] *Report* of the Deputy Administrator (annexed to the code).

[8] F.T.C., *Practices of the Steel Industry under the Code*, 17, 62. Hearings on the Iron and Steel Code. *United States Daily*, Aug. 6, 1933.

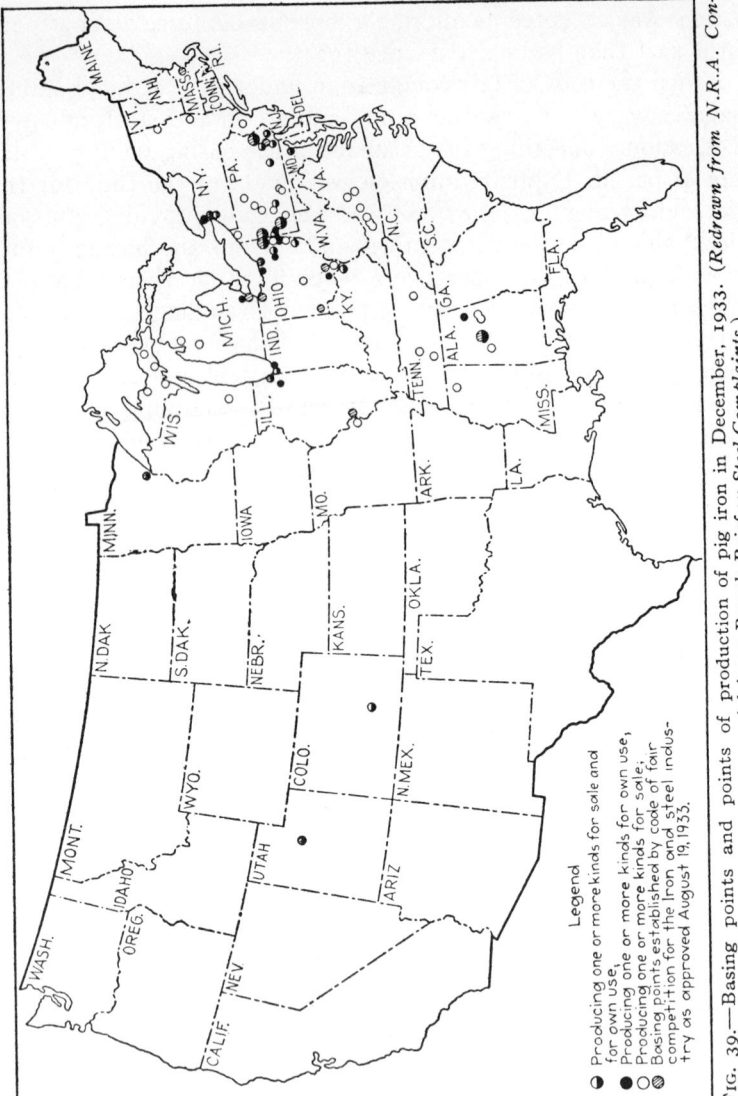

FIG. 39.—Basing points and points of production of pig iron in December, 1933. (Redrawn from N.R.A. Consumer Advisory Board: Brief on Steel Complaints.)

was the most important locality for the production of sheets in the country, yet, after the introduction of the code, all sheets were sold on a Pittsburgh base; only 0.2 per cent of the sheet manufacturing capacity of the area using Pittsburgh as a base was at Pittsburgh. Pittsburgh is 57 miles from Youngstown and the change involved an increase in the price of sheets of from $1.50 to $2.50 per ton to some purchasers.[1] Subsequently Youngstown was "granted a concession substantially restoring its previous position" and fabricators there did not press for a basing point lest it lead to the establishment of other basing points that would adversely affect them.[2]

The Federal Trade Commission contended that pig iron which had formerly been sold on an f.o.b. mill basis was placed on a multiple-basing-point system.[3] Figure 39 shows the basing points and points of production of pig iron in December, 1933. The secretary of the American Iron and Steel Institute stated, however, that pig iron had for some time been sold by reference to basing points and that the code merely made the base prices public and increased their number.[4] These and other changes in basing points[5] caused serious loss to some purchasers of iron and steel, and the Federal Trade Commission properly pointed out that "the power to select, discontinue, or increase the number of basing points involves the power of deciding what cities shall be handicapped and what cities shall be built up as centers for the remanufacture and processing of steel products"[6] because it is "the power to determine which mills shall collect a delivery charge from the purchaser which is not the equivalent of the actual cost of delivery."[7]

The remaining changes introduced by the code were mostly aimed at increasing the effectiveness of the basing-point system in securing uniformity in the delivered prices quoted by all steel producers. The base prices were themselves reduced to uniformity before or immediately after they were filed with the code authority owing to "cooperative action among the producers of competitive steel products organized as groups or committees, and to group

[1] F.T.C., *op. cit.*, 5, 17, 45.
[2] N.R.A., *op. cit.*, 91.
[3] *ibid.*, 8. This change had been unsuccessfully attempted by Judge Gary during the war of 1914 to 1918 (*ibid.*, 58, and see above, page 301).
[4] N.R.A., *op. cit.*, 50, 89.
[5] F.T.C., *op. cit.*, 16; *Basing Point System in the Steel Industry*, 30.
[6] F.T.C., *Practices of the Steel Industry under the Code*, 20, 45.
[7] *ibid.*, 16; *Basing Point System in the Steel Industry*, 30.

or code authority pressure."[1] The sums added to base prices to arrive at delivered prices were openly and rigidly standardized,[2] including transportation and delivery charges.

Basing-point systems can be maintained only if all sellers know precisely what prices will be quoted by rivals at each point. Such calculations require precise knowledge not only of base prices but also of the transportation charge from the base. Because the charges by railroads are published and relatively stable they offer the most convenient means of calculating the transportation charge. Prior to the code, railroad rates were very widely used in calculating delivered prices for steel. After the code adherence to the use of railroad rates was even more general. Uniformity of transportation charges was secured by the publication of freight tables which, pursuant to an amendment to the code, members were required to use in calculating delivered prices.[3] These tables followed, with a few unimportant exceptions, the published railroad tariffs. Switching charges were not always known in advance of shipment and arbitrary amounts were prescribed which sometimes exceeded and sometimes fell short of the actual charges.[4] Ocean rates were used from eastern to Gulf and Pacific ports[5] but as the use of actual rates "might result in unfair competitive conditions" arbitrary steamship charges were included in the freight tables; these rates were sometimes above and sometimes below the actual rates.[6] Apart

---

[1] F.T.C., *Practices of the Steel Industry under the Code*, 5, 9. "The level of prices under the present practice is not determined by the forces of competition but by the combined judgment of the organized industry of what the traffic will bear" (*ibid.*, 57). See also F.T.C., *Basing Point System in the Steel Industry*, 6. The harmony among steel producers was disturbed, however, in July, 1934, when subsidiaries of the National Steel Corporation filed new prices involving considerable reductions. Manufacturers were "astonished and dismayed at the action, as they had had no warning of the cuts" which were attributed to a desire to "favor the automobile industry" (*New York Times*, June 30, 1934).

[2] With the standardization of additions to and subtractions from the base price where the commodity sold departed from the standard commodity quoted (F.T.C., *Practices of the Steel Industry under the Code*, 9) and with the margins of jobbers (*ibid.*, 35) we are not here concerned. (Also F.T.C., *Basing Point System in the Steel Industry*, 7, 10.)

[3] *ibid.*, 34.

[4] F.T.C., *Practices of the Steel Industry under the Code*, 24. In large terminal areas a uniform switching charge was prescribed which was an average of actual charges. A small zone of uniform delivered prices was thus created. This practice was attributed to the necessity of placing fabricators and dealers in the area upon a uniform basis (N.R.A., *op. cit.*, 107). Presumably buyers taking delivery by truck would otherwise favor dealers nearest the mills and able to buy at a lower delivered price.

[5] N.R.A., *op. cit.*, 89; F.T.C., *Basing Point System in the Steel Industry*, 19.

[6] F.T.C., *Practices of the Steel Industry under the Code*, 22.

from these exceptions, the prescribed all-rail rates were used except where other charges were "previously approved by the board of directors and filed with the secretary."[1] The importance of the requirement to use rail rates lay in the availability of cheaper transportation by water and truck.

Prior to the approval of the code, prices had been calculated in a number of areas by reference to inland water transportation. The withdrawal of this practice naturally evoked protests from mills,[2] jobbers,[3] and fabricators[4] having access to navigable water. The code authority refused to exercise its power to permit the use of water rates except in a few minor cases.[5] In reply to the complaint that this policy nullified the attempts of the federal and state governments to provide cheap inland transportation by developing facilities for canal and river navigation, the manufacturers remarked that they did not dictate the kind of transportation used.[6] As, however, they required payment for rail transportation which was the most expensive as well as the speediest, water transportation was obviously handicapped and the water transportation companies protested, although abortively, against this interference with the development of their business.[7] Some steel manufacturers did, however, use water transportation.[8] The water transportation companies were not then obstructed, but the steel manufacturers were annexing the benefits of public expenditure on the development of water transportation facilities where such expenditure had been incurred.

Similar difficulties arose where truck transportation offered economies to buyers. The code authority endeavored to enforce prices including the cost of rail transportation although no transportation at all was provided,[9] but they were compelled to yield to protests to the extent of deducting 65 per cent of the carload

[1] Code Schedule E, Sec. 4.
[2] F.T.C., *Practices of the Steel Industry under the Code*, 21.
[3] *ibid.*, 28.
[4] *ibid.*, 27, 29 *ff.*; F.T.C., *Basing Point System in the Steel Industry*, 22.
[5] F.T.C., *Basing Point System in the Steel Industry*, 23. Local, temporary, and restricted departure was permitted in the case of pig iron owing to the failure of some concerns to file a base price at Granite City, Illinois, which was an approved basing point (F.T.C., *Practices of the Steel Industry under the Code*, 11, 27). In December, 1933, a number of deductions from the all-rail delivered price were recommended in connection with deliveries to certain ports on the Ohio, Mississippi, and Hudson rivers, the New York State Barge Canal, and the Atlantic seaboard, but the recommendations were not approved by the code authority (*ibid.*, 27).
[6] *ibid.*, 23.
[7] *ibid.*, 32; *Basing Point System in the Steel Industry*, 105, 106.
[8] F.T.C., *Practices of the Steel Industry under the Code*, 22, 30.
[9] *ibid.*, 33.

rate[1] for rail transportation; buyers taking delivery in trucks at the mill were thus still compelled to pay over one third of the cost of transporting their products by rail although the seller provided no transportation service at all. Protests from buyers[2] and trucking companies[3] produced no further concession. Thus where public expenditure on the improvement of road surfaces reduced the cost of transportation, at least a considerable part of the resulting benefit was annexed by the steel producers.[4] Where steel could be economically used as a return freight in the trucks of automobile and other manufacturers,[5] part of the economy accrued to the seller rather than to the buyer of steel. The steel manufacturers advanced the pseudo-benevolent defense usually offered in such cases that they wished to prevent unfair competition among both sellers and buyers of steel. If mills with access to water were permitted to use and charge for water transportation, buyers and sellers without such access would be handicapped.[6] Thus the industry was prepared to "impute to and enforce upon sellers, buyers, and localities having natural advantages making for low costs and lower prices the natural disadvantages of other sellers, buyers, and localities making for high costs and higher prices"[7] and thus prevent those with such advantages from sharing them with buyers in that locality. "It is in essence the monopolization by the sellers to the exclusion of the buyers of the natural advantages inherent in the natural resources of that territory."[8] There is little doubt, however, that the profits accruing to the manufacturers were a happy incidental consequence of a policy directed toward the restriction of price competition that might arise out of lack of uniformity in the

[1] Where less than carload lots were sold only 65 per cent of the carload rate was to be deducted although the less than carload rate was the higher, and had been used in calculating the delivered price from which the deduction was made (*ibid.*, 33). *Cf.* also F.T.C., *Basing Point System in the Steel Industry*, 24.
[2] F.T.C., *Practices of the Steel Industry under the Code*, 33.
[3] *ibid.*, 35; *New York Times*, Dec. 15, 1933.
[4] F.T.C., *Practices of the Steel Industry under the Code*, 33.
[5] *ibid.*, 34.
[6] *ibid.*, 28. The refusal to exclude all charges for transportation from prices when steel was delivered to trucks at the mill was defended partly on the ground that the movement of products to points within the mill where they could be picked up by truck involved costs, and partly because, if buyers for truck transportation were not charged some part of the cost of rail transportation they would benefit as compared with those not arranging for truck transportation, and the purpose of the practice was to "remove inequalities in the treatment of buyers" (*New York Times*, Dec. 15, 1933).
[7] F.T.C., *Practices of the Steel Industry under the Code*, 49.
[8] *ibid.*, 50. Where the advantage was in the form of improved roads or improved water navigation facilities the advantages were not entirely "natural" advantages.

charges for transportation by different sellers. Their principal immediate aim was the elimination of the use of trucks.[1] Nevertheless the industry did not find it entirely possible to secure price uniformity upon the simplest conceivable geographical structure of prices. Steel rails and a few other products[2] required special rules. The possibility of imports resulted in departures from the general system of basing points at Gulf and Pacific ports[3] where there were bases at points at which there was no production.[4] Local departures were also made upon a restricted basis in part of the pig iron market. The only notable concession obtained as a result of protest by buyers was obtained by the automobile manufacturers, some of whom bought steel on so large a scale that they were able to threaten to manufacture their own.[5] In consequence, the steel manufacturers permitted sales in Michigan alone at prices from three to five dollars per ton below the delivered prices arrived at by adding the cost of rail transportation to the basing-point prices.[6] The concession to buyers accepting delivery by truck has been mentioned. In order that the government might take advantage of its right to ship its purchases over land-grant railroads at less than the published transportation rates, sellers to the federal government were permitted to deduct the full transportation costs from delivered prices.[7] Concessions were also made to railroad buyers.[8]

[1] The steel manufacturers mentioned, for instance, that the use of cut-rate truck lines had in the past upset steel prices by allowing one steel mill to undercut another (*ibid.*, 35) and lack of uniformity in water transportation charges was open to the same objection. But "in that connection the question arises to what extent, if any, attainment of the objectives of this one industry for its own prosperity and recovery may be at the expense of other industries which cannot be ignored in the nation's struggle to restore normally prosperous conditions" (*ibid.*, 27).

[2] For example, hot rolled steel strip (*ibid.*, 11) and pipe and tubular goods.

[3] AMERICAN IRON AND STEEL INSTITUTE, *Basing Points and Competition in Steel*, 5.

[4] The N.R.A. committee stated that the use of such bases was "open to abuse and inequality" (*op. cit.*, 171).

[5] *ibid.*, 46, and see below p. 422. As the code for the iron and steel industry prohibited the building of new blast furnaces or open hearth capacity they would have been compelled to buy existing plants. They also diverted purchases from the larger to the smaller manufacturers "as a punitive measure" (*New York Times*, Feb. 2, 1934).

[6] *ibid.*, 10, 46. Manufacturers in Toledo, Ohio, finally protested against sales of steel in Detroit, Michigan, at $3\frac{1}{2}$ cents per hundred pounds less than in Toledo, which was nearer to Pittsburgh (*New York Times*, July 9, 1935). Minor concessions were permitted in California, Oregon, and North Carolina, where sellers were permitted to absorb the state sales tax. *Cf.* also F.T.C., *Basing Point System in the Steel Industry*, 18.

[7] The delivered cost to the government was then the base price plus the special land-grant transportation rate.

[8] F.T.C., *Practices of the Steel Industry under the Code*, 10.

As all these departures were subject to rigid rule, the uniformity of the delivered prices of the sellers was not disturbed. After a survey of the structure of base prices the Federal Trade Commission reported that "Pittsburgh, the basing point for 33 products,[1] is still the center and starting point for all basing-point calculations."[2] Five other cities were basing points for a number of products in 1934 but they were, in the main, secondary to Pittsburgh.[3] There were "indications that the price differentials between various basing points are recognized as standard and not subject to change by individual action."[4] Chicago base prices were generally one to two dollars per ton above those in Pittsburgh although the cost of production in Chicago was believed to be lower than in Pittsburgh, and, in the case of some products, so much lower that products could profitably be shipped from Chicago to Pittsburgh.[5] A similar complaint was made of the higher base price at Birmingham than at Pittsburgh.[6] The Board of Review appointed to discover whether the administration had fostered monopolistic practices or handicapped small enterprise, made scorching accusations of monopolistic control by the board of directors of the American Iron and Steel Institute acting as code authority for the industry. Its accusations were based largely upon the report of the Federal Trade Commission.[7] Counsel for the N.R.A. stated that this latter report was

[1] That is, practically all steel products.
[2] ibid., 17. Cf. also F.T.C., Basing Point System in the Steel Industry, 28.
[3] East and south of a line connecting Pittsburgh and Buffalo there were few basing points and those were principally for minor products; prices in a large part of the eastern, southeastern, and Gulf states and Pacific coast territory were determined, therefore, by Pittsburgh plus rail or combined rail and water rates. "Over all this area the essence of the Pittsburgh-plus practice applies on many products in its original effectiveness" (F.T.C., Practices of the Steel Industry under the Code, 17). From Chicago two-thirds of the way westward across the continent prices were "Chicago-plus" prices; the influence of Birmingham in the south was limited by high base prices.
[4] ibid., 19.
[5] ibid., 19, 56.
[6] F.T.C., Basing Point System in the Steel Industry, 21.
[7] The report of the ("Darrow") Board of Review was never published. An abstract will be found in New York Times, May 21, 1934. The board reported that counsel for the institute had charged that the report of the Federal Trade Commission on the operation of the steel code was a "tissue of falsehoods" but he had failed to substantiate the charge, from which failure the board concluded that "no answer was possible." After reviewing the report of the Federal Trade Commission it concluded that the practical consequence of the multiple-basing-point practice in the industry was "to hasten the exit of the small enterprise and foster the always growing autocracy of the greater" because it precluded price reductions by non-basing-point mills in sales to nearby purchasers, thus handicapping new and comparatively small concerns in obtaining a foothold in the industry. The practice involved "artificial, arbitrary . . . [and] uneconomic" discrimination between fabricators of steel and deprived the public of the benefits of price competition; the code "closes all discernible avenues to the entrance of price competition."

erroneous and unsound[1] but almost complete acceptance of the criticisms of the commission was implied in the proposal of the administration to recommend that the code be amended to provide for basing points "either at or within a short distance from the place of actual production . . . in no instance outside the immediate area of their actual production" and for the charging of only actual transportation costs or a fair approximation to them.[2] The amended code increased the number of basing points to take care of "outstanding complaints" and it was alleged that the provisions with regard to the calculation of transportation charges had been modified.[3] In promulgating the new code the President recognized the desirability of further modification of the basing-point system and ordered an investigation of the system by both the N.R.A. and the Federal Trade commission.[4]

[1] Counsel for the administration stated (*New York Times*, May 21, 1934) that the N.R.A. had "been from the beginning critical of the price provisions in the steel code including the setup of the basing-point system." While it was not contended that this system was socially or legally justifiable the administration was required to observe that in at least two anti-trust prosecutions where basing-point price systems were involved the Supreme Court has not held that such a price system was illegal *per se*. Owing to differences of opinion between competent legal and economic authorities the administration had felt that "the surest method of adjudicating the issue wisely would be to give these provisions a trial under close and continual public observation." The fruits of this observation had been offered to the Federal Trade Commission which had rejected them and produced an erroneous, unsound, and one-sided report. The commission had used the Recovery Administration "only in the gathering of evidence to support its legal and economic preconceptions"; its report made "ludicrous errors of fact," was unsound and inconsistent in some of its "conjectural conclusions," and unfair in its omission of all reference to the beneficent aspects of the code (*ibid.*).

[2] *New York Times*, May 31, 1934.

[3] The new code provided that when deliveries were not made by rail the code authority could authorize a charge for transportation less than the all-rail rate by an amount "equitable and necessary in order that competitive opportunities to producers and consumers shall be maintained," the administration of this clause being subject to review by the administrator. This clause involves no obvious change in the powers of the code authority except perhaps a more direct control by the administrator.

[4] Executive Order of May 30, 1934. It was stated in this order that "conditions of economic emergency make necessary the retention in a modified form of the multiple-basing-point system adopted in the original code and effective in the industry for many years." The increase in the number of basing points, and the alleged modification of the method of calculating transportation charges effected by the new code, while alleviating some of the inequities in the existing system, "illustrate the desirability of working towards the end of having prices quoted on the basis of area of production, and the eventual establishment of basing points coincident with all such areas, as well as the elimination of artificial transportation charges in price quotations." The investigation was to discover "in what manner the practices of the industry, particularly in regard to the multiple-basing-point system, may be improved so as to preserve for the benefit of all concerned the stabilizing effects of the existing system, and at the same time to insure full opportunity, through fair competition, to pass on to the consumers the benefits of increasing productive efficiency while continuing to improve labor and providing greater stability of employment." (*New York Times*, May 30, 1934.)

316   THE DECLINE OF COMPETITION

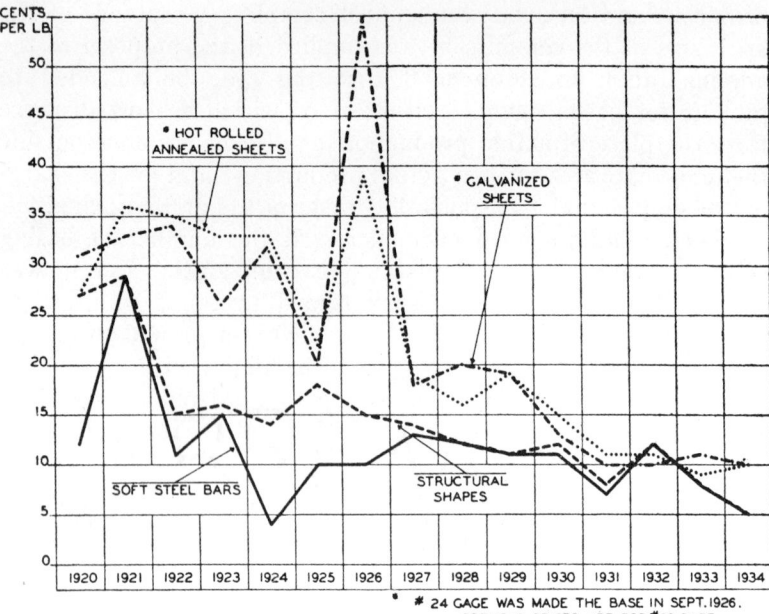

FIG. 40.—The differentials between the prices of soft steel bars, structural shapes, rolled annealed sheets, and galvanized sheets at Pittsburgh and Chicago, 1920 to 1934. (*Drawn from N.R.A. The Operation of the Basing Point System in the Iron and Steel Industry*, 44.)

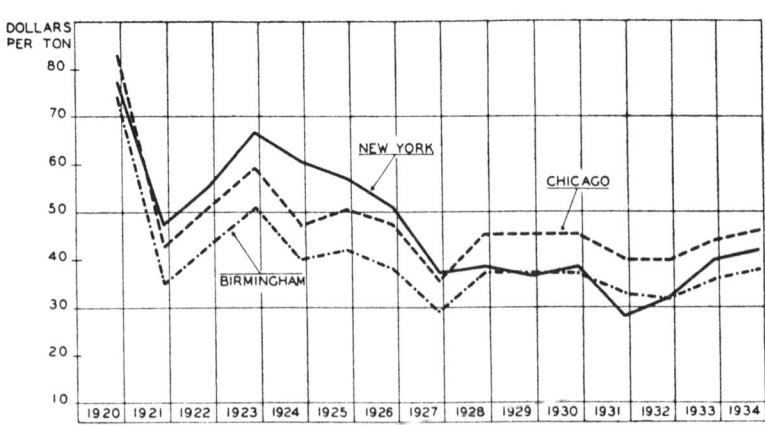

FIG. 41.—Annual average prices of cast iron pipe at New York, Chicago, and Birmingham, 1920 to 1934. (*Drawn from data in Steel.*)

The persistent modification of the basing-point system over a long period of years in the direction of increasing the number of basing points resulted in considerable transformation of the geographical structure of prices. Prices at the new bases were often considerably below the delivered price formerly prevailing there.[1] Chicago prices for heavy rolled steel products had been about $6.80 a ton above those at Pittsburgh when calculated on a Pittsburgh base; when the Chicago base was installed they were reduced to only $2.00 above Pittsburgh, a reduction sufficient to

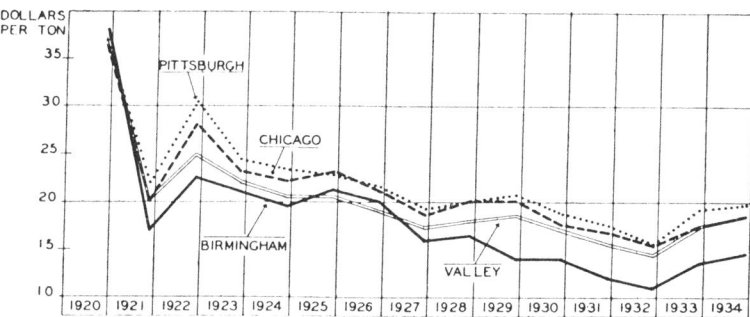

FIG. 42.—Annual average prices of pig iron at Pittsburgh, Chicago, Birmingham, and Valley Furnaces, 1920 to 1934. (*Drawn from data in Steel.*)

increase very considerably the profitability of fabrication at Chicago and points on the side of Chicago away from Pittsburgh. Even heavier reductions appear to have been made in the price of wire products at Duluth which were reduced from $12.00 to $2.00 per ton in excess of Pittsburgh.[2] Figure 40 showing the differential between the Chicago and Pittsburgh prices for a number of products indicates a narrowing of the differential on structural shapes and sheets. Figure 41 indicates that the price of cast iron pipe at Chicago and Bethlehem has preserved a fairly constant differential since 1923, while the price at New York, which was above the price at both the above centers in 1923, was below the price at both Chicago and Bethlehem in 1931. Figure 42 shows the annual average prices of pig iron at Chicago, Pittsburgh, and Birmingham.

c. The Cement Industry. The history of the basing-point system in the cement and steel industries is broadly parallel. The

---

[1] See diagram showing the reductions in the price of wire products at a number of points in FETTER, *op. cit.*, 159.
[2] FETTER, *loc. cit.*

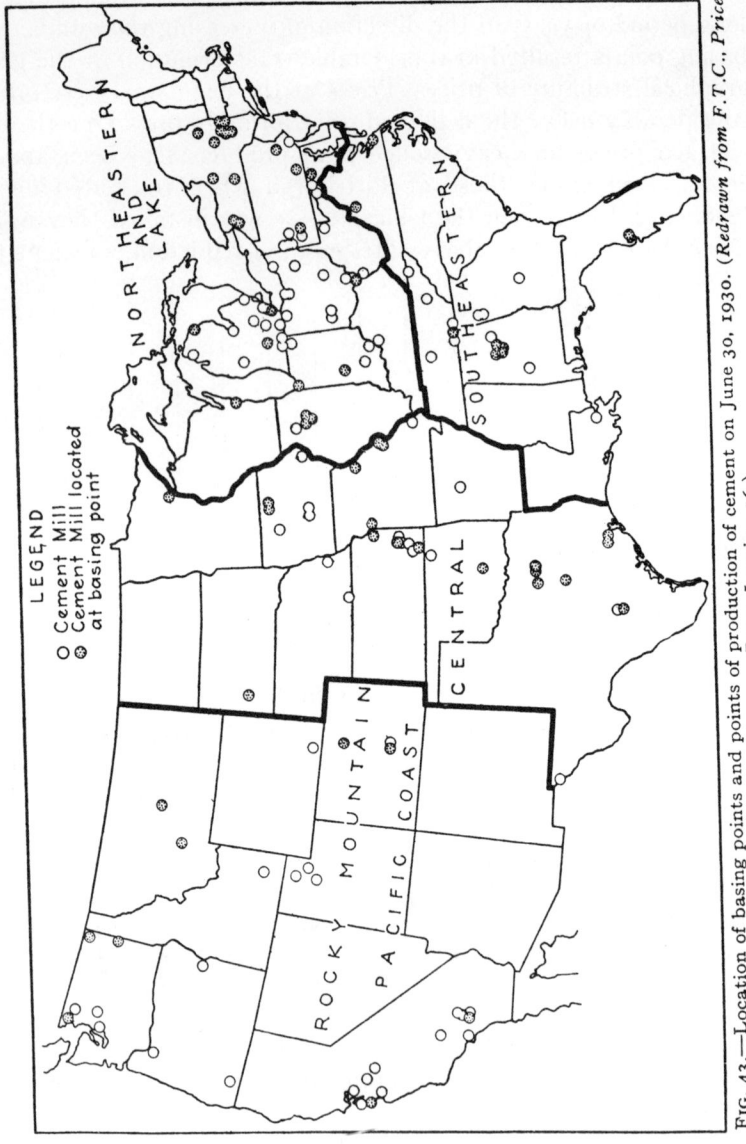

FIG. 43.—Location of basing points and points of production of cement on June 30, 1930. (*Redrawn from F.T.C., Price Bases Inquiry*, 16.)

cement industry was confined during the greater part of the nineteenth century to the eastern states and mainly to the Lehigh Valley. When new mills were established in the west and south prices were first made by reference to the Lehigh Valley as a base.[1] As capacity for production expanded at new points many were converted into basing points.[2] Figure 43 showing the location of cement mills throughout the United States, and distinguishing the basing-point from the non-basing-point mills, reveals that by 1930 in the northeastern and south central states most mills were at or near a basing point, but that in other parts of the country there was often a considerable distance between non-basing-point mills and their basing points. During the years 1921 to 1931 there were 69 basing points at which there were 107 cement mills and 2 silos,[3] but only 30 per cent of the cement output east of the Rockies was produced at basing points in 1927.[4] During the last half of 1931 and the early months of 1932 there were 30 different prices prevailing at these basing points.[5] There were thus more points of production and more basing points than in the steel industry.

There has been a high degree of correspondence between delivered prices calculated by reference to the basing points and those actually charged.[6] Sample investigations revealed over 90 per cent of the tonnage sold in accordance with the basing-point system.[7] Taking periods of time within which the price of cement

[1] F.T.C., *Price Bases Inquiry*, 7 note. Delivered prices appear to have been used by the Atlas Portland Cement Company as early as 1902, when the single-basing-point system had been used intermittently for some years for some steel products. It has been said that the United States Steel Corporation was responsible for introducing the basing-point practice when it acquired the Illinois Steel Company and, with it, the Universal Portland Cement Company (FETTER, *Masquerade of Monopoly*, 239) but the Federal Trade Commission was unable to verify the statement (*Price Bases Inquiry*, 30).
[2] The existence of a basing-point system is acknowledged by the sellers (F.T.C., *Cement Industry*, 33).
[3] F.T.C., *Cement Industry*, 1933, 37. At the close of 1930 there were 80 companies in the United States operating 166 mills producing Portland cement (F.T.C., *Price Bases Inquiry*, 16). Of these mills 80, or about one half, were non-basing-point mills (*ibid.*, 107).
[4] F.T.C., *op. cit.*, 89.
[5] F.T.C., *Cement Industry*, 1933, xiii.
[6] See diagrams at F.T.C., *Price Bases Inquiry*, 207 ff.
[7] An inquiry made by the Wisconsin Bureau of Markets concerning purchases of cement by dealers during 1927 amounting to more than 2.9 million barrels of cement (which was over half the total shipments to the state in that year) showed that deviations from basing-point prices plus freight affected less than 0.1 per cent of the total tonnage. The commission remarked that so high a percentage of agreement upon so large a volume of shipments by 14 manufacturers to 10 different shipping points was striking; no deviation exceeded 10 cents per barrel. The commission itself analyzed 66,157 sales of over 21 million barrels of cement to 21 different cities in

had remained unchanged, it was found that in all cities, with the exception of Baltimore and Detroit, complete harmony of actual prices with basing-point prices had existed for one or more such periods.[1] Only in the city of Detroit were there notably wide variations and even there 88.15 per cent of the tonnage sold conformed to the basing-point prices plus freight. Such deviations from basing-point prices as did exist ranged up to 35 cents per barrel. The greater proportion of tonnage sold at less than the basing-point price, however, was sold at from 6 to 10 per cent below that price, 4 per cent of the total tonnage being sold at prices within this range. A further 1 per cent was sold at prices from 11 to 15 cents under the basing-point price.[2] Of a little over 19 million tons of cement sold in 1929 to highway commissions for road building in a number of different states, 95.19 per cent was sold at prices conforming to the basing-point system; in 1930 of a similar tonnage about 97.60 per cent was sold on this basis.[3] The commission commented that these figures demonstrated "in a remarkable manner the strength and perfection of a system whereby producers maintained their mill prices for long periods in practically complete accord and in some more or less definite relation."[4]

Departures from basing-point prices did occur. Secret rebates have been made from the basing-point prices;[5] some mills have continuously offered openly to sell at prices from 10 to 20 cents per

---

the United States in the three years from 1927-1929. This analysis revealed that in 13 of the 21 cities, every sale had been made at a price corresponding to the basing-point formula, and that in 3 other cities approximately complete uniformity existed. Of all sales (made by different manufacturers) taken together, 93.95 per cent of the tonnage represented had been sold in accordance with the basing-point system. (*ibid.*, 57, 58.)

[1] Some of the departures were departures only in appearance because invoices represented deliveries under contracts made at an earlier date when the price of cement was below that prevailing at the time of the invoice. Had such invoices been referred to the date of the contract rather than the date of the invoice, greater uniformity would have been revealed.

[2] *ibid.*, 58, 59.

[3] *ibid.*, 63, and diagram at *ibid.*, 65. About one third of the total output of cement was used for road building and similar purposes in 1928 (*ibid.*, 17).

[4] *ibid.*, 64. It added that uniformity upon such contracts was more convincing than uniformity in prices to dealers, in view of the fact that "for a producer to be out of line on these gigantic state contracts by ever so little, if high, is to invite enormous losses in volume of business. . . . Yet such is the confidence of any member of the industry in his knowledge of the mathematical formula, base prices, and freight rates which the other members will use in arriving at their bids, that, when the system is smoothly working, as prior to 1931, he will bid a price calculated in that same way with an assurance born of experience that such a bid will enable him to share with a half dozen or so of others in the letting of contracts amounting to a total of from $2,000,000 to $6,000,000 and, in the case of one recent letting, to a total of more than $18,000,000." (*ibid.*, 64.)

[5] F.T.C., *Cement Industry*, 92.

barrel below the price calculated by reference to the governing basing point. This price cutting has apparently, however, been confined to certain delivery points, where mills believed that price cutting would "bring in more additional business with less risk of reprisal from the 'regular' companies."[1] One mill for some years maintained one base price for the state of Michigan and a higher base price outside the state,[2] and occasionally mills have arbitrarily restricted to a prescribed territory the application of a basing point.[3] Departures from basing-point prices have also been made in coastal markets around ports of entry to meet the competition of foreign producers of cement.[4] In California the multiple-basing-point system was abandoned in 1929 for a system of delivered prices based upon freight charges from the mill nearest the point of delivery.[5] Cement manufacturers, like steel manufacturers, have also departed from their general basing-point practice in dealing with railroads. They sold cement at a mill price wherever the mill was situated on a railway route.[6] They have also made arrangements similar to those in the steel industry to permit the federal government to take advantage of special land-grant rates available to it.[7]

As in the steel industry, the availability of cheaper methods of transportation than the railroad has caused pressure to modify the principle of adding railroad freight charges to the base price

[1] F.T.C., *Price Bases Inquiry*, 133; also *Cement Industry*, 1933, xiii.
[2] F.T.C., *Price Bases Inquiry*, 113.
[3] *ibid.*, 109; also *Cement Industry*, 51.
[4] F.T.C., *Cement Industry*, 46, 47.
[5] *ibid.*, 127.
[6] This mill price appears to be fixed by either the lowest basing-point price on the line, or the lowest total of base price from any point not on the line, and freight from such point to the nearest junction freightwise on the line, the lower of these two prices being the one set. Thus railroad buyers are in a position to secure for any point on their line "the lowest price prevailing commercially on their roads, all points considered," although railroad purchases of cement are not completely on a mill base. Wherever a purchase is made from a mill off the line the price charged is the same as the delivered price to a non-railroad buyer located at the nearest junction point on the railroad. Apparently in recent years railroads have pursued the policy of increasing their purchases from mills off their lines, but from which there is a through line to the destination on the line where the cement is required, the price of cement at the point at which it meets the line of the purchasing railroad being the lowest the company would have to pay at any point on the line. The freight from the mill to this junction point is deducted from the delivered price by the seller, the buying railroad pays the agreed proportion of the through rate to the railroad carrying cement to the junction point; as, however, this agreed amount is usually less than the sum deducted by the cement manufacturer on the invoice, the purchaser secures a gain upon such purchases. (F.T.C., *Price Bases Inquiry*, 102–103.)
[7] *ibid.*, 103, 104.

to arrive at the delivered price. With one[1] exception, however, the price was calculated by the use of railroad transportation costs even where water transportation was available. But cement was not always delivered by railroad; cement delivered by water yielded a higher price at the mill than sales to points equally distant freightwise to which water transportation was not available.[2] The availability of trucks resulted in the quotation of special prices for delivery by the buyer's truck.[3] These prices undermined the basing-point system because truck-delivered cement was cheaper than that delivered by rail. The code of fair competition for the industry under the National Industrial Recovery Act contained no reference to the basing-point system. Producers filed open prices for each delivery point in accordance with the system.

d. The Sugar Industry. The course of events in the sugar industry illustrates how efforts to regulate price cutting lead to the introduction of a basing-point system. Before 1928 (when the Sugar Institute began operations) the price of sugar at any delivery point was generally the price at the nearest refinery plus the cost of transportation thence to delivery points; the price of sugar at refineries at different points was approximately uniform.[4] Had sales been made to all buyers at uniform refinery prices, each refinery would have been limited to sales in the territories to which it could deliver more cheaply than any rival. Refiners were not willing, however, to accept this limitation upon their territories and had reached out into wider fields by "absorbing freight." The total absorptions by each were determined by the territories each decided to serve.[5] These freight absorptions

[1] The basing-point mill which determines the New York price has used a water transportation rate (*ibid.*, 25, 66).
[2] *ibid.*, 133.
[3] In some districts producers quoted mill prices when delivery was to be made to the buyer's truck about 15 cents per barrel above the prices for railroad deliveries (*loc. cit.; Cement Industry*, 55, 58, 59). In other areas, however, producers have ceased to quote any price for truck deliveries, thus establishing uniform prices based upon the all-rail cost of transportation (F.T.C., *Cement Industry*, 28, 57, 59, 62, 65).
[4] U.S. v. Sugar Institute, *Decision* of Judge Mack (mimeographed), 42.
[5] These decisions were embodied in their "freight applications," *i.e.*, the amount they added to the refinery price to arrive at the delivered price; the difference between the actual cost of transportation to a point and the refiner's "freight application" measured the amount of freight he "absorbed." The policies of refiners varied. "Some refiners would absorb no more than 10 to 15 cents per hundred pounds and normally even less; others like the California refiners would absorb as high as 30 cents. This they could afford to do because of certain advantages in purchasing raw" (*ibid.*, 43). (They purchased raw sugar from their parent company operating plantations in Hawaii.) In general, refiners did not refuse to sell at f.o.b. mill prices

resulted in an interpenetration of market areas involving lack of uniformity in mill-net realizations but left the structure of *relative* prices at different delivery points in conformity with what would be expected from a system of f.o.b. mill prices. In the territory east of the Mississippi River, north of the Ohio River, and west of a line from Buffalo to Pittsburgh, however, a "Philadelphia-plus" system prevailed.[1] In areas to which Texas refiners had most economical access, sales were made upon a New Orleans base and, in consequence, yielded a "pickup" to the Texas refiners who are said to have "substantially lived" on the "pickup" for many years.[2] The beet sugar producers are mainly located in Wisconsin, Michigan, Ohio, Indiana, Utah, and Colorado but, apparently since the beginning of the industry, beet sugar has been sold in each area at the prices at which cane sugar is offered there. As the cane sugar refineries are mainly on the coast, the beet sugar producers were able to "make a substantial profit on transportation,"[3] *i.e.*, to secure a freight "pickup."

The middle western states have traditionally been the most vigorously contested territory in the industry; water transportation was available and delivered prices were usually calculated by reference to the cost of transportation by water, even when sugar was actually transported by rail, either because the refiner did not have access to water, or for any other reason.[4] Similar conditions prevailed on occasion in Alabama, Tennessee, Kentucky, and the parts of Indiana reached by the Warrior River.[5]

The attempts of the Sugar Institute between 1928 and March, 1931, to standardize refinery prices and methods of doing business,[6] and to eliminate secret price making, diverted competition into more vigorous rivalry in making freight allowances. The institute then turned to strenuous efforts to eliminate this rivalry.[7] The outstanding difficulty of the industry lay in the existence of water transportation facilities, often considerably cheaper

---

but it is not clear whether these prices were uniform to all buyers irrespective of their location.
  [1] Deliveries into this territory from New York involved an absorption of freight of two cents per hundred pounds while deliveries from Baltimore yielded a "pickup" of one cent per hundred pounds (*ibid.*, 44).
  [2] *ibid.*, 44.
  [3] *Brief on the Facts for the Sugar Institute*, 177; U.S. v. Sugar Institute, *Decision* of Judge Mack (mimeographed), 44.
  [4] *Decision* of Judge Mack, 47.
  [5] *ibid.*, 47.
  [6] See p. 72.
  [7] *Decision* of Judge Mack, 45, 114.

than railroad transportation, although slower and more liable to cause deterioration of the product. After discussion, the institute decided that "absorbing freight means the selling of transportation at less than cost, which is unsound in principle and necessarily throws an undue burden on the consumers at and near the primary markets,"[1] a conclusion which, translated into action, would have completely reshuffled the market territories of the refiners. No effort was made to apply the new principle; the refiners sought "to prevent the breakdown of the freight structure chiefly in the Great Lakes[2] and Warrior River areas,"[3] *i.e.*, apparently to secure prices in those areas based upon the cost of railroad transportation. Similar but less successful efforts were made to establish a delivered-price system in other areas.[4] Thus the condemnation of local price discrimination by the institute in its ruling against freight absorptions was

[1] *ibid.*, 50.
[2] *ibid.*, 51. Desperate but abortive efforts were made during the early months of the institute to secure this end, and, by the summer of 1928, delivered prices in the middle west had fallen to the Philadelphia price plus the cost of combined rail and water transportation; the institute succeeded, however, in preventing their reduction to the still lower price arrived at by adding to the price in New Orleans the cost of transportation thence by barge (*ibid.*, 52). The refiners considered the desirability of zone prices and agreed delivered prices (*ibid.*, 53 *ff.*, and *Brief for U.S.*, 261, 262) and finally arrived at "a system of delivered prices with denial of the privilege of purchases f.o.b. refinery" (*Decision* of Judge Mack, 52). After drastic price cutting in the middle western states, the American Sugar Refining Company announced in April, 1929, that it would sell at the important lake ports, as well as at some nearby points, only at delivered prices. The prices announced were a little less than its refinery price plus the cost of railroad transportation and were, therefore, higher than the prices prevailing during the immediately preceding period of price cutting, as well as higher than those charged prior to the existence of the institute (*ibid.*, 59; *Brief for the U.S.*, 251). The extent to which refiners were thus enabled to "pick up" freight is indicated by the fact that refiners are said to have transported sugar to Chicago at a cost of 28 cents per hundred pounds while selling there at a price which included 51 cents per hundred pounds for freight (*Decision* of Judge Mack, 59. Cleveland purchasers paid 36 cents per hundred pounds for freight but could have transported their sugar for 23 cents per hundred pounds (*loc. cit.*)). In the litigation much importance was attached to the question whether or not the American Sugar Refining Company made this drastic increase in prices in the most competitive territory in the country with the assurance that its rivals would follow its lead. The refiners contended that the company acted on its own initiative and to meet price cutting by others (*Brief on the Facts for the Sugar Institute*, 208). It is difficult to see how the announcement of these prices above those prevailing can be attributed to previous price cutting. The Attorney General claimed that the company had been assured that its lead would be accepted and that its lead was, in fact, accepted; this new structure of prices prevailed until five weeks after the petition against the institute was filed (*Brief for the U.S.*, 251, 253, 262, 293). The judge in the Circuit Court decided that the adoption of the new price policy was greatly influenced by the collective activities of the refiners in the institute, and that the institute by concerted action maintained the policy (*Decision* of Judge Mack, 63).
[3] A similar policy of preventing the sale of sugar except at delivered prices was adopted in the area served by the Warrior River, in which also the delivered price was calculated by reference to the cost of railroad transportation although cheaper water transportation was available (*ibid.*, 63).
[4] *ibid.*, 71, 73.

completely forgotten when the new delivered-price system was discovered as a means of raising prices in the Great Lakes and Warrior River areas[1] where "freight pickups" were secured. Yet "pickups" involve discriminations as much as absorptions. The Circuit Court decided that the real purpose of the refiners was not to eliminate discrimination but "to solve in a manner advantageous to themselves and without consideration of the trade, a troublesome transportation problem."[2] The maintenance by the sugar refiners of freight applications departing from the actual cost of transportation stimulated the diversion of sugar in transit and the transiting of sugar (*i.e.*, the continuation of the transportation to a more distant point without transshipment) because buyers could thus, owing to the structure of transportation rates, evade the freight applications of the sellers.[3]

2. THE POLICY OF THE NATIONAL RECOVERY ADMINISTRATION

It has already emerged that the Recovery Administration took no determined stand against geographical price discrimination. Basing-point systems were used in the lumber and cement industries although not specifically authorized in the code.[4] In the bituminous coal industry "the determination of freight allowances by the marketing agencies . . . created a honeycomb of prices that has fostered discrimination between one buyer and another and uneconomic crosshauling of coal as well as its production at uneconomic points."[5] The steel industry, however, obtained explicit authority to compel adherence to the basing-point system and to control the selection of bases and methods of calculating transportation costs. Of the first 180 codes approved six[6] provided for zone systems, and five[7] for basing points. Some 33 other codes provided for delivered prices of some kind.[8] Some

[1] *ibid.*, 71.
[2] *ibid.*, 72.
[3] *ibid.*, 78. *Brief on the Facts for the Sugar Institute*, 252, 254, 258. Nevertheless the institute contended that it avoided placing any obstacles in the way of the free choice of methods of transportation by buyers and permitted buyers to purchase f.o.b. refinery (*op. cit.*, 193).
[4] The code for the cement industry prohibited the diversion of shipments, a provision indicating the intention to prevent sales on a mill basis.
[5] CONSUMER ADVISORY BOARD, *Fixing Coal Prices*, 5.
[6] Business furniture, storage equipment and filing supplies, fertilizer, petroleum, salt, and shovel drag line and crane. Zone prices for newsprint were vigorously opposed by newspaper publishers (*New York Times*, Feb. 2, 1934).
[7] Cast iron soil pipe, iron and steel, lime, refractories, reinforcing materials fabricating.
[8] For list see CONSUMER ADVISORY BOARD, Appendices to *Memorandum to General Johnson*, Feb. 19, 1934. The codes for the laundry and dry cleaning machinery and shovel drag line and crane industries provided for basing points only in the

specifically authorized the absorption of freight[1] and a few attempted to prohibit dumping[2] or to divide territory;[3] a number of codes, however, definitely required that all sales be made f.o.b. and that if the seller paid for transportation the whole cost thereof was to be charged to the buyer.

The Consumer Advisory Board criticized the acceptance of geographical discrimination[4] and suggested that, in general, market areas be adjusted to secure that each point be served from its nearest point of supply. The principal attacks upon basing-point systems were, however, leveled at the practices of the iron and steel industry.[5] It has already been stated[6] that when the amended code was approved in May, 1934, only minor modifications were made in the basing-point system[7] but that the Presidential order of May 30, 1934, stated that conditions of

---

Pacific coast territory. The cedar chest manufacturers were permitted to amend their code to establish Atlanta, New York, and Chicago as basing points.

[1] Sales below cost of production were permitted in the structural clay products industry to permit freight absorption to meet the published prices of a rival and in the sponge rubber and rubber sundries divisions of the rubber industry freight absorptions were permitted up to a maximum amount equal to the actual cost of transporting the commodity. The wallpaper manufacturing code permitted "freight allowances" but restricted them to amounts that would reduce the freight charge to the cost of railroad transportation from the nearest operating mill to the customer.

[2] The cast iron pressure pipe producers divided the whole of the United States into two "home markets" and ruled that quoting prices f.o.b. foundry in distant markets less than in the home market was destructive of sound business, and that it was unfair to sell in such distant markets at a foundry price less than that charged in the home market during the preceding fifteen days. The code for producers of funeral supplies made it unfair to sell outside the "normal" territory of a producer at prices lower than those charged in his normal territory. Sales of corrugated and solid fiber products outside the normal territory of each seller at prices below those prevailing in the other territories were prohibited.

[3] The code for automobile dealing provided that it was unfair to sell new cars in any area except through the regularly enfranchised dealer for the territory for the make of car concerned.

[4] It contended that although "such devices may be needed and fairly used in some industrial situations, their history is one of grave abuse" and suggested that they be permitted only under peculiarly close scrutiny by the administrator to guard against potential abuse (Memorandum on *Suggestions for Code Revision*, Feb. 19, 1934). The board sought information concerning the volume of output at each producing center and of shipments to each delivery point as a means of assessing the effect of these practices. Failing to obtain this information, partly because it was not in the possession of the code authorities themselves, it suggested that the latter be required to compile statistics that would reveal the effect of systems of dividing the market provided in the codes.

[5] After the attacks by the Federal Trade Commission (see p. 314) the administration announced a general policy of endeavoring to modify these systems until every important area of production was a basing point. In August, 1934, however, a code was approved establishing Pittsburgh, Chicago, and Birmingham as basing points for steel joists.

[6] See p. 315.

[7] *Cf.*, F.T.C., *Basing Point System in the Iron and Steel Industry*, 29.

economic emergency required the retention of the multiple-basing-point system in modified form and instructed the Federal Trade Commission and the National Recovery Administration "to study further and jointly the operation of the basing-point system and its effect on prices to consumers and any effects of the existing system in either permitting or encouraging price fixing or providing unfair competitive advantages for producers or disadvantages for consumers." The Federal Trade Commission[1] reiterated its previous criticisms of the basing-point system and recommended that the code be amended so as to withdraw the endorsement of the basing-point system by the government. The report of the National Industrial Recovery Administration,[2] however, while rejecting some of the criticisms of the system, agreed that it was desirable that producers be given a greater incentive to increase their market territories by reducing their base prices rather than by absorbing freight. Crosshauling was admitted to be wasteful and a burden upon purchasers. The committee decided that hostility to the system was such that piecemeal modification would not suffice and a comprehensive program aimed at a new system was needed. A system of uniform prices at the mill was too uncertain and disturbing in its effects to be recommended and would not meet the criticisms of the basing-point system unless freight absorption was also eliminated or restricted. Elimination was held to be undesirable and both elimination and restriction were believed to be unattainable by federal government compulsion. Where mills were close together uniform prices to all at each mill would involve unnecessary complications. It was accordingly recommended that in any revised code provision be made for the establishment of a basing point for every group of mills.[3] It was tentatively suggested that sales should be made to delivery points at which prices were determined by reference to any basing point other than that

[1] *ibid.*, 42.
[2] The report was presented by a committee consisting of Professor J. M. Clark, M. P. Sharp, R. W. Shannon, and B. T. Ansell.
[3] Group mill bases were to be established within 50 miles of each town with an annual ingot capacity of more than 20,000 tons and also containing facilities for rolling and shaping such ingots into primary or semi-finished forms. Existing basing points not thus qualifying as group bases were, however, to become group bases. Base prices were to be filed at such group bases for each product produced at plants nearer thereto than to any other base. (N.R.A., *The Operation of the Basing Point System in the Iron and Steel Industry*, 167.) This arrangement would have required the establishment of 19 additional group mill bases and would leave only $1\frac{3}{4}$ per cent of rolling mill capacity more than 50 miles from a group base (*ibid.*, 169, and Appendixes D and E).

governing the seller's mill only if they yielded at the seller's mill not more than $5.00 per ton less than sales within the territory in which his own base price determined delivered prices.[1] If these proposals appeared to be unacceptable the abandonment of the price features of the code was to be considered.

These principles were first applied in the amended code for the lime industry[2] which provided for the establishment of a multiple-basing-point system in which not all points of production need be basing points.[3] Water and truck transportation costs could, moreover, be standardized, but freight absorptions were limited to 20 per cent of the base price of the product.[4] Thus uniform mill nets with the resulting sharp separation of the market territories of each mill were rejected. The interpenetration of territories by freight absorption was, however, restricted to a band of territory.

We now turn to a discussion of the economic effects of basing-point systems.

[1] No information was given concerning the method of arriving at the figure of $5.00. An investigation of shipments of 1,534,000 net tons of steel products shipped during the three months ended June 30, 1934 (about 20 per cent of the total national output) by mills with 85 per cent of the national capacity within a fifty-mile radius of Pittsburgh), revealed actual freight charges paid in excess of freight charges passed on to buyers averaging $1.07 per ton (N.R.A., *op. cit.*, Supplement No. 1). This average freight absorption gives no indication of the number of tons shipped at absorptions exceeding $5.00 per ton. Total freight absorptions are distributed over all tonnage, including that involving no freight absorption.
[2] Code 31, Amendment 2, of Apr. 1, 1935.
[3] For hydrated finishing lime produced in Ohio a single base was established for the whole of the United States (Art. VIII, Sec. 2 (*b*)).
[4] Committees of the code authority were authorized to establish basing points in each district to govern all rail shipments (Art. VII, Sec. 2), every member of the industry being free, however, to establish his own plant as his basing point. Different basing points might be used for different products. These committees were also to designate for each basing point the territory (known as the "low-rate area") to "include all destinations from which such basing point has a minimum carload rail freight . . . lower than or equal to the minimum carload freight from another rail basing point" (Art. II, Sec. 9). The open-price clause provided that for all destinations within the "low-rate area" of a plant prices were to be filed "f.o.b. the rail basing point": the seller might also designate destinations outside this area to which such prices were to apply. In both areas delivered prices were to be the base price plus all-rail freight. Sales to other destinations were to be made at *not less* than the most favorable terms filed by any other member of the industry provided that the yield at the plant should be not less than 80 per cent of the filed base price (this latter proviso being stayed for 90 days). Art. VIII, Sec. 6, however, provided that a mill might deviate from its "filed" prices to meet the competition of sellers shipping into his area from outside, thus providing for a noncompliance with this clause. Prices for delivery at the mill or by truck or water might be filed provided they also specified the minimum quantity and area to which they applied and the charge for truck or water transportation. Provision was made for petitions for relief where this clause worked hardship (Article VIII, Sec. 3 (*g*)). The operation of this multiple-basing-point system was to be studied with a view to possible revision.

CHAPTER VII

PRICE DISCRIMINATION (*Continued*)

3. The effects of basing-point systems—*a*. The interpenetration of market territories—*b*. The non-basing-point producer—*c*. General effects of basing-point systems.

3. THE EFFECTS OF BASING-POINT SYSTEMS

The immediate effects of basing-point systems are upon the revenue of the sellers and the costs of buyers. These effects flow from both the absorption of freight even where all mills are basing points (*i.e.*, from the interpenetration of market territories), and from the presence of non-base producers. The more immediate effects of these two aspects of the systems will be discussed before their general effects are analyzed.

a. The Interpenetration of Market Territories. Freight absorptions originate in maladjustments between investment and demand. The ideal investment at each point would be such that, when fully utilized, its output, sold at a uniform mill net, would yield a revenue that covered the full costs of production, the scale of production being the most economical from a technical point of view. But the nature of demand and of methods of production obstructs such an ideal adjustment, with the result that the presence of unused capacity on the one hand impels efforts to secure the full utilization of plant, and, on the other, arouses fears of price cutting aimed at short-run gains.

Where the plant of a producer in an imperfect market is not being fully utilized the volume of production can be increased without incurring a proportionate increase in costs. A reduction in price to all purchasers (*i.e.*, in the base price) tends to increase sales revenue by increasing the volume of sales but this tendency is partly or wholly offset by the decline in the revenue per unit sold. A much greater reduction in price can be made to secure a given increase in the volume of sales if the reduced price can be restricted to a new class of customers; any price to this class that exceeds the marginal or direct cost of production increases the net revenue of the producer. It is largely because sales to purchasers more cheaply reached by a rival at another point of production appear to producers to fall into this category that they maintain prices to buyers in their existing territory and "absorb freight" to sell in the territories of others. In fact, however, freight absorptions stimulate similar absorptions by rivals. In consequence the firms seeking additional business from purchasers at new delivery points suffer a decline in business at points already reached more cheaply by them than by rivals. Freight absorptions may, therefore, prove altogether abortive as a device for increasing the rate of utilization of plant. They result in a mutual interpenetration of territories; if sellers charged uniform prices to all at the mill, market territories would be bounded by lines determined by transportation costs.[1] These absorptions are not an inevitable, but they are a usual, result of basing-point systems. Sellers prefer freight absorption to price competition partly because they believe that it can be more easily controlled than price competition, which may easily get out of hand.[2] They are probably also inclined to underestimate the elasticity of demand.

This interpenetration of territories is stimulated in a variety of ways. The desire to anticipate increases in demand induces firms to expand their productive capacity beyond the immediate demand for their product and results in pressure to utilize plant more fully. Fluctuations in demand over time also leave producers with unused plant at some periods and create a similar pressure. Changes in the location of production may have the same effect. The building of a new plant at a point which has a freight advantage in reaching part of the territory of an existing plant may increase unused capacity. If the new plant becomes a base the older plant may endeavor, by absorbing freight, to retain its business in the territory more cheaply reached by its new rival, more especially as it already has established connections with buyers there. Wherever it can reach its former customers more cheaply than its new rival it may, however, maintain its former level of prices. On the other hand, a new or small producer may seek thus to improve his position in the market (possibly with the object of attaining a more economical size); he may prefer to maintain prices in the territory in which he can reach pur-

---

[1] Cf. FETTER, *Masquerade of Monopoly*, 284. If transportation rates are not upon a mileage basis but are "blanketed" market areas may overlap.
[2] They may find it difficult to forecast the effect of a local price reduction on the whole structure of prices.

chasers more cheaply than rivals, but to attach new customers outside his existing territory by absorbing freight on sales to them, intending subsequently, perhaps, to reduce his base price. Changes in the cost of transportation may also stimulate freight absorption. If new and cheaper methods of transportation favor one seller as compared with another, the territory of the former is extended and that of the latter restricted. The latter firm, however, may seek to retain business in the affected area by absorbing freight on sales there, again partly because he has established connections with buyers.[1]

The foregoing maladjustments of investment tend over longer periods of time to disappear. Maladjustments may, however, be incapable of avoidance so long as present methods of production prevail. If demand is distributed sporadically, owing, possibly, to local concentrations of population, or the localization of an industry consuming the product in a few small areas, a single producer may be compelled, in order to keep his plant in full operation, to obtain business from more than one area of concentrated demand. A uniform price policy to all buyers might necessitate so low a base price (in order to reach the more distant markets) that the firm could not remain in profitable operation. This situation may be due to the plant being uneconomically located in relation to the existing geographical distribution of demand; local discrimination may enable the poorly located plant to continue in existence and, possibly, even in profitable existence, although in the long run it would be more economical for the plant to be relocated. But it may be that conditions of production suggest a scale of operation in excess of that necessary to supply demand from any one area of concentrated demand. If full freight were charged from A to B the delivered price in B might be so high that a plant of less than the most economical size might be attracted into existence at B, although a plant of the most economical size could supply both A and B. Partial absorption of freight to B may prevent this outcome and also permit sales in A at a lower price than would be necessary if separate plants existed at both A and B.[2] This argument may even apply if there is more than one plant at A; one plant of the

[1] *Cf.* SOUTER, "Modern Monopoly as the Gentleman Crook," *Polit. Sci. Quart.*, 48: 249 (1933).
[2] This argument is analogous to the argument that those who pay full rates to a public utility may be better off when lower prices are charged to some classes of purchaser because the plant as a whole can be operated on a more economical scale.

most economical size may be too few, and two too many, to permit the ideal adjustment.

In the same way the distribution of demand over time may prevent the ideal adjustment of investment. The demand for cement and steel, for instance, is subject to wide fluctuations in the territory most economically reached by each producer.

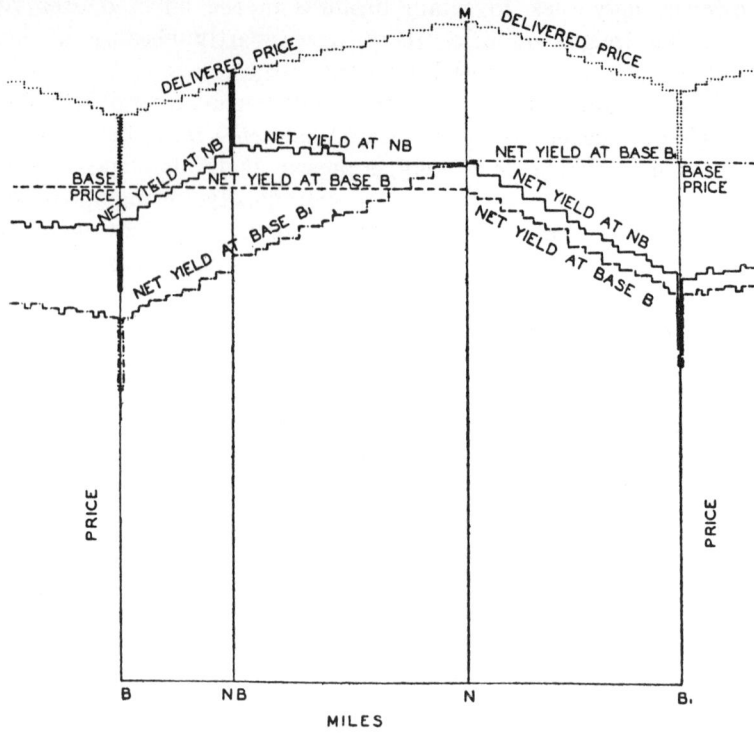

FIG. 44.—Net yields at base and nonbase mills under a basing-point system.

It depends upon the location of constructional activity, especially public works (including road construction). In any short period demand in the vicinity of a base may exceed the capacity of that base. Producers there might then raise their price until delivered prices in the area of heavy demand were sufficiently high for nearby mills to sell there without absorbing freight. The enlargement of local capacity might not occur because the probable demand throughout the life of a new plant would not suffice to make the investment remunerative. Shipments into the territories of other mills deter these sharp local price increases or uneconomic investments while providing a flexibility of supply otherwise unattainable. Similarly when demand in some territories declines much more than in others the mills closest to the depressed areas can reduce their losses by absorbing freight and selling in other territories.[1]

The most immediate effect of freight absorption is upon the revenues of sellers. Figure 44 shows the net yields obtained by base mills at B and B_1, upon sales to different places along a line joining the two mills. It assumes short-haul rates per mile higher than long-haul rates and that transportation costs per mile are approximately uniform. Each base mill obtains on all sales up to and including N a net yield equal to its base price. Shipments beyond N yield, at the mill, sums decreasing twice as fast as transportation costs increase.[2] These shipments reduce the average mill net obtained. The amount of these sales involving freight absorption depends upon the distribution of demand in the territory involving freight absorptions and the decision of the seller as to the territory in which he will endeavor to sell. It depends also upon the relative levels of prices at the two bases. The higher the price at a base in relation to that at other bases the smaller the territory in which sales involve no absorption of freight and the greater the tendency to obtain business by absorbing freight. Figures 45 and 46 show the actual variety of mill nets obtained by cement mills.

The effect of freight absorptions upon the local distribution of plants depends upon the extent to which the elimination of all sales from each base into the territories of others would affect their aggregate mill nets.[3] If aggregate mill nets would be unaffected by the complete abandonment of freight absorptions the geographical distribution of plants would be similarly unchanged. But where the sales revenue from shipments into territory governed by prices at other bases exceeds the revenue that

---

[1] *Cf.* the remark that freight absorptions permit producers to reduce their losses owing to purely local reductions in demand in the easiest way; "if he had to cut his base price in order to reach into adjacent districts the sacrifice might be so great that this resource would be of no value to him, and, in any case, its value would be very much less than if the same end could be gained by the less expensive method of freight absorption" (N.R.A., *op. cit.*, 144). *Cf.* also, AMERICAN IRON AND STEEL INSTITUTE, *Basing Points and Competition in Steel*, 13.
[2] The delivered price is falling and the cost of transportation is increasing at the same rate.
[3] It depends upon the volume of sales involving freight absorptions and the points to which they are made, *i.e.*, the mill nets upon each.

would be obtained if the mill took over the sales now made by mills shipping into its territory, the elimination of freight absorption would reduce its total sales revenue; it could maintain its revenue only by reducing its base price. The extent to which

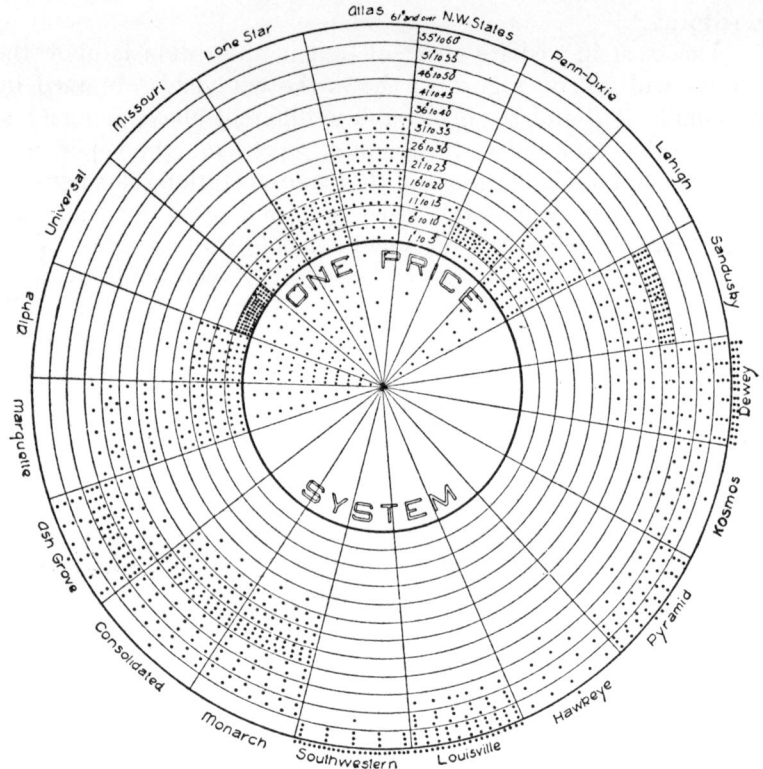

FIG. 45.—Net yields on bids submitted to the Division of Highways, Department of Public Works, State of Illinois for the sale of 3,000,000 barrels of cement to be delivered to 102 destinations, March 22, 1929. (F.T.C., *Price Bases Inquiry*, 198.)

NOTE:—Each dot represents a bid. Dots in the area marked "one price system" represent bids at prices yielding to the mill its "then current maximum mill net price." Dots in successive outer zones represent bids at prices which would yield less than the mill's maximum mill net by an amount within the range of cents indicated in each zone on the chart. (The delivered prices quoted by some firms at 56 of the 76 destinations were above that calculated in accordance with the basing-point system.)

sales revenues would be thus disturbed by abandoning freight absorption is unknown.[1] Apart from the possibility that the elimination of freight absorptions would change the relations between prices at different bases such absorptions leave the

[1] *Cf.* CONSUMER ADVISORY BOARD OF N.R.A., *Memorandum on Suggestions for Code Revision*, Feb. 19, 1934.

relative geographical structure of prices unchanged.[1] Prices increase with distance from base mills and increase in proportion to the cost of transportation from the mill to the delivery point.

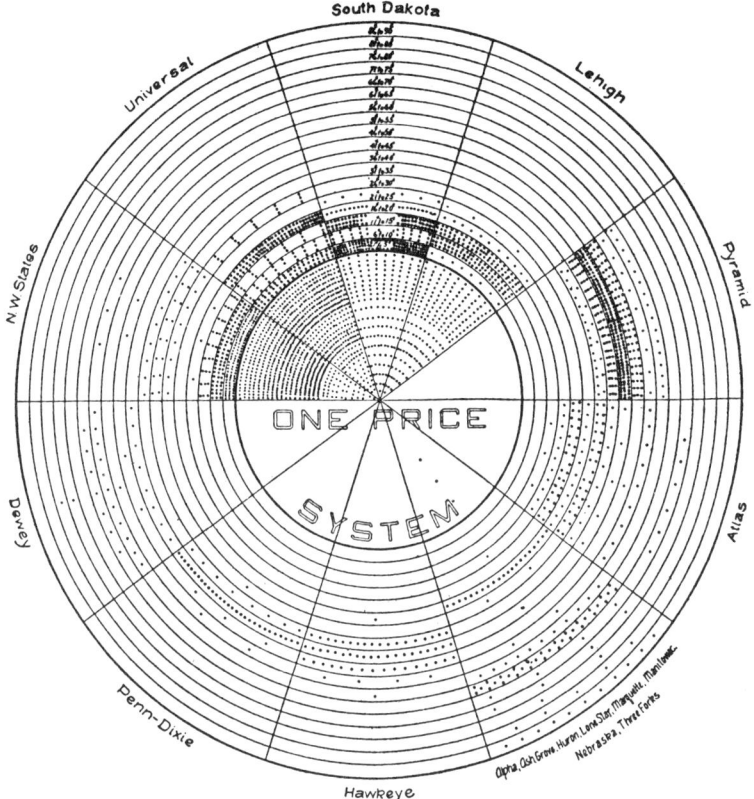

FIG. 46.—Net yields on the sale of 2,350 carloads (360,580 barrels) of cement to five Minneapolis line lumber companies at 210 destinations in Minnesota, Iowa, and North and South Dakota between July 1, 1927 and June 30, 1929. (*F.T.C. Price Bases Inquiry*; 206.)

NOTE:—Each dot represents one carload of cement. Dots in the area marked "one price system" represent sales at prices yielding to the mill its "then current maximum mill net price." Dots in successive outer zones represent sales yielding less than the mill's maximum mill net by an amount within the range of cents indicated within each zone on the chart.

Freight absorptions have no effect, therefore, upon the location of industries purchasing the product unless they affect the geographical structure of base prices.

[1] The use of railroad rates to calculate delivered prices where cheaper transportation is available necessitates a modification of this statement. This matter is discussed on p. 370.

The effect of freight absorption upon the relations between prices at different bases is far from clear. It permits a seller to maintain a high price to buyers in the vicinity of his mill without restricting his sales to the small territory in which his base price plus freight gives a lower delivered price than that calculated by reference to any other base. If neighboring bases reduce their price a mill can continue to sell in part of its former territory[1] without reducing its own base price. Sales into territory governed by the new lower base price yield less, but to respond by lowering its own base price would merely mean lower mill nets on sales to points in the vicinity of its mill.[2] But the maintenance of a base price when neighboring bases have reduced their price makes freight-absorbing sales by other base mills more attractive to them and may even induce quite distant mills to send salesmen into this high-price territory. Similarly, a relatively low base price discourages freight-absorbing sales.[3] Furthermore, where (as in the steel industry) a considerable proportion of all sales is made to fabricators, a reduction at one base gives a competitive advantage to fabricators there; steel manufacturers at other bases can protect fabricators in their own neighborhood (who are likely to be a large part of their non-freight-absorbing market) only by reducing their base price.[4] In the absence of freight absorption, however, the only means of increasing sales would be a reduction in base price which might increase sales within existing territory and (if rival bases did not respond) increase the territory served. The downward pressure upon prices would, therefore, be increased.[5]

b. *The Non-basing-point Producer.* Basing-point systems invariably establish fewer basing points than there are points of production. Commodities sold by the non-basing-point producers are sold at each delivery point at a price calculated by taking the *lowest* combination of base price plus transportation from the

---

[1] Reduction of neighboring base prices extends the territory they can reach without absorbing freight.
[2] *Cf.* F.T.C., *Price Bases Inquiry*, 145; N.R.A., *op. cit.*, 159.
[3] *Cf.* N.R.A., *op. cit.*, 155.
[4] *ibid.*, 161.
[5] *ibid.*, 155 *ff.*, 162. The inducement to extend territory by this means depends upon the rate at which freight rates increase with distance, the extent to which the base price exceeds direct costs, and the distribution of demand in neighboring territory. If freight charges are high in relation to existing margins between direct cost and prices, and demand is located near centers of production, the inducement is at a minimum. The probability that a price cut will immediately be met by nearby bases also deters such price cutting.

base to the delivery point, *i.e.*, as if they had been produced and shipped from that base, even though they may be sold at the door of the non-basing-point mill. The non-basing mill has no price policy of its own. Its revenues depend upon the price policies of the base mills governing prices at the various points at which it sells. It is in fact merely a limiting case of a base mill; it has a base price so high that there is no territory in which its price plus freight is lower than that of any other mill. Along a line joining the governing base with the non-base mill and projected in the direction away from the base its delivered price is *equal* to that of the base mill if transportation charges are proportional to distance. Thus practically all its sales involve mill nets below those on sales at its mill. As in practice transportation charges per mile are higher for long than for short hauls, there are few, if any, delivery points sales at which yield mill nets equal to those on sales at its mill.[1]

There is a number of possible reasons why a mill should set so high a price at its mill that it permits the base mill to deliver there without absorbing freight. In the last analysis, however, they are all traceable to maladjustments between investment and demand.[2] We have seen that in general the non-base mill is located at a point at which production was commenced later than at the base and that there is, over long periods, pressure to convert these mills into base mills. Mills are established at new points of production when it is believed that, at existing delivered prices in the territory expected to be covered by the mill, and taking account of the volume of business expected to be obtained there (by non-price competition), at least a normal return can be obtained upon the necessary investment, allowing also for the costs of production at the new point.[3] It may be that only upon this level of prices the mill can be built at all.[4] If it established a base price it might get no more business because existing mills would enter the territory in which it could sell most cheaply,

---

[1] *Cf.* Fig. 46.
[2] *Cf.* the statement that steel mills are often distant from supplies of raw materials or preferred markets, and that "changing industrial conditions may have brought about these dislocations" (AMERICAN IRON AND STEEL INSTITUTE, *Basing Points and Competition in Steel*, 4).
[3] In the cement industry it was claimed that the search for "freight pickups" led to the building of new plants in fresh areas at times when existing plants were not being used to full capacity, and this fact was offered as proof of the vigor of competition in the industry (U.S. v. Cement Manufacturers Protective Association, *Brief for the Cement Manufacturers Protective Association*, 125).
[4] N.R.A., *op. cit.*, 72, 128.

absorbing freight to do so. But, of course, so long as the new mill remains a non-basing-point mill purchasers obtain no benefit from the establishment of the new mill, except in speed of delivery and, possibly, other forms of service. With the growth of the local market, however, it may finally take the step of declaring a base price, thus reducing mill nets on business in its own neighborhood. Or it may declare a base price to attract fabricators near its mill.[1] Purchasers in this territory then benefit from the establishment of the new mill. The non-basing mill may thus be a transitional phenomenon characteristic of periods of relocation of industry.[2] But it is such, at least partly, because existing base mills, by absorbing freight, restrict the amount of business to be obtained by selling at a mill price.

Non-basing mills may, however, retain their status for long periods; they may do so (as did the steel mills in the Chicago area) when there is more than one non-basing mill in the same district. This policy may be due to its profitableness or to fear that the declaration of a base price would be regarded as cutting prices (or "undermining the price structure") and call forth reprisals. A firm already operating at a base may establish a non-base mill in territory already served by it and benefit by lower costs (of either production or transportation or both). It may do so because it is badly located in relation to the current geographical distribution of demand. The practice may give it abnormally high, normal, or subnormal profits[3] but in any event a revenue above what would be obtainable if it announced a mill price. Business obtained at high prices by expenditure on sales promotion is more profitable than business at lower prices involving equal expenditure on promoting sales. The only difference between this situation and one in which a new, well-located, mill remains a non-basing mill is that the latter has lower costs than the former and, therefore, higher profits. In either situation abnormally high profits continue only in the presence of barriers to increased

[1] *Cf.* below and N.R.A., *op. cit.*, 130, 161.

[2] It has been pointed out that before the basing-point system was authorized by a code of fair competition in the iron and steel industry any seller could transform a non-basing point into a base. Under the code, however, a three fourths vote of the producers of the country was needed to authorize the change. (N.R.A., *op. cit.*, 91, 128.)

[3] The Imperial Sugar Refinery at Sutherland, Texas, for instance, is said to have "picked up" freight to the extent of 0.453 million dollars in 1926 and 0.169 million dollars in 1931 because it sold on a New Orleans base price. Other companies obtained "pickups" in some years. (U.S. v. Sugar Institute, *Brief for the Sugar Institute on the Facts*, 180.) Beet sugar manufacturers also "picked up" freight in this way (*ibid.*, 177).

investment. It may be that the optimum scale of production is such that the addition of another mill of the most economical size would involve subnormal profits for both, or all the mills at the non-basing point. In any event the non-basing mill is a phenomenon of imperfect competition.

The restriction of the number of basing points affects the location of production through its effect upon the mill net obtained by sellers at non-basing points, and upon the size of the market territory in which basing-point mills can sell without absorbing freight. Figure 46 shows for a simple case the nature of the mill nets obtained by a non-basing producer NB. Shipments towards the base yield mill nets falling twice as fast as the delivered prices (ignoring the difference between long- and short-haul rates). Shipments away from the base usually yield higher mill nets than are obtained by the base mill. These shipments do not necessarily, however, make the non-base mill abnormally profitable. The *average* mill net of a non-base mill depends upon the territory it serves and the distribution of shipments within that territory. The greater the proportion of its total shipments made in the direction of the base the more does the average mill net fall below the maximum mill net. On the other hand, the profits of the non-base producer depend upon differences in costs of production at non-base and base mills: if the former are high-cost producers a higher average mill net is necessary to yield the same rate of return as at the base.

Where the deliveries from a non-base mill are such that a mill base price available to all buyers equal to the *average* mill net obtained as a non-base mill would result in equal aggregate mill nets, the location of production would not be changed by converting the mill into a base mill. The fact that the base mill can reach a wider territory without freight absorption than it could if all mills were base mills tends to encourage expansion of investment at the base[1] but the non-price competition of non-base mills tends to offset this tendency. As, however, the persistence of non-basing-point mills results in higher prices in the vicinity of the mills than might otherwise prevail, demand there is probably restricted. In so far as local mills would obtain a large part of this additional business investment there is somewhat discouraged.[2]

[1] *Cf.* VON BECKERATH, *Modern Industrial Organization*, 216.
[2] Local fabricators are for instance discouraged (F.T.C., *Basing Point System in the Steel Industry*, 25).

Conflicting opinions have been expressed concerning the effect of Pittsburgh-plus practice upon the development of steel manufacturing outside Pittsburgh. The Federal Trade Commission claimed that the Pittsburgh-plus practice had stimulated the development of the steel industry in Pittsburgh and retarded it in Chicago and the west, and to some extent in all places other than Pittsburgh,[1] and that the elimination of Pittsburgh basing would build up steel producing centers outside Pittsburgh.[2] Firms outside Pittsburgh insisted, however, that the Pittsburgh basing-point practice had stimulated the building of plants outside Pittsburgh and, moreover, that their survival depended upon the continuance of the Pittsburgh pricing practice.[3]

At first sight the opportunity to sell steel in Chicago at $6.80 per ton more than it would fetch in Pittsburgh, where the cost of producing it was about the same, suggests that production in Chicago might be so profitable that excessive development might be expected there.[4] But these maximum mill nets were obtained in a restricted territory. Chicago mills were able, for instance, to sell steel bars at a uniform and maximum net realization (which was above that obtained by Pittsburgh mills) only in portions of Illinois and Indiana, Wisconsin, Montana, South Dakota, Nebraska, Minnesota, Wyoming, Colorado, New Mexico, and Kansas.[5] Sales for delivery outside this area yielded less at

---

[1] F.T.C., *Statement on Pittsburgh Plus*, 318–319; *Annual Report*, 1924, 38.

[2] *Cf. Iron Age*, July 24, 1924, 205.

[3] Judge Gary contended that but for the practice plants would not have been built at Chicago or Duluth (F.T.C., *Statement on Pittsburgh Plus*, 888), and that the short interval of Chicago base prices in 1917 and 1918 threatened the existence of the high cost mills at Chicago (*ibid.*, 868). The Trumbull Steel Company of Warren, Ohio, claimed that its business had been built up in reliance upon the Pittsburgh pricing system and protested against any proposal to do away with it (F.T.C., *Applications, Answers, and Statements Concerning the So-called Pittsburgh Basing Point for Steel*, 1919, 173) and the Youngstown Sheet and Tube Company and others supported the argument (*ibid.*, 154). The American Iron and Steel Institute announced that "many steel plants have been located in places which have advantages as producing points under such a method of quoting prices, but which would not be desirable places from which to distribute steel products if the basing-point method of quoting prices were not continued" (*Basing Points and Competition in Steel*, 5).

[4] Professor Fetter suggests that fear of local price cutting prevented the establishment of firms at points where prices were high (*op. cit.*, 31). Capacity for independent production did, however, expand outside Pittsburgh (see p. 350).

[5] F.T.C., *Statement on Pittsburgh Plus*, 99, 318. The mill nets that would have been obtained by Chicago mills from sales on a Pittsburgh-plus basis had transportation in all directions from Chicago been on a uniform mileage rate are shown diagrammatically in Fetter, *op. cit.*, 122. It might be expected that Chicago mills selling on a Pittsburgh-plus basis would have been able to secure a maximum mill-net realization only on deliveries to points on a line joining Pittsburgh and Chicago and extended from Chicago in a direction away from Pittsburgh. In fact, however, transportation is not equally costly per mile in every direction. Moreover, Chicago would

the mill; those for delivery toward Pittsburgh yielded less owing to both falling delivered prices and rising transportation costs as Pittsburgh was approached.[1] Producers east of Chicago and west of Pittsburgh (e.g., Youngstown, Wheeling, and Columbus) were protected in the same way as Pittsburgh producers when shipping westward and producers east of Pittsburgh (e.g., Johnstown) were protected in the same way as Pittsburgh producers in competing with plants farther east at Bethlehem and Philadelphia.[2] In fact, moreover, most plants shipped in the direction of Pittsburgh. The Pittsburgh-plus system would induce a greater expansion of investment at non-basing points than a uniform f.o.b. system only if, after taking into account the geographical distribution of points to which delivery was made, and the amounts delivered to each point, the *average* realization at the mill exceeded the mill price that would have existed if all sales had been made upon a uniform f.o.b. basis. Figures 47 and 48 show that between 1916 and 1931 productive capacity outside Pittsburgh was growing faster than the capacity of the industry as a whole. Capacity for ingot production within sixty miles of Chicago increased from 3.230 million tons in 1908 to 8.545 million tons in 1923.[3]

---

be able to deliver at prices equal to those quoted by Pittsburgh mills on a line away from Pittsburgh only if the sum of the local rates from Pittsburgh to Chicago and Chicago to the point of delivery were equal to the rate for the whole distance from Pittsburgh to the point of delivery. As, however, the sum of the two local usually exceeds the through rate, the territory in which Chicago secured an advantage was more limited. (*ibid.*, 786.)

[1] In 1920 sales of steel bars in Chicago for delivery in Chicago yielded $7.60 *above* the Pittsburgh base price, sales for delivery in Pittsburgh yielded in Chicago $7.60 *less* than the *Pittsburgh* base price. Deliveries at other points yielded the following differentials:

	Dollars per Ton
Minneapolis	+7.10
Milwaukee	+6.50
Duluth	+6.40
Pacific coast terminals	+3.30
Indianapolis	+1.40
Muncie, Indiana	+1.10
New Orleans and Memphis	+0.80
Birmingham	+0.50
Galveston and Houston	0.00
Columbus, Ohio	−0.10
Buffalo, New York	−1.70
Toledo, Ohio	−1.80

(F.T.C., *Statement on Pittsburgh Plus*, 98.) Other similar calculations are given at *ibid.*, 97 and 832. These calculations all exclude switching charges. Similar calculations have been made for other products and for other points of production, but they reveal no new principle (see *ibid.*, 101, 102, 122, 244, 833, 837, 843).

[2] *ibid.*, 329.

[3] *ibid.*, 299. The total ingot capacity of the United States Steel Corporation outside Pittsburgh increased from 15.3 million tons in 1908 to 22.7 million tons in 1933,

Some light may be thrown upon the effect of Pittsburgh basing upon non-basing mills by an analysis of the consequences of the increases in the number of basing points between 1920 and 1924. The anticipations of the technical press were mixed. Youngstown producers regretted the acceptance of the order of the Federal Trade Commission by the United States Steel Corporation[1] either because they felt that control over price cutting would be weakened or for fear of the effect upon them of a redistribution

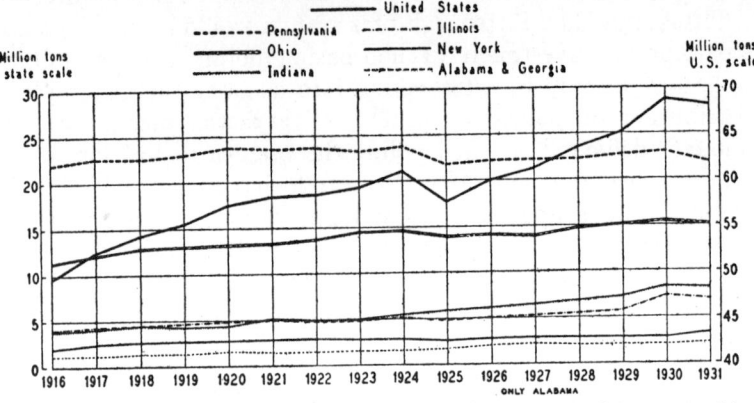

FIG. 47.—Productive capacity for steel ingots and castings and its geographical distribution, 1916 to 1931. (*American Iron and Steel Institute Statistical Reports.*)

of market territories. But it was also suggested that the abandonment of the practice would cause an expansion of capacity for production in Chicago, as well as the consolidation of independents. The latter anticipation has been realized.[2] The former suggests that capacity at Chicago had grown less fast than it would have grown in the absence of the Pittsburgh basing system. Figures 47 and 48 indicate that after the partial abandonment of the Pittsburgh-plus practice in 1921 the capacity for production of steel ingots and castings in Pennsylvania ceased to expand;

while its capacity in Pittsburgh increased only from 6.8 million tons in 1908 to 7.9 million tons in 1923 (*ibid.*, 325).
[1] *Iron Age*, Sept. 25, 1924.
[2] Since 1920 the Bethlehem Steel Corporation has absorbed the Lackawanna Steel Company (1922), the Midvale Steel and Ordnance Company (1923), the Pacific Coast Steel Company (1930), and the Southern California Iron and Steel Company (1930). The Youngstown Sheet and Tube Company has acquired the Brier Hill Steel Company (1923) and the Steel and Tube Company of America (1923); the Republic Iron and Steel Company has merged with the Trumbull Steel Company (1928) and acquired Steel and Tubes, Inc. (1928), the Central Alloy Steel Corporation, Donner Steel, Inc., the Bourne-Fuller Company, and a number of their subsidiaries (1930).

PRICE DISCRIMINATION

after the order of the commission in 1924 it declined slightly. Capacity in Ohio and Indiana continued to expand somewhat after 1921 and between 1924 and 1931 the expansion continued at most points outside Pennsylvania.[1] The proportion of the actual output of steel ingots and castings in the United States that was produced in Pennsylvania declined from an average

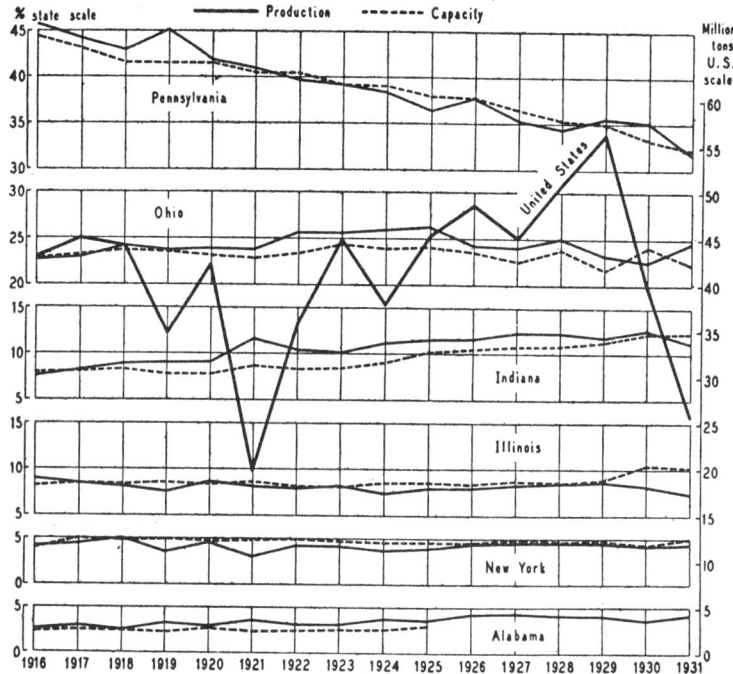

FIG. 48.—Production of steel ingots and castings and the geographical distribution of output and capacity, 1916 to 1931. (*American Iron and Steel Institute, Statistical Reports.*)

of 43 per cent in the period from 1917–1920 to 39 per cent in the period from 1921–1924 and 34 per cent in that from 1925–1931.[2] There is no evidence that the abandonment of Pittsburgh basing caused any great change in the profit prospects of the independent companies after 1921 or 1924. There is, however, no reason why their profits should have been reduced; where the points of production became basing points, *e.g.*, at Chicago, lower prices at the basing point and at points in the direction away from

---

[1] In 1929 the rolling mill capacity in the Chicago district for the first time exceeded that in the Pittsburgh district (*Iron Age*, July 31, 1930, 305).

[2] *Cf.* also N.R.A., *The Operation of the Basing Point System in the Iron and Steel Industry*, 21 ff. and 40.

Pittsburgh would be counterbalanced, at least in part, by higher yields than formerly on sales in the direction of Pittsburgh. Thus, although profits would be derived from different areas, the aggregate need not be changed.

Producers at the base are affected by the basing-point system because the fact that some mills are non-basing mills increases the territory reached by base mills without absorbing freight. Under a simple Pittsburgh-plus system, for instance, Pittsburgh producers could sell at any point in the United States at a price equal to that of any other producer without absorbing freight, the distribution of business between them depending upon the outcome of non-price competition. The base mills would, however, be likely to limit the territory in which they sought business by reference to the cost of canvassing very large territories. Producers with mills at a number of points[1] would be expected to minimize their transportation costs by shipping from the mill most accessible to the delivery point. Investment by these latter firms at each point would be regulated, therefore, by demand in each area; this demand would, however, be restricted by high prices resulting from the basing-point method of selling.[2] Prices at Chicago about $6.00 above those at Pittsburgh restrict demand and, therefore, investment at Chicago. Shipments by non-basing mills towards Pittsburgh, financed out of higher prices near to Chicago and in the territory on the side of Chicago away from Pittsburgh, tend to restrict sales from Pittsburgh and restrict investment there.

The net result of the Pittsburgh-plus practice upon Pittsburgh producers is, therefore, difficult to calculate. The selection of Pittsburgh as almost a sole base is explicable, as we have seen, in terms of the development of the industry. The attempt to maintain it in spite of the increasing proportion of the total productive

[1] The United States Steel Corporation having mills at a number of points might have set the base price on Pittsburgh below a level yielding a normal return upon investment there but have obtained a normal return upon its total investment because it obtained high returns from investment outside Pittsburgh. The absence of any signs of distress among producers operating only at Pittsburgh suggests that no such policy was followed. For this reason doubts must be reserved concerning the comment of the *Iron Age* on the abandonment of Pittsburgh-plus that "while under the new plan the buyer at Chicago may succeed in placing his tonnage at a price more nearly equal to that prevailing at Pittsburgh, he cannot be sure that the market at Pittsburgh would not have been considerably lower under conditions of country-wide competition" (*Iron Age*, Sept. 25, 1924). In fact, as we have seen, freight absorptions reduce the profits from base mills.

[2] In so far as the structure of transportation rates favored Pittsburgh fabricators (see p. 347) it induced fabrication there and, therefore, steel manufacturing also.

capacity outside Pittsburgh may have been due partly to the fear that permission to producers outside Pittsburgh to cut prices locally and establish other basing points might involve price movements that would get seriously out of hand. But the United States Steel Corporation was probably also more than acquiescent in the maintenance of the Pittsburgh base because of its very considerable investments in Pittsburgh, which were protected[1] by the maintenance of a practice which provided so wide a market for the output of its Pittsburgh plants.[2] The effects of the disturbance of this geographical price relationship in 1921 and 1924 were doubtless mitigated by the general prosperity of the industry between 1924 and 1929.[3] In 1935, however, the American Iron and Steel Institute believed that disturbance of the then existing basing-point system would "seriously decrease production in some of the largest producing centers such as Pittsburgh and Youngstown" and "increase production at plants that are favorably located in or near the large centers of steel consumption."[4]

The effect of the failure to make all mills basing points upon the location of the industries using the product sold under a basing-point system depends upon the effect of the system upon the geographical pattern of prices and the nature of the activities of the buyers. While freight absorptions leave the pattern of relative prices unchanged, the failure to make all production points basing points does not. Non-base producers are not surrounded by a "saucer" of concentric and rising price contours as they would be if they were basing-point producers. Buyers

[1] F.T.C., *Statement on Pittsburgh Plus*, 374.
[2] When Chicago base prices were temporarily set up in 1911 an official of the Carnegie Steel Company emphasized the seriousness of the change and refused to believe that "the corporation would so direct its affairs as to damage its Pittsburgh interests" (*Brief for Amici Curiae*, 72). In 1935 productive capacity within 75 miles of Pittsburgh was about 20 million tons a year or about three times as great as demand within that area (AMERICAN IRON AND STEEL INSTITUTE, *Basing Points and Competition in Steel*, 6). Nevertheless, by the time serious complaints were being made against the system, the corporation was probably willing to modify it although it had been deterred from doing so partly because some of the independents who thought their interest would be damaged by any change might have resisted, even to the extent of pursuing an independent price policy. The independent companies were manifestly disappointed when the United States Steel Corporation accepted without any challenge the order of the Federal Trade Commission requiring the corporation to abandon the practice. But there is no evidence that they suffered greatly from the modification of the system.
[3] *Cf.* N.R.A., *op. cit.*, 45.
[4] *Basing Points and Competition in Steel*, 8. Producers representing 97.9 per cent of the ingot capacity and 98.3 per cent of the finishing capacity of the industry favored the continuance of the existing system (*ibid.*, 8).

located near the non-base mill pay more than buyers at a distance from it in the direction of the governing base. This change in the geographical pattern of prices may exercise some but cannot exercise any great influence upon the geographical distribution of demand for cement or sugar. But it has greatly influenced the location of steel fabricating industries.

Rigid adherence to a simple Pittsburgh-plus basis of selling steel tends to induce the location of fabricating industries at Pittsburgh.[1] From thence they reach a wider market than from any other point. A fabricator at Chicago, for instance, would not be able to sell any more cheaply in Chicago itself or westward than a Pittsburgh fabricator, and at all points in the direction of Pittsburgh mill nets would be set by the price of the Pittsburgh fabricator and would be less than would be obtained by the Pittsburgh fabricator.[2] In other words, in so far as the only difference between the Pittsburgh and Chicago fabricator lay in differences in the cost of steel, those differences would be precisely equal to the difference in the cost of transportation from Pittsburgh and a Pittsburgh-plus price structure *for fabricated goods* would be expected to result even from competition in the fabricating industry, and, therefore, to give access from Pittsburgh to all markets. This broad tendency would be modified, however, if the cost of transporting fabricated goods were not always equal to the cost of transporting the constituent raw materials, by the pattern of transportation rates, and by differences in the other costs at different places.

---

[1] "There is a strong tendency for steel fabricating industries to locate at basing points" (F.T.C., *Practices of the Steel Industry under the Code*, 1934, 20).

[2] In consequence of the favorable effect of the Pittsburgh basing price practice upon fabricators in Pittsburgh (F.T.C., *Statement on Pittsburgh Plus*, 14) the United States Steel Corporation was able to call two hundred customer witnesses to testify that the practice was not harmful; the witnesses were almost entirely from the Pittsburgh district and occasionally from points eastward thereof (FETTER, *Masquerade of Monopoly*, 141). The Federal Trade Commission, on the other hand, had no difficulty in finding fabricators outside Pittsburgh prepared to testify to the adverse effect of the practice upon their business. Great numbers of western manufacturers testified that they were excluded by the price structure for steel from selling in eastern markets (F.T.C., *Brief on Pittsburgh Plus*, 117 ff.; *Statement on Pittsburgh Plus*, 12, 71, 932 to 1177). It would be expected, of course, that fabricators outside Pittsburgh would be unable to compete in Pittsburgh with fabricators there, but it was pointed out that they were at a disadvantage in selling to points only a short distance eastward (F.T.C., *Statement on Pittsburgh Plus*, 104, 789) and at many points north and south (*ibid.* 105–116, 124). Where their costs exceeded those of Pittsburgh producers by a sum equal to the cost of transportation from Pittsburgh they would be expected to be confined to deliveries along a line away from Pittsburgh.

Lack of complete correspondence between freight rates upon finished products and upon the steel used in their manufacture sometimes placed the fabricator at Pittsburgh at a positive advantage over rivals elsewhere and sometimes at a disadvantage, although not so great a disadvantage as he would have suffered under a system of uniform mill prices. Manufacturers of forgings in Pittsburgh had an advantage under the system over similar manufacturers at any other point because 20 to 65 per cent of the steel used does not emerge in the finished product. The Pittsburgh fabricator paid freight only upon the steel ultimately used in the forging while the fabricator at other points paid freight also upon the steel not appearing in the product.[1] The development of plants outside Pittsburgh must obviously have been discouraged. Indirectly expansion of facilities for steel production in Pittsburgh was encouraged, because of this localization of the demand for fabrication in Pittsburgh. Buyers of plates of irregular shapes were penalized in a similar manner.[2] Steel tanks, on the other hand, are *more* costly to transport than the raw material of which they are made. Nevertheless, a Milwaukee manufacturer of steel tanks buying steel on a Pittsburgh-plus basis and selling at delivered prices including actual freight paid, usually labored under a disadvantage over the Pittsburgh manufacturer; this disadvantage was, on deliveries at Pittsburgh, $1.015 per 100 pounds, at Chicago $0.165, at Duluth $0.025, at delivery points in Texas $0.215, at New Orleans $0.355, at Seattle and San Francisco $0.230. At Minneapolis and St. Paul he had an advantage of $0.01 and at Milwaukee of $0.18.[3]

[1] The Chicago forging manufacturer paying the freight rates prevailing from August, 1920, to June, 1922, was at a disadvantage compared with the Pittsburgh manufacturer of $3.20 per ton even when delivering in Chicago and as much as $10.70 per ton when delivering in Toledo, Ohio; had he paid in Chicago the same price for steel as his Pittsburgh rival he would have had an advantage in Chicago of $7.60 per ton (F.T.C., *Brief on Pittsburgh Plus*, 64, 112). The Chicago manufacturer would doubtless, however, obtain a higher price for his scrap than his Pittsburgh rival.

[2] The price for steel plates of irregular shapes (sketch plates) was calculated by adding together two amounts, *viz.*, a sum based upon the actual weight of the cut plate and a sum representing the price (at the rate charged for rectangular plates) of an amount of plate equal to the difference in weight between the smallest plate from which the sketch plate could be cut, and the actual weight of the sketch plate, after deduction of the scrap value of the waste. Thus an element of freight upon the scrap (which was not transported) was paid by all buyers outside Pittsburgh.

[3] F.T.C., *Statement on Pittsburgh Plus*, 943; also 940 and 931. The Chicago manufacturer of boilers and tanks buying materials on a Pittsburgh-plus basis was at a disadvantage as compared with the Pittsburgh fabricator upon deliveries to St. Louis of $0.215 per 100 pounds, to Duluth $0.19, to Minneapolis and St. Paul $0.14, and to Milwaukee $0.17 (*ibid.*, 946).

The structure of transportation rates also affects the position of the fabricator. Short-haul rates are in general higher per mile than long-haul rates. For this reason a fabricator not at a basing point is at a disadvantage compared with one at a basing point even in selling in a direction away from the base. He buys his steel at a price including freight charges from the base and, when he ships his product on, he pays a second freight charge. The fabricator at the base pays, however, for only one longer haul which costs less than the sum of the two shorter hauls. The fabricator not at the base must, if he sells at all, accept for his work less than the base fabricator. The committee of the National Recovery Administration contended that the privilege of "fabrication in transit" removed the worst effects of the system upon the location of fabricators using steel bars, plates, and shapes.[1] The committee added, however, that the privilege induces purchasing from distant mills.[2] If a fabricator in Pittsburgh buys from Buffalo he pays the same price for steel as if he bought in Pittsburgh but in the former case he can ship the product on at freight rates applicable to the extension of the first haul rather than at the rates applicable to a new haul.[3] But the committee did not refer to the efforts of the industry to eliminate this practice. The code provided that structural steel sold for fabrication in transit should be sold by calculating the delivered price at the place where the fabricator may erect an identified structure and not at the shop of the fabricator to which the material is actually delivered.[4] Even this regulation was not completely satisfactory and the steel manufacturers sought further control.[5] The fabricators resented the

[1] N.R.A., *The Operation of the Basing Point System in the Iron and Steel Industry*, 75. "Fabrication in transit" represents a concession by railroads permitting a fabricator to ship his material to his mill and his product from his mill to the market as if it were one continuous haul (plus a small charge for reshipping).
[2] *ibid.*, 95.
[3] The fabricator in Pittsburgh ships on to Detroit for the difference between the Buffalo-Detroit rate and the Buffalo-Pittsburgh rate plus a 3 cents stopover charge; for this second haul he pays $6\frac{1}{2}$ cents whereas if he bought steel in Pittsburgh it would cost $26\frac{1}{2}$ cents (F.T.C., *Basing Point System in the Steel Industry*, 98; also 76 ff., 80, 95). Even where the destination could not be reached by continuing the first haul the fabricator often held in stock steel bought from some other point on which a through rate could be obtained (*ibid.*, 93).
[4] *ibid.*, 21, 76, 87.
[5] Fabricators bought steel for jobs near their plant and then diverted it to distant jobs, thus securing freight advantages. The American Iron and Steel Institute sought to induce the railroads to make changes in the administration of the "fabrication in transit" privilege to eliminate this practice (*ibid.*, 85). These efforts were unsuccessful in part because it was explained to the railroads that the privilege as administered increased traffic partly by causing cross shipments of steel and partly by stimulating the decentralization of fabricating (*ibid.*, 98). The mills also claimed

power attained by the steel producers over the fabricating industry[1] and claimed that this power was being used to cripple the independents (*i.e.*, those not operated by subsidiaries of the steel producers).[2] The elimination of the advantages of fabrication in transit would, it was said, relocate fabrication at basing points and destroy the business of fabricators who relied on the privilege.[3] As the fabricating subsidiaries of the steel manufacturers were mainly located at basing points they would benefit from the change.[4] Fabricators also claimed that their business required them to hold stocks from which on the average about 20 per cent of their needs were supplied and that the ruling of the code authority would make the holding of such stocks onerous.[5] They contended, also, that their business was being disturbed by the steel manufacturers simply because the basing-point method of selling steel resulted in cross freighting which the steel manufacturers wished to avoid because it reduced their mill nets.[6]

It is evident, therefore, that the Pittsburgh basing-point system favored the establishment of steel using industries at Pittsburgh, although this tendency was partly offset by the "fabrication in transit" privilege, and by other differences in cost and convenience at different points. In so far as the practice was largely maintained by the United States Steel Corporation, the corporation was able to influence the rate of development of steel using industries in different parts of the country. The president of the corporation emphasized this power by implication when he agreed that occasionally local departures were made from the Pittsburgh-plus practice where it was decided to encourage a local industry. The Birmingham differential of $3.00 over Pittsburgh was quoted as a special example of the exercise of this power.[7]

---

that fabricators overbought for contracts and placed the excess purchase in stock, later shipping it on to a delivery point at a price less than that chargeable under the code (*ibid.*, 91, 97). The mills also desired to eliminate advantages possessed by fabricators able to ship their products by transportation cheaper than railroad transportation (*ibid.*, 91).

[1] *ibid.*, 81.
[2] *ibid.*, 95. It was claimed that the American Bridge Company and McClintic-Marshall Company did 50 per cent of the total fabricating business (*ibid.*, 97).
[3] *ibid.*, 91, 93, 98.
[4] *ibid.*, 98. It was stated that steel manufacturers had also taken contracts for fabricated products and sublet the fabrication as an indirect means of cutting the price for steel. The contract was taken at prices which did not exceed the cost of the steel by the cost of fabrication (*ibid.*, 86, 97).
[5] *ibid.*, 82, 91.
[6] *ibid.*, 98, 99.
[7] F.T.C., *Brief on Pittsburgh Plus*, 62. Professor Fetter points out that the steel

The Federal Trade Commission was, therefore, at least in part justified in claiming that the elimination of Pittsburgh basing would build up steel consumption outside Pittsburgh, return to western and southern producers the advantages of their location, save middle western farmers 30 million dollars per year, restore many western plants destroyed by Pittsburgh plus, and eliminate excessive prices for steel outside Pittsburgh.[1] The United States Steel Corporation argued that fabricators had always been free to locate where they wished, that they had selected their locations after the Pittsburgh-plus practice had been adopted,[2] and that they had prospered and multiplied outside Pittsburgh.[3] Some of these allegations were denied,[4] but, in so far as they are true, they ignore the question whether it was reasonable for fabricators to be forced to accept the price structure established by the corporation. As a natural corollary of this proposition it was claimed that the abandonment of the practice would involve unfairness to both steel producers and fabricators[5] by falsifying legitimate expectations. As fabricators had no alternative to accepting a practice which remained undisturbed by the government for so long they at least have some claim in equity to be protected for a time from serious loss if the system is eliminated.

The extent to which the multiple-basing-point system affected the location of industry depends upon the distance between the non-basing points of production and the basing points. This relationship is illustrated diagrammatically in Fig. 49 which shows that

---

manufacturers exercised a power of local discrimination of which railroads had been dispossessed by law (FETTER, *Masquerade of Monopoly*, 306).

[1] *Iron Age*, July 24, 1924, 205. Comment in the technical press at the time of the commission's order was very mixed. On the one hand it was said that the change came at a time when the Pittsburgh basing point was nonexistent as a market factor (*Iron Age*, July 31, 1924, 266); Cleveland consumers expected no relief (*Iron Age*, Sept. 25, 1924). On the other hand, it was said that Pittsburgh would continue visibly or invisibly "through its competition to furnish the yardstick by which market prices will be made," which was what it had done when it was formally established as a basing point. This situation would continue "until some other producing territory is so developed that it usurps Pittsburgh's position as the chief source of free surplus supply for the general market" (*Iron Trades Review*, Oct. 2, 1924, 856). The new pricing methods were not expected to cause any important reductions; it was argued that, while in years of great prosperity the United States Steel Corporation had been able to obtain higher prices under the Pittsburgh-plus practice than it would have otherwise secured, whenever competition developed, Pittsburgh plus had been ignored with the result that prices had been as low as were likely to be made without the practice (*Iron Age*, Sept. 25, 1924, 747 ff.).

[2] F.T.C., *Statement on Pittsburgh Plus*, 29, 1202.

[3] *ibid.*, 29, 1208.

[4] *Brief for Amici Curiae*, 45.

[5] F.T.C., *Statement on Pittsburgh Plus*, 505.

in 1934 about one quarter of the total capacity for producing iron and steel products was at basing points, about half within 50 miles, and the remaining quarter more than 50 miles from a basing point.[1]

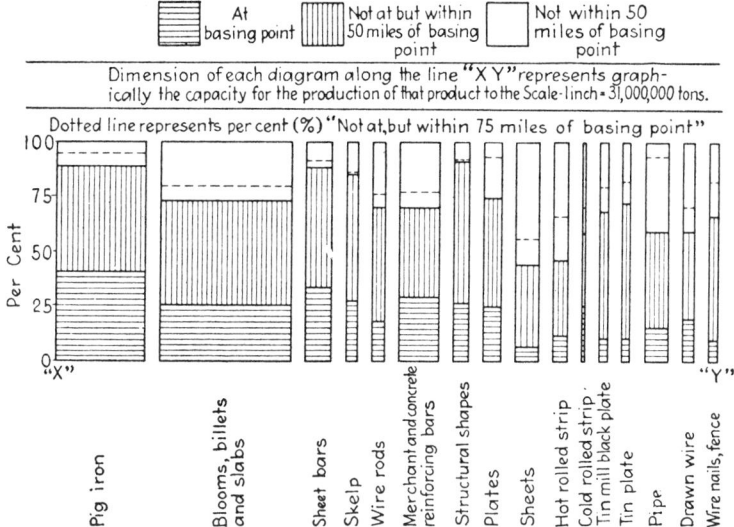

FIG. 49.—Location of productive capacity in the steel industry in relation to the basing points in 1934. (*Redrawn from N.R.A., Operation of the Basing Point System in the Iron and Steel Industry*, 55.)

The presence of non-basing mills within short distances of base mills is not open to serious criticism. Where mills are concentrated in groups and only one is a base mill the fact that the others are not

[1] The percentage distribution of productive capacity in 1934 was:

Product	Percentage of productive capacity		
	At basing point	Within 50 miles of base	More than 50 miles from base
Pig iron	40.85	47.58	11.57
Blooms, billets, and slabs	25.2	47.9	26.9
Merchant and concrete bars	29.1	41.0	29.9
Sheet and tin plate bars	33.5	55.0	11.5
Structural shapes	26.1	65.6	8.3
Plate	24.7	49.9	25.4
Sheets	6.3	37.6	56.1
Hot rolled strip	11.8	34.3	53.9
Cold rolled strip	21.3	36.9	41.3
Tin plate	10.6	61.9	27.5
Skelp	27.1	58.7	14.2
Pipe, etc.	15.5	43.7	40.8
Wire rods	18.1	52.4	29.5
Wire products	9.5	56.6	33.9
Wire	19.1	40.2	40.7

(N.R.A., *op. cit.*, 54, and Appendix C.) Approximately 6 per cent of the capacity of the United States Steel Corporation to produce code products and 44 per cent of the capacity of the Bethlehem Steel Corporation was more than 50 miles from an applicable basing point (*ibid.*, 43).

has little effect upon the geographical pattern of prices. Indeed, if each were required to become a base mill and give up absorbing freight, each would be compelled to sell only in the direction away from the group in which it had a freight advantage.[1]

It was also claimed that the Pittsburgh-plus practice favored fabricating units integrated with the United States Steel Corporation, such as the American Bridge Company.[2] This company in buying material from the plants of the corporation on a Pittsburgh-plus basis was on an equality with rival fabricators. It could afford, however, to quote prices lower than rivals, because it could cut into the profits being obtained by the parent corporation out of sales upon the Pittsburgh-plus basis, whereas unintegrated rival fabricators had no such opportunities. This policy was said to give it a great advantage in Chicago and the territory west thereof, and at Birmingham, Alabama, and in the territory south thereof.[3] This advantage was said to be reflected in the growth of the American Bridge Company's plant in Chicago to twenty times the size of that of its nearest competitor.[4] Similar advantages were secured in other branches of the fabricating industry by the United States Steel Corporation through the American Sheet and Tin Plate Company, the American Steel and Wire Company, and the Chickasaw Car and Shipbuilding Company (of Mobile, Alabama).[5] These advantages were expected by the Federal Trade Commission to disappear with the Pittsburgh-plus practice.[6] It has not been proven, however, that the Pittsburgh-plus practice directly results in high profits nor that the corporation accepted a subnormal rate of return on its fabricating activities.

The effect of the Pittsburgh-plus practice upon the price of the principal raw material of the industry, viz., pig iron, is difficult to estimate. Figure 42, showing the movements of the price of pig

[1] A mill in the center of the group would be compelled to quote a mill price sufficiently lower than its rivals to enable it to ship beyond them and might then be able to ship in more than one direction. If a shipper at the eastern edge quoted a mill price low enough to enable him to ship westward, shippers on the western edge could hardly ship at all. (Cf. N.R.A., *op. cit.*, 100.)

[2] The American Bridge Company was reported to fabricate more than 40 per cent of the structural shape material fabricated in the United States; its western plants fabricated probably ten times as much as any western competitor (F.T.C., *Statement on Pittsburgh Plus*, 288).

[3] *ibid.*, 288, 289.

[4] F.T.C., *Annual Report*, 1924, 38.

[5] F.T.C., *Statement on Pittsburgh Plus*, 289. The argument was more crudely expressed when it was stated that the American Bridge Company could afford to bid for jobs at cost (F.T.C., *Brief on Pittsburgh Plus*, 136).

[6] *Cf. Iron Age*, July 24, 1924, 205.

iron and the December prices for the years 1920 to 1931, reveals little immediate change in the geographical structure of pig iron prices during 1924 and 1925 owing to the abandonment of the Pittsburgh-plus practice.[1] The major portion of the pig iron used in steel manufacturing and about 80 per cent of all pig iron[2] is, however, produced by the steel manufacturers themselves.

 c. *The General Effects of Basing-point Systems.* At this point the attempt to segregate the consequences of freight absorption and the presence of non-base mills must be abandoned. The most striking general consequence of basing-point systems is the uniformity in the prices of all sellers at each point of delivery. The attainment of such a "one-price system" is the major immediate objective of the practice. Where production is decentralized, markets are wide, and overhead costs important, sellers especially fear secret and sporadic price cutting. It not only eats into their business unless expensive arrangements are made to meet it wherever it may occur, but it also undermines the general structure of prices. Openly declared base prices and uniformity of practice in calculating delivered prices from base prices provide a simple and certain method of avoiding unintentional and detecting intentional price cutting.[3] The steel producers repeatedly empha-

---

[1] Between 1921 and 1922, however, the Pittsburgh price rose much more than the price at Chicago, Mahoning, and Shenango Valley furnaces (on either side of the Pennsylvania-Ohio state line) or Birmingham, and fell much more than prices elsewhere during the years 1923, 1924, and 1925.

[2] U.S. TARIFF COMMISSION, *Iron in Pigs*, 1927, 3.

[3] The way in which basing-point systems develop to meet this need is illustrated by the difficulties encountered by some trade associations in establishing open-price systems. Price comparison is possible only if prices representing sales to different delivery points can be reduced to a comparable basis by the elimination of differences in freight charges. But the subtraction of freight charges from the delivered prices merely reveals the net yield of sales from each of a number of points of production. Consequently in some industries prices have been reduced to common terms by referring them to some central shipping point or "gateway." Freight charges from this gateway to the point of delivery are deducted from the delivered price at each point in the country to arrive at the "gateway" price. Information is then available in a form in which different sellers can most easily compare their prices with those of rivals, and, particularly, their prices for certain areas with those of rivals in the same area. The development of a basing-point system is not then inevitable; it occurs when this information leads, as it frequently does, to positive effort to equalize the "gateway" prices by all sellers to all buyers. (F.T.C., *Price Bases Inquiry*, 74–75.) Thus the lumber manufacturers in the west explained that as lumber mills had different freights to the principal consuming points, uniform f.o.b. prices would give rise to different selling prices in these principal markets. By uniform f.o.b. prices they meant prices uniform not as between all buyers from one mill but as between all mills at different points. The use of a basing point would avoid these differences between the prices of different sellers at the same delivery points only if the price of all sellers was equalized at the basing point. (F.T.C., *Lumber Manufacturers Associations*, 1922, 121.)

sized this function of the basing-point system,[1] often adding that it was a "stabilizing influence" and occasionally that buyers approved of the practice because they knew that their rivals were paying the same price for steel as they were.[2] This argument applied, of course, only to rivals at the same point of production.

This tendency towards uniformity of prices at each delivery point has been severely condemned as a device by which "price cutting of almost every conceivable sort appears to have been anticipated and proscribed."[3] The basing-point system in the steel

[1] A former vice president of the Carnegie Steel Company (a subsidiary of the United States Steel Corporation) testified that the Pittsburgh-plus system was adopted in order to secure uniformity of prices (F.T.C., *Findings on Pittsburgh Plus*, (Z — 19). A witness testified to the necessity of a basing point even prior to the formation of the corporation in order to stabilize the industry and keep it under control (F.T.C., *Statement on Pittsburgh Plus*, 644). Mr. Schwab stated in 1901 that a single basing point was essential even though steel was not all produced there (*Report of the Industrial Commission*, 13, 469, 470, cit. FETTER, *Masquerade of Monopoly*, 7). Colonel Bope, chairman of the Carnegie company, said that structural steel producers could not maintain uniform prices without a basing point; they had tried to do so in 1909 but failed so completely that they were glad to return to the old practice (F.T.C., *Statement on Pittsburgh Plus*, 545; *Brief on Pittsburgh Plus*, 15). Uniform prices were necessary to produce a stable market (F.T.C., *Brief on Pittsburgh Plus*, 60; *Statement on Pittsburgh Plus*, 929). If a base price were set up for each mill there would be a great variety of prices "without stability of any kind or without knowing what competition was or how we would be able to meet it. Therefore the mills themselves thought the proper thing to do was to have a basing point." (F.T.C., *Brief on Pittsburgh Plus*, 155.) The vice president of the Inland Steel Company (an "independent" company) said that, in the absence of a basing point, freight rates from all mills to all points would be difficult to get, with the result that some would quote "too high" and some "too low" (F.T.C., *Brief on Pittsburgh Plus*, 143); it was a matter of convenience to know what the price would be anywhere in the United States. The secretary of the American Rolling Mill Company agreed that the practice was aimed at the stabilization of business and prices (F.T.C., *Brief on Pittsburgh Plus*, 24). The National Association of Sheet and Tin Plate Manufacturers had the same object in view in adopting the practice (ibid., 40). Judge Gary recommended at a meeting of the price-fixing committee of the War Industries Board that Pittsburgh be restored as the sole basing point in the industry as the Pittsburgh pricing had done more to stabilize production, to increase production, and to bring about extension of the mills already established and, more particularly, the establishment of new mills, than anything else (F.T.C., *Statement on Pittsburgh Plus*, 868). At the preliminary meeting before the Federal Trade Commission he claimed that the practice was needed for the orderly conduct of business by both buyers and sellers (ibid., 84). The *Iron Age* spoke of an agreement to revert to strict adherence to the Pittsburgh pricing system as giving hope that irregularities in price which had been more or less general would be eliminated (ibid., 710). Finally, the president of the United States Steel Corporation agreed that the code of fair competition for the iron and steel industry under the National Industrial Recovery Act provided for a "one-day policy" (*New York Times*, Feb. 9, 1934. Cf. also N.R.A., *The Operation of the Basing Point System in the Iron and Steel Industry*, 32, and Appendix B).

[2] Mr. Gary pointed out that the fabricator of steel knew under the Pittsburgh-plus system what his rival was paying for steel (F.T.C., *Statement on Pittsburgh Plus*, 884). Professor Commons remarked that intermediate consumers of steel approved of this aspect of the basing-point system ("Delivered Price Practice in the Steel Market," *Amer. Econ. Rev.*, 14: 508).

[3] F.T.C., *Practices of the Steel Industry under the Code*, 12, 29, 33. Cf. also, "Sum-

industry "not only permits and encourages price fixing but . . . it is price fixing."[1] It has resulted, as we have seen, in the allocation of public contracts by lot in both the steel and the cement industries.[2] The steel producers while agreeing that the industry has a "one-price policy" deny the elimination of price competition.[3]

The basing-point system undoubtedly facilitates the elimination of price cutting aimed at short-run increases of business. But, on the one hand, it does not always completely eliminate such price cutting and, on the other, various kinds of pressure upon prices appear to survive. Reference has already been made to the "shading" of steel prices which has from time to time attained serious proportions.[4] Cutting below the delivered prices calculated in accordance with the basing-point system has also been a serious difficulty in the cement industry. Firms refusing to adopt the pricing structure conventional in the industry were sometimes dealt with by reducing the base price of the firm whose price most closely affected the delivered price of the offending firm.[5] This practice, however, throws a great deal of the cost of enforcement upon the firm required to reduce its price. Sometimes the delivered prices quoted by the firm cutting below the conventional price were met by rivals. This practice also was unsatisfactory, because, at least in the short run, it amounted to acceptance of the infringement of the convention and might prove demoralizing in other parts of the country. Occasionally a neighboring mill declared a

---

ming up this system of calculating delivery charges, it starts with an arbitrary basing point so that differences in actual delivery cost are merged into a fictitious common rate. Then it uses, but solely for calculating purposes, a higher cost mode of transportation than is frequently utilized. Then in some cases it substitutes arbitraries which are higher than the actual cost even of the calculated transportation. Thus the system is not one for determining actual freight costs. It is a device for automatically insuring that all mills will reach a given destination at identical delivered prices, and that the identity in their mill-base quotations will not be set at naught by differences in location and of actual freight costs." (*ibid.*, 23.) This uniformity of delivered prices the Federal Trade Commission held to be the "goal and object which motivated the initial step and each succeeding step in the process" (*ibid.*, 45). See also F.T.C., *Basing Point System in the Steel Industry*, 3, 4, 45 ff.; COMMONS, "Delivered Price Practice in the Steel Market," *Amer. Econ. Rev.*, 14: 508.

[1] F.T.C., *Basing Point System in the Steel Industry*, 35.
[2] See Chap. III. *Cf.* also F.T.C., *Cement Industry*, 73; *Basing Point System in the Steel Industry*, 5, 45 ff., 65; CONSUMER ADVISORY BOARD, Appendices to *Memorandum to General Johnson*, Feb. 19, 1934; *New York Times*, Jan. 6, 1934.
[3] The president of the American Iron and Steel Institute claimed that prices after the adoption of the code of fair competition "are bound to be dictated, as heretofore, by the laws of supply and demand" (F.T.C., *Practices of the Steel Industry under the Code*, 49).
[4] See Chap. III and present chapter, p. 302.
[5] F.T.C., *Price Bases Inquiry*, 84, 85.

base price at the point at which the offending mill was situated which had not until then been a basing point. Thus it made the base price for a mill at a point at which it was not producing. A mill showing marked independence of price policy was so dealt with,[1] as well as a plant operated by the state of South Dakota.[2] Such price cutting is clearly not to meet competition, as the commission pointed out. If no other mill was situated near by, the major part of the cost of such tactics fell upon the offender, although some necessarily fell upon the firms delivering at the new low prices. Freight absorptions in such cases *exceed* the amount necessary to meet the price of nearby rivals, but the departure from conventional practice is a short-term policy aimed at maintaining over a longer term the limitation of freight absorptions to the amounts necessary to meet such competition.[3] Finally, firms pursuing an independent price policy have found it desirable, or even necessary, to retire from the industry through mergers with existing firms.[4] These mergers, in the opinion of the commission, contributed to the smooth working of the basing-point system by providing an exit for the "bad actor," and by reducing the number of firms to be coordinated, thereby facilitating the acceptance of leadership.

That there is downward pressure upon prices even under a basing-point system is indicated by the history of such systems. Prices at newer points of production distant from the older have fallen and the number of basing points has increased. The ability to enter distant territory by absorbing freight relieves the pressure to reduce prices in nearby territory[5] and influences the price

---

[1] Outside mills made Marquette, Missouri, a basing point after a mill at that point had cut below the delivered prices of rivals in the vicinity of its own mill (*ibid.*, 125 note, and xix).

[2] *ibid.*, 130.

[3] *ibid.*, 91.

[4] The Federal Trade Commission reported that a state highway commission desiring to avoid the uniformity of prices in tenders for cement, endeavored to induce small independent corporations to quote below the conventional price, promising to concentrate awards on any producers following this suggestion. Some independents did accept the suggestion, and thereby caused so much ill feeling that the practice was discontinued. Of five companies selling to the highway commission below the conventional price, three have been absorbed by larger companies. The highway commission in question has found it difficult to secure a continuance of even such semi-competitive bidding because of the inability of the bidders to keep price concessions from the knowledge of their competitors and, therefore, to avoid the unpleasantness engendered, and because also of the tendency for such companies to be absorbed (*ibid.*, 92–93). In fact, the commission attributed the growth of several large cement manufacturing companies "as much to the buying out or merging with other companies as to their own building and enlarging of plants."

[5] *Cf.* F.T.C., *Basing Point System in the Steel Industry*, 17, and above p. 336.

policy of both the base and the non-base mill, even when there is more than one mill at a production point. But when demand declines there is a temptation to cut prices and make a bid for more local business; the repeated temporary departures from Pittsburgh basing in the Chicago area indicate the force of this temptation. Over longer periods there is a downward pressure on base prices or pressure to establish bases to attract fabricators or discourage freight-absorbing sales by distant mills.

The structure of prices at the different bases is, however, difficult to explain. Doubtless in industries in which basing-point systems develop there is a considerable measure of leadership. All freight-absorbing sales (which includes all sales by non-base mills) involve the acceptance of prices set by a rival. Control of prices at each base is generally in the hands of producers there. If producers at other points assumed the right to change prices at points at which they did not produce this element of leadership would be diminished. But base prices themselves are likely to be influenced by leadership. Leadership in the sugar and lumber industries is, however, unproven; trade associations have been influential in securing the common action essential to the maintenance of basing-point systems. In the cement industry acceptance of the system has been attributed in part to the emergence of a few large firms, which has provided effective mill-price leadership. At the commencement of 1930 the five companies possessing the largest plant capacity in the industry were together capable of producing 38 per cent of the cement which the country was equipped to produce, and in 1927 these companies in fact produced 42 per cent of the total output for that year. They were reported to operate between them 47 plants, all but two of which were located in strategic points throughout the territory east of the Rocky Mountains. Of the entire output of this territory they produced 47 per cent in 1927; a further 18 per cent was produced by mills at or near the basing-point mills of these five companies and a further 30 per cent was produced at non-basing point mills. Thus, if these five companies chose to cooperate they could influence directly the price of 95 per cent of the entire cement output east of the Rocky Mountains.[1] This leadership was presumably much strengthened by the merger in January, 1930, of the Universal Portland Cement Company and the Atlas Portland Cement

[1] F.T.C., *Price Bases Inquiry*, 89. These five companies produced 40 per cent of the total output in the United States in 1931 (F.T.C., *Cement Industry*, 12).

Company;[1] these two firms were responsible for about 17 per cent of the total domestic shipments of the country in 1927 and for a much higher percentage in the area in which they were influential. The tendency for troublesome firms to be absorbed has already been mentioned. Evidence that the largest firms cooperate is, however, lacking.[2]

Acceptance of the basing-point system in the steel industry may have been due to fear that if rivals cut much below the prices of the United States Steel Corporation at any point, the corporation would respond by damaging price cuts. The power of the United States Steel Corporation in this respect would depend partly upon the proportion of producing capacity at the more important points of production under its control, and partly upon the relation between its costs of production and those of rivals. It was said, for instance, that the corporation, being the largest producer in both Chicago and Pittsburgh,[3] could maintain a Pittsburgh-plus policy in spite of the independents.[4] It was also reported that steel producers in Chicago and Birmingham, at least, were convinced that the United States Steel Corporation was the lowest-cost producer in each area, and that it was, therefore, in a position to drive out competitors by price competition. This view appears to have been publicly expressed from time to time by officers of the corporation, and rivals believed that the corporation would, and indeed did, at times, punish price cutters.[5] Thus Mr. Gary's statement in February, 1909, that he would cease to publish the prices being quoted by the corporation and would make prices privately with customers without regard for their reaction upon rivals, resulted in the restoration of stable prices on a Pittsburgh-plus basis throughout the industry within sixty days.[6] Compliance with the policy of the corporation, on the other hand, insured

[1] F.T.C., *Price Bases Inquiry*, 94 and Exhibit 1.
[2] The Federal Trade Commission remarked that "fear of the large producer and even a degree of coercion may or may not be present" (*ibid.*, 88).
[3] The United States Steel Corporation controlled 59.7 per cent of the steel ingot capacity in Pittsburgh in 1923 (compared with 72.8 per cent in 1908) and 40.9 per cent of the capacity in the country as a whole (compared with 51.8 per cent in 1908) (F.T.C., *Statement on Pittsburgh Plus*, 325).
[4] *ibid.*, 377. The Federal Trade Commission claimed that the practice "produced a trend" towards certainty in fixing prices all over the United States" (*ibid.*, 761). The Western Association of Rolled Steel Buyers claimed that adherence to the practice by the United States Steel Corporation, which had a mill in every important steel center, induced rivals also to accept the practice with the result that competition among sellers was eliminated and the price of steel and steel products enhanced (*Brief for Amici Curiae*, 177).
[5] *ibid.*, 329.
[6] *ibid.*, 81.

protection from destructive price cutting by it. It also enabled independent producers at Pittsburgh to sell in any part of the United States.

In the tin plate branch of the industry it was contended that a general acceptance of the basing-point system was facilitated by a trade association consisting of practically all but the largest producer (the American Sheet and Tin Plate Company) whose quotation in Pittsburgh was used as the base price.[1] The American Sheet and Tin Plate Company published a book of freight rates and also a uniform list of extras and differentials which were used not only by the company but also by the independents in fixing Pittsburgh-plus prices.[2] One of the avowed objects of the association was to stabilize prices, and the Pittsburgh-plus practice was regarded as a means to such stabilization.[3] As in 1922 the members of the association produced from 60 to 65 per cent of the sheet steel of the country, and the American Sheet and Tin Plate Company, which was evidently cooperating closely with it, produced another 25 per cent,[4] the association was doubtless an effective mechanism for securing uniformity of price policy upon a Pittsburgh-plus basis.

Basing-point systems tend indirectly to generate conditions favorable to leadership. Firms controlling a number of widely

[1] The American Sheet and Tin Plate Company began selling on a Pittsbugh base after its formation in 1900, and the construction of new mills; its rivals followed its lead. Independents at that time sold at prices differing by small amounts from that of the American Sheet and Tin Plate Company. Prices were made in multiples of 5 cents; while Pittsburgh prices were quoted in multiples of 5 cents, freight rates were usually not in such multiples. In consequence, independents sometimes fixed their prices at the multiple of 5 cents next below the Pittsburgh-plus price. After 1912, as independents increased their volume of business, there was increasingly close adherence to the Pittsburgh-plus quotation. (F.T.C., *Statement on Pittsburgh Plus*, 225, 226.)

[2] *ibid.*, 233; *Brief for Federal Trade Commission*, 35. The American Sheet and Tin Plate Company lent to the association the printing plates for a book showing the weight of bars necessary to produce sheets in various sizes. When the National Association of Sheet and Tin Plate Manufacturers was formed in 1916, nearly all producers other than the American Sheet and Tin Plate Company (a subsidiary of the United States Steel Corporation) became members and the American Sheet and Tin Plate Company cooperated fully with the association, furnishing to it advance announcements of its prices, which the association published to its members in the form of bulletins. Some at least of the members of the association regarded these prices as minimum prices (*ibid.*, 226) and on a number of occasions between 1919 and 1921 independents notified their salesmen that they were following the prices of the American Sheet and Tin Plate Company (*ibid.*, 228).

[3] The president of the association believed that the abandonment of the practice would throw the industry into confusion "until some other means was found of serving the purpose served by the Pittsburgh-plus system" (F.T.C., *Statement on Pittsburgh Plus*, 236).

[4] *ibid.*, 236.

360   THE DECLINE OF COMPETITION

scattered plants are best able to ship from a fairly nearby plant and thus to minimize transportation costs. These systems, therefore, encourage mergers to obtain these economies.[1] Mergers in the steel industry and probably also in the cement industry[2] have been thus encouraged.[3]

The policy of the leader is mainly important because of his power to influence the selection of basing points from time to time and the structure of prices at these bases. There is, in fact, little

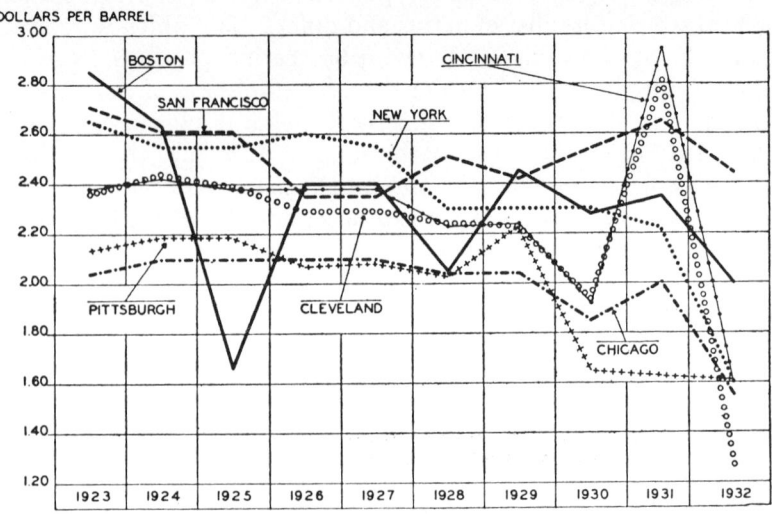

FIG. 50.—Prices of cement in seven cities, 1923 to 1932. (*Drawn from data in the Engineering News Record.*)

information concerning the influences affecting base prices under a basing-point system. The Federal Trade Commission confessed its inability to explain the factors influencing differences between base prices for cement[4] but suggested that basing-point practices in general increased costs owing to the disadvantageous location of plants in relation to raw materials, fuel, and labor,[5] and the protection of plants burdened with excessive overhead, obsolete equip-

---

[1] F.T.C., *Open Price Trade Associations*, 94.
[2] In the absence of such territorial integration sharing the market upon a geographical basis has at least the advantage that it tends to reduce transportation costs (*Cf.* VON BECKERATH, *op. cit.*, 244).
[3] FRASER and DORIOT, *Analyzing Our Industries*, 256. *Cf.* statement of a small steel producer that abandonment of the basing-point system would damage small steel companies who had only one or two producing points (AMERICAN IRON AND STEEL INSTITUTE, *Basing Points and Competition in Steel*, 11).
[4] F.T.C., *Price Bases Inquiry*, 88.
[5] *ibid.*, 142.

ment, and inefficient management.[1] Figure 50 showing the price of cement in a number of cities between 1923 and 1932 reveals a number of changes in the relation between prices in these cities arising doubtless out of changes in basing points, changes in the relations between prices at different basing points, and departures from basing-point pricing.

In the steel industry the United States Steel Corporation played a large part in opposing the abandonment of the modified Pittsburgh-plus practice and its possession of plants in most of the major production areas gave it considerable power. When the practice was modified the number of bases was increased. The Federal Trade Commission concluded, however, that prices at these bases were not competitively determined[2] owing to the lack of incentive to lower base prices. Base prices have, however, been lowered. But as new bases have been established prices have been maintained higher than those at Pittsburgh. Until about 1931 base prices for structural steel products were about $2.00 per ton above the Pittsburgh price (see Fig. 40) and those at Birmingham about $3.00 above Pittsburgh.[3] Such meager information as is available suggests that the costs of production outside Pittsburgh are not consistently above those at Pittsburgh; indeed, in 1920 costs of the United States Steel Corporation at Chicago were apparently less than at Pittsburgh and those at Birmingham little different.[4] It has been suggested that, as the cost of production is less in Chicago than in Pittsburgh, this price differential protects the

[1] *loc. cit.*
[2] F.T.C., *Basing Point System in the Steel Industry*, 16, 17, 103.
[3] *Cf. ibid.*, 21. Steel produced in California is sold virtually on a Pittsburgh price plus rail and water transportation although there are bases more accessible to California (*ibid.*, 19).
[4] An investigation by the Federal Trade Commission into steel costs and prices in 1920 revealed that, for the most important products, costs of production at Chicago were generally below and sometimes considerably below those at Pittsburgh and Birmingham, as it indicated by the following table:

Production point	Mill cost of production in dollars per ton in 1920			
	Structural shapes	Plates	Bars	Black sheets
Pittsburgh	52.207	48.659	50.319	85.891
Chicago	42.835	47.907	45.683	77.894
Birmingham	52.043	57.007	58.445	
Duluth			49.344	

(F.T.C., *Report on Steel Costs and Prices*, 110; *cf.* also F.T.C., *Practices of the Steel Industry under the Code*, 1934, 56.) These costs do not include general depreciation, administration expenses, selling expenses, taxes, or general overhead. The commission believed that overhead costs ran somewhat lower in the Pittsburgh district than in others. The figures include intercompany profits except at Birmingham.

Pittsburgh area from decline[1] and that with the disappearance of Pittsburgh plus "the Chicago district proper will become the quantity production area of the country."[2] The higher prices at bases outside Pittsburgh operate, therefore, to protect the local distribution of investment in steel production which grew up under the Pittsburgh-plus practice.[3] This policy is apparently conscious. The president of the American Iron and Steel Institute, protesting against a proposal to replace the basing-point system by f.o.b. mill prices, contended that the change would result in "the abandonment of a large part of the steel mills in the Pittsburgh district representing 25 per cent of the entire steel industry and would ultimately compel the relocation of many other industries using steel for their raw materials."[4] The Federal Trade Commission remarked, however, that "the growing weakness and comparative inefficiency of older plants in locations no longer best suited to the industry is bolstered up when they are assured a continued outlet into large areas at delivered prices not to be undersold by any present competitors or by newer, better equipped, and more efficient plants"[5] and that possibly the best preventive of excess capacity would be permission to "new mills in better locations, or more efficient, to supply the territory near them as fast and as far as they are able and permitted to do it by lower f.o.b. prices."[6] Some retardation of changes in the location of industry might be desirable to reduce the loss of capital on plants whose location is rendered relatively uneconomical by changing conditions.[7] But

[1] *New York Times*, Dec. 7, 1931.
[2] MacCallum, *The Iron and Steel Industry in the United States*, 52. *Cf.* also "Pittsburgh plus built the tremendous capacity that Pittsburgh has today and its abolition has left Pittsburgh with a surplus production for which it has no legitimate market" (*Iron Age*, Nov. 10, 1934). In consequence the Pittsburgh producers in 1927 sought an adjustment of freight rates that would extend their markets (*loc. cit.*).
[3] It has been reported that the United States Steel Corporation proposes to remove its Gary, Illinois, plant to the Pittsburgh area, owing partly to the high cost of assembling raw materials at Gary (*New York Herald Tribune*, May 19, 1933) but the report was denied (Standard Corporation Records, *Daily News Section*, May 20, 1933).
[4] F.T.C., *Practices of the Steel Industry under the Code*, 43. When an amended steel code was submitted to the President in May, 1934, it was admitted that "the multiple-basing-point system is designed to maintain existing areas of production and channels of distribution, and prevent violent dislocations proceeding from such unrestrained competition as has resulted in the past all too frequently in increasing concentration of business in the hands of large producers, with violent fluctuations in prices and wages, in a ruthless struggle to survive" (*New York Times*, May 31 1934).
[5] F.T.C., *Practices of the Steel Industry under the Code*, 43.
[6] *loc. cit.*
[7] See p. 547.

while the differential between Chicago and Pittsburgh, for instance, has been reduced during the past decade, there is no evidence of any intention over the longer period to induce the most economical location of the industry. In this manner the basing-point system may protect badly located investment or firms inefficient in other ways. Where the commodity affected is as important in the economic life of a country as steel, the leader, or the industry in council, exercises a far-reaching power over the rate of development of different parts of the country.[1] The Federal Trade Commission goes too far, however, in claiming that the effect of the basing-point system in the steel industry is "to neutralize and equalize all natural advantages and disadvantages of location as a factor in prices."[2]

The association of basing-point systems with leadership and the avoidance of short-run price cutting might be expected to result in stability of prices where such systems occur. Such stability has not appeared in the sugar industry[3] nor is it especially notable in the lumber industry. The price of cement is much more stable[4] and the discriminatory policy of the industry has been attributed to the desire to obtain additional business while preserving a rigid price structure.[5] The stability of steel prices has already been discussed.[6]

Basing-point systems react upon prices also through their effect upon costs. They affect the cost of selling and of transportation and may protect the less efficient producers. Sellers emphasize the fact that these systems increase the number of sellers at each delivery point; freight absorptions enable them, as we have seen, to penetrate each other's territory and the non-basing-point mill must meet rivals at every delivery point. The United States Steel Corporation defended the Pittsburgh-plus practice because it enabled Pittsburgh producers to compete for delivery in any part of the country and enabled less efficient rivals to enter the market;[7] thus more firms were offering to sell at any point than would offer if each mill had been a base mill.[8] The increase in the number of

---

[1] *Cf.* the protests against the abandonment of base prices at St. Louis (F.T.C., *Basing Point System in the Steel Industry*, 19, 20, 25).
[2] *ibid.*, 3, 18, 25.
[3] U.S. v. Sugar Institute, *Brief on the Facts for the Sugar Institute*, Exhibit O 3.
[4] *Cf.* F.T.C., *Price Bases Inquiry*, 56, 82.
[5] F.T.C., *Price Bases Inquiry*, 34, 89, 146.
[6] See Chap. V.
[7] *Brief for U.S. Steel Corp.*, 29.
[8] *Brief for Amici Curiae*, 51. *Cf.* also F.T.C., *Basing Point System in the Steel Industry*, 15, 16, and N.R.A., *op. cit.*, 148, where it was said that this increase in the number of sellers at each point "may be fairly important" and have the effect of

sellers at points distant from Pittsburgh was obtained, however, only because delivered prices were sufficiently above the Pittsburgh price to make shipment from Pittsburgh profitable. The number of sellers can always be enhanced by raising prices sufficiently.[1] The nature of the downward pressure upon prices was, as we have seen, seriously altered. There is little justification for the claim that costs were reduced[2] and good reason to believe that they were increased. The system rests upon the meeting, but not the cutting, of the prices of rivals and the maintenance of a "one-price policy." Business must be obtained by non-price competition except where public contracts are allocated by lot, and prices must, in the long run, cover these costs which tend to increase so long as any rivalry for business persists.[3] It is to be remembered, however, that the imperfectly competitive conditions that stimulate resort to basing-point systems tend also to increase the cost of selling even in the absence of basing-point systems.

Basing-point systems increase aggregate transportation costs. The interpenetration of market areas results in cross freighting. Local demands are no longer supplied from the most economical point of production taking account of costs of production and transportation. The commodity travels in both directions on the same railroad and may pass the doors of another mill. The wastefulness of such cross freighting (except where a mill is unable to supply the full demand in the territory most cheaply reached by it)

"definitely strengthening the force of competition" but it was admitted that "only those quoting on the home basing point are competing in a way tending very directly to reduce the price" (*ibid.*, 163). If every mill were a base mill and there were no freight absorptions there would be more than one seller at a delivery point only if there were more than one manufacturer at a point of production, if railroad rates were not on an equal mileage basis, or if the delivery points were just on the boundary between the territory of two points of production.

[1] "It is the effect of the monopolistic practice in enhancing prices which is condemned by the law and not the superficial consideration of the sum total of the number of competitors within a given area" (*Brief for Amici Curiae*, 53). It was also pointed out in this brief that the law is not concerned with the number of competitors (except in the rare circumstances in which all competition is eliminated) but with the restriction of the limitations upon competition to such normal and natural limitations as freight rates, proximity to raw materials, and markets (*ibid.*, 52).

[2] The American Iron and Steel Institute claimed that this widening of the "range of available sources of supply from which any user of steel may satisfy his needs without penalty of price" increased the freedom of competition among producers and made "actual costs of steel lower to the average user than would otherwise be the case" (*Basing Points and Competition in Steel*, 4).

[3] F.T.C., *Price Bases Inquiry*, 7, 142. Selling and administrative costs were reported to be 18.3 per cent of selling prices for the Lehigh Portland Cement Company and 12.20 per cent for the International Portland Cement Company (FRASER and DORIOT, *Analyzing Our Industries*, 309).

is acknowledged by the sellers.[1] If they are to obtain a normal profit these unnecessary transportation charges must be covered by prices.[2]

The extent of this cross freighting depends upon the territories which the various sellers decide to serve and there is practically no satisfactory information concerning this matter. The Illinois Steel Company, which produced near Chicago, sold considerable quantities of steel at prices yielding mill nets less than those obtained from sales in Chicago although it was a subsidiary of the United States Steel Corporation which was better able than any other seller to arrange for shipments from the nearest mill.[3] An investigation of shipments of 1,534,000 net tons of steel code products shipped during the three months ended June 30, 1934 (about 20 per cent of the total national output), by mills with 85 per cent of the productive capacity within a fifty-mile radius of Pittsburgh, revealed that the actual freight paid exceeded the freight charges added to basing-point prices by 1.639 million dollars or $1.07 per ton; the total delivered value of the shipments being 92.072 million dollars.[4] No information

---

[1] Mr. Schwab, addressing the American Iron and Steel Institute in 1928, commented that the "hunger for tonnage" arising from a desire to operate mills at full capacity had been one of the fundamental mistakes of the steel industry and the chief cause of the crosshauling of steel products. All steel manufacturers knew, he said, that they did not thus change their rates of operation as compared with competitors to any appreciable extent, but that they had merely dissipated part of their profit in unnecessary transportation. He admitted, however, that such wasteful crosshauling was paid for the consumer as well as the producer of steel products. (*Iron Trades Review*, May 31, 1928, 1410, cit. F.T.C., *Price Bases* Inquiry, 133.) The wastefulness of crosshauling has been recognized in the clay products industry, with the comment, however, that such crosshauling would not be so serious if all the freight charges could be passed on to the consumer (*Brick and Clay Record*, June 5, 1928, cit. F.T.C., *Price Bases Inquiry*, 134).

[2] Cf. F.T.C., *Brief on Pittsburgh Plus*, 798; *Iron Age*, July 24, 1924, 205.

[3] The shipments of the Illinois Steel Company yielding less than its maximum mill nets in 1919 were, in thousands of tons:

Territory	Heavy structural shapes	Plates	Bars	Total[a]
States east of Indiana-Ohio line and north of Ohio and Potomac rivers	.890	5.248	12.836	55.361
States south of Ohio River and of southern Missouri line (including Arizona and from Arizona east)	8.864	5.256	11.038	74.915
Pacific coast	34.268	149.065	9.949	206.942
Michigan	8.825	7.551	33.467	63.005

[a] The total includes commodities in addition to those included in the separate columns.

(F.T.C., *Statement on Pittsburgh Plus*, 300.) Similar figures are given for 1920.

[4] N.R.A., *op. cit.*, Supplement No. 1. No separate calculations were made for each product. Freight absorptions in this average are distributed over all tonnage including that involving no freight absorptions.

was obtained, however, concerning shipments into this area from outside.[1]

The aggregate net costs of freight absorptions in the sugar industry (after deducting "freight pickups" obtained by non-basing-point refiners) were reported by counsel for the refiners to have ranged between two and four million dollars between 1926 and 1931.[2] It was pointed out that since the formation of the Sugar Institute in 1928 losses on freight absorptions had increased by a little over a million dollars in four years, and that the amounts of the absorptions by individual refiners showed no harmony of movement.[3] If these losses on freight absorptions are computed by deducting the actual price obtained for sugar (after deducting any freight charges) from the price regarded as the ruling price at the refinery, and charged on a considerable volume of sales, they are not altogether satisfactory as a measure of unnecessary cross freighting, as will be evident from a consideration of the Federal Trade Commission's more complete analysis of the same problem in the cement industry.

The commission reported that in the cement industry the average manufacturing and selling cost of cement exclusive of interest charges in 1927 was $1.3145 per barrel while the average freight absorptions were $0.243 per barrel, or 44 per cent of the difference between average manufacturing and selling cost and average mill price.[4] It cannot be assumed, however, that all these sales involving freight absorptions involved cross freighting. Shipments from some market areas may have been very little offset by shipments in the opposite direction, owing, for instance,

[1] Examples of cross freighting of steel are described by the Federal Trade Commission in *Basing Point System in the Steel Industry*, 13.
[2] Freight ebsorptions were reported to have been:

	Million Dollars
1926	2.326
1927	2.974
1928	3.054
1929	3.152
1930	3.453
1931	3.974

These figures reveal only the *net* position for the country as a whole. (*Cf.* U.S. v. Sugar Institute, *Decision* of Judge Mack (mimeographed), 49).
[3] The heaviest absorptions were made by the California and Hawaii Sugar Refining Company which shipped from the Pacific coast: its total absorptions were 1.682 million dollars in 1926 and 2.071 million dollars in 1931, or considerably over half the total absorptions in the industry (U.S. v. Sugar Institute, *Brief for the Sugar Institute on the Facts*, 180). These figures are not comparable with those of other refiners as the company had an arrangement with those from whom it bought raw sugar to absorb freight (*Decision* of Judge Mack, 49). Its main supplier of raw sugar was its parent corporation which owned sugar plantations in Hawaii.
[4] F.T.C., *Price Bases Inquiry*, xiv, 90. Transportation charges on the average added 22 per cent and in some territories as much as 50 per cent to the mill price.

to temporary increases in demand in some areas. Comparison of freight actually paid with the freight from the nearest mill[1] is also a poor measure of the extent of uneconomic transportation. The nearer mill may be unable to supply the total demand at nearby points of delivery. Shipments from more distant points are, moreover, as economical as shipments from nearer mills when the cost of production at more distant points is sufficiently below that at the nearer mill to counterbalance any difference in transportation costs.[2] If, however, distant mills are less economical, the final economic costs are greater than these figures would suggest. In specific instances, however, the uneconomic effects of the system were evident.

Only one third of the sales of cement in Chicago, for instance, were made from the nearest mill, which was at the same time shipping considerable quantities to distant points, sales at which yielded mill nets below those on sales in Chicago.[3] Of sales in Milwaukee during the two-year period beginning on July 1, 1926, only 25 per cent came from the mill at the base upon which Milwaukee prices were calculated (which was also the mill by reference to which Chicago prices were calculated). A Wisconsin mill which was nearer than any other to Milwaukee, but which was not a basing point, provided only 6 per cent of the Milwaukee deliveries of cement and shipped the remainder of its output to Chicago, Minneapolis, and other more distant markets.[4]

The commission attempted to estimate "the burden of unnecessary production and distribution costs arising under imperfect competition" by calculating the difference between average mill nets and average prices in 1927,[5] and arrived at an estimate of

[1] The freight actually paid upon shipments of cement to 25 selected cities in the two years from July 1, 1926, to June 30, 1928, was compared with the freights that would have been paid had shipments been made from the mill nearest freightwise to the point of delivery. The average excess payment of freight upon these shipments (which were about 20 per cent of the total sales of cement during the period) amounted to 11.4 cents per barrel and to a total of about 7.2 million dollars. The amount of excess freight varied greatly for different cities, from 33.32 cents per barrel on shipments to Detroit, 31.92 cents per barrel on shipments to Davenport, Iowa, 22.42 cents per barrel on shipments to Philadelphia, and about 0.79 cents on shipments to Denver, to no excess at all on shipments to Seattle. (*ibid.*, 135.)

[2] *ibid.*, 136.

[3] The commission calculated that if the mill had sold at a uniform base price sales to Chicago could have been made at a price 22½ cents per barrel less than that actually paid. The quantity of cement actually supplied would have cost $800,000 less than it did in fact. (F.T.C., *Price Bases Inquiry*, 108.) It is assumed that if the mill price had been equal to the average mill net obtained under the basing-point system the volume of sales would have been the same.

[4] *ibid.*, 143.

[5] *ibid.*, 141.

$0.243 per barrel or a total of about 42 million dollars.[1] It does not follow, however, that, had all freight absorptions been eliminated, the same buyers could have purchased the same quantities of cement for $0.243 per barrel less than they paid without any loss of profit to the sellers. Some mills rely upon high base prices and a small volume of sales at these prices with a relatively large volume of sales involving freight absorptions. The non-base mill is the limiting case of such a policy. The elimination of freight absorptions would compel such mills to reduce their base prices by more than $0.243 per barrel if their sales were to remain unchanged. Non-base mills would also be compelled to declare a base price. The general structure of base prices would, therefore, be changed.[2] In fact, this estimate is affected not only by freight absorptions but also by attempts by mills to exploit local monopolies, possibly but not necessarily because they have abnormally high costs.[3]

In the last resort the difficulty of calculating the extent of uneconomic cross freight lies in the difficulty of establishing an ideal economic condition upon which to base comparisons. The problem might be approached by endeavoring to determine the market area of each plant by allocating each delivery point to

[1] It calculated the burden on 141 million barrels or 81 per cent of the total shipments for the year, and assumed that the remaining 19 per cent was sold under similar conditions.

[2] The commission states that its calculation rests upon "the assumption that the ratios of mill prices to costs are approximately alike" (*ibid.*, 139–141). Where a mill makes a mill price yielding a smaller margin over cost than its rivals at other production points, the territory of the mill is somewhat greater than it would otherwise be, with the result that some shipments which would otherwise involve freight absorptions do not involve them, and also the sum from which weighted net realizations are deducted is smaller than it would otherwise be. Thus the measure of "uneconomic freighting" for such a mill is less than it would be if its margin between cost and mill price were the same as for other mills. On the other hand, the measure of uneconomic freighting for producers shipping into the territory of this mill is increased, partly because more delivery points involve freight absorptions than would otherwise be the case, and partly because the average net realizations deducted from average mill prices are smaller (*loc. cit.*). These errors are somewhat offset, however, when all mills are taken as a group. The commission also states, however, that these statistics offer "an estimate of that part of production and distribution costs attributable to imperfect competition that would appear if a comparison of costs of all producers with the costs of the low-cost producer could be made" (*ibid.*, 140). There appears, however, to be no justification for the claim that these calculations indicate the extent to which costs exceed those of the low-cost producers.

[3] *ibid.*, 139, 141, 142. In its report on open price trade associations, the commission questioned whether crosshauling was as important under delivered-price systems as was commonly believed, partly because manufacturers naturally confined their major sales effort to territories within convenient reach of their plants, and partly because they naturally watch each other carefully and regard the invasion of their territory as provocative of retaliation (F.T.C., *Open Price Trade Associations*, 75).

the plant from which the sum of production and selling costs plus freight would be a minimum. It would then be possible to calculate from the total number of barrels of cement delivered to each point, the total sums that would have been paid for them had they been obtained from the mill in whose economic territory the delivery point was situated. This total for each delivery point could then be subtracted from the actual delivered prices charged under the basing-point system, and the extent of the uneconomic costs thus calculated. But such calculations would in some cases imply deliveries from a mill beyond its capacity to deliver, and in others, deliveries too small to maintain it in existence. Costs are not, moreover, independent of existing price policy. These difficulties might be attributable to temporary conditions. But high-cost mills might be unable to survive without the basing-point system. Yet any calculations based upon the best distribution of production in the light of present distribution of demand and costs at each point would be unfair because investment must be made in advance of knowledge of actual demand.

Basing-point systems exert, therefore, an upward pressure upon costs. In so far as profits tend to a normal level these increased costs are passed on to purchasers in prices.[1] The Federal Trade Commission remarked upon the significance of the "fact that the steel industry was able to show satisfactory profits for the first six months of 1934 without operating to more than half its producing capacity."[2] Over the longer period from 1925 to 1934, however, profits are said by the industry to have averaged only 2.5 per cent.[3] The average profit of 21 of the larger portland cement companies for the period from 1919 to 1928 was 14.2 per cent and for 64 of the larger lumber manufacturers 10.0 per cent.[4] There is no reason to suppose, therefore, that these additional costs were not passed on to buyers.[5]

[1] The contention that freight absorption tends to a lower average price for cement than would uniform mill prices (BROWN, "Economics of Portland Cement Prices," *Amer. Econ. Rev.*, 15: 77) appears to be untenable except where it permits technical economies in production (see p. 331).
[2] F.T.C., *Basing Point System in the Steel Industry*, 37; cf. also N.R.A., *op. cit.*, Appendix A, 10.
[3] American Iron and Steel Institute, *cit. New York Times*, May 14, 1935. The highest annual rate of return reported was 9.2 per cent in 1929. The average rate of return of 99 larger corporations in the metal castings and forgings industry (in which all iron and steel plants were included) for the period from 1919 to 1928 was 5.8 per cent (EPSTEIN, *Industrial Profits in the United States*, 287).
[4] EPSTEIN, *op. cit.*, 266, 284. The average profit of 26 larger planing mills was 17.7 per cent.
[5] The average profit for the same period for all manufacturing carried on by firms of moderate size was 10.8 per cent (EPSTEIN, *op. cit.*, 242).

These increased costs resulting from efforts to prevent shorttime price competition subject prices in increasing degree to the policy of sellers in the selection of sales territory and the determination of expenditure on sales promotion; these in turn show signs of group control. In the oil industry, for instance, refiners have been exhorted to keep to their normal marketing areas and adjust their operations to the probable demand from such areas.[1] A severe price war in the cement industry in the spring of 1931 was attributed to shipments by some mills outside their so-called "logical" markets.[2]

Basing-point systems react not only upon the industries selling and buying the product affected, but also upon the transportation industry. Uneconomical cross freighting increases the demand for transportation services in general and gives transportation agencies an interest in the maintenance of the practice. These systems also affect the demand for different kinds of transportation. Their use being principally stimulated by a desire to regulate price competition they must provide a simple and definite method of calculating transportation costs. Most frequently railroad transportation rates are used in calculating delivered prices; they are published and relatively stable and railroad transportation is the most generally available. It is unfortunate, however, that railroad transportation is not always the most economical. The availability of cheaper transportation is a constant source of difficulty, but also of profit. If delivered prices based on railroad rates can be maintained, but cheaper forms of transportation, e.g., by water or truck, used, mill nets of sellers are increased and sellers enabled to penetrate farther into rival territories, but there is no diversion of demand between different types of transportation. If, however, railroad transportation is used there is an uneconomical diversion of demand from the cheaper to the more expensive type of transportation but the mill nets of sellers are less than if the cheapest transportation were used.[3] In the steel and cement industries there have been attempts to dis-

[1] They were told that there was "no plainer or more persistent folly than the idea that a surplus can be gotten rid of for what it will bring without in turn affecting the home market. Inevitably these 'chickens come home to roost.' The original dumper must ultimately find his area invaded by some surplus if he initiates a policy of getting rid of his surplus in other territories at low prices" (*Oil and Gas Jour.*, Jan. 10, 1929).

[2] FRASER and DORIOT, *Analyzing Our Industries*, 310.

[3] *Cf.* the remark of the general manager of sales of the Republic Steel Corporation that abandonment of the basing-point system would "handicap railroads" (AMERICAN IRON AND STEEL INSTITUTE, *Basing Points and Competition in Steel*, 14).

courage the use of trucks by charging prices yielding higher mill nets when delivery is taken in trucks at the mill. Considerable effort is necessary, however, to maintain delivered prices based on the cost of railroad transportation where other and cheaper transportation is available. The first basing-point system for steel is said to have broken down because of the diversion of products to cheaper transportation.[1] If the system is modified to permit the calculation of delivered prices by the use of, say, water transportation, mills absorbing freight to reach points at which rivals have the advantage of access to water transportation must accept lower mill nets than if the base mill charged for railroad transportation. Furthermore, water transportation, being slower and more liable to cause deterioration of the product, the mill accessible to water and fixing its delivered price by the use of water transportation rates may be compelled to use railroad transportation, thus reducing its mill net. If it does not do so the greater speed by which the rival makes deliveries by rail, and the better condition of the product on arrival, may divert the major part of the business to him. In this manner, for instance, the delivered price of sugar in the Great Lakes territory, and occasionally in Alabama, Tennessee, Kentucky, and parts of Indiana served by the Warrior River, has been brought down to a level including the cost of only water transportation although other forms of transportation were used.[2] The use of water rates in calculating delivered prices for steel was resisted for fear of a similar outcome.[3] Similar action has been taken in the cement industry. The benefits of water transportation have, however, in a few places affected prices; silos and grinding plants have been established and made basing points, and prices at these bases appear to have been influenced by the fact that cement can be shipped there by water.

[1] A purchaser at Duluth arranged for delivery to Buffalo and transported thence by water.
[2] U.S. v. Sugar Institute, *Decision* of Judge Mack, 47, 48.
[3] F.T.C. *Basing Point System in the Steel Industry*, 23.

CHAPTER VIII

NON-PRICE COMPETITION

I. The origin and nature of non-price competition—II. The effects of non-price competition—*A*. Sales-promotion activities—1. Effects on the organization of production—2. Effect on the distribution of goods and services—*B*. Competition in quality and service—1. Effect upon the organization of production—2. Effect upon the distribution of goods and services—*C*. Competition in style—1. Effect on the organization of production—2. Effect upon the distribution of goods and services—III. The changing importance of non-price competition—*A*. Evidence of increasing importance—*B*. Evidence of declining importance.

I. THE ORIGIN AND NATURE OF NON-PRICE COMPETITION

The preceding discussion of the more important policies adopted as an escape from price competition has revealed that these policies almost all tend to deflect such rivalry as remains into what has been called "non-price competition." These policies are directed towards uniformity in the offer prices of sellers; those who seek to increase their volume of business must attract buyers by some means other than price cutting. Price leadership, price stabilization, and geographical price discrimination often lead, therefore, to non-price competition. Sharing the market, however, stands upon a different basis; all opportunity of obtaining an increased share in the market is cut off; if non-price competition occurs, it must be mutually neutralizing in its effect upon movements of business between firms. Thus although the increasing use of mechanical methods of production has made it possible to produce more homogeneous products, it has not, as might have been expected, brought the actual market more into conformity with the perfectly competitive market. Greater homogeneity has been attained by the conversion of a large proportion of the costs of production into overhead costs; unused plant is frequently present; in consequence price competition between sellers has been modified in the various ways already discussed and rivalry has been diverted into the channels of non-price competition.

Non-price competition has, however, been stimulated by other influences. The knowledge of buyers is imperfect; frequently they are fully informed concerning neither the offers of sellers, other than those with whom they have customarily dealt, nor the full range of varieties of products available. Sellers, in consequence, are induced to incur expenditure in order to make this information available. Sellers have also come into possession of knowledge of methods of influencing the attitudes of buyers to each product, of changing their estimates of the utility of a product. Sellers no longer accept the total demand for their product (at each price) as beyond their control. Realizing that they can influence the allocation of expenditure by individuals without reductions in price and thus increase the total demand for their product, and that efforts in this direction may be very profitable, they have, in some industries, so emphasized selling activities that the cost of selling exceeds the cost of manufacturing.

The distinction between price competition and non-price competition needs to be made with some care. The simplest and most direct basis of distinction may seem to be to regard price competition as a means of attempting to attract business by sacrificing revenue from sales, and to include under non-price competition all methods of attracting business involving additions to expenditure. This basis of distinction is, however, unsatisfactory; it involves entanglement in the bookkeeping practices of sellers. A seller may sell at a lower price to retailers who provide a special window display for his product, than to other retailers; it is unsatisfactory to classify this method of obtaining business as price competition when expenditures on advertising out of revenues obtained by charging a uniform price to all are classified as non-price competition.[1] A more satisfactory basis of distinction between price and non-price competition is suggested by the separation of costs into production and selling costs, selling costs being those costs which alter the demand curve and production costs those which do not.[2] Any deductions from the basic price made with the object of increasing the demand for the

[1] It is possible, of course, to regard the discounts for window display as expenditure which is, for convenience and economy, offset in settlement against revenue due from the same persons. But this adjustment is much more difficult to make when the price charged to all retailers is set on a lower level than would otherwise be charged, with the object, not of permitting a retail price lower than would otherwise prevail, but of increasing the margin of the retailer and thereby enlisting his services in pressing the commodity upon buyers.

[2] CHAMBERLIN, *Monopolistic Competition*, 123. Professor Chamberlin alternatively defines this distinction in the statement that "those [costs] made to adapt

product over what it would have been at that price (and all other prices) without such deductions, as well as all actual payments with the same object, are selling costs arising out of non-price competition. Production costs include not only costs of manufacturing and management but also costs of distribution (such as costs of transportation, handling, and delivery) which add utility to the physical commodity by making it more capable of satisfying wants.

Difficulties naturally arise in applying this criterion. If a price of ten cents is reduced to nine cents by making an advertising allowance of one cent, the dealer may contribute out of his resources of equipment or labor to furthering the sale of the product at the old price. But he may regard the allowance as a price reduction and reduce his resale price; it may be necessary, therefore, to regard the allowance as partly price and partly non-price competition. "Freight absorption" involving sales for delivery at some points yielding (at the point of production) less than sales at points nearer to the seller's point of production cannot be regarded as a cost incurred to increase demand at the existing mill price; it must be regarded as discriminatory price cutting. Reciprocal buying practices (buying on condition that the seller either buys some other product or service from the buyer or grants him some indirect benefit) present difficulties. Sales of steel rails to railroads at prices that can be maintained only because railroads are afraid of losing freight traffic if they actively seek rails at lower prices might be regarded as a covert rebate by railroads, *i.e.*, as price cutting in the market for transportation disguised as an enhancement of steel rail prices. But steel rail manufacturers may pay higher transportation costs in order to increase their sales of rails; such increases in freight payments are expenditures aimed at increasing the demand for the rails of each seller at the current price. The increased expenditures on rails by railroads may therefore reasonably be regarded as a cost of increasing the demand for transportation services at the current price. The extent to which the practice falls in the category of non-price competition depends upon the extent to which it is expected to result in an increase in total freight expenditures.

---

the product to the demand are costs of production; those made to adapt the demand to the product are costs of selling" (*ibid.*, 125). *Cf.* also BRAITHWAITE, "The Economic Effects of Advertisement," *Econ. Jour.*, 38: 17 (1928).

Expenditures on non-price competition fall into three classes which have very different consequences, *viz.*, (*A*) expenditures aimed at changing the attitudes of buyers to a commodity broadly similar to that sold by rivals and unaffected by considerations of style; (*B*) competition in quality and service, involving expenditure aimed at attracting buyers by offering incidental advantages not offered by rivals; (*C*) expenditure incurred to bring about changes in style which increase the demand for the commodity. These three types of non-price competition will be considered separately.

II. THE EFFECTS OF NON-PRICE COMPETITION

A. Sales-promotion Activities

Sales-promotion activities take a very great number of different forms. First, and most spectacular, is advertising involving expenditure upon publicity in newspapers and periodicals, on billboards, at radio broadcasting stations, expenditure on window displays and upon methods of packing intended solely to influence the purchaser. Manufacturers, wholesalers, and retailers making such expenditures tend to eliminate the market in which a homogeneous product is sold by a large number of sellers. In a perfect competitive market no seller advertises, because his product is indistinguishable from that of any other; he has, in consequence, no reason to expect that he will reap the fruits of advertising in any greater degree than his rivals; indeed, each seller assumes that he can increase his output and sales without any perceptible effect upon the market price and without any advertising. Whether or not advertising reduces the physical homogeneity of products is irrelevant if it induces among buyers a belief that products are not homogeneous. In the presence of this belief small reductions in price by one seller fail to shift all the business in a particular "product" to the price cutter.

Secondly, sales may be pressed through the employment of salesmen, who perform by word of mouth the functions expected in other circumstances to be performed by advertising. Salesmen may, however, also collect orders, adjust complaints, and act as instruments of service competition (as when they give technical advice). Salesmen approaching the final purchaser may also deliver the commodity and collect payment, thus performing some of the functions of production as broadly defined above.

Wherever the margin offered to a dealer is calculated to induce him to press goods upon his customers, such expenditure or loss of income must also fall under this heading. Thirdly, sellers attempt to change the attitudes of buyers by giving them an opportunity of experiencing, without payment, the utilities obtained from a product. Giving samples is naturally limited to products sold in units the cost of which is relatively low, such as soap, tobacco, and branded foods; it is not to be expected in the automobile or radio equipment industries. Fourthly, sellers may attempt to induce sales by giving buyers the right to participate in lotteries or in some other way to secure a chance of obtaining a prize. Fifthly, sellers may give coupons which are exchangeable in quantity for other commodities, a practice which has been common in the retailing of tobacco, candy, and some food products. Sixthly, sellers may bribe the agents of purchasers. Payments in money or in the form of entertainment are a source of considerable concern and regret in a number of industries. The attitude of the agent rather than that of the actual purchaser is influenced but the expenditure is believed to increase sales at each price or prevent their decline. Expenditure aimed at identifying the customers of rivals in order that sales campaigns may be concentrated upon those from whom the greatest response is likely are also a type of sales-promotion activity.[1]

The effects of expenditure upon sales promotion may be analyzed in terms of their effect upon the efficiency of production and upon the ultimate distribution of goods and services between the different classes in the community.

1. THE EFFECTS OF SALES PROMOTION ON THE ORGANIZATION OF PRODUCTION

When the expenditures of producers are increased by the inclusion of selling costs, the tendency for prices in the long run to cover no more than the costs of production ceases to operate. If there is any tendency to normal returns, prices must cover *both* selling and production costs. Expenditure on sales pressure

---

[1] Expenditures involving the "shadowing" of the salesmen of rivals, following their delivery wagons, or obtaining similar information from railroads by bribery or otherwise have in the past figured largely in condemnations of methods of large firms attempting to consolidate their position, e.g., oil (COMMISSIONER OF CORPORATIONS, *The Petroleum Industry*, I, 302, II, 58), and cash registers (SEAGER and GULICK, *op. cit.*, 164; *Petition* in U.S. v. National Cash Register Co. (1911), 12-29).

must, therefore, always result in costs higher than they would be under pure competition because under such competition "the individual firm is producing most effectively and without selling costs."[1] But it does not follow that sales promotion always increases total costs where competition is not pure and markets are not perfect. The organization of industry in the hands of firms "producing most effectively" may be hindered by the imperfections of competition and some of these hindrances may be overcome by sales promotion. The effect of sales pressure upon the total costs of business turns upon their effect upon production costs and upon the amount of the expenditure upon sales pressure.

In order to break up the problem into parts of manageable proportions, we may first consider the effect of sales pressure where the most economical scale of production, while not necessarily identical with the actual scale, is not changed by the introduction or intensification of sales pressure. Furthermore, we may first assume that sales pressure by one or more firms in an industry has no effect upon the total demand for the product of the industry; it merely shifts demand from one seller to another.

Where demand at prices equal to average total cost of production with full use of existing facilities[2] (*i.e.*, upon the scale at which the average costs of producing with the existing equipment are minimized) is insufficient to permit full utilization of resources, price competition causes prices to fall below average total costs. These conditions may prevail for considerable periods when total demand has fallen below its former level, until the resources allocated to the industry have been perfectly adjusted to the decline. They prevail also when allocations of resources have been made upon a too optimistic estimate of demand and until the excessive allocation has been corrected. If, however, competition is imperfect, sellers take into account the probable effect of changes in their price upon demand and the probable responses of rivals to their own changes in price (because there are but few very close rivals); they may be unwilling to change prices frequently, or take steps to prevent sellers from initiating price changes and securing additional business before others have followed suit. Prices may, in consequence, be maintained upon a level that

---

[1] CHAMBERLIN, *op. cit.*, 166.
[2] Whether or not these are of a size such as will permit production at the lowest costs possible with existing knowledge of methods of production.

prevents full utilization of resources.[1] Profits, however, may be kept down to normal by the appearance of new firms and a reduction in the volume of business done by each firm; their average costs increase and means of production are utilized below their full capacity. This condition is likely to be a continuing characteristic of imperfectly competitive industries and there is no tendency to the most economical use of the means of production.[2]

If sales pressure be substituted for price competition, the costs of the firms resorting to it are increased. If the total demand for the product is unchanged and the selling efforts of the various firms are mutually neutralizing, the amount of business done by each is unchanged; the costs of each being increased, profits are diminished or losses increased and the prospect of some firms being eliminated is enhanced.[3] In so far as the number of firms is thus diminished the amount of business done by each is increased and their average total costs are reduced again. Each must be operating upon a scale nearer to that at which average total costs are minimized than it formerly was; sales pressure has reduced the unused capacity of each surviving firm. But the average total cost of each of the remaining firms is likely to be higher than it would have been without sales promotion. In other words "selling costs per unit are greater than the decrease in production costs. The resources expended to achieve the result are, therefore, greater than those saved by achieving it. And of course the balance of excess capacity remains."[4]

The sales pressure of different firms may, however, react unequally upon their sales (owing to differences in the effectiveness of a given expenditure upon sales pressure). The period of adjustment is thereby further shortened; the firms that gain most business secure the greatest reduction in average costs and those that lose most business suffer the greatest increase in average costs and the greatest losses; the departure of these latter from the industry is hastened.[5] Thus expenditure upon sales pressure tends to cause firms to be expelled more speedily than they

---

[1] Even if competition were perfect, prices would not generally fall below marginal cost at which level plant might still not be fully occupied.

[2] *Cf.* CHAMBERLIN, *op. cit.*, 109. But see also KALDOR, "Market Imperfection and Excess Capacity," *Economica*, 2: 33 (1935).

[3] If sales promotion is resorted to contemporaneously with increases in investment the tendency to increase investment is at least partly offset by the rise in costs.

[4] CHAMBERLIN, *op. cit.*, 172.

[5] If greater increases in sales are obtained by a firm because of greater relative expenditures upon advertising (and not greater effectiveness or expenditures) the outcome depends upon a combination of both the above arguments.

would be if there were imperfect competition without selling pressure. They are probably,[1] but not necessarily, more speedily expelled than under price competition. From the point of view of the economy as a whole, greater efficiency in the use of resources is secured only where resources (such as labor and even some forms of not too highly specialized equipment) can be transferred to other uses.[2]

Where firms are using their existing facilities for production to the full it is quite likely in practice that the scale upon which at least some are organized is less than the optimum, *i.e.*, that which permits the lowest average costs if all existing knowledge of methods of production is utilized. Sales promotion may increase the demand for the products of firms below optimum size and enable them to attain it. If they can obtain sufficient business to keep their new and larger organization fully occupied, their average production costs will be reduced as a result of an increase in selling costs. These conditions are most likely to be present in new industries, and in those in which knowledge of more economical methods involving production upon a larger scale has been accumulating; its utilization may have been postponed by consideration of the cost (in the form of reductions of sales revenue) of attracting business by price cutting.[3] Sales promotion is rather more likely to facilitate the concentration of production in this manner than price cutting; it is probably less costly than price competition, and also it is regarded in many industries with less fear (price competition being regarded as the more difficult to control). The firm will, as we have seen, be unlikely to attain the same output as it would under perfect price competition. How nearly it is likely to approach that ideal as a result of sales promotion depends upon the rate at which average costs decline with an increase in capacity for production and upon the costs of sales promotion. If these latter costs fall short of the expected gains from economies of production, they merely diminish but do not eliminate the gains from reorganization upon a larger

---

[1] Because of the probability that some firms pressing sales will, in the present very partial state of knowledge of the effect upon sales of a given expenditure upon sales pressure (see p. 384), have greater success than others.

[2] If the number of firms is reduced as a result of mergers, some specialized resources that might otherwise be abandoned may be used; the purchase of new equipment to replace equipment wearing out may be postponed.

[3] The losses due to the obsolescence of plant when any serious reorganization is involved also obstruct changes in the scale of production, but they operate where reorganization is sought either through price cutting or through sales promotion.

scale; the firm will find it profitable to press sales and increase the scale of its organization. But expenditure on sales pressure is subject to disproportionate returns; up to a certain expenditure the marginal cost of attracting another unit of sales probably declines, but beyond that point it increases. If these marginal costs begin to increase at a volume of sales which is less than the amount of business necessary to permit production upon an optimum scale, the deterrent to the attainment of an optimum volume of production increases. The marginal cost of obtaining additional business may rise to a level which exceeds the gains from increasing the scale of production before the optimum is reached. The greater the resistance of other firms in the industry to such attempts at reorganization, the greater the sums they spend on sales promotion and the greater the obstacle in the way of any firm seeking by sales promotion to attract sufficient business to enable it to organize on an optimum scale.

Expenditure upon sales pressure, however, frequently increases the demand for the output of the whole industry. Indeed manufacturers occasionally cooperate to advertise with this end alone in view; the trade associations in the lumber, sugar,[1] and cement industries have undertaken such advertising. While some or all firms spend on sales promotion all may gain additional business. Firms already operating on an optimum scale will be faced with increased production as well as selling costs and their loss of profits is likely to weaken their position and reduce their expenditure upon selling efforts. But all the sub-optimum firms may reduce production costs, although not necessarily by the amount necessary to offset the increase in their selling costs. As a given expenditure upon sales promotion brings a greater increase in sales than in the earlier case, the hindrance to the attainment of the optimum size is diminished.[2] The scale of production is likely to be larger than where no increase in total demand results from efforts to promote sales, but the scale of production in both cases may be either larger or smaller than under perfect competition (without sales-promotion activities).[3]

---

[1] The Sugar Institute spent one and three quarter million dollars in four years on advertising products made from or consumed with sugar (U.S. v. Sugar Institute, *Decision* of Judge Mack (mimeographed), 101).
[2] Where advertising by one seller increases the sales of rivals who do not advertise at all the reaction of those who do not advertise to the policy of the advertiser is less drastic than it would otherwise be (*Cf.* CHAMBERLAIN, *op. cit.*, 153).
[3] *ibid.*, 162.

But even if no firm increases in size in the long run, and the increased output is provided by an increased number of firms, costs may be reduced. An increase in the industry as a whole may result in external economies; the resulting increase in the demand for equipment, semimanufactured materials, and subsidiary services (such as transportation) may make possible a reorganization of these subsidiary industries and a reduction in their costs. The expanding industry will secure reductions in cost, however, only when the industries serving it were not previously organized to produce on the most efficient scale; some measure of price competition is also essential in these industries to ensure that reductions in cost are reflected in reductions in price. An increased demand for the means of production may, of course, raise their cost of production; there may be external dis-economies.[1] The increased demand attracted by sales promotion is likely to be at the expense of industries away from which expenditure is deflected;[2] in shorter periods of time they suffer from operation below their full capacity; in longer periods they may either suffer a loss of external economies resulting from the shrinkage of their demands for specialized means of production or realize a gain because of the avoidance of dis-economies. Sales promotion, if it diverts spending, may either increase or decrease the relative importance of activities yielding either increasing or decreasing returns, and thus cause either a fall or a rise in other costs of production. In any event, the total costs of production will be higher than they would have been had the reorganization of production been possible without expenditure upon such pressure, although they may be lower than they would have been had there been no expenditure on sales pressure and no diversion of spending. These higher costs are the price paid for the imperfections of the market that lead producers to avoid price competition and buyers to respond to sales pressure.[3]

[1] That is, a rising long-period cost curve.
[2] Unless sales promotion leads to a change in the relative valuation of work and leisure resulting in an increase in total production (see p. 390).
[3] It has been said that purchasers have no one to blame but themselves for the largely wasteful expenditure on advertising because "if it were not true that a dollar spent on advertising brought in more orders than a dollar taken off the price of goods, manufacturers presumably would not advertise" (ROBINSON, E. A. G., *The Structure of Competitive Industry*, 69). But it is not true that resort to advertising is due solely to a greater readiness on the part of purchasers to respond to sales pressure than to price cutting. The very readiness of purchasers to respond to price cutting may necessitate a speedy response by all sellers to a reduction in price by one of them; where there is unused capacity prices may be pressed well below the average total

Sales-promotion activities have clearly played a part in facilitating the utilization of large-scale methods of production; they are one means by which a firm may increase the volume of its business. The resulting economies in production are frequently cited as one of the great benefits of sales promotion.[1] It is clear, however, that sales promotion is not the only means of attaining this end; price competition is a more effective means to the same end but the approach to large-scale production appears to involve a retreat from price competition.[2] In general, therefore, sales-promotion activities which divert demand from firm to firm or industry to industry may divert it in directions in which a larger demand facilitates the more economical utilization of resources and permits closer approach to the allocation of resources that yields the greatest net satisfactions (if we boldly ignore differences in the utility of dollars of income to different individuals). But sales promotion is equally capable of diverting demand into directions in which attempts to increase output encounter obstacles which raise production costs.[3] In any event such activities themselves attract the means of production from other uses. Probably the most frequent net result is that the total costs of production are increased, *i.e.*, that a given quantity of resources in a community yields less goods and services (in quantity but not value) than would otherwise be available.

The foregoing discussion has assumed that sales pressure does not itself affect the most economical scale of production. This assumption must now be removed. Sales pressure may originate in attempts to increase the scale of production more nearly to the optimum size, to increase the business of a firm even beyond that size because size itself is attractive to entrepreneurs, or to secure a position of leadership or market control. It appears, however, to attain a permanent place in the conduct of business; those who have not initiated it must adopt it and it becomes

---

cost of production for considerable periods; for that reason sellers may prefer advertising to price competition.

[1] *Cf.* VON BECKERATH, *op. cit.*, 193.

[2] It has been suggested that as countries develop in efficiency to the point at which less essential goods can be provided, continued reliance upon the choices of consumers as to their purchases will, as a result of untrained public taste, cause great instability of demand. It may even be necessary to control the production of these relatively nonessential goods in order to maintain an individualist organization in other fields of production (FISHER, A. G. B., "Capital and the Growth of Knowledge," *Econ. Jour.*, 43: 379 (1933)). The main causes of instability at present do not appear to lie, however, in the changeability of the attitudes of consumers.

[3] *Cf.* MARSHALL, *Principles of Economics*, 470 *ff.*

as much a means of defense as of offense. In many fields (*e.g.*, tobacco products, branded foods and drugs) it is becoming impossible to sell even at considerably lower prices than rivals unless demand is induced by sales promotion.[1] This addition to the functions of the entrepreneur may change the optimum size of business as a whole; the desire to organize continuing selling campaigns on the most efficient scale may lead to efforts to increase the volume of productive activities. It may result in concentration under a common control of a number of plants each of the most economical size for production. It may also lead to the combination in a single firm of the manufacturing of a variety of products calling for similar selling methods, *e.g.*, in the market for branded foodstuffs.[2] It may lead, as in the petroleum industry, for example, to the integration of manufacturing and distribution in a number of territories. Any of these methods of adjusting the size of the firm to the most economical scale for the promotion of sales is threatened, however, by the possibility that the resulting firm may be beyond the size that can be most economically managed, more particularly where increased integration is involved; these increases in costs may, however, fall short of the accompanying fall in the costs of sales promotion. If sales promotion could be avoided, not only would the expenditure directly involved be avoided, but also the accompanying inefficiencies of management. If these inefficiencies of management stimulate attempts to remove them the optimum scale of management may be increased; costs at the optimum may be reduced with the result that total average costs fall below the former average production costs.

Sales promotion not only affects costs by reacting upon the size of businesses; it also affects the costs of business at each scale of production for the firm and for the industry. In general a firm would be expected to expend upon sales-promotion activities up to the point at which additional expenditure would not be fully met by increased returns (total sales revenue *less* total production costs). The total expenditure so determined depends upon the nature and cost of the methods of sales pressure to

[1] "The problem for the manufacturer is becoming less and less the amount that he can produce at a given price and more and more the amount that he can sell. And the amount he can sell depends largely on his ability to create a reputation for his product." (BRAITHWAITE, *op. cit.*, 29.)

[2] *Cf.* Standard Brands, Inc., General Foods, Inc., Beech-Nut Packing Company, California Packing Company.

which buyers respond and the amount of their response. The amount of this response depends upon the success attending the attempt to influence the attitudes of former buyers and potential buyers, and the success of rivals in this respect, together with the amount of their expenditures. Total expenditure upon advertising also depends upon the manner in which production costs vary with output. In the long run the amount of these expenses must be such that the price charged will just cover both the average production and average selling costs of the output that can be sold at that price. The number of firms must be adjusted so that there is neither any excess above nor deficit below a normal return, and no firm can improve its position by increasing or decreasing selling costs.

Resort to sales promotion, in a world in which little scientific information is available concerning the effect of promotion activities upon sales, introduces an element of great uncertainty into costs. The probable amount and permanence of the addition to sales to be expected from any given expenditure are uncertain. So too is the reaction of rivals to such additions; rivals may spend on sales promotion but with unforecastable results. Advertising by one seller may even considerably increase the sales of his rivals. The effect of sales promotion upon total demand is also uncertain. Close rational planning by each firm is thus hindered and risks are increased. Where there is a small number of firms, the personal attitudes of a few individuals may play a dominant part in determining allocations for sales promotion, as they probably have in the tobacco, automobile tire, and similar industries. This lack of precise knowledge introduces an element of chance into the selection of firms for survival.

The distribution of business between firms depends partly upon luck where sales-promotion expenditures are important; the tendency for the most efficient producers to survive is modified by the tendency for the most fortunate, as well as, in some measure, the most skillful promoters of sales to survive. Potential competition is also likely to be obstructed; acquaintance with the costly and relatively unsuccessful attempt of the Lorillard Company to establish a brand of cheap cigarettes ("Old Gold") by advertising is a warning to potential competitors that they must be prepared to gamble with very large sums to bid for a position in the industry. The greater the amounts being spent upon advertising, the greater is the cost of creating a reputation for a new brand. The existence of firms specializing in the management of sales-promotion activities somewhat modifies these tendencies by enabling producers to attach to themselves for a period of time an already organized and experienced sales-promotion department; it also enables them to change their sales-promotion department without delay and difficulty; but sales promoters promote the sale of their own services and when one manufacturer succumbs others are often compelled to follow with the result that the total expenditure upon sales-promotion activities increases.

2. THE EFFECT OF SALES PROMOTION UPON THE DISTRIBUTION OF GOODS AND SERVICES

The distribution of the consequences of sales promotion must be traced in their effect upon the three classes of purchasers, investors, and sales promoters. The benefits obtained by these last are so obvious as to require little discussion. The emergence of a demand for the services of persons whose capacities, and often whose equipment and organization, qualify them to conduct sales campaigns enables this class to obtain an income from this source. Over long periods, however, such persons gain only to the extent that they are without equal capacity for undertaking other functions in connection with production.

Sales pressure affects purchasers through its effect upon prices, upon the allocation of spending by consumers, and upon the benefits directly obtained by purchasers from the methods of sales promotion adopted.

Sales pressure can, as we have seen, never result in prices lower than they would have been under perfect competition, *i.e.*, prices covering merely production costs and those at the technical minimum. But under imperfect competition, sales pressure influences prices through its effect upon both costs and profits. We have seen that the average total costs of production *may* be less than they would have been in the absence of sales promotion; in such circumstances consumers gain, provided that a tendency to normal profits persists even under imperfect competition. But where average total costs are increased, purchasers must pay more for the product[1] than they would otherwise have

---

[1] It is argued that advertising does not increase and may decrease the prices of products, because in the absence of advertising resort would be had to "personal selling" and other forms of sales promotion (STARCH, *Principles of Advertising*, 109).

paid if profits tend to a normal rate.[1] The tendency to normal profits is, however, often obstructed; if large sums are needed to build up a reputation for a product potential competitors are discouraged and abnormal profits may persist for a long time, more particularly where, owing to conditions of manufacturing or selling, the firm of the most economical size is very large. Over long periods, however, high profits will probably tempt new firms to try their luck.

The extent to which prices can be increased depends not only upon the behavior of average costs but also upon the responsiveness of purchasers, *i.e.*, upon the effect of sales-promotion activities upon the allocation of income by spenders. Spenders may be induced to reassess the utilities anticipated from each possible quantity of the product and thus to buy more at the same price as before, or the same amount at a higher price. These changes in the allocation of their incomes affect the total satisfactions obtained by consumers. Advertising may inform consumers of the existence of products which would have otherwise remained unknown to them, or of offers to sell goods similar to those which they have been buying but at lower prices than they have been paying; it then enables consumers to allocate their income so as to increase their total satisfactions. But there is little doubt that much advertising holds out to consumers false hopes of the satisfactions to be obtained from products; "truth in advertising" is no more truthful than any other advertising slogan.[2]

Interference with the allocation of spending is not limited to blatantly untruthful advertising. Advertisers endeavor to limit the benefits of advertising as far as possible to themselves, isolating their product in the minds of prospective purchasers

---

This argument merely concerns the different methods of sales promotion and has little bearing upon the effect of sales-promotion activities as a whole.

[1] Resort to branded goods is said to lead also to the stabilization of the prices of such goods and to the protection of purchasers from price increases because of the manufacturers' fear of disturbing the settled habits of buyers (VON BECKERATH, *Modern Industrial Organization*, 197). The consequences of the stabilization of prices have already been analyzed and it is to be remembered that stabilization denies purchasers the benefits of price reductions as well as protecting them from increases of prices.

[2] A bill (S. 1944, 73d Cong. 1st Sess.) requiring the more accurate and truthful labeling of food, drugs, and cosmetics, and prohibiting advertising either untrue or, by ambiguity or inference, creating a misleading impression (especially as to the curative qualities of drugs), aroused great opposition from the industrial interests concerned. The claim that the bill, if passed in its proposed form, "would seriously affect the advertising plans of manufacturers" (*New York Times*, Nov. 12, 1933) suggests that truth would be very damaging to advertising.

from the products of rivals; they establish brands easily identifiable by their appearance, often by their packing. Branded goods have rapidly increased in importance not only in the food, drug, cosmetic, tobacco, and automobile industries, but also in the sale of gasoline (identified by color), meat (identified by packing), and even coal (sold in identifiable bags).[1]

Advertising is aimed at creating the impression that one brand is superior to others[2] whether or not it is actually superior; wherever it is not sufficiently superior to counterbalance the higher price that is paid the total benefit obtained from his income by the consumer influenced by the advertising is reduced.[3] It is extremely difficult, however, to decide when the consumers' total satisfactions are in fact diminished; the allocation of spending that would have existed with advertising of the informative but without advertising of the persuasive types[4] offers a theoretical but hardly a practical criterion of the ideal allocation of spending.

It is impossible to ignore the fact that even after purchasers have yielded to advertising and, presumably, experienced the actual satisfactions obtainable from a commodity, they continue to purchase it; they may continuously pay a higher price for it

[1] This device is especially attractive to manufacturers where the distribution of the product is not in their hands (as it usually is not).

[2] It has been suggested that the monopoly of profits obtained by advertisers from the creation of brands might be diminished by a reversal of the present law with regard to trade-marks. If, instead of preventing the imitation of trade-marks, such imitation were permitted provided the imitator reproduced the product whose mark was imitated, monopoly profits would tend to be eliminated, and the inducement to advertising, in large part wasteful, also reduced. (CHAMBERLIN, *op. cit.*, 204.) The practical difficulties of such a policy are admitted as there has grown up under the present law a network of property rights in trade-marks largely but not entirely the result of advertising. If all the products sold under any mark were identical in quality there would be no danger that a purchaser buying on the basis of past experience of marked articles would suffer in any way, although the use of such marks would be discouraged. Even at present the qualities of branded goods do not remain constant.

[3] In the fertilizer industry formerly the same physical product was sold under a number of brand names as well as by a number of apparently, although not actually, independent sellers (*i.e.*, by "bogus independents") with the result that "the farmer . . . has had no means of knowing what company he was actually patronizing. As a result the larger fertilizer manufacturers have been able to divert to themselves, to the detriment of their competitors, considerable business which they would not otherwise have secured" (F.T.C., *The Fertilizer Industry*, 1916, 182, 221 ff.). Where experience suggested one fertilizer to be unsatisfactory, efforts to experiment with a different commodity were hindered by the fact that many commodities which seemed to be different were not so in fact. In the last resort this difficulty arises, of course, out of a sad lack of knowledge on the part of buyers concerning the qualities of the things they buy. The use of these bogus independents also enabled manufacturers to obtain the services of more dealers than would otherwise have been available to them.

[4] BRAITHWAITE, *op. cit.*, 19.

than for a physically identical unadvertised commodity, or pay the same price for advertised and unadvertised commodities, although the former are of lower quality. Either the advertised product yields more utility than the cheaper product, or the consumer allocates his income in the belief that it does. There is a very thin line between the realization of utilities and the belief that they have been realized. Advertising, by suggesting that certain satisfactions will be obtained, may induce the consumer to believe that he has obtained these satisfactions. The Federal Trade Commission, for instance, induced a seller of perfumes to agree to cease representing that its product was "irresistible and can captivate the soul or that it will enable the user to be exclusively attractive and to attract and win the love of any person desired" when, as the commission, with bureaucratic austerity, remarked, "such are not the facts."[1] The belief that one is irresistible is the important thing for the consumer and if she (or he) continues to hold this belief she (or he) may in fact have proved irresistible; had her (or his) experience conflicted violently with the belief, the perfume would not have been continuously purchased. Continued purchases suggest that the responses of individuals have been so changed (often by designed appeals to sex and other emotions) as to render the new allocation of income the most satisfying. To decide whether advertising has increased or reduced the total satisfactions of spenders, we must answer the difficult question whether the purchaser, as transformed by the advertiser, gets more satisfactions out of the allocation of income that appears most satisfying to him in his renovated condition than did the unreformed purchaser out of his allocation of spending.

Looked at from the point of view of the community as a whole, changes in the allocation of the spending of consumers brought about by persuasive and not informative sales promotion tend to diminish the national income in utilities; "reputation" is attached to commodities[2] with the result that purchasers are

[1] F.T.C., *Annual Report*, 1932, 238.
[2] Miss Braithwaite (*Econ. Jour.*, 38: 25) contends that where advertising fails to increase the total demand for a product, but shifts it to a seller whose prices are higher than those of his rivals (because of his expenditure on advertisement), and where economies in production do not offset the increase in selling costs, "the national dividend is made up of rather fewer other goods and services and rather more reputation than would have been the case had there been no advertisement." But if sales promotion increases the demand for the product as a whole, and does not bring economies in production, the total national dividend has been increased

induced to pay a higher price for the same quantity than they would without advertising. This tendency may be offset by increases in the efficiency of production. If decreases in cost of production do not offset increases in advertising costs, prices are higher with advertising than they would have been without; resources are diverted from the production of goods and services into the production of "reputation"; if the total demand for the advertised product is increased, some resources are also diverted from the production of other goods into the production of those successfully advertised. If the distribution of resources that would have occurred without advertising would have given greater satisfaction than the new distribution, aggregate satisfactions are reduced. Where economies in production resulting from large output exceed the costs of advertising, resources are diverted from the production of other commodities; resources saved as a result of the increase in demand provide for the creation of "reputation." The distribution of spending that would have occurred without advertising might nevertheless have yielded a greater aggregate of satisfactions. If the increased output is produced with less total resources than the smaller output sold without advertising, consumers must gain; they can purchase as much as before of all other commodities and also more of the advertised commodity, or as much as before of the advertised commodity and more of others. But it is probable that a greater total sum will be paid for the greater output of the advertised commodity and that resources will be transferred to the production of the advertised commodity. Where economies in production permit a reduction in cost, purchasers secure all the amount formerly obtained at a lower price per unit and thus gain. But they lose owing to the production of the units added to output resulting from advertising and which are produced at a price greater than their utility in the absence of advertising. This loss "is greater the greater is the increase in output due to advertisement and the more inelastic is the original demand curve.

because the shift in demand away from other commodities to the one advertised has been made "in order to produce a set of commodities which advertisement has induced people to consider more valuable than those which were previously being produced" and because "economics only takes into account the fact of subjective valuations as shown by the prices paid and does not consider whether these valuations are justified." Although the matter is of no great importance, it would be more consistent if value of product is accepted as a measure of the national dividend to accept the fact that as more is paid for the total product in the first case also, advertising can be said to have increased the national dividend in that case too.

On the other hand this loss is more likely to be offset the greater is the decrease in price brought about by advertisement."[1] Where advertising causes reductions in price, the adverse effects of diversion of demand away from the commodities that would otherwise be bought *may* be counteracted by gains from more economical production arising from standardization of output, and sometimes of savings in the cost of distribution.

Sales promotion is capable of changing the attitudes of purchasers not only to each brand of commodity and to each commodity, but also to the relative utilities of commodities in general and leisure. If it increases willingness to work to acquire more commodities, the resources for sales-promotion activities may be obtained without any diversion of resources from the production of other products and the national dividend of goods and services may be increased; but if the relative valuations of leisure and goods and services in general which prevails without advertising results in greater net satisfactions than the relative valuation resulting from advertising, purchasers are not benefited by the increase in the national dividend.[2]

Advertising like price cutting may also be a means to the attainment of monopoly by eliminating rivals; the American Tobacco Company, for instance, spent a much larger percentage of its revenue upon advertising when it was securing control of a tobacco product than it did after control had been secured.[3] If it assists the seller to attain a position from which he can more profitably restrict output,[4] purchasers bear a double burden.

Where there is a small number of firms in an industry and each considers the long-run interests of all those in the industry, *i.e.*, if each desires to maximize profits but, in doing so, takes into account the effect of sales pressure upon net income, both directly and through the reactions of rivals thereto, the total expenditure upon selling is determined in the same manner as if there were only one seller. A change in the sales-promotion policy of one firm affects rivals more directly when they are few than when they are numerous; each seller may, therefore, hesitate to increase

---

[1] BRAITHWAITE, *op. cit.*, 27.
[2] BRAITHWAITE, *op. cit.*, 29.
[3] COMMISSIONER OF CORPORATIONS, *The Tobacco Industry*, 1915, III, 4, 5. The decline in average selling costs was, however, partly due to the increased volume of output over which the expenses were distributed (*op. cit.*, III, 4), *i.e.*, to increased efficiency in the use of resources applied to advertising.
[4] For example, if it enables him to secure control of the whole market for cigarettes instead of the market for one brand.

selling costs unless a considerable increase in total demand is expected. Increased sales pressure is most likely where a seller takes a short view of the consequences of such a policy; he may have but a brief interest in the market; he may be shortsighted; he may be uncertain as to the effect of his action upon the markets of rivals and as to their probable response.[1] The greater the prospect of an increase in total demand, the greater the inducement to commence sales promotion. Where sales promotion by one would seriously affect the market of rivals, the amount spent on selling activities is indeterminate between zero and the amount that would be spent under monopolistic competition.[2] The market for tobacco products since the partition of the former tobacco trust into four companies in the more important branches of tobacco manufacturing offers the best practical example of this situation. Expenditure upon advertising increased rapidly until it was for years[3] practically the only form of competition. This emphasis upon advertising[4] was, however, greatly stimulated by a belief, justified by subsequent events, that the total demand for cigarettes could be greatly extended. The principal benefits to purchasers from the dissolution of the former tobacco trust have been, therefore, in the exhilarating effects of the advertising of the successor companies.

Purchasers may obtain direct gains from devices for promoting sales. The distribution of samples may give some satisfactions to those who receive and use the samples. The conduct of lotteries gives satisfactions to the winners if not to all the participants. The giving of coupons gives satisfaction to those with the assiduity to collect the coupons and convert them. When sellers bribe the agents of buyers, consumers obtain no benefits.[5] Traveling salesmen may bring technical advice with their sales talk and purchasers may secure information otherwise hard to come by.

Advertising presents a more subtle problem. It has been argued that advertising has a serious disturbing effect upon the consumer, driving him into "an increasing unrest and superficiality in the conduct of life" and endangering "the culturally and ethically

[1] CHAMBERLIN, *op. cit.*, 170.
[2] *ibid.*, 171.
[3] The appearance of 10-cent brands of cigarettes during the depression after 1929 reintroduced a measure of price competition.
[4] COMMISSIONER OF CORPORATIONS, *Tobacco Industry*, 1915, III, xxxii.
[5] The opportunity to obtain these bribes may reduce the remuneration paid by the employers to such persons (as the payment of tips affects the wages of waiters), but there is no reason why the final cost of the commodity or service to the buyer should be reduced.

valuable sense of harmony in the surroundings," inducing an "entirely impersonal striving for sensational change" and increasingly wasteful and uneconomical consumption.[1] Whether or not these moral and aesthetic judgments be accepted, the possibility of direct reduction of welfare must be faced. Benefits to purchasers are equally possible. When the International Harvester Company, in an effort to increase the demand for its products, operates experimental estates and engages in scientific research to enable it to suggest better methods of farm management involving the greater use of machinery,[2] it is likely to contribute to increased efficiency in farming, although its publicity is likely to be biased in the direction of greater mechanization.[3] In so far as the news and fiction sections of newspapers and periodicals are largely financed out of the advertising revenue obtained by the publishers, the readers of newspapers and magazines secure these services at less than their specific costs.[4] But the editorial and news policy of the press being considerably influenced by the views of their principal paymasters, the quality of the services is changed. The maintenance of radio broadcasting out of advertising revenues operates in much the same way. The cost of operating subways and taxicabs and the provision of matches and blotting paper is also partly met immediately by advertisers.

The incidence of the benefits of sales-promotion activities differs from that of price cutting; all buyers of the product benefit from the latter, but the benefits of advertising accrue to a larger class. Moreover, just as a price policy may be discriminatory, expenditure upon sales-promotion activities may be directed to one class of prospective purchasers. Those in a particular area or of a particular class may be approached. Sales promotion may be aimed directly at the customers of rivals and little attempt made to attract an increase in total demand.

Investors are the third class affected by sales promotion. They benefit principally from a reduction in the risks of investment arising out of the dangers of price cutting. But they shoulder

---

[1] Von Beckerath, *Modern Industrial Organization*, 192.
[2] *Cf.* Von Beckerath, *op. cit.*, 191.
[3] Analogous methods are said to have been used in the German coal and potash mining and chemical industries (*loc. cit.*).
[4] The benefits are distributed among readers but paid for, in so far as the payment can be traced at all, by the purchasers of each product or service contributing to advertising revenue. Advertising, however, is most extensively addressed to consumers who also provide the body of readers.

risks of another kind, *viz.*, those of shifting demands due to sales-promotion activities. These are in some industries considerable risks; the wide fluctuations in the distribution of business in the cigarette industry since 1912 appear to be mainly due to the varying degrees of success attending upon the advertising campaigns of the large cigarette manufacturing companies. The magnitude of these risks depends upon the extent to which rivalry persists in the industry, as evidenced by the amounts likely to be spent on promoting sales. We have seen that the amount of such expenditures is influenced by the nature of the commodity, and the extent to which preferences for one brand rather than another rest upon attitudes of mind created by advertising (because of the inability of consumers to assess their satisfactions apart from advertising activities). The following statistics of profits[1] (before deduction of federal taxes) as a percentage of capitalization (excluding funded debt) in a few industrial groups in which advertising has been important suggest, however, that during the whole period from 1919 to 1928 the profits of these industries were above the average rate of return in manufacturing in general:

TABLE XI

Industrial groups	Number of corporations	Profit as a percentage of capitalization (1919 to 1928)
Toilet preparations	9	31.6
Proprietary preparations	56	20.8
Confectionery	21	17.8
Bakery products	17	16.8
Package foods	19	16.2
Tobacco	23	14.2
Canned goods	16	13.8
Beverages	11	3.8
Meat packing	23	1.9
All manufacturing	2046	10.8

The figures relate, however, only to the medium and large-sized corporations that were continuously in business throughout the period.

[1] EPSTEIN, *Industrial Profits in the United States*, 242 ff.

In summary, therefore, the mixed régime of competition and monopoly tends, by reducing emphasis on price competition, to divert the lingering desires of firms to improve their position in relation to their rivals into expenditure upon the promotion of sales. This expenditure is encouraged by the imperfect rationality of buyers; it is further stimulated by some knowledge, although very imperfect, of methods by which sellers may play upon the psychological reactions of buyers and influence their assessment of the utilities obtainable from different products. Expenditure on sales promotion may be but is not necessarily offset by savings in production costs. It may yield benefits to consumers, more particularly by assisting them to allocate their expenditures with more correct regard for the utilities obtainable, but it is more likely to diminish their total satisfactions by holding out false expectations and diverting resources to the creation of reputation. Its general effect upon investors is uncertain; it replaces one risk by another.

B. Competition in Quality and Service

Non-price competition may also take the form of efforts to increase profits by adjusting the quality of the product or the extent of the services provided in connection with it. The offer of a higher quality product, or more service, for the same money is, in a sense, price cutting. But it differs from price cutting in that it presents the purchaser with a more complex choice than that between offers of identical products at different prices; buyers must choose between products varying from seller to seller in both their apparent utilities and their price.[1] This form of rivalry also affects costs and prices in a manner different from price cutting in a purely competitive market. Furthermore, adjustments of quality and service do not always involve the offer of more utilities for the same price; sellers may seek to increase their profits by offering less actual utilities than their rivals but at the same price.

Competition in quality and service is in general distinguished from sales promotion in that the former involves the open offer of actual benefits to the purchaser while the latter does not. But the distinction is difficult to make and is not always satisfactory. It

---

[1] In the wholesale dress market, however, there has been a tendency to set a series of fixed prices because retailers desire them "to fit into their established price lines" and to concentrate all competition upon quality (*New York Times*, Aug. 19, 1934).

is not applicable to the policy of deteriorating the product in the hope of gain during the period in which purchasers act without realizing that the product has been changed. Sales promotion and quality and service competition are frequently entangled in practice. Commodities of new colors, with different types of packing, or in containers of a new type, do not necessarily yield any greater utility to the consumer; if they do not, the cost of the alteration aimed at changing the attitudes of buyers is a selling cost; if the new container, for example, facilitates the use of the product or enables it to be used more economically, the cost of the change is in part at least a production cost. When a seller maintains an expensive selling organization which also renders advisory services to buyers, the additional costs are partly selling costs and partly the cost of producing more service.[1] It is equally difficult to segregate the expenses of retailers which increase their services to purchasers and those which influence the purchasers without increasing the utilities they obtain. Changes in quality and service may necessitate advertising to bring the changes to the notice of potential purchasers (or to induce them to believe that no change has been made); it is difficult, however, to analyze the costs of sales promotion into those necessary to make the changes in quality and service known, those which induce a false belief that the quality of the product is being maintained, and those which otherwise attract purchasers. Sales-promotion expenses are not, however, an inevitable accompaniment of changes in quality and service; better equipment and service in retail stores may attract purchasers without advertising, as may also better located retail stores. Competition between newspapers and magazines is mainly in terms of quality but involves little (although some) expenditure on acquainting prospective purchasers with the quality of the periodical.

1. THE EFFECT OF QUALITY AND SERVICE COMPETITION UPON THE ORGANIZATION OF PRODUCTION

Producers contemplating quality and service competition consider for each combination of quality and service likely to appeal to purchasers the cost of producing various quantities of

---

[1] The Commissioner of Corporations concluded, for instance, that the International Harvester Company had preferred to maintain an expensive selling organization rather than to reduce its prices (COMMISSIONER OF CORPORATIONS, *International Harvester Company*, 27).

each.[1] They also consider the prices at which different quantities of each product are likely to be sold[2] and endeavor to select the combination of product and service the conditions of demand and supply for which are such as to offer the highest profit. They do not necessarily select the product whose cost of production is lowest or produce the quantity of any product that permits the lowest cost of production.[3] If the products of different sellers differ in quality, the market for each is monopolized. The demand for each product is affected by the readiness of purchasers to shift from one quality to another. If the products differ so little that existing equipment can be adapted with little or no expense to produce a commodity of a different grade the costs of movement by producers from one market to another are reduced. If firms are operating below their full capacity and one changes the quality and price of its product, it may increase its profits without any disturbance of rivals; it may discover a type of product yielding for the same volume of output as before a price sufficiently increased to more than cover the increase in costs; costs may even be lower and prices unchanged. But, even so, purchasing power is withdrawn from some other direction, and temporary maladjustments of resources to demand will occur. The increased profits may, however, come from an increase in sales at the expense of rivals; the innovating firm operates more nearly to full capacity; it places rivals at a corresponding disadvantage and accelerates their expulsion from the industry. The firms whose changes in quality and service attract most business may be able to reorganize their plants upon a scale permitting lower costs than formerly; knowledge of more economical methods of production upon a large scale may be available but hitherto unused. Quality and service competition may bring about these adjustments more effectively than price competition in imperfect markets because the effects of quality and service competition are less feared than those of price competition. It may result in a speedier expulsion of firms because the innovation may react unequally upon the other firms; the products of some may be more firmly entrenched in the favor of purchasers than those of others. But firms thus threatened with expulsion are likely to make some effort to recapture their market. If they adjust the

[1] That is, they contemplate a series of cost curves each relating to a possible quality of product or combination of quality and service.
[2] That is, a series of demand curves.
[3] CHAMBERLIN, *op. cit.*, 80.

nature of their output to approximate to that of the successful firm and recover business before they fail, the old excess of capacity remains. Even if they fail, new rivals are to be expected, if the innovator makes high profits. We have seen that, when price competition is imperfect, excess capacity is to be expected, and while the extent of such capacity *may* be changed by resort to changes in product, there is no good reason to expect it to be less where rivalry is confined to quality and service.

Changes in quality and service do not necessarily operate in the same manner as sales-promotion activities; expenditure on changes in quality cannot always be adjusted gradually. The seller may be faced with a choice between one type of commodity or another; expenditure upon service can sometimes be more closely adjusted, although even here the seller must often choose, for instance, between offering the service of installing the product and not offering that service. The retail store may be able to adjust expenditure on service by relatively small amounts. In so far as such expenditures are capable of adjustment, the new scale of production depends upon the rate at which buyers respond to such expenditures, and the rate at which costs can be reduced as production is reorganized on an increasingly large scale, as in the case of competition in sales promotion.

Competition in service and quality is likely in some cases, however, to increase the total demand for the product. The provision of services which facilitate the repair and maintenance of automobiles tends to increase the demand for all automobiles; widespread facilities for the easy purchase of gasoline tend to increase the demand for it. Competition in the provision of such facilities may, therefore, benefit all firms, including those who do not participate in it; by increasing the response of buyers to such competition, it facilitates the organization of production upon a more economical scale. These gains in efficiency may, however, be immediately offset partly or wholly by changes in the opposite sense in the industries from which spending has been diverted.

Quality and service competition may, like sales promotion, react upon the optimum scale of production. Increasing attention to adjusting the product and the attendant services emphasizes one aspect of entrepreneur activities; the most economical scale for the production of such services may depart from that for any of the other functions and thus necessitate a recalculation of the most economical size of firms; the optimum scale of production under the new conditions may be larger or smaller than it was under the old.

But quality and service competition involves not only the managerial problem of seeking variations from the prevailing type of commodity and service and selecting the most profitable combination of quality and service. It affects also the problem of actual production; the technically optimum scale of production for the new product may be different from that for the old; the provision of more service may necessitate a larger scale of production; the provision of a traveling force for setting up and maintaining agricultural or shoe manufacturing machinery may be economical only if the sales in each area are large; the provision of service stations for automobiles, through ownership and through indirect control by petroleum refiners, may yield benefits only if such stations are generally available over wide areas; the provision of a rapid delivery service by a department store decreases in unit cost as the deliveries within each area increase in volume. The probability of a change in the most economical scale of production is, therefore, considerable.[1]

The effect upon sales of changes in quality and service is as uncertain as the effect of expenditure on sales promotion, with the result that risks are increased and the selection of firms for survival is subject to factors not related to efficiency of production in the narrow sense.

2. THE EFFECT OF QUALITY AND SERVICE COMPETITION UPON THE DISTRIBUTION OF GOODS AND SERVICES

The effects of quality and service competition upon different classes are very different from those of sales promotion. While sales promotion generates a demand for the services of sales promoters, there is no analogous class benefiting from quality and service competition;[2] those who plan changes in quality and service are performing functions traditionally included among those of the entrepreneur, although now more strongly emphasized. Quality and service competition favors the entrepreneur

---

[1] *Cf.* CONSUMER ADVISORY BOARD, *Statement at Hearings on the Operation of the Lumber Code,* Jan. 9, 1933, where it was argued that service competition was prejudicial to the small firms because of the heavy overhead costs of better selling and distributing services.

[2] Firms have, however, been established to advise concerning the attitudes of buyers to existing products and possible variant products.

most skilled in analyzing the probable attitudes of purchasers to variations in the commodity or to various combinations of commodity and service, compared with those whose skill lies mainly in improving the technique of producing and marketing an unchanging product.

The principal peculiarities of quality and service competition are to be found in its effect upon purchasers. In the first place, the statement that costs and prices must always be higher than they would be under free competition[1] loses much of its meaning; costs are increased but so are the utilities offered. If there is a tendency to normal profits, prices must cover the total costs of the commodity and service provided. But for any given price the product is inevitably somewhat inferior to what it would be under price competition, because of the tendency, where competition is imperfect, for resources to be used on less than the most economical scale. "The impossibility of selling all he pleases at the going price creates a tendency, not only towards higher prices, but also towards inferior products."[2] But in comparison with imperfect competition without competition in sales promotion or quality and service, the purchaser may gain; where existing facilities are more fully used or where reorganization permits lower costs, average costs are less than they were before the change in quality and services was made;[3] in other cases, average total costs and prices are higher than they would otherwise be.

The tendency to normal profits may, however, be obstructed by the provision of better quality or service. The provision of better credit facilities and services in connection with setting up and maintaining agricultural implements, is said,[4] for instance, to have given the International Harvester Company a great advantage in competition with its rivals. Where the optimum scale of production for a firm offering the same facilities as the International Harvester Company is very large in relation to the total market, the profits of the Harvester company may exceed a normal rate of return without attracting new firms of the same type because the total market may not be large enough to permit each of two such firms to secure a normal rate of return.

[1] See p. 377.
[2] CHAMBERLIN, op. cit., 100.
[3] In practice the cost of sales-promotion activities necessary to make known the higher quality or greater service will also be taken into account, i.e., the arguments of the present and preceding section must be combined.
[4] COMMISSIONER OF CORPORATIONS, The International Harvester Company, 27.

The extent to which quality and price competition affects prices depends also upon the response of purchasers. Spenders must be induced to reallocate their spending if this competition is to be a success. Sales-promotion activities may increase the utilities obtained by purchasers (by making them better informed) but they do not necessarily, or even frequently, have this effect. Quality and service competition, however, may increase the actual as well as the anticipated utilities obtained by purchasers. It does not follow, therefore, that any diversion of spending from the channels that would otherwise have been selected by purchasers must diminish their utilities. Their satisfactions are increased or diminished according as the gain in utilities exceeds or falls short of the increases in the price they pay. Wherever the price of a commodity has increased over a period of time and it is alleged that the commodity or the attendant services have been improved, it is difficult to decide whether the effect upon purchasers has been favorable or unfavorable. The large bakers, discussing the increase in the price of bread over a long period of time, argued that improvements in the quality of bread explained the increase in its price relatively to the prices of other commodities.[1] There is, however, no scientific criterion of quality; the quality of a food product cannot be judged entirely by its physiological effect; its psychological effect is extremely difficult to assess. The International Harvester Company claimed that part of the rise in the price of some of its products had been due to improvements in quality.[2] The president of the United States Steel Corporation similarly defended[3] the maintenance of the price of steel rails when most prices were falling. The manufacturers of sanitary enameled ware, who were accused of using a patent agreement as a means of fixing uniform prices upon a higher level than had formerly prevailed, argued *inter alia* that the quality had also been raised owing to the elimination of second-grade products;[4] they further argued that "with established prices a manufacturer would be enabled to devote his whole attention to improving the quality of the ware."[5]

[1] *Senate Hearings on Food Prices*, 1931, 59, 75.
[2] U.S. v. International Harvester Co., *Brief for International Harvester Co. (Reargument)*, 1916, 52.
[3] *New York Times*, May 23, 1931.
[4] U.S. v. Standard Sanitary Manufacturing Co. et al., 226 U.S. 20 (1912), *Brief for Standard Sanitary Manufacturing Co.*, 75.
[5] *ibid.*, 83, 78. The manufacturers' own argument that without a price agreement the difficulty of distinguishing first- from second-grade products led to the success of

Improvements in service have been cited as an explanation of the increasing margins obtained by retailers. Retailers may either operate more elaborate stores[1] or more stores. The number of retail outlets for gasoline and probably for many other products[2] appears, however, to be more an effect[3] than a cause of the size of the retailers' margin. The maintenance of the margin attracts so many firms that each is uneconomically small from the point of view of production alone, but, just as changes in quality may benefit purchasers even though they pay higher prices, so these increases in the number of sellers benefit purchasers where the increase in the number of retailers means easier access to goods.[4] But where price competition is eliminated as a result of control of resale prices or margins by manufacturers, by price leadership or custom, this type of competition, like competition in sales promotion, may operate to increase costs and reduce profits (to a normal rate or even less) without yielding to purchasers

---

producers of low-grade products and the decline of enameled ware into disrepute (*ibid.*, 81; U.S. v. Standard Sanitary Manufacturing Co., *Record in Circuit Court of Appeals*, A, 108) suggests that market conditions do not in fact encourage quality competition. The court remarked upon the failure to produce evidence of a decline in sales. Marking the different grades of product according to a uniform classification would have been expected had quality competition been desired.

[1] The increase in the retail margin for meat has been attributed to increasingly costly and elaborate equipment in retail meat stores (*Senate Hearings on Food Prices*, 327). A similar elaboration of equipment has obviously occurred in connection with the retailing of gasoline.

[2] Arguments in favor of permitting manufacturers to fix the retail prices of their products frequently rest upon the assumption that if retailers fix their own prices, some of them will indulge in price competition, with the result that the number of outlets will be diminished. Thus manufacturers seek to avoid price competition between retailers (including chain and department stores) precisely because they desire to maintain an increased number of outlets. A similar condition exists in England as a result of the reduction in the number of banks (but not banking offices) and presumably a reduction in price competition (which is, however, relatively rare in the field of banking in most countries); there has been a great increase in the number of branch banks and also in the cost of operating such banks ((Balfour) COMMISSION ON INDUSTRY AND TRADE, *Final Report*, 1929, 53).

[3] "The evils of the existing situation as regards distribution services are not due to profiteering or to the obtaining of large profits by distributers through the restriction of volume, but rather to the occupation of the field of distribution by too many concerns and the resulting low degree of utilization of facilities and labor, so that nobody gets more by reason of the undue spread between the wholesale and the retail price but there is merely great waste due to duplication and multiplication of distribution facilities" (F.T.C., *Open Price Trade Associations*, 365).

[4] In consequence of the fixing of the minimum combined charge to be made by the wholesaler and retailer of gasoline at 6 cents a gallon under the code for the petroleum industry, distributers complained that they could not compete with cooperatives distributing oil and paying a patronage dividend (CONSUMER ADVISORY BOARD, *Consumers' Cooperatives Distributing Oil and Gasoline*, Mar. 19, 1934). This situation arose partly from the fixing of the margin at a level which considerably exceeded the costs of operating stations in any way approaching their full capacity of operation.

increases in utility comparable with the difference between the prices they pay and those they would pay if price competition existed. This danger could be eliminated[1] if the consumer could continue to choose between the old commodity and its accompanying services at a price which just covered the total long-run costs of production, and each of the new commodities and combinations of quality and service at their corresponding long-run costs. But where price competition is eliminated and rivalry survives only in quality and service, this choice is also eliminated. Consumers may or may not, therefore, have suffered as a result of, for instance, the maintenance of the price of bread while its quality (whatever that may mean) has increased; it may be that they would have selected the former grade of bread at its old price and thus have obtained a greater total of satisfactions then hey now realize.[2]

Even competition in quality or service may, however, diminish the satisfactions obtained by purchasers by obstructing the rational allocation of spending. A seller may seek profit by offering a product of poorer quality or with less service at the same price as formerly;[3] if he sells the same output as before at the same price, but reduces his costs, he increases his profit. This increase in profits is limited, however, to the period of time required for purchasers to discover that their allocations of spending must be revised because the satisfactions yielded by the product are less than they formerly were. It is possible that a further depreciation of the product will offset part of the effect of the loss of business, but again the effect is temporary. The goodwill of a business may be deprived of all value by this policy of depreciation; it is conceivable that such a policy would be profitable where consumers awake slowly to changes in the satisfactions obtained from their continued purchases. This type of competition clearly diminishes the satisfactions obtained by purchasers during the periods in which the estimates of satisfaction upon which they base their allocations of spending are out of accord with the actual satisfactions they secure.

[1] Assuming that purchasers are capable of accurately estimating the utilities to be obtained from the acceptance of each offer.

[2] Similarly, were it possible to permit consumers to choose between a gasoline which was cheaper than other gasolines because the retail margin was lower but which was available at fewer filling stations, and a gasoline at a higher price which included the cost of maintaining a larger number of gas stations each of which did a smaller volume of business, it might be that they would choose the former.

[3] CHAMBERLIN, *op. cit.*, 73 *n*.

But even this competition aimed at short-run profits and originating in the deception of consumers is not wholly bad. If purchasers do not speedily transfer their demand to sellers who have not changed their product, the new product must appear to them to yield the same satisfactions as the old; as its cost of production is less than that of the old product, it represents a better adjustment of production to demand. Rivals or new firms are likely to enter production of the new type of product. If price competition occurs, prices will fall to the new costs and purchasers gain; if price competition is precluded by convention, the number of firms is likely to increase until costs have been raised to the point at which, even for the new type of product selling at the old price, profits are normal, but purchasers fail to share in the benefits of the adjustment of the product. If, however, as soon as they realize the product has been depreciated, purchasers transfer their custom to rivals who have not depreciated the product, the firm losing business may respond by reducing its price, hoping to regain business and secure at least normal profits. Should it succeed in recovering any considerable volume of business, it must be because purchasers consider that while the old product is preferable to the new so long as the prices of the two are equal, the new is preferable to the old when the difference in price is taken into account. The new situation is now comparable to that discussed in the earlier paragraphs of this section; purchasers must select from commodities offering different utilities at different prices.

If other firms continue to offer the old product, they fail to secure normal profits and if they refuse to supply what they often regard as flimsy or degraded products which purchasers *ought* not to purchase, some will in time retire from business. If they accept and adjust to the newly revealed demand, entering into competition in the production of the new product, its price is likely to fall towards the cost of producing it unless price competition is excluded and costs are adjusted to the price. Except in this latter case purchasers are enabled to secure a product which they regard as yielding more utilities per dollar than its predecessor, but whether the increase in satisfactions is as great as possible depends upon the degree in which this type of competition stimulates price competition.

The new product can hardly continue to be called a "depreciated" form of the old. It may be less durable or have less aesthetic attraction, but in so far as the change in spending rests upon any rational consideration of the relative virtues of the two products, the new represents a better adaptation of resources to demand than the old. Quality competition may, therefore, be introduced either by one firm raising the quality of its product above the quality of rival products or by a firm reducing it below the quality of rival products. But the two situations differ in that the former implies the absence of price competition, while the latter is more likely to lead to price changes.

There is a presumption that purchasers will gain from rivalry in quality and service over long periods of time. It stimulates experiments aimed at the closer adaptation of goods and services to the desires of the consumer. Some such changes are made simply to make an impression upon the consumer, and others are doubtless intended merely as a hook upon which the consumer may hang an unsubstantiated belief in the superiority of one seller's product or services over those of another; they are sales-promotion activities. But there remains a considerable residue of probability of benefit to the consumer. Changes that attract purchasers are likely to be imitated by rivals. Experimental changes not only tend to bring about a closer adaptation of products and services to demand as the more successful mutations supersede less successful types of product and service; they also tend to increase the variety of goods and services available, but only where there is considerable variety in the desires of buyers.[1]

[1] Professor Hotelling has denied this tendency ("Stability in Competition," *Econ. Jour.*, 39: 41 (1929)). He argues that there is a tendency to excessive homogeneity of products arising out of the desire on the part of each manufacturer to cover almost the whole market which his rival covers; there is "a tendency to make only slight deviations in order to have for the new commodity as many buyers of the old as possible, to get, so to speak, *between* one's competitors and the mass of customers" (*ibid.*, 54). This contention also appears to conflict with the suggestion often made that non-price competition aims at the subdivision of markets into partially noncompeting groups as a result of the efforts of each seller to mark off his customers from those of his rivals. Professor Hotelling admits that sellers in imperfect markets aim at a measure of differentiation of products, but contends that the measure aimed at is one just sufficient to make consumers feel that the product of one seller is different from that of another; if both commodities are believed to be identical a slight price cut by one will cause all the business available to shift to the price cutter. Furthermore, his conclusions apply only to special circumstances, which are not altogether in accord with practical conditions. Sellers are assumed to be very few. Buyers are assumed to be equally distributed in their tastes as between each grade of the product. To take Professor Hotelling's example, it is assumed that consumers can be regarded as varying by infinitesimal degrees in the sweetness of the cider they like. Should it appear that considerable numbers of buyers agree upon the degree of sweetness they prefer, *i.e.*, that there is a grouping about certain degrees of sweetness, then the approach to homogeneity of product cannot be expected. Furthermore, it is assumed that buyers, being regarded as varying by infinitesimal

This tendency to adapt products to the desires of purchasers may involve costs in the adaptation of plant, in the application of resources to the search for more profitable types of product, and the risk that changes will be unsuccessful. It may be possible to charge prices that cover these costs; they may, however, fall upon investors through failure to secure normal profits and even through loss of capital.[1]

Quality and service competition increases the complexity of the task of allocating income so as to maximize the satisfactions obtained by spending it. Purchasers are confronted not with a number of offers differing only in price but with offers differing in both commodity *plus* service and price. The variety of offers is now so great (and often information concerning the nature of the goods and services offered is so small) that rational selection is often beyond the powers of purchasers. Indirectly such competition induces expenditure upon sales pressure to crystallize the dazed minds of "prospects." But the variations in price and utilities also increase the difficulties of those who would eliminate price cutting; it is more difficult to identify price cutting where the variety of products and services is great. Each firm may aim at stabilizing the price of its own product, but the resistance to changes in price is reduced when they can be attributed to changes in product.

Quality and service competition reduces the risks of investment in so far as it operates effectively as a substitute for price competition. But it does not invariably so operate. The more differentiated products become, the greater is the probability of differences in price between sellers. Not only is it extremely difficult to distinguish between price cutting and differences in price due to differences in utilities offered, but also there is the new risk of shifts of business due to changes in quality and service. Rivals may discover a product or service that appeals to buyers;

---

degrees in the quality of the product that they prefer, do not diminish their demand because that particular quality of product is not available, that is, if there is a tendency for all cider to be of medium sweetness, those who prefer very sweet and those who prefer very acid cider buy just as much of the medium type as they would if the cider available were of precisely the grade which they prefer. In fact, therefore, this tendency operates only within limits in which departures from type of product most desired do not affect demand. Professor Hotelling agrees that "the elasticity of demand of particular groups does mitigate the tendency to excessive similarity of competing commodities, but not enough. It leads some factories to make cheap shoes for the poor and others to make expensive shoes for the rich, but all shoes are too much alike." (*ibid*, 57; *cf.* also the criticism of an analogous aspect of this problem at CHAMBERLIN, *op. cit.*, 194 *ff.*)

[1] See p. 396.

a firm may make expensive and unsuccessful experiments in quality and service competition. If the riskiness of the industry fails to restrict investment sufficiently to permit prices which in the long run cover all costs (including losses from these causes), purchasers secure some of their gains at the expense of investors.

In conclusion, quality and service competition may accelerate the adjustment of resources to demand; it may cause maladjustments in industries from which demand is deflected. It may change the most economical scale of production and reduce the average cost of production. It attaches increasing importance to the managerial function of adjusting products to the attitudes of consumers. It affects purchasers by changing both the prices they pay and the satisfactions they obtain, and the net result of the two changes is difficult to judge. Prices are likely to be higher than would yield normal profits if the new product were produced under the most efficient methods available. Quality and service competition may obstruct the most advantageous allocation of expenditure if products are depreciated, but even depreciation may facilitate the adjustment of products to demand and incidentally increase the variety of products available. Quality and service competition may obstruct the elimination of price competition, but at the same time increase the emphasis upon sales promotion; it may induce changes in appearance which are not in fact changes in quality; it may stimulate expenditure to emphasize changes which may or may not increase the satisfactions obtainable by purchasers. Investors may, but do not necessarily, free themselves from the risks of price competition and must accept new risks peculiar to quality competition.

C. *Competition in Style*

Competition in style partakes of some of the qualities of competition in quality on the one hand, and sales promotion on the other. Competition in quality involves changes in the nature of the product affecting its capacity to serve the purposes of the purchaser. If "quality" is limited to purposes for which scientific tests of capacity are at least conceivable,[1] style is concerned

---

[1] A better quality of automobile, for instance, usually implies in part an automobile offering less costly transportation per mile, and in part one offering greater comfort, still assessable, however, in terms of physical tests concerning such matters as noise, vibration, and seating space. Presumably a better quality loaf of bread is thought of in terms of physical tests, which may be stretched to include the physical effects of psychological reactions to a high-grade loaf.

with the aesthetic emotions of the purchaser. If the purposes of the purchaser be defined to include the desire for aesthetic satisfactions, style competition must be included as a special case of competition in quality. But competition in style differs from competition in quality in that changes in the physical qualities of the product are made more frequently and continuously, as a matter of deliberate policy, than where competition in quality is aimed merely at seeking more precisely and completely to satisfy demand. No sharp line of distinction is possible. In so far as changes in style are aimed at increasing the total demand for the product, they resemble sales-promotion activities except for the fact of accompanying changes in the commodity calculated to yield more direct satisfactions.

1. EFFECT OF STYLE COMPETITION ON THE ORGANIZATION OF PRODUCTION

Style competition reacts upon the organization of production most nearly like competition in quality. Changes in style, however, are generally made with greater frequency and often with greater regularity than changes in quality. Each change in style is doubtless made by producers after taking into account probable demand for each style at each price and the probable costs of production of each quantity; sellers endeavor to select the style and volume of output that will yield the maximum of profit. It is of course more difficult to estimate the demand for new styles than for new qualities. Moreover, success in selecting the most popular style is less likely to enable any firm to drive out competitors where excess capacity prevails; rivals are frequently able to imitate the successful style and avoid losing the whole of the business for the season; firms are likely to remain in the hope of recovering business in the next season, a prospect which is real enough in view of the lack of knowledge concerning the elements making for the popularity of new styles; only continued lack of success results in expulsion. Style competition, in so far as it leads to frequent and serious shifts of business, is more likely to increase the amount of unused capacity in an industry and thus raise the average cost of production above what it would be if all plant were continuously occupied. Furthermore, shifts in business arising from success in style changes are likely to facilitate a larger and more economical scale of production only where one firm is continuously and progressively more successful.

Changes in style in one industry often involve changes in the raw materials used; manufacturers of clothing may change their demands for cotton, wool, silk, rayon, leather, and other materials from season to season; shoe manufacturers may change their demand for leather, for different kinds of leather, and for textiles. These industries supplying raw materials suffer from the spasmodic use of their equipment, and their average costs are higher than they would be under continuous full operation.

Rapid changes in style also affect the costs of dealers and retailers by increasing the losses arising from the obsolescence of inventories. From these losses they have, however, found a partial escape in "hand-to-mouth buying," *i.e.* more frequent and smaller purchases; part of the risk is transferred to the producer who can sometimes reduce it by holding inventories in semimanufactured goods capable of being speedily finished in the style most in demand.[1] But hand-to-mouth buying tends to a more spasmodic production; it prevents continuous full utilization of plants and raises average costs (which are further increased by the greater expense of dealing with many smaller orders). The introduction of style changes in recent years into almost all branches of the cotton industry,[2] combined with the seasonal nature of the business (which necessitates the manufacture and purchase of goods further in advance than would otherwise be necessary), has very greatly increased its risks and its losses. The demands upon mills fluctuate more widely than formerly; their costs have increased owing to the greater capital needed.[3]

While over periods of time increasing emphasis upon style has doubtless increased the demand for some products, *sustained* competition in style does not attract continuously increasing demand. No continuous reactions upon the organization of production can, therefore, be expected from this source.

The effect of competition in style upon the most economical size of firms is not at all clear. If style designers are employed by manufacturers, a few very successful designers may secure large rewards and only the larger producers be able to employ them. Designing may, however, be so important that production must

[1] VON BECKERATH, *op. cit.*, 195.
[2] It is estimated that in 1914 only about 20 per cent of cotton goods were affected by style changes which, furthermore, were relatively slow. In 1932, however, practically all fabrics from flour bags to sheets and automobile upholstery were subject to changes in style. (MURCHISON, "Stabilization in the Cotton Textile Industry," *Proceedings of 45th Annual Meeting of American Economic Association*, 1932, 75.)
[3] *ibid.*, 76.

be easily and speedily adaptable to the ideas of the designer, or to rival designs that are proving successful; this flexibility may be difficult to secure in a large firm and the risks of adapting a large volume of production to the ideas of one or a few designers may be so great as to discourage production upon a large scale. Moreover, it is doubtful whether leadership in introducing style changes which are later successful is an important determinant of success. Such leadership may be very costly, involving as it does the expense of experimental work, some of which must prove unprofitable and involve heavy losses on inventories sold at low prices. "For most concerns the safest rule seems to be to carry what people want after their wants have been demonstrated."[1] The reactions of purchasers to various new styles offered are so incapable of forecast that the element of chance affecting survival is very great. But in many clothing industries changes from season to season are, at least in their main lines, uniform for most producers; the element of chance is, therefore, much less than it would be if every season brought from every seller an innovation unrelated to those of his rivals. Furthermore, it is not impossible that competition in style tends to reduce the costs of production in some industries; while there is rarely one style at any time, there is usually only a small number; fashion tends to restrict changes to a limited variety of styles and especially of colors of clothes available at any time.[2] This limitation reduces both the cost of production and the cost of distribution (by restricting the capital needed for inventories and the losses arising from their obsolescence).

2. THE EFFECT OF STYLE COMPETITION UPON THE DISTRIBUTION OF GOODS AND SERVICES

The effect of style competition upon different classes is again somewhat similar to the effect of quality competition. Style designers and managers skillful in selecting successful styles gain wherever style changes are frequently made.

Purchasers must necessarily pay a higher price for each product than they would if it were continuously demanded for long periods. Prices must cover the cost of employing designers and the cost of changing styles, including losses on inventories arising from the frequent obsolescence of products. In some

[1] NYSTROM, *Economics of Fashion*, 30.
[2] NYSTROM, *Fashion Merchandising*, 83.

industries the cost of designs alone is said to account for about one fourth of their entire income.[1] The risk that producers will make unfortunate selections of styles and have poor seasons or large inventory losses is sufficiently real to be taken account of by firms contemplating entry into the industry; the optimism of new competitors may, however, prevent the restriction of investment in the industry to an amount such that over long periods prices will cover total costs. But even so, prices are likely to be considerably higher than if these risks were not present.

Purchasers must pay higher prices than they would in the absence of style changes, but they are not necessarily worse off to the extent of the increase in prices. The response of many purchasers to style changes suggests that they secure additional satisfactions. It is true that their response is not the result of a free choice between an unchanging product and one with changing styles; frequently no such choice is available. Response to style changes is, moreover, an integral part of a complex social situation from which escape is difficult. But there is no reason to deny that frequent changes in the aesthetic qualities of products stimulate aesthetic appreciation and yield additional satisfactions. Changes in style also facilitate ostentation by reference either to economic superiority[2] or superiority in taste and again yield satisfactions. But there is no means of judging whether these satisfactions are proportioned to the increased costs of production involved in providing them.

Style competition also affects the distribution of spending by purchasers. It is often criticized because it induces consumers to abandon goods before they have lost their capacity to serve their purpose; clothes are abandoned before they are "worn out." This criticism is based upon a narrow definition of purpose and disapproval of the attitudes of consumers. It is not uneconomical for individuals to seek aesthetic satisfactions even at the expense of non-aesthetic. Changes in style serve also to introduce changes in quality; innovations conceived merely

[1] VON BECKERATH, *op. cit.*, 195. In the upholstery and drapery textile industry designs are said to cost from $500 to $800 each, plus the cost of experimental runs and further revisions (*Code of Fair Competition for the Upholstery and Drapery Textile Industry under NRA*, Report of Administrator, 262).

[2] Economic superiority may be indicated either by ability to keep pace with frequent changes in style (*i.e.*, ability to keep up to date) or by ability to purchase a variety of patterns of a commodity serving a single purpose in the narrower sense.

as style changes sometimes prove difficult to dislodge because purchasers obtain satisfactions other than purely aesthetic ones.[1] The simplification of clothing and its better adaptability to economic and physiological considerations may be traced to this source, although it is always hazardous to assume that such changes will persist. Changes in style also affect price competition. Like changes in quality, changes in style place great difficulties in the way of avoiding price competition because of the lack of standardization of products; industries in which style is important are often those from which there are complaints of drastic competition and frequent failures of firms.[2] Economies in production may therefore be more likely to be transmitted to consumers, although costs remain higher than they would be without style competition. Finally, style competition is in fact often accompanied by expenditure upon advertising intended to acquaint buyers with changes in style and to stimulate them to respond.[3] These expenditures on advertising tend also, therefore, to raise the level of costs and prices.

Style competition affects investors mainly through its introduction of a highly speculative element into demand for the product; it offers no escape from price competition or sales-promotion activities. The magnitude of the risks tends to increase the number of business failures in industries affected by style; the probabilities of high profits are probably overestimated by potential investors, with the result that prices do not cover the total costs of the industry as a whole over long periods.

In summary, style competition rarely operates to introduce economies of production, but tends to increase the costs of manufacturing and marketing above the level that would prevail without such competition. Purchasers must pay higher prices but the incalculability of the risks introduced may throw some of these costs upon investors, more particularly as style competition obstructs efforts to eliminate price competition. But in so far as purchasers seek aesthetic satisfactions and obtain

---

[1] For example, shirtwaists, introduced in the nineties, remained popular for twenty-five years, and wrist watches and low shoes, introduced during the World War, have persisted in use (NYSTROM, *Economics of Fashion*, 21).

[2] Resort to style changes has, however, been attributed to the desire to avoid cut-throat competition (BELL, *Fixed Costs and Market Price*, Quart. Jour. Econ., 32: 518 (1918)).

[3] Organized attempts to change fashions have, however, often been abortive, while great changes have spread without any aid from sales-promotion activities (NYSTROM, *Economics of Fashion*, 13).

them from frequent changes in style, their increase in satisfactions must be counted against the higher prices they pay.

III. THE CHANGING IMPORTANCE OF NON-PRICE COMPETITION

Earlier chapters have revealed an increasing tendency for manufacturers to limit price competition. Non-price competition frequently but not invariably facilitates this escape from price competition. Rivalry continues, although, as we have now seen, in forms that are by no means always profitable to producers or beneficial to purchasers. But is there any evidence that these forms of rivalry are in their turn being extinguished?

A. *Evidence of the Increasing Importance of Non-price Competition*

It is a commonplace of all recent criticism of the operation of the productive system that expenditure upon promoting sales has increased at an enormous rate in the past few decades.[1] Precise information on the subject is not available; there is no general information concerning expenditure upon sales promotion other than advertising, and information concerning advertising is often restricted to that involving payments to the publishers of newspapers and magazines. Expenditure on printed advertising appears to have remained fairly constant between 1911 and 1918,[2] after which year it began to increase sharply.[3] Information believed to cover 90 per cent of the total non-farm advertising in the United States but relating only to firms spending more than $10,000 per annum on advertising showed that expenditure on magazine advertising increased from 48.9 million dollars in 1918 to 107.7 million dollars in 1920 and declined to 77.4 million

---

[1] A brief summary of the history of advertising will be found at STARCH, *Principles of Advertising*, Chap. II.
[2] *ibid.*, Chap. III.
[3] Expenditure on printed advertising was estimated at about one billion dollars in 1923 (STARCH, *Principles of Advertising*, 36.) By 1927 expenditure on newspaper advertising alone had reached about one and a half billion dollars (NATIONAL BUREAU OF ECONOMIC RESEARCH, *Recent Economic Changes*, 402), and that on magazine advertising 178 million dollars by 1930 (CURTIS PUBLISHING COMPANY, *Leading Advertisers*, 1922–1931). The Federal Trade Commission estimated that in 1929 expenditure on advertising in the leading monthly and weekly magazines and representative farm magazines, together with radio advertising at the larger stations (but excluding daily newspapers), cost about 231 million dollars, of which 35.9 million dollars was on drug and toilet articles and 28.2 on food and food beverages (F.T.C., *Annual Report*, 1931, 111). About one billion dollars per annum is estimated to have been paid for advertising to the publishers of daily, weekly, and monthly periodicals between 1930 and 1933 (F.T.C., *Annual Report*, 1932, 43; 1933, 123).

NON-PRICE COMPETITION 413

dollars in 1922.[1] Similar statistics relating only to magazine advertising and including 36 leading periodicals in 1922 and 35 in 1930, and relating only to firms spending over $10,000 per annum on advertising, showed, among others, these changes:[2]

TABLE XII

Industry	1922 (millions of dollars)	1930 (millions of dollars)
Automobiles	12.1	27.7
Beverages	0.95	3.79
Candy and gum	0.68	2.46
Electrical products (including radio)	3.87	14.67
Foods	10.4	26.35
Furniture and floor coverings	2.15	5.17
Musical instruments	1.92	4.06
Office equipment	2.20	4.16
Toilet goods	6.9	22.56
Wearing apparel	5.2	7.92

Information as to total advertising expenditure, differing somewhat from year to year in the minimum expenditures included, and also in the number of magazines included (the number ranging from 30 to 36), shows an upward trend from 22.6 millions in 1915 to 178.9 millions in 1930, an increase of 691 per cent.[3] It is clear that there was a very great increase in expenditure on advertising during the decade from 1920 to 1930, although the amount of the increase cannot be measured.[4] The industries in which the greatest increases occurred were drugs, toilet products, foods, automobiles, and electrical products. But, as might

[1] Classification according to industries revealed the following notable increases (in millions of dollars):

Industry	1913	1922
Drugs and toilet articles	2.4	11.2
Foods	3.5	10.7
Automotive products	3.9	9.9
Clothing and dry goods	2.9	7.3
Furniture and furnishings	1.2	6.5

Advertising in these journals upon cigarettes and tobacco fell from 1.09 million dollars in 1918 to 0.95 million dollars in 1922 (CROWELL PUBLISHING COMPANY, *National Markets and National Advertising*, 1922, 60, 181).

[2] CURTIS PUBLISHING COMPANY, *Leading Advertisers*, 1922–1931.

[3] CURTIS PUBLISHING COMPANY, *Leading Advertisers*, 1922–1931. The total rose to 110.7 million dollars in 1920, fell to about 78 million dollars in 1921 and 1922, and then rose continuously until 1930.

[4] A summary of the estimates of expenditure upon advertising over a period of time will be found at STARCH, *Principles of Advertising*, Chap. III.

be expected, these expenditures declined with the general contraction of business after 1929. Payments by national advertisers to the publishers of 65 weekly and monthly magazines were estimated[1] at 192.3 millions in 1930 and 156.2 millions in 1931.

As the total value of products has increased during this period the percentage of unit costs attributable to advertising cannot have increased as fast as the aggregate expenditure on advertising. Sample investigations of the proportion of sales revenue spent on advertising have suggested[2] that 3 per cent or less of the sales revenue of manufacturers and 2 per cent or less of that of retailers was spent on advertising, making a total of between 4 and 5 per cent. Subsequent information obtained by the Federal Trade Commission from a sample of 450 manufacturers revealed that advertising costs increased between 1924 and 1926 more than any other element of costs; sales had increased 17.4 per cent and advertising costs 24.6 per cent, while profits had increased 29.7 per cent. Expenditure by these manufacturers for all industries and for the three years 1924, 1925, and 1926 taken together represented about 3 per cent of their revenue from sales, the highest percentage being found in the "other metals" group (7.1) and the lowest in the food products group (1.6).[3] The percentage of net sales spent upon advertising by wholesalers, however, showed no upward trend between 1924 and 1927.[4] During the same period the total sums spent on advertising by the chain stores more than doubled. The average percentage of sale price spent on advertising in 1927 by department stores was 3.97 and by chain stores 1.13.[5] The percentage of retail selling price that was spent on advertising by manufacturers,

---

[1] F.T.C., *Annual Report*, 1932, 43.
[2] STARCH, *Principles of Advertising*, 1926, 56. See also *ibid.*, 49, where information is given separately for a number of well-known branded and advertised products in 1916.
[3] F.T.C., *Resale Price Maintenance*, II, 23-25. High percentages were also found in chemicals and allied products (probably including petroleum products), 5.6; machinery, 5.4; clothing, 3.7; boots and shoes, 2.4; iron and steel, 2.4; automobiles, 2.1; and rubber products, 1.9.
[4] The highest percentage for the period of four years was found in the drug industry where it was 0.43 and the next highest in groceries and in plumbing supplies, in each of which it was 0.29 (*op. cit.*, II, 43).
[5] *op. cit.*, II, 125. In 1934, however, the Federal Trade Commission reported that the ratio of advertising expenditure to the value of sales of chain stores had been 1.15 per cent in 1919, 1.30 per cent in 1922, 1.42 per cent in 1925, and 1.52 per cent in 1928, an increase of nearly 17 per cent over the whole period (*Chain Store Advertising*, 1934, 10).

wholesalers, and retailers together in 1926 was 7.39 for dry goods, 6.34 for drugs, 2.30 for groceries, and 2.26 for hardware.[1]

The causes of this increase in expenditure are of course not difficult to discover. Firstly, it is predicated upon the existence of a cheap press, the price of which can be vastly reduced if it carries advertising. A cheap press in turn, of course, depends upon the existence of a large literate population. In more recent years radio broadcasting has provided access to the emotions of large numbers of people who need not even be literate. Practically the whole cost of this form of publicity is borne by advertisers. Secondly, such advertising is stimulated by the presence of a large number of people of changing economic status. A larger proportion of the income of such people is amenable to diversion by advertising than where incomes are almost constant and their allocation is dominated by habit. Thirdly, the introduction of new products stimulates advertising to make the new commodities known. Fourthly, advertising is doubtless related to the increased scale of production, although in a variety of ways. A great deal of magazine advertising is disseminated over a very wide area and, therefore, can be fully exploited only by firms able to distribute over areas of similar size. On the other hand, profits from the promotion of mergers have tended to develop firms large enough to be able to undertake advertising expenditures upon this scale. Fifthly, changes in the machinery of distribution have induced advertising, particularly by manufacturers. Manufacturers not controlling their own retail outlets are conscious of the power of the retailer to divert purchases to a particular brand of product (owing to the prevailing ignorance of the qualities of advertised products). Heavy expenditures upon advertising to induce purchasers to ask for a particular brand and to resist suggestions that others are better limit the influence of the retailer. Finally, increasing resistance to price cutting has led, as we have seen, where rivalry lingers on, to its expression in other forms, one of the most important of which is advertising.

Little or no evidence is available concerning the changing prevalence of other forms of sales-promotion activity.[2] Nor is there any satisfactory information concerning changes in attitude

---

[1] F.T.C., *Resale Price Maintenance*, II, 128.

[2] Salaries of traveling salesmen were crudely estimated in 1926 at two billion dollars, and the salaries and wages of retail stores at 10 to 15 per cent of sales revenue (STARCH, *op. cit.*, 57), but these expenses cannot be wholly classified as costs of sales promotion.

to quality and service competition, although, in so far as it is the outcome of reduced emphasis upon price competition, it has doubtless increased greatly in recent years. It is also certain that style competition has notably increased. The industrial revolution has replaced local and traditional methods of dress by clothing less durable and more frequently changed in style. New products, such as automobiles and radios, have also been subjected to style changes in the effort to increase demand for them; it has been prophesied that emphasis upon style will increase.[1] Increasing emphasis upon style changes has doubtless been facilitated by increases in the size of many of the smaller incomes, increasing literacy, increasing emphasis upon sales promotion, a more widespread desire on the part of those with smaller incomes to imitate the behavior of those with the larger incomes, and the adoption of more effective methods of cheaply reproducing new styles.[2]

B. Evidence of the Declining Importance of Non-price Competition

Scattered evidence of forces making for a decline in the importance of non-price competition is beginning to emerge. Branded articles supported by heavy advertising have produced their own reaction in the form of chain and department store brands much less advertised and sold at lower prices. Emphasis upon the heavy expenditure upon advertising other brands stimulates the demand for the less advertised. The passage of the Federal Trade Commission Act prohibiting "unfair competition" has produced a persistent campaign by the Federal Trade Commission against false advertising; it has been limited, however, to the elimination of the cruder sorts of advertising or minor falsities in the advertising of minor firms; advertising in general has been little affected. Trade associations sought to eliminate some forms of non-price competition, largely because their persistence undermines efforts to eliminate price competition;[3] the codes of fair competition under the National Industrial Recovery Act[4] provided

---

[1] NYSTROM, *Fashion Merchandising*, v. Professor Nystrom believes, however, that "we are now in an era in which business progress and success are much more dependent upon producing and offering consumers what they want than upon attempting to create new wants and new demands. Neither clever advertising nor high-pressure selling can in these days of sophisticated consumers make a profitable market for that which consumers do not want." (*ibid.*, iv.)

[2] NYSTROM, *Economics of Fashion* 25.

[3] See Chap. II.

[4] See Chap. X.

a better opportunity to pursue the same policy. Competition in quality and service is restricted by the standardization of products which has been sought by some trade associations for many years[1] and which was further provided for in a number of the codes under the National Industrial Recovery Act.[2] Attempts have been made to control competition in style by agreement between producers; a number of resolutions between 1910 and 1915, aimed at fixing styles, were passed by trade associations and similar bodies; attempts were made to fix the length and cut of coats and the cut and style of skirts for each season.[3] These efforts ceased, however, in 1915 and appear not to have been revived. The only limitations upon competition in style that are now of any importance are those incidental to the standardization of products; where products are standardized for all sellers it is difficult to arrange for speedy and frequent changes.

Non-price competition is falling in a small but increasing degree under control analogous to that affecting price competition wherever non-price competition expresses itself in forms likely to cover price competition. Such forms of non-price competition, as advertising, the employment of large numbers of salesmen, and the like, are as yet, however, completely unaffected by this tendency.

[1] See Chap. II.
[2] See Chap. X.
[3] NYSTROM, *Fashion Merchandising*, 57.

CHAPTER IX

THE INTEGRATION OF INDUSTRIAL OPERATIONS

I. Integration and the régime of mixed monopoly and competition—II. Imperfections in the capital market and integration—III. The principal patterns of integration—*A*. Vertical integration—1. Influences affecting such integration—2. The principal consequences—*B*. Integration of the production of commodities requiring similar selling organizations—1. Influences affecting such integration—2. The principal consequences—*C*. Integration of the production of substitute goods and services—1. Influences affecting such integration—2. The principal consequences—*D*. Territorial integration—1. Influences affecting such integration—2. The principal consequences—IV. Conclusions.

I. INTEGRATION AND THE RÉGIME OF MIXED MONOPOLY AND COMPETITION

The changes in the policies of industrial management outlined in the preceding chapters have been accompanied by changes in the variety of operations under common management, *i.e.*, by changes in the patterns of industrial integration. The present chapter is concerned with the relation between the changes in these patterns and declining emphasis on price competition and with the economic consequences of these changes. It is not a balanced analysis of industrial integration.

The operations integrated under common management fall into a number of patterns often crudely classified into vertical and horizontal. Vertical integration relates to combinations of operations such that the finished product of one is the raw material of another. Horizontal integration, on the other hand, relates usually to the scale upon which industrial operations are organized[1] and does not fall within the scope of the present chapter. Many combinations of operations under single control constitute neither vertical nor horizontal integration; a single management may manufacture products requiring a similar selling organization, products which serve as substitutes one for the other, and products marketed over a wide geographical territory. The forces which have given rise to these types of integration and their probable

[1] The word integration used in this connection sometimes relates also to the *process* by which *changes* in the scale of industrial operation are brought about (as when it is applied to the merging of firms conducting similar operations).

outcome are considered separately for each pattern of integration. Imperfections in the capital market affect integration, but as they do not induce any particular pattern in integration, they are discussed separately from the various patterns.

II. IMPERFECTIONS IN THE CAPITAL MARKET AND INTEGRATION

The allocation of capital between different uses is obviously not effected in a free market in which those responsible for supply and demand are entirely rational and completely informed. The imperfections of the market, particularly the imperfect knowledge of investors, and the inequality of access to capital, are a part[1] cause of promotion profits in times of general optimism. Promotion profits arise usually from the merging of existing firms; in the past these mergers have often increased the scale of management control within a market (*i.e.*, they have been horizontal combines). Promotion profits may originate, however, in the prospect of gains from integration. The profits from the promotion of the United States Steel Corporation flowed in part from the prospect of gains from vertical integration; the United Shoe Machinery Company offered gains from a different pattern of integration.

The inequality of access to capital is also reflected in the financial advantages of large firms. A large unit has access to the stock market and is usually also able to secure bank loans more cheaply than small firms. Frequently it also employs persons specialized in the financing of enterprises, and of whose services it wishes to make the fullest use. For both these reasons the large firm may be able to refinance firms in difficulty when they cannot finance themselves. It can also finance new enterprises more cheaply than adventurous business men seeking to give them an independent existence. Many of the largest firms, therefore, develop a series of subsidiary concerns engaged in lines allied to those of the parent company because of their easier access to capital (*e.g.*, the General Electric Company, Du Pont de Nemours

---

[1] Even if investors were fully informed, and all business men had equal access to capital, the imperfections of other markets would leave opportunities for promotion profits. If new methods of production make large-scale operations more economical, and if price competition is not perfect, it may pay to merge existing businesses rather than establish one of the new optimum size. If the new methods involve production on a scale which renders the market imperfect, the capitalized value of the expected income of the merger may exceed the total of the capitalized value of the merging enterprises, and someone can annex the difference.

and Company, the Standard Oil Company of New Jersey, and many others).

Inequality of access to capital is often combined with inequality of access to knowledge of profit opportunities, the large firm enjoying advantages in both respects. Firms of sufficient size to undertake technical research on a large scale may acquire a great deal of (often unexpected) knowledge concerning new products and new methods of production. If they utilize this information themselves, they develop a series of subsidiary firms and become an integrated unit whose pattern of integration is explicable only in these historical terms (*e.g.*, the General Electric and Westinghouse companies). Large firms often possess an advantage in financing research on a large scale. They are better able than small units to continue investment for a considerable, and often uncertain, period of time, in the hope of ultimately being able to utilize the results, a matter also requiring considerable capital. Research tends, therefore, to be conducted by large firms engaged also in production; the independent specialist inventor becomes less important.

The integration of research with more immediately productive activities facilitates the utilization of new knowledge. The difficulties in the way of the poverty-stricken inventor seeking to market his invention are too well known for comment. If the knowledge of a new product is born into the hands of a corporation with easy access to capital, the initiation of the new industry depends less than formerly upon access to the capital market, and, therefore, upon the opinions of bankers and investment houses. Moreover, as funds are available for promoting the new product the new industry is likely to be developed more rapidly than otherwise. The disadvantages of small firms in the capital market are somewhat reduced in significance by the tendency for new industries to develop within large firms in other industries.[1]

The now obvious separation of corporation management from ownership permits managers, within wide limits, to determine the portion of profit to be paid to the owners. It has become conventional to retain within the corporation a considerable share of the declared profits.[2] In part this policy arises from a well-founded

---

[1] The firm controlling the new knowledge may, however, also be interested in a branch of production in which its investment may be rendered obsolete if the new knowledge were immediately exploited.

[2] Between 1922 and 1927 corporations in the United States "saved" on the average 29.4 per cent of their net income (MEANS, "The Large Corporation,"

belief that what are called profits by accountants are not necessarily profits in an economic sense; intervals of a year are, in most industries, too narrow a basis for precise calculation of profits. Part of the so-called profit is transferred to a reserve intended to stabilize the incomes of stockholders and also to maintain the business in existence during periods of bad trade. This "conservative financing" tends, however, to develop into one of deliberate expansion out of profits. Desire for size as a direct means of satisfaction to managers may lead to ventures into allied lines when the number of firms in a market is so small that further expansion in that market may be difficult if not risky. Sharing the market through a cartel agreement or otherwise, may, at least temporarily, prevent expansion within the market in which it already operates. Thus desire for size may express itself in integration, without however compelling any particular pattern of integration; it is facilitated by the divorce of ownership from control.[1]

III. THE PRINCIPAL PATTERNS OF INTEGRATION

A. *Vertical Integration*

1. INFLUENCES AFFECTING VERTICAL INTEGRATION

Almost every business unit brings under a single management a series of operations performed in sequence upon each unit of material. Where the series is short, or there are no points in the sequence at which the product is commonly thought of as salable, the series is not usually regarded as an example of vertical integration although logically it is such. Where the product is thought of as salable at various stages in its progress through the series of operations the firm is regarded as vertically integrated, *e.g.*, a firm producing pig iron and converting the pig iron into steel. Vertical integration thus dictated by the opportunity to secure technical economies of production is not directly caused by the decline of price competition although it may contribute to that decline.

The decline of price competition may induce vertical integration where no technical advantages are to be obtained in produc-

---

Amer. Econ. Rev., 21: 29 (1931). See also WEIDENHAMMER, *Amer. Econ. Rev.*, 23: 36 (1933)).
[1] In Germany quota cartels have tended to induce vertical integration as a means of satisfying the desire for expansion partly cut off in other directions (VON BECKERATH, *Modern Industrial Organization*, 241).

tion. Where buyers believe that, as a result of the decline of price competition, the price of a product they purchase exceeds the cost at which they could produce it for themselves they are likely to produce it. Monopoly elements appeared early in the steel industry, and vertical integration subsequently became important. The reorganization of the industry between about 1888 and 1900 resulted in the establishment of a number of monopolistic or semi-monopolistic units fabricating crude steel into sheets, tubes, and the like, and of a small number of producers of crude steel also interested in the prior processes of mining and shipping. When, however, the National Tube Company decided to cease purchasing its crude steel from the Carnegie company, Carnegie responded with a threat to erect the finest tube works in the world.[1] The formation of the United States Steel Corporation resolved this conflict by integrating the fabrication of crude steel with its production. The International Harvester Company has found it very profitable to manufacture its own steel through the Wisconsin Steel Company.[2] After the acceptance of the code of fair competition for the steel industry under the National Industrial Recovery Act the raising of prices, the withdrawal of many discounts and allowances, and insistence upon the inclusion of transportation charges in delivered prices even when no transportation services were supplied, caused great opposition among one of the most important classes of steel users, viz., the automobile manufacturers. The General Motors Corporation considered the desirability of producing its own steel and is said to have negotiated for the purchase of a steel manufacturing business, with the result that special concessions were made to purchasers in portions of Michigan.[3] The Ford Motor Company announced an expansion of its steel manufacturing plant to "render it independent of all other manufacturers of steel."[4] Doubtless the ownership of ore railroads by the United States Steel Corporation, of pipe lines by the former Standard Oil

---

[1] *Cf.* SEAGER and GULICK, *Trust and Corporation Problems*, 219. The seriousness of the conflict was enhanced by the threat to integrate by adding to the existing facilities for production.

[2] COMMISSIONER OF CORPORATIONS, *The International Harvester Company*, 269; F.T.C., *The High Price of Farm Implements*, 670.

[3] F.T.C., *The Practices of the Steel Industry under the Code*, 1934, 46. The base prices of the products of most interest to automobile manufacturers were subsequently reduced (*New York Times*, June 30, 1934). See also *New York Times*, Feb. 2, 1934.

[4] *New York Times*, Aug. 31, 1934.

Company of New Jersey, and of stockyards by the large meat packers was in part motivated by the desire to avoid payment to others of high profits available in these fields. More recently high charges for the transportation of crude oil by pipe line led the Standard Oil Company (Indiana) to declare that it intended to cease using the pipe lines of the Sinclair Oil Company and to build its own. The Sinclair company accordingly offered to sell a one half interest in its pipe-line company to the Standard company which accepted the offer.[1] The number of cans made by packers for their own use has greatly increased since the formation of the American Can Company. High prices for electric motors for refrigerators after the approval of the codes under the National Industrial Recovery Act were reported to have placed the non-integrated producers at such a disadvantage compared with the integrated (*e.g.*, the General Motors Corporation, the General Electric Company, and the Westinghouse Electric and Manufacturing Company) as to cause the non-integrated to threaten to manufacture their own motors.[2]

Fear of unduly high prices for raw materials in the future may also induce the integration of the production of raw materials with their subsequent manufacture. Lumber and pulp mills commonly acquire sufficient stands of timber to provide supplies adequate to enable them to keep their mills in operation[3] until they are virtually exhausted. The International Harvester Company acquired stands of timber through the Wisconsin Lumber Company.[4] The former Standard Oil Company before its dissolution showed little interest in the hazardous business of drilling for oil; its control of distributing facilities and pipe lines assured it of supplies of crude oil. But the partition of the company by the court, and the appearance of a number of rival companies, together with uncertainty concerning the amount of crude oil in existence, and the peculiar legal institutions determining the title to oil have all stimulated vigorous efforts to integrate all stages in the production of petroleum products from the ownership of oil lands to the operation of retail stations.[5]

[1] F.T.C., *Prices, Profits, and Competition in the Petroleum Industry*, 1928, 41.
[2] This motive to integration has been important in Germany more especially in the presence of cartels (*Cf.* N.I.C.B., *Rationalization in Germany*, 56, 63).
[3] Acquisitions of timber have often, however, been speculations for a rise in the price of lumber. During the present century they have, in the main, proved unprofitable, because the expected rise in price has failed to materialize.
[4] COMMISSIONER OF CORPORATIONS, *The International Harvester Company*, 269.
[5] F.T.C., *Prices, Profits, and Competition in the Petroleum Industry*, 183.

In some industries desire for protection against losses rather than for a share in high profits stimulates vertical integration. Important elements in the physical plant are often exhausted in different periods of time and there is no moment at which production could be abandoned without considerable sacrifice of unexhausted assets. The imperfections of the market give to the sales connections and reputation of the firm a value which its managers are unwilling to abandon. Desire to insure the continuous utilization of production facilities or organization, together, doubtless, with a desire, not entirely rational, to provide for the continued survival of the firm, stimulate efforts to secure control of materials for very long periods in the future. This desire can be most easily satisfied where the material concerned is a mineral. At its formation the United States Steel Corporation controlled iron ore sufficient to meet all its requirements for 30 to 35 years,[1] and subsequently added to these holdings. The Aluminum Company has been reported to control practically all the supplies of bauxite in the United States[2] and some of the anthracite railroads controlled deposits of anthracite sufficient to meet estimated demands for 125 to 200 years.[3]

Fear of the failure of supplies in the necessary quantities is closely allied to fear of unduly high prices as a motive to vertical integration. Pursuit of the economies of large-scale production into the elaborate specialization of machinery characteristic of the automobile industry involves great risk of loss if the production unit as a whole is not completely synchronized. Failure of supplies of parts even for a few hours may bring the whole assembly plant to a standstill. Protection from this risk by holding large reserve stocks of each part increases costs by increasing interest charges on capital. In consequence, the producer may seek to avoid such risks by securing direct control of the supply of his own raw materials. Even in the automobile industry, however, this motive has operated with less effect than might have been expected;[4] the Ford company is the only producer making many of its own parts and it purchases many materials in the market. Manufacturers of bedding and automobile tires acquired or built

[1] COMMISSIONER OF CORPORATIONS, *The Steel Industry*, I, 225. Carnegie, however, regarded the production of iron ore as a risky business the integration of which with steel manufacturing was unnecessary and unwise (*ibid.*, 76).
[2] F.T.C., *House Furnishings Industry*, 1924, III, 91.
[3] F.T.C., *Premium Prices of Anthracite*, 50.
[4] FLÜGGE, "The Possibilities and Problems of Integration in the Automobile Industry," *Jour. Polit. Econ.*, 37: 150, 161, 170 (1929).

cotton mills between 1920 and 1930 apparently because there was a shortage of mills specializing in the manufacture of the products they needed and they wished to make sure of supplies. The decline of competition among the buyers of a product might also be expected to induce vertical integration where sellers believed that buyers were pressing down the prices they paid to a level which yielded them abnormal profits, while restricting sales and, therefore, the demand for the raw material. Pressure to such a "forward" integration, *i.e.*, a movement to bring under a single control processes nearer to the final purchaser, is undoubtedly present in a number of industries but it is frequently obstructed by other influences. Manufacturers of consumers' goods fear the outcome of the increasing scale upon which retailing is being organized. Yet subsequent steps on the way to the consumer often involve technical problems of such complexity that the advantages of specialization outweigh the advantages of integration with earlier stages. A manufacturer of toilet or drug products may vigorously desire to retail his products but he is dismayed by the necessity of entering the business of retailing soft drinks and sandwiches, cigarettes and corn poppers, in order to do so.[1] The economies of retailing obtained by mail-order and department stores handling a very wide variety of products further magnify this obstacle to the integration of retailing with manufacturing. It is, therefore, confined to products in the retailing of which specialization offers great advantages, as in the retailing of shoes, clothing, oil products, and automobiles.

Increasing emphasis upon non-price competition, resulting in part, as we have seen, from declining emphasis upon price competition, may in turn induce vertical integration. The continued tendency for steel manufacturers to absorb steel fabricators is due partly to the difficulties of completely eliminating price competition but also partly to the tendency, where efforts to eliminate it are successful, for non-price competition to determine the distribution of business.[2] Heavy expenditure upon advertising branded goods breeds a distaste upon the part of the manufacturer for price cutting in the retail market, *i.e.*, price competition at a

[1] Drug Incorporated did, however, integrate the operation of the Liggett chain of drug stores with the manufacture of such proprietary products as Bayer's Aspirin, Vitalis, Phillips' Milk of Magnesia, Cascarets, California Syrup of Figs, Diamond Dyes, etc. The integration was abandoned in 1933. The Beech-Nut Packing Company also held a stock interest in the United Cigar Stores.

[2] *Cf.* the reference to the proposed merger of the Truscon Steel Company and the Republic Steel Corporation, *New York Times*, Aug. 22, 1934.

later stage on the way to the consumer. It dilutes the direct advertising appeal to the emotions of purchasers and may lead to a reduction of the number of retailers[1] and thus hinder speedy and easy response to the advertising appeal. The manufacturer, moreover, often desires to utilize the sales-promotion capacity of retailers, their power to persuade the purchaser to buy the product of one manufacturer rather than that of another. Direct integration of retailing with manufacturing in the oil, shoe, clothing, and automobile industries has doubtless been largely stimulated by these considerations. But we have seen that there are serious obstacles to such integration. Types of partial vertical integration have been developed as a way of evading these obstacles to the integration of distribution and production. Manufacturers seek to prevent the retailer from handling rival products by making exclusive dealing contracts: they seek to control his price policy in the handling of their products through attempts to maintain the resale prices of products. In the oil industry retail outlets have been partly controlled through ownership and control by manufacturers and partly by "lease and license" or "lease and agency" agreements. The manufacturer leased the filling station from the owner; the manufacturer then licensed the owner to operate it to sell only the products of the manufacturer upon terms fixed in a sales agreement; or the manufacturer employed the owner on a commission basis (the commission being equal to the margin between the wholesale and retail prices of gasoline).[2] Manufacturers of electric lamps have secured control of the retail prices of their products by appointing the retailers their agents and retaining property rights in the retailer's stock until it is sold.[3] Special allowances for advertising for increasing the volume of sales, or for exclusive dealing, perform a similar function.

Vertical integration can often be attributed to a desire to secure a market without resort to either price or non-price competition. The acquisition of stock in, and the granting of loans to, newspaper publishing companies by the International Power

[1] Manufacturers also seek to maintain the number of dealers by the classification of chain stores for the purposes of determining discounts in such a manner as to hamper them in competition with independent firms.
[2] F.T.C., *Prices, Profits, and Competition in the Petroleum Industry*, 1928, 255 ff. The independent oil dealers objected strenuously to this practice at the hearings on the code for the industry under the National Industrial Recovery Act (*New York Times*, July 26, 1933) and the Secretary of the Interior, exercising his powers under the act, took steps to eliminate these contracts (Order of January 20, 1934, cit. *The New York Times*, Jan. 21, 1934).
[3] U.S. v. General Electric Co., 272 U.S. 476 (1926).

and Paper Company[1] appears to have been of this type. Integration of the control of automobile paints and automobile manufacturing, of automobile production and taxicab operation, and of airplane manufacturing and operation, at least in part also falls within this category.

Social control of industry has placed few obstacles in the way of integration. The Commissioner of Corporations reported that "in so far as the Steel Corporation's position in the entire iron and steel industry is of a monopolistic character it is chiefly through its control of ore holdings and the transportation of ore."[2] He reported of the Standard Oil Company that control of the tank-wagon wholesale delivery of oil products facilitated local price cutting which was one of the principal sources of its monopoly power;[3] its control of pipe lines was used to hinder the development of rivals.[4] Of the International Harvester Company he reported that vertical integration had been "a great element of strength," the adjusted rate of return upon its investment in the Wisconsin Steel Company having been 27.4 per cent in 1910 and 24.1 per cent in 1911, profits "extraordinarily large even for the iron and steel industry." Control of the Wisconsin Lumber Company, on the other hand, has been of no advantage to the company.[5]

The Federal Trade Commission has also commented adversely upon some examples of vertical integration. The distribution of meat products through branch houses and private-car routes was held to be "the bulwark of monopoly"[6] of the meat packers; it suggested that the control of the channels of distribution be separated from the control of beef packing in the narrower sense. After discussing the effect upon the oil industry of the partition of the Standard Oil Company of New Jersey it recommended

---

[1] *New York Times*, May 1, 1929. Under pressure resulting from the publicity attendant upon the hearings before the Federal Trade Commission on power and gas utilities, this integration was subsequently abandoned (*New York Times*, Mar. 21, 1931).
[2] *Summary of Report on the Steel Industry*, 1911, I, 60.
[3] COMMISSIONER OF CORPORATIONS, *The Petroleum Industry*, II, 27.
[4] COMMISSIONER OF CORPORATIONS, *The Petroleum Industry*, I, 24 (1907); INTERSTATE COMMERCE COMMISSION, *Report on Railroad Discrimination and Monopolies in Oil*, H. R. Doct. 606, 59th Cong. 2d Sess.
[5] *The International Harvester Company*, 269. The International Harvester Company stated that the rate of return upon its investment in the Wisconsin Steel Company had been 14.9 per cent in 1910 and 13.3 per cent in 1911.
[6] *The Meat Packing Industry*, 1919, I, 76. This view was reiterated by the commission in 1924 in *The Packer Consent Decree*, 31 (68th Cong. 2d Sess., Senate Doct. 219).

that the control of pipe lines be separated from the other branches of the industry.[1] It held that the maintenance of the monopolistic power of the International Harvester Company was aided by its control of a steel making subsidiary because the company either secured large profits from the subsidiary or secured its materials at cost, in either of which events it was placed in a competitive position superior to that of its rivals.[2]

Neither Congress nor the courts have, however, been especially concerned with vertical integration. The Sherman Act prohibits monopolies and restraint of trade. The "commodities clause" of the Hepburn Act of 1906 prohibits a common carrier from transporting a commodity in the production of which it is directly interested (in order to prevent the railroad so integrated from discriminating against non-integrated shippers of the same commodity). Although the same act declared pipe-line companies to be common carriers, the "commodities clause" was specifically restricted to railroads, thus leaving petroleum refiners and marketers free to integrate the ownership of pipe lines with these operations. The Air Mail Act of 1934 provided that no air transportation concern holding an air mail contract might directly or indirectly integrate its transportation service with the manufacture and sale of airplane parts or any phase of aviation (except the operation of the hangars and landing fields needed in connection with its transportation service.[3]

The courts when ordering the partition of the Standard Oil Company took no special steps to diminish the degree of integration between the refining and distribution of oil and the ownership of oil pipe lines, but in the partition of the American Tobacco Company, tin foil, liquorice paste, and retailing subsidiaries were separated from the successor manufacturing companies. In 1931, when two of the successor companies to the former Standard Oil Company of New Jersey sought to recombine, the Circuit Court of Appeals held that "the intent and purpose of the merger is solely to meet the normal and natural business necessities of the two companies brought about by the develop-

---

[1] *The High Price of Gasoline in 1915*, 164.
[2] *The High Price of Farm Implements*, 1920, 674, 675, 680.
[3] 73d Congress Public No. 308 (S.3170), Sections 7a and 7b. Companies holding air mail contracts were prohibited from any interest or control in another concern engaged directly or indirectly in *any* phase of aviation. No interest or control in a company holding an air mail contract might be held by a company interested in any phase of aviation or by a holding company.

ment of, and the changed competitive and business conditions in the industry," among which was the development of integrated companies exercising control from the production of crude oil to the retailing to the customer, and the merger was permitted.[1] While the Supreme Court does not appear to have referred to the scope and pattern of the integration effected by the United States Steel Corporation, the lower federal court accepted a desire for the economies of integration as a valid reason for the original establishment of the corporation.[2] A consent decree issued in 1920 under the Sherman Law enjoined the meat packers[3] from vertical integration by requiring them to dispose of their holdings in companies owning stockyards,[4] stockyard railroads, cold storage plants, and market newspapers: it also prohibited the operation of retail stores. When packers sought a modification of this decree in 1931 the Attorney General paid special attention to the probable effect of integrating meat packing with retail distribution; he admitted that chain stores had grown since 1920 and had themselves shown some tendency to integration[5] but claimed that their buying power had not greatly damaged the packers[6] by reducing their profits.[7] The packers continued to be the main source of supply of meat products to the chain stores; to permit the packers to engage in retailing would be to prepare the way for the meat packers to oust the chain stores from retailing[8] and "the complete annihilation of the independent retail grocer because of the many ways in which the packers could reduce the price of meat to their own stores."[9] The court, therefore, continued the prohibition upon the integration of meat packing with retailing. Thus a law aimed at the preservation of competition produced the strange spectacle of a court attempting to protect the retail grocer from competition arising, at least in part, from improvements in the technique of production.

[1] U.S. v. Standard Oil Co. of New York *et al.*, 47 Fed. (2d) 288 (1931).
[2] U.S. v. U.S. Steel Corp., 223 Fed. 178 (1915).
[3] U.S. v. Swift and Co. *et al.*, *Consent Decree* entered in Supreme Court of District of Columbia, Feb. 27, 1920.
[4] The stock interest of the packers in stockyard companies had not been completely severed by 1933 (*New York Times*, July 19, 1933).
[5] U.S. v. Swift and Co. *et al.*, 286 U.S. 106 (1931), *Brief for U.S.*, 21.
[6] *ibid.*, 21.
[7] *ibid.*, 16.
[8] *ibid.*, 22. A witness for Armour and Company admitted that if large buyers knew that the packer could get the business of the consumer the packer would be in a much stronger position in bargaining with them (*ibid.*, 68).
[9] *ibid.*, 18.

The commodities clause traveled a tortuous journey through the courts[1] which were mainly concerned with the application of the clause to coal mined by a company related through various types of stock control to a railroad company. In 1920, however, the Supreme Court decided that a railroad holding stock in a mining company for the purpose of making the coal company its agent contravened the commodities clause and that the mining and railroad companies must be restored to independence of each other.[2] Thus vertical integration of railroad operation and mining has at least been obstructed, although with difficulty.[3]

The integration of wholesaling and retailing resulting from the organization of chain and department stores and mail-order houses has not been directly attacked. Taxation penalizing chain stores has been approved[4] but it appears to be aimed more at territorial than at vertical integration.

The partial integration of manufacturing with distribution through resale price maintenance contracts empowering the manufacturer to determine selling prices at later stages in the journey of the product to the final purchaser, and exclusive dealing contracts empowering the manufacturer to limit the range of products handled by dealers in his product, have been the subject of litigation. The courts have been much influenced, however, by the forms by which the end is attained. Resale price maintenance attained by contract is unenforceable;[5] it has been upheld where achieved without contractual covenants but by urging retailers to maintain suggested prices, announcing that dealers failing to charge these prices will be denied supplies, and requesting information concerning price cutters.[6] Keeping records concerning the behavior of dealers and employing devices for tracing price cutting have been held to go beyond refusal to sell to dealers

---

[1] For a summary of the decisions concerning the integration of the ownership and operation of anthracite deposits with the ownership and operation of railroads see MCLAUGHLIN, *Cases on the Federal Anti-Trust Laws of the United States*, 139 note.

[2] U.S. v. Reading Co. *et al.*, 253 U.S. 26 (1920).

[3] Counsel for the United States in these cases remarked that vertical integration of mining and railroad operation was distinguished from other vertical integration because, railroads being regional monopolies, vertical integration broadened and extended that monopoly. To permit such integration would be to stimulate the use of monopoly power to coerce shippers. (GORDON, THURLOW M., in *The Federal Anti-Trust Laws*, Ed. Handler, 1932, 218.)

[4] See p. 458.

[5] Dr. Miles Medical Co. v. Park and Sons Co., 220 U.S. 373 (1911); Bauer & Cie. v. O'Donnell, 229 U.S. 1 (1913).

[6] U.S. v. Colgate and Co., 250 U.S. 300 (1919); U.S. v. Schraders Sons, Inc., 252 U.S. 85 (1920).

who will not resell at stated prices and practically to eliminate competition between dealers; this method of attaining resale price maintenance was, therefore, contrary to the Federal Trade Commission Act.[1] Where the manufacturer constitutes the distributor his agent he may, of course, instruct his employees concerning the price at which his property shall be sold.[2] He may also prevent these agents from handling the products of rivals,[3] although the courts are prepared to examine all the circumstances to insure the genuineness of the agency.[4] Again, apart from the form of the contract, the court condemns exclusive dealing arrangements where it believes that they will suppress competition among retailers[5] but not otherwise.[6]

2. THE PRINCIPAL CONSEQUENCES OF VERTICAL INTEGRATION

The consequences of vertical integration are not always sharply separate from its causes: the objectives of such integration, if achieved, become also consequences, as, for instance, when technical economies may be the spur to integration or a minor objective and a major consequence. Similarly vertical integration, whether or not aimed at the reduction of selling costs arising from non-price competition, may in fact reduce these costs. Increases in efficiency due to integration would display themselves in the form of reductions of costs. Although no measure of the economies thus obtained is available, there is no doubt that they have been secured in some instances. Where both integrated and less integrated firms continue in competition the explanation of the survival of both may lie in the fact that the direct economies are small, that they are offset by less direct dis-economies, or that imperfections of competition permit the survival of firms varying widely in their costs.

Vertical integration, however, diminishes the effectiveness of the market as a stimulus to the improvement of methods of production. Where little vertical integration occurs the efficiency of producers is checked at a great many points along the chain of operations from the production of raw material to that of

[1] Beech-Nut Packing Co. v. F.T.C., 257 U.S. 441 (1922); see also Cream of Wheat Co. v. F.T.C., 14 Fed. (2d) 40 (1926).
[2] U.S. v. General Electric Co. et al., 272 U.S. 476 (1926).
[3] F.T.C. v. Curtis Publishing Co., 260 U.S. 568 (1923).
[4] Standard Fashion Co. v. Magrane Houston Co., 258 U.S. 346 (1922); Butterick et al. v. F.T.C., 267 U.S. 602 (1925).
[5] Q.R.S. Music Co. v. F.T.C., 12 Fed. (2d) 730 (1926).
[6] Pearsall B. S. Butter Co. v. F.T.C., 292 Fed. 720 (1923).

finished product; costs of production are separated for each stage and the market facilitates the frequent comparison of costs and utilities. Where, however, a commodity is produced by a number of firms all vertically integrated, one may be efficient in one or two stages of production and others in other stages; the market affords opportunity for comparing only the aggregate cost of all stages of production. It is possible that no vertically integrated firm operates at the highest level of efficiency available in all the stages of production in which it is engaged. This difficulty can be minimized by the use of suitable recording devices and the preservation of a severely rational attitude by the management. But integration not always conceived in moments of severe rationality cannot be expected to be always rationally managed.

Vertical integration may diminish the responsiveness of the firm to changes in knowledge of methods of production. It assumes, within limits which vary from industry to industry, the use of certain materials and certain methods of production, and when changes occur, the vertically integrated firm is tempted to continue using the former raw material, in order to secure as great a return as possible from investment in prior processes which have now become partly obsolete. A corporation integrating the spinning of cotton yarn and the subsequent weaving of cotton textiles may be prejudiced against the substitution of rayon for cotton. The discovery of metal alloys more satisfactory than steel for the building of automobiles would place firms integrating steel and automobile manufacturing in a difficult position. The integration of the manufacture of automobile parts with the assembly of automobiles probably delayed abandonment of the "Model T" Ford.[1] If rival producers of the same commodity are not so integrated they will turn to the new method of production and reduce their costs. They are likely to find it profitable to increase their output and reduce their price somewhat. The integrated firms must then accept lower prices and lower returns upon the equipment now obsolete. They will continue to keep it in use,

[1] Consciousness of an analogous difficulty in the way of integrating bread baking with flour milling has been cited as the principal reason for the absence of such integration. "If a great baking corporation had its own mills it would have to use the output of those mills. Its raw materials would vary from season to season and thus difficulties would be introduced in standardizing the final bakery product. On the other hand, if a bakery concern is free to buy its flour where it pleases, it may shift the source of supply from year to year according to the quantity and quality of the crop in each wheat region. It will thus be able to secure a more uniform raw material—a vitally important matter in its manufacturing operations." (ALSBERG, *Combinations in the American Bread Baking Industry*, 97.)

however, so long as the additional (marginal) costs of production by the old methods do not exceed the total costs by the new; they thus recover some part of their investment in specialized equipment. If all firms are equally integrated and all seek the most profitable policy, in the long run they are likely to postpone both the utilization of the new methods and the reduction in price.[1] Capital is economized but purchasers must wait for the benefits of improving technique of production. The integration of two vertically related monopolies may stimulate innovations in production. Reductions in cost by one may suggest a reduction of the monopoly price but until the second has reduced his price the increase in sales which was the objective of the price reduction is not obtained and the innovator secures less gain from his innovation than he would if, being vertically integrated, he could make an immediate reduction in the final selling price.[2]

Vertical integration widens the scope of the control of single management; it thereby induces a more rational planning of industry. An independent firm producing machinery or raw materials for a subsequent process may, in imperfectly competitive conditions, fail to produce more durable commodities because of their tendency to reduce the later demand for its own products. A vertically integrated firm, however, is more likely to produce the equipment and materials most likely to minimize total costs. Furthermore, there is some chance that a vertically integrated firm will be somewhat better informed concerning the qualities and types of product needed for each stage of production because of its primary interest in the efficiency of the whole chain of production rather than of any separate stage.

For the same reason vertical integration tends to a more perfect synchronization of production. In the cotton industry there is little vertical integration;[3] the separate organization of

[1] Unless the marginal cost of production by the old exceeds the total cost of production by the new methods.
[2] If "each of two monopolies is essential for the performance of a given public service, and if there is no chance that any effective competition will be offered to either, then it is generally in the public interest that they should be amalgamated. For when separated the benefit of any outlay made by either for the improvement of its efficiency will accrue partly to the other until new terms for the division of the earnings of their joint work have been agreed upon; whereas a single monopoly would get at once the whole reward of its enterprise." (MARSHALL, *Industry and Trade*, 420.)
[3] Rubber tire manufacturers, Marshall Field and Company, and the Simmons Company produce their own textiles (MURCHISON, "Stabilization in the Cotton Textile Industry," *Proceedings of the 45th Annual Meeting of the American Economic Association*, 1932, 79).

spinners, weavers, converters, commission merchants, piece goods buyers, and garment manufacturers has resulted in what is "tantamount to a series of speculative mechanisms" each of which clouds the judgment and obstructs the activities of other divisions and stimulates interest in "profits from fortuitous circumstances and shrewd forestalling." Production schedules are controlled by men not even remotely associated with the market and wholly ignorant of the forces shaping market tendencies.[1] In the absence of vertical integration, a change in the demand for the final product is transmitted back through the preceding stages of production only as each firm changes its policy in purchasing raw materials or as such changes are foreseen. Non-integrated firms may, therefore, plan production in anticipation of the continuance of demand upon the same level as before but if the anticipation proves erroneous their inventories increase or decline according to the direction of the change in demand; subsequent production is reduced or increased to restore these inventories. The production of pig iron and even of raw steel products, for instance, is said to have fluctuated more widely before steel production was integrated with the production of pig iron and crude steel than since. Rising prices for cotton goods induce the covering of anticipated requirements upon an excessive scale. Increases in demand are pyramided as they are transmitted back to the mills with the result that fluctuations in prices and output are magnified. The partial integration of automobile manufacturing with retailing has led to the adoption of systems of control by which the various stages of production are closely adjusted to changes in the demand for the final product. Gains and losses on inventories tend thus to be diminished by vertical integration. Whether a vertically integrated industrial organization is better able than a non-integrated one to adjust its long-term investment in prior processes, including mining, to harmonize closely with its policy in later stages of production is not clear.

It has been suggested that integration tends to reduce the cyclical fluctuations of business.[2] The effect of vertical integration upon the business cycle is, however, far from clear. Changes in

---

[1] MURCHISON, *op. cit.*, 76 *ff*. Mr. Murchison concludes that the most hopeful path to greater stability in the industry is the establishment of a form of control that will supply continuity of supervision "all the way from the spinning process to the final disposition of the finished product." *Cf.* also COPELAND and LEARNED, *Merchandising of Cotton Textiles*, 5.

[2] FRANK, "The Significance of Industrial Integration," *Jour. Polit. Econ.*, 33: 179 (1925).

the demand for final products would be expected to be more rapidly transmitted through the whole productive organism where vertical integration is common than where it is not, i.e., cyclical changes would be more sudden both in times of increasing and in times of decreasing business activity. The price policies of vertically integrated firms are, however, the most vital determinant of the effect of vertical integration and these are discussed below.[1]

Some indirect light is thrown upon the effects of vertical integration by statistics of profits. Where prices are uniform from seller to seller differences in return reflect differences in costs. The Federal Trade Commission found that in the steel industry (excluding the United States Steel Corporation) during the years 1915 to 1918 "the greater was the extent of integration the less was the return."[2] The United States Steel Corporation, which was more highly integrated than its rivals, had, in three of the four years, a rate of return less than the average returns of its rivals taken in four broad classes on the basis of the degree of their integration. An investigation of the relation between vertical integration and profits in the petroleum industry[3] yielded the following results during the four years from 1922 to 1925:

Functions Performed	Rate of Return[1] (per cent)
Crude oil production and refining	9.4
Refining	4.5
Refining and marketing	9.5
Crude oil production, refining, and marketing	8.5

[1] Rate of return is an average of annual average rates of return.

Differences in integration were, however, correlated with differences in size; the rates of return differed from class to class for this reason as well as because of differences in integration. The available statistics are, however, too sparse and uncertain a basis for any generalizations concerning the consequences of integration upon profits.

The rate of return obtained by vertically integrated firms naturally tends to be lower than the highest return obtained in any of the separate operations in which it is engaged, because

[1] See p. 437.
[2] *Wartime Costs and Profits of the Steel Industry*, 1925, 32. In general the most highly integrated companies had considerably lower direct costs but, chiefly because of their proportionately higher investment of capital, their rate of profit was not higher.
[3] *Prices, Profits, and Competition in the Petroleum Industry*, 1928, 293.

the best results are offset by poorer results in other operations; the returns of firms engaged in producing crude oil and refining and marketing it were reduced by the poor results in refining. Similarly, in so far as the different stages of production involve different degrees of risk, the vertically integrated firm, by pooling profits from all these operations, is likely to secure a rate of return fluctuating less than that of a firm interested in only one stage of production; this consequence has appeared in the petroleum industry.[1] Indeed the integration of crude oil production, refining, and marketing has been attributed to "the lack of security in obtaining profits in any one branch of the industry." Cheap crude oil, for instance, may mean low profits in the production of crude oil, but high profits in refining and marketing.[2]

Vertical integration is said to have resulted in a greater fixity of costs of production for the United States Steel Corporation than for producers who buy their coke and ore or even their iron. Labor being the only element in cost capable of variation, the profits of the corporation were *more* sensitive to price changes than those of non-integrated producers; the latter benefited from reductions in the price of their raw materials when the price of the finished product declined.[3] It may be true that the profits of the United States Steel Corporation fluctuated more than those of non-integrated firms engaged in steel manufacturing; they must, however, have been more stable than those of firms engaged in the production of ore and coke. In other words, the profits of the vertically integrated firm fluctuated less than those of specialized firms in the branches of the industry subject to the widest fluctuations, although they fluctuated more than those of non-integrated firms engaged in the branches of the business subject to the narrowest fluctuations.[4] It is evident, however, that as a device

---

[1] F.T.C., *op. cit.*, 293.
[2] Evidence of the Chief of the Petroleum Section, Minerals Division, Bureau of Foreign and Domestic Commerce, U.S. Department of Commerce, in U.S. v. Standard Oil Co. of New York and Vacuum Oil Co., *Summary of Evidence*, District Court, 30.
[3] MEADE, "The Price Policy of the United States Steel Corporation," *Quart. Jour. Econ.*, 22: 457.
[4] The same point of view was implied in the statement that "In the case of a non-integrated business, proportionate decline in profits as a result of the fall in price is much less than when little compensation for falling prices is afforded by decreasing cost of materials." But even a non-integrated firm, *e.g.*, one producing iron ore, may benefit little in a period of declining prices from a decline in the cost of its materials. If the average return obtained by an integrated firm on operations A, B and C fluctuates more than the return to non-integrated firms engaged in operation C, the return on either B or A or both must fluctuate more than the combined return

for stabilizing profits vertical integration is open to the objection that all the operations brought under single control are subject to a common risk, viz., of variations in the demand for the final product.

Vertical integration may affect prices by affecting either or both of costs and profits. If vertically integrated firms obtain a normal return, prices are lower than they would be without vertical integration where vertical integration enables producers to secure technical economies in production, or to coordinate the various stages of production more effectively, or to reduce selling costs. They are higher than they would otherwise be where pressure to improve methods of production is diminished and where integration introduces positive obstruction to the adoption of such methods. There remains the question how vertical integration may affect price policy apart from its effect upon the level of costs of production.

It has been argued that the competitive strength of a vertically integrated unit is greater than that of a non-integrated unit because the profit per unit in an integrated firm is greater than in a non-integrated: all the profits on intermediate processes are summed up in one total profit for the integrated firm whereas for non-integrated firms the profits on prior processes are included in the price paid for its raw materials. For this reason "the operator has a much greater possible reduction in price before he must go out of business than his less integrated competitors."[1] The proportion of total unit costs represented by overhead costs is, however, the relevant consideration. As this proportion is greater for the vertically integrated than for the non-integrated firm, the range within which prices may fluctuate is wider for the former than for the latter. If the price of the final product falls it will meet the direct costs of the non-integrated firm before it meets those of the integrated. It does not follow, however, that the non-integrated will be the first to be expelled from the industry; non-integrated firms press their suppliers for a reduction in the price of materials; these suppliers must either lose business to the vertically integrated firm or respond to the pressure, thus reducing the direct costs of those producing for the final market.

---

on all three operations. Therefore the inference that "a conservative policy is evidently far more necessary in the capitalization of an integrated than of a nonintegrated company" is invalid. (MEADE, "The Capitalization of the United States Steel Corporation," *Quart. Jour. Econ.*, 16: 214 (1902).)

[1] THORP, *Integration of Industrial Operation*, 257.

In so far, therefore, as the total overhead costs of the integrated firm equals the sum of the overhead costs of the non-integrated firms engaged in the same series of activities, the extent to which the former can survive a greater reduction in price than the latter depends upon the relations between the non-integrated firms at each stage of production. There may be no advantage in integration in this respect. In fact, if non-integrated firms are able to secure reductions in the price of their materials commensurate with the decline in the price for finished goods they can maintain normal profits while the vertically integrated firm cannot. Where all firms are vertically integrated the only market in which competition can persist is of course the final market.[1]

Vertical integration may itself cause market imperfection. The most economical scale of production at some stages of production is larger than at others; the longer the chain of processes integrated the greater is the probability that it will include one which will induce large-scale organization of that process and, therefore, also in preceding and succeeding processes. In these other stages the number of firms may be reduced below the number that would have persisted without integration, and fall so low as to restrict competitive conduct. The move toward such integration may originate in the industry operated on a large scale; the desire to expand its existing operations is obstructed by high costs and serious risks where the number of firms is already small. The initiative may come from industries purchasing from, or selling to, those who are so large in relation to the total market in which they operate that serious departures from the competitive price are suspected or feared. The large size of firms in this latter market may discourage integration by those engaged in industries in which relatively small-scale organization prevails; but if sufficient inducement is present the smaller firm may be compelled to reorganize and increase the size of the firm in its present market in order to facilitate integration. The whole chain of integrated processes need not, however, be completely self-contained. The process performed on a large scale may be partly supplied with raw materials purchased on the market; part of its output may be sold on the market.[2] If the excess product is sold at prices yielding a normal return above technically necessary costs the

---

[1] *Cf.* VON BECKERATH (*op. cit.*, 258) who remarks that vertical integration may transfer price wars to the finished goods markets.

[2] The Ford Motor Company is said to have sold part of the output of its glass making plant to other automobile manufacturers.

THE INTEGRATION OF INDUSTRIAL OPERATIONS 439

integration does not cause a large optimum scale of production at one stage to affect the number of firms at other stages. If the price charged is above this level, non-integrated rivals buying the material suffer and may be eliminated; they suffer not because of the integration, but because of the imperfection in the market in which the number of firms is small. Even then they suffer only if the integrated firm sells the final product at a price which exceeds that of the intermediate product by a differential insufficient to permit profitable operations at later stages.[1] It is sometimes impossible, however, to sell part of the output of the process economically organized only on a large scale. The bulwark of such monopoly as the large meat packers enjoyed was said to be their superior transportation facilities and particularly their ownership of refrigerator cars[2] and organization of "peddler-car routes."[3] These transportation services were economically operated only on a large scale and the difficulties of arranging for the performance of this service by the large packers for non-integrated meat packers as well as for themselves are obvious. In consequence, large-scale operations at other stages were in the hands of the integrated firms with resulting complaints concerning the only partially competitive condition of the market.[4] Similarly the former Standard Oil Company integrated the tank-wagon wholesale delivery of oil with refining. This function was economically performed only on a very large scale with the result that it was difficult for a rival service to be established when the Standard Oil Company had established itself.[5] It would be absurd to expect the company to deliver the oil of less integrated rivals in its tank wagons.

Vertical integration may, however, undermine attempts to secure monopoly prices. German cartels attempting to control output and prices have encountered a tendency for firms whose expansion is thus hindered to integrate the performance of subsequent functions with those controlled. The cartels have, more-

[1] See p. 440.
[2] F.T.C., *The Meat Packing Industry*, I, 42; III, 193.
[3] *ibid.*, III, 125.
[4] It has never been satisfactorily shown, however, that a smaller unit could not operate such cars over perhaps a smaller geographical area with equal economy. What appears to be more probable is that, whether or not the packers integrated into this business, they were such important purchasers of railroad transportation that they could apply great pressure to the railroads to secure favorable treatment for themselves and sometimes apparently also unfavorable treatment for their rivals and for any refrigerator cars that the latter might own. (*ibid.*, I, 41.)
[5] COMMISSIONER OF CORPORATIONS, *The Petroleum Industry*, I, 329.

over, frequently been compelled either to exclude from production control output to be used by the producer in subsequent operations, or to place less severe restrictions upon such output. Where the later stages of production are not cartelized the vertically integrated producer escapes the cartel control and thereby undermines its effectiveness. Vertical integration is thereby encouraged[1] although it offers no technical advantages. In the making of codes of fair competition under the National Industrial Recovery Act similar conflicts emerged. The companies integrating the mining of coal and the production of steel resisted adoption of the proposed code for the coal industry partly because they sought the exemption of "captive mines" (*i.e.*, those controlled by the steel companies) from the sales agency and price fixing clauses in the code for the coal industry.[2] In the textile industry producers of rubber tires resisted limitations upon the number of hours during which their fabric mills might be operated; their non-integrated rivals objected to integrated firms being allowed to continue to obtain fabric at costs based on full utilization of plant unless they were permitted to do the same.[3] The vertically integrated firm may, however, be satisfied to share the profits of the stage of production thus controlled and not undermine the control.

Vertical integration by providing for the pooling of profits from a series of operations makes possible discrimination analogous to the geographical price discrimination facilitated where profits from sales over a wide area are pooled.[4] A vertically integrated firm might permit the sale of a product at one stage of production at less than cost, making up the loss on other products sold at prices much above cost.[5] An integrated steel manufacturer is unlikely to sell pig iron at "less than cost" because by doing so he would be placing his non-integrated rivals in a position in which, if they secured normal profits on the processes in which they were engaged, they could sell their finished products at a price which would yield less than a normal return on all the

[1] *Cf.* VON BECKERATH, *op. cit.*, 241; BRADY, *The Rationalization Movement in German Industry*, 97. In times of business activity the vertically integrated favor their own plants in disposing of raw materials and in times of recession they may force sales of finished products in order to dispose of their raw materials, thus damaging the business of the non-integrated cartel members and thrusting upon them a large part of the burden of restricting output (*ibid.*, 257).
[2] *New York Times*, Sept., 26, 1933.
[3] *New York Times*, June 28, 1933.
[4] See Chaps. VI and VII.
[5] FETTER, *The Masquerade of Monopoly*, 422.

operations of the integrated firm. The integrated firm would be subsidizing its own rivals. If, however, the United States Steel Corporation chose to set prices upon the finished products sold through its subsidiary, the American Bridge Company, which yielded less than a normal return on the operations of that company, it could undersell its rivals. But the parent company could secure a normal return on all its operations only if the prices set at some of the earlier stages yielded more than a normal return on the operations in those stages; it could continuously obtain such prices only in the absence of competition in these earlier stages of production. Discrimination between products in the sense that the price of each product is not set to cover its cost of production does not follow, therefore, from vertical integration alone. It has been claimed, for instance,[1] that the Aluminum Company having control of the price of ingot aluminum has maintained for ingots a price which approaches too nearly the prices of its fabricated products to permit non-integrated firms to buy ingot from it and compete with it in fabricating.

Vertical integration combined with monopolistic or quasi-monopolistic conditions at some stages of production has given rise to serious complaints. If a firm secures control of the market in one of the earlier stages and integrates subsequent operations with those at the earlier controlled stage it can impose a levy upon the output of its less integrated rivals; the fact that it pays the same high level of charges for its own raw products is, of course, a matter of no importance to it as the payment is made to one of its own subsidiaries.[2] For a considerable time the Standard Oil companies controlled the pipe lines for the transportation of crude oil. These lines could be economically operated only where a large volume of business could be secured. Partly because rival concerns were too small to be able to supply such a volume of business, and partly because the Standard Oil companies obstructed the establishment of rival pipe lines, the Standard pipe lines often monopolized the pipe-line transportation for a field; the competition of railroads was of limited effect because the cost of railroad transportation was very much higher than

[1] N.R.A., *The Aluminum Industry* (mimeographed), 1935, 10.
[2] In Germany vertically integrated firms have been interested in cartelizing the earlier stages of production especially where by securing more favorable treatment than non-integrated cartel members they have been able to avoid some of the burdens of cartel control of output (VON BECKERATH, *op. cit.*, 257).

that of pipe-line transportation. Pipe-line rates of transportation were in consequence maintained on a level high in relation to costs.[1] Small independent refiners were thus hindered in the development of their business.[2] The Hepburn Act of 1906 declared pipe lines (other than those transporting water and gas) to be common carriers subject to the supervision of the Interstate Commerce Commission. For a number of years after the Supreme Court had upheld the constitutionality of this declaration[3] onerous shipping requirements by the pipe-line companies nullified the attempt to make the pipe-line companies common carriers so far as shipments east from the mid-continent field were concerned.[4] In 1922, however, the Interstate Commerce Commission ordered the Prairie Pipe Line Company to reduce the minimum shipment it would accept. By 1928 the Standard companies with refineries on the eastern seaboard were finding it cheaper to ship crude oil from California by way of the Panama Canal than by pipe line from the mid-continent field. The Prairie company then sought shipments from independent companies to replace those of the Standard companies which it had lost.[5] The Federal Trade Commission recommended[6] that, unless the Standard lines running eastward from the mid-continent field voluntarily accepted common-carrier shipments on terms that enabled both Standard and independent companies to use them freely, there should be absolute dissociation of pipe-line ownership from interests engaged in producing and refining crude petroleum.

The United States Steel Corporation owned two railroads in the Lake Superior ore region which handled two thirds of the ore traffic there. Upon these roads profits were reported to be "extraordinary" and "undoubtedly excessive, thus not only contributing large revenue to the Steel Corporation, but at the same time imposing a burden upon such of its competitors as

[1] COMMISSIONER OF CORPORATIONS, *The Petroleum Industry*, 1907, I, 24, 38.
[2] INTERSTATE COMMERCE COMMISSION, *Report on Oil* (H. R. Doct. 606, 59th Cong. 2d Sess.). They were also hindered by high minimum shipments and rate structures discriminating in favor of shipments to points where the refineries of the companies also controlling the pipe lines were located.
[3] "The Pipe Line Cases," 234 U.S. 548 (1914).
[4] F.T.C., *Prices, Profits, and Competition in the Petroleum Industry*, 1928, 40. Beginning in 1914 these lines refused to accept shipments of less than 100,000 barrels: their rates were also reported to be exorbitant. The Federal Trade Commission concluded that "the prosperity and perhaps even the existence of many small concerns depend on lower pipe line rates and reasonable minimum shipments"(F.T.C., *Pipe Line Transportation of Petroleum*, 1916, 32).
[5] F.T.C., *Prices, Profits, and Competition in the Petroleum Industry*, 1928, 42.
[6] *loc. cit.*

THE INTEGRATION OF INDUSTRIAL OPERATIONS 443

are forced to ship their ore over these roads."[1] Rival roads did, however, exist and the control of ore roads, although it had conferred great advantages upon the United States Steel Corporation, had not prevented the growth of its rivals.[2] The large beef packers integrated the part ownership of stockyards with beef packing. The packers claimed that the prospect of profit in the operation of stockyards was not sufficient to stimulate efficient operation;[3] on the other hand, the stockyard companies have been accused of excessive charges for their services.[4] These charges fall immediately upon the sellers of livestock; in the long run they tend to express themselves in the price paid for livestock by non-integrated firms as well as those integrating packing with stockyard operation.

While these situations are objectionable, the objection does not arise out of the integration. If pipe lines or stockyards are monopolized and conditions permit charges in excess of those which will yield a normal return on investment the owners of the monopolized facility benefit, but they do not benefit more because they are engaged in subsequent processes. The effect upon stages of production subsequent to that monopolized depends upon the policy of the integrated firm. If it sets prices at each subsequent stage with the object of securing a normal return, non-integrated firms do not suffer as a result of the integration. If the integrated firm uses some of its monopoly profits to subsidize its operations at later stages of production, setting prices at those later stages at levels which do not yield a normal return, non-integrated firms will find profitable operation difficult. If rivals to the United States Steel Corporation[5] and Standard Oil companies suffered

[1] COMMISSIONER OF CORPORATIONS, *The Steel Industry*, 1911, I, 60, 375.
[2] *ibid.*, 377.
[3] F.T.C., *The Meat Packing Industry*, I, 428. The packers offered a similar explanation of their financial control of livestock market newspapers (*loc. cit.*).
[4] F.T.C., *The Meat Packing Industry*, 1919, III, 58. The most serious complaints appear to have concerned the price of hay and grain for feeding animals (*Hearings on H.R. 13324*, 1919, 206, and F.T.C., *op. cit.*, III, 58) and the prices paid for dead animals (*Hearings on H.R. 13324*, 198, 199 (1919), and F.T.C., *op. cit.*, III, 61).
[5] It was argued, for instance, that the United States Steel Corporation was able to use its profits from the sale of steel in the middle west at the high prices resulting from the Pittsburgh-plus practice to permit subsidiaries like the American Bridge Company, the American Sheet and Tin Plate Company, and the American Steel and Wire Company to sell at prices too low to permit non-integrated rival producers purchasing crude steel at Pittsburgh-plus prices to survive (F.T.C., *Statement on Pittsburgh Plus*, 288, 289).

Judge Gary of the United States Steel Corporation referred to the ability of the corporation to drive rivals out of business and attributed it partly to "Our ownership in the independent concerns such as the railroads, the steamship lines, and so forth, which gives a large credit from the United States Steel Corporation's stand-as a result of the integration, the integrated companies must have pursued this latter policy. The average rate of profit of the integrated firm may be normal or even above normal although not so high as if it had exacted its full monopoly profits, and at other stages secured a normal rate of return. It is not clear why the integrated firm should sacrifice part of its monopoly profits in this way. If it hopes thus to drive out rivals in subsequent stages of production and in the longer run secure a monopoly or a quasi-monopoly position there the advantages of doing so are not clear; the major monopoly profits available from control of the supply of a given commodity are obtained by control of one stage in its production.[1]

Vertical integration combined with control of natural resources gives rise to similar questions; again, the monopoly element and not the element of integration is the main source of complaint. The Commissioner of Corporations reported[2] that "the Steel Corporation does occupy a position in the iron ore industry which, while by no means constituting a monopoly,[3] is clearly indicative of a monopoly influence." The commissioner contended that the corporation had kept up the prices of ore, thus forcing rivals to pay high prices for pig iron: while it paid the same prices itself, the payment was a mere transfer raising profits in the ore and pig iron departments at the expense of the steel departments.[4] The Aluminum Company of America, with its almost complete monopoly of the production of aluminum in the United States, fortified by a high protective tariff on imports, controls the domestic price of sheet aluminum to utensil manufacturers.[5]

---

point" (Testimony before Committee on Ways and Means of the 60th Congress, on Dec. 18, 1908, cit. F.T.C., *Statement on Pittsburgh Plus*, 405).

[1] Control of one stage does not always suffice. The output that will yield the maximum monopoly profit may require a charge for the operation monopolized (*e.g.*, pipe-line transportation for oil) that will call into use rival methods of performing that operation (*e.g.*, railroad transportation of oil); as soon as the price of the finished product is raised to a level that offers normal profits to non-integrated firms using the substitute (*e.g.*, railroad transportation) such firms are attracted into the industry.

[2] COMMISSIONER OF CORPORATIONS, *The Steel Industry*, 1911, I, 377.

[3] In 1909 it was believed that the United States Steel Corporation controlled over 75 per cent of the known deposits of workable ore in the Lake Superior region (*ibid*, 380).

[4] *ibid.*, II, 2, 3, 132. Attention has been drawn to the great reserves of ore of which the corporation secured control often without any immediate capital investment. The president of the Bethlehem Steel Corporation has argued that large reserves are necessary to give to a steel company sufficient security of future supplies to justify the investment necessary for economical production (*Brief for U.S.*, 6214, I, 390; COMMISSIONER OF CORPORATIONS, *op. cit.*, I, 382).

[5] N.R.A., *The Aluminum Industry*, 1935, 4, 5: See also p. 230.

The monopolistic position of the company arose out of the ownership of patents and the acquisition during the life of these patents of "practically all the known commercial deposits of bauxite (the mineral from which aluminum is obtained) in the United States."[1] Here also there is no obvious reason for a monopolist to interest himself in the subsequent manufacture of the monopolized product, although by setting a margin between the price of the raw material and the price of the finished product insufficient to yield a normal return he could obstruct if not expel rivals.

The effect of vertical integration upon the distribution of goods and services between profit receivers and others turns upon its effect upon costs and prices. Production costs may be reduced by the better coordination and synchronization of processes and selling costs by the reduction in the number of occasions upon which the product passes through a market on its way to the final purchaser. On the other hand, costs may be raised by inefficiency resulting from the temptation to expand operations in some fields beyond the most economical scale and by obstacles to the improvement of processes. The effect of these influences upon profit receivers depends upon the extent to which they are forced immediately to transmit economies to purchasers, and the extent to which increases in cost can be passed on. The broadening of the comparison of costs and prices resulting from the diminished frequency of resort to the market alleviates the pressure upon inefficiency and diminishes the tendency to transmit economies to purchasers. Profit receivers are able to pool the risks of different stages of production and thereby diminish the fluctuations of profits. The pursuit of discriminatory price policies is facilitated with the result that monopolistic or semi-monopolistic positions in one market can be used as a base for the capture of similar positions in other markets although the profitability of such operations is doubtful. On the other hand, vertical integration undermines attempts to secure monopoly positions. It may stimulate competition by buyers from or sellers to those seeking monopoly profits, provided such new integrated competitors do not merely share in the monopoly profits. Vertical integration tends to intensify price wars although this tendency has been much overrated. The effect of vertical integration on the trade cycle is not clear.

[1] F.T.C., *House Furnishings Industry*, 1925, III, xxvii.

B. Integration of the Production of Commodities Requiring Similar Selling Organizations

1. INFLUENCES AFFECTING SUCH INTEGRATION

Integration of the production of commodities calling for a similar selling organization has come to be one of the most important of all patterns of integration. Integration of the ownership and operation of the arrangements for the physical distribution of goods with the production of those goods has been discussed as an example of vertical integration. The organization for the physical distribution of goods may, however, not only be such as can be most economically operated on a large scale but also such as can be economically applied to the distribution of a variety of goods. Meat packers owning refrigerator cars could transport perishable foodstuffs other than meat, often without payment of additional freight, and could secure more expeditious transportation than rivals not controlling such facilities. Groceries and canned goods could be handled by the branch houses of the packers with practically no increase in distributing expense or overhead cost,[1] partly because branch house capacity was excessive for business in meat alone. Under these circumstances there is an inducement to integrate the production of a variety of products such as meat, canned foods, and groceries in order to make the most economical use of distributing facilities. Incidental services other than physical distribution may give rise to similar integration. The integration by the United Shoe Machinery Company of the manufacture of various kinds of machinery for making shoes facilitated, according to the court, the maintenance of local repair crews.[2] The International Harvester Company supplied similar services in connection with its full line of implements. Integration of this type is aimed at and may secure technical economies of production but has little direct relation to the declining importance of price competition.

The growth of selling costs has stimulated efforts comparable to those discussed above to reduce unit selling costs by making the fullest use of the organization for selling. Increasing emphasis upon advertising necessitates the employment of a personnel specializing upon this function. A personnel that has successfully

---
[1] SWIFT AND COMPANY, *Statement,* Aug. 19, 1918; U.S. v. Swift and Co. *et al.,* 1931, *Brief for U.S.,* 21, 45.
[2] U.S. v. United Shoe Machinery Co. *et al.,* 247 U.S. 32 (1918).

handled one product can often be more effectively and economically utilized if it handles a range of similar products. Similar economies in the use of services of traveling salesmen are also to be obtained by providing salesmen with a wider variety of products if they can be sold to a single class of buyers. The meat packers became interested in the production of fruit syrups because they found it necessary to send salesmen to sell meat extracts to drugstores and then found it economical to give these salesmen a wider variety of drugstore supplies to sell.[1] Late in 1931 when modification of the Consent Decree was being sought it was argued that selling costs could be reduced if "the salesman who sells meat products can also take orders for groceries."[2] The International Harvester Company also claimed[3] economy from the integration of the production of a variety of agricultural implements because it enabled salesmen to handle a "full line." Both these considerations must have played a large part in determining the range of the activities of firms engaged in producing drugs, cosmetics, groceries, tobacco, and many similar products.[4] Integration in retailing in the sense that retailers handle a wide variety of products tends, therefore, in the direction of a similar integration in wholesaling and manufacturing although, as we have seen, it may be, and frequently is, obstructed by technical difficulties. A manufacturer attempting to supply all the needs of drugstores would face a variety of technical problems too great to be solved at present.

The relation between the increasing importance of sales promotion or non-price competition and integration involves, however, further subtleties. The increasing importance of advertising induces efforts to economize expenditures in this direction; emphasis upon brand names being an inevitable accompaniment of advertising, attempts to increase the return per unit of advertising expenditure sometimes lead to the use of a brand name for a

[1] *Hearings on Government Control of the Meat Packing Industry* (H.R. 13324) before House Committee on Interstate and Foreign Commerce, 1919, 143. The chairman of the Federal Trade Commission, however, attributed this integration to a desire to secure control of competing products (*Hearings on Proposed Merger of Meat Packing Corporations* (S.R. 389) before Senate Committee on Agriculture and Forestry, 1923, 9, 10).
[2] *Cit.* U.S. v. Swift and Co. et al., *Brief for U.S.*, 51.
[3] U.S. v. International Harvester Co., *Brief and Argument for International Harvester Co.*, 1925, 3.
[4] It probably also explains the formation of firms like Standard Brands, Inc. (selling coffee, tea, yeast, baking powder, vinegar, and gelatin) and General Foods (selling prepared breakfast foods and desserts, prepared flour, syrups, coffee, cocoa, chocolate, and salt) in the course of the merger movement in 1922-1929.

variety of products. The advertising of each product tends, not only to promote the sales of that product, but also to make the brand name under which it is sold more familiar, and to promote the sales of other products of the same name. In recent years, therefore, there has been a tendency to extend the use of names such as "Beech-Nut," "Del Monte," and "Heinz" (boastfully applied to "57 varieties") to an increasingly wide range of products. The same tendency is evident in the allusion in the advertising of the General Motors Corporation to the fact that a commodity is "a product of General Motors."

Declining emphasis upon differences in price increases the importance of inducements to dealers to persuade buyers to purchase one brand rather than another. Manufacturers successful in securing the allegiance of retailers seek to provide them with a "full line" in order to utilize their persuasiveness to the maximum. Counsel for the Standard Oil Company of New York and the Vacuum Oil Company placed great emphasis upon this consideration in arguing in favor of the merger of the two companies. They contended that the production of lubricating oils is commonly integrated with the production of gasoline and that lubricating oils are usually distributed through the filling stations distributing the gasoline. The Vacuum Oil Company, which had specialized in the production of a wide range of lubricating oils, was encountering difficulty in selling its oils, because it had little gasoline to offer to the filling stations and considered it impracticable to establish a new nationwide system for distributing gasoline. "The only practicable way to meet the needs of the Vacuum brands for nationwide distributing facilities in connection with gasoline is the union of the Vacuum lubricating business with a company such as the Standard Oil Company of New York having the present typical organization of crude supply, refining capacity, and a widespread system of distributing facilities for gasoline."[1] The growing tendency of integrated manufacturers to secure direct control of retail outlets increasingly excluded the lubricating oils of the Vacuum company from sale by distributors also dealing in the gasoline and lubricating oils of the producers controlling them.[2] The Vacuum Oil Company

[1] U.S. v. Standard Oil Co. of New York and Vacuum Oil Co., *Answer to Supplemental Petition* (District Court), 18–20.
[2] It was reported that the number of distributors of Vacuum products had decreased by 20 per cent in four years and that the sales of the Vacuum company had decreased in about the same proportion, although the number of motor vehicles

on the other hand possessed a world-wide organization for the distribution of marine lubricants, and the great increase in the use of fuel oil in marine transportation made available great economies in the distribution of the fuel oil of the Standard Oil Company if it could use the outlets of the Vacuum Oil Company.[1]

It was argued that the large percentage of all the sales of the more complicated farm implements in the hands of the International Harvester Company had been used to promote its sales of other implements. The company pointed, however, to the diminishing importance of the sales of these implements in its total business after 1913.[2] It contended that success in the manufacture and sale of plows provided as good a basis for stressing other lines as success in harvesters, particularly as it placed salesmen in touch with farmers early in the season, and that tractors also provided good leaders; in neither of these lines did the company predominate.[3] Similar situations occur in the meat packing and other industries.

Social policy has presented no serious obstacle to integration of this type except in the meat packing industry. Mergers producing this pattern of integration have been neither obstructed nor disintegrated. No attempt has been made to deprive the International Harvester Company of its "full line." In a decision concerning the United Shoe Machinery Company which integrated the manufacture of machines needed by shoe manufacturers for performing different processes in the manufacture of shoes, the Supreme Court remarked that it could see no greater objection to one corporation manufacturing 70 per cent of these noncompeting groups of patented machines collectively used for making a single product than to three corporations making the same proportion of one group each.[4] The Consent Decree con-

---

in operation had increased by about 20 per cent (U.S. v. Standard Oil Co. of New York and Vacuum Oil Co., 1930, *Brief for Standard Oil Co. and Vacuum Oil Co.*, 26–27).

[1] *ibid.*, 30–31, and *Rejoinder Brief for Standard Oil Co. of New York and Vacuum Oil Co.*, 22.

[2] U.S. v. International Harvester Co., *Brief for International Harvester Co. (Reargument)*, 120. The decline in demand for harvesting machinery was attributed to a decline in the initial demand owing to the filling up of the western grain territory (the demand from which was shrinking to replacement proportions), the diversification of crops, the increasing life of the machines made, and the increasing efficiency of machines (*e.g.*, harvesting machinery drawn by tractor could deal with crops from a larger area than when drawn by horse traction). (*Brief for the International Harvester Co.* 15).

[3] *loc. cit.*

[4] U.S. v. Winslow, 227 U.S. 202, 217 (1913). The case is complicated, however, by the presence of patents.

cerning the larger meat packers in 1920[1] enjoined the packers from dealing in "unrelated lines" which included wholesale groceries, fresh, canned, or salt fish, and a hundred other enumerated commodities. In 1931,[2] however, the decree was modified to permit wholesale, but not retail, dealings in a number of food products. Not until 1933, however, were dealings in "unrelated lines" finally abandoned.[3]

2. THE CONSEQUENCES OF SUCH INTEGRATION

The effects of this type of integration are complex. It tends to reduce the unit costs of sales promotion and thereby to minimize the effect upon costs of the development of non-price competition.[4] It induces the more effective use of personnel and, indirectly, utilizes the potentiality of sales of one product to induce sales of another. In common with all forms of integration, however, this type hinders the comparison of costs and prices for each separate branch of production. Selling costs are incurred for a number of products and there is no satisfactory means of calculating the selling cost of each; there may, therefore, be wide variations in efficiency in the production and sale of different commodities. The market applies only the cruder comparisons of profits on the whole set of operations in which each firm is engaged. Where some firms remain highly specialized a more detailed check is possible; its effectiveness depends upon the importance of price competition. If the cost of production by specialized firms is higher than by integrated firms even this check is not severe.

The effect of this integration upon profits depends largely upon the competitiveness of the market. There is, however, a

---

[1] U.S. v. Swift and Co. *et al.*, *Consent Decree* entered in the Supreme Court of the District of Columbia, Feb. 27, 1920. During the years 1927, 1928, and 1929 Armour and Company's sale of "unrelated lines" were, however, still over $6,750,000 annually (U.S. v. Swift and Co. *et al.* (1931), *Brief for U.S.*, 12, 20), and not until July, 1933, did the court appoint a trustee to dispose of Swift and Company's 60 per cent stock interest in Libby, McNeill, and Libby (*New York Times*, July 12, 1933).

[2] U.S. v. Swift and Co. *et al.*, 286 U.S. 106 (1931). This case is complicated by the consent of the packers to restrictions upon their activities which may well have been more severe than the court would have imposed and also by the fact that they "had abused their powers so grossly and persistently" (U.S. v. Swift and Co. *et al.*, 286 U.S. 106, 119). Subsequent litigation turned partly upon the reasonableness of efforts by the packers to modify a bargain they had previously made in consideration of the abandonment of proceedings by the Attorney General under the anti-trust laws.

[3] *New York Times*, July 12, 1933.

[4] It is likely to disturb existing forms of organization. *Cf.* the attempt of the Drug Institute to prevent the sale of drugs "through other than legitimate drugstore channels" (*New York Times*, May 2, 1935).

THE INTEGRATION OF INDUSTRIAL OPERATIONS 451

tendency to less fluctuation in profits simply because of the pooling of risks in a number of markets; as the markets are less subject to a common risk than are those with which a vertically integrated firm is concerned, greater stability of profits is to be expected.

This type of integration affects prices in so far as it reduces unit selling costs and such reductions are reflected in prices. On the other hand, arising as it does out of non-price competition, it is accompanied by all the effects of such competition.[1] In itself, moreover, it gives rise to opportunities for price discrimination in the sense of selling individual products at prices exceeding or falling short of the total costs of producing and selling. The difficulty of segregating the management and selling costs of each product allows such discrimination from inadvertence. The pooling of the profits from the production and sale of a number of commodities also facilitates deliberate discrimination in this sense. The inducement to discriminate is most likely to be present when the integrated firm enjoys advantages in one market; it may exploit these advantages and divert part of the monopoly profits thus obtained to subsidize sales at less than apparent cost in other markets. The Commissioner of Corporations contended, for instance, that the International Harvester Company used the profits arising from the large scale of its operations and its semi-monopolistic position in the market for the more complicated agricultural implements to increase its trade in other agricultural implements, rather than to reduce the price of harvesting machines; he feared that when the Company had obtained a strong position in the market for other implements, it might then proceed to a policy of monopolistic prices in those markets as well.[2] The cost of producing harvesting machines by the Harvester company was so far below the costs of its rivals that it could charge prices that they could not meet and yet obtain sufficient profit to enable it to attack their business in other implements. The Federal Trade Commission also suggested that the relatively low average rate of profit obtained by the large

---
[1] See Chap. VIII.
[2] COMMISSIONER OF CORPORATIONS, *The International Harvester Company*, 288, 289. The Harvester company argued, however, that the development of what is called a "long line" resulted in the prices of a whole line of implements moving up and down together, and argued that if a high price were charged for a particular machine, buyers might buy the whole line elsewhere. Thus it was argued that purchasers were protected against high prices and competitors against low prices. (U.S. v. International Harvester Co., *Brief for International Harvester Co.*, 55.)

meat packers was due to the fact that high profits on meat had been used to finance ventures into new fields,[1] some of which might, in their initial stages even have involved losses, and added that low profits and even losses in new lines being invaded might be "an indication of the sort of competition waged in the invasion of unrelated distributing and manufacturing lines." Within short periods of time the profits of the integrated firm are diminished by this policy. But over the longer period it may extend its position of monopoly or leadership into new fields and obtain monopoly profits from them also. The profits available to the vertically integrated firms from this source are, as we have seen, very limited. The same limitations do not apply, however, to firms integrated according to the pattern at present under discussion. There are, however, limits, and possibly severe limits, to the profit possibilities of this policy. If non-integrated firms can be driven out only by price discrimination involving sales below the cost of production it is likely that new non-integrated firms will be attracted into the industry as soon as any attempt is made to depart from this policy.

A firm thus integrated may pursue the same objective by a different route, *viz.*, that of "full line forcing." Having secured a powerful position in the market for a product by economies in production, or by fortunate advertising, it may refuse to sell the product in general demand except to dealers who agree to handle and press the sales of its other products. It may even insist upon exclusive dealing in all of its products. In its early years the International Harvester Company pursued this policy.[2] Reference has been made also to the attempts of oil companies to tie the sale of other petroleum products to the sale of gasoline. Wholesale slaughterers complained that "occasionally we have competition from large packers who demand that their customers patronize their entire line of products, otherwise they will not sell an exclusive line."[3] The most notable example of such forcing is offered by the policies of the United Shoe Machinery Company. This company, having a virtual monopoly of the manufacture of the machines used for certain processes in the manufacture of shoes,

---

[1] *The Meat Packing Industry*, 1920, V, 16.
[2] COMMISSIONER OF CORPORATIONS, *The International Harvester Company*, 304. The effect of this practice was intensified by the fact that the company integrated the manufacture of a number of brands of the more important products and allocated each brand to a separate dealer, insisting upon exclusive dealing by each.
[3] F.T.C., *The Meat Packing Industry*, I, 488.

inserted tying clauses in its leases and attempted by other means to prevent shoe manufacturers from obtaining machinery for performing any of the processes of shoe manufacturing from rival producers of machinery: it thus obtained a virtual monopoly of the production of all shoe manufacturing machinery.[1] This policy differs in its effects from that of price discrimination directed to the same ends in that it involves no sacrifice of profits from sales in the controlled market. Where, however, the products tied to a product already in great demand are inferior to other similar products and more difficult to dispose of, pressure from dealers may necessitate price reductions which do involve such a sacrifice. Again integration is not the sole cause of these attempts to secure monopoly positions. It is merely a useful instrument for that purpose when control has been secured in one market.

The general consequences of this type of competition upon the distribution of goods and services between buyers and investors are largely identical with those already discussed as resulting from non-price competition. While sales expenditure may be more economically applied, there is a risk of reduced efficiency; unless price competition also prevails, the consumer is unlikely to benefit from any economies obtained. Furthermore, in so far as one product tends, or is deliberately used, to "sell" another, the buyer is confused in his distribution of expenditure; products sold under the same brand name are not necessarily equally desirable. Moreover, the risk of the application of high profits in some fields to the building up of positions in other fields which could not be acquired merely by more direct competitive methods is a matter of considerable importance. It may mean the introduction of more vigorous competition into other fields but that competition may be temporary and give place later to a semi-monopolistic régime.

C. *The Integration of the Production of Substitute Goods and Services*

The pattern of integration adopted by a business organization may be such that one product is a substitute for another. This type of integration is not always easy to identify; substitutability is a matter of degree; commodities which may substitute one for

---

[1] See SEAGER and GULICK, *Trust and Corporation Problems*, 290. These clauses were held not to violate the Sherman Act in U.S. v. United Shoe Machinery Co., 247 U.S. 32 (1918) but were held to contravene Sec. 3 of the Clayton Act in U.S. v. United Shoe Machinery Co., 258 U.S. 452 (1922).

the other may also have other characteristics which stimulate integration. The manufacture of airplanes and automobiles is sometimes integrated and while they are, within narrow limits, substitute commodities, the fact that they involve similar technical problems of production has probably played the larger part in inducing the integration of their production. Cigars, cigarettes, and pipe tobacco are commonly produced by a single firm, and, while each is within limits a substitute for the others, the fact that they involve similar problems in the purchasing of raw materials, manufacturing, and (in recent years) marketing, has probably been the most important inducement to integration. The meat packers were charged with "rapidly extending their control over all substitutes for meat"[1] when they undertook the distribution of poultry and dairy products and other foods. The packers, however, argued with reason that this integration was motivated by the similarity of the conditions of marketing these various products and by the possibility of realizing economies in the physical distribution of products.[2] The classification of patterns of integration into mutually exclusive classes is, therefore, not always possible.

1. INFLUENCES AFFECTING SUCH INTEGRATION

A monopolist whose profits were restricted by a high degree of elasticity in the demand for his product because of the presence of nearby substitutes would benefit if he could widen the scope of his control until there was no nearby substitute to which buyers could turn. Actual examples of integration thus motivated are difficult to find.

Integration of this type occurs, however, without monopoly. It is most commonly motivated by a desire to reduce risk, which is closely related to the desire to secure the survival of the business unit. The firm is impelled to enter the production of goods and services likely to displace its existing products. Capital losses owing to a decline in the demand for these latter products are counterbalanced by abnormal profits for a time upon activities in the field in which demand is growing. The Studebaker company, making carriages and wagons, entered the production of automobiles. Other possible examples of integration thus motivated

[1] F.T.C., *The Meat Packing Industry*, I, 35.
[2] See p. 446.

are offered by the integration of gas and electrical utilities,[1] and of railroad, airplane, and road transportation. The integration of telephone and radio with telegraph communications would probably have been wise from this point of view. When a firm seeks to control patents upon alternative methods of production, which may render existing methods less profitable or even obsolete, it is impelled by an analogous motive. The Standard Oil Company of New Jersey, for instance, controls patented processes of distilling oil from coal, and the General Electric and American Telephone and Telegraph companies are reputed to control patents covering processes having in some cases only a distant possibility of superseding existing processes.

Social control has little effect upon this type of integration. The Consent Decree concerning the large meat packers is of some relevance, so far as it affects unrelated lines, although fear of the probable effects of such dealings upon the distributors of other products appears to have been the dominant consideration rather than the, always visionary, possibility of the packers securing a monopoly of all food products. The Radio Act of 1927 prohibited the common control of radio transmission and cable and wire transmission of telegraph or telephone messages.[2]

2. THE CONSEQUENCES OF SUCH INTEGRATION

The main effects of this type of integration are suggested by the motives inducing it. It may be an effective instrument for strengthening the position of a monopolist if it is used to secure control of substitute products. Conditions in all the markets affected must, however, be favorable to the attainment and maintenance of monopoly. A railroad securing control of road transportation will be severely restricted in making price policy if new road transportation services are brought to birth whenever prices attain the level at which non-integrated road transportation services can be profitably operated. The probability that manufacturers controlling alternative methods of production will hinder the introduction of better products or the utilization of improved methods of production has already been discussed.[3]

[1] Here, however, there are also technical problems common to both and more economically handled by common control, *e.g.*, the handling of public utilities commissions.
[2] Sec. 17.
[3] *Cf.* p. 16. The Standard Oil Company of New Jersey has placed the control of the patents upon the hydrogenation of crude oil (acquired jointly with the I. G. Farbenindustrie, *i.e.*, the German dye trust) under the control of the refining indus-

456   THE DECLINE OF COMPETITION

In the absence of monopoly conditions such integration facilitates the pooling of the profits of a group of industries where increased profits in one are likely directly to cause decreased profits in the other; the profits of an integrated firm will fluctuate less than those of non-integrated firms. The opportunity for postponing the introduction of new products or the utilization of new methods depends upon the degree of imperfection of the market. If new substitute products are made but sold at a high price with the object of maintaining the sales of older types, new non-integrated firms with no losses arising from obsolescence may enter the market. Moreover, if the new product is introduced by non-integrated firms, integrated firms whose sales are likely to be reduced may, as we have seen, fight for survival by entering the new field of production and may even hasten the decline of prices there.

D. Territorial Integration

Territorial integration occurs when a firm distributes its products over a wide area. This definition implies the existence of a number of territories, distribution in each of which is integrated under a common management. Territories are not, however, capable of definition and the concept lacks complete precision. In fact the extension of the areas of distribution of products may be described either as an extension of market territories or as an increasing integration of distribution in different territories.

I. INFLUENCES AFFECTING SUCH INTEGRATION

Several causes may induce this change. Increasing resort to division of labor and the use of specialized equipment involve the increasing local concentration of production and, consequently,

---

try as a group. The new process increases the output and reduces the cost of the lighter oils (including gasoline) obtained from crude oil. The Standard Oil Company leased its rights on a royalty basis to a new company. But by offering stock in the new company to producers owning about 80 per cent of the crude oil refining capacity of the country in proportion to their productive capacity, it transferred to the industry at large the determination of policy concerning the time at which the new process should be utilized and purchasers begin to receive benefits. If the company sets high royalty payments it postpones exploitation of the process and maintains the price of gasoline. Low royalty payments encourage the utilization of the process. (The rate of royalty to be paid by the managing company to the Standard company and the I. G. Farbenindustrie presumably set the minimum royalty payment.) The Standard company thus denied itself the opportunity to improve its relative position in the industry, by price cutting, doubtless because of the resistance it expected to encounter. It was admitted at the time that control of the process was likely to play a large part in the control of competition in the industry. (*New York Times*, July 14, 1930.)

an increasingly wide marketing area for the production unit. Vertical integration inducing larger scale production intensifies this effect. Falling transportation costs lower one of the barriers to increasing the scale upon which production is locally concentrated. Desire to utilize to the full knowledge of the economies of large-scale production is not, however, the sole explanation of increasing territorial integration. Business units controlling the production of a single commodity or group of commodities in a number of plants have evidently expanded beyond the size necessary to secure plant economies. If the optimum size of a management unit is in excess of the optimum size of a production unit, considerations of economical management suggest the maintenance of production units in different localities under common control.

Territorial integration may be stimulated by the desire to diminish risks. A firm confining itself to a narrow territory links its fortunes with those of that territory. There appears, for instance, to have been a strong tendency in recent years for steel producers to obtain control of plants so located that they can secure business over a large part of the whole country. It has already been suggested that the abandonment of the Pittsburgh-plus method of calculating prices may possibly have stimulated this policy.[1]

The increasing importance and the nature of non-price competition are probably a more important reason for territorial integration. Where sales-promotion expenditures take the form of expenditure on advertising in periodicals which circulate throughout the whole country, the greatest return will be obtained from expenditures upon such advertising if the commodity is available in all the places reached by the advertising. The development of very large marketing territories for petroleum products has been attributed partly to this cause and partly to the fact that, as many purchasers travel over wide territories, the product they have been induced to buy must be made available wherever they go.[2] Where local price discrimination occurs those selling in the low-price areas are induced to enter the high-price areas; where some firms are operating in restricted areas and others over wider areas the former may fear local price cutting by the

---

[1] See Chap. VII.
[2] U.S. v. Standard Oil Co. of New York and Vacuum Oil Co., *Brief for Standard Oil Co. of New York and Vacuum Oil Co.*, 22, 23.

latter and seek to prevent it by enlarging their own areas. It was argued in favor of the merger of the Standard Oil Company of California and the Standard Oil Company of New Jersey that, since one marketed on the Atlantic seaboard and the Gulf coast and the other west of the Rockies, they were handicapped by being able to meet only locally competition offered by other large corporations with nationwide systems of distribution (a complaint ironically enough once made by the rivals of the Standard Oil Company against its practice of local price cutting). Each desired, therefore, to enlarge its territory and they sought a merger to avoid the waste that would result if each established a new marketing organization in the market territory of the other.[1]

There has been no deliberate social control of territorial integration. The partitioning of the former Standard Oil Company of New Jersey resulted in the establishment of a series of successor companies each concerned with an almost separate market territory, but this result was an incident to the elimination of the former Standard concern as a holding company. The Supreme Court has, however, maintained the constitutionality of state legislation designed to place chain stores at a disadvantage compared with retailers less integrated on a territorial basis.[2]

2. THE CONSEQUENCES OF SUCH INTEGRATION

The main consequences of territorial integration are suggested by the forces motivating it. It may permit production or even management upon a scale nearer to the optimum. In so far as demand fluctuates differently in different territories costs may be reduced by the utilization of productive equipment at a more uniform rate. It may reduce the average cost of selling.[3] On the

[1] STANDARD OIL COMPANY OF NEW JERSEY, *The Lamp*, October, 1931. This proposal has subsequently been abandoned.

[2] In Tax Commissioners (of Indiana) v. Jackson, 283 U.S. 527 (1931) the court decided by a circuitous route that a tax graduated according to the number of stores operated by a single firm did not contravene the guarantees of the fourteenth amendment to the Constitution; it reaffirmed its position in relation to a law of the state of North Carolina (Great Atlantic and Pacific Tea Co. v. Maxwell, 284 U.S. 575 (1931). A Florida law imposing taxation dependent upon the number of counties in which the stores operated was held, however, to be unconstitutional (Liggett Co. et al. v. Lee, 288 U.S. 517 (1933)). The exemption of gasoline filling stations and "voluntary chains" was upheld. A vigorous dissenting opinion was written by Mr. Justice Brandeis. The inclusion of gas stations in a similar West Virginia law was upheld (Fox v. Standard Oil Co. of New Jersey, 55 S. Ct. 333). State legislation affecting chain stores is summarized in F.T.C., *Chain Stores* (Final Report), 1935, 78.

[3] The Federal Trade Commission found that chain store expenditure on advertising per dollar of sales in general varied inversely with the number of stores operated. Chains of six to ten stores spent 4.18 per cent of their sales revenue on

other hand the desire for size for its own sake may induce territorial integration leading to rising production, management, and selling costs. Firms with more restricted markets which are able to avoid these rising costs might be expected to triumph over the more integrated. Their triumph depends, however, upon the competitiveness of the market, *i.e.*, upon the effect of such integration upon price policy. Territorial, like all forms of integration, renders more vague and general the check upon efficiency afforded by the market price. Some services are supplied generally in connection with business in a number of different territories and the precise cost of doing business in each cannot be calculated. Variations in efficiency from one market to another are absorbed into a general average, and not clearly recognized. Local discrimination arising not out of ignorance of the cost of each type of business but out of deliberate policy is, however, more important.[1]

Broadly speaking, local price cutting during the first period of the consolidation movement in America was aimed at the expulsion of rivals. Territorial integration facilitates but does not necessarily induce such a policy. It is most probable where some firms are much more integrated than rivals, as, for instance, when the former Standard Oil Company of New Jersey marketed throughout the United States while its rivals were confined within narrow geographical limits. The policy of the Standard company "of price discrimination or predatory competition" was in fact "one of the main bulwarks of its monopoly power."[2] This policy is greatly facilitated if monopoly prices can be charged in some areas; the resulting profits can be in part allocated to financing low prices in areas where competition is threatened. Local price cutting tends, however, as we have seen, to stimulate greater territorial integration with the object of preventing local price cutting; when all sellers are equally integrated there is little inducement to local discrimination to drive out rivals. If an impregnable monopoly is acquired in one territory it may be used as a base from which to acquire monopolies elsewhere but,

---

advertising in 1928 and those operating over 100 stores only 0.58 per cent. (F.T.C., *Chain Store Advertising*, 1934, 61.)

[1] See Chap. VI

[2] COMMISSIONER OF CORPORATIONS, *The Petroleum Industry*, I, 328. Local discrimination was facilitated by the vertical integration of refining with the wholesale distribution of oil. Tank-wagon delivery was so costly that it was economical only on a large scale and the prospect of profitable operation by a new firm seeking to compete with the Standard company was small. (*op. cit*, I, 330.)

if in other markets new competitors arise as soon as any monopoly policy is pursued there, continuous local price discrimination is necessary to retain business; this discrimination reduces the otherwise unassailable monopoly profits.

In the more recent period local price discrimination has accompanied the transformation of price policy into a matter for joint administration by all the large firms in an industry operating in different areas. The operations of different firms are integrated but without a merger of all property rights. The Federal Trade Commission has, however, remarked of chain stores that they have rarely required each store to yield the average rate of profit established for the chain as a whole. Had they done so they would have limited price cutting and denied the chain

the competitive advantage which results from the power of the chain to draw upon the profits of some of its stores for the funds with which to wage a drastic price war in highly competitive localities. . . . By far the greater number of chains . . . meet local competitive conditions as they arise and . . . the profits obtained in all the localities where they operate are automatically averaged.[1]

IV. CONCLUSIONS

In conclusion, integration may result from attempts to secure economies in production and marketing. In a large measure, however, it is explicable in terms of considerations that would be absent from a purely competitive world. The emergence of monopoly or quasi-monopoly conditions may induce vertical integration as a form of protection, or as a means of sharing in the monopoly profits; it may induce other types of integration in the hope of using a monopoly position in one field as a base from which to attain monopoly in another or to strengthen a monopoly by securing control of nearby substitutes. The increasing importance of non-price competition may stimulate vertical integration to reduce the number of times a commodity passes through the market, or the integration of the production of goods requiring similar selling organizations or territorial integration in order to minimize the unit cost of sales promotion. The imperfection of the market which cannot be relied upon to supply the products most suited to the needs of the buyers or to supply them precisely when they are needed stimulates vertical integration. The desire to

---

[1] F.T.C., *Chain Store Price Policies* (Senate Doct. 85, 73d Cong. 2d Sess.), 1934, 117.

avoid what Marshall regarded as the normal fate of business units, *viz.*, that, like the trees of the forest, they should rise to maturity and then decline and pass from the scene, leads to efforts to reduce risk. Integration satisfies this desire by permitting the pooling of the profits of a variety of operations, some patterns giving promise of greater stability of profit over both long and short periods than others.

The principal effect of integration alone is to carry a number of stages further the blurring of unit costs of production: this blurring began with the use of durable equipment for mass production. While integration may permit economies of production, management, or selling, this blurring of costs reduces the pressure to efficient production, although where many large non-integrated firms persist and price competition survives this pressure remains. Integration may obstruct innovations in production. It tends to more rational planning in the adaptation of products to processes, in the synchronization of production, and in the adaptation of production to changing knowledge of technique and the changing attitudes of consumers. But in this last respect its effectiveness depends upon the absence of non-integrated firms. Integration may undermine attempts to secure monopoly profits. Wherever non-integrated firms are easily established it is not very effective as a means of extending monopoly power from one field to another by price discrimination.

CHAPTER X

INDUSTRIAL POLICIES UNDER THE NATIONAL INDUSTRIAL RECOVERY ACT, 1933

I. The provisions of the law—II. The concentration of power to make policy in the hands of industry groups—*A*. Control of output—1. Direct control—2. Indirect control through regulation of hours of plant operation—*B*. Control of prices—1. Direct control—2. The prohibition of sales at prices below the cost of production—3. "Open-price" provisions—*C*. Control of non-price competition—1. Methods of selling—2. Quality and service competition—*D*. Control of long-term investment—III. Summary.

For 43 years social control of industry rested upon the assumption that an individualism not sufficiently rugged to maintain itself could be compelled by law to survive. This pretense was temporarily abandoned in 1933 when the National Industrial Recovery Act was passed. It was restored as the rule of social control a little less than two years later when the Recovery Act was declared unconstitutional.[1] The life of the act was, however, rich in contributions to the study of both the evolution of industrial policy and the problems of social control of industry. Promising to restrict the legal prohibitions upon cooperation between firms, the act encouraged the open and frank discussion of the new business policies analyzed in the foregoing chapters, and the attempt to secure their enforcement by law. Provision for public hearings before any code was approved made these discussions of policy more generally available. The attempt to secure the speedy adoption of codes throughout the industrial system made available information concerning business attitudes over a far wider range of productive activities than ever before; litigation and government reports, the main source of information prior to the new act, were richly supplemented. The energy with which the campaign to secure general cooperation was organized encouraged publicity concerning industrial policy.

[1] U.S. v. Schechter Poultry Corporation *et al.*, 55 S. Ct. 844 (1935). The Supreme Court held that the act attempted an unconstitutional delegation of legislative power and that the Constitution placed severe limits upon even the power of Congress to regulate industry. The court while agreeing that Congress might regulate intrastate commerce affecting interstate commerce, drew a line between direct and indirect effects which prevented any effective federal control of industry.

I. THE PROVISIONS OF THE LAW

The National Industrial Recovery Act[1] itself contained few innovations in law; it was built upon already established institutions and legal concepts. One of its objectives was "to eliminate unfair competitive practices";[2] such practices had been forbidden by statute for twenty years. The declaration of intention

to induce and maintain united action of labor and management under adequate governmental sanctions and supervision . . . to promote the fullest possible utilization of the present productive capacity of industries, to avoid undue restriction of production (except as may be temporarily required), to increase the consumption of industrial and agricultural products by increasing purchasing power, to reduce and relieve unemployment . . . and otherwise to rehabilitate industry and conserve national resources[3]

foreshadowed, however, an enlargement of the concept of "unfair competitive practices." The major departures from former policy were introduced as a result of this enlargement.

The principal device for administering the new policy was also some fifteen years old. It was the Trade Practice Submittal, later renamed the Trade Practice Conference; this procedure was taken over from the Federal Trade Commission[4] by the new administration. The act followed a new principle, however, in delegating the widest powers to the President. He was empowered[5] to approve of codes of fair competition submitted by trade or industrial associations or groups subject to such conditions as he might impose.[6] He might approve of any code provided that it would not permit monopolistic practices and would effectuate the policy of the act. The policy of the act was very widely defined and the power to determine whether codes would effectuate that policy was vested in the President. He had no power, however,

---
[1] H.R. 5755, 1933.
[2] Sec. 1.
[3] loc. cit.
[4] The act also provided that nothing contained in it should impair the powers of the Federal Trade Commission (Sec. 3, b), a proviso the significance of which did not emerge during the period under review.
[5] Sec. 3.
[6] His approval might "impose such conditions (including requirements for the making of reports and the keeping of accounts) for the protection of consumers, competitors, employees, and others, and in the furtherance of the public interest, and may make such exceptions to and exemptions from the provisions of such code as the President in his discretion deems necessary to effectuate the policy herein declared."

to approve of codes that would permit monopolies.[1] Heavy penalties were provided for the breach of any clause in an approved code "in any transaction in or affecting interstate or foreign commerce" (*i.e.*, by *any* firm in an industry for which a code had been approved, whether or not the firm was a party to the code). Finally it was provided[2] that during the operation of the act, and for sixty days thereafter, any action in compliance with an approved code "shall be exempt from the provisions of the anti-trust laws of the United States."[3]

II. THE CONCENTRATION OF POWER TO MAKE POLICY IN THE HANDS OF INDUSTRY GROUPS

The act was, therefore, an invitation to trade associations to place before the President plans, as limited or as far reaching as they could agree upon, for the centralized control of their respective industries; the President held the ultimate power to determine the degree of centralization to be permitted.[4] The policies pursued represented the demands of trade groups modified by the Recovery Administration. Reliance upon trade associations as the chief instruments for the regulation of industry enabled these associations to influence very markedly the policy of the administration during the period when the first codes were being adopted. This influence is not surprising. Producers interested in a small range of commodities are more willing and better able than consumers interested in a wide range of products to form strong organizations

---

[1] The President was authorized to approve codes provided (1) that such associations or groups were truly representative of their trades and imposed no inequitable conditions upon membership and (2) that the "codes are not designed to promote monopolies or to eliminate or oppress small enterprises and will not operate to discriminate against them and will tend to effectuate the policy of this title." Thus the President was himself empowered to determine the representativeness of trade associations submitting codes and the tendency of codes to give rise to monopolies or to damage small firms, except that it was separately "provided that such code or codes shall not permit monopolies or monopolistic practices."

[2] Sec. 5.

[3] The act also empowered the President to impose a code upon an industry (Sec. 3, d), to regulate imports (Sec. 3, e), to make agreements with trade, industrial, and labor organizations (Sec. 4, a) and to require producers to obtain a license to continue in operation (Sec. 4, b) (this clause expired on June 16, 1934). These powers were used either not at all or only rarely. The power to prescribe limited codes of fair competition concerning conditions of labor (Sec. 4, a) was the basis of the President's Reemployment Agreement but is not relevant to the present study. The requirement that codes should provide for the right of workers to bargain collectively and that workers should not be required to join a company union or to refrain from joining any other union (Sec. 7, a) was the cause of bitter dispute, but is also irrelevant to the present study

[4] This Presidential power was exercised largely by an administrator appointed under the act (Sec. 2) and advised by boards representing respectively the interests of industry, labor, and the consumer.

to protect their interests. In particular, they can afford to hire able counsel. Moreover, most business men felt justified in exacting a *quid pro quo* for the wage increases they were asked to make.[1] In consequence, the initial codes approved under the act revealed in the most striking manner the objectives towards which trade associations had been striving, often with little success, during the preceding twenty years. The legal sanctions behind the codes of fair competition not only forced into the associations or code authorities most of the producers in each industry, but also permitted the more direct attainment of their ends; they were no longer limited to devices that would avoid the prohibitions of the anti-trust laws. Reliance upon the provision of statistical information and suggested interpretations as a means of controlling prices was replaced by devices for more direct control of output and prices, although outright and explicit cartelization was, in general, resisted by the administration. Statistics concerning prices remained of great importance, but were adapted more openly to the control of price competition. The broad lines of policy will be discussed by reference to its effect upon control of output, prices, non-price competition, and long-term investment.

A. *Control of Output*

1. DIRECT CONTROL

Although a number of industries, stimulated by a model code drawn up by the National Association of Manufacturers,[2] presented draft codes providing for complete regulation of output and the distribution of production quotas by the code authority, the administration in general refused to approve such direct control of output.[3] The principal industries in which output or sales control was approved were lumber and timber products, petroleum, and copper; these industries, being concerned with the

[1] Lyon and others, *The National Recovery Administration*, 563.
[2] *United States News*, June 10–17, 1933.
[3] The codes of a miscellaneous group of industries (including iron and steel, cement, piano manufacturing, paper and pulp, cotton garment, and folding paper box) provided for consideration of the matter and the later presentation of plans for controlling output should they be thought necessary. Proposals for control of the output of newsprint were later advanced but bitterly opposed by the newspaper publishers (*New York Times*, Aug. 4, 1934). The code authority for the cement industry was authorized to draw up and submit to the administrator plans for "the equitable allocation of available business among all the members of the industry," provided that such plans did not reduce the total output below what was necessary amply to supply demand. No such plan was ever agreed upon.

marketing of a natural resource, were thought to require special treatment.[1] No control of output (or prices) was provided, however, in the lead,[2] zinc, or aluminum industries, and no code was ever approved for the anthracite coal industry.

The code authority for the lumber and timber products industry was authorized to estimate every three months the consumption and exports of each division of the industry and establish a maximum output, or quota of imports, for each division in order to balance production and consumption; it was also authorized to allocate the total permissible output between all the producers in each division according to a complicated formula, every person known to be operating a plant being entitled to a quota; quotas were not transferable from one producer to another. Actual production generally fell short of the quotas set by the code authority, doubtless because of its price policy;[3] inventories, however, were greatly reduced.[4] In April, 1935, the Attorney General withdrew an appeal lodged with the Supreme Court which would have tested the constitutionality of the code because the government was unwilling that the

---

[1] Output control was also approved, without any such justification, in the glass container industry where so long as the industry was operating below 70 per cent of its registered capacity "the principle of sharing available business equitably among the members of the industry shall be recognized, not to restrict production, but to maintain a reasonable balance between production and consumption of glass containers, and to assure adequate supplies thereof." This program was attributed to a desire "to maintain competitive conditions." The demand for containers was to be estimated every six months and the total quota distributed "equitably" among the producers, due consideration being given to the productive capacity and past performance of each and to the greater difficulties of curtailment of output by small producers. Output control was also approved in the Atlantic mackerel industry. The executive committee was authorized to "estimate consumer demand" and limit the catch of mackerel to that figure. Immediately prior to restriction 1.5 million pounds of mackerel had been landed per week. The catch was restricted first to 614,000 pounds and later to 445,000 pounds. Whenever production was reduced to the point where the price exceeded three cents a pound (compared with 1.3 cents per pound immediately before restriction) the aggregate return to fishermen fell below the weekly return before restriction commenced. The Consumer Advisory Board decided that "the only ones to benefit from the code program were the mackerel themselves" (*Price Control through Limitation of Production in the Mackerel Fishing Code*, 6). The demand for mackerel was elastic because of the availability of nearby substitutes. The restriction program was abandoned in October, 1934 (*ibid*).

[2] The code authority was empowered to consider the matter; not even open-price clauses were included for either metallic or pig lead.

[3] The index of wholesale lumber prices generally, which by March, 1930, was about 42 per cent below that of 1926, increased between March and December, 1933, over 50 per cent; in December, 1934, however, it was only 40 per cent above its level in March, 1933. The price of Douglas fir lumber increased nearly 100 per cent at the mill, that of yellow pine flooring 123 per cent at the mill, and cedar shingles about 75 per cent between March and December, 1933.

[4] *Cf. New York Times*, Mar. 2, 1935.

constitutionality of the act should be first tested by reference to a code giving to a code authority final power to determine output.[1]

The provisions for control of the output of petroleum were broadly similar[2] but they also led to legal difficulties, and the delegation to the President of power to prohibit interstate shipments of oil produced in excess of the quotas fixed by the states was held unconstitutional by the Supreme Court.[3]

Control of sales of copper was imposed upon the industry over the protests of some of its members.[4] Broadly speaking, the producers, refiners, and smelters who accepted (with regard to copper sold in the United States) the restriction of sales, the allocation of sales quotas, and the allocation of orders by a single marketing agency,[5] were permitted to call their product "blue eagle copper";

[1] In consequence, the code authority threatened to abandon all efforts to apply the code (*New York Times*, Mar. 30, 1935, and Apr. 2, 1935).

[2] A federal agency nominated by the President was to estimate "the required production of crude oil to balance the consumer demand for petroleum products," due account being taken of "probable withdrawals from storage and of anticipated imports." The Secretary of the Interior (who was nominated as the agency to control the industry) was authorized to allocate this allowable total output for the country equitably between the various states; arrangements were also made for the further allocation of quotas to each pool, lease, or well within each state. Production in excess of these quotas was an unfair practice. Further power to enforce the restriction of output was given through the power vested in the President by the National Industrial Recovery Act to regulate the shipment of petroleum and petroleum products from any state to the extent necessary to effectuate the purposes of the act where any state exceeded its total quota of production or failed to make an allocation of quotas within the state. Both the act and the code empowered the President to regulate imports of oil and the code empowered the code authority (the Planning and Coordination Committee) to regulate withdrawals of oil from storage. The supply of crude oil for refining was, therefore, intended to be completely controlled. The code authority was also authorized to specify to all refineries the crude runs to stills necessary to maintain a proper ratio between inventories and sales in each district, and production of gasoline in excess of these quotas was an unfair trade practice, as well as the maintenance of inventories of gasoline in excess of those necessary to provide for necessary fluctuations in working stocks and to meet seasonal variations in demand. The prices of oil products rose after the adoption of the code but, in considering the increases, the unusually low levels of price prevailing in the immediately preceding period must be taken into account. (See F.T.C., *Gasoline Prices*, 1934, *passim*.)

[3] Panama Refining Co. v. Ryan, 55 S. Ct. 241 (1935).

[4] *New York Times*, Apr. 24, 26, 1934. The refiners, smelters, and fabricators, having been unable to agree upon a basis for the control of output, requested authority subsequently to make voluntary agreements aimed at raising the price of copper and reducing stocks.

[5] Absolute monthly and annual quotas of sales were provided for each primary producer by name. Quotas were based on annual capacity for production, except for smaller companies which were allowed to produce at a higher ratio of capacity than the larger (*New York Times*, Apr. 26, 1934). The administrator was empowered to change the quotas from time to time and an aggregate quota was set aside for secondary producers (*i.e.*, those producing copper obtained by reworking scrap copper, scrap brass, and scrap alloys containing copper), this quota to be distributed between individual producers "by some equitable method agreed on by such producers and approved by the code authority and, failing any agreement, by the

this copper alone was eligible for use in any article to be sold to the federal government.¹ Any or all of the marketing provisions might be suspended if the price of copper became unreasonably high in the opinion of the code authority or the administrator. Immediately after the approval of the code, the price of copper was raised from 8½ to 9 cents per pound. Within a few weeks similar copper fell in foreign markets to about 7.25 cents per pound.² The quotation of "non-blue eagle" copper at a price below that of "blue eagle" copper caused difficulties which were met partly by the surrender of part of their quotas by producers not operating, and partly by drastic efforts to eliminate "non-blue eagle" copper by destroying the market for it.³ Attempts were later made to maintain the price by the restriction of output

---

administrator." As these producers failed to agree, the administrator allocated quotas (*New York Times*, May 16, 1934). Temporary provision was also made for custom smelters and refiners. Those receiving sales quotas were required to accept allocations of sales made to them by a sales clearing agent, provided they had copper available for sale within the delivery period covered by the allocation, sales being proportionately applied to the quotas for the current month. Sales in any month in excess of the quota for the current month were to be allocated to succeeding months, and only after the quotas for the two succeeding months were exhausted were stocks to be drawn upon. The code authority was to propose a plan to deal with these withdrawals from stocks which, when approved by the administrator, would provide for the orderly liquidation of stocks. Sales of copper by members of the industry in contravention of the plan were a violation of the code. Provision was made for the monthly adjustment of sales to sales quotas by purchases and sales between holders of quotas. When the Phelps Dodge Corporation absorbed the United Verde Copper Company the code was amended to permit the former company to take over the sales quota of the latter (Approved Code 401, Amendment No. 1, of Apr. 26, 1935).

[1] Copper held by those without such quotas and unable to obtain such quotas, and the output of smelters and refiners in excess of their quotas, was non-blue eagle copper. Direct regulation of output (and prices) was provided for only in the event of an emergency in the industry "in that destructive price cutting and/or excessive production is being engaged in to such an extent as to endanger the effectuation of the purposes of this code or the act."

[2] *New York Times*, June 24, 1934; July 29, 1934; Aug. 9, 1934. While producers of raw copper were left free in their production for export, fabricators were seriously affected. The import duty of 4 cents per pound was sufficient to prevent imports, apart from the obstacles placed by the code authority in the way of the use of "non-blue eagle" copper, (which included imported copper). This differential persisted, therefore, and seriously handicapped American fabricators exporting products containing a substantial amount of copper in competition with foreign fabricators (*New York Times*, July 24, 1934) until the code authority permitted purchases of copper at the foreign price for use solely in products to be sold abroad (*New York Times*, Aug. 1, 1934).

[3] *New York Times*, May 23, 1934. The code authority, exercising its power to make regulations defining "blue eagle" copper, decided to class as "non-blue eagle" copper the whole output of a plant using any "non-blue eagle" copper; the use of any "non-blue eagle" copper by one subsidiary of a copper fabricating plant would contaminate the output of all other subsidiaries. Thus members of the code were prevented from using any "non-blue eagle" copper (*New York Times*, May 10, 1934). The agreements for the sale of copper to fabricators drawn up by the code authority provided that fabricators should neither fabricate on toll nor purchase "non-blue eagle" copper (*New York Times*, Aug. 1, 1934).

beyond the sales quotas prescribed in the code.[1] Finally, when the National Industrial Recovery Act was declared unconstitutional,

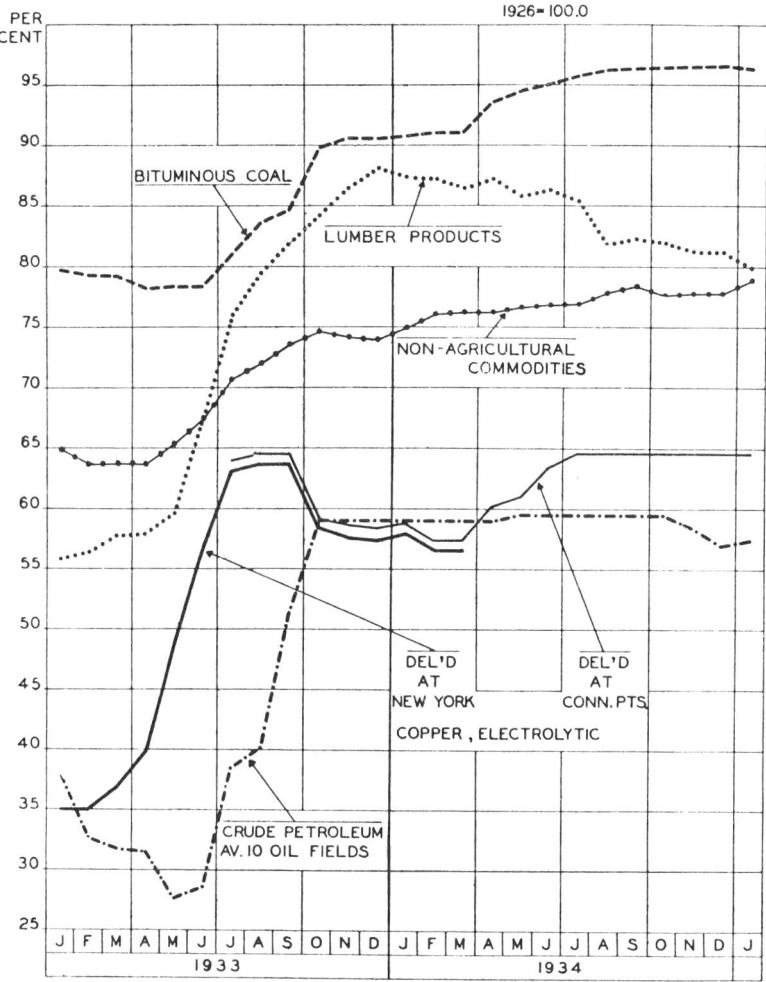

FIG. 51.—The prices of commodities the output or prices of which were directly controlled under the National Industrial Recovery Act, in 1933 and 1934. [*Drawn from data in United States Bureau of Labor Statistics: Wholesale Prices (coal and lumber). "Oil Paint and Drug Reporter" (oil) and "American Metal Market" (copper).*]

the price was maintained for a time and then, following upon a

[1] Primary producers agreed to forego their sales quotas for six weeks in order that all sales might be allocated to secondary, custom, and by-product producers and approved the principle of restricting output to actual sales (*New York Times*, September 28, 1934).

period of stagnation in the market, reduced from 9 to 8 cents.[1] The behavior of prices in the principal industries in which control of output was permitted is indicated in Fig. 51.

2. INDIRECT CONTROL THROUGH REGULATION OF HOURS OF PLANT OPERATION

Output was indirectly controlled in about 60 codes which prescribed the maximum number of hours for which plant might be operated. The cotton textile industry had experimented unsuccessfully with this device as early as 1930 and it led the way in securing compulsory restrictions upon plant operation; its code required the limitation of operations to two shifts of forty hours a week.[2] Forty-three of the 60 codes including similar restrictions were for the special branches of the textile industry where 80 hours a week was commonly prescribed as a maximum, although 40 was not uncommon. So long as the possible output of the whole industry, operating at the maximum rate permitted, exceeds the actual output, control of plant operation need not affect prices or production; it operates (as it probably did immediately after the approval of the cotton textile code) to distribute production more evenly among producers, *i.e.*, it is a "share the work" movement applied to plant equipment, and assists the less efficient to obtain business, more particularly if the entry of new capital is discouraged or prevented by control.[3]

Control of the hours of plant operation can, however, be use to control total output if the maximum is set sufficiently low. It then automatically sets quotas for each producer in proportion to his capacity to produce. Policy did in fact develop in this direction. On a number of occasions the administrator approved temporary reductions in the permitted number of hours of opera-

---

[1] *New York Times*, June 19, 28, 1935. The United States Copper Association decided to take over the functions of the copper code authority but there was little doubt that the control of output was illegal.

[2] This rule was approved over the objection of some firms, especially those making surgical dressings, and rubber tire manufacturers producing their own fabrics. The clause was approved for the cotton industry to "prevent both undue market stimulation and undue market demoralization," to avoid the accumulation of "diseconomic surpluses," and (it was alleged) to aid large numbers of small firms which, lacking resources for more than two shifts, would otherwise be at a disadvantage. The clause was not expected to interfere with the fair competition of efficient producers or with the interests of workers or consumers. The report of the administrator (annexed to the code) stated that two shifts were not likely to be used by more than half the mills.

[3] The entry of new capital was controlled under the code for the cotton textile industry (see p. 509).

tion or even temporary closing down of all plants where demand had declined and inventories had increased.[1] Used in this manner this power became a means of restricting output to demand at the current price and sharing the available business.[2] On at least one occasion an industry was permitted temporarily to increase its hours of operation to enable it to meet a seasonal increase in demand.[3]

B. Control of Prices

Soon after he took office the administrator announced that, although conduct in accordance with approved codes was exempt from prosecution under the anti-trust acts, it was not intended to authorize price agreements. Nevertheless, 560 of the first 677 codes contained some provision relating to minimum prices or

---

[1] Further curtailments of the hours of plant operation were approved in December, 1933, and thereafter in various branches of the textile industry; in the hosiery industry the number of days of operation was restricted (CONSUMER ADVISORY BOARD, *Cotton Textiles*). In May, 1934, the administrator permitted the restriction of plant operation in the cotton textile industry to sixty hours a week for twelve weeks owing to a decline in demand and an increase in inventories. The synthetic yarn staples industry was permitted to close down for eight weeks (*New York Times*, May 23, 1934). In July, 1934, the code authority for the silk textile industry voted to operate on a single shift of forty hours a week provided the rayon weaving industry adopted a similar restriction (*New York Times*, July 18, 1934). Wholesale exemptions from the order are said to have been granted by the administration to avoid accusations of unfairness or monopoly (*New York Times*, Sept. 9, 1934). The code authority for the upholstery and textile fabrics industry considered the abandonment of the regulation of the hours of loom operation and its replacement by a rule permitting full operation provided the inventory of the mill did not exceed 20 per cent of its sales for the preceding year (*New York Times*, Aug. 12, 1934). (This rule was criticized as likely to cause less regularity of operation and employment.) The code for the lumber and timber products industry was amended to permit control of output in terms of allowable hours of operation where two thirds of the branch of the industry concerned so requested (Amendment No. 11 of June 5, 1934). It was later reported that the administration was unwilling further to restrict the output of cotton goods by this means (*New York Times*, Sept. 9, 1934). In March, 1935, however, some branches of the textile industry were authorized to reduce the hours of plant operation by not more than 25 per cent for an emergency period of twelve weeks. This action was in accordance with recommendations of the Textile Planning Committee and arose out of a serious decline in demand and increase in inventories (*New York Times*, Mar. 27, 1935).

[2] An approach to the sharing of the market is also suggested by the provision in the code for the structural steel and iron fabricating industry that the code authority, in determining whether to investigate in detail complaints that members had sold at prices below "reasonable estimated cost of production," should consider, *inter alia*, whether the member of the industry complained of "had, since the effective date of the code, contracted for more than its fair share of the business of fabricating products used in and for doing erection work in the United States." It will be recalled that the American Institute of Steel Construction had proposed earlier to adapt its method of charging membership fees so as to levy fines upon those doing more than their "fair share" of business (see p. 153).

[3] The warp knit fabrics group was permitted to operate three forty-hour shifts a week for a few weeks (*New York Times*, Apr. 26, 1935).

costs.[1] These various provisions fall into a number of classes which can be grouped under (1) direct price control (2) prohibition of sales at prices below the cost of production, and (3) "open-price" clauses.

1. DIRECT CONTROL OF PRICES

Only 12 of the first 677 codes empowered the code authority, with or without the approval of the administrator, to establish minimum prices without reference to the cost of production.[2] The most important codes permitting direct control of prices were those for three industries concerned with the marketing of natural resources, in which "cutthroat competition has led to public disaster,"[3] *viz.*, soft coal, lumber, and petroleum. The code for the soft coal industry authorized the establishment of marketing agencies in each regional division and empowered them to determine the "fair" market price for coal necessary to enable operators to pay the minimum wage rates and to furnish employment.[4] No reference was made in the code to costs of production. By March, 1934, coal prices had been raised above their 1929 level and continued to advance even during the summer. But while prices in November, 1929, were 6 per cent above their 1929 level, production was 37 per cent and employment 20 per cent below the 1929 level. Accumulations of slack threatened the whole structure of prices. Serious conflicts occurred within the industry[5]

---

[1] N.R.A., *Prices and Price Provisions in Codes*, Jan. 9, 1935, Part III.
[2] *loc. cit.*
[3] *Release* by Consumer Advisory Board, Oct. 4, 1933. No direct price control was provided, however, in the copper, lead, zinc, or aluminum industries.
[4] If the member of the code authority representing the President failed to approve of any change in price it did not become effective without the consent of the administrator. In the determination of this "fair price," competition with other kinds of fuel and sources of heat production was to be taken into account. No provision was made at the outset for the coordination of the price policies of the agencies in different divisions: the administration members of the several marketing agencies served as an informal coordinating committee until a formal committee was appointed for the purpose; finally an arbitration committee was established by an amendment to the code (LYON and others, *op. cit.*, 177). The price fixing provision was thought by the deputy administrator submitting the code to the President to be likely to relieve the industry of much cutthroat competition, to obviate the dumping of coal at ruinous prices, reduce materially uneconomic and destructive competition between fields, and do much to restore equilibrium between fields and promote the development of markets related geographically and economically to the producing centers (Report annexed to the code). A price war was, however, subsequently reported in Pennsylvania, West Virginia, Ohio, Illinois, and Indiana (*New York Times*, Jan. 13, 1934).
[5] The setting of a minimum price without regard for differences in sulphur content, although coal with a high sulphur content had commonly been sold at a lower price than coal containing less sulphur, was said to discriminate against small firms.

and code prices were widely evaded.[1] Several districts formally withdrew from the inter-district price correlation procedure.[2] Prices were sufficiently attractive to have induced the opening up of "gopher hole" mines in some areas. The differentials between different grades were sometimes discriminatory and calculated to limit the sales of efficient producers and protect the less efficient.[3]

The code authority in the lumber and timber products industry was authorized to establish minimum f.o.b. prices "to protect the cost of production" whenever it was satisfied that it could determine the cost of production, and that the setting of minimum prices would contribute to the accomplishment of the declared purposes of the code.[4] Minimum prices for imported lumber might be set by reference to the minima for the same or competing items, grades, sizes, or species of domestic production. It has already been remarked that very considerable increases were made in the prices of some types of lumber with the result that sales fell short of the quotas of output. The power to fix minimum prices was withdrawn in July, 1934, and replaced by a clause empowering the administrator to set minimum prices based upon "reasonable cost" wherever he adjudged an emergency to exist.[5] In the almost complete absence of accurate information concerning costs "the minimum prices represented little more than guesses."[6]

The setting of a margin between the prices of washed and unwashed coal insufficient to cover the cost of washing, handicapped small enterprises selling unwashed coal. (("DARROW") BOARD OF REVIEW, *Report, cit. New York Times*, May 21, 1934.)

[1] The survival of the machinery for fixing prices was attributed to the ease of evasion. Code prices did not affect pre-code contracts and the code is said to have been evaded by making contracts as of dates prior to the code (CONSUMER ADVISORY BOARD, *Fixing Coal Prices*, 2. The code was also evaded by contracts providing for forfeits if coal failed to comply with standards known to be impossible of fulfillment, by excess shipments, and deliveries of superior grades. Lack of control of forward prices under the code necessitated an amendment on Jan. 25, 1935 (Amendment No. 6).

[2] CONSUMER ADVISORY BOARD, *op. cit.*, 2.

[3] *ibid.*, 4 ff.

[4] The minima were to be established "with due regard to the maintenance of free competition among species, divisions, and subdivisions, and with the products of other industries, and other countries, and to the encouragement of the use of said products." The code set limits, however, to the minima that might be established (except for goods for export). The upper limit was "the current weighted average cost of production" in each division, the items to be included in costs being set out. The lower limit was the weighted average of costs excluding all depreciation and amortization charges and all charges for logs and other raw materials.

[5] Amendment 15, code for lumber and timber products industry, approved July 16, 1934. This clause embodied a new policy adopted by the administration (see p. 489).

[6] CONSUMER ADVISORY BOARD, *Price Fixing in the Lumber Industry*, 1935, 1. The difficulties of price fixing in the industry are indicated by the fact that the lumber price list included about 5,000 different items, for each of which there were

In the first ten months of 1934 lumber prices "averaged 53 per cent higher relative to general wholesale prices than before 1914."[1] Demand in the second half of 1932 was lower than during any six-month period of the twentieth century; it rose during 1933 but declined again in 1934[2] and inventories increased again. The minimum prices attracted into operation 5,000 additional sawmills.[3] Violation of the minimum-price provision became common and the industry itself finally requested the discontinuance of minimum prices, which was granted.[4]

The code for the petroleum industry contained far-reaching provisions for control of the prices of oil and oil products, which were not unanimously approved in the industry[5] and were disapproved by the Consumer Advisory Board.[6] During periods in which the production of crude petroleum in any state was within the quota allocated to it, the sale of crude oil of a basic specification[7] at a price less than 18.5 times[8] the price per gallon of a basic specification of gasoline[9] (to the nearest cent) during the preceding month[10] was prohibited. Fair and equitable differentials were to be provided for other grades, and oil in other locations. This device merely fixed the relationship between crude oil and gasoline, but further provision was made for the fixing of the absolute level of prices. During an initial period of ninety days the President was empowered to establish detailed schedules of minimum prices for petroleum and petroleum products; sales below these prices were unfair. In the subsequent period, petroleum might not be sold below its recovery cost[11] and petroleum products

---

six different prices (*loc. cit.*). Variations in grades, rebates, lack of uniformity in granting discounts also caused difficulties.

[1] *ibid.*, 2. Furniture manufacturers protested but had apparently succeeded in buying at less than code prices (*ibid.*, 5).

[2] *ibid.*, 3.

[3] *ibid.*, 4.

[4] *ibid.*, 6.

[5] *Cf. New York Times*, Nov. 12, 1933. Some of the larger and most of the smaller firms objected to this policy.

[6] Letter to the Secretary of the Interior, Oct. 9, 1933, in which the board appealed for a postponement of price fixing until a more comprehensive study of the problem had been made.

[7] Mid-continent crude petroleum of 36° to 36.9°A.P.I. gravity.

[8] The constant of 18.5 represented the relationship during the period 1928 to 1932 between the average price per barrel of crude oil of the basic quality prescribed and the average price per gallon of gasoline of the prescribed quality.

[9] Group 3 tank-car price per gallon of U.S. motor gasoline of 60 to 64 octane rating.

[10] This average price was to be ascertained and declared by the Secretary of the Interior.

[11] In determining this cost the federal agency was to determine the average cost of

might not be sold at prices which did not cover their average cost of production.¹ The President was also authorized to set *maximum* prices for petroleum and its products but did not exercise the authority. Thus the price of crude oil might not fall below the average cost of producing it nor the price of oil products below their cost of production. The price of gasoline might fall below neither its cost of production nor the price arrived at by applying the multiplier 18.5 to the price of crude oil. The Secretary of the Interior issued an order fixing the prices of oil products in detail as to type of product, grade, and location,² but energetic protests resulted in the postponement of its operation and, finally, its abandonment. The Secretary of the Interior decided to delegate control of the price of petroleum products to a marketing agency³ consisting of the refiners, which was to purchase gasoline "which threatens the stability of the oil price structure" and dispose of it in an "orderly" manner so as to maintain the above relationship between the prices of crude oil and gasoline.⁴ Later the Secretary of the Interior announced that he was considering an amended plan for restricting gasoline supply to demand and establishing agencies to achieve this end. Pooling agreements were proposed under which the participants would keep their own "surplus" gasoline off the market and thus assure the small independent refiner of an outlet for his product "at a fair price."⁵ Subsequently he approved of an agreement among the refiners on the Pacific coast not to handle crude oil produced in excess of the "allow-

---

production of crude petroleum "and the fair economic limit of the cost of production in 'stripper' well areas (*i.e.*, areas in which wells needed to be pumped) which must be met to prevent the premature abandonment of such 'stripper' wells as may be found to be economically practicable of operation."

[1] The federal agency was instructed to determine the "average costs" of economically refining, transporting, and distributing petroleum and its products "for different areas and for different methods of marketing." The prices set for different localities and different grades "shall bear such relations as shall be fair and equitable." The Secretary of the Interior called for the information necessary to make these calculations on Dec. 7, 1933.

[2] *Order* of Secretary of Interior, Oct. 16, 1933. The prices were to be experimental for a period of ninety days and were said to have been based upon the statistics of cost.

[3] *Order* of Secretary of the Interior, Jan. 19, 1934.

[4] In February, 1934, companies handling more than 95 per cent of the gasoline sold in Pacific coast territory made a cartel agreement dividing the market between them (*New York Times*, Feb. 20, 1934). In March, 1934, however, the major oil companies selling in California were charged with secretly cutting the price of third-grade gasoline by selling it under different brand names through subsidiaries ostensibly in competition with their controlling companies and at prices lower than those charged by the controlling companies (*New York Times*, Mar. 24, 1934).

[5] *New York Times*, Apr. 6, 1934.

ables" set, to sell all gasoline at posted prices, and to purchase all gasoline in the hands of independent refiners which they were unable to sell "in the regular course of their business." A similar agreement aimed at maintaining the price of gasoline was negotiated in the east Texas field[1] and it was later announced that this device was to be applied to the whole territory east of the Rockies.[2] Explicit control of prices thus gave place to the restriction of sales to amounts that would permit the maintenance of prices accepted as satisfactory by the refiners and the Secretary of the Interior.[3]

The behavior of prices in the soft coal, petroleum, and lumber industries is shown at Fig. 51 on page 469.

Among the remaining attempts to set minimum prices the most troublesome was the power given to the code authority in the cleaning and dyeing industry to prescribe "fair and reasonable minimum wholesale and retail prices by regions and/or local areas for the several services comprised within the definition of cleaning and dyeing." The administrator hoped that this clause would terminate ruinous price competition which had resulted in wage cutting, poor quality of service, and the threat to the existence of small shops—a plea which, no doubt, might have been advanced in many other fields.[4] This clause proved

---

[1] *New York Times*, June 24, 1934.
[2] *New York Times*, Sept. 1, 1934.
[3] The order setting minimum prices brought to light a host of difficulties. It was claimed that the proposed minima discriminated against small companies. Uniform prices were set for both advertised and unadvertised gasoline, thus preventing the small company from attracting business by lower prices rather than by advertising. The margin between the price of gasoline at Gulf ports and on the eastern seaboard was insufficient to permit the purchase of gasoline at Gulf ports and its resale in New York and Boston; the margin between the price in east Texas and at Atlantic seaboard ports was also insufficient to permit transportation from the former to the latter (*New York Herald Tribune*, Nov. 26, 1933). The price in east Texas was said to be the same as at Gulf ports, although transportation alone from the east Texas field to the coast cost 79 cents per barrel. The ratio of 18.5 between the price of crude oil and that of gasoline was attacked because it was based upon conditions prevalent during the period between 1928 and 1932 when operations were said to have been unprofitable; the margin between crude oil and gasoline being fixed as a ratio of the price of crude oil, the principal gains were likely to be obtained by integrated firms and owners of oil rights. The price set for gasoline would cause an increase in the price of crude oil and the non-integrated refiners would be "squeezed." The decline in the price of oil products other than gasoline since the base period from 1928 to 1932 also made the margin thus fixed unprofitable to the non-integrated firms. "Skimming plants" *i.e.* those not "cracking" oil) would suffer because, the octane rating of their product being below that on which the formula was based, they would have to sell at a price below that set for gasoline of the standard rating. (See *United States News*, Aug. 19-26, 1933.)
[4] He also referred to the racketeering with which the industry had been afflicted, although there was no obvious reason why the clause should eliminate racketeering.

unenforceable and the major part of the code was finally abandoned with considerable ill feeling.[1] The code for the cigar container industry permitted the code authority to establish minimum prices;[2] that for the graphic arts industries permitted the issue of "price determination schedules" to serve as "guides of fair value"; that for the cigar manufacturing industry set a minimum price in the code itself.[3] Modified authority to set minimum prices was also provided in the fur dressing and dyeing, domestic freight forwarding, and wholesaling and distributing industries. In the course of the hearings upon the code proposed for the electrical products industry, however, the administrator refused to authorize the code authority to fix fair prices because such power meant "arbitrary price fixing on the products of an individual manufacturer by a jury of his competitors."[4]

In the distributing trades the price of the service of the dealer is his "mark up," or the margin between the price at which he buys and the price at which he sells. Although attempts were made in some branches of the industry to set minima which would be generally applicable, the policy generally adopted in dealing with retailers was to set the minimum "mark up" so low that it merely obstructed the use of "loss leaders," *i.e.*, sales at prices which did not return to the retailer a reasonable proportion of his total costs of operation. The principal retail code prohibited sales at prices which did not cover the costs of the commodity to the retailer plus "an allowance for actual wages of store labor to be fixed and published from time to time" by the code authority. Similar clauses appeared in the codes for drug retailing, jewelry

---

[1] Resistance to the tariff of minimum prices set was so great that this code accounted for more than half the "blue eagles" removed (*New York Times*, May 28, 1934). When the service industries were freed from all clauses in their codes except those concerning labor conditions (unless 85 per cent of those in any locality agreed to other provisions) (*Executive Order*, May 27, 1934) price cutting was intensified (*New York Times*, May 29, 1934) and the maintenance of the labor conditions in the code was imperiled. Finally the code authority "turned back its code to General Johnson," charging the administration with bad faith in suspending the fair practice clauses (and especially the price fixing clause) without a hearing (*New York Times*, June 22, 1934).

[2] The minimum might be neither more nor less than the weighted average cost of production, but was also to take account of the competition between different kinds of containers and competition with other industries.

[3] It provided that no member of the industry should distribute any cigars or stogies made by employees under the wage and labor conditions prescribed in the code unless they were packed in containers stating that they were intended to sell to consumers at not more than two for five cents (Code for cigar manufacturing, approved June 19, 1934).

[4] *New York Times*, Jan. 5, 1934.

retailing, retail food and grocery, wholesale grocery, and paper distributing, although they were generally subject to a number of exceptions.[1] Subsequently the administrator virtually established the minimum charge for the services of retailers when he set the allowance for wages of store labor at not less than ten per cent of the cost to the merchant of the article sold.[2] While there is an obvious danger in fixing the minimum price for retailing services in general, or even for specific products, there is little objection so long as the minimum is set so low that it could not be applied equally to all the goods sold by a retailer. The "loss leader" tends to mislead purchasers concerning the general efficiency of the seller, although it is a form of advertising that, unlike most, directly benefits consumers.

The code for the retail lumber industry provided for a minimum "mark up" by retailers based upon the "modal" cost of distribution.[3] The average "mark up" was set by the administrator at 41 per cent of the cost of the product, but, in June, 1934, this percentage was reduced by order of the administrator to 29 per cent to permit reductions in the retail price of lumber, not, apparently, because the modal cost of handling lumber had changed, but to facilitate plans to stimulate the building industry. Reduction for this reason indicates that the cost of doing business was not the basis upon which the price of the services of lumber dealers was fixed. This "mark-up" provision lapsed altogether in March, 1935.[4] The minimum discounts to be allowed for wholesaling and retailing cigars might be set by agreement between the code authorities for cigar manufacturing, wholesale

[1] For example, exempting storekeepers in places with less than 2,500 inhabitants and not part of a larger trading area; permitting lower prices to meet the prices of rivals complying with the clause, and also permitting lower prices for food and other perishable products, or in *bona fide* clearances of discontinued lines, sales upon final liquidation, sales in large quantities, and sales to institutions and public relief agencies.

[2] *Administrative Order* of April 6, 1934. This order did not apply to drugs and allied products; the code for drug retailing was subsequently amended to prohibit the sale of drugs, cosmetics, and toilet preparations at a price below the manufacturers' wholesale list price per dozen (*N.Y. Herald Tribune*, Apr. 8, 1934). The only available explanation of the basis upon which 10 per cent was arrived at is the administrator's own statement that "after an extensive inquiry extending over years I know of no legitimate merchant who sells at an expense of less than 10 per cent on cost" (JOHNSON, *The Blue Eagle from Egg to Earth*, 182).

[3] Art. VIII, 8. The mode is a peculiarly unsuitable average, as no clearly marked mode may exist. There may be more than one mode, and if the "mark up" of each product is separately calculated by the selection of the mode, the resulting pattern of "mark ups" may be unworkable. (See TERBORGH, *Price Control Devices in N.R.A. Codes*, 12.)

[4] *New York Times*, Mar. 2, 1935.

tobacco, and tobacco retailing, subject to the concurrence of the administrator.[1]

It is evident that explicit continuous control of prices was not generally permitted; where it was authorized it was not generally a success. In the oil industry control of sales replaced the proposed control of prices; in lumber and timber products continuous price control was replaced by control restricted to periods of emergency; only in the bituminous coal industry did it survive and there with much difficulty. It collapsed completely in the cleaning and dyeing industry. The codes for the distributing trades usually prescribed minimum margins between purchase and resale prices, sometimes, but not always, aimed at preventing any item from being used as a "loss leader." The administration placed increasing reliance upon the prohibition of "destructive" price cutting and the setting of minimum prices during "emergencies." These experiments can, however, be discussed only after the attempts to prevent sales at "less than cost of production."

2. THE PROHIBITION OF SALES AT PRICES BELOW THE COST OF PRODUCTION

Although the administrator was opposed to price fixing, he was strongly in favor of the prohibition of sales at prices below the cost of production. Business interests were persuaded to cooperate in the administration of the act by the prospect of limiting price competition. Having been induced to increase their payrolls they made speedy demands for the approval of clauses declaring "less-than-cost" selling to be unfair. In consequence 403 of the first 677 codes prohibited sales below cost. In 352 of these codes in the non-distribution industries the costs of the individual seller set his minimum price.[2] Differences in the costs of different firms result in differences in minimum price. Where the products of the different sellers are comparable the lowest-cost seller is able to obtain all the business (if he chooses to charge the minimum price) except where ignorance on the part of buyers prevents their discovering the lowest prices, or differences in transportation costs protect some firms. Thus the less efficient suffer not only from their higher costs, but also from the loss of business to rivals, which is likely either to accelerate their departure from business or, more probably, their recapitaliza-

[1] Code for tobacco retailing trade.
[2] N.R.A., *Prices and Price Provisions in Codes*, 1935, Part III.

tion at lower levels.¹ In fact, however, there was little doubt that sellers would refuse to comply with the rule rather than expose themselves to such dangers and little pressure was brought to compel them to comply.

In 267 of these codes the less efficient were protected from these risks by a provision that they might sell at prices below their own cost of production to meet the prices of a rival.² Where the output of all producers was uniform, a single minimum price was thus set for the whole industry. As, however, the only firm permitted to resort to this price was the lowest cost firm, the clause protected sellers only from the price cutting of high cost, and not from that of low cost, firms within the limit set by the costs of the lowest cost firm. In 78 codes the rule was simplified by merely prohibiting sales at prices below the cost of production by the lowest cost firm, thus permitting any firm to initiate price reductions down to this level.³

Rigid adherence to prohibitions upon sales below cost in one or other of these forms would cause difficulty to sellers whose products had gone out of fashion, who had overestimated demand and were forced to sell in order to obtain liquid funds, who wished to liquidate their businesses, or who desired to dispose of discontinued lines or of second-grade products necessarily occurring in the normal course of production. In 323 industries sales under such conditions or under some of them were excepted from the prohibition on sales below cost; two thirds of these codes provided that such sales should be reported to the code authority and the remaining one third required the approval of the code authority.⁴ These

---

[1] In the baking industry firms in higher cost areas were protected from the competition of those in lower cost areas by a provision that the administrator might require firms invading a higher cost area to sell at not less than the lowest price filed by any producer in the high-cost area. In the salt industry a producer might not sell in another zone below the lowest price filed by producers in that zone.

[2] N.R.A., *loc. cit.* In 111 codes the authority to meet the prices of a rival was limited to meeting prices which did not themselves contravene the rule against selling below cost; in 36 codes prices in violation of the rule might be met provided they were reported to the code authority, or pending the taking of action thereon by the code authority. In some, firms were prohibited from meeting price cuts which they had themselves instigated. Twelve codes required the approval of the code authority to sales below cost. (N.R.A., *loc. cit.*)

[3] Where the products of different sellers were not identical, a code authority applying a clause permitting firms to sell at prices below their own costs to meet the prices of a rival had to decide how competitive were the different products and determine the differences in price justified by the differences in the products, *i.e.*, set price differentials between all types of product, a task of enormous magnitude and difficulty in some industries. *Cf.* TERBORGH, *Price Control Devices in N.R.A. Codes*, 24).

[4] N.R.A., *loc. cit.*

exceptions were obviously a source of great weakness in the control of sales below cost, but without them the rule would have been impossible of compliance in most industries.

The level of minimum prices resulting from the application of this clause depends entirely upon the method of calculating costs. In 361 of these codes provision was made for the establishment of uniform methods of cost accounting; 92 per cent required the approval of the administrator of the accounting systems. Methods of calculating costs were prescribed in some 87 non-distribution codes but there was no uniform basis of calculation. A few codes prescribed whether raw materials should be entered at their replacement or their original cost.[1] Ten non-distribution codes provided for the addition to factory costs of an arbitrary percentage, uniform for all firms, to cover general management, taxes, selling costs, and the like.[2]

During a period of subnormal operation average costs depend greatly upon the method of calculating overhead costs including the depreciation and obsolescence of plant. If the full amount[3] of these costs is distributed over actual output, the minimum price must be one which enables the lowest-cost firm to cover all its costs excluding interest.[4] The resulting minimum price may be considerably above the existing prices; there may, of course, be no price that will enable the firm to cover all its overhead costs. In some industries a "standard burden"[5] for overhead costs was adopted. For instance, the amount to be included in unit costs for overhead might be calculated upon the assumption that the plant was being utilized to 65 per cent of its full capacity. This device would affect the distribution of the recovery of overhead costs over time; less than the annual amount calculated in accordance with the firm's rule concerning depreciation and obsolescence is recovered from sales in periods when plant is operated at less than the standard rate, and more is recovered in periods when it is operating at more than the standard rate. The higher this standard rate of operation the lower, of course, is the average cost of production which sets the minimum price. Some codes prescribed this standard burden by reference to the actual rate of operation

[1] For example, paint, varnish, and lacquer.
[2] Structural clay products, paint, varnish, and lacquer (Amendment No. 1).
[3] That is, the share of overhead costs for the year or other period calculated according to the rules adopted by the firm concerning depreciation and obsolescence.
[4] Even interest was included in the calculation of the cost of producing lumber.
[5] Six of the first 400 codes required overhead calculated on a uniform base (*New York Times*, June 10, 1934).

during a past period,[1] others by reference to the rate of operation of "reasonably efficient" plants during a past period.[2]

Departures from the setting of minimum prices by reference to the costs of the lowest cost firm were implied in these calculations of the standard rate of overhead burden by reference to the experience of the "reasonably efficient" or any other class of firms. In fact there were many other such departures. In eight industries the minimum was set by reference to "lowest reasonable costs," in ten to "reasonable costs," and in eight to the "lowest representative" costs. The definition of representativeness was occasionally given, as for instance, that it might not exclude more than 10 per cent of the firms,[3] that it should exclude all firms whose capitalization was unduly low,[4] or that the representative firm was one engaged in a full line of activities including research and sales promotion.[3] Five set the minimum price by reference to the average of the cost of production by all firms.[5] Where the costs of the representative firm were above the lowest costs in the industry the minimum price was, of course, higher than it would have been if the costs of the lowest cost firm had been used; the use of a weighted average obviously also yielded a higher minimum than the costs of the lowest cost firm. Little or no attention appears to have been paid to the valuation placed upon plant,[6] which valuation determines the amount of depreciation and obsolescence charges, which are a large part of the annual overhead charge. Where the costs of the lowest-cost firm set the minimum price this matter was of least importance; that firm was least likely to be carrying its assets at inflated values, but where representative or average costs were used such inflated capital values might raise the minimum price.

Minimum prices cannot, of course, be determined by reference to actual costs; they must be calculated by reference to the past

[1] In the canning and packaging machinery industry a firm might, with the consent of the administrator, use the costs for the last year in which it made profits. In the resilient flooring industry the code authority was to determine the lowest reasonable percentage of overhead costs during 1927 to 1932 and, if approved by the administrator, this figure was to be used in calculating costs.

[2] In the cement industry these costs were to be allocated by reference to the average rate of utilization by the one third portion of the industry reporting the lowest average cost per unit in the period from 1927 to 1932.

[3] Refractories.

[4] Rubber manufacturing.

[5] A weighted average in lime, cigar containers, lumber and timber products; an average excluding at least 40 per cent of the members with the highest costs in the slate industry.

[6] Among the possible causes of "unduly low" costs in the rubber industry, "the acquisition of plant at less than fair appraisal value" was cited.

cost of producing similar commodities. Although minimum prices are influenced by the frequency with which cost calculations are made, few codes prescribed the periods to be used in calculating costs, whether one, three, or twelve months should be the basis of calculation.

The practical importance of prohibitions upon less-than-cost selling is difficult to estimate. They probably had no widespread effect for by February, 1935, only 37 cost estimating or accounting systems had been approved by the administrator.[1] Nevertheless, in some industries cost determinations were made effective though not approved.[2] In the wallpaper manufacturing industry informal minimum prices were agreed upon although no method of calculating costs had been approved.[3] The price of common brick was said to be about a third higher in 1935 than in 1929 partly owing to a provision in the code for the structural clay products industry forbidding prices below individual direct factory costs plus a weighted average of indirect cost determined by the code authority.[4] Minimum processing costs to be used in calculating minimum prices had been approved for the paint and varnish industry on the basis of very inadequate information.[5] Sellers filing prices lower than their competitors were occasionally reminded that they could be called upon to show that they were not selling below cost and that this procedure might be unpleasant and costly.[6] In some industries declines in demand and an increase in sales at below-code prices prevented the restriction of price competition.[7]

By the end of 1933 the increases in the prices of many products since the act was adumbrated were causing widespread criticism of the administration.[8] It was widely claimed that, directly or

[1] N.R.A., *Prices and Price Provisions in Codes*, Part III. In fact 244 industries had not even submitted any cost accounting system for approval.
[2] *Cf.* Lyon and others, *op. cit.*, 587.
[3] Consumer Advisory Board, *Experience with Price Fixing under the Codes*, Jan. 9, 1935, 8.
[4] *ibid.*, 2. The National Recovery Administration had not reviewed these determinations of indirect cost and had obtained information concerning the basis of their calculation from only one district.
[5] *ibid.*, 4. Permanent approval was, however, denied (statement of chairman of Consumer Advisory Board to Senate Finance Committee, Apr. 1, 1935). A proposed fair minimum price for lead pencils was found to be likely to yield as much as 60 per cent profit to the lowest cost producers and was disapproved (Consumer Advisory Board, *Experience with Price Fixing under the Codes*, 4).
[6] *ibid.*, 7.
[7] *ibid.*, 8, 9. In the machined waste industry prices were filed by brand name and "a producer wishing to make a special price had only to file a price for a new brand" (*loc. cit.*).
[8] *Cf.* also Lyon and others, *op. cit.*, Chap. XXXVIII.

indirectly, the Recovery Administration was facilitating the restriction of production.[1] The administration accordingly set out to revise its policy. It attempted to meet the charge that it assisted price fixing in the interest of higher profits. But it was unwilling to antagonize business by withdrawing protection from price competition. It announced that it would attempt to limit the setting of minimum prices to emergencies. New codes and amendments to old codes would authorize code authorities in whose industries there was destructive price cutting to declare the existence of an emergency "such as to render ineffective or to seriously endanger the maintenance of the provisions of . . . the code." Thus were recognized emergencies within the greater emergency which called for the National Industrial Recovery Act. After notice and hearing the code authoriy could determine "the lowest reasonable cost of the product" by reference to "plants of average efficiency." During the period of the emergency sales at prices below this "reasonable cost," provided it was accepted by the administrator, contravened the code and the act.[2] This policy was severely criticized by the Consumer Advisory Board.[3]

Again in June, 1934, the administration announced[4] a policy with regard to price fixing which was said to be "the product of

---

[1] In February, 1934, the Federal Trade Commission was recalled to service; it was instructed to investigate the effects of the code for the iron and steel industry and price increases in the oil industry (*Cf. New York Times*, Feb. 6, 1934).

[2] *New York Times*, Feb. 20, 1934. This new policy was referred to at the first of a series of public meetings, called in Washington to ventilate criticism of the policy of the administration, as "a more equitable and uniform rule of national price stabilization in those cases where it is necessary to maintain wages at a decent standard against the certain results of predatory and cutthroat competition and further insurance against increase of price faster and further than increase of purchasing power." The administration promised *inter alia* "a more effective rule on costs for the purpose of maintaining rules against sales below cost of production," "certainty of protection against monopoly control and oppression of small enterprise," and the better coordination of the terms of different codes (*New York Times*, Feb. 28, 1934).

[3] *Release* of Mar. 4, 1934. The board commented that permission to code authorities to fix minimum prices in periods of emergency tended to make emergencies attractive. The use of "lowest reasonable costs" as a basis for such minimum prices had permitted increases calculated to diminish general purchasing power and shifted business from efficient firms (able to make money by selling at less than average costs) to high-cost producers. It commented upon the inclusion in costs of excessive charges for plant, and recommended the use of individual rather than average costs as a basis for minimum prices, and the provision of a formula for calculating costs which would exclude selling and financial costs and include overhead costs calculated by reference to a normal rate of operation.

[4] *N.R.A. Office Memorandum* 228 of June 7, 1934; *New York Times*, June 8, 1934.

months of economic study" but which reiterated the program of setting minimum prices during periods of emergency. It was, however, somewhat elaborated. An emergency was defined by reference to "(a) impairment of employment or wage scales, (b) particularly high mortality of enterprises, especially small enterprises, or (c) panic in an industry or other special conditions thought by the administrator to require stabilization by means of a minimum price." The Research and Planning Division was to examine the evidence of these conditions, "analyze the probable effects of various possible minimum prices,"[1] and render a written report thereon. On the basis of this report the administrator might declare an emergency to exist and prescribe a minimum price.[2] The minimum price was to "be reasonably calculated to mitigate the conditions of such emergency and to effectuate the policy of the National Industrial Recovery Act."[3] Emergencies were to be "declared only for particular products and for a stated period not longer than ninety days, subject to earlier termination or to extension upon decision of the administrator,"[4] and "remedial provisions" were "to be put into effect."[5]

The new policy was announced as a definite rejection of price fixing which would require the revision of scores of codes to permit greater freedom in competition and obstruct attempts to maintain prices.[6] Code authorities inferred that prohibitions upon sales

[1] It was to analyze their effects "on total national production, general employment and general recovery, production and consumption of the product of the industry in question, other phases of national life, and the interests of the industry in question to the extent compatible with the foregoing" (*ibid.*).
[2] The declaration of any emergency was to "be accompanied by a statement of the facts upon which the declaration is based and an explanation of the plan which is being applied" (*ibid.*).
[3] *ibid.* Clauses in these terms appeared in some codes, *e.g.* shoe and leather finish, etc., umbrella (Amendment No. 1), industrial oil burning equipment, bedding (Amendment No. 3). It was announced to the press that these emergency minimum prices would be based upon "the lowest reasonable cost not a profit covering figure for the majority of enterprises" (*New York Times*, June 8, 1934). "Historically we believe the concept of 'emergency price' to have been the product primarily of an emergency within the ranks of the N.R.A. itself—a fear grown to panic proportions that minimum-price procedures were becoming too firmly entrenched in formal code provisions. Refuge was sought in a ceremony to be invoked only on rare occasions when, by virtue of an emergency proclamation and the recital of an appropriate cost incantation, price practices hitherto suspect were to emerge wholesome and pure." (CONSUMER ADVISORY BOARD, *Emergency Price Experience*, 1.)
[4] *ibid.*
[5] These "provisions" were to be "subject to a plan of supervision which it shall be the duty of the Research and Planning Division to devise which will include the requirement of such financial, operating, employment, and other reports as shall be necessary to indicate the effect of the provisions" (*ibid.*).
[6] *New York Times*, June 8, 1934.

at prices below the cost of production were to be withdrawn and the administrator was inundated with requests for the declaration of emergencies; he then announced that he could not "use too much emphasis in saying that this policy does not affect codes already approved." As some 459 codes covering 90 per cent of the industries subject to the N.I.R.A.[1] had then been approved, the announcement of a new policy was far less important than had appeared at first sight.[2] Some industries were expected to resist the withdrawal of the less-than-cost selling clause because they relied upon it to enable them to meet the higher labor costs imposed under the act; others were said to be disillusioned as to the effectiveness of such clauses as they had proved unworkable and were widely violated.[3] In fact, however, codes continued to be approved during June and July containing clauses forbidding sales at prices below the cost of production.[4] Occasionally the emergency price fixing clause appeared as well.[5]

The administration never succeeded, however, in adapting the majority of the codes already approved to its new policy and probably could not have done so if the codes were to remain voluntary.[6] The new policy began to take effect, however, when the amended code for the steel industry was approved; the section of the code (Schedule E, Sec. 5) empowering the code authority to set aside an "unfair" price filed with it, and to fix a "fair base price" was removed and the new code contained no price fixing clause and none prohibiting sales at prices below the cost of production. Yet some time later a code was approved for the structural steel and iron fabricating industry[7] providing for the imposition of penalties upon firms charging prices less than the reasonable estimated cost of the work performed or commodities pro-

---

[1] Measured by "actual 'gainfully occupied'" (*cit.* LYON and others, *op. cit.*, 739).
[2] *New York Times*, June 9 and 10, 1934. The new policy was to be applied to existing codes "only as a result of negotiations with and agreement by the interested code authorities." "Divisional administrators shall seek through agreements with code authorities of approved codes to amend them to conform with these policies and, wherever resistance is encountered, the subject shall be taken up with the administrator." (*N.R.A. Office Memorandum* 228 of June 7, 1934.)
[3] *New York Times*, June 8 and 10, 1934.
[4] For example, cocoa and chocolate, lift truck and portable elevator, commercial vehicle body, resilient flooring, light sewing, complete wire and iron fence, dental goods, candy manufacturing.
[5] Automobile hot-water heater, replacement axle shaft, leaf spring manufacturing.
[6] By January, 1935, only about twelve codes had been amended in accordance with the announcement of June 7, 1934.
[7] Code No. 480 approved July 11, 1934.

vided.[1] However, in two other codes[2] the operation of clauses prohibiting sales at prices less than cost of production was suspended by the administrator when approving the code or amendment.

Emergency price fixing clauses also began to appear; of the first 677 codes 187 included such clauses.[3] The clause in the codes for the lumber and timber products industry authorizing the fixing of minimum prices was replaced by such an emergency clause. The decline in business activity during the summer of 1934 resulted in many applications for the setting of minimum prices under these emergency clauses. Applications were granted, however, only in the agricultural insecticide and fungicide,[4] cast iron soil pipe, ice[5] (in three territories), lumber and timber products, retail tobacco, wholesale tobacco, retail solid fuel (approximately 150 local emergencies), automobile tire, and waste paper industries.[6] These declarations were justified in a variety of ways; the promised explanation of the basis of the calculation of the minimum price and the plan to terminate the emergency was, however, not provided.

The emergency in the cast iron soil pipe industry was attributed to the entry of new firms, mainly in the south, and the attempt of the older firms to eject them by price cutting. Any attempt to guarantee prices was denied; the administration sought to act as a "stabilizer" and regarded the declaration as an experiment which "will not apply to the majority of cases."[7] What

[1] The code provided that if any member complained that any other member had performed work or sold products for prices less than their reasonable estimated cost, the code authority should determine whether to investigate the complaint. In making this determination the code authority was to consider whether the member complained of had, during the operation of the code, "contracted for more than its fair share of the business" of fabricating or erecting and whether the difference between its price and those of rivals warranted further investigation. In the event of the authority deciding after investigation that this clause had been violated, the offending member was required to pay a sum for liquidated damages not exceeding twice the difference between the price charged and the authority's estimate of the reasonable cost of the work, *plus* the cost of the investigation. If the authority decided that no violation had occurred, the complaining member was required to pay the cost of the investigation. The basis of the allocation of overhead and general and selling expenses was to be determined by the code authority.
[2] Cotton textile (supplementary code for cotton thread), warm-air register (which had prohibited sales below "allowable" cost).
[3] N.R.A., *Prices and Price Provisions in Codes*, Part III.
[4] "The only result reliably reported from the current insecticide emergency to date is that sales have been completely stopped" (CONSUMER ADVISORY BOARD, *Emergency Price Experience*, 7).
[5] No usable cost data were available and the minimum prices were "patently arbitrary" (*ibid.*, 4).
[6] N.R.A., *op. cit.*
[7] Amendment No. 2 to code for the cast iron soil pipe industry, July 10, 1934, and *New York Times*, July 19, 1934.

it sought to stabilize and the basis of the calculation of the minimum price[1] were not revealed. The declaration of emergencies in the retail solid fuel industry and the setting of minimum retail prices for coal in 150 areas led to complaints from retailers that the minimum prescribed was excessive[2] and to resistance to its enforcement.[3]

The declaration of an emergency in the tire retailing trade was avowedly aimed at the protection of the independent dealers and small manufacturers against company-owned distributors and large selling organizations.[4] The administration failed, however, to attain its objective and pressure was applied to raise the emergency minimum and exempt tires sold by mail and also certain brands; smaller dealers asked either for the abandonment of the minimum or a differentiation between the advertised and unadvertised brands[5] which was subsequently granted.[6] The emergency in the wholesale and retail tobacco industries was originally declared for ninety days, but was twice renewed.[7] Minimum wholesale and retail prices were set which were "calculated to establish a fair minimum price for the retail sale of cigarettes which, at the same time, will not raise existing prices except for stores which have used cigarettes as 'bait.'"[8] The National Industrial Recovery Board finally acknowledged, however, that "the causes of this emergency do not yield to treatment on an emergency basis and are perhaps of a more permanent nature than was originally believed." But as the emergency order had benefited the retail tobacco trade and especially the small

---

[1] The minimum price was set "without benefit of cost data worthy of the name" (CONSUMER ADVISORY BOARD, *op. cit.*, 4).

[2] The prices set were from 7 to 27 per cent below those proposed by the trade in various territories (EDWARDS, *Experience with Price Fixing under the Codes*, 4); *cf.* also, CONSUMER ADVISORY BOARD, *Fixing Coal Prices*, 10.

[3] *New York Times*, July 21, 22, 1934. When the National Recovery Administration, over the violent protests of the industry, undertook to review the minimum prices it encountered great difficulty in obtaining information concerning costs (CONSUMER ADVISORY BOARD, *Fixing Coal Prices*, 10; *cf.* also CONSUMER ADVISORY BOARD, *Emergency Price Experience*, 7, and LYON and others, *op. cit.*, 618). The code authority for the industry subsequently resigned in a body largely as a protest against the attitude of the administration to price fixing (*New York Times*, Sept. 4, 1934). The administration announced that the resignation did not affect the operation of the code (*New York Times*, Sept. 5, 1934). The minimum prices were stayed from May 1, 1935, to May 31, 1935, and the industry was required to submit factual evidence in support of the existence of an emergency before minima were again prescribed (*New York Times*, Apr. 26, 1935).

[4] *N.R.A. Release*, May 4, 1934.

[5] *New York Times*, Aug. 4, 1934.

[6] *New York Times*, Aug. 26, 1934.

[7] *New York Times*, Mar. 30, 1935.

[8] *New York Times*, July 13, 1934.

retailers the code was amended to prevent the sale of cigarettes at retail at more than 9.1 per cent below the manufacturer's list price. The prices of other tobacco products which had previously not been controlled were also to be maintained at or above 7.1 per cent below the manufacturer's list price.[1] It was further provided that the minimum retail price could be set in excess of the amount above prescribed by the addition of an allowance for the cost of retail distribution. The board accordingly issued an order setting such an allowance for retailing cigarettes with the result that the minimum price was identical with that under the emergency order.[2]

The declaration of an emergency in the lumber and timber products industry was followed by an order *reducing* the mill prices of lumber products used in house construction by 8 to 10 per cent.[3] Thus although the emergency clause was originally stated to be intended to deal with destructive price cutting[4] it appeared that it could be used also to deal with prices believed by the administrator to be excessive. The Consumer Advisory Board condemned the whole experiment with emergency price fixing as a failure, an "idea too narrowly conceived and far too trustingly administered."[5] Reliable cost data were completely absent and no more than lip homage was ever paid to costs in fixing prices.[6] There was no policy in the determination of justifiable costs. The board regarded the experiment as futile because the troubles of the industries in which emergencies were declared to exist were no less when, after bickering and violation of the minimum price orders, they were finally rescinded. Industries torn by strife were merely given a breathing period, which was

[1] Approved Code 466, Amendment No. 1 of Apr. 23, 1935.

[2] *Cf. New York Times*, Apr. 24, 1935.

[3] *New York Times*, July 17, 1934. "The price reduction was arbitrary and had no relation to costs" (CONSUMER ADVISORY BOARD, *Price Fixing in the Lumber Industry*, 1935, 2). It "brought nothing but violations, curtailment of buying and revolt in the industry" (CONSUMER ADVISORY BOARD, *Emergency Price Experience*, 6).

[4] The amendment to the code for the lumber and timber products industry inserting this emergency provision (Amendment No. 15 to Approved Code No. 9, July 16, 1934) makes no reference to destructive price cutting but merely to conditions endangering the provisions of the code or the act. As the prices set in the emergency are merely minimum prices, they can be made actual only if a sufficient number of firms is prepared to resort to them.

[5] CONSUMER ADVISORY BOARD, *Emergency Price Experience*, 2.

[6] In one area retail solid fuel prices were based upon cost returns made by 3 out of 800 dealers there. In another district the code committee looked over the cost reports received and then turned their backs upon them and "drew on their own experience and trade knowledge" (CONSUMER ADVISORY BOARD, *Fixing Coal Prices*, 8).

itself sometimes disturbed by new difficulties, and might merely impose undesirable delay upon desirable adjustments.[1]

The new policy of June, 1934, which was to eliminate price fixing also provided, however, for the prohibition of "destructive price cutting."[2] Clauses forbidding such price cutting and occasionally also "willfully destructive price cutting" began to appear in June, 1934, and by February, 1935, 51 codes included such clauses.[3]

In applying the new poclicy clauses were inluded in some 51 codes providing that "when no declared emergency exists there is to be no fixed minimum basis for prices. It is intended that sound cost estimating methods should be used, and that consideration should be given to costs in the determination of pricing policies."[4] The administrator announced that while

codes should contain clauses recommending principles of cost finding appropriate to the industry and approved by the administrator, . . . no such methods shall be obligatory, and none shall suggest uniform additions to total sales cost in the form of percentages or differentials designed to bring about arbitrary uniformity in costs or prices.

Clauses providing for the establishment of standardized cost accounting systems continued to be approved; 75 codes provided that when the cost accounting and estimating system had been formulated and communicated to producers, "all employers shall determine and/or estimate costs in accordance with the principles of such methods."[5] Finally some industries announced in their codes that they "recognized that price increases such

---

[1] For example, in the retail solid fuel and tobacco retailing industries to new methods of distribution. In lumber and cast iron soil pipe the trouble was only superficially diagnosed as a case of "fallen prices" (*ibid.*); *cf.* also LYON and others, *op. cit.*, 605.

[2] The model clause proposed provided that "willfully destructive price cutting is an unfair method of competition and is forbidden. Any member of the industry or of any other industry or the customers of either, may at any time complain to the code authority that any filed price constitutes unfair competition as destructive price cutting imperiling small enterprises or tending toward monopoly or the impairment of code wages and working conditions. The code authority shall within five days afford an opportunity to the member filing the price to answer such complaint and shall within fourteen days make a ruling or adjustment thereon. If such ruling is not concurred in by either party to the complaint all papers shall be referred to the Research and Planning Division of the N.R.A., which shall render a report and recommendation to the administrator." (*N.R.A. Office Memorandum* 228 of June 7, 1934.)

[3] N.R.A., *Prices and Price Provisions in Codes*, Part III.

[4] *Cf. N.R.A. Office Memorandum* 228 of June 7, 1934.

[5] For example, gas powered industrial truck, safety razor, envelope machinery.

as may be required to meet individual cost should be delayed and, when made, should, so far as possible, be limited to actual additional increases in sellers' costs."[1]

Thus, clauses prohibiting sales at prices below the cost of production were widely sought and widely granted during the first year of the National Recovery Administration. The administration made little progress, however, in defining costs; indeed, its tardiness in approving methods of cost calculation indicates that these clauses must have been of limited practical significance. In the face of criticism it sought to reduce the emphasis upon minimum prices. Many of the first 400 industries to obtain codes retained their clauses prohibiting less-than-cost selling. Industries obtaining new codes were pressed to accept clauses providing for the setting of minimum prices only during emergencies and then by the administrator. Many also accepted prohibitions upon willfully destructive price cutting and clauses requiring the calculation of individual costs according to a standardized system and the calculation of prices with reference to these costs. Only the first of these three clauses was of practical importance and that only in some nine industries. Even so, the definition of an emergency was never made clear nor were the methods of calculating minimum prices during emergencies. There is no evidence that the setting of prices could be expected to remedy the conditions inducing these industries to seek protection nor that it did in fact remedy them.

3. "OPEN-PRICE" PROVISIONS

The "open-price" policy which had been so important an element in the work of the trade associations for twenty years prior to the establishment of the National Recovery Administration was urged upon the administration and accepted by it. Of the first 709 codes and supplements approved 422 contained an "open-price" clause. This clause usually stated that it was unfair to sell at prices other than (or occasionally **only at** prices *less* than) those published by the seller. Almost **invariably** full lists of the prices of all products, with all discounts (including quantity and trade discounts) and sometimes the special charges made for delivery at different points, or departures from the

---

[1] For example, lift truck and portable elevator, cocoa and chocolate, wholesale monumental marble, bicycle, vegetable ivory button, candy, open steel flooring, etc., public seating, and others.

standard products, were required to be lodged with the code authority[1] and no price departing from this list might be charged unless a new list or notice of the change had been lodged.[2] The filed prices were, therefore, usually actual, not minimum, prices.[3] Of the above codes and supplements 274 provided that a firm notifying a change of price might not change its actual price until after the lapse of a period varying from twenty-four hours to twenty days (usually ten days) after the notice of change had been lodged. The code authority was required, as soon as it received notice of change, to circulate the notice to all its members. A few codes left the provision for publicity concerning prices at this point, but a greater number provided also that any firm desiring to change its price in response to a notice of change received and circulated by the code authority, might give notice of intention to so respond, and that such price change should become operative at the same time as the change first notified. A few industries permitted sales at below the price lodged in order to meet competition provided the price then charged was not less than the lowest price filed. In some industries discontinued lines, stocks that must be liquidated, damaged products, and the like,[4] might be disposed of at less than the announced prices, although often subject to the supervision of the code authority.[5] The arrangements authorized in these clauses differed from those permitted prior to the act mainly in their requirement that notice of future prices should be given; formerly information concerning past prices alone could legally be exchanged.

[1] The code for the petroleum industry merely required the conspicuous posting of prices at the point from which deliveries were made and that all prices should remain in force for at least twenty-four hours.
[2] In some industries these provisions for open prices applied only to those branches of the industry or products for which it had been customary to use net price lists, or price lists with discount sheets, and in some the code authority might order the application of this clause to branches or products in which such lists had not previously been used but to which it decided that they were appropriate.
[3] The announcement of a new policy concerning open-price clauses provided that they should be only minimum prices (*New York Times*, June 8, 1934) but the official record provides that "no member of the industry shall sell or offer to sell except at filed terms and conditions" (*N.R.A. Office Memorandum* 228 of June 7, 1934). The prices filed in the steel industry were, however, minimum prices (Art. VII of code for iron and steel industry).
[4] The baking industry found it necessary to regulate sales of stale products including those returned by distributors.
[5] Although it would appear to be unnecessary if the open-price clause was effective and set actual prices (and not minimum prices) most codes provided also that it should be unfair to sell at discriminatory prices, *i.e.*, to charge for similar products different prices to individuals in the same class. The falsification of invoices as to date or description of product was also usually pronounced unfair.

These clauses were attacked at a very early stage in the administration of the act. As the Consumer Advisory Board pointed out, the "waiting period," together with the revelation of the identity of the firm lodging notice of change of price, exposed firms desiring to cut prices to coercion by those who preferred a policy of high prices.[1] Few code authorities, moreover, were prepared to make price information available to buyers as well as to sellers. The board charged that prices had often been raised by amounts exceeding the additional costs imposed on industry under the act and calculated to imperil general recovery. "The tendency in some industries to forget the recovery program in their own interests is, of course, strengthened by any arrangement which makes the determination of prices a matter of agreement among the members of the industry." Most critics were prepared to accept some price reporting service but pressure was exerted to secure the filing of prices with a confidential agency that would reveal only the range of prices without identifying sellers and to eliminate the requirement that notice be given of changes in price.[2] At the end of January, 1934, it was ordered that provision for a waiting period be stayed in all future codes[3] and a little later that no such clauses be approved.[4]

The new policy of June, 1934,[5] already referred to, embodied also a decision that future "open-price" clauses should require that prices be reported to a confidential disinterested agent of the code authority or, if none existed, with an agency designated by the Recovery Administration, that the waiting period was to be abolished so far as reductions in price were concerned[6] but that forty-eight hours' notice of increases of prices would be required. It was also proposed to include a rule that

. . . no member of the industry shall enter into any agreement, undertaking, combination, or conspiracy to fix or maintain price terms nor

[1] *Release* of Mar. 4, 1934, cit. *New York Times*, Mar. 5, 1934.
[2] *Cf. Release* of Consumer Advisory Board of Mar. 4, 1934. The Distribution and Consumer Service Trades Committee appointed by the administrator following the general meeting of representatives of code authorities in March, 1934, defended the open-price policy as a means of restricting cutthroat competition. It recommended, however, that the prices filed be available for inspection by any interested person, that prices be filed with the administration as well as with the code authority, and that members filing increased prices be required to produce statistics of costs in support of the increase (*New York Times*, Mar. 29, 1934).
[3] *N.R.A. Administrative Order* of Jan. 27, 1934.
[4] *New York Times*, Feb. 2, 1934.
[5] See *N.R.A. Office Memorandum* 228 of June 7, 1934.
[6] The administration was prepared to consider exemptions from this provision (*N.R.A. Office Memorandum* 228 of June 7, 1934).

cause or attempt to cause any member of the industry to change his price terms by intimidation, coercion, or any other influence inconsistent with the maintenance of the free and open market which it is the purpose of this article to create.[1]

As such conduct was authorized by no code this latter rule merely restated the law on the books since 1890. The new policy, it will be remembered, applied only to new codes and to existing codes where voluntarily accepted by the code authority.[2]

Open-price clauses continued to be approved but the provision for a "waiting period" was invariably stayed by order of the administrator. In February, 1935, of 274 codes providing for waiting periods the provision was stayed in 182 and in operation in 92. The filing of prices with a neutral confidential agent was occasionally required[3] but more frequently provision was made either for the prices filed to be open to the inspection of all interested parties or all buyers,[4] or for information concerning the prices filed to be circulated to those interested parties prepared to reimburse the code authorities for the cost of the service.[5] The requirement of forty-eight hours' notice of price increases appeared in a few codes but applied only to prevent the filing of an increased price within forty-eight hours after any change in price.[6] This provision was principally aimed at the filing of reduced prices for very short periods to permit lower prices on particular orders.[7] The prohibition upon coercive control of the

---

[1] *New York Times*, June 8, 1934; *N.R.A. Office Memorandum* 228 of June 7, 1934.

[2] *New York Times*, June 9, 10, 1934.

[3] Wholesale monumental marble, woven wood fabric shade, wholesale tobacco, retail tobacco, cigar manufacturing (in the last three codes the operation of the whole clause was stayed until arrangements satisfactory to the administrator had been made for the confidential treatment of prices filed). In some the disinterested agent was appointed by the code authority and, failing an appointment by it, by the administrator (*e.g.*, steel joist, sheet metal distributing). The director of research and planning announced, however, on July 19, 1934, that the administration would require the filing of prices with a neutral confidential disinterested agency for distribution to all members, and customers willing to pay for the service (*New York Times*, July 19, 1934).

[4] For example, lift truck and portable elevator, sulphurated oil, automobile hot-water heater, cotton ginning machinery, school supplies and equipment, open steel flooring.

[5] For example, construction machinery distributing, wholesale monumental marble, candy, wholesale tobacco, retail tobacco, cigar (in the last three of which the operation of the whole open-price clause was stayed until such arrangements had been made).

[6] Wholesale monumental marble, woven wood fabric manufacturing, electric hoist, and monorail. One code (steel joist) provided that a price filed should prevail for at least twenty days except that it might be earlier reduced to meet the prices of a rival.

[7] The code for the iron and steel industry as revised in May, 1934, prohibited seeking orders by promising subsequently to file new prices. It also provided that

prices filed was rarely insisted upon[1] and a very few codes provided that the administrator might suspend them if he found they were used to fix prices[2] or unduly enhance them.[3] A few codes provided that nothing in the open-price clause "shall constitute a limitation upon the right of any employer to file revised lists fixing his own prices, discounts, and terms of sale and payment which prices and discounts may be either more or less favorable than those contained in any other price list."[4]

Toward the end of June, 1934, the administration attempted to modify the open-price policy.[5] It ordered that persons operating under codes with open-price provisions should be held to have complied with these provisions if, in bidding to supply to public authorities, they quoted prices not more than 15 per cent below those filed under the code, provided that the reduced prices were filed with the code authority immediately after the bid was opened. If the administrator found that this "tolerance" of 15 per cent induced destructive price cutting he was authorized to reduce it, although not below five per cent. The administrator was also directed to study the effect of the introduction of the tolerance "upon the maintenance of standards of fair competition in sales to public and private customers." The object of this order was never made clear. On the one hand it was attributed to a desire to "eliminate difficulties" arising out of the receipt of numbers of identical bids, owing to the operation of the "open-price" clauses.[6] On the other hand, it was said to be aimed at the creation of an area of price competition with a maximum of 15 per cent for all governmentally used materials (*i.e.*, practically all commodities); thus pressure was to be applied to those indus-

---

reductions but not increases in price might be filed in any quarter (to prevent brief reductions to secure particular orders). As, however, the prices filed in this industry were merely minimum prices the effect of the provision was not clear.

[1] For example, wholesale monumental marble, woven wood fabric, electric hoist and monorail, steel joist, sheet metal distributing. The code for the iron and steel industry, as revised in May, 1934, prohibited coercion to induce a manufacturer to withdraw or change a base price filed by him. This code also permitted manufacturers to quote as their own the lowest price filed by any competitor at a base at which they had not filed prices. When a producer filed a lower price at any basing point *any* member might change *any* contract previously made for sales by reference to such basing point to permit charging for all products subsequently shipped under the contract at the lower price filed as soon as it became operative (Schedule E, Sec. 3).

[2] For example, sulphurated oil.
[3] For example, school supplies and equipment.
[4] Hoist builders' industry.
[5] *Administrative Order* 6767 of June 29, 1934.
[6] *New York Times*, June 30, 1934.

tries which, having codes, had resisted attempts to amend them in accordance with the policy announced on June 8, 1934, restricting price fixing to periods of emergency.[1] The administration interpreted the order to permit the filing of bids at reduced prices "for information only" thus preventing them from affecting sales to other than public authorities, an interpretation suggesting more a desire to facilitate the making of public contracts than to resuscitate limited price competition.[2] The new policy was resisted[3] and exemptions were reported to have been granted.[4] The order failed, however, to attain either of the alleged objectives. Sellers almost universally refused to take advantage of the order[5] and there was "practically no evidence that the order secured to the public exchequer even a fraction of a per cent of the potential savings which it was hoped a 15 per cent discount upon governmental purchases would achieve."[6] Moreover, there was "no objective evidence to indicate that the order promoted even a semblance of the price cutting predicted by industries objecting to the order."[7] The order had "not served to loosen at all the grip of strongly organized industries upon the prices and upon the consumers of their products." Such industries had "organized under the codes to such an extent as to bring

[1] There having been no evidence of a general desire to amend the existing 400 codes in accordance with the new policy "it became necessary for the government to act to make the new rule effective and release the brakes being applied to recovery by restrictions and limitations" (*New York Times*, July 8, 1934).

[2] *New York Times*, June 30, 1934, July 15, 1934.

[3] It was reported that the code authority for the iron and steel industry would seek exemption from the order on the ground that the code constituted a contract which could not be abrogated without mutual consent (*New York Times*, July 4, 1934). Tenders for iron and steel early in July, 1934, were at prices five to ten per cent below the filed price (*New York Times*, July 15, 1934).

[4] For example, to the coal industry (*New York Times*, July 5, 1934).

[5] *Report of Research and Planning Division of N.R.A.*, cit. *New York Times*, Apr. 23, 1935. Only half a dozen industries took advantage of the order with any frequency and less than a dozen more industries took occasional advantage of it. "Almost universally bidders upon public contracts failed to offer a discount." The percentage of tie bids increased notably in steel, paper and pulp, and building materials, decreasing in asbestos, scientific apparatus, and cement, and remaining about the same in automobiles, paint, chemicals, and glass containers. The secretary of the code authority for the rubber manufacturing industry, for instance, instructed his members to "adhere to currently fixed prices" (*New York Times*, Apr. 2, 1935).

[6] *Report of Research and Planning Division of N.R.A.*

[7] *loc. cit.* The order "failed to make the slightest impression upon the seemingly irresistible trend toward uniformity of prices and bids in the iron and steel industry" (*loc. cit.*). The National Industrial Recovery Board was more cautious; it concluded from the information available that the order "appeared to have had no great effect upon tie bids in one direction or another" and that it could arrive at no conclusion concerning its effect on prices. "In the opinion of the 102 purchasing agents who replied to the questionnaires the order has not had any substantial effect on prices." (*Report on the Effects of Executive Order 6767, 5.*)

about rigidity and gradual petrification in the price structure."[1] In April, 1935, the National Industrial Recovery Board announced a "new definition of policy" to the effect that open-price filing should be administered "to serve the ends of a free and open market." In fact, however, it added little to existing policy.[2]

Open-price reporting facilitates the elimination of differences in price between sellers.[3] Even in the absence of a "waiting period" information concerning price changes usually travels so speedily that differences in prices are likely to be eliminated. Making information concerning filed prices available to buyers increases this probability of uniformity. After codes were adopted and up to July, 1934 (when the "tolerance" order became effective), the Procurement Division of the treasury and the Bureau of Supply and Accounts of the navy both experienced in industries with open-price clauses an increase in the number of commodities upon which identical prices were quoted by two or more bidders; after July, 1934, the frequency of "tie bids" declined somewhat.[4] "Tie bids" were also the lowest bids in an increasing number of cases handled by the treasury throughout the whole period[5] but declined somewhat in frequency in the cases handled by the navy after July, 1934. Apart, however, from the paper and pulp and iron and steel industries,[6] "tie bids" at the lowest price generally declined after the "tolerance" order. The Navy Department

[1] The National Industrial Recovery Board was reported to have recommended the rescission of the order (*New York Times*, May 24, 1935).

[2] It emphasized the necessity for filing with a confidential body which would impartially distribute price lists to members of the industry and their customers. Any private agencies undertaking these functions should be subject to the immediate oversight of the government. Filed prices should be actual and not minimum prices. Waiting periods were inadvisable as a general rule and the burden of proof was upon the industry wishing to employ them. Requirements that prices once filed must remain in force for a stated minimum period might be necessary "in rare cases to impose some limit upon the frequency of price change." (*Cit. New York Times*, April 24, 1935.)

[3] It was stated by the Consumer Advisory Board that open-price filing in the plumbing fixture industry had furnished large manufacturers with full information concerning the selling prices for the unbranded goods of the small firms and enabled them to meet these prices and threaten the existence of the small firms (*Regulating Channels of Trade in the Plumbing Fixtures Industry*, 6).

[4] N.R.A., *Prices and Price Provisions in Codes*, Part VI. In industries without open-price clauses "tie bids" handled by the treasury did not increase in frequency until after the "tolerance" order but by February, 1935, were about as common as in industries with open-price clauses; those handled by the navy increased throughout the whole period but were less frequent than in the industries with open-price clauses.

[5] A similar increase occurred in the bidding on commodities not affected by open-price clauses (*ibid.*).

[6] It has already been noted that the president of the United States Steel Corporation agreed that the code for the iron and steel industry provided for a "one-price policy" (*New York Times*, Feb. 9, 1934).

resorted to the allocation of contracts by lot as a result of this uniformity.[1] Lack of complete homogeneity in the output of all producers modifies this tendency to uniformity of prices[2] but may lead to efforts to standardize products and remove this obstacle. Where codes provide that firms not filing prices shall be governed by the most favorable prices and terms filed price leadership is implemented if only one or a few large firms file prices.[3]

In various ways this policy is also calculated to discourage price cutting[4] and, therefore, to induce a greater stability of prices. Even if price cutters are relieved from intimidation during the "waiting period" the inducement to price cutting in the form of gains from business attracted from rivals in the period within which their prices are below those of rivals is reduced to small dimensions if not eliminated. Neither can new firms secure a footing in the industry by temporary price cutting. Doubtless, however, the mere presence of heavy overhead costs and excess capacity was a strong deterrent to short-term price cutting, even

[1] *New York Times*, Jan. 6, 1934. *Cf.* also *New York Times*, Oct. 30, 1933, and May 18, 1934, and Consumer Advisory Board, appendices to *Memorandum Submitted to General Johnson*, Feb. 19, 1934.

[2] It has been suggested (TERBORGH, *Price Control Devices in N.R.A. Codes*, 28) that permission to firms to sell below their filed prices to meet the competition of rivals without giving notice of change of price required in the code (*i.e.*, during the "waiting period") makes it necessary to determine what goods are competing goods and how great a difference in price is permissible in view of differences in the products concerned; the code authority would be required to calculate justifiable differences. Such problems arise, however, only during the waiting period and if that period is eliminated these problems are also eliminated.

[3] For example, in the tag industry (CONSUMER ADVISORY BOARD, *Experience with Price Fixing under the Codes*, 6).

[4] The president of the Bond Electric Corporation, who was also chairman of the Dry Battery and Flashlight Section of the National Electric Manufacturers Association, however, announced that his company had revised its opinion of the open-price clause of which it had formerly approved. He stated that in practice it had operated to throw the minimum prices of the manufacturer open to everyone and had thereby "given his most vital information to every 'gyp' in his industry." It had also instructed the unscrupulous as well as the small manufacturers "as to where to look for business" with the result that "unscrupulous producers today approach all channels of trade offering goods at the lowest price," facing the legitimate manufacturer "with nervous competition." His company accordingly announced its intention of allowing any discount below its published price "down to the actual cost of production . . . necessary to obtain business against the unscrupulous price competition which has developed in our particular industry under the open-price plan." (*New York Times*, Feb. 27, 1934.) This complaint throws little light on the nature of the difficulty but suggests that the company filed a minimum price but resented the resulting pressure to apply it to all sales. A number of rubber companies resisted the rule requiring the filing of prices also on the ground that it permitted "competitors to know and meet respondents' prices and to appropriate their customers by rendering such customers services and advantages which respondents cannot render" (*New York Times*, Aug. 4, 1934).

in the absence of these clauses. The following table[1] suggests

TABLE XIII. OPEN VERSUS NON-OPEN PRICES

Classification relative to codes	Number of prices	Mean percentage movement		
		Decline, 1926 (average) to February, 1933	Advance February, 1933, to August, 1933	Advance August, 1933, to August, 1934
Codes with waiting period.........	73	25.7	8.5	7.7
Codes without waiting period......	84	33.1	16.7	5.4
Codes with past price reporting....	24	40.2	55.7	−0.51
All open-price codes..............	181	31.1	18.5	4.9
Other codes.....................	130	39.8	35.2	0.5
Prices not under approved codes...	52	40.0	23.3	8.2
All nonagricultural prices.........	707	36.3	13.0	8.1

that prices declined least and advanced least in industries with open-price clauses and waiting periods; where there were open-price clauses but no waiting period prices declined more and advanced more, while in industries without open-price reporting prices fell and rose still more. Open-price reporting does not, however, eliminate price cutting; the price of steel was reduced by the National Steel Company in June, 1934, much to the dismay of most producers, especially as they had no warning of the proposed reduction.[2] Again in April, 1935, a reduction in the price of cold finished bars was initiated by a small Detroit producer.[3]

In some industries adherence to filed prices proved impossible of attainment.[4] In general, however, the open-price clause probably obstructed downward changes of price. As no firm was likely to raise its price without some assurance that the rest would follow, prices tended to be brought under the control of

[1] N.R.A., *Prices and Price Provisions in Codes*, Part VI.
[2] See *New York Times*, June 30, July 1, 2 and 15, 1934. The reduction is believed to have been made as a result of pressure from the automobile manufacturers.
[3] *New York Times*, Apr. 8, 1935.
[4] For example, in the canvas industry where the provision was stayed (CONSUMER ADVISORY BOARD, *Experience with Price Fixing under the Codes*, 5); also machined waste, cork insulation, commercial refrigerator, lumber manufacturing (*ibid.*, 9).

collective opinion in the industry.¹ The all-inclusiveness of the code authorities facilitated this control although discussions of price changes were not likely to be part of the official procedure of the authority.² The flexibility of the price structure was probably also diminished owing to the importance attached in each industry to stable prices. For this dangerous consequence the National Industrial Recovery Act was not to be blamed although it facilitated rather than obstructed it. On the other side, it was claimed that the limitation of price cutting directed competition into the channels of service and quality. Even such a deflection withdraws from the purchaser the choice between better quality and more convenience at the old price and the old quality and convenience at a lower price. In fact, however, the code authorities often endeavored also to restrict these types of competition.

C. Control of Non-price Competition

Having severely circumscribed price competition, the codes proceeded to the elimination of other methods of attracting purchasers by offering indirect advantages. Such advantages undermine efforts to restrict competition; they either offer a disguise for price competition or provide alternative channels for rivalry. These measures may be broadly classified according as they are concerned with methods of selling or quality and service competition.

1. METHODS OF SELLING

Many industries provided for the standardization of discounts. In some industries this end was attained by providing that the code authority might draw up a standard form of selling contract and that sales on other terms should be unfair;³ these contracts might then embody the standardized terms as to trade and credit

---

[1] *Cf.* the report that an expected increase in the price of iron and steel products did not materialize because "support of all producers was needed for the change" and could not be obtained (*New York Times*, Feb. 25, 1935).

[2] In the canvas industry the code authority gave its approval to the use of a price list prepared by a trade association (CONSUMER ADVISORY BOARD, *Experience with Price Fixing under the Codes*, 5).

[3] Of the 731 codes and supplements approved in February, 1935, 340 provided for the regulation of the forms or terms of contracts (N.R.A., *Condensed Information Based on the Operation of the National Industrial Recovery Act*, 5).

discounts. In a number of industries the lists of prices that were required to be filed with the code authority included either the trade discounts or the prices separately for each trade classification (jobbers, wholesalers, retailers, etc.) in the industry.[1] Thus net prices after allowance of trade discounts could be standardized for all firms. In some industries[2] the code authority was empowered to regulate trade discounts, the basis of classification of firms for purposes of trade discount being often also closely regulated by the code authority[3] either by definitions in the code itself or authorization to the code authority to draw up such definitions. In some[4] the code authority was authorized to draw up a list of all purchasers classified for the purpose of such discounts, or sellers were required to lodge a list of those in each class with the code authority.[5]

Provision for the standardization of quantity discounts[6] was similarly included in a number of codes and gave rise to great difficulties.[7] The refusal of quantity discounts on steel purchases was reported to have caused one automobile manufacturer to

[1] For example, in the petroleum industry prices were required to be posted separately for each trade classification.

[2] For example, furniture manufacturing, funeral supplies, pyrotechnics, fire extinguishing appliances (in which industry they were set by reference to differences in the cost of selling). The code for the floor and wall clay tile industry limited such discounts to 15 per cent.

[3] Floor and wall clay tile, cement, ladder manufacturing, fire extinguishing appliances, most branches of rubber manufacturing, iron and steel, lumber and timber products, wholesale automotive.

[4] Asphalt and mastic tile, reinforcing materials (in which industry the code authority might require the modification of the list if it believed that such allowances were a means of departing from published prices).

[5] Retailers objected to the discounts based on trade status and claimed that discounts should be based upon volume of business, size of order, and the value of the services rendered and also that the restriction of quantity discounts was undesirable because such discounts induced earlier commitments, the promotion of the products of certain manufacturers, and the reduction of the costs of distribution (*Cf. New York Times*, Oct. 30, 1933). Vigorous objection was also voiced against the classification of the state of New York as a retail buyer, thus increasing the cost of petroleum products purchased by it by $750,000 a year (*New York Times*, Jan. 10, 1934).

[6] For example, funeral supplies, pyrotechnics, buffing and polishing compositions, motor fire apparatus, hot-air furnace (in which the granting of quantity discounts not earned was proscribed as unfair), retail jewelry (where they were prohibited if they exceeded the savings obtained by the seller from selling in quantities), petroleum. Sales at carload rates to purchasers who pool their orders were regulated in the American match and lumber and timber products industries. After the codes lapsed it was said that quantity discounts were likely to be restored in the steel industry to encourage larger orders "on the score that they are more economical to roll" (*New York Times*, June 6, 1935).

[7] Quantity discounts can be disguised; those who place large orders are likely to be given the first opportunity to purchase a desirable "close out" or to obtain

contemplate the purchase of a steel plant to manufacture his own steel.[1] On the other hand, the granting of quantity discounts was said to hamper small firms.[2] Where the rate of discount increased with an increase in the size of order the formation of cooperative buying groups was encouraged.[3]

Rivalry might also persist in the granting of credit where price competition is largely eliminated. In so far as higher discounts might be allowed for payment before the expiration of the stated period of credit, they would reduce the net cash price of the firm offering them. Firms all selling for the same price after deduction of discounts may, however, rival each other in the period of credit granted, a form of competition with very real dangers. Again, this matter was regulated by proscribing as unfair sales not made upon a standard form of contract which included a statement of credit terms. In some industries power was given to the code authority, or its district committees, to draw up uniform terms of credit[4] but 282 codes[5] set out the maximum terms of credit to be allowed. In some industries the minimum initial payments and the maximum period of credit for sales on the installment plan were also prescribed in the code.[6] In addition to these provisions 553 codes specifically ruled as unfair the payment of secret rebates and allowances of all kinds.

There remained a variety of devices under cover of which financially more advantageous bargains might be offered by one firm than by others. Deductions from quoted price in return for advertising facilities or activities by the purchaser were regulated

---

superior materials or workmanship—advantages quite as lucrative in some fields as discounts (*New York Times*, Sept. 1, 1934).

[1] *New York Times*, Feb. 2, 1934.

[2] The ("Darrow") Board of Review reported that small manufacturers of rubber footwear had been thus handicapped (*New York Times*, May 21, 1934).

[3] A proposed arrangement for cooperative buying by a number of chains operating over 14,000 grocery stores was announced and attributed to the economies obtainable because of the quantity discounts provided in the codes (*New York Times*, July 28, 1934). It was promptly met, however, by a proposal to set maximum quantity discounts to prevent the concentration of purchasing in the hands of a few super-buying groups (*New York Times*, Aug. 5, 1934). The carpet and rug manufacturers sought the elimination from their code of a provision authorizing quantity discounts but their proposal was strongly opposed by retailers (*New York Times* Apr. 18, 1935).

[4] Concrete masonry.

[5] This and succeeding statistics concerning the frequency of particular clauses relates to February, 1935, when 731 codes and supplements had been approved, and is cited from N.R.A., *Condensed Information Based on the Operation of the National Industrial Recovery Act*.

[6] Shovel, drag line and crane, motor fire apparatus manufacturing, commercial refrigerators.

in 133 industries[1] in spite of protests from retailers' organizations.[2] The splitting of commissions with brokers and jobbers[3] (which means a sale at below the open price) or the storage of goods in a customer's warehouse[4] were sometimes ruled to be unfair. Sales to cooperative organizations of retailers or industrial consumers whereby the members secure the product at a price other than the open price were unfair in the bituminous coal industry although farm cooperative organizations were expressly accepted as buyers in the codes for the petroleum industry and for retail stores. Subsequently, however, all cooperatives, whether farm or consumer, were exempted from clauses forbidding rebates or sales at other than filed prices.[5] Sales with repurchase agreements were occasionally pronounced unfair.[6] Trade-in allowances were altogether prohibited in some[7] and regulated in others.[8] Elaborate arrangements were made to set maximum trade-in allowances for automobiles[9] and the motor fire apparatus industry provided also for the notification to the code authority of full information concerning the sale of repossessed equipment and

[1] *Cf.* beauty and barber shop mechanical equipment manufacturing industry. Any such allowances were to be granted only in pursuance of written contracts providing for specific services and filed with a confidential and disinterested agent of the code authority by whom they were to be made available to all sellers and buyers (Approved Code 286, Amendment No. 2 of Apr. 15, 1935).

[2] These organizations claimed that such allowances develop the interest of consumers, accelerate distribution, and permit profitable distribution at economical advertising rates (*New York Times*, Oct. 30, 1933).

[3] For example, lime, bituminous coal, American match.

[4] For example, rubber flooring, American match, smelting secondary metals into brass and bronze ingots.

[5] *Executive Order*, Oct. 23, 1933. *Cf.* statement of chairman of Consumer Advisory Board to Senate Finance Committee, Apr. 1, 1935.

[6] For example, gas appliances. Repurchase agreements provide a means by which manufacturers selling through independent distributors can relieve their distributors of inventory losses when they reduce their prices. The prohibition of such agreements handicaps the independent dealer and benefits manufacturers operating their own distribution system (*Cf.* LYON and others, *op. cit.*, 654).

[7] Rock crusher industry (sellers might assist in finding buyers for old machinery), washing and ironing machines, shovel drag line and crane.

[8] For example, canning and packing machinery, road equipment, gas appliances, motor fire apparatus manufacturing, industrial instrument and laboratory supplies, sections of the scientific instrument industry, commercial refrigerators.

[9] The automobile dealers undertook to collect in each district the actual prices paid by the public for each model, of each make of used car of each year. The 20 per cent of sales at the lowest prices were then excluded and the remainder averaged for each class separately. It was unfair for any dealer in any district to make a trade-in allowance for any car which exceeded the above class average for the period of approximately sixty days preceding the allowance, less a minimum handling, selling, and reconditioning charge (ranging from 5 to 15 per cent varying with the age of the car). In each district lists of the maximum trade-in allowances calculated in this manner were printed and circulated and special arrangements were made for dealing with cars of types of which very few sales occurred in any period. There was no

for the prohibition of the sale of show cars at less than the open sales price.

Some industries[1] prohibited the acceptance of stocks, bonds, and securities, in part or full payment; some, however, permitting their acceptance at their market value. The concrete masonry industry prohibited the sale of a grade superior to that ordered if only the price for the lower grade was charged, but the gear manufacturing industry permitted the seller to offer a substitute product which he felt to be equal or superior to that specified provided he declared that the commodity did not meet the specification. The substitution of any other article for that ordered was prohibited in 141 codes. Lump sum or combination prices (*i.e.*, the making of prices without setting out the price of each item)[2] were forbidden in 118 codes and some authorized the code authority to standardize methods of bidding.[3] The code for the retail drug industry prohibited advertising by druggists that they would fill all prescriptions at a uniform price, and that for the retail jewelry severely circumscribed the circumstances under which jewelry could be sold at auction.[4]

Long-term contracts were felt in many industries to obstruct the maintenance of uniform prices because buyers who had made such contracts might continue to purchase at prices below those being charged to other firms after the price had been increased;

---

reason why a dealer should not allow less than the maximum amount thus calculated. The interests of the dealers in this matter conflicted with those of automobile manufacturers and a reduction of trade-in allowances meant a virtual increase in the net price of new cars to the public which might result in a reduction of the prices of new cars by manufacturers and the narrowing of the margin allowed to the dealers. It was claimed that the arrangement was unfair to the owner of a car in unusually good condition and that it had proved unenforceable. (*New York Times*, August 3, 1934.)

[1] For example, cement, vitrified clay sewer pipe, structural clay products, reinforcing materials, scientific instruments (where they might be accepted in payment of insolvent accounts), silverware, refractories.

[2] In the reinforcing materials industry it was provided that wherever a contract exceeded $300 in value, and there was in the district an approved estimating bureau, contract bids should be arrived at by lodging with the bureau the bidder's list of prices which were to be applied by the bureau to the quantities as calculated by the bureau. This latter arrangement prevented any differences in bids due to differences in the calculation of quantities but also saved the cost of more than one calculation of quantities.

[3] Scientific instruments.

[4] Such sales were permitted only for the purpose of liquidation or in case of dire need, and then only with the permission of the local retail jewelry trade committee; no special purchases might be made for sale at the auction and the stock auctioned was required to be legitimately owned by the seller and an inventory of the goods to be sold was to be lodged with the local committee at least fifteen days before the date of the sale. The Appellate Division of the New York State Court in Brooklyn upheld this clause (*New York Times*, June 22, 1934).

fear of dissatisfaction thus arising might deter sellers from raising prices. Maximum limits to the period of contracts were, therefore, set in the steel[1] and a number of other industries.[2]

Guarantees against decline of price before the completion of a contract (carrying the liability to make reductions of price on all outstanding contracts if reductions were made upon new contracts) tend somewhat to discourage price cutting, but the offer of such contracts tends also to induce buyers to purchase larger quantities than they otherwise would; such guarantees were prohibited in 187 codes.[3] The provisions in the codes aimed at the regulation of price competition between producers in different parts of the country by the use of basing-point systems have already been discussed at length.[4]

Some codes permitted manufacturers to control the resale price of their products. Thus contracts for the maintenance of resale prices which had hitherto been held to contravene the anti-trust laws were enforceable with the aid of the government. Refiners, distributors, and jobbers of petroleum products could require buyers for resale to charge a prescribed price. Jobbers of steel products[5] might not resell them at prices lower than would have been paid by the buyer had he bought from the manufacturer.[6] Distributors of machine tools and equipment, retailers

---

[1] The original code for the iron and steel industry, for instance, provided that no contracts might be made for shipment later than the end of the quarter ending not more than four months after the date of the contract (except where the product was required by the purchaser for a specified and definite contract with a third party at a fixed price). This provision, together with a further requirement that contracts in force at the time the code became operative should be completed by December 31, 1933, gave rise to an uneconomical rush to complete orders in the closing weeks of the year 1933 and to consideration of the desirability of modifying this rule to prevent the recurrence of such a rush at the end of each quarter (*New York Times*, Jan. 1, 1934, and *Steel*, Jan. 1, 1934). This limitation on long-term contracts was attributed to a desire to prevent speculative buying (*New York Times*, May 31, 1934). The revised code for the industry, however, permitted contracts for the delivery of steel after the end of the next calendar quarter if the products were required for an identified structure, railroad cars, locomotives, or a definite public contract.

[2] Petroleum (for fuel oil), lime, floor and wall clay tile, buffing and polishing compositions, reinforcing materials (except for specific jobs), lumber and timber products, American match.

[3] These guarantees facilitate the operations of manufacturers selling through independent distributors in much the same way as repurchase agreements (See p. 503).

[4] See Chaps. VI and VII.

[5] This provision is said to have been "indifferently observed under the code" and was expected to be drastically modified when the code lapsed (*New York Times*, June 6, 1935).

[6] Similar arrangements were made in the package and pasteurized blended and process cheese industry.

of parts and accessories for automobiles, and wholesalers and retailers of automobiles were required to sell at the manufacturer's published prices and discounts. The "cigar merchandising plan" virtually prohibited the sale of cigars at retail at other than the prices set by manufacturers.[1] Some codes prohibited selling to jobbers and other dealers unless they had agreed not to resell in violation of the code for the manufacturing branch of the industry. In some industries manufacturers were authorized[2] and in others required[3] to enforce the maintenance of resale prices by boycotting offending distributers. Control by the manufacturer of the retailer's policy in deciding what products to sell gave rise to difficulties in the petroleum industry where "lease and agency" and "lease and license"[4] devices had enabled refiners to limit retailers to the sale of one brand of gasoline or petroleum products. The federal oil administrator prohibited new contracts of this type and authorized the cancellation of those already in force.[5]

The prohibition upon sales on consignment which appeared in 277 codes was presumably also aimed at preventing retailers from being loaded up with inventories held on consignment and tempted to indulge in price competition which might ultimately result in pressure upon manufacturers to reduce their prices.

[1] Codes for cigar manufacturing, wholesale tobacco, and tobacco retailing.
[2] For example, petroleum, copper and brass mill products, gasoline pump.
[3] For example, asbestos, buff and polishing wheel, rock crusher, warm-air furnace, saddlery. In the plumbing fixtures industry an attempt was made to control and raise prices by a combination of resale price maintenance, control of discounts, and open-price filing. The attempt failed largely because of the resistance of the mail-order houses. (CONSUMER ADVISORY BOARD, *Regulating Channels of Trade in the Plumbing Fixtures Industry*.)
[4] The retail filling station was leased by the refiner for a rent based upon the estimated sales of the filling station; this rent virtually constituted a price rebate to the owner of the station, who was then licensed or appointed agent of the refiner to sell his products and no others (*Cf.* F.T.C., *Prices, Profits, and Competition in the Petroleum Industry*, 1928, 256).
[5] The industry was unable to agree concerning the prohibition of the practice and the execution of new agreements of this type was prohibited pending a decision by the Federal Trade Commission. In the event of the commission failing to render a decision within sixty days, the President or any agency appointed by him was authorized to make a decision or temporarily to prohibit such arrangements pending a decision by the courts. The order of the Secretary of the Interior of Jan. 19, 1934, approving a marketing agreement aimed at the control of the prices of oil and oil products, provided that contracts expiring prior to Aug. 19, 1934, were not to be renewed and those with a cancellation clause were to be canceled as soon as possible. All future contracts for the sale of gasoline were to be made in an approved form giving the retailer the right of cancellation on thirty days' notice and no new exclusive contracts were to be made for the sale of oil. Finally, in an order of Mar. 5, 1935, the federal oil administrator authorized the cancellation of all exclusive dealing contracts (*New York Times*, Mar. 6, 1935).

Advertising was rarely controlled except where it was false.[1] The provision in the code for the lead pencil industry regulating the number of pages that might be printed in color in catalogues was a step in this direction but was unusual. Where selling expenses were excluded from calculations of cost upon which minimum prices were set there was an indirect discouragement to advertising when the minimum was operative. Other types of behavior which had long been regarded as undesirable were prohibited in many codes, e.g., commercial bribery in 531 codes, defamation of competitors in 500, false marking or branding in 398, imitation of trade-marks in 198, piracy of style or design in 117, false invoicing in 378, espionage upon competitors in 147, enticement of employees in 76, and the giving of premiums and prizes in 144.

A large number of codes specifically exempted sales for export from all the clauses of the code, or specifically from the open-price clauses and those concerning sales below cost. One[2] ruled it to be unfair to sell for export unless the buyer had agreed not to resell the product in the United States (a clause which indicated that the product was being dumped abroad).[3] An effort was made, on the other hand, to boycott foreign goods through clauses in the codes pronouncing it to be unfair for any manufacturer to deal in foreign goods or to sell to a customer dealing in goods of foreign origin,[4] but no such clause appears to have been approved.

The variety of rules adopted by code authorities arose from the variety of disguises under which price competition might occur. Few of these methods of selling, however, were developed simply to disguise price cutting: many had their separate economic justification. Producers, in their efforts to prevent their use as disguises, were forced into preventing their use under all circumstances. In consequence the control of price competition was facilitated at the expense of obstructing changes in the organization of industry and of methods of doing business which might be more economical than those prevailing. It was, moreover, frequently claimed by representatives of retailers that manu-

[1] In 550 codes misrepresentation by advertising or otherwise was prohibited. In the retail industry an attempt was made to prohibit advertising claiming a continuous policy of underselling rivals but, after a long and bitter dispute, the code was finally approved, merely prohibiting such advertising when it was inaccurate.
[2] Asbestos.
[3] The National Export Trade Committee announced in November, 1933, that in one form or another 62 of the codes exempted export business from the operation of the codes (*New York Times*, Nov. 20, 1933).
[4] Proposed code for the cordage industry (*cit. New York Times*, Nov. 12, 1933).

facturers had taken the opportunity offered by the drafting of codes not only to standardize selling practices but also to standardize them on a basis more favorable to themselves than had previously prevailed, especially in the matter of discounts and shipping practices.[1] The discounts allowed in fifteen industries concerned with apparel and house furnishings were said to have been reduced by the codes by an aggregate annual total of $50,000,-000.[2] New discount terms proposed in the cloak and suit industry involved an increased annual charge of $18,000,000, and those in the fur industry of $10,000,000.

2. QUALITY AND SERVICE COMPETITION

Quality and service competition were regulated in a number of codes. In some[3] the products of all sellers were to be standardized. Forty-eight codes authorized the regulation of the marketing of second-grade products.[4] In some industries[5] additions to and deductions from the prices of standard products because of departures from basic specifications were standardized for all firms.[6] The conditions under which allowance might be made for goods returned were standardized in 112 codes. The basis of standardization was criticized especially where credit was given only when goods were returned within a few days; where goods were passed on unopened the responsibility for faulty goods was transferred to the dealer, with the result that slovenly production is said to have been encouraged.[7]

In a considerable number of industries limitations were placed upon the incidental services that might be rendered by the seller

[1] *New York Times*, Oct. 30, 1933; Jan. 10, 1934. *Cf.* statement by National Retail Dry Goods Association, *cit. New York Herald Tribune*, Mar. 4, 1934.
[2] *New York Herald Tribune*, Apr. 1, 1934.
[3] Floor and wall clay tile, cement, pyrotechnics, excelsior and excelsior products, motor fire apparatus, cleaning and dyeing (in which industry these provisions occurred together with the power to fix minimum prices), rubber tire, lumber and timber products. In 261 codes the maintenance of standards of quality was in some way regulated.
[4] In the floor and wall clay tile industry the proportion of output that might be sold as second grade was restricted. In the hair and jute felt industry the combined total of discontinued lines that might be sold as discontinued lines and "seconds," *i.e.*, below the filed price, was limited to one per cent of the value of the previous year's sales (Amendment of July 22, 1934).
[5] For example, iron and steel, refractories.
[6] For example, business furniture (*cf.* Consumer Advisory Board, *Experience with Price Fixing under the Codes*, 3).
[7] *New York Herald Tribune*, May 20, 1934. The return of shopworn, damaged, or obsolete merchandise was controlled in the beauty and barber shop mechanical equipment manufacturing industry (Approved Code 286, Amendment No. 2 of Apr. 15, 1935).

without cost to the buyer, especially estimating services, surveys, and the like.[1] In 105 industries the guarantees that might be given concerning the performance of the product were also limited, in either scope or duration, or both. Demonstrations were regulated in some and the use of samples in 79. The code for the petroleum industry provided for the elimination of the practice of providing retailers with free filling-station equipment and also prohibited the repair of such equipment except where repairs could be made without removal of the equipment.[2]

The limitations on quality and service competition may, as we have seen, reduce the cost of production in the broad sense. Standardization in particular may have this result. On the other hand, they not only tend to diminish a form of rivalry that may benefit purchasers by inducing experimentation in the introduction of new products or new methods of business organization, but they facilitate (as they are often intended to) the elimination of rivalry in all forms.

D. *Control of Long-term Investment*

Although the National Industrial Recovery Act was initially operative for not more than two years, a considerable number of industries sought and obtained power to control long-term investment. For the most part they aimed at the restriction of entry into their respective industries. Regulations issued under the first code approved, *viz.*, that for the cotton textile industry, required all producers to register their productive equipment with the code authority; the installation of new equipment that would add to the total capacity of the industry was prohibited unless a certificate had been obtained from the administrator that such installation would be consistent with the policy of the act, exceptions being made for installations "for replacement of a similar

[1] For example, floor and wall clay tile, steel joist, miscellaneous steel castings, cement, radio broadcasting. Suppliers of heating oils might not supply free burner service.

[2] It was unfair for refiners, distributors, jobbers, wholesalers, or retailers to lease oil pumps, tanks, air compressors, or to replace equipment already lent. When a retailer ceased the sale of the products of one refiner and commenced the sale of the products of another, equipment installed by the first refiner was to be sold to the second at prices fixed in an elaborate schedule attached to the code. Refiners might, of course, provide such equipment for stations which they owned. They might also provide it to stations leased by them, provided that, at the time of the lease, the property was not equipped as a filling station, or the lease had run for at least five years and provided for a substantial rental not dependent upon sales. (These latter provisions were intended to prevent the provision of such equipment to stations controlled by refiners through a "lease and agency" arrangement.) The provision of paint and the construction, repair, lease, or loan of driveways, buildings, canopies,

number of units of productive equipment, or to bring the operation of existing productive machinery into balance."[1] In the steel industry the initiation of the construction of any new blast furnace, open hearth, or Bessemer steel (but not rolling mill) capacity was prohibited and the code for the lumber and timber products industry was amended to prohibit the award of production quotas to new firms until the firms holding quotas were running at full capacity. In fact 34 of the codes and supplements in force in February, 1935, restricted the installation of new machinery or increases in productive capacity,[2] and in seven others such restrictions became effective when initiated by the code authority. Some codes required the consent of the administrator to the installation of any additional plant,[3] while others required notice of intent to increase the capacity of the industry to be filed with the code authority which was authorized to advise the administrator concerning the desirability of the increase.[4] One provided for the delimitation by the code authority of the areas in which ample supplies were available from existing facilities.[5] In three, not only was the installation of new plant subject to control but also the reopening of closed plants.[6] Some codes,[7] however, exempted investments made with the object of improving the quality or reducing the cost of the product. Many code authorities were merely authorized to make proposals for the control of new investment,[8] and one for control by mutual agreement.[9]

---

air compressors, grease lifts or pits, grease equipment, towers, light poles, and flood lights was also prohibited under similar conditions.

[1] *New York Times*, Oct. 19, 1933. Up to the end of 1934 the committee of the cotton textile code authority had refused no request for permission to expand plant capacity.

[2] N.R.A., *Tables on the Operation of the National Industrial Recovery Act*, Table 32. These clauses occurred mainly in the textiles, basic materials, and chemical divisions.

[3] For example, pyrotechnics.

[4] For example, floor and wall clay tile, glass container, cement (in which industry the code authority was authorized to investigate capacity for production and demand in the area affected and to petition the administrator not to permit the installation if it was expected to increase the problem of overcapacity or overproduction in the area).

[5] Crushed stone, sand gravel and slag. If the administrator approved of the conclusions of the code authority the district committee might recommend him to withhold his approval of increases in capacity where they would obstruct the attainment of the purposes of the act.

[6] For example, structural clay products (except where the plant had been owned by the firm desiring to reopen it prior to Oct. 1, 1931).

[7] For example, structural clay products, crushed stone, sand gravel and slag, cement.

[8] For example, fertilizer, limestone, piano manufacturing, rubber footwear, paper and pulp (in which industry the code authority might also propose regulations for control of the shifting of equipment from one kind or type of product to another).

[9] In the motor vehicle storage and parking industry any group of members might

Restriction upon new investment in industries already suffering losses owing to excessive equipment was not generally of serious moment because there were so few new investors to deter. The restriction was not without influence, however. Firms desirous of commencing the manufacture of a new "flake ice" were obstructed by firms, already entrenched, who advised the administrator that additional investment was undesirable.[1] Although the allegation was denied,[2] it suggests the possibility that control of plant investment even in times of depression may obstruct improvements of methods of production. Control over the construction of new blast furnace, open hearth, or Bessemer steel capacity was said to obstruct the building of plants at low-cost points, protect existing plants, and thereby retard cost reductions.[3] Control of plant investment also placed obstacles in the way of changes in the distribution of business. The efficient firm could expand its business until its plant was fully occupied, but no further, without the consent of the administrator,[4] who might be advised by rivals to disapprove the proposed new investment because of the presence of unused plant. Indeed, the clause was alleged to have caused bitter complaint by small firms.[5] The administration appears, however, to have continued to approve of such clauses.[6] Thus, in so far as it operated to restrict the entry of new firms and obstruct the expansion of existing ones, this clause gave legal protection to those who had secured a position in an industry prior to the adoption of the clause. The suggestion that new investment should be obstructed until all existing plant was in operation was tantamount to protection from any new competition likely to undermine a selected price policy (except where demand at the price chosen exceeded the capacity of existing plant) no matter how far

---

agree not to increase capacity "except where needed," such agreements binding only the parties to them and being subject to interpretation by the administrator.

[1] ("DARROW") BOARD OF REVIEW, *Report, cit. New York Times*, May 21, 1934.

[2] Reply of counsel to National Recovery Administration, *ibid*. The constitutionality of the rule was contested in enforcement proceedings before the Federal Trade Commission (F.T.C., *Annual Report*, 1934, 5).

[3] F.T.C., *Basing Point System in the Steel Industry*, 27.

[4] If, however, transfers of equipment from firm to firm were unaffected by the rule (*e.g.*, excelsior products, silk textiles) additional equipment could be purchased from a rival or obtained by merger.

[5] ("DARROW") BOARD OF REVIEW, *Report, cit. New York Times*, May 21, 1934.

[6] Such a clause was added to the code for the silk textile industry by an amendment approved on July 17, 1934, which was curiously worded, however, to apply only to "any employer now in the industry." The association of wool manufacturers recommended a prohibition upon the installation of new machinery or the operation of machines that had been idle for two years except under license from the administrator (*New York Times*, Feb. 18, 1934).

the price exceeded the cost of production in an efficient plant employed to a reasonable percentage of capacity. In so far as the restriction was operative it tended, of course, to diminish the demand for capital goods.[1]

A few moves were made in the direction of reducing the capacity of some industries but none was successful. The code authority for the cement industry was authorized to submit proposals for the closing down or amortization of the less economical plants in an area where there was a permanent excess of capacity but it took no action. Twenty-one companies, controlling about 50 per cent of the output of paper board, submitted to the administrator a plan to form a corporation to buy up plants that could not "operate successfully under normal business conditions," and withdraw them from the industry; the companies concerned promised to produce "a sufficient supply of paper board to meet the demand." The proposal met, however, with a severe opposition and was characterized by one critic as a "plan to tax consumers to pay for their own chains."[2] Such policies look to a more sustained and serious restriction of output than the mere obstruction of new investment.

III. SUMMARY

The history of the National Industrial Recovery Act is the resultant of two sets of forces, the policies urged by business managers, on the one hand, and those of the administration, on the other. The policies urged by business interests were those developed by trade associations prior to the act; they rested ultimately upon the restriction of competition and control of output by each industry group. The act gave fresh hope to the supporters of these policies by promising emancipation from the limitations of the anti-trust laws and offering the aid of the state in enforcing uniform policies. The state, on the other hand, was dominated during this first year by a desire to secure the speedy acceptance of codes in all industries. This anxiety resulted in a large measure of acquiescence in the plans of trade associations. The very magnitude of the task of securing the universal adoption of codes and its delegation to a new and hastily assembled administrative machine contributed to this docility on the part of the state. The absence of any clear plan resulted in shortsighted policies as well as incon-

[1] *New York Times*, July 8, 1934.
[2] *New York Times*, Feb. 16, 18, 1934.

sistencies in the codes.[1] The initiation of the new program at the low point of a depression turned immediate attention to the acceleration of business activity and the reversal of the downward trends of wages and prices, and away from the long-run implications of industrial regulation.

The net result of these two sets of forces was a large measure of open concentration in each industry of the functions performed by the individual entrepreneur in a régime of competition; *viz.*, the functions of determining the volume of output, prices, the nature of output produced, methods of selling, and long-term investment. The degree in which these functions were actually concentrated varied greatly from industry to industry, more particularly with the number of firms in each and the relations between them.

Direct control of output was denied to industry at large. Some (but not all) industries marketing exhaustible natural resources were granted such control and all that can be said of the policy pursued in the exercise of this power is that it was aimed at increased prices. Indirectly, however, control of production and the rationing of output in proportion to capacity to produce gained in importance through the regulation of the maximum hours of plant operation. At first applied to few industries and in such a way as to leave total output unaffected, these regulations gradually came to affect total output and to apply to an increasing number of industries.

Explicit authority to fix prices was sought by many industries but obtained by few. Those who obtained the power were usually concerned with exhaustible natural resources, but even their experience was not encouraging. In the bituminous coal industry price fixing resulted in widespread evasion. In the lumber industry the power was given but subsequently withdrawn and replaced by "emergency" price fixing. In the copper industry reliance was placed at the outset upon control of sales, and the oil industry, setting out with explicit powers to fix prices, moved towards the organization of cartels to control sales. In the cleaning and dyeing industry price control proved unenforceable. In the distributing trades minimum margins between purchase and resale prices were usually fixed, sometimes with the object of preventing the use of any commodity as a "loss leader" and sometimes merely to "stabilize competition."

[1] *Cf.* National Industrial Recovery Board, *Code Revision Memorandum No. 1: Evolution of Trade Practice Policies.*

In spite of the difficulties that emerged when attempts were made to administer clear and continuing powers to fix minimum prices, price fixing found its way into a number of codes by an indirect route. Prohibitions upon "destructive price cutting" and the power to set minimum prices during "emergencies," came to apply to an increasing number of industries, these powers being, however, clearly placed in the hands of the administrator. The prohibition of sales at prices below the cost of production appeared in the early codes and survived all attacks during the first year of the administration: failure to secure approval of methods of calculating costs, however, rendered most of them inoperative.

The open-price policy of the trade associations was early entrenched in the codes and was blamed for increasing the uniformity of prices among sellers. Coercion upon those giving notice of intention to reduce prices was charged, with the result that efforts were made to amend, but not to abolish, the open-price clause. Policy moved in the direction of the elimination of notices of changes in price, the elimination of information concerning the identity of the seller quoting each price, and the obstruction of short-period price cutting by filing a reduced price to prevail only for a very short period (covering one important sale).

The standardization of products and methods of selling which had been increasingly sought by trade associations prior to the act as a means of avoiding disguised price competition and non-price competition was extensively provided for in the codes. Finally, the trade associations sought and often obtained the concentration of authority over long-term investment as a means of attacking the problems of cutthroat competition at their source.

The immediate effects of this relocation of authority over economic resources are impossible to segregate from movements in world economic conditions or from the consequences of the policies of the federal government with regard to monetary conditions, agriculture, the relief of the unemployed, and public works. Accurate measurement is, of course, impossible because of the absence of adequate statistics of output, wages, employment prices, and profits. Nevertheless the general measures of economic conditions summarized at Fig. 52 throw some light upon the matter. The immediate objectives of policy were the stimulation of business activity by increasing payrolls and between March and July, 1933,[1] payrolls increased by 35 per cent, employment in manufacturing by 23 per cent, while manu-

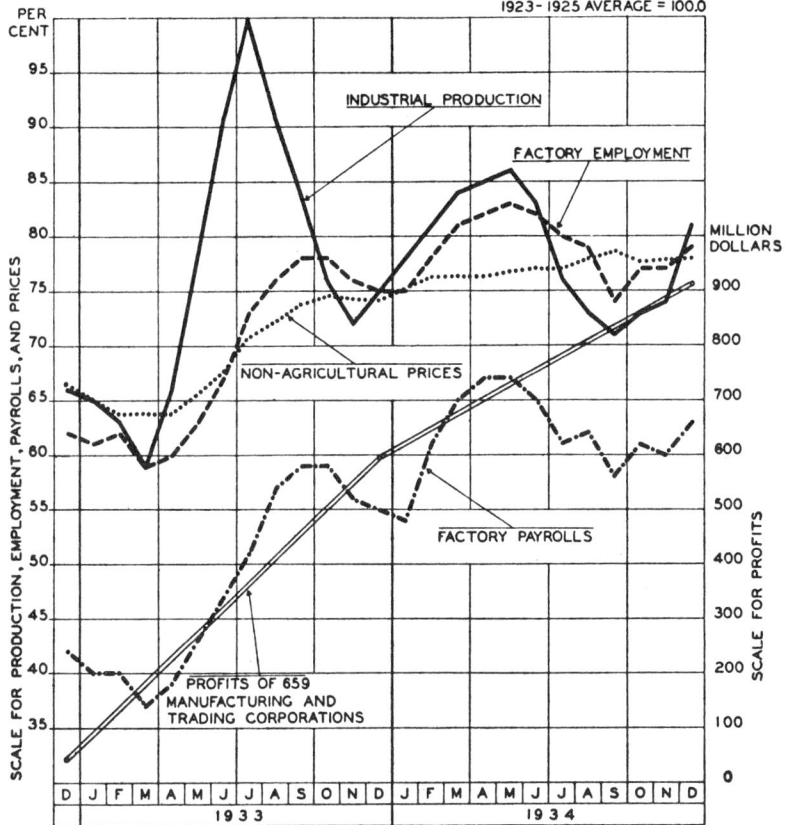

FIG. 52.—Industrial activity, payrolls, prices, and profits, 1933 and 1934. (*Drawn from data in Federal Reserve Bulletin.*)

facturing activity rose by 66 per cent and the wholesale prices of non-agricultural products on the average 11 per cent.[2] Between July, 1933, and December, 1934, factory payrolls increased a

[1] The sharp upturn in business activity before the National Industrial Recovery Act became operative on June 16, 1933, cannot be dismissed as unrelated to the act because it was in part stimulated by anticipation of the effects of the act (as well as of the effects of the monetary policy of the administration) in raising both prices and labor costs. Efforts were made to increase production before labor costs increased, in order to sell when prices had been raised.

[2] A fuller analysis of these statistics will be found at BURNS, "The First Phase of the National Industrial Recovery Act," *Polit. Sci. Quart.*, 49: 161 (1934).

further 23 per cent, and factory employment (adjusted) 8 per cent. Industrial production (adjusted) however, after falling in November, 1933, to 28 per cent below the July, 1933, figure rose in May, 1934 to 14 per cent below it, then fell to 29 per cent below in September, 1934, and by December, 1934, was again 14 per cent below it. The wholesale prices of non-agricultural products rose 10 per cent between July, 1933, and December, 1934. These statistics indicate that increases in output and payrolls were accompanied by increases in prices, the most rapid rise occurring between March and July, 1933. The marked increase in the volume of production during this period was accompanied, however, by an increase of 8 per cent in stocks of manufactured goods, an increase in harmony with the assumption that dealers and manufacturers were speculating on increases in prices and costs. But when sales at the higher price level failed to carry off all current production, prices were not reduced; they were further increased[1] with the result that between August, 1933, and December, 1934, production averaged 21 per cent below its level in July, 1933, but 34 per cent above its level in March, 1933.[2] These increases in price resulted in considerable increases in profits, 659 manufacturing and trading corporations which had reported aggregate profits in 1932 of $41,000,000 reporting profits of $598,000,000 in 1933 and $911,000,000 in 1934.[3] Doubtless part of this improvement in profits was due to the introduction of more efficient methods of production and organization, and

[1] The index of wholesale prices is far from a perfect measure of increases in prices. There was considerable complaint that the custom of adding a fixed percentage to cost to cover distributing costs at each stage of the process of distribution resulted in increased charges for distribution whenever the wholesale price of the product increased and irrespective of changes in the actual cost of distribution. In some industries the elimination of sales at less than the announced price, as well as the reduction and elimination of discounts and allowances of various kinds, caused considerable increases in actual prices not included in these figures. It was also claimed that actual increases in the cost of paper, for instance, exceeded those suggested by these averages because the prices of the important types were drastically raised, while those of the less important were raised very little.

[2] The raising of prices and restriction of output were most notable in the building materials industries where prices were by 1935 only 9 per cent below their level in 1929. The composite index of the cost of construction compiled by the *Engineering News-Record* was in October, 1934, only 1½ per cent below the average for 1929. Construction awards were only 20 per cent of their average for 1923 to 1925 (CONSUMER ADVISORY BOARD, *The Effect of Price Control and Price Stabilization on the Construction Industry*).

[3] These statistics relating to large corporations are probably not typical of industry in general. The National Bureau of Economic Research has called attention to a remarkable inverse correlation between size of firm and rate of return in 1931 and 1932 (*Bulletin* 55, April, 1935).

part to the fuller utilization of plant, but it is hard to reject altogether the suggestion that prices were increased to an extent more than necessary to cover increases in payrolls. The deficiencies of statistics of profits are too obvious and numerous to specify; but there is no reason for rejecting the general conclusion to which they point, *viz.*, that prices were raised sharply between March and July, 1933, and more slowly between July and December, 1934, and that production was adjusted to the rising level of prices. The particular admixture of collectivism and individualism established by the act failed to secure compliance with the President's plea for temporary sacrifices in the hope of later gain from the fuller utilization of the means of production. The maintenance of production in December, 1934, at a level some 30 per cent above that in December, 1932, must be attributed in large part to other aspects of government policy. Beginning in September, 1933, considerable amounts of purchasing power were placed in the hands of farmers in the form of crop allotment payments, and a little later the distributions made for Civil Works projects, Public Works, and the Civilian Conservation Corps attained sizable proportions.[1] Thus the elevation of the trade association to a position of control in industry and the larger measure of acquiescence in their policies by the state resulted in the use of the new concentration of authority to seek immediate profits in increases in prices rather than in the acceleration of business activity.

It is difficult to attribute this outcome to any particular clauses in the codes except where explicit and effective control of output, sales, or prices has been permitted and proved enforceable. Although the open-price clauses probably exert an upward pressure upon prices, they do not, as we have seen, determine prices. It is unlikely that the elimination of these clauses would have resulted in a fall in prices;[2] producers were schooled in the processes of cooperative price making and would be unlikely to revert to short-run price cutting. Nor were the clauses prohibiting sales at prices below cost of production of primary importance in determining prices. They were not brought into general operation because of the time required to establish uniform methods of

[1] The Consumer Advisory Board concluded in 1935 that if rents had not lagged behind other elements in the cost of living "the subsidy of consumers by the federal government would be the only source of the increased physical volume of sales" (*Prices in Relation to the Consumer's Income*, 2).
[2] *Cf.* CONSUMER ADVISORY BOARD, *Private Price Control and Code Policy*, 1.

calculating costs; many of the codes, moreover, required that the administrator approve of proposed methods of calculating costs and the machinery for examining and approving proposed cost accounting systems was slow in being established. In any event the policy of the administration in interpreting the phrase "cost of production" could at best set the minimum and not the maximum price. The administration avoided the use of its power to license industries and had little other direct power to reduce prices[1] or prevent their increase except where firms were willing to reduce actual prices when minima were reduced. It is nevertheless probable that considerable pressure could have been exerted by the threat to withdraw approval of the code in an industry whose price policy was disapproved; the industry would then become subject to the anti-trust laws.[2]

The Board of Review established to investigate the extent to which the National Industrial Recovery Act had induced monopolistic practices or hampered small businesses concluded that

"monopoly sustained by government . . . is clearly the trend in the . . . National Recovery Administration. . . .

"Fair competition is merely a resounding and illusory phrase . . . what the powerful producer calls fair his weaker rival fiercely denounces as most unfair; and there is no way to reconcile the difference. All competition is savage, wolfish, and relentless; and can be nothing else."[3]

A supplemental report concluded that no power under the act was showing itself able to protect the small producer and that

"there is no hope for the small business man or for complete recovery in America in enforced restriction upon production for the purpose of maintaining higher prices. . . . To give the sanction of the government to sustain profits is not a planned economy but a regimented organization for exploitation. . . . The tendency to raise prices while forcing down wages reduces the purchasing power which alone can balance production and consumption."[4]

There is little doubt that the programs in the main successfully urged by business managers were not even in their own interests

---

[1] The power to fix minimum prices in an emergency was used to secure a reduction of retail lumber prices but this case stood alone and untested.

[2] The labor clauses would then also have ceased to operate unless a limited code applying to them alone had been imposed or only the clauses affecting prices and output withdrawn.

[3] ("DARROW") BOARD OF REVIEW, *Report, cit. New York Times*, May 21, 1934.

[4] *loc. cit.* Counsel for the administration charged that the board was partial in its attitude and incorrect in its facts.

as a group. It may be argued that their failure to bring to the solution of the problems of depression nothing more than their old policies writ large and plain was due partly to the fact that the full consequences of these policies had never been revealed in the earlier period because of the impotence of trade associations. Yet general reasoning suggests very forcibly that, while restriction of output by some groups may benefit them at the expense of the remainder, the policy cannot be generalized for all groups simultaneously. A society is not generally better off the less it produces. Rather the explanation lies in the fact that business managers were, as would be expected, still motivated by the pursuit of private profit. They had broadened the basis of their calculation of profit to compass the interests of each industry as a group, but no further. They were beginning to resemble very closely in their policies the craft guilds of the middle ages. This measure of concentration, however, possesses neither the merits of the wide distribution of authority implied in free competition nor those of its complete concentration in the state.

The President announced that "we have created a permanent feature of our modernized industrial structure" which will prevent both ruinous rivalries in industry and monopoly and restraint of trade "under the supervision but not the arbitrary dictation of the government itself."[1] The gesture was cramped at the outset, however, because policy was directed to considerations no more far reaching than an estimate of what representatives of industry would accept without protest. Essential reform must necessarily involve from time to time the imposition of policies distasteful to the class that is most highly organized and articulate. During the first year of the act the administration, however, spoke with two voices, one for business and another for critics of its policy. Repeated references were made to the abandonment of price fixing and the maintenance of a free market; in fact it merely changed the forms of control of prices and output without reducing the extent of the control although during its second year clauses permitting price control became less important.

The declaration that the National Industrial Recovery Act was unconstitutional[2] brought to an end an experiment in industrial control estimated to have cost for its administration about

[1] *Message to Congress* of President Roosevelt, Jan. 3, 1934.
[2] U.S. v. Schechter Poultry Corp., 55 S. Ct. 837 (1935).

94 million dollars.¹ It was received by industrialists with mixed feelings. They were gratified by the decision of the Supreme Court to obstruct greater government control of industry but conscious, for the most part, that the control hitherto exercised under the act had been very helpful to them. There were signs, however, of the development of a more critical attitude within the administration.² A number of trade associations and large corporations sought to avoid a general exodus from the promised land by declaring publicly their intention to continue adherence to the codes now unsanctified by law.³ General adherence to the wage levels set in the codes was expected to prevent general price reductions. Plans were made for voluntary codes to be enforced by resort to arbitration.⁴ The remnant that remained of the National Recovery Administration moved warily in encouraging the adoption of voluntary codes. It was aware that the government, being no longer able to offer immunity from the anti-trust laws, had little to offer as a reward for the acceptance of clauses distasteful to industry.⁵ It was made clear that voluntary codes must comply with the anti-trust laws⁶ and industries were invited to submit codes to the Federal Trade Commission which would deal with them in cooperation with the National Recovery Administration under its former Trade Practice Conference procedure, although possibly the commission might "modernize" some of its rulings concerning the acceptability of trade practice rules.⁷ The first voluntary code under the new regime of cooperation between the National Recovery Administration and the Federal Trade Commission was obtained by the wholesale tobacco distributing trade on Sept. 30, 1935. The Trade Practice Division of the commission accepted as rules which it was prepared to enforce prohibitions on "loss leaders," and selling below cost with intent to injure a competitor "and where the intent may be to lessen competition, or tend to create a monopoly, or unreason-

---

[1] Estimate of National Industrial Conference Board (*cit. New York Times*, June 10, 1935). The expenditures of code authorities included in this figure were estimated at 71.8 million dollars.

[2] *Cf.* National Industrial Recovery Board, *Code Revision, Memorandum No. 1: Evolution of Trade Practice Policies*; LYON and others, *op. cit.*, Chap. XXIX.

[3] *Cf. New York Times*, June 4, 1935; address of president of U.S. Chamber of Commerce, *cit. New York Times*, June 15, 1935; *cf.* also *New York Times*, July 19, 1935.

[4] *New York Times*, June 13, 1935.

[5] *New York Times*, June 20, 26, 1935.

[6] *New York Times*, June 8, July 4, 1935.

[7] *New York Times*, July 4, 1935.

ably restrain trade." Price discrimination, secret rebates, allowances, and services were prohibited under similar conditions.[1] In some industries, however, there was evidence that part of the ground gained under the act would have to be evacuated. The declaration of the American Iron and Steel Institute of the intention of its members to continue to act in accordance with its code diminished the prospect of price reductions but greater flexibility of prices was expected; the prohibitions on quantity discounts and the requirement of resale-price maintenance were expected to be modified and the rules governing fabrication in transit[2] to be materially altered.[3] There was grave doubt whether the rationing of sales of copper could be continued under any voluntary code.[4]

The abandonment of the National Industrial Recovery Act provided no solution to the problem of adapting economic institutions to an industrial system diverging increasingly from free competition. Under the act even where there was no explicit sanction of control of output and prices the aspects of sales other than prices were often so closely regulated that informal regulation of prices was relatively easy.[5] Return to the régime prevailing prior to the act may somewhat hinder such regulation but the preceding chapters have shown how persistent is the trend away from competition under existing law. The state cannot by refraining from positive control obtain the benefits of free competition. On the other hand, state participation in price policies presents profound and complex problems both economic and political. Yet some such participation is inevitable.

[1] *New York Times*, July 20, 1935.
[2] See p. 348.
[3] *New York Times*, June 6, 1935.
[4] *New York Times*, June 19, 28, 1935.
[5] *Cf.* CONSUMER ADVISORY BOARD, *General Statement* by Dexter M. Keezer on Jan. 9, 1935.

CHAPTER XI

THE PROBLEM OF SOCIAL CONTROL—OBJECTIVES

I. The requirement of competition by law—*A*. Without industrial reorganization—*B*. Industrial reorganization to restore competition—II. Acceptance of the concentration of economic power—*A*. Without state participation—*B*. With state participation—1. Considerations of productive efficiency—*a*. Shifts in demand—*b*. Shifts in the demand for natural resources—*c*. Cyclical fluctuations in demand—*d*. Changes in methods of production—*e*. Changes in conditions of supply of the means of production—*f*. Maintaining the efficiency of productive units—2. Considerations of the distribution of the produce between different classes and individuals—*a*. Within a given period of time—*b*. Over time—3. Considerations of the non-financial burden of productive activity—III. Conclusions.

In the preceding chapters we have surveyed industrial price and production policies from the years preceding the Sherman Anti-Trust Act of 1890 to the end of the effective life of the National Industrial Recovery Act of 1933. That survey reveals, on the one hand, the development of conditions increasingly unfavorable to fully competitive behavior and, on the other, the development of policies not easily explicable in terms of theories of imperfect competition. Unstable and partial concentration of economic power has resulted in policies dominated by fear; price competition has been restricted and evaded in a variety of ways.

We now turn to discuss the problems of state control; this discussion serves more than a practical purpose; it compels the sharp focusing of our analysis of the régime of the past forty-five years. Attempts to reform are often couched in terms of changes in administrative machinery, of proposals to establish a commission to decide what is fair and just. The more urgent problem, however, is the clarification of objectives; administrative forms can then be devised with reference to the functions to be performed. The objectives of social control will, therefore, be discussed before turning to the means of control.

Social control of economic activity is as old as private property. Laissez faire is itself a policy of social control. The contrast between economic planning and laissez faire lies in the nature and scope of the economic functions to be centralized in the state. The changes in industrial conditions set out in the preceding chapters have seriously undermined faith in laissez faire. Choice in the matter of social policy now appears to lie between the preservation of competition by law (a paradoxical policy of social control) and state participation in the exercise of the already concentrated economic authority.

I. THE REQUIREMENT OF COMPETITION BY LAW

The anti-trust laws in force from 1890 to 1933 were an attempt to maintain competition by law. The Sherman Law prohibited monopolies and restraint of trade, and the legislation of 1914[1] was intended to implement this policy by somewhat elaborating and clarifying the meaning of "restraint of trade" and improving the machinery for administration. During this period great concentrations of economic power occurred; an increasing number of vital industries were transformed from a mainly competitive to a quasi-monopolistic condition. Although these industries may be less important in the whole field of industry than the publicity concerning their activities suggests, the urge to centralize some of the entrepreneur functions is present even in industries where control is organized in relatively small units. The foregoing studies of trade associations before and after the passing of the National Industrial Recovery Act have revealed how widespread is the movement to centralize economic authority. The unwisdom of applying the general property laws as well as the anti-trust laws to exhaustible national resources has been officially acknowledged.[2]

The anti-trust laws have been a notable failure as a means of maintaining competition. Many support their preservation, however, on the ground that they failed, not because the laws were deficient, but because enforcement was lax; the remedy, therefore, is more vigorous and more competent enforcement.[3]

---

[1] The Clayton Act and the Federal Trade Commission Act.

[2] Evidence of Secretary of the Interior Wilbur at *Hearings Pursuant to Senate Resolutions 2626, 2627, and 2628 on the Amendment of the Federal Trade Commission Act*, 1932, 221, 222.

[3] *Cf.* letter signed by Professor F. W. Fetter and over one hundred economists in *Amer. Econ. Rev.*, 22: 467 (1932), contending that the weakening of the Sherman Anti-Trust Act would involve consequences inconsistent with the principles of private industry and that the extension of public price fixing would impose upon government agencies impossible tasks of control and irreparable injuries to the political, social, and economic interest of the nation. They opposed any amendment of the anti-trust laws that would "weaken them as agencies for preserving the policy of free markets," reaffirmed the principle of fair competition, rejected the contention

But can vigorous application of the law maintain competitive conduct in the industrial system as now organized or must the system be reorganized in harmony with a pattern calculated to induce competitive behavior?

A. Legal Requirement of Competitive Conduct without Industrial Reorganization

It has been suggested that the development of monopolistic behavior has been an inevitable consequence of the development of large-scale production involving the use of durable equipment and productive organization incapable of instantaneous creation or abandonment. Business managers, being fully conscious of the dangers of price competition based upon a short and narrow view of its consequences, seek to avoid it. The policies they have adopted are, however, difficult to eliminate unless the causes giving rise to them are also eliminated. It is obviously impossible to prohibit price leadership. Even under competitive conditions there is a tendency for the prices charged by different sellers to attain a uniform level; it would obviously be absurd to attempt to prohibit such uniformity, or to compel sellers to change their prices when others do not. It is equally impossible to insist that changes in price shall not always be initiated by the same firm. Price stabilization is equally difficult to prevent unless the state is prepared to determine when prices ought to be changed. Policies of sharing the market could be attacked only if the state were prepared to decide the proper distribution of business between existing firms; it would also find itself compelled to determine how the distribution of business should be changed from time to time. Direct attacks upon integration would necessitate determination of the proper degree and pattern of integration. Control of non-price competition would necessitate the determination of the proper methods of securing business and, particularly, the proper amounts to be spent upon advertising and other methods of promoting sales. Prevention of the discussion of prices and production by all the producers in an industry is a hopeless task. Thus attempts to restore competition by direct

---

that the anti-trust law by inducing excessive plant expansion and production was one of the causes of the depression. They referred to the inadequate enforcement of the law and demanded genuine and effective enforcement. *Cf.* also Professor FETTER, *The Federal Anti-trust Laws* (ed. Milton Handler), 14 *ff*. "Let the anti-trust laws be obeyed and enforced. Competition as the principle and policy of industrial pricing has merits which remain undimmed by all the slanders cast upon it."

attack upon policies departing from competition lead perversely into the very planning of industrial organization by the state to which the plan is intended to supply an alternative.

B. Industrial Reorganization to Restore Competition

If competitive behavior cannot be induced by legal means unless the organization of industry is changed, what changes are necessary to resurrect competition? The size of business units is the outstanding, although not the only, cause of departure from competition. The first change required would be, therefore, a reduction in the size,[1] and an increase in the number, of firms, either by positive prohibitions or the imposition of heavy taxes upon large firms. This change would affect production costs. Much of the recently acquired knowledge of methods of production involves mass production: if firms are reduced in size some of the benefits of mass production must be abandoned. The amount of these losses is impossible to calculate and it is probable that the economies of large firms are frequently exaggerated. Moreover, given sufficient time, business could adjust to the compulsion to use smaller units. In recent years, a considerable amount of the energy, initiative, and resources devoted to the improvement of methods of production has been directed to discovering better methods of large-scale production. If these resources were diverted into the investigation of the economies of smaller-scale production, smaller firms might ultimately be made as economical as larger ones.[2] Nevertheless, considerable reductions in efficiency would follow upon increases in the number and reductions in the size of firms in some industries. The transition from the present to the new régime would also involve costs. There is doubtless much plant and equipment, and considerable business organization, that can be fully utilized only when large-scale methods are permitted; the reorganization of industry to utilize smaller-scale methods would render this equipment and organization obsolete.

The principal objective of this regulation of the size of firms is to attain the fruits of competition without planning. Yet it requires planning of a peculiarly cumbrous kind. The state must

---

[1] *Cf.* BRANDEIS, *The Curse of Bigness*, 107 and *passim*.

[2] Opportunities to make very large profits from the promotion of mergers have led to subsequent attempts to make large firms more efficient; frequently there has been little social gain from these attempts. *Cf.* BURNS, "The Process of Industrial Concentration," *Quart. Jour. Econ.*, 47: 289 (1933).

evolve criteria of competitive conduct in order to be able to calculate the minimum number of firms likely to induce competition. It would be necessary to keep a constant watch upon the behavior of producers and to increase the minimum number of firms whenever quasi-monopolistic behavior appeared. The state might find it necessary to seek some means of adjusting the actual number of firms to the minimum number desired when voluntary entrants into the industry did not attain the required number.

But the fatal objection to this policy is that it is self-defeating; it is fundamentally inconsistent with the maintenance of competition. Wherever a business attained the maximum size permitted under the law, the stimuli present under free competition would operate only in a very modified form. The inducement to improve methods of production in order to reduce prices and thereby capture an increasing share of the total business in the industry is eliminated. There is no further inducement to price competition by such a firm.

Attempts to restore competitive behavior by law offer no prospect of dealing with the developing element of monopolistic control in industry.

II. ACCEPTANCE OF THE CONCENTRATION OF ECONOMIC POWER

The alternative to the foregoing policies is for the state to acquiesce in the concentration of control over economic resources. It may then either permit the unregulated exercise of monopoly power or participate in exercising that power.

A. *Without State Participation*

Vague but resounding claims for "the American tradition of free enterprise" have frequently been little more than pleas for the minimization of state interference with economic activity (except where foreign competitors and labor unions are concerned). The outcome of laissez faire when industry is organized on a small scale is very different, however, from the outcome when industry has been transformed by the impelling force of the economies of mass production. The conventional objection to private monopolies that the interest of the monopolist is often in conflict with the interest of society as a whole is undeniable. Maximum profit frequently derives from a volume of production less than could be sold at a price covering all costs of production, including the minimum remuneration for which the entrepreneur would serve.

The foregoing chapters suggest, however, that the calculation of the monopoly policy necessitates extremely difficult estimation. Many monopolists, moreover, are severely limited in the profits they can obtain by the presence of nearby substitutes. They become anxious to avoid dangerous price wars between monopolists and possibly to avoid public criticism. In consequence they have resorted to policies which are workable, but which are often not in the general interest, and often not to the ultimate benefit of those who adopt them. There is a general resistance to price cutting which develops into the stabilization of prices. This type of policy increases the tendency for the industrial organism to react excessively to declines in demand. It tends also to prices high enough to yield returns upon plant excessive in relation to production and to reward inefficient management. Group monopolies able to control output and prices are relieved from competitive pressure to maintain efficiency; fear of price cutting by those with the lowest costs is removed. The level of efficiency in each industry tends to be administratively determined by those in the industry, and they do not voluntarily subject themselves to competitive pressure to keep down costs. Efforts to increase efficiency induced under competition by a prospect of profit or fear of loss are also diminished by group monopoly. These policies may be due to the unsteadiness of the concentration of economic power through trade associations and leadership. They may be the policies of a transition; open concentration of power backed by the force of law might free the industrial dictator from fear of price wars and permit a more farsighted policy.

There is, however, no reason to believe that more power would induce a greater sense of responsibility, a greater regard for the broad social interest, and a greater realization that the fate of an industry is bound up with the fate of all the others. The ideal of service said to be developing among business managers implies that some such broadening of the basis of their industrial policy has occurred. Discussion of this ideal among business men springs more probably from a suspicion that the lack of such a viewpoint exposes them to criticism than from a willingness to adopt it.[1]

[1] The development of an ideal of social service, of course, undermines the foundation of economic thought based upon the assumption that the primary drive to economic activity is the maximization of individual income but that assumption is

Bankers are often expected to be guided by motives other than those of self-interest.[1] Much of the bitter criticism of bankers during the years following the collapse of business at the end of 1929 flowed from a resentful realization that bankers had failed to conduct their business with a view to the general social welfare. Yet neither the declarations of bankers nor the records of their past conduct justified the assumption that they would so behave. It is nevertheless true that business management has modified its behavior since the days of industrial brigandage at the end of the nineteenth century, partly because of fear of public criticism, and partly because of a realization that ferocious attacks on rivals may draw return fire that may lead to bloody battles. But the conflict between private and public interest remains. Furthermore the leaders of industry may not see even the interests of their own industries very clearly.[2]

Even if those in each industry desired to further the general social interest, they would encounter serious obstacles. The policy in each industry likely to have the best reactions upon society as a whole is clearly dependent upon the policies being pursued in other industries. Not only would information be necessary concerning the policies of other groups but also all these policies would require coordination.[3] These interrelationships are so many and complex, however, that effective coordination is attainable only through an organization which covers the whole political territory; and the state is the most appropriate group organization for this purpose.[4] Separate industry groups may

---

already open to considerable question. It is seriously undermined by the conduct of the major part of industrial activity, by corporations whose managers do not directly secure all the gains arising out of profitable policies or suffer all the losses resulting from unprofitable ones.

[1] In England, where the central bank is legally a corporation with private stockholders, there is an increasing claim that it should conduct its operations with a view to their effect upon the country as a whole, and not with a view to their effect upon its own profits; private banks are expected to cooperate in this policy.

[2] Mr. James Dole, who participated on the side of the administration in the making of the early codes under the National Industrial Recovery Act, remarked: "Strangely enough we found ourselves in many cases trying to protect the industry against itself and unwise and shortsighted practices which the sponsors were trying to impose on themselves." "It was surprising to find the confidence which many business men felt in what they could do for their industry if only they could create a monopoly." (*New York Herald Tribune*, Mar. 4, 1934.)

[3] Many of the codes of fair competition under the National Industrial Recovery Act empowered code authorities to coordinate their codes with those of related industries.

[4] In fact, in so far as the industries of different territories are interdependent, the argument indicates the necessity for international control.

well conceive of the social interest in different and conflicting terms and this conflict again requires the coordinating services of a body representing the whole economic group. Finally, the long-term planning necessitated by present methods of production, whether it be in the hands of individuals, groups, or the state, involves the estimation of future demand and future sources of supply and methods of production. The material for making estimates is often so tenuous that the estimates rest more upon individual and group bias than upon inferences from the observed past. If bias cannot be avoided, considerable supervision over these estimates should be transferred to the state which is responsible for taking account of the interests of all conflicting groups.

B. *Acceptance of Concentration of Economic Power and State Participation in its Exercise*

All efforts to deal with the unsatisfactoriness of the outcome of the present organization of industry lead in the end to the acceptance by the state, in some form or other, of responsibility for participating in the exercise of economic power. That power is now concentrated, in spite of the past policy of the state, to a degree rendering assumptions of competitive behavior completely unreal. Striving after individual competition as a neat self-regulating device is fruitless because, by its nature, it cannot be established and maintained by law. We are compelled to pass beyond to the direct selection of economic objectives as a basis for the policy of the state. The economist has no exclusive claim to lay down the objectives of society. He is, as an economist, concerned with the probable consequences of attempts to pursue particular ends, basing his prophecies upon such past experience as appears relevant. Any policy must rest ultimately, however, upon decisions concerning the volume of output or efficiency of production, the distribution of output between classes, and the types of activity individuals should undertake.

The effect of any policy upon the output of society is not, of course, a paramount consideration.[1] There are many ways in which the output of society could be increased but which would

[1] In the last resort it is impossible to conceive of the volume of production apart from a particular distribution of incomes; the production of heterogeneous commodities can be added only in value terms and values are influenced by the distribution of income. The argument of the remainder of this chapter rests upon the assumption that no great changes in the distribution of incomes occur.

be rejected on the ground, either that they resulted in an undesirable distribution of income, or that they placed undue physical and mental burdens upon some or even all members of the group. Nevertheless, the effect of any policy upon total output is a matter of considerable importance, and one to be calculated in order to determine, after consideration of other probable economic consequences of the policy, whether it is desirable or not. Any kind of state participation leads ultimately to considerations of this kind. Under the National Industrial Recovery Act the state "demanded of many citizens that they surrender certain licenses to do as they pleased in their business relationships; but we have asked this in exchange for the protection which the state can give against exploitation by their fellow men or by combinations of their fellow men."[1] The account in the preceding chapter of the problems resulting from this policy will serve as a ready means of revealing the implications of state participation in the utilization of economic resources.

I. CONSIDERATIONS OF PRODUCTIVE EFFICIENCY

Productive inefficiency in the recent past arose out of changes in demand and conditions of production which had not been anticipated. Attempts to deal with these economic changes by embryonic planning by business have proved wasteful, and the problem of social control is that of finding a way of avoiding these wastes. The state may increase the efficiency of the industrial organism in two ways. It may seek to minimize maladjustments in the allocation of resources or, once the maladjustments have occurred, to minimize the waste of resources.

Events drive the state along this path. Investment and management interests are both troubled by the unemployment of plant, which involves loss and is a potential stimulant of destructive price competition. The efforts of private interests to prevent such competition have been shown to be so unsatisfactory that it is in the general social interest that the state should intervene. Moreover, where private interests fail to eliminate such competition they themselves press for state intervention. The spectacle of unemployed labor indirectly leads also to demands for state action.

[1] *Message to Congress* of President Roosevelt, Jan. 3, 1934.

The state may begin by supervising the fixing of prices as in the lumber and timber products, oil, coal, cleaning and dyeing and a few other industries under the National Industrial Recovery Act, but it must then decide upon the proper criteria of price policy. It may supervise the administration of clauses intended to prevent prices from falling below the cost of production; but how is cost of production to be calculated? After the manner of the National Recovery Administration it may set out to eliminate destructive price competition; but how is it to distinguish "destructive" from constructive or desirable competition? If it attempts to "stabilize the trade" it can do nothing until this aim is translated into more specific terms; if it concerns itself with price cutting that destroys some of the existing producers it must discriminate between price reductions aimed at transmitting economies of production to purchasers (and incidentally destroying less efficient firms), and that aimed directly at destroying rivals. It may attempt to fix minimum prices during "emergencies"; but what are the stigmata of an "emergency"? If the state defines an emergency by reference to events causing a "particularly high mortality of enterprises and especially small ones" it is beset by all the difficulties of attempts to deal with destructive price cutting. If an emergency is defined in terms of price reductions imperiling wage scales, it must investigate how far any given reduction does imperil wage scales and what is the proper wage policy. If, in the emergency, it attempts to use "lowest reasonable costs" as a basis for setting minimum prices the interpretation of "reasonable" is the determinant of its whole policy. The use of these phrases by the National Recovery Administration indicates merely the need for planning and not the selection of a plan.

The types of economic change responsible for the most difficult problems of control are shifts in demand, cyclical fluctuations in demand, changes in methods of production, and changes in the conditions of supply of the means of production (*i.e.*, changes in costs other than those due to changes in methods of production). These problems are discussed separately.

The demand for protection from competition that presses prices down below the cost of production cannot be passed by without a glance. The maintenance of prices at or above the cost of production is, of course, incompatible with competition. If costs include remuneration to investors and managers sufficient to enable them to continue in business no firm can ever fail; the inefficient as well as the efficient survive, indeed; increasing inefficiency must be covered by rising prices. The forces regulating the direction of new investment or the readjustment of past allocations of resources are suspended; investors become pensioners. New machinery would be needed to maintain efficiency and direct the allocation of resources.

We now turn to the problems of policy that arise when the state participates in making industrial policy. These problems are far reaching and difficult and it is not suggested that the state should undertake immediately to solve them for the whole of industry. In some industries competitive pressures remain as a real force but in others they have been largely transformed. The present chapter is not concerned with what should be done in any particular industry or class of industry. It is concerned merely with the implications of state intervention in the organization of production.

a. Shifts in Demand. Changes in the direction of demand which have not been fully anticipated and allowed for by investors, or changes which have been expected but have failed to materialize, cause an excess or deficiency of specialized equipment in an industry. Excess of plant capacity, rather than deficiency, leads to complaints by investors and managers because of the pressure upon producers, acting individually, to reduce their prices in order to increase the volume of their business. Taking account of changes in their own price policy upon those of rivals and upon demand, they endeavor to stabilize prices or follow the policy of a leader. Seeking relief in monopoly profits they prevent equipment from being fully utilized. The state may seek to reduce waste of this kind in two ways, *viz.*, by influencing price policy after an unanticipated decline in demand has occurred, or by exercising control over long-term investment so as to prevent uneconomical allocations of capital.

Two extreme policies are possible with regard to prices after demand has declined. The state may refuse to protect industry from price competition or even attempt to induce such competition; if price competition occurs output will be higher and prices lower than they would otherwise have been. If prices fall so low that they fail to cover more than the direct costs of production (thus contributing nothing towards the overhead costs) and aggregate demand is even then insufficient to maintain

THE PROBLEM OF SOCIAL CONTROL—OBJECTIVES 533

all plant in production, some is likely to be abandoned.[1] The balance of the plant may remain in use yielding some repayment of the original investment and possibly some earnings on that investment. Investors carry the major burden of the maladjustment of investment; some part of the burden may, however, be passed on to workers and especially administrative employees who cannot, easily transfer to other fields. On the other hand, purchasers gain by being able to obtain goods at prices less than the average costs of production in an efficient plant occupied to a reasonable percentage of full capacity. The great merit of this policy is that it tends to a fuller utilization of specialized equipment than a policy of avoiding short-run price competition. It has, however, important secondary effects. The risk of heavy losses when demand declines may deter investors from entering the industry until prices rise to a level offering a normal return after allowing for the probability of these losses, *i.e.*, in the longer run investors seek to pass these greater risks of loss on to purchasers in higher prices. If there are prospects of high profits during periods of deficient plant capacity, and investors take these prospects also into account, the risks of loss may be counted against the chance of abnormal gains. However, by increasing the penalties of investment based upon inaccurate forecasts of demand this policy intensifies the stimulus to careful forecasting.[2]

The extreme alternative to the foregoing policy is to accept and implement the policies recently developed by producers in self-defense. The state might permit producers in times of declining demand to maintain, or even raise, prices in the effort to secure in each year the contribution towards their overhead costs upon which they relied when the investment was made. Conditions of demand may, of course, often prevent a normal return upon all existing investment no matter what price is charged. Immediately, this policy involves a smaller output and, therefore, a greater waste of specialized equipment than the policy of price cutting. More of the burden of the unanticipated change in demand is placed upon purchasers; they may pay prices yielding a return upon unused as well as upon used plant. Investors carry

[1] In fact, some may remain in production for short periods even if prices remain on this low level but, on the other hand, some firms are likely to fail even before this level is reached. Their plant may, however, be recapitalized on a lower level and remain in production.
[2] The general effect of this policy upon savings should also be taken into account but to do so would require more facts and more space than are at present available.

a smaller burden, but unless demand is sufficiently inelastic they are unable to escape all loss. This policy also has important secondary effects. The risks of losses in times of falling demand having been diminished, investors enter the industry in response to a somewhat smaller prospect of profit; on the other hand, if the state, having protected them in adverse circumstances, denies them special profits in times of deficient capacity for production, this tendency is modified. The stimulus to careful calculation of probable changes in demand before investments are made is diminished; the burden upon purchasers of unanticipated reductions of demand, therefore, tends to be increased.

Between these two extremes lie, of course, a great number of policies the effects of which are composed of a mixture of the consequences of the extremes. Prohibitions upon sales at prices below the cost of production in the codes under the National Industrial Recovery Act suggested a variety of policies. The definition of "cost of production" determines the level of the minimum price. If the minimum is set by reference to the total costs of the highest-cost firm and a normal profit, no firms need bear any burden and none need be expelled (provided demand at this price is sufficient to yield the desired return). If the costs of other than the highest-cost firm (*e.g.*, the costs of a "representative firm") or some average of costs is used as the basis of the minimum price some losses fall on some firms. If the costs of the lowest-cost firm are used (as they were in some of the codes) an increased burden of loss is thrown upon investors. If profits, interest, selling, or other selected elements of cost are excluded the burden is also increased. The extent of the protection involved in any given level of prices depends upon the extent of the decline in demand in relation to the existing capacity of production, and the elasticity of demand under the new conditions.

The effects of these two extreme policies must be pursued further; the distribution of this burden within the class of investors reacts upon the efficiency of production. A policy of enforcing price competition in the face of excessive capacity for production, if it succeeds, sooner or later expels producers from the industry. Where the specialized equipment of some firms is almost worn out they, being the first to have to decide whether the industry can offer attractive profits to new investment, might be expected to be the first to be expelled. This method of reducing the amount of resources applied to the industry appears to involve the minimum of sacrifice of the potentialities of past allocations of capital to the industry. But the selection of firms for survival by reference to this accidental element, *viz.*, the date at which their principal resources have reached the end of their economic life, cannot also insure selection by reference to their efficiency in production. While considerations of the age of equipment are doubtless of some importance they are, in fact, minor. Firms rarely have an opportunity to retire from business without abandoning capital.[1] Plant consists of a number of units expiring at different times and management and selling organizations often have no calculable economic life. In consequence firms fight for survival and make new investments even when their probable average rate of return is low;[2] the survival of firms depends more, therefore, upon the financial structure of firms than upon the date of the expiration of their major specialized equipment. Here too, the ejection of firms, in the sense of the management unit, is determined by reference to considerations other than efficiency in production.

Departure from price competition of the foregoing type results in a different distribution of the burden within the industry group; this distribution depends upon the manner in which business is distributed between the firms in the industry. If price competition ceases to operate as a means of distributing business between firms some alternative determinant must operate. Pools and cartels usually involve the distribution of quotas. The codes of fair competition under the National Industrial Recovery Act providing for the direct regulation of prices or output usually provided also for the allocation of quotas of production or sales.[3] The aggregate burden falling upon producers is determined by the price policy imposed upon the industry; the distribution of that burden depends then upon the basis upon which quotas are allocated.[4] In a number of industries (mainly concerned with textiles) the National Recovery Administration permitted control of output by regulation of the hours of plant operation. The aggregate burden falling upon producers was determined by the

[1] Individuals may do so by transferring their ownership.
[2] Whenever a portion of equipment requires renewal the reinvestment will be made if the probable costs of continuing in production (including the cost of renewals) fall short of probable revenues; *i.e.*, if the renewal will permit production yielding revenue that will cover all direct costs, the renewals, and something for other overhead.
[3] For example, lumber and timber products, copper, petroleum.
[4] The code for the lumber and timber products industry provided for the calculation of quotas upon the basis of an elaborate formula, but that for the copper industry based their calculation upon the productive capacity of the producers.

price ruling when it was decided to adjust supply to demand; this burden was distributed among firms partly[1] according to the plant capacity of each. There was no tendency to eject the highest-cost firms. Where, as in many codes, provision was merely made for a minimum price, which became the actual price, the distribution of business between firms depended upon their existing business connections, upon competition in quality and service, and upon competition in sales promotion. Where competition in quality and service was severely circumscribed (as it frequently was by other clauses in the codes) expenditure upon sales promotion offered the only possibility of changing the existing distribution of business. Emphasis upon sales promotion aimed at undermining existing business connections involves costs which in the longer run must be passed on to purchasers. The resulting distribution turns, therefore, upon the relative effectiveness of different firms in this type of competition which appears to be in considerable part a matter of chance.[2] The selection of firms for survival is again not on the basis of their general efficiency.

Policy in times of unanticipated reductions in demand cannot, however, be considered apart from that in periods of unanticipated increase. The periods in which demand at a price covering average total costs of production exceeds the capacity of an industry to produce are generally shorter than those in which capacity exceeds demand at this level of prices; the periods within which plant investment can be expanded are shorter than those in which it can be contracted. While plant is wearing out all the time, whole business units are, as we have seen, continuously faced with problems of partial replacement rather than with complete recommitments to the industry. State control of long-term investment may, however, by restricting investment in periods of activity, increase the importance of periods of deficient capacity.

Two extreme policies of control during such periods may be analyzed. Prices may be permitted to rise until demand is reduced to the capacity of the existing plant. Investors gain as a result of the increased demand for the produce of their specialized plant and equipment; purchasers bear a corresponding burden in the form of either prices in excess of the average total costs of produc-

---

[1] Some firms were unable to operate at the maximum number of hours permitted.
[2] *Cf.* BURNS, "The Process of Industrial Concentration," *Quart. Jour. Econ.*, 47: 277 (1933).

tion or inability to purchase. The prospect of such profits may attract investment into industry at a somewhat lower level of selling prices for the product than would otherwise attract it. This prospect also stimulates efforts to anticipate changes in demand and prepare for them: the periods within which such profits are available and burdens are placed upon purchasers are thus curtailed. Alternatively, social policy may be aimed at the restriction of prices to those which cover the average total costs of production (including normal profits). The profits of producers are prevented from rising above normal and the corresponding burdens upon purchasers are eliminated. The level of prices at which new investment is attracted is somewhat raised and the stimulus to anticipate increases in demand is reduced. But price competition being removed as the mechanism for the allocation of restricted supplies among those willing to pay for them, an alternative mechanism must be established.[1] Rationing is possible but extremely cumbrous. Prices may be permitted to rise to the level at which demand equals supply and the difference between the average total costs of production and the price that adjusts demand to possible supply in the short run appropriated by taxation. The price mechanism continues as a means of rationing limited supplies. Producers unwilling to bear the losses resulting from unanticipated declines in demand can hardly object to being deprived of the profits of unanticipated increases. The proceeds of the tax might be paid in subsidies to reduce the amount of equipment withdrawn from production by firms faced with a decline in demand.

Attempts to relieve producers of the risks of shifts in demand may seriously increase uneconomical allocations of investment. Relief from the losses arising from unanticipated shifts in demand retards the reduction of investment in these industries. Deprivation of profits from unanticipated increases in demand retards increases in investment. In a perfectly competitive system the price of the commodity the demand for which is falling declines to the marginal cost of producing it; this decline in price diminishes the demand for the product that is replacing it. Thus specialized investments once made are utilized so long as the revenue from sales exceeds the *additional* costs of production. Investments in the production of the new commodity are made

---

[1] Just as when, competition being removed as a means of distributing sales among sellers, a substitute must be found.

only if it is expected that prices will cover the *total* costs of production. In imperfectly competitive markets, existing specialized equipment is less fully utilized when the demand for the commodity declines because of the various attempts to maintain prices. Taxes and subsidies of the type above suggested are defensible, therefore, in an imperfectly competitive world because they tend to a more economical use of resources. It is evident, however, that while a retardation of adjustment of investment to the new direction of demand can be justified, complete prevention of adjustment cannot. Taxes and subsidies must, therefore, be planned so as to taper off with the passage of time.

It is very doubtful, however, whether the reallocation of the gains and losses owing to shifts in demand can be effected entirely by taxes and subsidies which enter into private calculations of cost and probable demand. These calculations have been made in the past and yet excessive investments of capital have occurred; some of the causes of this uneconomical investment remain, *e.g.*, difficulties of estimating demand and lack of coordination of the plans of different investing groups. Direct control of long-term investment appears, therefore, to be a necessary auxiliary to taxes and subsidies. Regulation of investment involves control of the acquisition of new equipment not only out of the proceeds of stock and bond issues by existing firms in each industry, and by new firms proposing to enter it, but also out of accumulated profits and reserves. Experiments in the regulation of industry have already led to such control, *e.g.*, in railroads[1] and public utilities generally[2] and banking.[3] More recently in the general industrial field business men have themselves urged control of long-term investment; a considerable number of codes of fair competition under the National Industrial Recovery Act provided for such control. Hitherto this power has been confined to the limitation of expansions of plant capacity,[4] replacements

[1] The Interstate Commerce Commission already supervises the issue of securities and the assumption of obligations (in the form of leases and otherwise) by the common carriers subject to its jurisdiction (Transportation Act, 1920, Sec. 20, a).

[2] Most public service commissions have a comparable control over investment in public utilities. It is generally provided that no new corporation may be established in these industries until a certificate of "convenience and necessity" has been obtained from the commission.

[3] Persons desiring to establish national banks are required under the National Banking Act to obtain the consent of the Comptroller of the Currency before the bank may be established.

[4] Even control of increases in plant investment may present a practical problem; the state may permit such increases but its permission will be ineffective if investors refuse to avail themselves of the permission.

of existing plant being exempted from control; such restricted control is, however, inadequate to deal with changes in demand over long periods.[1]

Control of investment can be exercised only when criteria of desirable investment are set up. In the discussion of the initial codes under the National Industrial Recovery Act there was a tendency to assume that if there was any unused plant there should be no new investment in the industry. This criterion is obviously inadequate. Increasing demand might be met by increasing prices sufficiently to keep some plant out of use and thus continuously prevent any new investment. It is also extremely difficult to define existing plant. Plants may be out of use because they are out of date in their equipment or in their location. To prevent new investment until such plants are in full use would be to deny purchasers for long periods the benefits of improvements in methods of production, including improvements in the location of the industry. In so far as the state aims at the maximization of industrial efficiency it must calculate the price at which the most technically efficient plant can sell and secure a normal return when it is occupied to what is regarded as a reasonable percentage of its capacity. Whenever the state decides that the probable sustained demand at this price exceeds the present capacity of the industry, additional investment should sooner or later be permitted.[2] Additional investment may be permitted when present plants are only partly occupied, either because the existing price yields a profit above that upon which the calculations have been based, or because some plants fail to reach the standard of efficiency assumed in these calculations. Additional investment will sometimes be prevented although demand at current prices exceeds the total capacity of the existing plant. It would be prevented if demand were not expected to continue on its existing level long enough to justify investment in resources that can be fully utilized only over long periods of time; the state would thus prolong periods of deficient capacity.

If, however, calculations of probable sustained demand reveal a considerable excess of capacity the state must decide for how

[1] The code for the cement industry made tentative provision for the withdrawal of plant; it was also proposed that an agreement be made among kraft board and paper board producers to purchase mills and withdraw them from production (*New York Times*, Feb. 16, 1934). This device has been employed in the British shipbuilding industry.

[2] See discussion concerning control of the timing of the utilization of new methods of production, p. 547.

long it will attempt to protect those who have secured a position in the industry. Its policy in the control of both investment and prices must be coordinated. Both will be controlled by the dates when large units of equipment are exhausted. But we have already seen that whole complexes of investments can rarely be abandoned without loss. It would often be necessary to prevent replacements of existing plant with the object of gradually reducing the investment in the industry. In doing so the state attempts to bring about by direct means the adjustments that are enforced under price competition, but made only very slowly and in a very unsatisfactory manner in an imperfectly competitive system. Proposals such as that in the code for the cement industry for the closing down of redundant plants suggest a method of distributing the losses of abandoned plants among the survivors in the industry. If the survivors contribute towards the purchase of inefficient plants they are able to obtain higher prices because the sales of each are likely to be increased. Their capital costs are increased by the sum paid virtually for the additional business. If these payments are regarded as costs in the sense that surviving firms may restrict output to secure revenues that will cover them, as well as other costs, part of the burden of unwise past investments is placed upon purchasers of the product.[1] This transfer of risk should then be remembered in calculating permissible rates of profit.[2]

The disadvantage of direct planning of these adjustments is, of course, that it will encounter bitter opposition from those required to abandon their industrial position. There would be someone to blame for this abandonment whereas under a competitive system there is no one. Any planning aimed at the elimination of the inefficiencies of the present system must face this difficulty. Opposition may be mitigated by the realization that the losses resulting from uneconomic investment will be reduced as well as shifted.

b. Shifts in the Demand for Exhaustible and Irreplaceable Natural Resources. Changes in the demand for exhaustible and irreplaceable resources present problems similar in many, but not all, respects to those already discussed. Proposals to balance

---

[1] It can be so placed only if prices can be raised to a level at which revenue from sales covers all costs, *i.e.*, only if the demand for the product is sufficiently inelastic.

[2] The risks still fall partly upon investors if the price at which redundant plants are purchased is based upon their earning power in an industry in which there is excess capacity.

THE PROBLEM OF SOCIAL CONTROL—OBJECTIVES 541

production with consumption[1] are, of course, a shallow pretense. It is desirable to avoid the accumulation of unwieldy inventories but the major problem is the price at which supply shall be adjusted to demand.[2] Demands for state assistance are heard when changes in demand reduce the prospect that existing holders will secure the profits expected at the time of their investment. "Conservation" by the state is then urged.

Again two extreme policies of state control are possible. The state may endeavor to enable investors to secure a normal rate of return upon their investment together with the repayment of that investment as the product is marketed. It must then endeavor to retard the utilization of the resource sufficiently to raise prices so as to yield the expected revenue upon sales extending over a longer period of time than was anticipated.[3] When demand increases beyond that anticipated at the time of investment prices must be kept below those anticipated because of the speedier return of capital. The problem of rationing among buyers does not in this case arise; the utilization of the resource is accelerated and the date of exhaustion advanced. Alternatively, the state may seek to induce vigorous price competition; it may seek a decline in prices in response to a decline in demand and an increase in response to an increase in demand. As prices fall the resources with the higher recovery costs cease to count as reserves. The resulting level of prices depends upon the new conditions of demand and the amount of the resource that can be marketed at each price, taking account of (often wide) variations between firms in the cost of recovery and marketing. The level of prices where demand increases is similarly determined.

Price policy cannot be determined (as in the first case discussed) in terms of the desirable speed of adaptation of the quantity of the resource to the shift in demand. Its quantity cannot be increased at all. The expectations of investors at the time the resource was acquired cannot provide a basis for policy, least of all when the expectations of investors have been falsified by subsequent events. Investors, moreover, may be unwilling to engage in wars to reduce prices to the level desired; purchasers,

[1] *Cf.* Code for the petroleum industry and the various orders of the Secretary of the Interior in administering the code.
[2] The various orders under the code for the petroleum industry to provide for orderly marketing and to "keep distress gasoline off the market" were a means to the maintenance of the prevailing price level. In the longer run the desirability of this price level must be questioned.
[3] Whether this result can be secured depends upon the elasticity of demand.

on the other hand, may rebel against fortunes arising out of unanticipated increases in demand due to increases in population, changes in consumption habits, or methods of production for which those receiving the profits were in no way responsible. The state cannot, therefore, avoid resting its price policy upon a consideration of the desirable distribution of the use of the resource over time.[1] The higher the price in the present, the slower the rate of marketing and the greater the amount of the resource left for future consumers. Calculation of the desirable rate of exploitation raises, however, serious problems of ethics rather than economics. Rapid exploitation reducing the remaining supplies raises future prices. If the increased price fails to stimulate the discovery of substitutes, industrial activity may contract. But

. . . even if such an eventuality should occur and a reduction in the population be necessitated, is it certain that the characteristics of our descendants will be so superior to our own that it becomes the duty of the present generation to refrain from exploiting the natural resources of the country in order that a restriction of their own numbers should postpone the necessity for a similar restriction in a later age?[2]

Furthermore, the rate of realization selected after considering the relative importance to be attached to the utilities of future persons as against those of the present persons, and the desirable distribution of population over time, may or may not permit a price that will return all past investments in the resource.

c. Cyclical Fluctuations in Demand. Cyclical fluctuations in demand throw into spectacular relief the general inefficiency of the existing organization of production. Demand at existing prices falls below the capacity of most industries when business recedes and very large amounts of plant are left unused. The policies of the existing imperfectly competitive system, *viz.*, maintenance of prices and restriction of output, result in a sharp reduction of the disbursements of a number of industries, more

---

[1] In the oil industry some, but not all, distributors of oil products integrate distribution with the holding of reserves of crude oil with the result that attempts to arrive at a price policy under the National Industrial Recovery Act gave rise to very considerable friction between various producers in the industry. Producers (mainly the largest) owning large stocks of crude oil were less anxious to pass on to purchasers the benefits of reductions in the current price of crude oil, while those who did not own such stocks were particularly interested in reductions of price which might induce additional business.

[2] (British) Royal Commission on the Coal Industry, *Report* (Cmd. 2600), 1926, 20.

particularly upon payrolls, with the result that restriction of output is redoubled. Calculations of costs usually rest upon the assumption that overhead costs should be fairly equally distributed between yearly periods in the life of the investment. Attempts to cover costs in years of receded demand then suggest the raising of prices. Selling at prices which do not cover total costs, thus calculated, involves "losses." The period of one year is conventionally taken to avoid difficulties arising out of seasonal variations in demand. The same logic, however, suggests calculations of cost for periods long enough to include whole cycles. There is a tendency to modify this distribution over time of the recovery of overhead costs. Firms draw, in times of depression, upon open or secret reserves accumulated in times of business activity, thus redistributing the burden of overhead costs throughout the period of the cycle. There is, however, much resistance to "losses" during depression;[1] there are claims for protection against destructive price competition and selling at prices "below the cost of production";[2] cost accounts are produced to show that, within short periods, prices do not cover average costs. The state may attempt to diminish the amount of unused equipment during depressions; it may seek to improve the basis for estimating the profitability of long-term investments or it may actually control such investments. During expansions of business it must decide how far to permit prices to rise and investment to be increased. During depressions it must decide how far prices shall be reduced to reduce unemployment of plants and labor.

The state, unlike a cartel, influences prices in a large number of industries. The price policy for each is an integral part of the desirable policy for society as a whole. If the state participates in the maintenance of prices it must take account of the aggregate effect of its policy upon the demand for commodities in general

[1] The level of prices in the steel industry in 1934 was reported to be such that most companies could obtain profit if they operated at 50 per cent of their capacity. (*New York Times*, Aug. 15, 1934).

[2] The National Recovery Administration in supervising calculations of cost for the purpose of setting minimum prices adopted a "standard burden" in the calculation of costs in some industries. When the plant is used at the rate assumed to be the standard rate of operation and prices just cover the costs so calculated, the year's quota of the cost of durable means of production is just secured; when it operates at less than this rate less than the quota is secured, and when at a greater rate more than the quota is obtained. The pressure to reduce output when demand falls off is reduced and with it the wastage of existing specialized equipment; the overhead element in unit costs is stabilized independently of the volume of business. The amount of the standard burden determines the level of costs; the lower the standard burden the higher the general level of average costs.

through its effect upon the incomes of those participating in production. A cartel for a single industry can often afford to ignore this matter because the demand for its products is little reduced by a decline in its payments to its employees and to producers of its equipment. General restriction of output, however, means lower payroll disbursements and postponed expenditures on capital goods, which result in still less payrolls and cause a further recession of demand. The National Recovery Administration was bitterly criticized for the increases in prices that occurred after its establishment and some of which it directly authorized. If prices had been lower the volume of business activity would probably have been greater and existing resources more fully used. Industry being left largely under private control there were, however, narrow limits to practicable policy. In some industries lower prices would have increased the volume of sales sufficiently to yield returns as high as upon a smaller volume at a higher price. In other industries where demand is little affected by price, or average costs are little affected by volume, no such hope could be held out. Moreover, costs were increasing, and the prevention of price increases might have caused failure and a redistribution of business favoring those with the lowest costs (owing either to greater efficiency or lower capitalization); more probably it would have caused a reduction of the capitalization of the weaker firms. Such an adjustment of capital values to current prices and other cost levels is, however, painful and discouraging to business. Return to profitable operation was said to be the surest stimulus to business recovery. Recovery is marked by the return of profits, but their return is due to increased demand and sales. In so far as the National Industrial Recovery Act, taken alone, implemented the policy of seeking higher profits in higher prices and consequently less output, high profits indicated a shift in the distribution of the real national income (which the operation of the act tended to reduce) rather than expansion of demand and output. Higher profits might offer a better chance for the recovery of industries making producers' goods because more profits provide more funds for investment; the profits originated, however, in policies which increased the amount of unemployed plant.

During periods of business activity abnormally high profits are available to many firms. If firms are protected from loss in time of depression they cannot expect to receive these abnormal profits when demand increases. But if they are compelled to reduce prices as demand increases, business expansion is likely to be further stimulated and, possibly, the rationing of products required. The resulting reduction in profits and savings would, however, result in higher interest rates which would somewhat retard expansion. Taxes might be levied to mitigate this effect and the proceeds used to subsidize industries in time of depression. An unemployment insurance fund for plant might be established.[1]

The determination of the proper price policy throughout business cycles calls for a general dynamic economic theory which will permit more detailed forecasting of the effects of each policy and, particularly, more accurate timing; it calls also for consideration of the long-time consequences of each policy, more especially upon the distribution of resources and the probability that they will be fully and continuously used. It is obviously undesirable in times of depression to seek to restore profits to existing industry; continued business stability may be impossible while, for example, the lumber,[2] steel, cement and building industries remain of their present size. They may be overexpanded by reference to the probable total savings out of which their products can be bought. Some of them may be overexpanded because techniques of production have changed adversely to them. It is necessary to estimate, therefore, the probable future demand for their products over considerable periods of time. This estimate involves estimates of the future distribution of income and willingness to save and of methods of production. If demand is expected to revive, it is obviously uneconomical to abandon equipment which must be later replaced. Purchasers should be denied the low prices that would prevail if all equipment were utilized; equipment would be worn out which might yield greater benefits to purchasers if its use were postponed.[3] The importance of even this consideration depends, however, upon the extent to which plant is likely to deteriorate either physically or economically (owing to obsolescence). The greater the probability

---

[1] Such a fund would, like a personal unemployment insurance fund, raise questions concerning the investment of the accumulating fund.
[2] The productive capacity of the lumber industry, for instance, was calculated in 1933 to exceed the actual output in any past period.
[3] Economies are obtained at a later date because demands for equipment are reduced, but if the industries manufacturing equipment are themselves dependent upon the use of a large amount of specialized and durable plant these economies are not realized; they translate themselves into waste in the form of unused plant in the equipment or raw material industries and the unemployment of workers.

of such deterioration, and the longer the period before which demand can be expected to revive, the stronger is the case for utilizing present plant to the full (provided purchasers will pay for the product anything beyond the direct costs of production). The possibilities of direct control of industrial policy are well worth investigation as a means of controlling cyclical fluctuations in view of the inadequacy of indirect control through monetary policy.

d. Changes in Methods of Production. Investors also carry the risk of changes in the methods of production (including changes in the location of industry). Wherever production involves the use of plant equipment capable of use for a long period of time, there is a possibility that the discovery of new and cheaper methods of production will prevent the owners of the now obsolete equipment from recovering their investment together with a normal return thereon. If the introduction of innovations could be timed to coincide with the wearing out of existing plant no such losses would occur. They arise when a new firm, with no equipment to become obsolete, enters the industry and seeks business by price cutting; it may reduce the price until it covers only a normal return upon investment in up-to-date plant, which means less than a normal return upon obsolete plant. Even if the new firm obtains business without price cutting other firms lose part of their sales and suffer losses; the industry then suffers from excessive capacity, the obsolete plant being included with the most up-to-date. If the state accepts responsibility for controlling prices and long-term investment, it must decide whether prices may cover costs that include reserves for probable losses due to obsolescence, and whether it will protect investors from price cutting arising out of the adoption of improved methods of production. Again two extreme policies are possible.

If the state encourages price competition the extent of the probable fall in prices depends upon the addition to the capacity of the industry. Prices may fall below the average total cost of production but they will tend to return to this level as investment in the industry is adjusted; purchasers obtain the benefits of the improvement as soon as it is utilized if not before.[1] Alternatively

---

[1] If the innovator fixes his price upon a level that will yield a normal return over costs only when the new plant is utilized to a reasonable proportion of its capacity, but must wait for the demand for his product to increase sufficiently to permit the utilization of his plant at this rate, purchasers benefit before the new methods are in full and effective use.

investors may be relieved from all losses due to obsolescence; they may be permitted to maintain prices that insure the return of all their investment and a normal return upon it, even though it has become obsolete. Reductions in price are postponed and, therefore, the transmission to purchasers of the benefits of the innovation. The inducements to improve methods of production are magnified by this maintenance of prices. But if the new firm must charge the same price as others it cannot attract business by price cutting; and how will business be distributed in the absence of the competitive market mechanism? Resort to sales promotion is the most probable device but it increases the costs of both the new and the old firms and, in the long run, places an additional burden upon purchasers.

The main problem is that of timing the adoption of new methods so as to minimize the cost of transition.[1] Not all improvements in methods of production should be utilized immediately they become available if the greatest efficiency of the economic system as a whole is desired. Individuals continue to use automobiles that are obsolete because they balance the cost of abandoning the old car against the increased utilities offered by the new, and the principle is obviously sound. It may be argued, however, that it has not been consistently applied in industrial production. If an innovator can secure the gains resulting from better methods and thrust the losses owing to the abandonment of plant upon others the change is made; individual accounting does not include as a cost of the change the losses imposed upon other firms, or upon other industries. The argument is, however, not altogether valid. Under perfect competition innovators charge prices that cover only the full cost of production by the most up-to-date methods. Less up-to-date rivals must accept the same price and

[1] In one peculiar and isolated case under the Sherman Law, the Supreme Court considered this problem. As a result of inventions, there was a strong tendency for machine-made window glass to replace hand-made glass, the cost of production of the former being half that of the latter. Furthermore, the addition of the machine plants to the industry resulted in a great increase in capacity for production. It became evident that hand-made glass could not be sold except at a price as low as that of machine-made glass and, furthermore, that it was now impossible for all the plants adapted mainly to manual operation to be kept in production. Instead of permitting the competitive process to work itself out and expel a number of producers of hand-made glass from the industry together with their employees, the owners of hand-operated plants and their organized workers came to an agreement to operate the factories in rotation. Thus these plants rationed the available business between them. The Supreme Court decided that the arrangement was *not* an illegal restraint of trade. It was doubtless largely influenced by sympathy with the workers in the industry, and it emphasized that not more than 2,500 workers were left in the industry. (U.S. v. National Window Glass Manufacturers, 263 U.S. 403 (1923).)

the resulting losses due to the obsolescence of their plant. But, unless the new prices fail to cover the *direct* costs of production with the older equipment, there is no reason why that equipment should not remain in full use. There is no necessary waste of equipment. But the increasing scale upon which commitments must be made for productive equipment and the increasing life of the equipment direct greater attention to the prospect of losses due to obsolescence. Sellers include in their accounts reserves to meet losses due to obsolescence when their methods shall in turn have become out of date. If prices are not permitted to be maintained on a level that covers the full prospective losses due to obsolescence, the period within which innovators benefit from their superior efficiency disappears; the inducement to exploit new methods is minimized. Investors are likely to be deflected from those industries in which losses due to the obsolescence of equipment appear most probable; they thus indirectly shift to purchasers in advance the probable cost of innovations. Investors fail to enter the industry unless prices appear to cover the risk.

These efforts by investors to protect themselves against this risk reduce the losses due to obsolescence and also the benefits obtained by purchasers. But sellers have already been impelled to efforts toward still greater self-protection. They attempt to secure control of newer methods of production, especially where they are protected by patent. They sought to use the machinery of the National Industry Recovery Act to obstruct the transmission to buyers of the benefits of new methods. Changes in methods of producing rival fuels were necessarily taken into account in fixing the minimum prices set for soft coal[1] and a representative of the National Coal Association on one occasion urged an increase in the price of fuel oil, low prices for which had been "raising havoc" in the coal industry.[2] The association also opposed federal financial assistance in the development of hydroelectric power projects.[3] The National Industrial Recovery Act also brought into the open the conflict in the distributing trades between new and old methods. The chain and department stores integrated wholesaling and retailing and also increased the scale of retailing. The former hierarchy of distributors sought provisions in the

[1] *New York Times*, June 17, July 14, 1933.
[2] *New York Times*, July 31, 1934. Between July, 1933, and July, 1934, fuel oil prices had increased from 200 to 400 per cent (*ibid.*).
[3] *New York Times*, Aug. 19, 1934.

THE PROBLEM OF SOCIAL CONTROL—OBJECTIVES 549

codes setting margins between the prices of products at each stage of distribution such as would cover the costs of distribution by the older methods.[1] Those committed to the newer and larger-scale methods favored discounts based upon the volume of business, size of order, or the services rendered by the distributor.[2] Manufacturers also were interested in preventing the prices of their products from being driven down by the bargaining power of large distributors.[3] The administration yielded, however, to the drastic pressure to secure differentials based upon the type of distributor and thus tended to prevent rather than postpone the introduction of improved methods. The relocation of industry was somewhat hindered by approval of the basing-point system in the steel industry.[4]

Clauses in codes preventing extensions of plant capacity without the consent of the administrator raised similar problems. New investment might permit production by newer methods at lower costs than those of the existing producers. New investment might permit changes in the location of production. It was necessary to decide whether new investment might be made in new localities or to permit the use of new methods although it would involve losses to owners of existing plants. The protection of small firms (which was required in the National Industrial Recovery Act) obstructs the introduction of new methods when-

[1] The Wholesale Dry Goods Institute claimed that unless manufacturers with power to fix minimum prices set definite and equitable differentials between minimum prices to the wholesale and the retail trades, small enterprises would be oppressed, monopolies promoted, and "our national economy greatly disturbed, disorganized, and demoralized" (*New York Times*, June 28, 1933).

[2] The National Retail Dry Goods Association in *New York Times*, Oct. 30, 1933.

[3] The drive for differentials based upon the class of distributor was attributed by the Consumer Advisory Board partly to the desire of jobbers and wholesalers "to operate upon a margin protected by law from the competition of more direct methods of distribution" and partly to the desire of manufacturers "to avoid having their prices driven down by the bargaining strength of large buyers." It added that while it was desirable to prevent large buyers from clubbing unreasonable discounts out of manufacturers it was "very undesirable to freeze the present system of distribution by setting up arbitrary price differentials to apply to the different stages of distribution." (*Release* of Mar. 5, 1934.)

[4] *Cf.* p. 362. Regulation of minimum wages under the codes also raised the question whether the relocation of industry was to be stimulated or retarded. Lower minima were claimed for the small towns and the south. If the differentials prevailing prior to the act were maintained the broad lines of the location of industry would be maintained. If that location was not the most desirable, the foregoing arguments would suggest that change might be timed so as to minimize its cost. But the necessity for wage differentials may arise out of a variety of causes, out of local differences in the productivity of labor (arising out of differences in both efficiency and the value of the product), in the purchasing power of money, or in the effectiveness with which industry is organized. In so far as differentials are permitted to offset this latter element adaptation to the most economical location is obstructed.

ever they involve an increase in the scale of production.[1] The differential taxes imposed upon chain stores by an increasing number of states are aimed at the preservation of those distributing goods upon a small scale although larger-scale operations are more economical. Again innovation is prevented rather than regulated.

In this world of imperfect competition, therefore, control of the timing of the introduction of new methods of production can be justified. Control could be administered by the imposition of taxes upon innovators and the use of the proceeds to pay subsidies to those whose plant is rendered obsolete. Prices could then be reduced without imposing the full loss of obsolescence upon the owners of obsolete plant, the state endeavoring to avoid both excessive encouragement of production by obsolete methods and excessive discouragement to innovators.[2]

e. Changes in the Conditions of Supply of the Means of Production. Investment is also subject to risk of changes in the conditions of supply of the means of production, *i.e.*, to changes in costs of production due to causes other than changes in the technique of production. Long-term investments in specialized plant are based in part upon estimates of the future cost of production as well as upon estimates of future prices. Failure of the former to fulfill expectations causes losses as great and profits as troublesome as a similar failure on the part of demand. Changes in costs react upon profits and upon prices. A rise in prices when costs rise may fail to preserve normal profits because demand falls off. In the long run changes in costs are, of course, likely to be passed on to the purchaser although he may run for a very long time before he succeeds in getting them. The more serious problems are presented by the process of adjustment to the new conditions.

[1] In justifying the setting of minimum wholesale and retail prices for cigarettes the recovery administrator stated that "in a trade so characterized by small enterprises a reasonable minimum of income should be insured to the small storekeepers for whom at the end of the week such income as may be earned is tantamount to wages" (*New York Times*, July 13, 1934), a gospel which the unemployed might argue should apply equally to them. The supplemental report of the Board of Review (*cit. New York Times*, May 21, 1934), moreover, saw no hope for the small man in a return to unregulated competition.

[2] As soon as any part of the supply is made by more efficient methods some reduction in price can be made, although the price must remain above that which covers the average cost of production by the new method. If the old price were maintained no subsidies would be needed; if the price were reduced to the cost of production by the new methods no taxes could be levied. The price will presumably cover the weighted average cost of production and decline as the new methods are more widely used.

By influencing the time at which changes in price shall be made owing to changes in costs the state influences both the total costs of adjustments to such changes in cost and their distribution between purchasers and investors and between different investors.

The extreme policies available to the state are suggested by the controversy over the question whether the price policies of public utilities shall be regulated to give a fair return upon their actual investment or upon the replacement costs of their investment. If the prices of products are to follow their replacement costs, changes in price must be made simultaneously with any changes in the costs of new firms setting up in business without any past commitments. When costs increase this policy means a profit to existing firms wherever the means of production have been purchased on the former lower level of costs. An increase in prices simultaneously with an increase in wages yields a profit on all work in progress and inventories of finished goods. An increase in prices simultaneously with an increase in the cost of raw materials means a profit on all existing inventories of such materials (including those in partly or wholly manufactured form).[1] Where some firms integrate manufacturing with the control of large reserves of minerals such as oil, iron ore, bauxite (for aluminum), copper, and the like, these profits may be considerable and long sustained. If prices are increased simultaneously with increases in the cost of equipment, firms with unexhausted equipment secure special profits. Each firm can argue that these profits are necessary to enable it to continue in business on its existing scale and, indeed, that further working and fixed capital is usually required; if, for instance, equipment is half worn out when the increase in its replacement cost occurs, although prices are immediately raised to the new level, one half of the increased cost of equipment must be supplied by the investors when the time for replacement arrives.

Consistency demands that when costs fall prices should be immediately reduced imposing losses upon producers. They may be informed that continuance in the industry requires less working and fixed capital than formerly, and that the losses imposed on them by the pursuit of this policy still leave to them some profit.[2]

[1] Inventory profits are, however, frequently the resultant of two causes, *viz.*, price increases based on replacement rather than actual cost and price increases permitted or induced by conditions of demand in excess of even increases in replacement costs, *i.e.*, failures to anticipate changes in demand.

[2] If plant were half exhausted when the decline in its replacement cost occurred at least one half of its original cost has been recovered.

This policy stimulates investors to forecast as accurately as they can changes in the costs of production and to adjust their investment policy accordingly.[1] In fact, however, the response to the stimulus of actual or anticipated profits from changes in costs has often been excessive. Inventory profits frequently also modify the pressure to maintain efficiency; inventory losses, on the other hand, while they increase the stimulus to maintain and even increase efficiency, tend to restrictive policies of production. Increases in wage or other costs frequently impel producers to improve their organization and methods of production because they are unwilling or unable to recover all the increase from purchasers through increases in price.[2]

The extreme alternative to basing prices on replacement cost is to base them upon actual increases in cost. This policy is beset with practical difficulties owing to the vagueness of costs; replacement costs are, however, almost equally vague. When costs increase producers may be required to continue selling at their old prices until the goods being sold are those produced as a result of disbursements on the higher level. When costs decline producers must be permitted to continue to secure the old price until the goods being sold have actually involved disbursements on the lower level. Thus inventory profits and losses are eliminated. If complete elimination is possible a further step is made towards assuring investors a normal return upon their investment. The stimulus to advance adjustment of investment to changes in costs is removed, but the danger of excessive responses to the stimulus in periods of activity is also removed. The transmission to purchasers of the benefits of the fall in costs as well as of the burden of an increase in costs is retarded as compared with a policy of permitting prices based on replacement costs. When it has become easier to obtain some of the means of production, purchasers must wait for the benefits until investors have secured their expected

[1] If costs other than those of specialized equipment are expected to fall investors are induced to anticipate an increased demand by increasing plant investment in the expectation of a decline in the price of the finished product; if an upward trend is expected they are induced to make anticipatory reductions of investment in the expectation of a lower demand at the higher level of prices necessary to cover the new costs. If the costs of equipment are expected to fall investors are induced to postpone investment until equipment can be more cheaply purchased and then to base investment upon demand expected at the lower price for the product; if the cost of equipment is expected to rise they are induced to purchase before the increase occurs.

[2] Contemporary methods of accounting generally reveal losses and profits due to changes in wages and raw material costs more speedily than those due to increases in the cost of equipment.

return on previous commitments. When it becomes more difficult to obtain the means of production, purchasers bear the increased burden only when those acquired when conditions were more favorable have been exhausted.

State policy in the control of prices and long-term investment must also rest upon the timing of the adaptation of the productive system to the new conditions. The state must seek to minimize unemployment of equipment when the means of production required to be used with it become more difficult to obtain; equity suggests that it should prevent investors from obtaining special profits when the means of production required to utilize existing equipment become cheaper; sellers should immediately pass on the benefits to purchasers. Investors protected from losses due to the appearance of new competitors when the cost of specialized equipment declines must in return abandon the prospect of windfall profits when the cost of equipment increases. Control might again be applied through taxes upon producers sufficient to appropriate the advantage of a new firm incurring the costs of production upon current levels over firms who committed themselves earlier and paid higher prices. Such a tax raises the total costs (including the tax) of new firms, and of firms reequipping themselves or purchasing materials, to the costs of existing firms already committed. In other industries, or at other times, when costs are increasing subsidies should presumably be paid to new firms to reduce their net costs (allowing for the subsidy) to the costs of existing firms. Total costs and prices are thus adjusted to the actual costs of firms in the industry at the time of the change. But if costs are changing prices must sooner or later give effect to the change; if they do not, industries continue at their old size regardless of the increasing difficulty or ease of obtaining the means of production. Taxes in some industries and subsidies in others would become a permanent institution and increasing inefficiency develop in the industrial system as a whole. Taxes and subsidies must, therefore, be tapered off to effect the necessary transition at the most economical speed and control of long-term investment be applied on the same basis. The more nearly the state succeeds in protecting existing investment without stimulating replacements tending to perpetuate the allocation of investment based upon the past prices of the means of production, the less will be the cost of adjusting investment to the new scale of costs. The more nearly it succeeds when costs are falling in protecting existing investment without discouraging extension of plant, the less is the probability of periods of deficient capacity.

The National Recovery Administration encountered this problem early in its career. The administration made it very clear that its new opportunity to coordinate industrial action would be most speedily exercised by an attempt to control the broad lines of wage policy. Producers having sought during the depression to limit the losses resulting from declining demand by reducing payrolls (both by reducing wage rates and by discharging workers), had progressively restricted the market for goods. No individual firm could maintain or raise wages in the hope of maintaining sales because none could be assured that all would pursue the same policy; any single firm pursuing this policy would raise its costs more than it would increase its own sales, except in the odd case that the increases of pay granted to its workers were all spent on the goods made by their employers. But if employers could be assured that all would increase payrolls simultaneously, the policy would appeal to all or most of them. In consequence, the President exhorted employers to shorten the hours of work and raise rates of pay in order to increase total payrolls. The President's Reemployment Agreement was intended to operate as a temporary general code which would have this effect and the initial special codes all contained clauses fixing minimum rates of pay and maximum hours of work. But it was immediately realized that the concentration of control over prices and production in each industry might lead to higher prices to cover the higher costs of labor and that it was necessary to "put some control on undue price increases so that prices will not move up one bit faster than is justified by higher costs."[1] The administration sought to minimize the tendency of increases in direct costs to diminish the extent to which plant was used. But it was unwilling to bear the costs of the experiment by paying subsidies; it endeavored to persuade producers to bear it in the hope of greater profits in the future resulting from a greater volume of business. There was, however, widespread evasion of the wage clauses in the codes and of the President's Reemployment Agreement, both directly and through the de-

---

[1] N.R.A. *Release* No. 11, June 25, 1933. In the words of the President, "if we now inflate prices as fast and as far as we increase wages the whole project will be set at naught. We cannot hope for the full effect of this plan unless in these first critical months, and even at the expense of full initial profits, we defer price increases as long as possible."

THE PROBLEM OF SOCIAL CONTROL—OBJECTIVES 555

motion of workers and by "stretching out" and speeding up of workers.[1]

f. Maintaining the Efficiency of Productive Units. Attempts to protect investors from losses arising out of unanticipated reductions in demand lead almost necessarily to claims that they be relieved also of the windfall profits arising out of unanticipated increases in demand. The state is compelled to attempt to direct the adjustment of investment to shifts in demand and, as far as possible, to make the adjustment by anticipation. Attempts to protect investors from losses arising out of changes in methods of production lead in the same way to efforts to control the introduction of the new methods to minimize the incidental losses. Attempts to relieve investors from losses due to unanticipated changes in costs of production due to other causes suggest also that they be relieved of the windfall profits available when costs change so as to make such profits possible. Again the state is impelled to direct the process of adaptation. In thus attempting to increase the efficiency of the system as a whole the state is faced, however, with the problem of segregating losses or subnormal profits due to such causes from those due to inefficiency within the individual firm.

Competition having failed to maintain efficiency some substitute must be devised. Tests of efficiency in terms of the costs of production of individual firms must be devised. The National Recovery Administration was pressed by industry groups to prohibit sales at prices which did not cover the cost of production. Protection from such competition, if fully obtained, would relieve investors not only of the burden of changes of the types above discussed but also of the penalty of declining inefficiency within individual firms. The interpretation of "costs of production" determines the amount of protection obtained. Sometimes minimum prices were based, as we have seen, upon the costs of the lowest-cost firm and sometimes upon an arbitrary figure compiled from the costs of a number of firms. The use of any costs above those of the lowest-cost firm reduces the pressure upon all firms to increase their efficiency and reduce their costs.[2] The extent to which prices are permitted to exceed the costs of the lowest-cost

---

[1] It has already been pointed out (p. 516 and Figure 52) that the relation between the movements of costs and prices was such that profits, far from being temporarily diminished, were increased.

[2] Unless differences arise from differences in methods of calculating costs or marketing conditions permit differences in selling prices.

firm determines the pressure applied to the less efficient. Too great pressure may result in failures and prices above the costs of the most efficient firm. Too little pressure means increasing divergence from the efficiency promised by the competitive system.

The National Industrial Recovery Act provided for special consideration of the effect of the codes of fair competition upon the small enterprise. The President in determining whether to approve of codes was required to consider, *inter alia*, whether they were designed or would operate to "eliminate or oppress small enterprises" or discriminate against them.[1] The administration repeatedly avowed its desire to protect the small enterprise. This policy involves departure from the efficiency promised by competition wherever the small firms are those with the highest costs. They may be adolescent producers who will be the most efficient of the future but, even so, they are most likely to become efficient if they must measure up continuously to the attained efficiency of rivals expressed in the prices they charge. On the other hand, the small firm is a constant check upon the growth of firms because of the attractiveness of size for its own sake, or because of desire to control the market, provided, of course, price competition continues.[2] The economic soundness of attempts to support the small firm depends partly upon the extent to which it is actually or potentially more efficient than the larger; it depends also upon the extent to which price competition transmits the benefits of that efficiency to purchasers. The Board of Review, which was especially charged to investigate this aspect of the policy of the administration,[3] charged that the codes had hampered small businesses more particularly through the fixing of prices for the benefit of the large companies, prohibitions on the expansion of plant capacity, and the use of basing-point systems and discounts on large purchases.[4] Fixing prices to benefit large firms as compared with the small might be expected to hamper the latter only when the former

---

[1] Sec. 3, a.
[2] *Cf.* the conclusion of the ("Darrow") Board of Review that the small firm is often the "consumer's sole barrier against complete grasping and irresponsible monopoly" (*cit. New York Times*, May 21, 1934). It added that the "chiseler" is not always a public enemy; he may be "struggling to prevent the total absorption of an industry into a monopolistic organization against which the public has no other protection" (*loc. cit.*).
[3] Appointed Feb. 19, 1934, and popularly known as the "Darrow Board" after its chairman, Clarence Darrow. The reports of the board were not made generally available. The first report was released May 20, 1934; an abstract will be found in *New York Times*, May 21, 1934.
[4] See p. 502.

were the more economical. In fact, however, the products of the large and the small firms are frequently not completely homogeneous and a code authority representing mainly the large units may either fail to provide any differential (although the price of the product of the small firm has customarily been lower than that for the product of the larger) or fix differentials favoring the product of the large firm.[1] The protection of the small firm is, however, a serious political issue and, as we have seen, often represents the resistance of established firms to improvements which threaten to replace them.

The costs of the lowest-cost firms cannot, however, be accepted as a standard of efficiency to be accepted by the state. We have seen that, in their efforts to avoid price competition, producers have resorted to a variety of practices making for a decline in the efficiency of all producers. The costs of even the lowest-cost firms must be examined to determine what costs are acceptable. The amount to be included for overhead costs is a matter of primary importance, especially in view of the tendency outlined in the preceding pages to the development of excessive capacity for production.

In the first place, it is necessary to decide how high a charge may be included in prices for the use of equipment throughout its whole life; the valuation placed upon equipment by its owners cannot be accepted without inquiry. Not only must it be asked whether the sum at which the equipment was valued represents its cost, at the time of its acquisition, to a prudent and honest buyer, but also whether, in view of later events, prospective demand justifies continued efforts to secure full repayment of these costs in the long run. The answer to this question lies in the policy adopted to deal with unanticipated changes in demand, in methods of production, and in costs due to other causes. When the total amount to be recovered has been thus determined the distribution of the recovery over time depends upon the policy of the state in dealing with cyclical fluctuations in demand. These matters have already been discussed.[2]

[1] For example, the ("Darrow") Board of Review contended that differentials between the price of washed and unwashed coal insufficient to cover the cost of washing handicapped small firms selling unwashed coal; the absence of any differential based upon sulphur content handicapped small firms producing coal with a high proportion of sulphur. The fixing of uniform prices for advertised and unadvertised goods in the oil and automobile tire industries is said to have handicapped smaller producers.

[2] See p. 542.

We have seen that in recent years an increasing amount of the means of production has been allocated to activities in the nature of non-price competition, more particularly to methods of pressing sales in which advertising plays a large part. Payments for this type of rivalry appear in the costs of firms; in attempting to regulate prices by reference to costs, to prevent destructive price cutting, or to prevent sales at prices that do not cover the cost of production, it must be decided whether these costs are to be covered by the minimum price or not. The National Recovery Administration usually, but not always, excluded them. In the automobile tire and oil industries, however a single minimum price was set for both advertised and unadvertised brands. The minimum price apparently permitted continued advertising and the unadvertised products lost their appeal. If competition is to be regulated, the state must take a stand as to the desirable amount of resources to be allocated to promoting sales. This decision is not easy because, as we have seen, some advertising supplies needed information, facilitates the rational allocation of income, and reduces the disparity between expected and realized satisfactions. Much advertising, however, has the reverse effect. It is doubtful, moreover, how far such services as are rendered by sales promotion are commensurate with the price paid for them. A great deal of such expenditure is mutually neutralizing and doubtless many firms would submit to the limitation of advertising expenditures if they were sure that their rivals would be similarly treated. It would also be necessary to decide how much expenditure upon sales promotion is to be permitted to enable new products to be marketed or to permit new firms to secure a footing in the industry.

Style competition raises problems which go to the root of social mores. Yet, in determining the reasonableness of total costs, the reasonableness of the costs of designing, manufacturing, and marketing of new styles of product and those arising out of losses on inventories rendered obsolete by the change in style must be decided. Decision is impossible, however, without facing such aesthetic and moral questions as whether it is desirable for people to obtain those satisfactions that arise from changes in the aesthetic aspects of the commodities they purchase. Should individuals be compelled to continue wearing their clothes until they have reached an arbitrarily determined stage of physical deterioration? Or should they be permitted the satisfactions arising out of changes in the aesthetic qualities of such commodities?

THE PROBLEM OF SOCIAL CONTROL—OBJECTIVES 559

The wide separation of control from ownership of large corporations has given rise to the problem of determining the reasonableness of the remuneration of the managers and higher executives. The salaries of such persons[1] have received considerable attention but there is little doubt that their effect upon average costs is usually small and in planning for the maximum of production this question need cause little economic difficulty.

Closely associated with any consideration of the attainment of maximum satisfactions is the problem of providing for the improvement of the efficiency of production. The stimulus to the improvement of methods of production has been diminished by some of the recent changes in industrial conditions. How large a sum may be included in current costs, and imposed upon current purchasers, to cover the cost of devising new products or new methods of organizing production or distribution? Competition (interpreted somewhat loosely) stimulates the reduction of costs; failure to allow some expenditure of the above type obstructs improvements in efficiency. A fundamental decision must be made, namely, how much of the present means of production shall be withdrawn from immediate production in order to improve future production.

Control of long-term investment also presents the problem of securing the greatest efficiency of individual firms. Where reduction of investment is required maximum efficiency is likely to be secured in the longer run, not by sharing the business between existing firms, but by the elimination of the least efficient, a most delicate operation for the state to undertake. Similarly when increased investment is permitted the most efficient of the applicants should be selected to enter the industry. Difficult as this selection may be it is inherent in the control of investment unless resort is had to the crude device of selection according to priority of application.[2]

[1] The Supreme Court has already accepted responsibility for controlling the bonuses paid to the higher officials of corporations in order to prevent misuse and waste of the property of the corporation. "If a bonus has no relation to the value of the service for which it was given it is in reality a gift in part and the majority stockholders have no power to give away corporate property against the protest of the minority" (Rogers v. Hill, 289 U.S. 582, 591 (1933)).

[2] This problem has already been met by the Comptroller of the Currency in exercising his powers to control the establishment of national banks. The Comptroller in dealing with applications for permission to establish banks takes account of the general character and experience of the organizers and proposed officers of the bank, the need for further banking facilities and further banking capital, the probable growth of the town or city in which the bank is to be established, the methods and practices of the existing banks, the interest rates they charge, the character of the service which as quasi-public institutions they are rendering to the community, and

2. CONSIDERATIONS OF THE DISTRIBUTION OF THE PRODUCE BETWEEN DIFFERENT CLASSES AND INDIVIDUALS

In the making of policy for the social control of industry the probable effects of policy upon different classes would have to be kept in view. The political dangers of laxity in this direction are obvious and are illustrated by the two safeguards suggested by the National Industrial Recovery Act, *viz.*, that it should not be used to further monopoly or hamper small businesses. Monopoly not only restricts the total output of society, but also enlarges the share (and the absolute amount) of that total obtained by the monopolist. Maintenance of the small firm is supported because it limits the policy of monopolists as well as because small firms although economically inefficient may be numerous and politically powerful.[1]

Control of industrial policy involves the power to determine broadly the distribution of the produce of industry between classes, groups, and individuals. The extent of the changes that can be introduced depends, however, upon the measure of liberty and privacy of property that is maintained. Drastic changes can be made only if the state *de jure* or *de facto* operates the industrial system; the implications of such policies are best studied by reference to the history of the Russian Soviet state. Less drastic enlargement of the functions of the state restricted to attempts to minimize the more obvious inefficiencies of an imperfectly competitive system also raises problems of distribution. If the state regulates the losses and gains accruing from the changes already discussed it must decide their proper incidence. In the preceding section we have been concerned with the control of this incidence with a view to securing the maximum efficiency of production. It cannot be taken for granted, however, that this incidence should be regulated with regard to efficiency alone.

At the outset these problems of distribution fall into two categories. On the one hand, each policy of control must be considered in relation to its effects upon the distribution of produce between the various classes in a community within any given period of time. On the other hand each policy must be considered with reference

---

the reasonable prospects of success for the new bank if efficiently managed (*Instructions of the Comptroller of the Currency Relative to the Organization and Powers of National Banks*, 1928, 5).

[1] *Cf.* the opposition of the individually operated store to the chain store.

to its effect upon the distribution of economic well-being between persons and classes in different periods of time.

a. Distribution within a Given Period of Time. The most convenient classification of members of society for the purpose of the present discussion of distribution[1] consists in division into investors, managers, and purchasers, it being obvious that these groups do not consist of individuals belonging exclusively to one group, but that they afford merely a means of segregating different aspects of the economic life of the same individuals. If the larger equity of the distribution resulting from the present industrial organization be excluded from discussion, it remains only to consider the distributional aspect of the changes already discussed in connection with the maintenance of efficiency.

The burdens and benefits of shifts in demand tend ultimately to fall upon purchasers. Over shorter periods, and within particular industries, however, there are considerable departures from this tendency. State control of prices or investment requires that the state decide whether it is equitable for sellers to secure windfall profits when demand increases although when demand declines investors are protected from loss. If investors receive these benefits without carrying the corresponding burdens the ability of investors, and the willingness of actual and potential investors, to save and invest is increased and the rate of interest reduced. The state must then decide, on other than economic grounds, whether the resulting change in the general distribution of income is desirable.

The detailed effect of various possible social policies upon purchasers and investors and upon production groups (*e.g.*, corporations) within the class of investors has already been suggested. It must be decided whether the benefits and burdens exceed or fall short of the amounts necessary to stimulate the changes in behavior which will increase efficiency. Increased profit may stimulate increased investment, but does the increase in profit exceed the minimum necessary for this purpose? If this minimum falls short of the profit obtainable, considerations of efficiency cannot determine the proper disposal of the excess.

Similar ethical problems arise in connection with the distribution of losses. If plant investment is excessive the distribution of losses may be determined by the distribution of quotas; these

[1] The class of workers, is, for the most part, here excluded from consideration, solely in order to reduce the scope of the analysis to manageable proportions. For the same reason, distribution between subgroups within the conventional classes and between individuals is excluded.

quotas, however, are usually calculated on some basis selected for its simplicity (*e.g.*, past production or plant capacity) rather than because of its ethical desirability. If price, quality, and service competition are restricted (as in many industries under the National Industrial Recovery Act), business is distributed according to the success of each firm in promoting sales. This policy diverts resources into activities which yield little in the way of economic satisfactions and diminish the capacity of the industrial system to yield satisfactions. The ethical desirability of the resulting sharing of business requires also to be questioned.

The introduction of new methods of production or adaptation to changes in costs due to other causes also presents ethical questions. If investors are protected from losses is it equitable that they should obtain the profits resulting from changing costs? Protection from loss due to innovation shifts the burden to purchasers and retards innovation. While it is clear that innovation can be too speedy, especially where it imposes serious unemployment upon workers, the protection of investors benefits some by hindering others. It is necessary to calculate the net effect of this policy upon general distribution and to establish ethical criteria for appraising the result. The reward necessary to induce innovation is probably considerably less than the rewards often obtained. The spectacular profits of some are a bait impelling others into experimentation but there may be waste of bait. Where changes in the technique of production take the form of changes in the location of industry, the losses and rewards may exceed those necessary to secure the desired increase in efficiency; the proper distribution of the excess losses and benefits between those in different industries must then be determined.

There remain a number of changes the incidence of the benefits and burdens of which under a laissez faire system is so unsatisfactory that intervention is demanded more on ethical than on economic grounds. Floods, earthquakes, and droughts distribute benefits and burdens which do not in any important measure stimulate effort to take advance account of them. Considerations of efficiency, therefore, provide little or no criterion of the proper incidence of these profits and losses. State and federal subsidies in aid of the primary sufferers are based upon the view that the incidence of these losses is a matter for state regulation. Finally, unforecastable social phenomena also give rise to difficult problems concerning the proper distribution of their benefits and burdens.

Changes in the attitude of buyers to particular goods and services are of such importance that they have been considered above. Consideration of the distribution of the benefits and burdens resulting from war would involve too extended an analysis to be embarked upon here. A state participating in industrial policy in time of war must, however, decide whether producers in industries producing war supplies shall be permitted to raise prices sufficiently to reduce demand to that which can be met with existing means of production. In fact, during the war of 1914-1918 in most of the participating countries this problem was faced, and attempts were made, at least in the later stages of the war, to reduce prices and to annex by taxation profits attributable to war. In part this problem is merely a special example of the general problem of determining the proper distribution of the consequences of unforeseen changes in demand.

b. Distribution over Time. The analysis of the problems of state control aimed at the maximization of efficiency resolved itself into a discussion of the timing of the response of the industrial organism to various stimuli. The discussion inevitably, therefore, rested in part upon considerations of the distribution over time of the burdens and benefits of economic change. In the main the period of time in view was relatively short. State control of industrial policy presents, however, problems of distribution over the longer sweep of time the solution of which turns in considerable part upon ethical rather than economic considerations.

Wherever any price policy, by changing the prospective benefits or burdens of investors, affects the general rate of saving, the relative well-being of people at that time and in the future is affected. Any policy that discourages saving increases direct satisfactions from goods and services but diminishes the amount of material equipment available for production in subsequent periods when total output is also diminished. Wherever price policy reacts upon the accumulation of knowledge of methods of production, the relative well-being of people in different intervals of time is affected. If research be discouraged, the consumption of goods and services in the period in which the change occurs is increased, but knowledge of methods of production and the volume of output in subsequent periods is less than it would otherwise be. State control of the amount of resources to be allocated to the accumulation of knowledge of methods of production must take account of this redistribution of economic well-being over time. Consideration of the proper distribution of goods and services over time is also essential to the determination of the proper price policy for exhaust ble natural resources such as coal, oil, copper, etc. This matter has, however, already been discussed.[1]

3. CONSIDERATIONS OF THE NON-FINANCIAL BURDEN OF PRODUCTIVE ACTIVITY

As industrial controller the state must decide what types of activity its citizens may be required to undertake in the course of production. This matter cannot be here considered at length. The state and federal governments have long been concerned with "social legislation" aimed at setting the maximum of pain, unpleasantness, and risk that workers shall be required to bear. The National Recovery Administration encountered the same problem. The limitation of the hours of operation of cotton mills was defended partly because it would eliminate the "graveyard shift," although as we have seen its principal motivation came from other sources. Before accepting such a rule its effect in reducing the social output (or increasing costs) must be weighed against the desirability of eliminating night work. Clauses setting the minimum age of workers with the object of eliminating child labor involve similar considerations.

III. CONCLUSIONS

Centralization of authority to make economic policy raises very serious problems and nothing is gained by minimizing them. Changes in methods of production have, however, so transformed the environment in which business managers make policy that Adam Smith's "unseen hand" has already been brushed aside by the half-seen hand of "self-government in industry"; competition is being increasingly regulated by leaders or groups of mutually considerate individuals. The unseen hand cannot be restored by law. It has, moreover, always been overrated, needing as it does the guidance of the visible hand of the state.

Contemporary developments all point in one direction, *viz.*, that "leaving it to competition" is a state policy with which no one is satisfied and upon the meaning of which there is no general agreement. There is even less agreement concerning the nature of the desirable departures from individualism. Business managers have developed devices for regulation and planning within each

[1] See p. 540.

industry. These developments lead on to proposals to regulate inter-industrial competition. They also lead to efforts to introduce order into the transactions of industry groups related as buyer and seller. The recurrence of business cycles drives home with crude force the interdependence of all economic groups. Planning or the regulation of competition cannot stop short at the frontiers of each "industry."

State participation in the administration of economic resources is urged as a means of securing greater efficiency than the partially competitive and partially monopolistic system of the past has been able to offer. It requires the frank recognition of the conflicts of interest between groups and individuals and serious effort to compromise these conflicts. This compromise can be made, however, only on the basis of a clear conception of the objectives of society. The subtlety of this problem has been indicated. What pressure are we prepared to exert for the maintenance and improvement of industrial efficiency? What is the most economical and equitable incidence of the benefits and burdens of economic change? Recent experiments in the use of the taxing power of the state with the deliberate object of directing the allocation of the means of production in agriculture suggest the more general use of taxes and subsidies as a means of controlling the incidence of the benefits and burdens of economic change to maximize the general efficiency of the productive system.

In both the political and economic sphere the greatest of all contemporary problems is that of deciding how great a concentration of power shall be permitted. The choice is not a simple one between complete individualism and complete collectivism, neither of which terms has any precise practical application. The dangers of drift towards either extreme are now too obvious to be ignored. Rather the problem is one of designing patterns for the distribution of power that will minimize the evils of either extreme. At this point we turn from the ends to the means of social control.

CHAPTER XII

THE PROBLEM OF SOCIAL CONTROL—MEANS

I. The problem—II. The distribution of authority within the administration of the state—*A*. Control by legislative bodies—*B*. Control by judicial bodies—*C*. Control by administrative bodies—III. The sanctions—*A*. The state as conciliator—*B*. The state as administrator of a veto power—*C*. The state as controlling authority—1. Types of coercion—2. The underlying influences determining the effectiveness of sanctions—IV. Conclusion.

I. THE PROBLEM

The foregoing study of the changing location of control of economic resources and of the consequent problems of social policy must finally come to earth in the discussion of administrative aspects of social control. Exhaustive treatment would be neither appropriate nor possible, but to avoid any discussion is to stand too remote from practical issues.

The ultimate problem of industrial organization is one of deciding the proper location of authority over economic resources. This authority must inevitably be distributed in some measure among all the participants in production. We are here principally concerned, however, with the location of the functions of general management. The foregoing discussion has indicated the nature of the powers that must be transferred from individual owners, from the managers of group organizations of owners (such as corporations), and from the leaders of groups of such organizations. The most vital of these powers is that of determining output; this power involves, directly, the power to determine prices, and, indirectly, the power to control the allocation of the means of production to different uses through control of long-term investment. Among the other functions to be transferred are the determination of standards of efficiency of operation, of the proper rewards of each of the classes contributing to production, the proper distribution of well-being over time, and the other matters discussed in the preceding chapter. If these powers are to be transferred to the state where should they be located within the administrative machinery of the state? Some past experience of this type of problem is available. Some of the powers above referred to have been transferred to the state from industries arbitrarily classified as "affected with a public interest," but the National Industrial Recovery Act presented this problem on a vaster scale.

In transferring these functions to the state it is generally assumed that they will not be exercised by individuals who will use them to maximize their own incomes; the object of the transfer is to secure decisions in the interests of the social group. We have seen, however, at how many points and how subtly the interests of the members of this group conflict. The primary requirement of effective state control is, therefore, that those with authority shall be exposed to the reactions of all the affected groups. But once having decided, they must be able to implement their decisions in circumstances in which there will usually be opposition. In other words, in devising instruments of state control there are two basic problems, *viz.*, the distribution of authority within the state and the sanctions to which resort can be had in enforcing decisions.

II. THE DISTRIBUTION OF AUTHORITY WITHIN THE ADMINISTRATION OF THE STATE

A. *Control by Legislative Bodies*

Members of legislative bodies appointed by ballot are more exposed than any other public administrators to the play of all the interests in society. They suggest themselves, therefore, as most appropriate to lay down the broad lines of policy. The federal Congress has, however, consistently evaded decisions even on the broad lines of policy. It has repeatedly vested regulatory powers in commissions and launched them on their careers with no more guidance concerning their ultimate objectives than a few benevolent but vague phrases. The Interstate Commerce Commission, established to investigate violations of the act to regulate commerce,[1] had as its only guide pronouncements condemning "unreasonable and unjust" charges, "discrimination" between shippers, "undue and unreasonable" preferences, more particularly between localities and particular descriptions of traffic.[2] The Transportation Act of 1920 elaborated the instruction concerning "just and reasonable" rates but the commission remained

[1] Interstate Commerce Act, 1887, Sec. 13.
[2] *ibid.*, Secs. 1, 2, 3.

without any precise statement of policy.[1] The Sherman Anti-Trust Act prohibited without defining "monopolies" and "restraint of trade." The Federal Reserve Board which was empowered to review the discount rates charged by the federal reserve banks was instructed to see that such rates "shall be fixed with a view of accommodating commerce and business."[2] The administrative, as apart from the investigatory, functions of the Federal Trade Commission were embodied in a phrase empowering and directing it to prevent the use of "unfair methods of competition in commerce."[3] The Federal Power Commission, which was to issue licenses for development of water power in connection with navigable waters, public lands and reservations, and government dams was to secure "reasonable" payments for the enjoyment of the lands and dams of the government and secure the expropriation to the United States of "excessive" profits accruing to those developing resources until state governments prevented or expropriated such profits. When the resulting electric power entered into interstate commerce the charges therefor were to be "reasonable" and "nondiscriminatory."[4] The Federal Radio Commission was appointed "to regulate all forms of interstate and foreign radio transmission and communication." Licenses under conditions set out in the act were to be granted to any applicant "if public convenience, interest, or necessity will be served thereby." In allocating wave lengths, times of station operation, and power among different states and communities the commission was to endeavor "to give fair, efficient, and equitable radio service" to

[1] The commission was to apply its authority so that carriers as a whole, or as a whole in large freight territories, would earn a "fair" return on the aggregate value of their railroad properties "under honest, efficient, and economical management" and after making "reasonable" expenditures for maintenance of way, structures, and equipment (Transportation Act, 1920, Sec. 422). The commission was left to determine a "fair rate of return," giving due consideration among other things to the transportation needs of the country and the necessity of enlarging railroad facilities "in order to provide the people of the United States with adequate transportation." As to the valuation of railroad properties upon which rates were to yield a "fair" return, the commission was to "give due consideration to all the elements of value recognized by the law of the land for rate-making purposes." Similar undefined authority appears elsewhere in the act where the commission is required to do what is "just and reasonable" (*ibid.*, Secs. 405, 418), "just, reasonable, and equitable" (*ibid.*, Sec. 418 (6)), what will be "in the interests of better service to the public," "in the public interest" (*ibid.*, Sec. 407), and what will attain "the public interest and a fair distribution of the traffic" (*ibid.*, Sec. 420).

[2] Federal Reserve Act, 1913, Sec. 14 (d). The Banking Act of 1935 (Sec. 204) required that open market operations "be governed with a view to accommodating commerce and business and with regard to their bearing upon the general credit situation of the country."

[3] Federal Trade Commission Act, 1914, Sec. 5.

[4] Federal Water Power Act, 1920, Sec. 4.

each state and community.[1] Congress has, therefore, generally left to administrative bodies the determination of what is in the public interest, of what is "fair," "just," or "reasonable."

The National Industrial Recovery Act of 1933 suggests at first glance a clearer definition of objectives but, in the final definition of policy, it relied as we have seen, upon phrases already accepted by the courts. The act was avowedly aimed *inter alia* at the inducement and maintenance of "united action of labor and management under adequate governmental sanctions and supervision."[2] It vested in the President the power to approve of codes of fair competition and to impose conditions upon his approval of codes "for the protection of consumers, competitors, employees, and others and in furtherance of the public interest."[3] In him also was vested the power to impose codes where none had been submitted and approved by him,[4] to regulate imports,[5] to enter into agreements with trade associations and labor organizations,[6] to require that producers obtain licenses to continue operating,[7] and to impose limited codes with regard to labor conditions.[8] His powers were limited in two ways. He might approve of codes submitted by trade associations only if the associations were, in his opinion, truly representative of their industries and imposing no inequitable restrictions on admission to membership, and if also, in his opinion, such codes would not promote monopolies or eliminate small enterprises.[3] He was also prevented from approving codes permitting monopolies or monopolistic practices (irrespective of his opinion in the matter).[9] In the last resort, therefore, Congress defined policy merely in terms of the requirements of "fair competition" and the prevention of monopoly and the oppression of small enterprises.

Legislative bodies engage in too wide a range of activities to be able to define policy other than in terms of brief general formulae. They cannot participate continuously in the interpretation of the formula; they may indirectly and intermittently do so by criticism of policies or by inquiries ventilating criticism of them. They are

[1] Radio Act, 1927, Sec. 9.
[2] National Industrial Recovery Act, 1933, Sec. 1.
[3] *ibid.*, Sec. 3 (a).
[4] *ibid.*, Sec. 3 (d).
[5] *ibid.*, Sec. 3 (e).
[6] *ibid.*, Sec. 4 (a).
[7] *ibid.*, Sec. 4 (b). This clause expired one year after the Act was passed.
[8] *ibid.*, Sec. 7 (c).
[9] *loc. cit.*

handicapped because their formulae become the playthings of courts distrustful of interpretation by reference to their spirit and intention.[1] The growing importance of social control of economic activity and the greater willingness of the courts to allow Congress to make policy justifies some hope, however, of a more responsible attitude by Congress.

B. *Control by Judicial Bodies*

Judicial bodies participate in the administration of policies of social control not only because the vague formulae of the legislature must be interpreted, but also because their conformity with a written Constitution delimiting the powers of the federal and state governments must be decided. The extent to which the power to "interpret" has developed into a major power to legislate is now evident enough, and the courts have already assumed considerable power to make policy. Open surrender to the courts of the power to make economic policy has, however, been suggested. Among the many plans for amending the anti-trust laws prior to the passing of the National Industrial Recovery Act one[2] was urgently commended, largely because it placed the function of making policy in the hands of the federal courts and not in those of administrative boards or commissions.[3]

Control by courts means control by persons with a particular training and one that is often a positive hindrance to effective control. Emphasis upon interpretation as the function of courts suggests the application of fairly fixed rules in times of slow changes. The rule of precedent emphasizes the desirability of continuity with the past. But when rapid and far-reaching change is needed the judiciary is ill equipped to guide and most likely to retard that change. The relatively mild reforms of the Federal Trade Commission Act were, for instance, largely nullified by the courts.

Judicial officers lack the training necessary to handle problems of economic control. In interpreting the Sherman Act the courts have often preferred to contemplate the probable intent of the parties rather than to analyze the consequences of behavior. Bad consequences do not, unfortunately, flow only from bad intentions.

[1] In the interpretation of the Sherman Law courts have concerned themselves overmuch with the "intent" of business firms and too little with that of Congress.

[2] By Gilbert H. Montague, on behalf of the Merchants Association of New York, to a committee of the American Bar Association on Apr. 12, 1933.

[3] It was proposed to exempt from the anti-trust laws "any arrangements" for the restraint of trade and the limitation of production "if such arrangements are in the public interest," leaving the interpretation of "the public interest" to the courts.

THE PROBLEM OF SOCIAL CONTROL—MEANS 571

The criteria of bad intention have, moreover, been loose and conventional. It is agreed that the act was intended to maintain a competitive régime in industry, yet the courts have also held that the mere size of a firm is no offense against the act. But it cannot be denied that the increasing size and diminishing number of firms are among the major immediate causes of the decline of competition. The courts similarly refuse to hold price leadership to be contrary to the act.[1] Much unreason has been wasted upon the "rule of reason" in connection with restraint of trade. A fantastic verbalism has been constructed upon naïve notions of competition and the courts have consistently avoided technical analysis and disdainfully rejected technical evidence.[2] They have realized the impossibility of enforcing competition, and they have been unwilling to oppose strong economic and social pressure, *i.e.*, they have been unprepared to make any positive policy. The protection of conduct imputed to motives respected in the past and the condemnation of behavior not so motivated is a weak and uncertain foundation for policy,[3] but it is comprehensible in terms of the body making policy. Legal training is essential to any administrative process in order to secure the consistent application of principles of policy, but it is not a necessary qualification for policy making. Judicial bodies are not especially qualified for the functions of selecting desirable ends or analyzing the means of attaining them.

C. *Control by Administrative Bodies*

Congress being incapacitated from giving more than general guidance (if even that) and the courts being concerned more with the facts of the past than the needs of the present, the delegation of control to a new authority is indicated. This authority can avoid the inadequacies of legislatures and courts by being, on the one hand, permitted to specialize in the business of economic control, and, on the other, constituted of persons selected with more direct reference to the functions to be performed.

---

[1] "The fact that competitors may see proper, in the exercise of their own judgment, to follow the prices of another manufacturer does not establish any suppression of competition or show any sinister domination" (U.S. v. International Harvester Co., 274 U.S. 693 (19127)).
[2] U.S. v. International Harvester Co., 274 U.S. 693 (1927); U.S. v. U.S. Steel Corp., 251 U.S. 417 (1920).
[3] See BURNS, "The Process of Industrial Concentration" *Quart. Jour. Econ.*, 47: 277 (1933).

The most important problem is that of providing for the claims of the interested groups to enter into the deliberations leading to decisions. Should the policy-making body be constituted of persons deliberately selected to represent the affected classes, or of persons with as little community of interest as may be with any of these parties? It may be decided that there are no impartial persons; the best body is, then, one whose membership represents the groups whose claims it must compromise. Representation of political groups (which has been commonly provided in the regulating commissions established in the past[1]) is clearly not based upon this principle. It may minimize friction and changes in personnel owing to shifts of power between the parties, but the necessity for the arrangement arises partly out of the political spoils system and partly out of interparty frictions irrelevant to the underlying economic conflicts.

Representation of the major conflicting economic interests has been provided for in connection with the Federal Reserve Board; in making appointments under the original act the President was to "have due regard to a fair representation of the different commercial, industrial and geographical divisions of the country." The interests of the federal government were represented by the Secretary of the Treasury and the Comptroller of the Currency who were made *ex officio* members.[2] An amendment of 1920 increased the number of board members and required that agriculture be added to the interests to be borne in mind in making policy; in fact, the amendment was aimed at securing the representation of agricultural interests on the board.[3] The Banking Act of 1935[4] provided for the removal of the Secretary of the Treasury and the Comptroller of the Currency from the board and required

[1] When the Interstate Commerce Commission was established not more than three of its five members were to be of the same party (Interstate Commerce Act, 1887, Sec. 11). No such limitation was placed on the selection of the members of the Federal Reserve Board (Federal Reserve Act, 1913, Sec. 10). Not more than three of the five members of the Federal Trade Commission (Federal Trade Commission Act, 1914, Sec. 1), three of the six members of the Tariff Commission (Revenue Act, 1916, Sec. 700), three of the five members of the Federal Radio Commission (Radio Act, 1927, Sec. 3), or three of the five members of the reorganized Federal Power Commission (Federal Water Power Act, 1930, Amendment) were to be of the same political party.

[2] Federal Reserve Act, 1913, Sec. 10. The requirement that at least two of the appointed members were to be experienced in business and finance may be interpreted either as an attempt to secure representation of their interests or to secure persons aware of the implications of policy.

[3] 42 Statutes at Large, 620, and HARDING, *The Formative Period of the Federal Reserve System*, 244 ff.

[4] Sec. 203.

the President in making appointments to "have regard" for the various interests.[1] Conflicts of interest between different geographical areas have also been recognized in the membership of the Federal Radio Commission; not more than one of the members of the commission may be appointed from any of the five zones into which the country was divided for the purposes of the act.[2]

Conflicts of interest cannot, however, be painlessly and completely resolved by any neat device of administration. If decisions are made by bodies constituted of representatives of a number of interests, the location of ultimate power then depends upon the number of representatives of each interest and the manner in which they align themselves on each issue. There is much to be said, therefore, for segregating the responsibility for making policy from the function of making available the information in the light of which policy must be made. This segregation can be effected by placing the representatives of interested groups in an advisory capacity. Power to make policy can then be concentrated in a few persons accountable for their decisions and able to devote all their time and energy to the task, without routine administrative responsibilities.[3] This arrangement expresses the actual situation, *viz.*, that the state must make final policy but must do so after consideration of all the possible consequences of its decisions. Appointments of administrative commissions in the past have more frequently followed this principle than that of securing representation of the conflicting interests. Attempts have been made to prevent administrators from being financially interested in the industries they are to regulate, either by specific prohibition of such interests[4] or by a requirement that none may engage in any other business, vocation, or employment (which does not, however, exclude property interests in the corporations controlled).[5] Occasional attempts have been made to provide positive qualifications for membership. Of the five members to be appointed to

---
[1] "In selecting the members of the board, not more than one of whom shall be selected from any one federal reserve district, the President shall have due regard to a fair representation of the financial, agricultural, industrial, and commercial interests and geographical divisions of the country."
[2] Radio Act, 1927, Sec. 3.
[3] *Cf.* CURRIE, *The Supply and Control of Money in the United States*, Chap. XVI; LYON and others, *The National Recovery Administration*, 82.
[4] Interstate Commerce Commission (Interstate Commerce Act, Sec. 11), Federal Reserve Board (Federal Reserve Act, 1913, Sec. 10), Federal Radio Commission (Radio Act, 1927, Sec. 3), and the Federal Power Commission (Federal Water Power Act, Amendment, 1930).
[5] Federal Trade Commission Act, 1914, Sec. 1; Tariff Commission (Revenue Act, 1916, Sec. 700).

the Federal Reserve Board by the President, two were originally required to be experienced in business and finance; this requirement disappeared, however, in 1922.[1] Since 1930 those appointed to the Tariff Commission must, in the opinion of the President, be possessed of the qualifications required for developing expert knowledge of tariff problems and efficiency in administering the functions of the act,[2] an amendment reflecting upon the appointments of past Presidents. If the executive is not anxious to secure able administrators there is of course no effective means of compelling him by statute to secure them.

There is no single type of training which alone can be regarded as a prerequisite to appointment. Regard for all the probable reactions of a decision can best be attained by securing the advice of lawyers, economists, and persons trained in the technical aspects of the more important industries. For making decisions concerning the relative importance of efficiency and other social aspects of production, the most desirable distribution of income, and, more particularly, of the benefits and burdens of unforecastable disturbances of economic conditions, neither a training in law nor one in economics will suffice. A high degree of impartiality and general competence can be secured only if attractive conditions are offered, not only in terms of salary, but also in terms of prestige and power. An administrative body hampered as the Federal Trade Commission has been by the judiciary cannot attract able men. If its power is limited by political pressure, only those whose interests are narrowly political can be attracted. If, on the other hand, its members operate in a setting of reasonable security of tenure, real power, and public anticipation of disinterested pursuit of the general social welfare, an entirely different policy will result. Such a policy involves dangers in the short run but is the only means of insuring capacity and vigor in the long run.

The initial administrative procedure established under the National Industrial Recovery Act is remarkable in that it vested the control of policy in the President alone. The range of his discretionary power has been partly described. In addition to the prohibition upon the approval of codes permitting monopoly or monopolistic practices, he was required to include in every code of fair competition, agreement and license, clauses preserving to workers "the right to organize and bargain collectively through

[1] Federal Reserve Act, Sec. 10, and amending act of 1922, 42 Statutes at Large, 620.
[2] Tariff Act, 1930, Sec. 330.

representatives of their own choosing" and protecting them from coercion to join company unions or to refrain from joining labor organizations of their own choosing.[1] Statutory safeguards were also imposed with the object of insuring the presentation of the views of interested groups. Persons engaged in other stages of the economic process whose services and welfare were affected were entitled to be heard prior to the approval of codes.[2] A code could not be imposed upon an industry until after such public notice and hearing as the President should specify[3] and a similar limitation was placed upon his power to require producers to obtain licenses to continue in operation.[4] He was also to afford every opportunity, so far as practicable, for employers and workers to establish labor standards by mutual agreement,[5] and limited codes with regard to labor standards were to be imposed in the absence of mutual agreement "after such hearings as the President finds advisable."[6] Thus the statute relied upon the public hearing as a means of ventilating opposing views; there was, however, no obligation to be guided by what was heard.

The details of the administrative machinery established and the procedures followed are not important here,[7] but their main outlines are relevant. The administrator appointed to exercise the powers vested in the President was advised by boards representing the views of industry, labor, and the consumer.[8] A procedure was developed for dealing with the establishment of initial codes and code authorities[9] in the course of which the three advisory boards were consulted. These boards were in fact, as well as in title, advisory: their opinions were not published except in so far as they were ventilated at the public hearings.

The major power was in the hands of the deputy administrator, subject to the supervision of the administrator, and ultimately to that of the President, who made numerous decisions on matters of policy. The Business Advisory Board was reinforced by

[1] Sec. 7 (a).
[2] The act provided that it did not deprive such persons of this right to be heard (Sec. 3 (a)).
[3] Sec. 3 (d).
[4] Sec. 4 (b). He was required also to find that the industry was suffering from "destructive wage or price cutting or other activities contrary to the policy of this title."
[5] Sec. 7 (b).
[6] Sec. 7 (c).
[7] They are admirably described by DEARING and others, *The A.B.C. of the N.R.A.*, Chaps. IV, V, and VI.
[8] *ibid.*, 49 ff.
[9] *ibid.*, 81 ff.

an organized group with clear, if mistaken, objectives. Failure to secure acceptance of its advice could be followed up with real pressure. The Labor Advisory Board was immeasurably weaker in this respect, but it was not helpless. The Consumer Advisory Board was in the peculiar position of having so large a constituency that it had none at all.[1] Consumers were the members of the business and labor groups when they came to face the consequences of their policies in terms of output and prices. The board became the one branch of the administration interested in the broad social consequences of policy.[2] Its membership was, with a number of notable exceptions, inadequate to its task. It was powerless to implement its criticism. It was restricted as to both funds and publicity because of its advisory status. During the initial period of the act the administrator, to whom its advice was tendered, was so anxious to secure the adoption of codes throughout industry that he did not welcome criticism. After a life of turbulent obscurity the board secured the public release[3] of criticism of the provisions of the first 180 codes and played an important part in the modifications of policy which have already been discussed.[4] From that time its influence steadily grew. The Research and Planning Division of the National Recovery Administration, which might have been expected to influence the broader social aspects of policy, appears to have been diverted into other channels of activity although not without some protest.[5]

In February, 1934, a new administrative device was tested. There was a public belief that the codes had, in spite of the provisions of the law, fostered monopolistic practices. The administrator called a series of public meetings in Washington to ventilate public opinion; an impressive volume of criticism was offered and in the subsequent months there were efforts to give the impression that the policies of code authorities were being severely restricted;

---

[1] The administrator held to the view that "the real consumers' representative is the President himself" (Speech at meeting for criticism of the N.R.A., cit. *United States News*, Mar. 5, 1934).

[2] In the long run a consumer representative would take as partial a view of policy as the other groups; he would tend in pressing for low prices to induce inefficiently low wages or long hours.

[3] *Release* of Mar. 4, 1934. This release was made immediately prior to the meeting of the delegates of code authorities in Washington.

[4] See Chap. X.

[5] *Cf.* the remark of Alexander Sachs, first director of the division, that "as a matter of economy in the unparalleled stress and speed of rushing through uncharted economic waters, map making and instrument making was apparently deemed too much of a diversion" (BERLE and others, *America's Recovery Program*, 165).

the code authorities succeeded, however, in preventing serious changes.[1]

The application of decisions of general policy to specific industrial situations raises a number of problems that cannot be fully analyzed here. Congress in the National Industrial Recovery Act avowed, as we have seen, a desire to provide for the joint administration of industry by industrial management, labor, and the state. Some business groups saw clearly that "the tendency towards monopoly and the oppression of small enterprises is more likely to spring from administration than the actual provisions of the code."[2] The principle of joint administration was introduced into the membership of the code authorities only in the mildest and most tentative form. The early codes usually provided for government representatives, frequently three, upon the code authority but without power to vote; representatives of consumers and labor were practically nonexistent.[3] The competence and effectiveness of these government representatives were seriously questioned and, at the meeting of those invited to Washington to ventilate criticism of the policies of the administration, the administrator announced his intention of providing for "adequate labor and consumer representation in an advisory capacity on code authorities" and "uniformly of governmental representation on code authorities."[4] The difficulties of obtaining a sufficient number of competent representatives of consumers are obvious and the efficacy of such representation can easily be overemphasized.[5] The "Darrow" Board of Review contended that the powers of the directors of the American Iron and Steel Institute as the code authority for the iron and steel industry, were "more drastic than have ever been reposed, so far as we know, in any branch of the federal government" and, "if given at all, should be conferred only on an organization having governmental char-

---

[1] See Chap. X. In fact, although not required to do so by law, "in order to preserve the spirit of cooperation between industry and the National Recovery Administration it has been the policy of the President to obtain the assent of the industrial or trade association to the amendments which he has attached to codes" (Dearing and others, *op. cit.*, 91).

[2] Distribution and Consumer Service Trades Committee appointed by the administration (*cf. New York Times*, Mar. 29, 1934).

[3] It was held that the government representatives were consumer representatives. The code authority for the retail trade did, however, include a representative of the consumer.

[4] *New York Times*, Feb. 28, 1934.

[5] The Consumer Advisory Board commented upon the lack of adequate financial rewards to consumer representatives, the lack of positive power and assistance, and the disadvantages of appointments for only one year (*Release* of Mar. 4, 1934).

acter." The code authority was a body "perfectly equipped to exercise monopolistic control," yet its members were "not only untrained for functions which are judicial in character, but they are also persons interested financially through their companies in various important questions that come up for determination by the board acting as code authority."[1] The board also commented upon the anomaly of permitting industries to govern themselves; "monopolistic combinations are expected to enforce against themselves a law to prevent monopoly," the fact finding that would reveal violations being largely under the control of the code authorities.[2]

The personnel of the code authority was also open to attack because it failed adequately to represent conflicting interests within the business group, e.g., the integrated and the non-integrated and especially the large and the small firms. The Board of Review concluded that small enterprises had been very generally oppressed and that one of the most important immediate causes of this oppression was the domination of the code authorities by the large firms in each industry (which frequently, of course, were responsible for the greater part of the output of the industry). The board attacked especially the constitution of the code authorities for the iron and steel and the moving picture industries.[3]

As an experiment in industrial control the National Recovery Administration suggests a number of conclusions concerning matters of administration. The views of the representatives of the interested groups should be freely available, but so also should the reasons for important decisions. Greater access to the proceedings of code authorities should be granted to advisory boards. The interest of the consumer being so widespread that it is difficult to organize, the state must accept the function of representing the consumer; his interest being, in the main, identical with the general

---

[1] *Cf. New York Times*, May 21, 1934.

[2] *loc. cit.* The board added that "the Federal Trade Commission is far superior to the National Recovery Administration as an enforcing and fact-finding agency" in spite of its progressive weakening since the war (*ibid.*). Subsequently moves were made to make greater use of the commission as an enforcing agency, provision for which was made in the act, but they appear to have been abortive (*Cf. New York Times*, Aug. 4, 1934).

[3] Eight of the ten members of the code authority for the moving picture industry were connected with the large firms in the industry. The deputy administrator in charge of the code for the moving picture industry was alleged to be prejudiced against the independent producers. Similar charges of control of the code authority by the large firms were made with regard to the soft coal, rubber footwear, hard coal, and ice industries; control of the expansion of plant capacity mainly exercised by the larger ice manufacturers was said to have wrought serious injustice.

efficiency of production, the state should be prepared to grant far more financial and administrative recognition to him than was granted under the National Industrial Recovery Act.

III. THE SANCTIONS

The method of enforcing the policy of the state is of great political importance; it is the application of sanctions that makes evident the real degree and nature of the authority over economic resources that has been transferred to the state. For this reason it is the starting point of violent conflict. The available sanctions may be roughly classified by reference to the nature of the relationship between the state and private groups and individuals. The state may be a conciliator, the administrator of a power of veto, or a regulatory and controlling authority.

A. *The State as a Conciliator*

If the state undertakes to conciliate, its representatives establish contact between the various classes interested in production and endeavor to induce them to arrive at a policy acceptable to all of them. A conciliator has no power of compulsion. The chance of arriving at decisions is less than if the representatives of the state could impose a policy, but the chances of any decision thus reached being accepted by all are greater. For this reason effort has been made in recent years to restrict state interference with industry as far as possible to conciliation. The new policy adopted by the Federal Trade Commission in 1925 was broadly aimed at reducing to a minimum the coercive power of the commission and developing its capacity to assist business managers to agree with each other upon a code of fair competition. The minimization of publicity concerning alleged offenses and the increased emphasis upon Trade Practice Conferences were steps in this direction. The administration of the Sherman Law has revealed a similar trend. Recent attorneys general have called for the private and secret submission of plans for proposed mergers in order that they may signify whether or not they see in them any present reason for prosecution. The administration of the National Industrial Recovery Act in its first year appears also to have been ultimately dominated by a desire to find formulae that "could be worked," which in fact meant rules that business managers would accept without excessive opposition and obstruction; it showed great unwillingness to exert its powers of compulsion. The clause permitting the President to require producers to obtain licenses to continue in operation was never used and was allowed to lapse at the end of one year after the act became operative. The power of legal coercion to enforce decisions was resorted to slowly and with extreme reluctance. This policy was doubtless in part due to a desire for the speedy establishment of some kind of code in every industry; such a code would provide a basis for regulation and could subsequently be amended. The attitude of the courts was also in doubt. Above all, however, this policy sprang from a prevailing distaste for what has often been called the "big stick" method of administration. These efforts to minimize resort to coercion inevitably resulted in the domination of policy by the group most ready and able to obstruct decisions of which it did not approve.[1]

There are three major difficulties in the way of a policy of conciliation. In the first place, it assumes that conflict arises from an inadequate understanding by each group of the attitude and interests of the others. The state need merely bring the representatives of the interests to the same table and serve as a catalytic agent facilitating an interchange of views; reason must then triumph in the adoption of a decision recognized by all as being in the interests of each. Conciliation is a way of inducing concessions by each group to the demands of the others by emphasizing that the major interest of all is the continuance of economic activity. But it is useless to evade the fact of real conflicts of interest between the groups. The concessions required to induce agreement may be so great that they involve greater loss than at least a temporary suspension of economic activity. The policy adopted by the National Recovery Administration during its first year resulted in 1934 in the most costly outbreak of labor disputes for over a decade. Great damage may be done, moreover, if the process of conciliation is protracted. Attainment of the general social interest by way of a series of concessions by each group calls for a clear conception of the social interest by the conciliator.

In the second place, reliance upon conciliation assumes equally effective organization of all the interested groups. The outstanding difficulty of conciliation in industrial control is, however, that only one class, business management and ownership, is effectively organized. It can and does organize to employ skilled and effective

[1] See BURNS, "The First Phase of the National Industrial Recovery Act of 1933," *Polit. Sci. Quart.*, 49: 194 (1934).

negotiators. Workers are only very partially organized. Individuals in their capacity as purchasers (often consumers) are completely unorganized. The essentials to conciliation are, therefore, lacking. In agriculture the state has in recent years encouraged, by financial aid and otherwise, the organization of producers' cooperative associations. The National Industrial Recovery Act was aimed at at least removing barriers to the organization of workers,[1] but the stimulation of voluntary organizations of consumers is hopeless. Consumers are affected by the prices of such a wide variety of products that their interest broadens out into an interest in the efficiency of the whole industrial system. The state suggests itself, therefore, as the proper organization for the representation of consumers. Real conciliation is possible only when the state not only acts as conciliator but also represents one of the parties to the conflict. In other words, the state while acting as conciliator must determine the outcome by deciding the claims it will press and the concessions it will make on behalf of the consumer. In the National Recovery Administration the President was held to be the protector of the consumer while he was also endowed with powers to supervise the terms of the codes. It has been shown how still and small was the voice speaking for the consumer.

In the third place, decisions must be made concerning the broad lines of social policy affecting the relative positions of the major economic interests of purchasers, workers, owners, and managers. Organization along these broad lines hardly exists except perhaps of organizers and managers.[2] The lack of organization of this type is more than a special case of the previous argument. It involves considerations so much more sweeping as to be different in kind. The organization of interests on this grand scale must inevitably fall in large part upon the state. The stimuli to economic efficiency are operating more fitfully and less effectively than formerly and efficiency is not to be increased alone by the removal of minor frictions in particular industries. Moreover the interests of the major groups would often conflict with those of subdivisions of the group. If the state lays down the underlying principles controlling the relations between the economic classes, the principle of conciliation is abandoned in regard to the most fundamental decisions. Yet the attempt to adhere to the principle involves

---

[1] In Sec. 7 (a).
[2] Such organizations of workers as exist are in fact representative only of a small and highly selected group of workers.

fundamental political reorganization and increased chances of destructive conflict.

If the state undertakes the functions of an arbitrator between conflicting interests without power to enforce its decisions it differs from a conciliator only in the compulsion placed upon it to state clearly what it believes to be a desirable policy. The shortcomings of conciliation apply equally to this type of arbitration. Arbitration by the state, backed by the power of legal coercion, amounts to state control.

B. *The State as the Administrator of a Veto Power*

The desire to minimize the effective authority of the state without going so far as to reduce the state to a conciliator has resulted in various suggestions that the state be armed with a mere power of veto. It should stand aside leaving the parties interested in production to solve their own problems, with the proviso that it may intervene and veto developments of which it disapproves.

Among the various proposals for the amendment of the antitrust laws prior to the passing of the National Industrial Recovery Act was one[1] that producers desiring to make contracts restricting output and sharing business should be permitted to do so,

> but in order to protect the public against unreasonable prices, these contracts should be filed with some federal commission and should be subject to the approval or disapproval of that commission. . . . A contract is filed. It takes effect within a reasonable time, say two weeks or a month, unless in the meantime someone is objecting or unless in the meantime the federal supervisory commission takes up the matter of its own accord.[2]

A fundamentally similar proposal was made after a few months of experience of the operation of the National Recovery Administration. When attitudes to the proper functions of the state began to crystallize, it appeared that business men generally desired the continuance of the concentrated control of industrial policy but a curtailment of the powers of the state. This movement expressed itself clearly, if prematurely, in a plan proposed by Gerard Swope, the chairman of the Business Advisory and Planning Council of

---

[1] Presented by Harry I. Harriman (as chairman of Committee on the Continuity of Business and Employment of the United States Chamber of Commerce) at the *Hearings on the Establishment of a National Economic Council*, before a subcommittee of the Committee on Manufactures of the U.S. Senate, 1931, 161 *ff.*

[2] *ibid.*, 167.

the National Recovery Administration at its opening meeting.[1] He contended that "much of the great adventure of the National Industrial Recovery Act should be made permanent"; on the foundations it had built should be erected "a better structure—more in keeping with our democratic philosophy and traditions . . . where the employer and employee will work together." Accordingly he proposed that "commerce and industry organize themselves into definite and compact units and that these organizations be self-governing and include such representation on their governing boards so that the public interest will be protected."[2] Upon the body governing each trade or industry was to be "one or more" representatives of the state to protect "the public and consumer interest" and to "receive all data and information that is available to the board or executive committee as well as the minutes of the meetings." Compliance was to be secured by referring complaints to some arm of the government. Finally, "there shall be a national chamber of commerce and industry located in Washington which may well be an enlargement of and development of the present Chamber of Commerce of the United States with the necessary reorganization along the lines of this program." The board of this national chamber would elect a panel to sit "as a board of appeals on any questions that may arise in the interpretation and enforcement of the national code provisions." On this board would also sit members appointed by the President of the United States. The president of the (existing) Chamber of Commerce, while denying that the plan had been evolved by the chamber, endorsed it as "thoroughly in accord with the views of the chamber's membership,"[3] and the administrator of the National Industrial Recovery Act added his endorsement.[4] Although it was not explicitly provided in the plan, it was later stated that the government would possess a veto power and great importance was attached to the distribution of authority between business and the state. The president of the Chamber of Commerce remarked that "there is a vast difference between the possession of power that is seldom used and constant spying by the government to see to it that observance is had."[4] Principal reliance for enforcement was to be placed on public opinion.

[1] Cit. New York Times, Nov. 2, 1933.
[2] "If industry does not organize and govern itself either the state or federal government will, with the consequent paralyzing effects on initiative and progress."
[3] New York Times, Nov. 2, 1934.
[4] loc. cit.

The assumption that the governmental power of veto would be rarely used is, of course, gratuitous. The history of the Chamber of Commerce does not justify the assumption that its policies would meet with so little opposition that there would rarely be pressure upon the government to exercise its power of veto. The vitally important matter of the balance of power within the board of appeals between the representatives of industry and the government is undefined. Most important of all, however, the veto is too weak and unsatisfactory an instrument of government regulation. Mere veto without power to make constructive rules is likely, if vigorously applied, to be irritating to industry. Nevertheless it is well to remember that so long as government control takes the form of the regulation of the exercise of private rights, it must be largely a power to prohibit rather than a power to compel. It is possible to prohibit new investment but not to compel it, to prohibit price reductions or increases of output but not to compel them. The greatest danger, however, is the practical one that financial starvation of the branch of the government exercising the power of veto may result in the rare use of the power, which is precisely the aspect of the program most commended. Financial starvation of an administrative service whose positive endorsement of policies is required is less likely because delays and inaction would hinder changes of policy desired by business men.

C. *The State as Controlling Authority*

If the state is to control it must not only establish policy but secure its general acceptance. The discussion of the difficulties of conciliation has indicated that policy can be established only when machinery has been set up to secure equally effective presentation of the interests of all parties. At least the consumer interest must be represented by the state itself while it also acts as final arbiter. This duality of function presents no serious difficulty provided the different functions are exercised by separate arms of the state.[1] Indeed this duality has the sanction of tradition. The state both prosecutes and adjudicates infractions of the criminal law. While administering the general laws of property and labor with a view to smooth and effective cooperation, it has also passed special laws aimed at the protection of particular classes regarded as in-

---

[1] *Cf.* the criticism of the Federal Trade Commission on the ground that it acts as both prosecutor and judge (SEAGER and GULICK, *Trust and Corporation Problems*, 522 *ff.*).

capable of securing satisfactory treatment by their own efforts. There is now need in the field of industrial regulation for a counsel entrusted with the active prosecution of behavior damaging to the interests of purchasers, e.g., attempts to charge unreasonably high prices (either in the hope of abnormally high profits, or in the presence of high costs due to inefficiency or over-investment), failure to improve the methods of production at a satisfactory rate, the placing of undue burdens upon the purchasers of the present in order that those of the future may benefit.

1. TYPES OF COERCION

The principal types of coercion call for only the briefest treatment. The most obvious and direct coercion is the deprivation of property or liberty where individuals fail to accept the policy selected by the administrative body. The extent to which this type of coercion can be used depends upon the attitude of the courts interpreting the Constitution. The coercive powers provided in the anti-trust laws have been severely limited by the courts in the past. The extent to which coercion is used depends also upon the attitude of the executive; the attorney general need not prosecute unless he chooses; the policies of the Federal Trade Commission have been molded by the careful selection of its personnel and by pressure from the executive arm of the state.[1] Ultimately, however, policy in this matter depends upon the pressure to which the legislature, the executive, and the judiciary are exposed. To class these pressures as "public opinion" is to give them too vague a name. But to be more specific would be to travel too far afield.[2] The varying degrees of activity of different attorneys general in seeking out and actively prosecuting infringements of the anti-trust laws are in part correlated with changes in the tone of public opinion, expressing itself only partly through the type of legislator and President elected. Even the judiciary appears to be affected by changes in "public opinion." We have seen that although the National Industrial Recovery Act provided for enforcement by the infliction of fines and imprisonment these sanctions were little used during the first year of the act, partly because of doubt concerning the attitude of the courts, partly because public opinion was believed to be averse to the "big stick," and partly because industrial

---

[1] Cf. BLAISDELL, The Federal Trade Commission, 77 ff.
[2] It is obvious, however, that some classes are more articulate, more urgent, and more effective in expressing their opinions than others.

management was hostile to vigorous enforcement and able to apply effective pressure.

Coercion by means of public boycott was developed as a sanction for the National Industrial Recovery Act. The "blue eagle" was devised by the administration (not by Congress) to facilitate a general public boycott of firms refusing to subscribe to codes of fair competition or to the President's Reemployment Agreement. It doubtless stimulated the speedy adoption of codes. Enforcement by general boycott is, however, obviously dependent for its effectiveness upon the attitude of the general body of purchasers to the policy of the administration. If purchasers are out of sympathy with the objective they are unlikely to boycott. This type of coercion, therefore, demands not only machinery for the identification of those to be coerced into accepting the policy of the administration but also machinery for developing the will to coerce. The emotional appeals of the first few months of the act were designed to develop this will.

The National Recovery Administration developed also a third type of coercion, *viz.*, boycott by the state. This device was probably the most effective sanction operating during the first year of the act. The extension of the scope of state activity has rendered the state an increasingly important purchaser in a growing number of markets. Refusal by the state to purchase any goods from those who do not in all their activities accept its policy is, therefore, a powerful means of coercion.[1] The President ordered,[2] soon after the act became operative, that government contracts be made only with firms complying with the code approved for their industry.[3] The code for the copper industry indicates the possibilities of this policy. Only "blue eagle" copper was eligible for supply to the government. "Blue eagle" copper was that produced by firms accepting a restriction of sales and allocation of quotas. The code

---

[1] The state has also utilized its coercive powers as a purchaser of transportation service in its administration of the post office. Payments for marine transportation have been in part used to secure compliance with a national policy of developing a merchant marine. Payments for air transportation have been used to encourage aviation and more recently to influence the organization of the industry.

[2] *Executive Order* of Aug. 19, 1933.

[3] The Comptroller General held that the requirement that firms comply with codes was a reasonable one in government contracts but not a requirement that firms agree to comply with codes (*New York Times*, Nov. 12, 1933). This sanction was also indirectly used when it was ordered that tenders for supplies to public authorities should be held not to contravene the open-price clauses in codes provided the prices quoted were not more than 15 per cent below those filed under the clause. This order was interpreted as we have seen as a means of inducing the acceptance of modifications to codes.

authority, being permitted to make rules defining "blue eagle" copper, determined that if any non-blue eagle copper was used by a fabricator in any of his plants all his output should be classified as non-"blue eagle" copper.[1] Thus upon the basis of a government boycott a virtual control of imports and of all sales was built.

But even a boycott by the state is limited in its application. It is subject to all the influences brought to bear upon the state in the use of its power to apply direct coercion, such as the limitations set by the judiciary and by "public opinion." It is also subject to the particular limitation that it is applicable only in the event of some firms in an industry accepting the policy of the state. It was reported, for instance, that the producers of steel and automobiles were considering the abandonment of their codes of fair competition in order to avoid the requirement to bargain collectively with labor unions representing their workers.[2] If all producers united to take this action the state would be compelled to boycott all producers and either manufacture its own steel and automobiles or import them.

2. THE UNDERLYING INFLUENCES DETERMINING THE EFFECTIVENESS OF SANCTIONS

All these methods of coercion depend for their potency in the long run upon acquiescence in their use by effective public opinion. Public support may be sought by emotional appeals to national feeling, class or group frictions, and the like; such appeals are, however, difficult to sustain. Appeal may be had to reason; attempts may be made to elucidate the facts and the general basis of policy. The force of reason in such matters is often belittled; yet a broad dissemination of information concerning the nature of the problems which the state is endeavoring to solve, and the ultimate objectives it seeks to attain, appears indispensable if we are to avoid both complete centralization of authority based upon crude force and economic waste of the type now growing to considerable proportions. Publicity in such matters not only adjusts the behavior of individuals to the policy of the state but also tends to adjust policies to the attitudes and interests of those affected. It cannot be denied, however, that many of those affected are incapable of individual assessment of the policies of the state. The underlying problems are, however, in essence no more complex

[1] See Chap. X.
[2] *New York Times*, Aug. 19, 26, 1934.

than those which arise in other fields of state activity. Publicity must obviously be designed to clarify only broad trends of development and the basic objectives of the state.

In one respect the traditions of the courts may well be borrowed. All important legal decisions are in writing and at least pretend to reveal the reasoning by which the decision has been arrived at. This principle has been adopted by some administrative bodies such as the Interstate Commerce Commission. Its general adoption is essential if policies are to be made clear to those affected. It is essential even to the development of sound theories upon which to base policy. Tribute has been paid by an eminent jurist and student of the judicial process to the contribution of academic critics to the development of legal principles.[1] This criticism has been sharpened and facilitated by the compulsion upon the judiciary to rationalize its decisions. The Federal Reserve Board, on the other hand, undoubtedly suffered prior to 1935 because of the secrecy in which its decisions in the matter of credit policy were made. Objectives were undefined and the reasons for the selection of means to desired ends unrevealed. Written decisions after the manner of legal decisions would have exposed the board to even more criticism than it encountered, but the criticism would have been directed to revealed weaknesses in aims or methods and the development of the technique of control would have been more speedy. The secret submission of proposed industrial mergers to the attorney general is open to the same criticism. The Banking Act of 1935, however, required the board of governors to keep a record of voting upon open market and other policies and of the reasons underlying its decisions and to report annually to Congress upon these matters in full and including a copy of the records of votes and reasons for its decisions.[2] Only able administrators are likely to accept the responsibility of thinking and deciding in the open and they will be constantly stimulated to clear thinking by the prospect of criticism.[3]

These considerations apply in every detail and with equal force to the control of industry. The administration of the National Industrial Recovery Act suffered from lack of explicit statements of the reasons for policy shorn of reliance upon such unmeaning terms as "stabilization," "monopoly," "free market," and the

[1] CARDOZO, *The Growth of the Law*, 13.
[2] Banking Act, 1935, Sec. 203.
[3] *Cf.* CURRIE, *The Supply and Control of Money in the United States*, 161.

like. In particular, the views of the Consumer Advisory Board received little publicity and were slow to find expression in policy. Had the views of each interested group, as seen by the administration, been summarized and the reasoning by which decisions were reached been revealed, a foundation would have been laid for the development of the technique of control as well as the discussion of objectives.

IV. CONCLUSION

The administration of the powers of the state over industry raises two major questions; *viz.*, the location of these powers within the machinery of the state, and the sanction by which their exercise is to be made effective.

Administrative bodies able to devote their full time to the making policy in the control of industry appear to be the best instrument of social control. Legislatures have too wide a variety of activities to be able to make policy in any detail. The judiciary has, in the past, been saddled with impossible tasks in the regulation of industry. It is, moreover, inappropriate to the tasks of selecting social ends or analyzing the methods of attaining those ends in industry. In its present form it has proved unsuitable to the task of making adjustments to rapidly changing conditions. Administrative bodies can avoid these difficulties if they are permitted to specialize and their personnel is selected with full consideration of the functions they are to perform. Bodies representative of all the interests in conflict offer a less satisfactory organ of administration than those consisting as far as possible of impartial persons required to consider the views of the interested parties. In the last resort the kind of policy pursued will be determined largely by the type of person appointed.

The extent of the sanctions to be applied to implement decisions in matters of policy is determined by the status of the government in relation to industry. Dislike of the "big stick" method of administration suggests that the state act as a conciliator. This status is, however, unsatisfactory; there are real and deep conflicts which demand the imposition of some policy; conciliation requires equally effective presentation of the views of all the interests (which is impossible without the aid of the state) and the attainment of greater general economic efficiency and the solution of the broader group conflicts requires an organization of large groups which does not exist. If the state is vested with a power of veto over private conduct a less continuous interference is suggested although in fact continuous control is essential. The mere power to veto is irritating and is too easily rendered impotent by financial starvation. If some industrial functions must be transferred to the state to secure their more effective exercise the administrative machinery should frankly represent the true situation. The administrative body should make positive policy and be responsible for it.

A compromise between complete centralization of power, reenforced by crude compulsion and a wide distribution of liberty to exercise economic power must be sought partly in indirect types of sanction but mainly in the full ventilation of views as a precedent to the making of policy. General public boycotts and boycotts by the state have already been used. These sanctions, as well as the direct deprivation of liberty and property rest ultimately upon a broad measure of support for the policies pursued and, therefore, suggest general publicity concerning the main outlines of the problems to be solved as well as of the underlying objectives by reference to which solutions are sought. To rely upon emotional appeals to national or other group frictions is to divert attention from the principal problem and, over long periods, cannot succeed.

The courts have developed a technique of social control by reasoned decisions applying general rules to specific cases which, like all other administrative devices, falls short of perfection but is vastly superior to administration by bald announcements of the sort made up to 1935 by the Federal Reserve Board and the National Recovery Administration. Reasoned decisions publicly available are the best means of providing for the evolution of an effective technique of control and for the minimization of resistance to policy.

BIBLIOGRAPHY

I. BOOKS AND PERIODICAL ARTICLES

ALSBERG, CARL L. *Combination in the American Bread Baking Industry*, Food Research Institute, Stanford University, California, 1926.

AMERICAN BUREAU OF METAL STATISTICS. *Yearbooks*, New York.

AMERICAN IRON AND STEEL INSTITUTE. *Annual Statistical Reports*, New York. *Basing Points and Competition in Steel*, New York, 1935.

AMERICAN PETROLEUM INSTITUTE. *Recent Rises in the Price of Petroleum*, annual meeting, 1927.

ANDREWS, E. B. "Trusts According to Official Investigations," *Quart. Jour. Econ.*, 3: 117 (1889).

BARNEY AND COMPANY. *The Tobacco Industry*, New York (annually).

BEATY, A. L. "The Petroleum Triangle," at annual meeting of American Petroleum Institute, 1924.

BEDFORD, A. C. (Chairman of Board of Standard Oil Company of New Jersey). "The Oil Industry," at annual meeting of American Petroleum Institute, December, 1922.

BELCHER, W. E. "Industrial Pooling Agreements," *Quart. Jour. Econ.*, 19: 111 (1904).

BELL, S. "Fixed Costs and Market Price," *Quart. Jour. Econ.*, 32: 511 (1918).

BERGLUND, A. Discussion in *Proceedings of the American Economic Association*, 1931. "The United States Steel Corporation and Industrial Stabilization," *Quart. Jour. Econ.*, 38: 607 (1924).

"The United States Steel Corporation and Price Stabilization," *Quart. Jour. Econ.*, 38: 1 (1923).

BERLE, A. A., and G. C. MEANS. *The Corporation and Private Property*, New York, 1932.

BERLE, A. A., and others. *America's Recovery Program*, New York, 1934.

BLAISDELL, T. C. *The Federal Trade Commission*, New York, 1932.

BRAITHWAITE, D. "The Economic Effects of Advertisement," *Econ. Jour.*, 38: 17 (1928).

BRANDEIS, L. D. *The Curse of Bigness*, New York, 1935.

BROWN, G. S. "Economics and Portland Cement Prices," *Amer. Econ. Rev.*, 15: 77 (1925).

BUREAU OF RAILWAY ECONOMICS. *Commodity Prices* (Bulletin 28), Washington, 1927.

BURNS, A. R. "The Process of Industrial Concentration," *Quart. Jour. Econ.*, 47: 277 (1933).

"The First Phase of the National Industrial Recovery Act of 1933," *Polit. Sci. Quart.*, 49: 161 (1934).

CARDOZO, B. N. *The Growth of the Law*, New Haven, 1924.

CHAMBERLIN, EDWARD H. *The Theory of Monopolistic Competition*, Cambridge, 1933.

CLARK, E. W. *Presidential Address*, meeting, American Petroleum Institute, 1927.

CLARK, J. M. *Studies in the Economics of Overhead Costs*, Chicago, 1923.
CLEMEN, R. A. *The American Livestock and Meat Industry*, New York, 1923.
CLEVELAND TRUST COMPANY, *Business Bulletin*, May, 1927.
COMMONS, J. R. "Delivered Price Practice in the Steel Market," *Amer. Econ. Rev.*, 14: 505 (1924).
COMPTON, WILSON. *The Organization of the American Lumber Industry*, Chicago, 1916.
"Price Problems in the Lumber Industry," *Amer. Econ. Rev.*, 7: 582 (1917).
"Will the Lumber Industry Settle Up or Down?" Annual Conference of National Lumber Manufacturers Association, Chicago, 1925.
"Is the 'Future' of Lumber Ahead or Behind?" National Lumber Trade Extension Conference, Chicago, Ill., Feb. 15, 1926.
COPELAND, M. A. "How Large Is Our National Income?" *Jour. Polit. Econ.*, 40: 1 (1932).
COPELAND, M. T., and E. P. LEARNED. *Merchandising of Cotton Textiles*, Boston, 1933.
COX, R. *Competition in the American Tobacco Industry*, New York, 1932.
CROWELL PUBLISHING COMPANY. *National Markets and National Advertising*, New York, 1922.
CURRIE, L. B. "The Failure of Monetary Policy to Prevent the Depression of 1929–1932," *Jour. Polit. Econ.*, 42: 162 (1933).
CURTIS PUBLISHING COMPANY, *Leading Advertisers 1922 to 1931*, Philadelphia, 1932.
DEARING, C. L., and others. *The A.B.C. of the N.R.A.*, Brookings Institution, Washington, D.C., 1934.
DEWING, A. S. *Corporate Promotions and Reorganizations*, Cambridge, 1914.
"A Statistical Test of the Success of Consolidations," *Quart. Jour. Econ.*, 36: 84 (1921).
Financial Policy of Corporations, New York, 1926.
DUNCAN, C. S. "The Chicago Milk Inquiry," *Jour. Polit. Econ.*, 26: 321 (1918).
DURAND, E. D. *The Trust Problem*, Cambridge, 1915.
EDDY, A. J. *The New Competition* (5th ed.), Chicago, 1916.
EDGERTON, C. E. "The Wire Nail Association of 1895–1896," *Polit. Sci. Quart.*, 12: 246 (1897).
ENGINEERING NEWS-RECORD. *Construction Costs 1910–1929*, New York, 1930.
EPSTEIN, R. C. *Industrial Profits in the United States*, New York, 1935.
FETTER, F. A. "The Economic Law of Market Areas," *Quart. Jour. Econ.*, 38: 520 (1924).
The Masquerade of Monopoly, New York, 1931
FLÜGGE, E. "Possibilities and Problems of Integration in the Automobile Industry," *Jour. Polit. Econ.*, 37: 150 (1929).
FRAME, S. T. "Planning for the Newsprint Industry," *Harvard Bus. Rev.*, 10: 447 (1932).
FRANK, L. K. "The Significance of Industrial Integration," *Jour. Polit. Econ.*, 33: 179 (1925).
FRASER, C. E. "The Readjustment of Retail and Wholesale Operating Expenses," *Harvard Bus. Rev.*, 1: 212 (1923).
FRASER, C. E., and G. F. DORIOT. *Analyzing Our Industries*, New York, 1932.
HAMILTON, W. H., and H. R. WRIGHT. *The Case of Bituminous Coal*, New York, 1926.

HANDLER, M. "The Jurisdiction of the Federal Trade Commission over False Advertising," *Columbia Law Rev.*, 31: 527 (1931).
"Industrial Mergers," *Columbia Law Rev.*, 32: 179 (1932).
(Editor). *The Federal Anti-Trust Laws*, New York, 1932.
HANEY, L. H. "Price Fixing in a Competitive Industry," *Amer. Econ. Rev.*, 9: 47 (1919).
HANSEN, A. H., and H. TOUT. "Investment and Saving in Business Cycle Theory," *Econometrica*, 1: 147 (1933).
HOTELLING, H. "Stability in Competition," *Econ. Jour.*, 39: 41 (1929).
JAVITS, B. A. *Business and the Public Interest*, New York, 1932.
JENKS, J. W. "The Development of the Whisky Trust," *Polit. Sci. Quart.*, 4: 296 (1889).
"Recent Legislation and Adjudication on Trusts," *Quart. Jour. Econ.*, 12: 461 (1898).
JENKS, J. W., and W. E. CLARK. *The Trust Problem* (5th ed.), Garden City, New York, 1929.
JOHNSON, H. S. *The Blue Eagle from Egg to Earth*, New York, 1935.
JONES, ELIOT, *The Anthracite Coal Combination in the United States*, Cambridge, Mass., 1914.
"Is Competition in Industry Ruinous?" *Quart. Jour. Econ.*, 34: 473 (1920).
The Trust Problem in the United States, New York, 1921.
JONES, F. D. *Trade Association Activities and the Law*, New York, 1922.
KALDOR, N. "Market Imperfection and Excess Capacity," *Economica*, 2: 33 (1935).
KIESSLING, O. W. *Cooperative Development of Oil Pools* (Technical Publication 28, American Institute of Mining and Metallurgical Engineers), 1927.
KING, W. I. *Employment Hours and Earnings in Prosperity and Depression*, New York, 1923.
LIEFMAN, R. *Cartels, Concerns, and Trusts*, New York, 1932.
LYON, L. S., and others. *The National Recovery Administration*, Brookings Institution, Washington, D.C., 1935.
MACCALLUM, E. D. *The Iron and Steel Industry in the United States*, London, 1931.
MACGREGOR, D. H. *Industrial Combination*, London, 1906.
"Rationalization of Industry," *Econ. Jour.*, 37: 521 (1927).
MARQUAND, H. A. *Dynamics of Industrial Concentration*, London, 1931.
MARSHALL, ALFRED. *Principles of Economics* (8th ed.), London, 1920.
Industry and Trade, London, 1920.
MCLAUGHLIN, J. A. *Cases on the Federal Anti-Trust Laws of the United States*, New York, 1930.
MEADE, E. S. "The Capitalization of the United States Steel Corporation," *Quart. Jour. Econ.*, 16: 214 (1902).
"The Price Policy of the United States Steel Corporation," *Quart. Jour. Econ.*, 22: 452 (1908).
MEANS, G. C. "The Large Corporation," *Amer. Econ. Rev.*, 21: 29 (1931).
Review of Fetter, F. W., *Masquerade of Monopoly*, *Columbia Law Rev.*, 32: 389 (1932).
Industrial Prices and Their Relative Stability (Senate Doc. 13, 74 Cong. 1st Sess.) 1935.
MILLS, F. C. *The Behavior of Prices*, New York, 1927.
Economic Tendencies, New York, 1932.

MITCHELL, W. C. *Business Cycles*, New York, 1927.
MONTAGUE, G. H. *The Rise and Progress of the Standard Oil Company*, New York, 1903.
MONTGOMERY, D. E. "Government and the Theory of Competition," *Amer. Econ. Rev.*, 15: 440 (1925).
MURCHISON, C. T. "Stabilization in the Cotton Textile Industry," *Proceedings of American Economic Association*, 1932, 77.
NATIONAL ASSOCIATION OF COST ACCOUNTANTS. *Yearbook*, 1923.
NATIONAL BUREAU OF ECONOMIC RESEARCH. *Recent Economic Changes in the United States*, New York, 1929.
Business Cycles and Unemployment, New York, 1923.
Bulletin 44 (1933).
Bulletin 50 (1934).
NATIONAL INDUSTRIAL CONFERENCE BOARD. *Trade Associations*, New York, 1925.
Public Regulation of Competitive Practices, New York, 1925.
Mergers in Industry, New York, 1929.
Rationalization of German Industry, New York, 1931.
NATIONAL LUMBER MANUFACTURERS ASSOCIATION. *Brief*, 1916.
Bulletin, Washington, D.C., 1922 to 1926.
NELSON, M. N. *Open Price Associations*, Urbana, Ill., 1923.
NICHOL, A. J. *Partial Monopoly and Price Leadership*, Philadelphia, Pa., 1930.
NOURSE, E. G., and associates. *America's Capacity to Produce*, Brookings Institution, Washington, D.C., 1934.
NYSTROM, P. H. *Economics of Fashion*, New York, 1928.
Fashion Merchandising, New York, 1932.
ORCHARD, J. E. "Proposal for Regulation of Coal Industry," *Quart. Jour. Econ.*, 39: 196 (1925).
PIGOU, A. C. "An Analysis of Supply," *Econ. Jour.*, 38: 238 (1928).
Industrial Fluctuations (2d ed.), London, 1929.
POGUE, JOHN E. *The Economics of Petroleum*, New York, 1921.
READ, T. T. "Valorization in the Metal Industry," *Polit. Sci. Quart.*, 47: 238 (1932).
RIPLEY, W. Z. *Railroad Rates and Regulation*, New York, 1912.
(Editor). *Trusts, Pools, and Corporations*, Boston, 1905.
ROBINSON, E. A. G. *Structure of Competitive Industry*, New York, 1932.
ROBINSON, JOAN, *The Economics of Imperfect Competition*, London, 1933.
"What is Perfect Competition?" *Quart. Jour. Econ.*, 49: 104 (1934).
SAKOLSKI, A. "Price Making and Price Stability," *Harvard Bus. Rev.*, 3: 204 (1925).
SCHULTZ, H. "Theoretical Considerations Relating to Supply," *Jour. Polit. Econ.*, 35: 437 (1927).
SEAGER, H. R., and C. A. GULICK. *Trust and Corporation Problems*, New York, 1929.
SHARFMAN, I. L. "The Trade Association Movement," *Amer. Econ. Rev.*, Supplement, 1926, 203.
SLOAN, L. H. *Corporation Profits*, New York, 1929.
SMITH, A. *Wealth of Nations* (Editor Edwin Cannan).
SOUTER, R. W. "Modern Monopoly as the Gentleman Crook," *Polit. Sci. Quart.*, 48: 240 (1933).
SPURR, J. E., and F. E. WORMSER (Editors). *The Marketing of Metals and Minerals*, New York, 1925.
STARCH, D. *Principles of Advertising*, New York, 1923.

BIBLIOGRAPHY

STEPHENS, GEORGE A. "Determinants of Lumber Prices," *Amer. Econ. Rev.*, 7: 289 (1917).
STEVENS, W. S. *Industrial Combinations and Trusts*, New York, 1913.
Unfair Competition, Chicago, 1917.
STOCKING, G. W. *The Oil Industry and the Competitive System*, New York, 1925.
SUMMERS, N. B. "Comparison of the Rates of Earnings of Large Scale and Small Scale Industries," *Quart. Jour. Econ.*, 46: 463 (1932).
SWIFT AND COMPANY. *Statement on the Summary of the Report of the Federal Trade Commission on the Meat Packing Industry*, Aug. 19, 1918.
Rejoinder to Statement of Federal Trade Commission, Oct. 29, 1918.
Analysis and Criticism of Part II of Report of Federal Trade Commission on the Meat Packing Industry, Apr. 5, 1919.
Prices of Pork Products: Hams and Bacon, 1923.
Prices of Pork Products: Pork Loins, 1922.
Prices of Pork Products: Lard, 1923.
Seasonal Influences on Receipts and Prices of Cattle and Beef, 1921.
TAUSSIG, F. W. "Price Fixing as Seen by a Price Fixer," *Quart. Jour. Econ.*, 33: 205 (1919).
"Is Market Price Determinate?" *Quart. Jour. Econ.*, 35: 394 (1921).
TERBORGH, G. *Price Control Devices in N.R.A. Codes*, Brookings Institution, Washington, D.C., 1934.
THORP, W. L. *The Integration of Industrial Operation* (Census Monograph III), Washington, D.C., 1924.
TOSDAL, H. R. "The Tobacco Industry Since the Dissolution of the Trust," *Quart. Jour. Econ.*, 29: 848 (1915).
UNITED KINGDOM OF GREAT BRITAIN AND NORTHERN IRELAND.
ROYAL COMMISSION ON THE COAL INDUSTRY.
Report (Cmd. 2600), 1926.
(BALFOUR) COMMISSION ON INDUSTRY AND TRADE.
Factors in Industrial Efficiency, 1929.
Final Report, 1929.
UNIVERSITY OF ILLINOIS, AGRICULTURAL EXPERIMENT STATION. *Marketing of Milk in the Chicago Dairy District* (Bulletin 269), 1925.
VANDERBLUE, H. B. and W. L. CRUM. *The Iron Industry in Prosperity and Depression*, New York, 1927.
VAUGHAN, F. L. *Economics of Our Patent System*, New York, 1925.
VINER, J. "Objective Tests of Competitive Price Applied to the Cement Industry," *Jour. Polit. Econ.*, 33: 107 (1925).
VON BECKERATH, H. *Modern Industrial Organization*, New York, 1933.
WALKER, F. "The Beef Trust and the United States Government," *Econ. Jour.*, 16: 491 (1906).
WALLACE, H. C. "Livestock, the Basic Raw Material of the Packing Industry," in *The Packing Industry*, Institute of American Meat Packers, Chicago, 1923.
WARRINER, D. *Combines and Rationalization in Germany*, London, 1931.
WATKINS, M. W. "The Federal Trade Commission," *Quart. Jour. Econ.*, 40: 561 (1926).
Industrial Combinations and Public Policy, Boston, 1927.
WELCH, L. M. *The Recent Increases in the Prices of Petroleum and Its Products*, American Petroleum Institute, 1920.

WELD, L. D. H. "The Meat Packing Investigation," *Quart. Jour. Econ.*, 35: 412 (1921).
"The Packing Industry, Its History and General Economics," in *The Packing Industry*, Institute of American Meat Packers, Chicago, 1923.
WHITNEY, S. N. *Trade Associations and Public Policy*, New York, 1934.
WILLIS, H. P., and J. R. B. BYERS. *Portland Cement Prices*, New York, 1924.

II. PUBLICATIONS OF THE UNITED STATES GOVERNMENT

COAL COMMISSION. *Report*, 1923.
COMMISSIONER OF CORPORATIONS.
  The International Harvester Company, 1913.
  The Lumber Industry, 1914.
  The Petroleum Industry, 2 vols., 1907.
  The Steel Industry, 3 vols., 1911 to 1913.
  The Tobacco Industry, 3 vols., 1905 to 1915.
CONGRESS, HOUSE OF REPRESENTATIVES.
  Preliminary Report on Communications Companies (pursuant to H.R. 59, 72d Cong.), 73d Cong. 2d Sess., 1934.
  COMMITTEE ON AGRICULTURE.
    Hearings on Meat Packer Legislation (Anderson Bill), February, 1920.
  COMMITTEE ON INTERSTATE AND FOREIGN COMMERCE.
    Hearings on Government Control of the Meat Packing Industry (H.R. 13324), 65th Cong. 3d Sess., 1918, 1919.
CONGRESS, SENATE.
  COMMITTEE ON AGRICULTURE AND FORESTRY.
    Hearings on the Amendments to the Packers and Stockyards Acts (S.R. 3676 and 4387), 1926.
    Hearings on the Packer Consent Decree (S.R. 211), 1923.
    Hearings on the Price of Food Products (S.R. 374), 1931.
    Hearings on Proposed Merger of Meat Packing Corporations (S.R. 389), 1923.
  COMMITTEE ON INTERSTATE COMMERCE.
    Hearings on the Control of Corporations (S.R. 98), 1912.
  COMMITTEE ON JUDICIARY.
    Hearings on the Aluminum Company of America (S.R. 109), 69th Cong. 1st Sess., 1926.
    Hearings on the Amendment of the Federal Trade Commission Act (S.R. 2626, 2627, 2628), 72d Cong. 1st Sess., 1932.
  COMMITTEE ON MANUFACTURES.
    Hearings (Subcommittee) on the Establishment of a National Economic Council (S.R. 6215, 71st Cong.), 72d Cong. 1st Sess., 1931.
    Report on High Cost of Gasoline and other Petroleum Products (S.R. 295), 1923.
  SENATE DOCUMENTS.
    Fluctuations in Wheat Prices (No. 135, 69th Cong. 1st Sess.), 1926.
    Letter from the Chairman of the Federal Trade Commission re Mergers of Iron and Steel Companies (No. 208, 67th Cong. 2d Sess.), 1924.
    Open Price Trade Associations (No. 226, 70th Cong. 2d Sess.), 1930.
    Report of Special Assistant to the Attorney General on the Aluminum Company of America (No. 67, 69th Cong. 1st Sess.), 1926.

BIBLIOGRAPHY 597

DEPARTMENT OF AGRICULTURE.
Agricultural Cooperative Associations (Technical Bulletin 40), 1928.
American Forests and Forest Products (Statistical Bulletin 21), 1927.
Factors Affecting the Price of Hogs (Bulletin 1440), 1926.
Farmers' Cooperative Associations in the United States (Circular 94), 1929.
Geographical Phase of Farm Prices: Oats (Bulletin 755), 1919.
Geography of Wheat Prices (Bulletin 594), 1918.
Legal Phases of Cooperative Associations (Bulletin 1106), 1922.
Lumber Cut of the United States, 1870–1920 (Bulletin 1119), 1923.
Secretary of Agriculture v. Armour & Co. before the Secretary of Agriculture. *Conclusion and Order* (Docket 19), 1925.
Some Economic Aspects of the Marketing of Milk and Cream in New England (Circular 16), 1927.
Some Public and Economic Aspects of the Lumber Industry (Report 114), 1917.
Summary of Cases and Decisions on the Legal Phase of Cooperation (mimeographed), Numbers 1–5; 1924–1928.
Timber Depletion, Lumber Prices, Lumber Exports, and Concentration of Timber Ownership (Forest Service), 1920.
DEPARTMENT OF COMMERCE.
Trade Association Activities, 1923.
DEPARTMENT OF COMMERCE, BUREAU OF MINES.
Mineral Resources of the United States.
DEPARTMENT OF JUSTICE.
Decrees and Judgments in Federal Anti-Trust Cases, 1918.
Federal Anti-Trust Laws with Amendments, 1926.
Report of Special Assistant to Attorney General Concerning Alleged Violation by Aluminum Corporation of America of Decree Against It, 1926.
DEPARTMENT OF LABOR, BUREAU OF LABOR STATISTICS.
The Trend of Wholesale Prices, June, 1929, *to* 1933 (mimeographed).
Wholesale Price Series and Retail Price Series Covering the Period 1914–1933.
Wholesale Prices 1913–1928, 1929 (Bulletin 493).
FEDERAL FARM BOARD. *Annual Reports*, 1930–1932.
FEDERAL TRADE COMMISSION.
Advance in Prices of Petroleum Products, 1920.
Annual Reports.
Applications, Answers, and Statements Concerning the So-called Pittsburgh Basing Point for Steel, 1919.
Bakery Combines and Profits, 1927.
Basing Point System in the Steel Industry, 1935.
Calcium Arsenate Industry, 1923.
Canned Foods: General Report on Canned Vegetables and Fruits, 1918.
Canned Milk, 1921.
Canned Salmon, 1918.
Cement Industry, 1933.
Chain Store Advertising, 1934.
Chain Store Price Policies, 1934.
Chain Stores, 1932.
Chain Stores (Final Report), 1935.

Combed Cotton Yarns, 1921.
Commercial Feeds, 1921.
Commercial Wheat Flour Milling, 1920.
Competition and Profits in Bread and Flour, 1928 (Senate Doc. 98, 70th Cong. 1st Sess.).
Competitive Conditions in Flour Milling, 1926.
Cost Reports: Copper, 1919.
Cotton Trade, 1924.
Digest of replies in response to an inquiry of the F.T.C. relative to the practice of giving guarantees against price decline, 1920.
Fertilizer Industry, 1916.
Fertilizer Industry, 1923.
Flour Milling Industry, 1926.
Fundamentals of a Cost System for Manufacturers, 1916.
Gasoline Prices in 1924 (Letter of Submittal).
Gasoline Prices (Senate Doc. 178, 73d Cong. 2d Sess.), 1934.
Grain Trade, 7 vols., 1920–1926.
High Prices of Farm Implements, 1920.
House Furnishings Industries, 3 vols., 1923, 1924, 1925.
Leather and Shoe Industries, 1919.
Lumber Manufacturers Trade Associations, 1922.
Meat Packing, report of July 3, 1918.
Meat Packing Industry, 6 vols., 1919.
Milk and Milk Products, 1921.
Newsprint Paper Industry, 1917.
Newsprint Paper Industry, 1930.
Northern Hemlock and Hardwood Manufacturers Association, 1923.
Open Price Trade Associations, 1929.
Pacific Coast Petroleum Industry, 2 vols., 1921.
Packer Consent Decree, 1924 (Senate Doc. 219, 68th Cong. 2d Sess.).
Petroleum Industry, 1920.
Petroleum Industry in Wyoming and Montana, 1922.
Pipe Line Transportation of Petroleum, 1916.
Pittsburgh Plus: Federal Trade Commission v. U.S. Steel Corp., before the Federal Trade Commission (Docket 760).
    Statement of Case.
    Brief for F.T.C. (1924).
    Brief for U.S. Steel Corp.
    Brief for Amici Curiae.
Practices of the Steel Industry under the Code, 1934.
Premium Prices of Anthracite, 1925.
Price Bases Inquiry, 1932.
Price of Gasoline in 1915, 1917.
Prices, Profits, and Competition in the Petroleum Industry, 1928.
Prices of Tobacco Products, 1922 (published in 1926 as Senate Doc. 34, 69th Cong. 1st Sess.).
Resale Price Maintenance, 2 vols. 1929 and 1931.
Shoe and Leather Costs and Prices, 1921.
Southern Pine Lumber, 1922.

BIBLIOGRAPHY

Sugar Industry, 1917.
Sugar Supply and Prices, 1920.
Tobacco Industry, 1920.
Wartime Costs and Profits of Southern Pine Lumber Companies, 1922.
Wartime Costs and Profits of the Steel Industry, 1925.
Wealth and Income in the United States, 1926.
Western Red Cedar Association, 1923.
Wheat Flour Milling Industry, 1924.
Wholesale Marketing of Food, 1920.

FUEL ADMINISTRATION. *Prices and Marketing Practices for Gasoline*, 1919.

INTERSTATE COMMERCE COMMISSION.
Railroad Discriminations and Monopolies in Oil (H.R. Doc. 606, 59th Cong. 2d Sess.), 1907.
Reciprocal Purchasing Agreements (Docket 22455), 1932.

NATIONAL RECOVERY ADMINISTRATION (all mimeographed).
Operation of the Basing Point System in the Iron and Steel Industry (Report, Supplement No. 1, and Appendices A, B, C, D, and E), 1935.
BOARD OF REVIEW ("DARROW BOARD"). *Reports* (unpublished, cit. *New York Times*, May 21, 1934).
CONSUMER ADVISORY BOARD.
Brief on Steel Complaints, 1933 (?).
Consumers Cooperatives Distributing Oil and Gasoline, March, 1934.
Effect of Price Control and Price Stabilization on the Construction Industry (statement by J. M. Hadley at price hearing on Jan. 9, 1935).
Emergency Price Experience (statement by Ben W. Lewis at price hearing Jan. 9, 1935).
Experience with Price Fixing under the Codes (statement by Corwin D. Edwards at price hearing Jan. 9, 1935).
Extras on Tool Steels, 1933 (?).
Fixing Coal Prices (statement by W. L. Chandler at price hearing Jan. 9, 1935).
General Statement for the Consumer Advisory Board at price hearing on Jan. 9, 1935, by Dexter M. Keezer.
Memorandum on Suggestions for Code Revision, and Appendices, Feb. 19, 1934.
Oil Price Fixing, 1933 (?).
Paper Complaints, 1933 (?).
Price Control through Limitation of Production in the Mackerel Fishing Code (statement by George M. Haddock at price hearing on Jan. 9, 1935).
Price Fixing in the Lumber Industry (statement by Constant Southworth at price hearing Jan. 9, 1935).
Prices of Bituminous Coal, 1933 (?).
Prices in Relation to Consumer Income (statement by L. F. Boffey at price hearing, Jan. 9, 1935).
Prices and Standards of Quality (statement by T. C. Blaisdell at price hearing Jan. 9, 1935).
Private Price Control and Code Policy (statement by Ruth Ayres and Enid Baird at price hearing on Jan. 9, 1935).
Regulating Channels of Trade in the Plumbing Fixtures Industry (statement by Leander Lovell at price hearing on Jan. 9, 1935).

Statement by chairman of Consumer Advisory Board before Finance Committee of the U.S. Senate, Apr. 1, 1935.
Statement at hearing on Lumber Code, Jan. 9, 1934.
NATIONAL RECOVERY BOARD.
Code Revision Memorandum No. 1: Evolution of Trade Practice Policies, 1935.
Report on the Effects of Executive Order 6767 upon the maintenance of standards of fair competition in sales to public and to private customers, Apr. 8, 1935.
RESEARCH AND PLANNING DIVISION.
Aluminum Industry, April, 1935.
Building Material Prices, January, 1935.
Charts on the Operation of the National Industrial Recovery Act, 1935.
Condensed Information Based on the Operation of the National Industrial Recovery Act, February, 1935.
Tables on the Operation of the National Industrial Recovery Act, 1935.
TARIFF COMMISSION.
Aluminum, 1921.
Cement, 1932.
Cotton Sewing Thread and Cottons for Handwork (Tariff Information Survey), 1927.
Red Cedar Shingle Industry, 1927.
TREASURY.
BUREAU OF INTERNAL REVENUE. *Statistics of Income.*
COMPTROLLER OF THE CURRENCY. *Instructions of the Comptroller of the Currency Relative to the Organization and Powers of National Banks*, 1928.

III. COURT PAPERS

Addyston Pipe and Steel Co. v. U.S., 175 U.S. 211 (1899).
Brief for U.S.
Brief for Addyston Pipe and Steel Co.
Supplemental Brief for Addyston Pipe and Steel Co.
American Column and Lumber Co. *et al.* v. U.S., 257 U.S. 377 (1921).
Supplemental Brief for U.S.
Bandini Petroleum Co. *et al.* v. Superior Court of the State of California, 284 U.S. 8 (1931).
Bauer et Cie. v. O'Donnell, 229 U.S. 1 (1913).
Beech-Nut Packing Co. v. F.T.C., 257 U.S. 441 (1922).
Bigelow v. Calumet-Hecla, 167 Fed. 704 (1908).
Blount Manufacturing Co. v. Yale and Towne Manufacturing Co., 166 Fed. 555 (1909).
Butterick *et al.* v. F.T.C., 267 U.S. 602 (1925).
Cement Manufacturers Protective Association *et al.* v. U.S., 268 U.S. 588 (1925).
Record.
Brief for Cement Manufacturers Protective Association.
Brief for U.S.
Champlain Refining Co. v. Corporation Commission of the State of Oklahoma *et al.*, 286 U.S. 210 (1932).
Chesapeake and Ohio Fuel Co. v. U.S., 115 Fed. 610 (1902).
Continental Paper Bag Co. v. Eastern Paper Bag Co., 210 U.S. 405 (1908).
Continental Wall Paper Co. v. Voigt and Sons, 148 Fed. 947 (1906), 212 U.S. 227 (1909).

BIBLIOGRAPHY

Brief for Respondents.
Petitioners' Points.
Cream of Wheat Co. v. F.T.C., 14 Fed. (2d) 40 (1926).
De Forrest Radio Co. v. Radio Corp. of America *et al.*, 24 Fed. (2d) 565 (1928), 28 Fed. (2d) 257 (1928), 35 Fed. (2d) 962 (1929), 283 U.S. 847 (1931).
Dr. Miles Medical Co. v. Park Sons Co., 220 U.S. 373 (1911).
Ellis v. Inman Poulsen and Co., 131 Fed. 182 (1904).
Evart Manufacturing Co. v. Baldwin Cycle Chain Co., 91 Fed. 262 (1898).
F.T.C. v. Curtis Publishing Co., 260 U.S. 568 (1923).
F.T.C. v. Mennen Co., 288 Fed. 778 (1923).
F.T.C. v. National Biscuit Co. and Loose-Wiles Biscuit Co., 299 Fed. 733 (1924).
F.T.C. v. Paramount-Famous Players-Lasky Corp. 57 Fed. (2d) 152 (1932).
F.T.C. v. Thatcher Manufacturing Co., 5 Fed. (2d) 615 (1925).
Fox v. Standard Oil Co. of New Jersey, 55 Sup. Ct. 335 (1935).
Geddes v. Anaconda Copper Mining Co., 254 U.S. 590 (1921).
Brief for Appellees.
Great Atlantic and Pacific Tea Co. v. Cream of Wheat Co., 224 Fed. 566 (1915), 227 Fed. 46 (1916).
Great Atlantic and Pacific Tea Co. v. Maxwell, 284 U.S. 575 (1931).
Halloran v. American Sea Green Slate Co., 207 Fed. 187 (1913).
Heaten-Peninsular Button Fastener Co. v. Eureka Specialty Co., 77 Fed. 288 (1896).
Henry v. A. B. Dick Co., 224 U.S. 1 (1912).
Hoe v. Knap, 27 Fed. 204 (1896).
Indiana Manufacturing Co. v. J. I. Case Threshing Machine Co., 154 Fed. 365 (1907).
International Harvester Co. v. Kentucky, 234 U.S. 216 (1914).
International Shoe Co. v. F.T.C., 280 U.S. 291 (1930).
Liggett and Co. v. Lee, 288 U.S. 517 (1933).
Maple Flooring Manufacturers Association v. U.S., 268 U.S. 563 (1925).
Brief for U.S.
Brief for Maple Flooring Manufacturers Association.
Petition by Attorney General for Rehearing.
Reply Brief for Maple Flooring Manufacturers Association.
Mennen Co. v. F.T.C., 288 Fed. 774 (1923).
Montague v. Lowry, 193 U.S. 38 (1904).
Motion Picture Patents Co. v. Universal Film Manufacturing Co. *et al.*, 243 U.S. 502 (1917).
National Association of Window Glass Manufacturers v. U.S., 263 U.S. 403 (1923).
National Biscuit Co. v. F.T.C., 299 Fed. 733 (1924).
National Harrow Co. v. Bement, 186 U.S. 70 (1902).
Northern Securities Co. v. U.S., 193 U.S. 197 (1904).
Panama Refining Co. *et al.* v. Ryan *et al.*, 55 Sup. Ct., 241 (1935).
Pearsall B.S. Butter Co. v. F.T.C., 292 Fed. 720 (1923).
Pipe Line Cases, 234 U.S. 548 (1914).
Q.R.S. Music Co. v. F.T.C., 12 Fed. (2d) 730 (1926).
Raladam Co. v. F.T.C., 42 Fed. (2d) 430 (1930).
Rogers v. Hill, 289 U.S. 582 (1933).
Schechter Poultry Corp. *et al.* v. U.S., 55 Sup. Ct. 837 (1935).
Sears, Roebuck and Co. v. F.T.C., 258 Fed. 307 (1919).

Standard Fashion Co. v. Magraine Houston Co., 258 U.S. 346 (1922).
Standard Oil Co. of Indiana v. U.S., 283 U.S. 163 (1931).
Standard Sanitary Manufacturing Co. v. U.S., 226 U.S. 20 (1912).
Brief for Standard Sanitary Manufacturing Co.
Brief for U.S.
Tax Commissioners (of Indiana) v. Jackson, 283 U.S. 527 (1931).
Temple Anthracite Coal Co. v. F.T.C., 51 Fed. (2d) 656 (1931).
Thatcher Manufacturing Co. v. F.T.C., 272 U.S. 554 (1926).
U.S. v. Aluminum Co. of America.
Petition in District Court of Western Pennsylvania.
Reply Brief for Aluminum Co.
U.S. v. American Can Co. *et al.*, 230 Fed. 859 (1916).
Summary of Evidence.
Brief for American Can Co.
Brief for U.S.
U.S. v. American Linseed Co. *et al.*, 262 U.S. 371 (1923).
Record.
Brief for American Linseed Co.
Brief for Amici Curiae.
Brief for Ankeney Linseed Co.
Brief for U.S.
U.S. v. American Thread Co., *Petition* in Equity.
U.S. v. American Tobacco Co., 164 Fed. 700 (1908), 221 U.S. 106 (1911).
Record.
Brief for U.S.
U.S. v. Appalachian Coals, Inc., 288 U.S. 344 (1933).
U.S. v. Colgate and Co., 250 U.S. 300 (1919).
U.S. v. Corn Products Refining Co. *et al.*, 234 Fed. 964 (1916).
U.S. v. Delaware and Hudson Co., 213 U.S. 366 (1909).
U.S. v. Delaware, Lackawanna and Western Railroad Co., 238 U.S. 516 (1915).
U.S. v. E. I. Du Pont de Nemours and Co., 188 Fed. 127 (1911).
Pleadings.
U.S. v. General Electric Co.; *Decree* of Circuit Court of Oct. 12, 1911, *cit.* U.S. Dept. of Justice, *Decrees and Judgments in Anti-Trust Cases.*
U.S. v. General Electric Co., 272 U.S. 476 (1926).
U.S. v. Hollis *et al.*, 246 Fed. 611 (1917).
U.S. v. International Harvester Co., 214 Fed. 987 (1914), 10 Fed. (2d) 827 (1926), 274 U.S. 693 (1927).
Record.
Brief and Argument for International Harvester Co.
Brief for U.S.
Brief for U.S. (Reargument).
Reply Brief for International Harvester Co. (Reargument).
Appendix to Defendant's Brief.
U.S. v. Joint Traffic Association, 171 U.S. 505 (1898).
U.S. v. Keystone Watch Case Co., 218 Fed. 502 (1915).
Petition in Equity.
U.S. v. E. C. Knight and Co., 156 U.S. 1 (1895).
Brief for U.S.

BIBLIOGRAPHY

U.S. v. Lehigh Valley Railroad, 254 U.S. 255 (1920).
U.S. v. National Association of Window Glass Manufacturers, 263 U.S. 403 (1923).
U.S. v. National Cash Register Co.; *Petition*, 1911.
U.S. v. New Departure Manufacturing Co., 204 Fed. 107 (1913).
U.S. v. Patten, 226 U.S. 525 (1913).
U.S. v. Quaker Oats Co., 232 Fed. 499 (1916).
Brief for Quaker Oats Co.
Petitioner's Summary of Evidence.
U.S. v. Radio Corp. of America *et al.*
Decree in Federal District Court of the District of Delaware, Nov. 21, 1932.
U.S. v. Reading Co., 226 U.S. 324 (1912).
Record.
Brief for Enterprise Coal Co.
Brief for Reading Co.
Brief for U.S.
U.S. v. Reading Co., 228 U.S. 158 (1913).
U.S. v. Reading Co., 253 U.S. 26 (1920).
Record.
Brief for U.S.
Brief for Reading Co.
U.S. v. Reading Co., 259 U.S. 156 (1922).
U.S. v. Schechter Poultry Corp. *et al.*, 55 Sup. Ct. 837 (1935).
U.S. v. Schraders Sons, Inc., 252 U.S. 85 (1920).
U.S. v. Standard Oil Co. of New Jersey, 173 Fed. 177 (1909), 221 U.S. 1 (1911).
Brief on Facts for Standard Oil Co. (Circuit Court).
Brief for Standard Oil Co.
Brief for U.S.
Supplementary Brief for U.S.
U.S. v. Standard Oil Co. of New York and Vacuum Oil Co., 47 Fed. (2d) 288 (1931).
Brief for Standard Oil Co. and Vacuum Oil Co.
Brief for U.S.
Rejoinder Brief for Standard Oil Co. and Vacuum Oil Co.
Answer to Supplemental Petition.
Summary of Evidence.
U.S. v. Standard Sanitary Manufacturing Co. *et al.*, 226 U.S. 20 (1912).
Brief for Standard Sanitary Manufacturing Co.
Brief for U.S.
Record in Circuit Court of Appeals.
U.S. v. Sugar Institute.
Brief for Sugar Institute on the Facts (District Court).
Brief for U.S.
Decision of Judge Mack in U.S. District Court for Southern District of New York (1934) (mimeographed).
U.S. v. Swift and Co. *et al.*, 196 U.S. 375 (1905).
Brief for Swift and Co.
U.S. v. Swift and Co. *et al.*
Consent Decree in Supreme Court for the District of Columbia, Feb. 27, 1920.
U.S. v. Swift and Co. *et al.*, 276 U.S. 311 (1928).

Brief for Swift and Co. and Armour and Co.
Brief for U.S.
Record in Circuit Court of Appeals.
U.S. v. Swift and Co. *et al.*, 286 U.S. 106 (1931).
Brief for Swift and Co. et al.
Brief for U.S.
U.S. v. Tile Manufacturers Credit Association.
Decree of Nov. 26, 1923, in U.S. District Court for Southern District of Ohio.
U.S. v. Trenton Potteries *et al.*, 273 U.S. 392 (1927).
U.S. v. Union Pacific R.R. Co., 226 U.S. 61 (1912).
U.S. v. United Shoe Machinery Co., 222 Fed. 349 (1915), 247 U.S. 32 (1918).
Brief for U.S.
U.S. v. United Shoe Machinery Co. *et al.*, 264 Fed. 138 (1920), 258 U.S. 451 (1921).
U.S. v. United States Steel Corp. *et al.*, 223 Fed. 55 (1915), 251 U.S. 417 (1920).
Brief for U.S.
Brief for United States Steel Corp.
Record.
Summary of Evidence.
Petition for Rehearing.
U.S. v. Winslow, 227 U.S. 202 (1913).
Brief for U.S.
U.S. v. Wool Institute, Inc.
Petition.
United States Seeded Raisin Co. v. Griffin and Skelly Co., 126 Fed. 364 (1903).
Van Camp and Sons v. American Can Co., 278 U.S. 245 (1929).
Westmoreland, etc. Co. v. Dewitt, 130 Pa. St. 235 (1875).

INDEX

A

Adaptation, of goods, quality competition and, 404
  of production, style competition and, 410
Addyston Pipe case 149, 150
Administrative bodies, personnel of, 572
  social control and, 571
Advertising, 375
  allowances for, 502
  branded goods and, 387
  cooperative, Trade Associations and, 47
  duopoly and, 390
  effect on purchasers, 391
  elasticity of demand and, 27
  false, 416
  increasing expenditure on, 412
  monopoly and, 390
  N.I.R.A. and, 507
  rationality of buyers and, 386
  selling integration and, 446, 447
  social control of, 524, 558
  style competition and, 411
  territorial integration and, 457
  total satisfactions and, 389
  valuation of leisure and, 390
  vertical integration and, 425
  willingness to work and, 390
Agreements, on prices, export trade, 21
  marine insurance, 21
  shipping, 21
  on prices and output, 17, 18, 40
  anti-trust laws and, 3, 20
  on prices and production, in steel industry, 78
Agricultural Adjustment Act, 8, 22
Agricultural Cooperative Marketing Act, 1929, 22
Agricultural implements, cost, 114
  decline in demand, 113
  premium prices, 109
  price leadership, 109-118
  price setting, 198
  price trend, 117
  profits, 116
  quality competition, 400
  selling integration and, 446, 447, 449, 451, 452
  share of International Harvester Company, 111
  size of firms and costs, 115
  stabilization of prices, 217
  and production, 254
  uniformity of prices, 109, 111
  vertical integration, 422, 423, 427, 428
Agriculture, cooperative marketing and, 22
Air Mail Act, 1934, 428

Alcohol, price leadership, 135
  profits, 136
  stability of prices, 136
  trade associations, 135
  trend of prices, 135
  zone prices, 283
Allocation of spending, quality competition and, 402, 405
  sales promotion and, 386
  style competition and, 410
Aluminum, anti-trust laws and, 230
  concentration of control of raw materials, 39
  division of territory, 150
  investment in natural resources, 37
  price discrimination, 276
  stabilization of prices, 229
  trade-association statistics of production, 58
  vertical integration, 424, 441, 444
Aluminum Company of America, 11, 229
American Bell Telephone Company, 16
American Can Company, 11, 17, 129
American Institute of Steel Construction, 83
American Iron and Steel Institute, 79
  price cutting and, 81, 83, 215
American Marconi Company, 12n.
American Petroleum Institute, 100
American Steel and Wire Company, 16
American Telephone and Telegraph Company, 12n., 13
American Tin Plate Company, 17n.
American Tobacco Company, 11, 16, 17, 20
  effect of partition of, 6
Anthracite, concentration of control of, 39
  pools, 147
  potential competition, 188
  premium prices, 120, 126
  price cutting, 120
  price leadership 118-122, 129
  price setting, 198
  price trend, 124, 189
  rationing of mine utilization, 154
  reciprocal purchasing, 172
  reserves, control of, 123, 188
  seasonal discounts, 28
  sharing the market, 123, 166
  stabilization of prices, 216
  uniformity of prices, 119
Anti-trust laws, 2, 523
  agreements on prices and production, 17, 20
  agricultural cooperative marketing, 22
  aluminum, 230
  concentration of industrial control, 19
  conciliation as a means of administration, 579
  cooperative selling, 152
  cooperative selling agency, 18n.
  criteria of control, 568
  dissolutions, 20

605

606 THE DECLINE OF COMPETITION

Anti-trust laws, distribution of business, 19
  exclusive dealing and, 430
  exemptions from, 21
  export trade, 21
  judicial interpretation of, 570
  lack of definition of policy, 588
  marine insurance, 21
  meat packing and, 165, 185
  mergers and, 18, 20
  motive as criterion, 18
  National Industrial Recovery Act and, 22, 464
  partitioning of firms, 20
  patent consolidations and, 14
  patent pooling, 12
  price cutting, 18, 20
  price leadership and, 18, 20, 144, 571
  public opinion and, 585
  resale price maintenance and, 430
  sales promotion, 18
  selling integration, 449
  sharing of market and, 165
  shipping, 21
  size of firms and, 17–20, 571
  territorial integration and, 458
  trade associations and, 44, 54
  tying contracts, 14, 15
  vertical integration, 427
Appalachian Coals, Inc., 18n.
Arbitration by the state, social control and, 582
Asphalt and mastic tiles, zone prices, 282
Asphalt roofing, basing-point prices, 299
Automobile tires, price leadership, 140
  price trend, 233
  vertical integration 425, 440
Automobiles, price policy and production, 251
  price setting, 198
  seasonal price stability, 243
  selling integration, 448
  threat to abandon code under N.I.R.A., 587
  vertical integration and, 422, 424, 434
Aviation, vertical integration, 428

B

Bait sales (*see* Loss leaders)
Bananas, stabilization of price, 231
Basing-point prices, 290–371
  asphalt roofing, 299
  bolts, nuts, and rivets, 299
  building tiles, 299
  cement, 319–321
  comparison of prices and, 63
  consequences, 328
  copper, 296
  corn gluten feed, 294
  cost of production and, 360, 363, 369
  fabrication in transit and, 348
  fertilizers, 297
  foreign competition and, 313
  government purchases and, 313, 321
  interbase-price competition, 357, 361
  interpenetration of territory, 329
  iron, 301, 309, 352
  lead, 299
  leadership and, 357, 359
  level of prices and, 336
  lime, 328

Basing-point prices, location of production and, 330, 331, 333, 335, 337–340, 344, 345, 349, 350, 360, 362
  lumber, 291, 292, 296
  market territory and, 344, 369
  mergers and, 356, 360
  metal laths, 299
  mill nets and, 333
  N.I.R.A. and, 293, 297, 307, 309, 314, 322, 325
  non-basing-point producers, 336
  number of bases, 314, 315, 319, 336, 342
  petroleum, 298
  pig iron (*see* Iron)
  price competition and, 355
  production at basing points, 319, 351
  profits and, 338, 369
  railroad purchases and, 300, 313, 321
  secret rebates, 320
  selling costs and, 364
  sewer pipe, 299
  stability of prices and, 363
  stabilization of cement prices and, 222
  standardization of transportation charges, 310, 312
  steel, 81, 283, 299 ff.
    number of bases, 304
    Pittsburgh plus, 300 ff.
  sugar, 322
  trade associations and, 295, 322, 357, 359
  transportation costs and, 364
  transportation industry and, 370
  truck transportation and, 311, 322, 370
  uniformity of prices and, 301, 309, 319, 353
  unused capacity and, 362
  vertical integration and, 352
  water transportation and, 310–312, 322, 323, 370, 371
  zinc, 295
  zone prices and, 288n.
Bathtubs, quality competition, 400
  zone prices, 283
Bauxite (*see* Aluminum)
Berle and Means, 9n.
Bethlehem Steel Corporation, 89
Bituminous coal, cooperative selling, 152
  methods of production, changes in, 33
  National Industrial Recovery Act and, 548
  price control under N.I.R.A., 472
  reciprocal purchasing, 172
Blue Eagle, 586
Bolts, nuts, and rivets, basing-point prices for, 299
Book print, long-term contracts, 200
Boycott, public, as a means of social control, 586
  state, as a means of social control, 586
Branded goods, 28, 416, 447
  advertising and, 387
  price setting, 199
  sales promotion and, 383
Bread, price setting, 199
  price stabilization, 234
Bread prices, and flour prices, 236
Bribery, 376, 391
Brokerage charges, control of, sugar, 72
Business cycles, excess capacity and, 34
  overhead costs and, 543
  social control of prices and, 542–545

INDEX

Business cycles, stabilization of prices and, 245, 262
  taxation policy and, 545
  vertical integration and, 434

C

Calcium carbide, division of market, 150
California, petroleum prices in, 101
  State control of petroleum, 24
Canning, price setting, 198
Cans, leader's share of business, 131
  patents, 11
  price leadership, 129
  stabilization of prices, 204, 225
  trend of prices, 130
  uniformity of prices, 129, 130
  vertical integration, 423
Capacity, productive, newsprint, 132
  trade-association statistics, 59
Capital market, integration and, 419
Capper Volstead Act, 1922, 22
Carpets, price setting, 198
Cartels (see Agreements, on prices and output; Pools)
Cash registers, patents, 11
Cattle, railroads sharing transportation of, 171
Cement, basing-point prices, 319–321
  fluctuations of demand, 332
  government purchases and, 321
  interbase price structure, 361
  N.I.R.A., 322, 325
  railroad buyers and, 321
  transportation costs and, 366
  truck transportation and, 322, 371
  water transportation and, 321, 371
  distribution of business by formula, 175
  effect of price reductions, 201
  investment control under National Industrial Recovery Act, 540
  leadership and basing-point prices, 357
  mergers, 137
  price cutting and basing-point system, 355
  price leadership, 136
  profits, 369
  quantity discounts, 279
  reciprocal purchasing and, 172, 175
  secret rebates, 320
  selling costs, 269
  stabilization of prices, 222
  uniformity of prices, 136
  unused capacity, 267, 268
Chain stores, advertising and, 414
  differential taxation of, 550
  local price discrimination, 460
  territorial integration and, 458
  trade discounts and, 278
  vertical integration and, 430
Chemicals, stabilization of prices, 240
Cigarettes, price policy and production, 252
Clark, J. M., 28, 49n.
Clayton Act (see Anti-trust laws)
Cleaning and dyeing, price control under National Industrial Recovery Act, 476
Coal, anthracite (see Anthracite)
  bituminous (see Bituminous coal)
  geographical price discrimination, 325
  price discrimination, 277, 277n.
  reciprocal sales, 175

Coal, vertical integration, 430, 440
Coffee, zone prices, 283
Collusion, anti-trust policy, 3
Commodity, definition of, 4
Commodities clause, 428, 430
Common buying agents, 6
Competition, decline of, 1
  definition of, 3
  maintenance by law, 523
  regulation of, 1
Concentration, industrial, 2
  anti-trust laws and, 19
  effects, 527
  social control and, 528
Conciliation, by the state, social control and, 579
Consent decrees, electric lamps, 15
  Radio Corporation of America, 13
Conservation of natural resources, 541
Consignment sales, 506
Consumer Advisory Board (see National Industrial Recovery Act, Consumer Advisory Board)
Consumer interest, social control and, 578, 581
Continental Wall Paper Company, 17
Cooperative buying, 503
Cooperative marketing, milk, 7
Cooperative Marketing Act, 1926, 22
Cooperative Marketing Associations, 22
Cooperative sales promotion, 380
Cooperative selling, 151
  anti-trust laws, 151, 152
  bituminous coal, 152
Cooperative selling agency, 18n.
  for petroleum, 151
  for salt, 151
  for wallpaper, 151
Copper, basing-point prices and, 296
  concentration of control of, 39
  production control under N.I.R.A., 467
  stabilization of price, 63
  state boycott as a means of control, 586
Copper Exporters, Inc., 63
Copper Institute, 63
Cordage industry, pools, 147
Corn gluten feed, basing-point prices, 294
Corn products, price leadership, 132
  prices, 133
  stabilization of, 221
  zone prices, 283, 289
Corn Products Refining Company, 18, 20, 76n., 132
Corporation laws, size of firms, 9
Cost accounting, control of, 37
  overhead costs and, 49
  price policy and, 48
  profit, inclusion of, 50, 52
  standardization, 48
  under N.I.R.A., 481
  by trade-association, 47
Cost of production, agricultural implements, 114
  average, calculation by trade associations, 51
  basing-point prices and, 360, 363, 369
  changes in, and price policy under N.I.R.A., 554
  social control and, 550–590
  differences in, price leadership and, 144

Cost of production, meat packing, 182, 186
  petroleum industry, 107
  price policy and, 551, 552
  prohibition of prices below, under N.I.R.A., 479, 483, 486, 491, 513, 531, 533, 534, 555
  publication of, 51
  quality competition and, 396, 399
  reciprocal purchasing and, 193
  selling costs and, 377
  sharing the market and, 190
  stabilization of prices and, 244, 257, 258, 266
  steel industry, 90
  style competition and, 408–410
  taxation and, 553
  territorial integration and, 458
  trade associations and, 68
  vertical integration and, 431, 437, 445
Cost of transportation, changes and interpenetration of territory, 331
Cotton bagging pool, 150
Cotton Textile Institute, 66
Cotton textiles, control of investment under N.I.R.A., 509
  plant-utilization control, 154
    under N.I.R.A., 470
  production control, 66
  style competition, 408
  vertical integration, 434, 440
Cotton thread, division of market, 150
  zone prices, 282
Crackers, price leadership, 138
  stabilization of prices, 225
Credit information, provision of, by trade associations, 47
Criteria of control, legislative, 567
Cross freighting (*see* Interpenetration of territory)

D

Delivered prices for lumber, 292
  sugar, 72
Demand, fluctuations and interpenetration of territory, 332
  prices and, in imperfect markets, 26
  shifts in, social control and, 532
Department stores, trade discounts and, 278
  vertical integration and, 425
Deterioration of products, 402
Differentiation of products, cost calculation and, 50
  price cutting and, 36
  price policy and, 35
  prices and, 36
Discounts, quantity, cement, 279
  discrimination and, 278
  N.I.R.A. and, 501
  petroleum, 279
  standardization, by trade-association, 71, 72
    under N.I.R.A., 501, 508
  steel, 279
  sugar, 279
  Sugar Institute policy, 72
  trade status and, 549
Discrimination, 70, 273–353
  aluminum, 276

Discrimination, geographical 280–353
  (*See also* Basing-point prices; Zone prices)
  price, chain stores, 460
  coal, 277, 277*n.*, 325
  consequences, 277
  glass, 276
  grapes, 275
  investment and, 277
  milk, 274
  wheat, 276
  sales promotion, 392
  selling integration and, 451
  territorial integration and, 457, 459
  trade-association elimination of, 73
  trade status and, 277, 280
  use of product and, 274
  vertical integration and, 440
  (*See also* Quantity discounts)
Distributing trades, changing methods in, N.I.R.A. and, 548
  control of "mark-up" under N.I.R.A., 477
Distribution of business, anthracite, 166
  anti-trust laws, 19
  meat packing, 156, 180, 184
  sales promotion and, 384
  sewing thread, 229
Distribution of goods and services, sales promotion and, 385
Distribution of income, social control and, 560
  stabilization of prices and, 270
Division of territory (*see* Territorial division of market)
Drugs, price setting, 199
  stabilization of prices, 240
Duopoly, sales promotion and, 390
Dupont de Nemours Company, 20
Durability of plant, excess capacity and, 32
  price competition and, 37

E

Eastman Kodak Company, 17
Economies of production, vertical integration and, 421
Eddy, A. J., 44, 60, 64*n.*
Efficiency, meat packing, 181
  of firms, social control and, 555
  standards of social control, 557
  of production, leadership and, 144
  selling integration and, 450
  social control and, 534
  stabilization of prices and, 266, 268
  territorial integration and, 459
  vertical integration, 431
Electric lamps, patents on, 11
Entry, freedom of, 5
  N.I.R.A., 509
Entry of capital, petroleum industry, 106
Envelopes, patents for, 11
Ethics, codes of, 70
"Eveners" of railroad traffic, 171
Excess capacity, 5, 30
  business cycles and, 34
  changes in demand and, 32
  changes in location of industry and, 33
  changes in methods of production and, 33
  durability of plant and, 32
  extent of, 31
  size of firms and, 32

INDEX 609

Excess capacity, trade associations and, 67
   trade-association statistics of capacity and, 60
Exclusive dealing, 17, 426, 430, 506
Explosives, pools, 147, 150,
Export corporations, 21
   sulphur, 229
External economies, sales promotion and, 381

F

Fabrication in transit, 348
Fashion (*see* Style)
Federal Oil Conservation Board, 24*n*.
Federal Power Commission, legislative criteria of policy, 568
Federal Radio Commission, legislative criteria of control, 568
   personnel, 573
Federal Reserve Board, lack of publicity concerning policy, 588
   legislative criteria of policy, 568
   personnel, 572, 573*n*., 574
Federal Trade Commission, conciliation as a means of control, 579
   judiciary and, 574
   policies of, 585
Federal Trade Commission Act, judicial interpretation of, 570
Federal Water Power Commission, personnel, 573*n*.
Fertilizers, basing-point prices, 297
   price leadership, 134
   stabilization of prices, 240
Flour milling, change in location of, 33
   changes in methods of production, 34
   vertical integration, 432*n*.
Flour prices, bread prices and, 236
   wheat prices and, 235
Fluctuations of production, vertical integration and, 434
Follow the leader (*see* Leadership, price)
Foreign competition, basing-point prices and, 313
Formulae for distribution of purchases, cement, 175
Freight absorption, 284, 329, 374
   (*See also* Zone prices; Basing-point prices)
Freight allowances (*see* Discrimination, geographical)
Freight pickups (*see* Discrimination, geographical)
Frequency of price changes, 242
Fruit brokers, sharing the market, 169
Full-line forcing, 452
Furniture, average costs, publication of, 52
   cost accounting, 49
   differentiation of products, 35
   open prices, 60
   seasonal price stability, 243

G

Gary, Judge, 80
Gary dinners, 78, 79
Gasoline cracking patent pooling, 12
General Electric Company, 11, 13–16
Geographical distribution of demand, unused capacity and, 33

Geographical price discrimination (*see* Discrimination, geographical)
Ghost competition (*see* Phantom competition)
Glass, distribution of business, 224
   plant-utilization control, 154
   price discrimination, 276
   sharing the market, 170
   stabilization of price, 224
Glass bottles, division of market, 150
Glucose (*see* Corn products)
Government purchases, basing-point system and, 313, 321
Grain, sharing transportation of, 171
Grain elevators, sharing the market, 169
Grapes, price discrimination, 275
Guarantee against price decline (*see* Price decline, guarantee against)
Gunpowder, division of market, 150

H

Hand-to-mouth buying, 408
Hardwood Manufacturers Association, 66
Hardwood trade association, control of production, 65
Hepburn Act, 442
Hides, price trend, 238
"Holding off" the market, 6
Homogeneity of products, 4
Horizontal integration (*see* Integration, horizontal)
Hours of plant-operation control (*see* Plant utilization control)

I

Imperfect markets, demand conditions and, 28, 29
   supply conditions and, 29
Imperfection of market, consequences of, 527
Improvement of technique of production, price stabilization and, 269
   sharing market and, 190
Initial demand, unused capacity and, 32
Integration, 418–461
   capital market and, 419
   causes of, 460
   consequences of, 461
   horizontal, 418
   mergers and, 419
   patterns of, 421
   promotion profits and, 419
   research and, 420
   reserved profits and, 420
   sales promotion and, 383
Integration, selling, 446–453
   agricultural implements, 446, 447, 449, 451, 452
   anti-trust laws and, 449
   automobiles, 448
   consequences, 450–453
   discrimination and, 451
   efficiency of production and, 450
   food products, 448
   meat packing, 446, 447, 449, 450, 452
   monopoly and, 451, 453
   petroleum, 448, 452
   prices and, 451
   profits and, 450
   selling costs and, 446, 450

Integration, selling, shoe machinery, 446, 449, 452
  size of firms and, 419
  social control of, 524
  stabilization of prices and, 27
  substitute goods, 453–455
    meat packing, 454
    methods of production and, 456
    monopoly and, 454–455
    new products and, 456
    patents and, 455
    profits and, 456
    risk and, 454
  territorial, 456–460
    anti-trust laws and, 458
    chain stores, 458
    consequences, 458–460
    costs and, 458
    discrimination and, 459
    efficiency of production and, 459
    local price discrimination and, 457
    monopoly and, 460
    non-price competition and, 457
    petroleum, 457, 458
    prices and, 459
    risk and, 457
    selling costs and, 458
    size of firms and, 457, 458
  types of, 418
  vertical, 418, 421
    advertising and, 425
    agricultural implements, 422, 423, 427, 428
    aluminum, 424, 441, 444
    anti-trust laws, 427
    automobile tires, 425, 440
    automobiles, 422, 424, 434
    aviation, 428
    basing-point system and, 352
    cans, 423
    chain stores, 430
    coal, 430, 440
    consequences, 431, 445
    costs and, 431, 437, 445
    cotton textiles, 434, 440
    department stores and, 425
    discrimination and, 440
    economics of production and, 421
    efficiency of production, 431
    exclusive dealing and, 426, 430
    flour milling, 432n.
    fluctuations of production and, 434
    mail-order houses and, 425
    market for products and, 425
    meat packing, 423, 427, 429, 439, 443
    methods of production 432, 433
    monopoly and, 433, 441, 443
    monopoly prices and, 422, 439
    N.I.R.A. and, 422, 423, 440
    natural resources and, 444
    newsprint, 427
    overhead costs and, 437
    paper, 423
    petroleum 422, 423, 427, 428, 435, 436, 439, 441
    prices, 437
    profits, 435
    raw materials and, 423
    resale price maintenance, 426, 430
    risk and, 436

Integration, vertical, selling costs and, 431, 445
    size of firms and, 438
    stabilization of production and, 434
    steel, 422, 424, 427, 429, 434, 435, 440, 442, 444
    tobacco, 428
Interest rate, as regulator of investment, 34
Interlocking stock ownership, petroleum industry, 100
International Harvester Company, 19n., 20
  leadership of, 109–118
  share of business, 111
International Paper Company, 132
Interpenetration of territory, basing-point prices and, 329, 330, 364
  changes in cost of transportation and, 331
  fluctuations in demand and, 332
  size of plants and, 331, 339
Interstate Commerce Commission, 567
  personnel of, 573n.
Iron, basing-point prices, 301, 309
Iron ore, guarantee against price decline, 201
  pool, 149
  stabilization of price, 209
Inventories, price stabilization and, 244
  trade-association statistics of, 59
Inventory speculation, price cutting and, 28, 29
Investment, natural resources, price control and, 541
  obsolescence of plant and, 548
  price discrimination and, 277
  sharing the market and, 192
  social control of, 532, 533, 536–539, 543, 548
  stabilization of prices and, 256, 266
  valuation of, social control and, 557
Investment control, efficiency of firms and, 559
  N.I.R.A. and, 509, 549

J

Joint production, price policy and, 34
Judicial bodies, social control by, 570

L

Laths, metal, basing-point prices, 299
Lead, basing-point prices, 299
  price leadership, 138
Leadership, price, 20, 76–145
  agricultural implements, 109–118
  alcohol, 135
  anthracite, 118–129
  anti-trust laws, 2, 18, 20, 144, 571
  basing-point prices and, 357, 359
  can industry, 129
  canned salmon, 139
  cement, 136
  consequences, 140
  corn products, 132
  crackers, 138
  definition of, 76
  differences in cost and, 144
  efficiency and, 144
  evidence of, 77–140
  fertilizers, 134
  lead, 138
  leaders' share of business, 142

INDEX

Leadership, price, meat packing, 140
  mergers and, 145
  newsprint industry, 132
  non-ferrous metals, 138
  "open prices" and, 498
  petroleum industry, 93-109
  prepared oats, 138
  price level and, 141
  price uniformity and, 81
  rubber tires, 140
  sales promotion and, 382
  selling costs and, 142, 144
  size of firms and, 77
  social control of, 524
  stability of, 145
  stabilization of prices and, 142, 204
  steel industry, 77-93
  sugar, 138
  tobacco manufacturing, 140
  trade associations and, 67, 76
  uniformity of prices, 142
  zone prices and, 288, 289
  style, 409
Leather, price trend of, 238
Leather products, price policy and production, 252
  zone prices, 282n.
Legislative bodies and social control, 567
Leisure, valuation of, and advertising, 390
Lime, basing-point prices, 328
Linseed oil, trade association and price stabilization, 202
  zone prices, 284, 289
List prices, actual prices and, 81
Livestock markets, competitive conditions in, 5
Local price cutting, 8, 282
  petroleum, 459
  territorial integration and, 457
Location of production, basing-point prices and, 292, 330, 331, 333, 335, 337-340, 344, 345, 349, 350, 360, 362
  changes in, unused capacity and, 33
  zone prices and, 289
Long-term contracts, 72, 200, 504
Loss leaders, 477, 488
Lotteries, 376, 391
Lumber, adjustment of output of products, 35
  basing-point prices, 291, 296
  changes in location, 33
  control of output under N.I.R.A., 466
Lumber distributing, control of "mark-up" under N.I.R.A., 478
  investment in natural resources, 37
  open prices, 60
  output control, 65, 154
  price control under N.I.R.A., 473, 489
  production statistics of trade associations, 56
  profits, 369
  shifts in population and demand for, 32n.
  trade associations, 40, 44, 55, 65
  uniformity of prices, 292, 293

M

Mahogany, zone prices, 282
Mail-order houses, vertical integration and, 425
Management and ownership in corporation, 10

Maple flooring, average cost, publication of, 52
  basing-point prices (see Lumber, basing-point prices)
  cost accounting, 50n.
  trade-association activities, 65n.
Marine insurance, anti-trust laws and, 21
Market (see Perfect market)
  imperfect, 4
Market territory, basing-point prices and, 370
Marshall, A., 1, 29, 35
Matches, price stabilization, 238
Means, G. C., 10n.
Meat packing, adjustment of output of products, 35
  anti-trust laws and, 19, 165, 185
  branch houses, 182, 183
  chain stores and, 183
  change in location of, 33
  competitive conditions in livestock markets, 6
  cost of production, 186
  distribution of business, 180, 184
  division of market, 150
  efficiency, 181
  integration of substitute goods, 454
  joint products in, 35
  overhead costs, 182
  peddler-car routes, 182, 183
  pools, 147, 148
  price leadership, 140
  prices, sharing of market and, 177
  profits, 180, 185
  quick-freezing process, 184
  reciprocal purchases, 173
  refrigerator cars, 182, 183
  selling integration, 446, 447, 449, 450, 452
  sharing the market, 156
  vertical integration, 423, 427, 429, 439, 443.
Meat products, trend of prices of, 186
Merchant Marine Act, 1920, 21
Mergers, advertising and, 415
  anti-trust laws and, 18, 20
  basing-point systems and, 356, 360
  cement, 137
  cost of patent litigation and, 16
  integration and, 419
  price leadership and, 145
  sharing the market and, 191
  size of firms and, 8, 10
  steel, 89n.
Methods of production, changes in, and control by taxation, 550
  excess capacity and, 33
  N.I.R.A. and, 548
  price competition and, 546
  sales promotion and, 547
  social control, 546
  timing, 547
  improvement, and social control, 559
  integration of substitute goods and, 456
  investment control and, 511
  social control of rate of change, 562
  vertical integration and, 432, 433
Milk, canned, guarantee against price decline, 201
  control of, 7
  discriminatory prices, 274
  stabilization of prices, 232
Milk distribution, concentration of, 7

612 THE DECLINE OF COMPETITION

Mineral resources, concentration of control, 39
  taxation of, and price competition, 24
Misrepresentation, 70
Monopoly, 3
  advertising and, 390
  growing importance, 3
  integration of substitute goods and, 454, 455
  policy of, 5
  selling integration and, 451, 453
  social control and, 560
  territorial integration and, 460
  vertical integration, 433, 441, 443
Monopoly price, 5
  vertical integration and, 422, 439
Monopoly profits, 527
Morris and Company, 19
Motion picture industry, patents for, 11

N

Nail pools, 147, 149, 150
National Binding Company, 17
National Cash Register Company, 17
National Electric Lamp Company, 17
National Harrow Company, 17
National Industrial Recovery Act, 71, 462–512
  administration, 574
  advertising allowances, 502
  anti-trust laws and, 22
  basing-point prices, 293, 297, 307, 309, 314, 322
  Business Advisory Board, 575
  changing methods of production and, 548
  code authority personnel, 577
  coercive enforcement, 580, 585
  conciliation as a means of administration, 579
  consequences of policy, 514
  consignment sales, 506
  Consumer Advisory Board, 326, 484, 489, 493, 576, 589
  consumer interest and, 579, 581
  cooperative buying, 503
  cost of production, definition of, 481
  destructive price cutting, prohibition of, 490
  discounts, standardization of, 501
  emergency price fixing, 484, 487, 489
  exclusive dealing, 506
  government purchases and, 495, 497
  guarantees against price decline, 505
  investment control under, 509, 538, 539
  Labor Advisory Board, 576
  lack of definition of policy, 588
  legislative criteria of policy, 569
  long-term contracts, 504
  non-price competition and, 416, 500–509
  "open price" clauses, 491, 497, 517
  "open prices," consequences of, 497
  overhead costs and minimum prices under, 481
  petroleum industry, 24, 108
  plant utilization control, 470, 535
  policy of administration, 512–521
  prices and, 516, 544
  price control, 471, 479, 485, 535
  price policy, changes in cost of production and, 554
  prices below cost of production, prohibition of, 479, 483, 486, 491, 513, 531, 534, 555

National Industrial Recovery Act, production control, 465, 535
  production under, 516
  profits and, 516, 544
  proposed amendments, 582
  provisions, 463
  quality and service competition, 508
  resale price maintenance, 505
  research and planning, 576
  sales promotion and, 500, 536
  secret rebates, 502
  standard cost burden, minimum prices and, 481
  standardization of cost accounting, 481, 490
  standardization of discounts, 508
  steel industry code for, 84, 486
  threats to abandon codes, 587
  trade associations and, 577
  trade discounts and, 549
  vertical integration and, 422, 423, 440
  wage policy and price policy, 554
Natural gas, prevention of waste, 24
  property rights in, 22
Natural resources, anti-trust laws and, 523
  investment in, price control and, 541
  price and production policy, 38
  production control under N.I.R.A., 467
  social control and, 540–541
  vertical integration and, 444
New products, integration of substitute goods and, 456
  unused capacity and, 32
Newspapers, advertising and, 392
Newsprint, leader's share of business, 132
  leadership, 132
  location of, changes in, 33
  long-term contracts, 200
  methods of production, changes in, 34
  productive capacity, 132
  profits, 132
  stabilization of price, 220
  trade associations and, 203
  vertical integration, 427
  zone prices, 285, 289
Nickel, stabilization of prices, 231
Non-ferrous metals, price leadership, 138
Non-financial burdens of production, social control and, 564
Non-price competition, 372–417
  causes, 372
  changing importance, 412–417
  definition, 373
  effects, 375–412
  N.I.R.A. and, 416, 500–509
  social control of, 524, 558
  territorial integration and, 457
  trade associations and, 416, 417
  (*See also* Advertising; Quality competition; Sales promotion; Service competition; Style competition)
Northern Hemlock and Hardwood Manufacturers Association, production control, 66
Number of firms, 4
  competitive behavior and, 5
  decline of, 8
  livestock markets, 6
  milk distribution, 7
  milk production, 7
  social control of, 524

INDEX 613

Number of firms, social policy, 9
tobacco-leaf markets, 6

O

Oats, prepared, price leadership, 138
  zone prices, 284
Obsolescence of plant, 545, 546, 548
Oil (*see* Petroleum)
Oklahoma, state control of petroleum, 24
Open-price system, N.I.R.A. and, 491, 497, 517
  trade associations and, 44, 48, 60
Opening prices, 198
Optimum firm, quality competition and, 397
  sales promotion and, 382
Output (*see* Production)
Overhead costs, 29, 41
  business cycles and, 543
  cost accounting and, 49
  distribution over time, 543
  meat packing, 182
  minimum prices and, under N.I.R.A., 481
  petroleum, 23
  railroads, 31
  vertical integration and, 437
Ownership and management in corporation, 10

P

Paper, trade associations, 203
  unused capacity, 203, 268
  vertical integration, 423
Patent law, size of firms and, 11
  exclusive dealing, 17
Patent litigation, size of firms and, 16
Patents, 548
  cost of litigation, 16
  integration of substitute goods and, 455
  mergers and, 13
  pooling, 12
  suppression, 15
Perfect market, 4
Personnel of administrative bodies exercising control, 572
Petroleum, adjustment of output of products, 35
  basing-point prices, 298
  cooperative selling agency, 151
  costs, 107
  demand, growth of, 105
  entry of capital, 106
  exclusive dealing, 426
  interlocking stock ownership, 100
  investment in natural resources, 37
  leadership, effects of, 102
  local price cutting, 459
  long-term contracts, 200
  N.I.R.A. and, 108
  premium prices, 97
  prevention of waste, 24
  price changing initiative in, 98, 100, 101
  price control under the N.I.R.A., 474
  price cutting, 97, 99
  price leadership, 93–108
  price policy, 102
  price setting, 198, 199
  price trend, 106, 219
  production control under N.I.R.A., 467

Petroleum, profits, 106
  property rights in, 22
  quantity discounts, 279
  resale price maintenance, 426
  selling integration, 448, 452
  share of Standard Oil companies, 103
  sharing of market territories, 101
  sharing transportation of, 170
  stabilization of price, 218
  territorial integration and, 457, 458
  uniformity of prices, 99
  vertical integration 383, 422, 423, 427, 428, 435, 436, 439, 441
  zone prices, 285, 289
Petroleum lands, distribution of control of, 104
Phantom competition, 60
Philadelphia and Reading Company, share of anthracite business, 122
Photographic materials, patents, 11
Pig iron, basing-point prices for steel and, 352
  price trend, 92
Pig-iron production, steel prices and, 246, 249
Pipe, cast iron, pool, 149, 150
  sewer, basing-point prices, 299
Pipe-line transportation, 423, 428, 442
Pittsburgh-plus system (*see* Basing-point prices-Steel)
Plant utilization (*see* Excess capacity)
Plant-utilization control, 154
  anthracite, 154
  cotton textiles, 154
  glass, 154
  N.I.R.A. and, 470, 535
  trade associations and, 66
Plate glass (*see* Glass)
Pools, 2, 146, 147
  cast-iron pipe, 149, 150
  coal, 147
  cordage, 147
  cotton bagging, 150
  explosives, 147, 150
  iron ore, 149
  iron and steel, 147, 148
  nail, 147, 149, 150
  patent, 12
  salt, 147
  territorial division of market, 150
  whisky, 147
  (*See also* Agreements on prices and output)
Population shifts, distribution of demand and, 33
Premium prices, agricultural implements, 109
  anthracite coal, 120, 126
  petroleum, 97
  steel, 82
Potential competition, anthracite, 188
  sales promotion and, 384
  sharing the market and, 176
Price competition, changes in methods of production and, 546
  durability of equipment and, 37
  "open prices" and, 498
  shipping subsidies and, 25
  style competition and, 411
  unused plant and, 533
Price control, cost accounts and, 49
  N.I.R.A. and, 471, 485, 535
  emergency control and, 484, 487, 489

Price control, natural resources, 541
  size of firms, 8
Price cutting, anthracite, 120
  anti-trust laws and, 18, 20
  basing-point prices and, 355
  discouragement of, 41
  distribution of demand over time and, 28
  increase in size of firms and, 8
  petroleum industry, 97, 99
  steel industry, 82
  trade associations and, 67
Price decline, guarantee against, 72, 200, 505
Price discrimination (*see* Discrimination)
Price leadership (*see* Leadership, price)
Price level, stabilization of prices and, 244
Price policy, changes in costs, 554
  N.I.R.A. and, 544
  production and, leather products, 253
  in textile industry, 253
Price setting, 197
  agricultural implements, 198
  anthracite, 198
  automobiles, 198
  branded goods, 199
  canning, 198
  carpets, 198
  petroleum, 198
  tin plate, 198
  trade associations, 198
  woolen industry, 198
Price stabilization (*see* Stabilization of prices)
Price trend, agricultural implements, 117
  alcohol, 135
  anthracite, 124, 189
  automobile tires, 233
  cans, 130
  meat products, 186
  paper, 203
  petroleum, 106, 219
  pig iron, 92
  rayon, 233
  shoe machinery, 233
  steel, 90, 211
  tobacco products, 227
Price uniformity, sharing the market and, 175
  trade associations and, 53
Price wars, 27, 30
Prices, basing-point systems and, 336
  corn products, 133
  criteria of, under social control, 531, 536
  discrimination and, 277
  meat packing and sharing the market, 177
  minimum, trade associations and, 53
  N.I.R.A. and, 516
  reciprocal purchasing and, 193
  sales promotion and, 385
  selling integration and, 451
  sharing the market and, 177
  style competition and, 409
  territorial integration and, 459
  trade-association statistics of, 60
  vertical integration and, 437
Printing and publishing, zone prices, 282*n*.
Production, N.I.R.A., and, 516
  stabilization of prices and, 244, 245
  trade-association provision of statistics of, 55
Production control, anthracite, 154
  glass, 154
  lumber, 154
Production control, N.I.R.A. and, 465, 535
  sharing the market and, 176, 177
  trade associations and, 64
  (*See also* Plant-utilization control)
Profits, normal, 5
  agricultural implements, 116
  alcohol, 136
  basing-point prices and, 338, 369
  cement, 369
  cost accounting and, 50, 52
  integration of substitute goods, 456
  lumber, 369
  meat packing, 180, 185
  N.I.R.A. and, 516, 544
  newsprint, 132
  petroleum industry, 106
  quality competition and, 399
  reservation of, 10
  sales promotion and, 386, 393
  selling integration and, 450
  social control and, 561
  stabilization of prices and, 262, 265, 266, 271
  steel industry, 369
  vertical integration, 435
Promotion profits, integration and, 419
  size of firms and, 10
Public opinion, social control and, 585-587, 590
Pullman cars, patents on, 11
"Putting patents to sleep" (*see* Suppression of patents)

Q

Quality and service, competition in, 394-406
  N.I.R.A. and, 508
  difficulty of adjusting, 397
Quality competition, adaptation of goods and, 404
  agricultural implements, 400
  allocation of spending and, 402, 405
  bath tubs, 400
  changing importance of, 415
  consequences, 406
  cost of production and, 396
  costs and, 399
  deterioration of products, 402
  effect on buyers, 400
  effect on organization of production, 395
  optimum firm and, 397
  price competition and, 394
  profits and, 399
  risks, and, 398, 405
  sales promotion and, 394
  steel, 400
  unused capacity and, 396
Quantity discounts (*see* Discounts, quantity)

R

Radio Corporation of America, 12, 13, 14
Radio equipment, reciprocal purchasing and, 173
Radio industry, patents for, 12
  tying contracts in, 14
Railroads, basing-point prices and, 300, 313, 321
  overhead costs and, 30
  reciprocal purchasing and, 172
Rationality of buyers, advertising and, 386

INDEX 615

Raw materials supplies, vertical integration and, 423
Rayon, price trend of, 233
Reaction time of buyers, price competition and, 27
Reading Company (see Philadelphia and Reading Company)
Reciprocal purchasing, 170, 374
   anthracite coal, 172
   bituminous coal, 172
   cement, 172, 175
   coal, 175
   consequences, 193
   costs and, 193
   meat packing, 173
   prices and, 193
   radio equipment and, 173
   railroads and, 172
   steel rails, 171, 206
Replacement costs as basis of price policy, 551
Republic Iron and Steel Company, 89
Resale price maintenance, 401*n*., 426, 430, 505
Research, integration and, 420
   social control and, 559, 563
Reserved profits, integration and, 420
Reserves, corporate, and distribution of overhead costs over time, 543
Retail margins, 401
Risk, integration of substitute goods and, 454
   of investment, stabilization of prices and, 270
   quality competition and, 398, 405
   sales promotion and, 384, 392, 393
   style competition and, 411
   territorial integration and, 457
   vertical integration and, 436
Rubber products, zone prices, 282*n*.

S

Sales promotion, 375-394
   allocation of spending and, 386
   anti-trust laws, 18
   benefits to purchasers, 391
   causes, 373, 394
   consequences, 394
   cost of, 383, 384, 391
   discriminatory, 392
   distribution of business and, 384
   distribution of goods and services and, 385-394
   duopoly and, 390
   effect on organization of production, 376-385
   external economies and, 381
   general economic efficiency and, 382
   increasing expenditure upon, 412
   methods of production and, 547
   N.I.R.A. and, 500, 536
   optimum firm and, 382
   potential competition and, 384
   price leadership, 382
   prices and, 385
   profits and, 386, 393
   risk and, 384, 393
   size of firms and, 383
   style competition and, 411
   trade associations and, 380
   unused capacity and, 378
Salmon, canned, price leadership, 139

Salt, cooperative selling agency, 151
   pool, 147
   stabilization of prices, 240
   zone prices, 283
Samples, 376, 391
Sanctions of social control, 579
Saving, social control and, 561, 563
Scale of production, increase of, 8
Seasonal prices, 28*n*., 243
Secret price cutting, steel, 214
Secret prices, steel, 79, 80, 305
Secret rebates, 70, 502
   basing-point prices and, 320
   cement, 320
"Seesawing" market, 6
Selling costs, amount of, 391
   basing-point prices and, 364
   cost of production and, 376
   duopoly and, 390
   price leadership, 142, 144
   price stabilization and, 244, 269
   retail margins and, 401
   selling integration and, 446, 450
   sharing the market and, 175
   size of firms and, 377, 379, 380, 382
   territorial integration and, 458
   vertical integration and, 431, 445
   zone prices and, 288
Selling methods, trade associations and, 69, 71
Service competition (see Quality competition)
Sewing machines, stabilization of prices, 231
Sewing thread, distribution of business, 229
   stabilization of price, 229
Share of market, leader's, agricultural implements, 111
   cans, 131
   newsprint, 132
   petroleum, 103
   price leadership and, 142
   steel, 85
Sharing the market, 146-194
   anthracite, 122, 123, 166, 188
   anti-trust laws and, 153, 165
   consequences, 175, 188, 194
   conventions for, 155
   cooperative selling, 151
   definition, 146
   fruit brokerage, 169
   glass, 170
   grain elevators, 169
   improvement of technique and, 190
   meat packing, 156, 177
   mergers and, 191
   plant utilization, control of, 154
   potential competitors and, 176
   price competition and, 175
   price uniformity and, 175
   prices and, 177
   production and, 176, 177
   sales promotion and, 175
   social control of, 524
   steel, 168
   steel construction, 153
   tobacco, 169
   trade associations and, 58, 152
   zone prices and, 288
Sharing market territories in petroleum industry, 101
Sherman Law (see Anti-trust laws)

Shipping, anti-trust laws, 21
 subsidies and, 25
Shipping Act, 1916, 21
Shipping-point prices, 281
Shoe machinery, patents for, 11, 13
 selling integration, 446, 449, 452
 trend of prices, 233
 tying contracts, 14, 15
Shoes, prices of, and leather and hide prices, 238
 stabilization of prices, 238
Singer Sewing Machine Company, 11
Size of firms, advertising and, 415
 agricultural implements, 115
 anti-trust laws, 2, 18, 20, 571
 efficiency and, 9
 excess capacity and, 32
 growing importance of, 40
 improvement of technique and, 190
 increase, cause of, 8
 integration and, 419
 leadership and, 77, 80
 monopoly and, 527
 patent laws, 11
 promotion profits, 10
 quality competition and, 396
 reservation of profits and, 10
 selling costs and, 377, 379, 380, 382
 social control of, 9, 525
 steel industry and, 89
 style competition and, 407, 408
 technological change and, 25
 territorial integration and, 457, 458
 trade associations and, 46
 United States Steel Corporation, 88
 vertical integration and, 438
Size of plants, interpenetration of territory and, 331, 339
Smelting, adjustment of output of products and, 35
Soap, zone prices, 283
Social control, 564
 advertising, 524
 administrative bodies and, 571
 personnel of, 572
 coercive enforcement, types of, 585
 conciliation as a means, 579
 consumer interest and, 578, 581
 costs, as basis of price policy, 552
 costs of production and, 550–554
  and taxation, 553
 distribution of income and, 560, 563
 efficiency of firms and, 555
 efficiency of production and, 534
 integration and, 524
 investment, 532, 533, 536, 539, 543, 548
  and selection of firms, 559
 judicial bodies and, 570
 legislative bodies and, 567
 management, remuneration for, and, 559
 means, 566–590
 methods of production and, 546, 559, 562
 monopoly and, 560
 natural disasters and, 562
 natural resources, 540–542
 non-financial burdens of production and, 564
 non-price competition and, 524, 558
 number of firms and, 524
 objectives of, 522–565

Social control, price leadership and, 524
 price policy, criteria of, 531, 536
 prices, and business cycles, 542, 544, 545
  and taxation, 537, 538, 545
 productive efficiency and, 530–560
 profits and, 561
 public boycott as a means, 586
 replacement costs as basis of price policy, 551
 research and, 559, 563
 sanctions and, 579–589
 saving and, 561, 563
 sharing the market and, 524
 shifts in demand and prices, 532
 size of firms and, 9, 525
 stabilization of prices and, 52
 standards of efficiency and, 557
 state arbitration as a means of, 582
 state boycott as a means of, 586
 style competition and, 558
 taxes to control innovation and, 550
 unused plant capacity and, 532, 534, 539
 valuation of investment and, 557
 veto by the state as a means of, 582
 war and, 563
 written decisions, 588
Socony-Vacuum merger, 98
South Improvement Company, 170
Southern Pine Association, production statistics, 56
Speculation and stabilization of prices, 246, 256
Spoiling the market, 28
Stability, price, of alcohol, 136
 anti-trust policy, 2
 basing-point prices and, 363
 open prices and, 61
 trade associations and, 62
Stabilization of prices, 195, 220, 224
 agricultural implements, 217, 254
 aluminum, 229
 anthracite, 216
 automobile production and, 251
 bananas, 231
 bread, 234
 burden of depression and, 261
 business acceleration and, 264
 business cycles and, 245, 262
 cans, 204, 225
 cement, 222
 chemicals, 240
 cigarette production and, 252
 consequences of, 243
 constructional goods, 259
 corn products, 221
 cost of production and, 246, 257, 258, 266
 crackers, 225
 distribution of incomes and, 270
 drugs, 240
 duration of cycles, and, 254
 efficiency of production and, 266, 268
 evidence of, 196
 extension of sales territory and, 270
 fertilizers, 240
 general business fluctuations and, 259, 260, 263
 guarantee against price decline, 200, 201
 integration and, 270
 inventories and, 244

INDEX

Stabilization of prices, investment and, 244, 256, 266
 iron ore, 209
 linseed oil, 202
 long-term contracts, 200
 matches, 238
 milk, 232
 nickel, 231
 overhead costs and, 260
 paper, 203
 petroleum, 218
 price leadership and, 142, 204
 price level and, 244
 price setting, 197
 production and, 244, 245
 profits and, 262, 265, 266, 271
 risks of investment and, 270
 salt, 240
 selling costs and, 244, 269
 sewing machines, 231
 sewing thread, 229
 shoes, 238
 social control of, 524
 speculation and, 246, 256
 spread of, 264
 steel, 204, 205, 209
 steel rails, 205
 sulphur, 229
 tobacco products, 225
 trade associations and, 58, 59, 202, 204
 unused capacity and, 266
 wages and, 265
Stabilization of production, vertical integration and, 434
Standard cost burden, minimum prices and, under N.I.R.A., 481
Standard Oil Company of New Jersey, 12
Standard Oil Company of New York, leadership of, 98
Standard Oil companies, 93–109
 relations between, 100
 share of business, 103
Standardization of cost accounting, N.I.R.A. and, 490
Standardization of products, style competition and, 417
 trade associations and, 68
Starch (*see* Corn products)
Statistics, trade association provision of, 55–64
Steel, agreements on prices and output of, 78
 basing-point prices, 81, 299*ff*.
 fluctuations in demand and, 332
 government purchases and, 313
 location of production and, 340, 345
 N.I.R.A. and, 325
 number of bases and, 314, 315, 342
 price uniformity and, 354
 railroad buyers and, 300, 313,
 water transportation and, 311, 312, 371
 code authority personnel, 577
 code for, under N.I.R.A., 84, 486, 497, 499, 501, 505, 510, 521
 costs, 90
 effect of price reduction on, 201
 fabrication in transit, 348
 foreign competition and basing-point prices, 313
 Gary dinners, 78, 79
 guarantee against price decline, 200

Steel, inter-base price structure, 361
 investment in natural resources, 38
 leadership and basing-point prices, 358
 mergers, 89*n*.
 N.I.R.A., and basing-point prices, 326
 pools, 147, 148
 premium prices, 82
 price control, 78
 price cutting, 79, 80, 82
 and basing-point prices, 355, 358
 price leadership, 77–93
 price policy in, and production, 245, 248
 price trend, 90, 211
 production of, at basing points, 351
 and price policy, 245, 248
 profits in, 369
 quality competition, 400
 quantity discounts, 279
 secret price cutting, 214
 secret prices, 305
 sharing the market, 168
 size of firms, 89
 and leadership, 80
 stabilization of prices, 85, 204, 205, 209
 standardization of transportation charges, and basing-point system, 310-312
 territorial integration, 457
 threat to abandon code, under N.I.R.A., 587
 trade association and basing-point prices, 359
 transportation costs, and basing-point prices, 365
 truck transportation, and basing-point prices, 311, 371
 uniformity of bids, 84
 uniformity of prices, basing-point prices and, 301, 309
 unused capacity for production, 268
 vertical integration, 422, 424, 425, 427, 429, 434, 435, 440, 442, 444
 zone prices, 283, 289
Steel construction, sharing the market, 153
Steel rails, division of market for, 150
 long-term contracts for, 200
 price policy and production, 245, 248
 reciprocal purchasing and, 171
 stability of price of, 205
Stoves, zone prices, 282
 cost accounting, 49*n*., 50*n*.
Style competition, 406–409
 adaptation of products and, 410
 allocation of spending and, 410
 consequences of, 411
 costs and, 408-410
 distribution and, 409
 increase in, 416
 organization of production and, 407
 price competition and, 411
 prices and, 409
 risks and, 411
 sales promotion and, 411
 social control and, 558
 standardization of products and, 417
 size of firms, 407, 408
 unused capacity and, 407
Subsidies, price competition and, 24
 shipping, 25
Substitute goods integration (*see* Integration, substitute goods)

Sugar, basing-point prices and, 322
   water transportation, 323, 371
   price leadership and, 138
   price setting and, 199
   quantity discounts on, 279
   transportation costs, and basing-point prices, 366
   zone prices, 283
Sugar Institute, 58, 72, 322
   production statistics, 58
Sulphur, stabilization of price, 229
Suppression of patents, 15
Swope, Gerard, 153, 582

T

Tariff Commission, personnel of, 574
Taxation, chain stores, 550
   changing costs of production and, 553
   price competition and, 24
   rate of innovation and, 550
   social control of prices and, 537, 538, 545
Territorial division of market, 150
   aluminum, 150
   calcium carbide, 150
   cotton thread, 150
   glass bottle, 150
   gunpowder, 150
   meat, 150
   steel rail, 150
   tobacco, 150
Territorial integration (*see* Integration, territorial)
Texas, state control of petroleum, 24
Textiles, location of production, 33
   plant-utilization control, 470
   price policy and production, 253
   zone prices, 282n.
Tile, building, and basing-point prices, 299
Timber, concentration of control of, 39
   taxation of, and price competition, 24
Timber Conservation Board, 40n.
Time, distribution of incomes over, and social control, 563
   distribution of overhead costs over, 543
   distribution of utilization of natural resources over, 542
   of buyers' reactions, and price competition, 27
Time period, monopoly price and, 27
Tin plate, price setting, 198
Tires (*see* Automobile tires)
Tobacco, cost of selling, 391
   division of market, 150
   patents for, 11
   price leadership, 140
   prices of, and price of leaf, 227
   sharing the market, 169
   stabilization of prices, 225
   vertical integration, 428
   zone prices, 282
Tobacco leaf markets, competitive conditions in, 5
Trade Associations, 43–75
   alcohol, 135
   anti-trust laws and, 44, 54
   attitude of state toward, 43
   basing-point prices and, 295, 322, 357, 359
   capacity statistics of, 59
   cooperative advertising, 47

Trade Associations, cost accounts, standardization of form of, 47
   costs effect upon, 68
   definition of, 43
   excess capacity and, 67
   history of movement, 43
   industrial distribution of, 44
   inventory statistics of, 59
   leadership and, 76
   lumber industry and, 40
   meetings of, discussing prices, 53
   minimum prices and, 53
   N.I.R.A. and, 464, 512, 517, 577
   non-price competition and, 416, 417
   open prices and, 60
   paper, 203
   plant-utilization control and, 154
   policies of, 74
   policies of, and their effects, 74
   power of, to control output, 64, 66
   price agreements, difficulties of, 54
   price cutting and, 54, 67
   price leadership and, 67
   price policies of, 67
   price setting by, 198
   price uniformity and, 53
   production control by, 66
   provision of credit information by, 47
   provision of information by, 45
   publication of average cost by, 51
   sales promotion by, 380
   selling methods and, 69, 71
   sharing the market and, 58, 152
   size of firms and, 46
   stabilization of prices and, 202, 204
   standardization of discounts by, 71
   of products by, 68
   unfair competition and, 69
   War Industries Board and, 45
Trade-association statistics, manipulation of, 65
   of prices, 60
   of production, 55
   of unfilled orders, 59
Trade discounts (*see* Trade status)
Trade Practice Conferences, 70, 463, 579
Trade Practice Submittals, 70
Trade status, discounts, 549
   price discrimination and, 277, 280
Transferable quotas, 191
Transportation Act, 1920, criteria of control, 567
Transportation charges, standardization of, basing-point prices and, 310–312, 321, 323, 370
Transportation costs, basing-point prices and, 364
Transportation industry, basing-point prices and, 370
Truck transportation, basing-point prices and, 311, 322, 370
Trusts, 40
Tying contracts, 14, 453

U

Unfair competition, 19
   N.I.R.A. and (*see* N.I.R.A.)
   trade associations and, 69

INDEX

Unfilled orders, trade-association statistics, 59
Uniformity of prices, 4
  agricultural implements, 109, 111
  alcohol, 135
  anthracite, 119
  basing-point system and, 319, 353
  cans, 129, 130
  cement, 136
  corn products, 132
  fertilizers, 134
  government bids and, 84
  leadership and, 81, 142
  lumber, 292, 293
  newsprint, 132
  open prices and, 61, 497
  petroleum industry, 99
  steel, and basing-point prices, 301, 309
  zone prices and, 288
United Fruit Company, 12n., 13
United Shoe Machinery Company, 11, 13, 16, 17
  tying contracts, 14, 15
United States Chamber of Commerce, amendment of N.I.R.A. and, 582
United States Industrial Alcohol Company, 76n.
United States Shipping Board, powers of, 21
United States Steel Corporation, 19, 20, 76n.
  price leadership by 77–84
  profits, 88
  share of business, 85
Unused plant, basing-point prices and, 362
  causes of, 31
  changes in methods of production and, 546
  geographical distribution of demand and, 33
  initial demand and, 32
  new products and, 32
  paper, 203
  price competition and, 533
  quality competition and, 296
  sales promotion and, 378
  social control and, 532, 534, 539
  stabilization of prices and, 266
  style competition and, 407

V

Vacuum cleaners, trade association statistics of production of, 58
Vertical integration (see Integration, vertical)
Veto, state, as a means of social control, 582

W

Wages, stabilization of prices and, 265
Wallpaper, cooperative selling, 151
War, social control and, 563
War Industries Board, trade associations and, 45
Washing machines, patents on, 11
  trade-association production, statistics of, 58
Water transportation, basing-point prices and, 310–312, 322, 323, 370, 371
Webb Pomerene Act (see Export corporations)
Westinghouse Electric Company, 12n.,13, 14
Wheat, price discrimination, 276
Wheat prices, flour prices and, 235
Whisky, pool, 147
  taxation of, investment policy and, 24
Window glass (see Glass)
Wire, steel, patents for, 11
Woolen industry, price setting, 198

Z

Zinc, basing-point prices, 295
Zone prices, 282–290
  alcohol, 283
  asphalt and mastic tiles, 282
  basing-point systems and, 288n.
  bath tubs, 283
  coffee, 283
  consequences, 288
  corn products, 283, 289
  cotton thread, 282
  linseed oil, 284, 289
  location of production and, 289
  mahogany, 282
  N.I.R.A. and, 325
  newsprint, 285, 289
  oats, 284
  origin, 288
  petroleum, 285, 289
  price leadership and, 288, 289
  printing and publishing, 282n.
  rubber products, 282n.
  salt, 283
  selling costs and, 288
  sharing market and, 288
  soap, 283
  steel, 283, 289
  stoves, 282
  sugar, 283
  textiles, 282n.
  tobacco products, 282